# LITERARY CULTURES AND DIGITAL HUMANITIES IN INDIA

This book explores the use of digital humanities (DH) to understand, interpret, and annotate the poetics of Indian literary and cultural texts, which circulate in digital forms—in manuscripts—and as oral or musical performance. Drawing on the linguistic, cultural, historical, social, and geographic diversity of Indian texts and contexts, it foregrounds the use of digital technologies—including minimal computing, novel DH research and teaching methodologies, and critical archive generation and maintenance—for explicating poetics of Indian literatures and generating scholarly digital resources which will facilitate comparative readings.

With contributions from DH scholars and practitioners from across India, the United States, the United Kingdom, and more, this book will be a key intervention for scholars and researchers of literature and literary theory, DH, media studies, and South Asian studies.

**Nishat Zaidi** is Professor of English at Jamia Millia Islamia, New Delhi. As a scholar, critic, and translator, she is a recipient of several prestigious grants and has conducted collaborative research with the Centre for Indian Studies in Africa, University of Witwatersrand, SA; South Asia Institute, Heidelberg University, Germany; and Michigan State University, USA. Her publications include *Day and Dastan* translated by Nishat Zaidi and Alok Bhalla (2018); *Purdah and Polygamy: Life in an Indian Muslim Household*, by Iqbalunnisa Hussain, edited and introduced by Nishat Zaidi (2018); *Between Worlds: The Travels of Yusuf Khan Kambalposh* translated and edited by Mushirul Hasan and Nishat Zaidi (2014) among others. Her forthcoming work is *Karbala: A Historical Play* (translation of Premchand's play *Karbala* with a critical introduction and notes) to be published in 2022.

**A. Sean Pue** is Associate Professor of Hindi Language and South Asian Literature and Culture at Michigan State University, USA. He is the author of *I Too Have Some Dreams: N. M. Rashed and Modernism in Urdu Poetry* (2014). An Andrew W. Mellon New Directions Fellowship allowed Pue to study linguistics and computer/data science and to develop "Publics of Sound: Data Driven Analysis of the Poetic Innovation in South Asia," which includes an extensive sound archive of South Asian poetry and analytical and methodological writings. Pue holds a PhD degree in Middle East and Asian Languages and Cultures and Comparative Literature and Society from Columbia University.

# LITERARY CULTURES AND DIGITAL HUMANITIES IN INDIA

*Edited by Nishat Zaidi and A. Sean Pue*

Routledge
Taylor & Francis Group
LONDON AND NEW YORK

Cover image: © Getty Images

First published 2023
by Routledge
4 Park Square, Milton Park, Abingdon, Oxon OX14 4RN

and by Routledge
605 Third Avenue, New York, NY 10158

*Routledge is an imprint of the Taylor & Francis Group, an informa business*



*British Library Cataloguing-in-Publication Data*
A catalogue record for this book is available from the British Library

ISBN: 978-1-032-05673-9 (hbk)
ISBN: 978-1-032-40675-6 (pbk)
ISBN: 978-1-003-35424-6 (ebk)

DOI: 10.4324/9781003354246

Typeset in Bembo
by Apex CoVantage, LLC

# CONTENTS

## PART IV
## Forms in Flux II: Born Digital 245



## PART V
## Digital Atmospheres 313

# ACKNOWLEDGEMENTS

This edited volume emerged out of the two-day international conference "Confronting the 'Global', Exploring the 'Local': Digital Apprehensions of Poetics and Indian Literature(s)," hosted by the Department of English, Jamia Millia Islamia, on 21 and 22 December 2020 with Michigan State University. This conference was a part of the collaborative project "Digital Apprehensions of Poetics" funded by the Ministry of Education, Government of India, through its Scheme for the Promotion of Academic and Research Collaboration (SPARC) with Nishat Zaidi (JMI, INDIA) as the Indian PI and A. Sean Pue (MSU, USA) as the foreign PI. We would like to express our gratitude to the Ministry of Education, Government of India, for funding the project and enabling this research. We would also like to express our gratitude to the administration of Jamia Millia Islamia, especially the Vice Chancellor and conference patron Professor Najma Akhtar, who always supported the project. Finally, we are grateful to the research scholars of the Department of English, JMI, for their unconditional support and hard work in organizing the conference. Zahra Rizvi, Indrani Dasgupta, and Asra Mamnoon deserve a special mention for their help in organizing the volume material.

# ILLUSTRATIONS

## Figures

## Tables

# NOTES ON CONTRIBUTORS

**Mohd Aqib** is a PhD scholar at the Department of English, Jamia Millia Islamia, New Delhi, India. He is currently working on self-translations of Urdu fiction into English. He did his master's degree from Delhi University.

**Parthasarathi Bhaumik** is Associate Professor of Comparative Literature at Jadavpur University, Kolkata, India, and Visiting Associate Professor at the Tokyo University of Foreign Studies, Tokyo, Japan. He is the author of *Bengalis in Burma: A Colonial Encounter (1886–1948)* published by Routledge in 2021. He worked with the British Library, UK, as Chevening Fellow, and built a database on "Nationalism, Independence, and Partition in South Asia (1900–1950)." He is former Joint Director of the School of Cultural Texts and Records, Jadavpur University, and engaged in various digital archiving projects pertaining to the history and cultures of South Asia.

**Spandana Bhowmik** is Head Archivist at Wipro Archives and Resource Centre, Bangalore. Spandana has a PhD degree in digital humanities from Jadavpur University, Kolkata. Her research was on textual transmission of a cluster of plays by Rabindranath Tagore and creation of an interactive multimedia archive representing the textual changes and other documentations surrounding it. She was Charles Wallace Fellow in 2008, visiting the Centre for Textual Scholarship, De Montfort University, UK. In 2014, she was Visiting Fellow at the Scholars' Lab, University of Virginia; and the British Library, UK. She was part of the School of Cultural Texts and Records (SCTR), Jadavpur University, where she worked on various DH and archival projects. She was an essential member of the three-person Digital Development Team which created the Bengali Collation software "Prabhed" for *Bichitra Online Tagore Variorum* project (bichitra.jdvu.ac.in). She also taught modules in the "Digital Humanities and Cultural Informatics," the one-year PG diploma course run by the SCTR. Previously, she was Archivist at the India Foundation for the Arts (IFA), Bangalore, responsible for creating and maintaining the IFA Archive.

**Aibhi Biswas** has completed his graduation and post-graduation in English at University of Delhi. His MPhil degree on magical realism in Indian cinema was completed at Central University of Haryana. He is currently pursuing his PhD degree at Central University of Haryana on the topic Contemporary Indian Graphic Novels—A Socio-Cultural Study. Biswas is deeply interested in topics such as digital humanities, cultural studies, comparative literature, comic studies, film studies, and popular literature. He has written and presented several papers on the topics such as anti-heroes in superhero movies, the idea of villainy in popular cinema, representation of homosexuality in Indian cinema, and the role of Indian comics for social awareness. Alongside, he has written a few poems as well.

**Avanti Chhatre** is currently pursuing her PhD degree in socio-cultural anthropology at Indiana University Bloomington. Prior to enrolling at IU, she completed her MPhil degree in sociology at Jawaharlal Nehru University, New Delhi. Located within the wider domain of performance studies, her MPhil dissertation focused on the cultural politics of realism in Marathi theatre during the 1970s–1980s. She wishes to continue to work in areas such as performance studies, sociology of popular culture, Dalit studies, and media studies.

**Debashree Dattaray** is Associate Professor of Comparative Literature and Deputy Coordinator of Centre for Canadian Studies, Jadavpur University. She is a recipient of Fulbright Alumni Award, Shastri Mobility Programme Fellowship, CICOPS Fellowship, Fulbright-Nehru Visiting Lecturer Fellowship, Erasmus Mundus Europe Asia Fellowship, and Fulbright Doctoral Fellowship. Her areas of research are Indigenous studies, ecocriticism, digital humanities, and comparative literature methodology. She is the author of *Oral Traditions of the North East: A Case Study of Karbi Oral Traditions* and has co-edited *At the Crossroads of Literature and Culture, Following Forkhead Paths: Discussions on the Narrative, Ecocriticism and Environment: Rethinking Literature and Culture* and has been Issue Editor for a volume on Indigenous studies for *Littcrit: An Indian Response to Literature*. She has been Principal Investigator for the Jadavpur University RUSA 2.0 Project on "Locating Indigeneity in the Global South: Revival, Conservation, Sustainability." She is currently working on a book project on narratives of Northeast India.

**Maya Dodd** received her PhD degree from Stanford University and subsequently did her post-doctoral fellowships at Princeton University and JNU, India. At FLAME University, Pune, India, she currently serves as Director of the FLAME Centre for Legislative Education and Research. She also teaches Literary and Cultural Studies in the Department of Humanities at FLAME University, where she has been exploring tools for cultural archiving via techniques from the digital humanities. She serves as an editor for the Routledge series on Digital Humanities in Asia. She has also been part of several initiatives such as the Milli consortium dedicated to nurturing archives in India, the TOPHI project for working on public history in India, and service to building digital humanities scholarship via the DHARTI collective.

**Michael Falk** is a digital humanist and scholar of 18th-century literature. He is an interdisciplinary scholar, who works with computer scientists, designers, historians, and linguists around the world, to determine how AI can enrich the study of literature, and how literature can reshape the science and design of AI systems. He has published on colonial Australian literature, the history of the sonnet, design fiction, artificial stupidity, quantitative book history, character network analysis, and the evolution of modern tragic drama. He is currently developing a new project, which uses digital methods to explore how Swahili, Hindi-Urdu, and Australian English developed as literary languages from 1700 to 1900.

**Nishat Haider** is Professor of English at Jamia Millia Islamia, New Delhi, India. She is the author of *Tyranny of Silences: Contemporary Indian Women's Poetry* (2010). She has served as the director at the Institute of Women's Studies, University of Lucknow. She is a recipient of many academic awards, including the Meenakshi Mukherjee Prize (2016), C. D. Narasimhaiah Award (2010), and Isaac Sequeira Memorial Award (2011). She has lectured extensively on subjects at the intersection of cinema, culture, and gender studies. Her current research interests include postcolonial studies, translation, popular culture, and gender studies.

**Tanya Jaluthria** is conferred with an MPhil degree in English Literature, with her research in the domain of performance studies. Currently working in the field of language assessment, she looks forward to building a career that caters to her interests in theatre, literature, cinema, and research. Apart from studying the theoretical background of drama, she has also practiced in theatre for about five years. Subsequently, her experience in acting, direction, and backstage support gave roots to her fascination for analysing theatrical performances, and reading their verbal and non-verbal cues, images, and structure, making her choose theatre as a field of research.

**Justy Joseph** is a doctoral student at Digital Humanities and Publishing Studies Research Group, IIT Indore, India. Her current research attempts to develop a linguistically informed bias prediction system that can identify narrative biases. Cognitive studies and partition literature are her other areas of research interest.

**Abiral Kumar** is Assistant Professor at the Department of English, St. Stephen's College, Delhi University. His graphic narrative *Fragrance of Time* based on the Hamzanama tradition was recently awarded by the Barzinji Foundation, USA. He is currently pursuing his PhD degree in early Hindi novels and the creation of a public sphere at the Department of English, University of Delhi.

**Nirmala Menon** leads the Digital Humanities and Publishing Research Group at the Indian Institute of Technology (IIT), Indore, India. She is Professor in the School of Humanities and Social Sciences (HSS), Discipline of English, IIT Indore. She is the author of *Migrant Identities of Creole Cosmopolitans: Transcultural Narratives of Contemporary Postcoloniality* (Peter Lang Publishing, Germany, 2014) and *Remapping the Postcolonial Canon: Remap, Reimagine, Retranslate* (Palgrave Macmillan, UK, 2017). She has published in numerous international journals, and speaks, writes, and publishes about postcolonial studies, digital humanities, and scholarly publishing. She directs PhD students in their projects and runs DH projects from the research lab at IIT Indore. Her primary area of research is postcolonial literature and theory. Her focus is on the comparative study of 20th-century postcolonial literatures in English, Hindi, and other languages. Digital humanities, gender studies, globalization, and translation studies are additional areas of research. Her interests are multilingual but also interdisciplinary; her research examines the ways in which literatures from different non-Western languages influence and can redefine and reframe postcolonial theoretical concepts. She has also served on the Advisory Board of the Open Library of Humanities (OLH), as Chair (2016–2017) of the CLCS Global South Forum of the Modern Language Association (MLA), and as Editor of Post-Colonial Indian Literature at litencyc.com, The Literary Encyclopedia. She has published in well-known international journals and books and is currently working on her third book titled *Decolonizing Knowledge Structures: Digital Humanities in India.*

**Souvik Mukherjee** is Assistant Professor of Cultural Studies at the Centre for Studies in Social Sciences, Kolkata. He is the author of two monographs, *Videogames and Storytelling: Reading Games and Playing Books* (Palgrave Macmillan 2015) and *Videogames and Postcolonialism: Empire Plays Back* (Springer UK 2017), and many articles and book chapters in national and international publications. He has also been an advisor on an archive on the "Plaques of Presidency" project. He has been a board member of the Digital Games Research Association (DiGRA) and a founder member of DHARTI, the Digital Humanities Group in India. Souvik has been named a "DiGRA Distinguished Scholar" in 2019. He is also an affiliated senior research fellow at the Centre of Excellence, Game Studies at the University of Tampere.

**A. Sean Pue** is Associate Professor of Hindi Language and South Asian Literature and Culture at Michigan State University. He is the author of *I Too Have Some Dreams: N. M. Rashed and Modernism in Urdu Poetry* (University of California Press, 2014). An Andrew W. Mellon New Directions Fellowship allowed Pue to study linguistics and computer/data science and to develop "Publics of Sound: Data Driven Analysis of the Poetic Innovation in South Asia," which includes an extensive sound archive of South Asian poetry and analytical and methodological writings. Pue holds a PhD degree in Middle East and Asian Languages and Cultures and Comparative Literature and Society from Columbia University.

**Roopika Risam** is Associate Professor of Secondary and Higher Education and English and Faculty Fellow for Digital Library Initiatives at Salem State University.

**Samya Brata Roy** is a PhD student in the Department of Humanities and Social Sciences at IIT Jodhpur and a HASTAC scholar (2021–2023). His interests lie in and around literary studies, digital humanities, remediation, pedagogy, and promoting access via networks. His other roles include filling in as part of the Anti-Racist Task Force with *Alliance of Digital Humanities Organisations*, as Technical Advisory Member with *Humanities Commons*, an executive member with *Digital Humanities Alliance for Research and Teaching Innovations*, as a transcriber with *The Canterbury Tales Project*, as Liaison with *The Association for Computers and the Humanities*, and as the founding member of *Electronic Literature India*.

**Yousuf Saeed** is a Delhi-based independent filmmaker and researcher. He has produced documentary films and write-ups on South Asia's shared cultural traditions, art, and media practices. His films such as *Khayal Darpan*, *Basant*, and *Campus Rising* have been screened worldwide. Yousuf worked at *the Times of India* and *Encyclopaedia Britannica*. He is the author of *Muslim Devotional Art in India* (Routledge, 2012–2019) besides other publications. Being an archivist of popular art, Yousuf co-founded *Tasveer Ghar*, a digital archive of South Asia's popular visual culture. Yousuf has been Sarai/CSDS Fellow (2004), Margaret Beveridge Senior Research Fellow at Jamia Millia's Mass Communication Research Centre (2009), and a grantee of the Asian Scholarship Foundation (2005–2006) and India Foundation for the Arts for research and documentation projects. Yousuf has made lecturing tours in universities such as the Harvard, Boston, Chicago, Columbia, and Austin (in the USA), besides Heidelberg (Germany) and Amsterdam and Leiden (the Netherlands).

**Shruti Sareen** earned her PhD degree from the Delhi University on the topic *Indian Feminisms in the 21st Century: Women's Poetry in English* which is now forthcoming from Routledge, UK, as two monographs in 2022. She has had over 100 poems and a handful of short stories published in journals and anthologies. She is currently seeking publishers for her novel, *The Yellow Wall*, and is working around a hybrid manuscript around lives of queer artists, on themes of queerness and mental health. Her debut poetry collection, *A Witch Like You*, was published by Girls on Key Poetry (Australia) in April 2021.

She was an invited poet at global poetry festival, hosted by Russia, Poeisia-21. Having earlier taught at Dyal Singh College (Delhi University), she currently teaches at the Department of English, Jamia Millia Islamia.

**Shanmugapriya T**'s research and teaching interests include an interdisciplinary focus in the areas of digital humanities, digital environmental humanities, and digital literature. She is particularly interested in building and applying digital tools and technologies for humanities research. She completed her PhD degree at Indian Institute of Technology, Indore, India. She was AHRC Postdoctoral Research Associate at Lancaster University, UK. She is currently working as a postdoctoral scholar at University of Toronto, Canada. She has published papers in national and international journals such as DSH, DHQ, and EBR. She is one of interim executive committee members of DHARTI.

**Devika Singh Shekhawat** is a writer, educator, and researcher in the field of sociology. She is a published author with Zubaan Publications on the history and memory of migration of tea plantation workers of Assam and a co-author of a book chapter with the Programme of Social Action's The Research Collective on the Ecological Crisis of Shrimp Aquaculture and discourses of migration and infiltration in Coastal Odisha. She completed her bachelor's degree in history and political science at St. Stephens College, New Delhi. She went on to pursue her master's degree in sociology from Jawaharlal Nehru University, New Delhi, and is currently pursuing her PhD degree in questions of health and labour in tea plantations of Assam at Ambedkar University, Delhi. She has a keen interest in writing, teaching, curation, and research work, and her expertise lie in the field of gender and sexuality studies with a close emphasis on intersections of gender and labour, ecology, cultural studies, sociological theory, oral histories, folklore studies, migration, and developmental issues.

**Amardeep Singh** teaches at Lehigh University in Pennsylvania in the U.S. He has published on postcolonial literature and film, including a 2018 book on the filmmaker Mira Nair. Since 2015, he has been developing digital collections mostly using the Scalar platform. Some notable projects include "Claude Mckay's Early Poetry," "The Kiplings and India," and "Women of the Early Harlem Renaissance."

**Deborah Sutton** teaches Modern South Asian History at Lancaster University. She is interested in the fields of cultural, environmental, and urban histories and heritage.

**Dhanashree Thorat** is Assistant Professor of English at Mississippi State University. Her research is situated at the intersection of Asian–American studies, postcolonial studies, and digital humanities. Broadly, she examines how colonial and racial ideologies shape the technological imagination, specifically in technical infrastructures, platforms, and policies. Dhanashree is a founding executive council member of the Center for Digital Humanities, Pune, India. She is currently working on a monograph that argues for decolonizing infrastructural development and, in particular, highlights new modes of regional co-building, ownership, and management of Internet infrastructures in the Global South.

**Nishat Zaidi** is Professor of English at Jamia Millia Islamia, New Delhi. As a scholar, critic, and translator, she is a recipient of several prestigious grants and has conducted collaborative research with the Centre for Indian Studies in Africa, University of Witwatersrand, SA; South Asia Institute, Heidelberg University, Germany; and Michigan State University, USA. Her publications include *Day and Dastan* translated by Nishat Zaidi and Alok Bhalla (2018); *Purdah and Polygamy: Life in an Indian Muslim Household*, by Iqbalunnisa Hussain, edited and introduced by Nishat Zaidi (2018); *Between Worlds: The Travels of Yusuf Khan Kambalposh* translated and edited by Mushirul Hasan and Nishat Zaidi (2014) and *Karbala: A Historical Play* (translation of Premchand's play *Karbala* with a critical introduction and notes). She has also co-authored monographs *Dreaming of the Digital Divan: Digital Apprehensions of Poetry in Indian Languages (2022)* and *Ocean as Method: Thinking with the Maritime (2021).*

# INTRODUCTION

*Nishat Zaidi and A. Sean Pue*

"If you do not write in English, people think you do not write," said Egyptian author Nawal El Saadawi in one of her interviews. As the default language of digital technologies, English holds on to its historical position of global power. And yet, languages other than English do thrive within the digital space, with literatures in hundreds of languages circulating across digital media. With this in mind, questions of methodology arise: How does the global reach of digital tools transform and transmute local/regional literary cultures, particularly from the Global South? What are the best methods for archiving, assessing, and understanding these shifts? How can scholars committed to the methods of the digital humanities address inequalities in digital knowledge production? This collection of essays, focused on the literary cultures and digital humanities of India, addresses these and other questions.

In doing so, this book's authors join a growing critique of normative forms of "digitality" in the digital humanities (DH) as a field of scholarship. In her 2016 pathbreaking study of Digital Humanities in India, P. P. Sneha has drawn attention to the long history of predominantly Anglo-American narrative of DH which mostly ignores the work in DH emerging from countries in the "Global South," notably India and China and the need to understand and address better the questions that may emerge from the practice of DH in these spaces. She writes,

> The efforts to map different histories of DH in the last couple of years, seen in the emergence of fields such as postcolonial DH and feminist DH, then point to diverse locations, and more intersectional perspectives from which the discourse around the field is being shaped. This is an important opportunity to better contextualise the debates around the digital as well—where conditions and hierarchies of access and usage, transition from analogue to the digital, and the notion of "digitality" itself need to be defined and understood better.
>
> *(Sneha 2021, n.p.)*

DOI: 10.4324/9781003354246-1

Equally critical, Roopika Risam's works have consistently drawn attention to colonial violence in digital archives, highlighting the colonialist dimensions of the global organizations that support digital humanities and calling for decentring the Global North in digital knowledge production (cf. Risam 2018; Risam and Josephs 2021; Risam and Gairola 2020). They are joined in these calls by scholars of digital humanities from other parts of the world (cf. Dodd and Kalra 2020).

The chapters in this volume focus on Indian digital cultures, outside of English, by consistently embedding the study of literature in culture and society. They explore literary cultures in the sense promulgated by Sheldon Pollock, in which language and literature are in constant dialogue with history. Pollock's work points towards negotiations and contestations involved in the intricate connections between power and literary production which are mostly inter-disciplinary, crosscutting between many disciplines and approaches (Pollock 2003). Authors of chapters privilege experiences of reading, listening, and/or viewing. The text is treated not as an object for a separate and singular subject to interrogate; rather, the experience made possible by the digital artefact is a focus of many of the chapters. Just as games are not isolated from gameplay, the social practices of literary cultural consumption and production are topics of study. These include the formation of digital literary communities and the production and sales of literary commodities. The chapters consider the role of scholars and archivists as social and cultural beings, addressing the ethical implications of digital and literary scholarship, whether in India or the United States. There is an obvious reflexivity in most of the chapters that follow: a contextualization of the scholar as situated in the world, an imbricated participant in literary culture and in society.

The authors in this book find their point of departure in Kathleen Fitzpatrick's definition of DH:

> It has to do with the work that gets done at the crossroads of digital media and traditional humanistic study. And that happens in two different ways. On one hand, it's bringing the tools and techniques of digital media to bear on traditional humanistic questions. But it's also bringing humanistic modes of inquiry to bear on digital media. It's a sort of moving back and forth across those lines, thinking about what computation is, how it functions in our culture, and then using those computing technologies to think about the more traditional aspects of culture.
>
> *(Lopez* et al. *2015, n.p.)*

The value Fitzpatrick places on "traditional humanistic study" is also shared by DH theorists Nyhan and Flinn, who argue that DH "takes place at the intersection of computing and cultural heritage." As they describe,

> [DH] aims to transform how the artefacts (such as manuscripts) and the phenomena (such as attitudes) that the Humanities study can be encountered,

> transmitted, questioned, interpreted, problematized and imagined. In doing so it tends to differentiate itself from now routine uses of computing in research and teaching, for example, email and word processing.
>
> *(2016, p. 1)*

Indeed, Schreibman, Siemens, and Unsworth describe as the field's "central concerns" "the representation of knowledge-bearing artifacts," for, as they write, "The process of such representation—especially so when done with the attention to detail and the consistency demanded by the computing environment—requires humanists to make explicit what they know about their material" (Schreibman *et al.* 2004, p. xxvi).

Unfortunately, engagements with humanistic sentences are increasingly rare. We share these authors' continuing commitment to humanistic questions, one that is often dismissed from educational and scholarly models emphasizing science and technology, sometimes with the addition of the arts. We acknowledge the shaping role played by the consistent undervaluing of the domain of culture. By bridging computation with cultural and historical thoughts, DH offers a profoundly different approach. It "brings the values, representational and interpretive practices, meaning-making strategies, complexities, and ambiguities of being human into every realm of experience and knowledge of the world," resulting in "a major expansion of the purview of the humanities" as a "global, transhistorical, and transmedia approach to knowledge and meaning-making" (Burdick *et al.* 2012, p. 8).

This volume addresses the failure of DH to grapple effectively with the challenges that the global circulation of digital technology and culture poses to its methods and underlying assumptions. Not only do few of DH's so-called global institutions have serious footholds outside of the West, but also few studies of global DH question the assumptions built into the term "global," as do theorists such as Gayatri Spivak, who advocates instead for the category of the "planetary." She writes,

> I propose the planet to overwrite the globe. Globalization is the imposition of the same system of exchange everywhere. In the gridwork of electronic capital, we achieve that abstract ball covered in latitudes and longitudes, cut by virtual lines, once the equator and the tropics and so on, now drawn by the requirements of Geographical Information Systems. . . . The globe is on our computers. No one lives there. It allows us to think that we can aim to control it. The planet is in the species of alterity, belonging to another system; and yet we inhabit it, on loan.
>
> *(72)*

In her view, the "global" carries with it a concept of homogenous space, ready to be classified and described, by a separate, independent subject, as either nature or culture. In other words, the global perpetuates the biases and monolithic assumptions associated with colonial modernity. Spivak continues,

> If we imagine ourselves as planetary subjects rather than global agents, planetary creatures rather than global entities, alterity remains underived from us; it is not our dialectical negation, it contains us as much as it flings us away. And thus to think of it is already to transgress, for, in spite of our forays into what we metaphorize, differently, as outer and inner space, what is above and beyond our own reach is not continuous with us as it is not, indeed, specifically discontinuous.
>
> *(73)*

Planetary thinking is among the most powerful models for unravelling the conventional self/other—or agent/object—dichotomy, allowing for a more expansive sense of collectivity and of responsibility. The chapters in this volume explore local digital cultures and local approaches to Digital Humanities in order to confront the biases and monolithic assumptions of the epithet, global.

A central object of the volume's critique is the network, which has served as the motivating structure for organizing global digital humanities as an academic formation, and one of the field's signal methodological approaches. To expand definitions of cognition, N. Katherine Hayles makes a useful distinction between the assemblage, which she associates with Deleuze and Guattari, and the network. Glossing cognition as "a process of interpreting information in contexts that connect it with meaning," she includes nonhuman actors alongside human ones, recognizing the role of "processes occurring at multiple levels and sites within biological life forms and technical systems." The analytical advantages of assemblages over network, she explains, are numerous; they allow "for arrangements that scale up" and the ability to "lose or add parts." Their materiality is different, too, as Hayles explains:

> Networks consist of edges and nodes and are analyzed through graph theory, conveying a sense of a spare, clean materiality. Assemblages, by contrast, allow for contiguity in a fleshly sense—touching, incorporating, repelling, mutating. When analyzed as dynamic systems, networks are sites of exchange, transformation, and dissemination, but they lack the sense of these interactions occurring across complex three-dimensional surfaces, whereas assemblages include information transactions occurring across membranes, involuted and convoluted surfaces, and multiple volumetric entities interacting with many conspecifics simultaneously.
>
> *(Hayles 2016, p. 33)*

The "spare, clean materiality" of the network/graph model consists of nodes/vertices and edges between them. Its edges can be represented as a two-dimensional matrix, activating the toolkit of linear algebra. The graph brings with it the ordered certainty of quantifiability against the multidimensional—and potentially sticky—messiness of the assemblage. The network graph, through various algorithms, provides metrics and measurability; the model falls into the realm of discrete math, based on countable, separate elements. The assemblage, on the other hand, resists simple, clean mathematical representation and the certainty of logic-based operations. Digital Humanities has also been accused of reduction of human culture to the "spare, clean materiality" of the graph—to a realm of numbers. The insights into literary cultures that can be gained from numbers are important. Even so, the studies in this volume prefer the multidimensional complexity of the assemblage over the clean abstraction of the graph.

Accompanying this movement towards assemblages is an attention to the role of atmosphere in the aesthetics of the digital literary artefact and in the social life of its consumer or producer. Atmosphere, as Gernot Böhme has argued, has a "peculiar intermediary status" that lies "between subject and object"; as a result, "[w]e are not sure whether we should attribute them to the objects or environments from which they proceed or to the subjects who experience them." We do, however, have a vocabulary to describe atmospheres—as "serene, melancholic, oppressive, uplifting, commanding, inviting, erotic, etc." (Böhme 1993, p. 114). Earlier aesthetic theory has focused on aesthetic "judgment" and, as a result, developed a preoccupation with "language" in descriptions of art.

When understood as the "production of atmospheres" (116), however, aesthetics might expand to include the other domains besides art, such as political life. To do so requires an undoing of the subject–object dichotomy. Instead of information processed by an autonomous subject, perception can instead be expanded to include "the affective impact of the observed, the 'reality of images', corporeality." In other words, perception is "the manner in which one is bodily present for something or someone or one's bodily state in an environment." This expansion of aesthetic discourse moves from the realm "aesthetic pleasure" to also include "aesthetic manipulation." It is to expand from the "aesthetics of the work of art" to "the aesthetics of everyday life, the aesthetics of commodities and a political aesthetics" (125).

While the approach of the authors here in is not explicitly aligned with this new aesthetics, it is clearly operating, especially in discussions of digital communities. The role of aesthetic experience is considered not only in relation to the literary artefact but also in relation to the feelings accompanying digital sociality. Consequently, even YouTube or other social media comments are taken up as revelatory for gauging atmospheres.

The consideration of atmospheres as aesthetic experience affirms the relevance of literary studies to the digital realm. Returning to Kathleen Fitzpatrick's useful definition of DH, it is not only in the use of digital tools to study traditional aesthetic objects but also in using the toolkit of the humanities, including aesthetics, to study the digital.

## The Chapters in This Book

This volume is an intervention into the field of Global Digital Humanities by virtue of its examination of the idea of the "global" and how such an epithet impacts and complicates Digital Humanities. Believing that explorations of local digital cultures and local approaches to Digital Humanities can confront the biases and monolithic assumptions of the epithet of the "global," this book takes into account the linguistic, cultural, historical, social, and geographic diversity of a particularly fascinating localization—that of the poetics of Indian literatures and cultures in DH.

With contributions from DH scholars and practitioners from across India, the United States, Australia, the United Kingdom, and more, this volume explores the use of digital technologies to understand, interpret, and annotate the poetics of Indian literary and cultural texts which circulate in digital forms, in manuscript, and as oral or musical performance. In Kathleen Fitzpatrick's view, digital humanities involves

> the work that gets done at the crossroads of digital media and traditional humanistic study. And that happens in two different ways. On one hand, it's bringing the tools and techniques of digital media to bear on traditional humanistic questions. But it's also bringing humanistic modes of inquiry to bear on digital media.

Accordingly, our contention is that computational technology can enhance both scholarly analysis and pedagogical explanation of the poetics of Indian literatures.

Some of the questions we hope to both ask and explore through this volume are: Can modelling formal processes allow for computer-assisted scholarly analysis across the variously related languages and literary histories of India? What are the exigencies involved in applying digital tools to languages other than English? Can different forms of graphical visualizations be used to determine the most effective modes to convey poetics to new generations of students and scholars? What role can computational technology play in facilitating understanding of poetics?

This volume hopes also to foreground the use of digital technologies such as minimal computing, novel DH research and teaching methodologies, critical archive generation and maintenance, to mention a few, for explicating poetics of Indian literatures and generating scholarly digital resources which may facilitate comparative readings. Including "born digital" materials, in English, Hindi, and Urdu, this volume also considers how to channel the affordances of digital technologies to engage a generation of readers both within academia and beyond. In doing so, the contributors strive to uncover exciting contemporary projects and possibilities of localized DH now and for the digital futures of Indian poetics. Acknowledging the ongoing work of localized global DH, this volume offers a novel contribution to the field, seeking to open up future conversations and engagement. The volume includes chapters that engage with the thematic and practical concerns of DH localization including, but not limited to, minimal computing and poetics, case studies of ongoing DH projects in the domain of Indian Literatures, literary modelling and comparative Indian poetics, digital futures of Indian literatures, text encoding for Indian languages, digital cultures in India, localization of tools and technologies for apprehensions of poetics in Indian literatures, digital diasporas, decentring global DH, postcolonial DH, media archaeology of Indian literatures online, and DH pedagogy and Indian literatures.

Addressing India's sprawling and complex literary cultures, rather than literary histories, the realm of literature is conceived as part of culture and of society, rather than a separate or transcendent realm. Several chapters in the volume embrace "lower" or "popular" genres often still dismissed as unfit for study. Regional Indian languages feature prominently in the volume, alongside those focused on English. Digital art forms are also addressed with rigor: audiobooks, electronically transmitted plays, graphic novels, and videogames, including those based on Bollywood movies, are all considered as literary artefacts. Indeed, the transformations of genres and poetics that digitalization affords are a central concern of this book.

The chapters in this volume are arranged in five parts. Part I comprises three chapters that explore the conceptual questions related to digital humanities from the sidelines of the mainstream practices, especially from the postcolonial locations such as India where multilinguality, caste, regulatory regimes, and digital literary pose unique challenges to digital humanists. Chapters in Part II consider the scholarly and critical response necessitated by shifts in form and community participating in digital cultures. Parts III and IV analyse the transformations and amalgamations of "traditional" literary forms—poetry, plays, short stories, and novels—occasioned by the introduction of digital technologies, alongside those of natively "born digital" forms, including video games. Part V gathers chapters that consider the phenomenology and dynamics of digital literary communities and other affinity groups, often attending to experiences of the digital. In one way or another, all the chapters take on a perspective grounded in or applicable to India, understood broadly.

## *Digital Humanities From the Sidelines: Theoretical Considerations*

While the digital dust of social media connections is plagued by questions of privacy and data sovereignty, there still exists the possibility of a new public sphere of radical democracy and social engagement. Basing her arguments on this promise of Google's "next billion users," Maya Dodd argues in "Digital Cultures in India: Digitality and Its Discontents" that the COVID-19 pandemic has revealed the possibility of transcending earlier industrial-age constraints through digital extensions. Against a predominant focus on questions of surveillance, privacy, and regulatory concerns within digital culture studies in India, Dodd focuses on emergent sites of participatory culture on digital platforms. Wishing to recuperate the digital platform as a site of possibility, Dodd stresses the importance of open culture and open education in India as she describes the multilingual and multiregister expansion of the digital public sphere in India through the social web.

Dhanashree Thorat's paper, "Digital Literary Studies in Uncertain Times," focuses on the democratizing potential of digital humanities' emphasis on open-access publishing, sharing texts and archives with broader and new audiences, and destabilizing canonical formations. Acknowledging the limits of these techniques in challenging the structural dominance of the Euro-American canon, Thorat revisits the affordances of digital humanities methods and platforms in our present moment. Situating herself in the diasporic and trans/national contexts of India and the United States, the author makes a case for postcolonial and anti-caste praxes to ground work in digital literary studies. This includes taking up the broader question of how DH practitioners can respond to socio-political emergencies in their local and national communities. Against the backdrop of a pandemic unfolding amidst state and systemic violence, Thorat underlines that DH scholars and teachers can enact radical and transformative practices and pedagogies at the intersection of digital humanities and literary studies.

However, "multilingual DH" is mostly confined to the problem of translation. One of the prominent aspirations of Digital Humanities is to model the emergence of modern literature. In "Three Models of World Literature," Michael Falk addresses the shifts in approaches to world literature within digital literary studies over the last 20 years. He observes how 20th-century computational scholars focussed on details, compiling exhaustive concordances of classic texts, densely tagged databases of stylistic examples, or comprehensive digital editions of famous writers. Later, scholars aspired to data mine the archive, in order to model world literature as a whole. Falk contrasts three such models: the canon, the cosmopolis, and the archive, and their accompanying method as assisted or transformed by digital technology. The tools most prized by distant readers, such as bibliometrics, topic modelling, and sentiment analysis, are ill-suited to the study of heterogeneous documents in multiple languages from distinct literary traditions. Drawing on Kath Bode and Roopika Risam's powerful materialist critiques of digital literary scholarship, Falk suggests that scholars should accept *orthogonality*—the search for axes—as the underlying principle of world literary history. Instead of a singular map of world literature, Falk proposes a profusion of literary maps, each with their own gridlines, as a method for a new kind of planetary distant reading.

## Archives, Ethics, and Praxis

Parthasarathi Bhaumik goes on to examine the Digital Archives for Indian Literatures in his chapter. Parthasarathi Bhaumik's chapter, "Digital Archives for Indian Literatures and Cultures: Challenges and Prospects," is based on his own experience of working in various digital archiving projects in the United Kingdom's British Library and Jadavpur University's School of Cultural Texts and Records. Taking a comparative approach, Bhaumik considers how the shift in digital cultures in India, vis-à-vis those of the outside world, poses particular ethical concerns. He considers the role that resource and infrastructural constraints might play in the production of decentralized archives. Against the centripetal model of the digital archive, Bhaumik proposes instead a digital archive using the affordances of hypertext to operate within a larger social ecosystem. The chapter argues that the personal digital archives in place of big and expensive libraries and physical archives may turn to be of advantage for a developing country like India, provided that technologies can be harnessed for Indigenous purposes and ingenious ways found for their visualizations.

Spandana Bhowmik's chapter examines one of the biggest success stories of DH in the context of Indian literatures, which is the online variorum of Rabindranath Tagore's works titled *Bichitra*, developed at the School of Cultural Texts and Records (SCTR), Jadavpur University. Bhowmik explains how deploying a unique collation software titled *Prabhed* ("difference" in Bengali) helps to assemble text at three levels: (a) chapter in novel, act/scene in drama, and canto in poem; (b) paragraph in novel or other prose, speech in drama, and stanza in poem; (c) individual word. The variorum allows for the critical reading of literary oeuvre of the great writer by making it possible to trace variations across different editions.

Prakruti Maniar's paper, "Presenting Purple Pencil Project as a Case Study of Digital Humanities Project in Practice in the Field of Indian Literatures," describes how the problem of multilingual searching led to the formation of the Purple Pencil Project, a website which aims to increase access to and awareness of Indian literature. The project encourages the discovery of non-Anglophone Indian writers through crowdsourcing techniques, in order to create digital representations of Indian literary works and authors and stakeholders such as bookstores and publishers, across the different regions and languages featured on the website. Privileging the knowledge of lay-readers who read in many different languages and talking about them on the Purple Pencil Project's platform, they draw attention to marginalized authors. Second, the platform seeks to diversify the content broadcast across and by social media and search engines. In all, the project aims to create a self-sustaining cultural ecosystem, where readers will be organically interested in reading regional literatures, thereby incentivizing publishers to engage with regional literatures, and, in turn, encouraging writers to write these stories.

Debashree Dattaray explores the relevance of digital technologies in the archiving and preservation of Indigenous oral-literary traditions and art practices. In her paper, "Archiving 'Community's Voices' in Karbi Anglong: Collective Memory and Digital Apprehensions," Dattaray examines the work of the Centre for Karbi Studies and the Karbi Lammet Amei in Karbi Anglong, Assam, to textualize and preserve oral tradition. Karbis, the largest hill community in Assam, India, have struggled to retain their cultural identity and sovereignty. Dattatray traces the cultural preservation activities of individuals and organizations, such as Dharamsing Teron, Sikari Tisso, and the Karbi Lammet Amei, who have documented oral traditions as embedded cultural experience and Indigenous knowledge. Dattaray's paper discusses the opportunities and challenges of the long-term preservation and access to Karbi oral traditions, and it explores issues of research integrity and curriculum plans in the context of the "archive." This carves a space for dialogue between theory and practice and proffers new readings/frameworks of Karbi artistic practices.

Nishat Zaidi and Aqib Sabir, in their chapter, "Rekhta to Rekhta.org.: Digital Remapping of Urdu Literary Culture and Public Sphere," undertake a close examination of the archiving and digitization of Urdu books, a work being carried out by the Rekhta Foundation-owned website rekhta.org to examine the ways in which digital technology is transforming Urdu literary and public sphere. Their study employs a qualitative research method involving document review, interviews, and personal observation of the Rekhta Foundation office, workspace, and their digitization process.

### *Forms in Flux I: Digitalization of Indian Literatures*

Literary studies, especially English studies, have been the fulcrum of Digital Humanities all over the world. While digital technology has transformed the form, production, and circulation of literature, this section studies the conventional literary genres such as poetry and the novel, in Indian languages and in the Indian writing in English, to gauge the impact of digitalization on literary texts.

In "Digitizing Derozio: Exploring Intertext to English Romanticism in *Collected Poems of Henry Derozio*," Amardeep Singh offers a response to what he terms the "Archive Gap": the disparity in the availability and quality of archival and digital resources for the study of authors outside the white, Euro-American canon. Creating the first digital edition of Henry Derozio, the first Indian poet to write in English, offers an opportunity, Singh argues, to revisit Derozio's work for its local references to both Bengal and Calcutta, where he lived and taught, and for the global imaginative geography of his poetry. Derozio wrote in dialogue with British Romantic writers, such as Thomas Moore and Lord Byron, who were themselves engaged in a global project, setting poems in Greece, Turkey, and other versions of "the Orient." How, Singh asks, did Derozio repurpose the global scope of Romantic Orientalism for his own, local ends? And how can we use digital tools, including visualizations and maps, to reinscribe Romantic poetry as a globalized project?

Shruti Sareen's essay, "The Internet in the Context of Indian Women's Poetry in English," describes how digital connectivity involves processes of becoming, flux, and hybridization that blur the conventional boundaries of text, author, and reader. Sareen describes how the internet, especially social media, enables the formation of poetic "discourse communities," furthered by literary fests, poetry readings, and slams. Through small poetry publishing houses, grants, awards, residencies, and online and print not-for-profit journals, Sareen argues, Indian women have formed these online poetic communities as "gift economies" that are non-capitalistic, self-sustaining, cooperative, engaged, and empowering. Hypertext and hypermedia blur the boundaries of author and reader, enabling new potentialities for poetry. In dialogue with biological-feminist critique, Sareen explores how Indian women poets writing in English foreground issues of embodiment and materiality that break down the boundaries of animal, human, and machine.

Aibhi Biswas's "Putting the Local in the Global: Indian Graphic Novels, the New Vogue of Indian Writing in English" addresses the phenomenon of Indian graphic novels, especially those developed for online reading, which quickly have gained in popularity since the early 2000s. Biswas contextualizes the rise of the graphic novel within the context of the liberalization of India's economy. As a hybrid form—simultaneously literary and visual, elite and popular, Indian and international—the graphic novel functions as a work of art often with socio-cultural and political themes, such as gender-based violence and Dalit suffering at the hands of dominant social groups. A glocal (global and local) and cosmopolitan form, the graphic novel, Biswas argues, offers an alternative to mainstream media that can have a positive impact on society.

Shanmugapriya T., Nirmala Menon, and Deborah Sutton's chapter "Quantitative Stepwise Analysis of the Impact of Technology in Indian English Novels 1947–2017" uses a computational text analysis to study the imprint of technological artefacts—particularly, telephones, radios, televisions, and computers—in Indian English novels for the 70 years following Independence/Partition. After weighing existing DH methods of distant reading, macroanalysis, and critical stepwise formalization for text analysis, the authors propose quantitative stepwise analysis (QSA) as a complement to existing method. QSA allows for the study of a predetermined or identified discourse in a corpus of texts. Following QSA, text mining and visualizations tools, such as Keyword-in-Context (KWIC), are deployed to extract and visualize the frequent appearances and discourses of technological artefacts in the selected corpus of novels. The authors create and analyse two types of visualizations: scatter plot charts for the frequency of technological artefacts in Indian novels from 1947 to 2017, and bubble charts for discourses of technological artefacts in the novels' narration.

There are various digital modes available to enhance readers'/audience's access to non-Anglophone literatures. For instance, unlike audio media, such as podcasts, and song streams which are not rooted in pre-existent textual forms, an audio book works as a translation between the analogue and digital, between the ocular and the aural. Through an attention to audio recitation of Hindi-Urdu literature on social media, Abiral Kumar's "(Un)scripting Hindustani: The Special Case of Hindi-Urdu Audiobook" considers the possibilities of denaturalizing the large script- and vocabulary-based separation of Hindi and Urdu and restoring an experience of one language, Hindustani, among listeners. Kumar returns to the writings of Devakinandan Khatri, who defended his language as Hindustani against the association of Urdu with Muslim and Hindi with Hindu identity. Discussing freely available audiobooks on YouTube, usually associated with either Hindi or Urdu, Kumar argues that the boundaries between the languages dissolve in the spoken register, enabling a return of Hindustani as a shared, inclusive, and common heritage, thus enabling Hindi-Urdu, or Hindustani, as a singular world language, despite current associations.

## *Forms in Flux II: Born Digital*

Videogames have emerged as an important pillar in the realm of popular culture and literature. Souvik Mukherjee attempts to arrive at the subaltern poetics in Indian video games. Using a well-worn but very relevant term from postcolonial discourses, Mukherjee probes the implications of assumptions of self-hood in video games when the game is about the subaltern. Subaltern studies of video games, Mukherjee argues, have been overdetermined by an Aristotelean poetics that favours heroic action. In "Journeying against the Heroes: Subaltern Poetics in Indian Video Games," Mukherjee considers the possibilities for representing the position of the subaltern, the oppressed, and the non-heroic in video game poetics. Mukherjee reads two videogames from India, *Missing: Game for a Cause* and *Somewhere*, as challenging the typical game poetics of agency and selfhood. Instead of heroic action, these games represent multiple perspective that acknowledge the displacement of choice and the absence of self-representation that characterize subalternity. It is only through a non-Aristotelean poetics that these games approach the representation of the othered and the oppressed.

Nishat Haider delineates the aesthetic connections between Bollywood films and video games to critically engage with issues of interactivity in consumer culture, film aesthetics, spectatorship, and narrative. In "Narrative and Play: Some Reflections on Videogames Based on Bollywood," Haider examines the ways in which games construct conceptions of spatiality, political systems, ethics, and society. The coalescence of Bollywood cinematic images with the transmediated "text" in the form of the videogame opens the possibility of alternative modes of identification for the spectator/participant. Haider analyses videogames accompanying both the films *Krrish 3* and *Dhoom 3* as social construction and as textual practice. Haider stresses, however, that an ideological or textual analysis alone is insufficient. Because of the participatory nature of videogames, gameplay—as an immersive, interactive, and emotional experience—must also be considered a constitutive element of videogames and their analysis.

In "*Hitman 2 and Its Spectre of Mumbai: A City Lost in Translation*," Samya Brata Roy addresses the (mis)representation of India and Mumbai in a popular North Atlantic videogame. Roy aligns his methodology with the critical technocultural discourse analysis (CTDA) method associated with Andre Brock. Roy also draws from work by Soraya Murray to address race and gender in the gamic space. Lisa Nakamura's study of racial behaviour in online spaces, especially her idea of identity tourism, informs Roy's approach to the videogame character. To understand the history of India's representation in gamic space, Roy utilizes Souvik Mukherjee's work on postcolonialism in video games. Penix-Tadsen's study of game semiotics, especially of Brazilian favelas, provides a model for Roy's analysis of Mumbai's slums. In his article, Roy confronts and contextualizes the exoticization of Mumbai in the Hitman series. He finds it to be perpetuating stereotypes of India as the "Orient" that assumes a White and Anglophonic perspective.

In their chapter "Electronic Literature in India: Where Is It? Does It Even Exist?," Justy Joseph and Nirmala Memon consider the state of electronic literature in India in 2020, especially following the COVID-19-inducted lockdown that classified books as non-essential goods. Whereas electronic publication previously accompanied print publication or served as a method of testing the market for what would be a print book, digital-only publication has now gained popularity, and a 2020 book consumption survey confirms that over 71% of the year's reading in India was on digital platforms. Through a survey sampling of publishing houses, small-scale digital publishing platforms, authors who published their works in 2020, and readers, the authors study Indian responses to the shift to digital publishing in English and regional languages. Acknowledging a lack of effective publishing strategies, Joseph and Memon posit that changes in archaic government policy, favourable internet access across the nation, and an academic orientation of digital publication are some of the ways in which the COVID-19 lockdown has unfettered the significant potential of digital publication in India.

## *Digital Atmospheres*

In "The Cult of Youtube Mushairas in India's Small Towns," Yousuf Saeed considers the possibility that YouTube fan clubs of mushairas (Urdu poetry gatherings) are, in fact, adding a new dimension to Urdu poetics. Saeed posits that, while mushairas are an age-old and popular tradition, attracting thousands of attendees in rural communities and small towns across India, irrespective of religious affiliation, the Internet and social media have lately provided a new platform for this tradition to flourish. All over Urdu-knowing India, especially in the qasbas of Uttar Pradesh, Madhya Pradesh, Haryana, Punjab, Maharashtra, Telangana, Karnataka, etc., real mushairas are video-recorded and uploaded to social media platforms, such as YouTube and Facebook, where they are watched and shared by millions of fans of young and local poets, such as Nikhat Moradabadi, Danish Ghazal, Qamar Ejaz, Shabana Shabnam, Saba Balrampuri, Shabina Adeeb, and Lata Haya. Saeed considers these mushairas and their circulation as videos from multiple angles—local politics, multimedia companies, and audience reactions in person and online. He calls for an embrace of popular multimedia forms, even at the expense of linguistic purity.

Literature in India has played a crucial role in articulations of subaltern voices. Entwining of digital cultures with literary outpourings has recast those articulations, mostly amplifying them, and forging a liberating space for them. In "Performative Politics in Digital Spaces: An Analysis of Lokshahiri (People's Poetry) on YouTube," Avanti Chhatre examines the role of the folk performative/musical tradition of Lokshahiri in Dalit cultural mobilization in Maharashtra, in its present digital form. Chhatre establishes the continuing role in anti-caste resistance of Lokshahiri songs, which engage with Ambedkar's thought and personal/political struggles, Dalit struggles for social justice, and contemporary socio-political realities. She then explores the reinvention of Lokshahiri through technology, as artists alter their repertoires for digitally enabled platforms and embrace new idioms like "Dalit Pop." Amateur participation in YouTube cultures helps to democratize the Dalit public sphere and allow Lokshahirs to fashion their music as part of everyday soundscapes. Finally, Chhatre considers how new media technologies enable solidarities that straddle caste divides within Dalits in Maharashtra and open up shared spaces for the oppressed across the subcontinent at large.

Devika Singh Shekhawat in "Encountering the Digital: Jhumur Folk Songs, Memory, Migration and the Digital Spheres" traces the history of the migration of tea plantation labour and the role of the migrant population in shaping the histories and cultures that can be seen in *Jhumur* songs and performances. Shekhawat explores the complexity and implications of the intermingling of *Jhumur* songs and music with popular culture and digital archiving to understand the way *Jhumur* has taken shape as a popular folk culture. For example, the *Jhumur* song "*Chol Mini Assam Jabo*," which traces the journey, life, and experiences of a worker, seems to have become a statement in popular culture, with legends like Bhupen Hazarika singing renditions of the song and Adivasi youth from the tea tribe community remixing the song and uploading it on different music streaming sites. Similarly, the song "*Axom Deshe Bagisare Sowali*," from the 1974 movie *Sameli Memsahib*, and the *Jhumur* song *Ranchi Che Bhejar Kuli*, collected by cultural activist Kali Dasgupta in the 1960s, have also been able to mark their places in the digital realm through archiving projects or by finding a place in various remixes or covers. Digital archiving gives the songs a new kind of popularity and space, as the terrain of oral traditions shifts through such a documentation process.

Adaptation of literary texts into visual and performative arts is an age-old practice, reinventing the text, broadening its horizon, at times even twisting it to alternative ideological agendas. However, when this performative culture is wedded to digital culture, literary texts morph into multivalent forms that transmute, translate, transform, or reconfigure aesthetic principles binding that text. These transformations are often reflective of transformations in performative lives of people and society instrumental in carrying these adaptations/transformations. In "Infusing Digital Media Into Theatre in Contemporary Indian Performances," Tanya Jaluthria examines the use of digital technologies in Indian theatre and their effects on theatrical performances and on audiences. The chapter has two foci: the Delhi-based digital theatre of Amitesh Grover and Abhilash Pillai, and the newly emerging form of cineplay—theatre consumable at home on the internet—introduced in India by Subodh Mascara and Nandita Das. Digital media, Jaluthria argues, not only adds visual spectacle to theatre but also makes the semantics of the form more complex, as it becomes an integral part of the narrative. Jaluthria observes that digital technology is used strategically to retain—and reinvent, to some extent—the essence of the source text, as may be seen in adaptations like Pillai's *Blindside* and Grover's *Strange Lines*, the latter based on a graphic novel. Cineplay, by blurring the boundaries between cinema and theatre, expands the reach and possibilities of Indian theatre.

## *Afterword*

In her Afterword, "Rethinking Digital Colonialisms: The Limits of Postcolonial Digital Humanities," Roopika Risam provides a critical insight on how far the terrain of digital humanities has developed in the South Asian context. From listing the impressive work being done by Bichitra: Online Tagore Variorum, Iqbal Urdu Cyber Library, and Project Rekhta in terms of straddling multiple genres and multilingual formats, these projects have served to cut across boundaries of varying aesthetic notions and sites. Risam's chapter considers the possibilities inherent in this digital humanities field with projects like Umang based in Karachi and Nitartha Digital Tibetan fostering transcultural connections and enabling language preservation. In varying ways, these projects have facilitated in countering dominant historiography to resurrect subaltern voices and histories. Focusing on the scholarship underpinned in postcolonial digital humanities, Risam's afterword raises crucial questions on home, nation, belonging, diaspora, violence against women, and uses of memory. Her chapter highlights the omissions and gaps in the present-day scholarship on Dalits and Denotified Tribes. Risam's chapter documents the way forward for digital humanities scholarship by opening it up to questions of authorization, legislation, the ideological basis of the making of any archives, and re-envisaging the methodological practices practiced in this terrain.

****

This volume gathers contemporary work by scholars engaged in addressing the issues identified by Risam. Focused on literary cultures and Digital Humanities in India—the view from the Global South; issues of archives, ethics, and praxis; the changing forms of digitalized and born-digital artefacts; and the digital atmospheres of affinity groups—the essays bring the affordances of digital technologies to the literary realms of India, understood capaciously. At the same time, the articles bring the toolkit of the humanities and literary studies to analyse digital technology itself. As such, this volume is a humble effort at complicating the assumptions of what constitutes "digitality" in the global Digital Humanities through a form of localization—engaging with challenges and exploring the possibilities that exist in this rich field.

## References

Böhme, Gernot. (1993) "Atmosphere as the Fundamental Concept of a New Aesthetics." *Thesis Eleven* 36.1: 113–26.

Burdick, Anne, Johanna Drucker, Peter Lunenfeld, Todd Presner, and Jeffrey Schnapp. (2012) *Digital_Humanities*. Cambridge, MA: MIT Press.

Dodd, Maya and Nidhi Kalra. (2020) *Exploring Digital Humanities in India: Pedagogies, Practices and Institutional Possibilities*. New Delhi. Routledge.

Hayles, N. Katherine. (2016) "Cognitive Assemblages: Technical Agency and Human Interactions." *Critical Inquiry* 43: 32–55.

Lopez, Andrew, Fred Rowland, and Kathleen Fitzpatrick. (2015) "On Scholarly Communication and the Digital Humanities: An Interview with Kathleen Fitzpatrick", *In the Library with the Lead Pipe*, 14 January. www.inthelibrarywiththeleadpipe.org/2015/on-scholarly-communication-and-the-digital-humanities-an-interview-with-kathleen-fitzpatrick/. Accessed 26 October 2021.

Nyhan, J. and Flinn, A. (2016) *Computation and the Humanities: Towards an Oral History of Digital Humanities*. New York: Springer.

Pollock, Sheldon (2003) *Literary Cultures in History: Perspectives from South Asia*. Berkeley, CA: University of California Press.

Risam, Roopika. (2018) *New Digital Worlds: Postcolonial Digital Humanities in Theory, Praxis, Pedagogy*. Illinois: Northwestern University Press.

Risam, Roopika and Kelly Baker Josephs, ed. (2021) *The Digital Black Atlantic*. Minnesota, MN: University of Minnesota Press.

Risam, Roopika and Rahul K. Gairola, ed. (2020) *South Asian Digital Humanities: Postcolonial Mediations Across Culture's Canon*. New Delhi: Routledge.

Schreibman, Susan, Ray Siemens, and John Unsworth, ed. (2004) *A Companion to Digital Humanities*. Oxford: Blackwell.

Sneha, P. P. (2021) "Mapping Digital Humanities in India." *The Centre for internet & Society*. https://cis-india.org/papers/mapping-digital-humanities-in-india. Accessed 26 October.

Spivak, Gayatri. (2003) *Death of a Discipline*. New York: Columbia University Press.

# PART I

# Digital Humanities From the Sidelines

## Theoretical Considerations

# 1

# DIGITAL CULTURES IN INDIA

## Digitality and Its Discontents

*Maya Dodd*

### Introduction: The Analogue and the Digital

The formats of culture in India span the analogue and the digital. From the vantage point of the present moment, while it may seem that today's contemporary cultures shall inevitably transform into a total digital future, the brute fact, especially true of India, is that we live in multiple time zones of history. Thus, from novels to screens (Vikram Chandra's *Sacred Games* from 2006 as, published in 2006 and then screened as a series on novel to Netflix in 2018), Twitter to historiography (Prashant Bhushan's tweets that interplay in the news cycle with the after-shocks of Ram Guha's historical chronicles), and the changed media of poetry (Urdu poetry on *Rekhta* that digitally co-exists alongside Rupi Kaur's Instagram poetry), Indian digital cultures are marked by parallel lives and occasional points of intersection. Just as the lyrics of Majrooh Sultanpuri retain enduring popularity alongside *Gully Boy* rap remixes, we have to acknowledge the twinned realities of an Indian digital culture that is simultaneously marked by both mobile phones *and* a frequent lack of electricity. To understand how much the circumstances of digital cultures differ, we must read in multilingual, multimodal, and polyvocal terms. When attending to the popular cultural texts of our current times, we are reading them not only for content but also as milestones of *how* forms shape content and subsequent meaning.

While COVID-19's aftermath will be remembered as the forced dawn of the digital for many (leaving behind an additionally disadvantaged population), as we were suddenly made to live online, it is also true that its effects have made us realize that the constraints of an industrial age and its limitations *could* be transcended—especially if there is a platform effect.[1] Just as television relayed the spectacle of sports beyond an immediate audience,[2] suddenly, all across the world, museums, zoos, and concerts—all of which had used a paying-customer model as a barrier to entry—had to re-think their funding models and audiences. This questioning

DOI: 10.4324/9781003354246-3

of why we do things the way we have—be it the carbon-expensive daily commute through tedious traffic or inflexible study schedules—was underlined by the pandemic's disruptions. Initial challenges to living digitally continue on with disruptions that re-frame human existence differently than the intended subject of industrial societies. However, the experience of being human is suddenly in clear focus. One thing has become evident: there is a new awareness of an extended ability into the digital. In a strange way, it is the digital copy of offline life that has allowed many institutions—especially educational ones—to persist through this pandemic at all.

## Living Online: Engagements and Divisions

Of course, access to digital life is still framed by issues of the digital divide, as it is this divide which fundamentally structures inequality and asymmetric baselines to access. Especially since the COVID-19 pandemic, questions raised on the digital divide have been further complicated in the Indian context, since they are linked to variances in economic, social, gendered, and historical access, and, hence, access to any kind of online life *at all*. While we might suggest that the "challenges of the digital" function not just as limitations in the present, we must also acknowledge that these realities will persist and even expand in the future. We must also recognize that, while only some in India participate in digital cultures, the number of such participants will continue to grow, in size and significance, in the fast-arriving future.[3]

Indications of this future are already alive in our present. At the time of writing, Indian social media usage is estimated at 530 million users on WhatsApp[4] (of a 2.7 billion global subscriber base). Facebook's largest userbase is similarly composed of 290 million Indians.[5] Likewise, the 17 million Indian users of Twitter's global 330 million userbase[6] have a disproportionately wide impact on their comparatively narrow slice of the platform pie.[7] Why does this matter? Without overstating the influence of social media in India, we are no doubt witnessing the dawn of a new age of communication and society with its own forms of inscription and culture. While the digital dust of the social web is plagued by questions of privacy and data sovereignty, there is also the real possibility (despite many valid reasons for scepticism) of a new public sphere of radical democracy and social engagement. And it is in this sense that digital cultures offer a new space of participatory possibility in India if the languages of participation expand to include more and more people.

Through several illustrations of digital engagement across media and education, and by describing how digital cultures are shaping up in India alongside what is yet possible, we can trace the contours of the emergence and discontents of digital cultures in India. Though questions of surveillance, tracking, and regulatory concerns seem to predominate the focus of the discontents of digitality in India, another view can also be gleaned. Especially from a Humanities perspective, viewing some sites of digital practice as efforts in *creating participatory cultures* may afford new possibilities for cultural practice and study. Aspects of open and participatory cultures instantiate digital culture's trysts with what it means to be human, especially in times of technological possibility and transformation.

## The Texts of Digital Cultures: Archival Deficits

In keeping with the legacy of cultural studies methods, the first question to ask of digital cultures is, "What is the text?" The second is "What did digitality do to it?" In scholarship, the Humanities has been flirting with the possibilities digital tools afford for textual study for some time.[8] Perhaps that focus on DH as an extension of literature has obscured attention away from this fundamental question. The digitization of several literary texts has of course afforded new insights, but several of these efforts have supported canonical authors. While many digital tools treat texts as "data" to be mined, mapped, or inter-linked, these are just some of the applications of the digital onto the textual. Although many digital tools treat texts in the same vein as "data," such methodologies of marrying the digital and the literary constitute but a few of digitization's possibilities. This chapter deviates from the idea that "data-mining" texts are the ultimate quest for humanities scholars, who already attend to both questions of text and context, whether through digital tools or otherwise.

On this point though, what is noteworthy for Indian academia is that the tools of digital humanities (or "DH/dh") are revolutionary in terms of *multilingual* textual study. So, in terms of translation, what is new is the development of recent tools—like optical character recognition (OCR)—and also a new conversation among Indian literatures across languages. Enabled by the digital, this constitutes an exciting frontier that is emerging. Additionally, the application of machine learning, natural language processing, and other computational tools holds great promise for reading texts to answer specific questions. That being said, the question of "how" DH can be gainfully applied to existent literary study needs also to be understood with the "what" of future study. That is to say, the "texts" of humanities scholarship exceed the canonical works of great authors to also include the smaller voices that animate cultural histories. Since the time of Father Bussa,[9] literary studies have been intensified through the application of digital methods. To explore how this turn will also impinge on our reading of digital cultures, I'd like to return attention to the preliminary query of "why DH" to parse this question further.

Given the hybrid realities and circumstances of Indian scholarship, one of the prominent reasons for a spotlight on the tools and techniques of DH has been related to the creation of digital archives. In the first instance, it is the idea of *greater access* that underwrites the need for DH, and the subsequent application of this access to cast a new light on cultural memory and engagement. So we see the "why" question has, as its obvious answer, one overwhelming rationale—an archival deficit. Traditionally in India, the access to online or offline libraries, databases, or catalogues has been limited. Hence, it is no surprise that this barrier to entry should find an extension in the digital world. In fact, so basic is this deficit that much isn't even made of our long-standing denial of archival access to mainstream or non-mainstream histories in India. So, the first case for digital scholarship is related to the *need for digital archives* and invoked to address this deficit first as a corrective.

## Humanities New Publics: Archival Abundances

This need for access can not only be linked to scholarly needs as a carry-over from the analogue. As mentioned earlier, the initial access rendered through digitization remains skewed in favour of the canonical. The difference here is that instead of accessing a particular edition of a Tagore text in print, I now seek access online—as has been made possible *to anyone* through the DH Jadavpur project, *Bichitra* (Jadavpur University, School of Cultural Texts and Records, n.d.).[10] However, from a greater public standpoint follows the next question: how will we decide what is "worthy" of digitization and access? Related to the analogue curatorial choices for textual study are the basic questions of who will fund these new infrastructures, and who will narrate these stories. The ecosystem in the Indian academic and/or GLAM (galleries, libraries, archives, and museum) spaces is hardly straightforward, and so any untangling of these questions must clarify not just the formalities of funding but who the *audience* itself is today.

While there is no *singular* public—especially in a nation where youth and digitality speedily intersect—given that India's population is skewed towards a young demographic (amounting to approximately a billion people under the age of 30), such numbers comprise many publics. So the goals to address these new publics must also span the distance between the concrete and the exemplary. More than the rhetorical gestures of inclusivity, it is often the contemporary *relevance* for a certain public that frames the meaning of cultural attention. As much as history is an act of translation, archival returns are invariably about our present, and in times of an attention economy, the narrator's point of view must be viewed in relief.

To draw from the example of archival choices, we can extend the questions asked in an earlier context by historian Antoinette Burton. In thinking through what was specifically recorded of Indian women's history in the archives, she names so much that can be counted but is left out. From memoirs to letters, the materials that exist outside of official archival spaces speak louder than what institutional memory lets on. The archival legacy is challenged when we turn our gaze away from the canonical to view the many forms of evidence that lie outside of institutionally sanctified spaces. With one eye on the present and one on the past, Burton writes,

> What makes a historically positivist project like History vulnerable in this context is precisely the democratization—some would say, the vulgarization—of "the archive" that has followed from the intersections of mass production, consumer culture, and postmodern modes of analysis in the post-1968 period. It is not simply a matter of oral testimony—or comic books, or pottery, or chat rooms—disrupting traditional standards of archival evidence. It is equally the problem of archival proliferation, especially in the wake of

> the new information technology: that "windless region of hyperspace" that offers new possibilities for a poetics of the archive and new frontiers.
>
> *(Burton 2003, p. 8)*

On a related note pertaining to digital archives, Renee Sentilles (2005, p. 141) quotes Roy Rosenzweig's suggestion that simply "reading around" is inadequate in the age of abundant information. He asserts that we may have to "learn to write complex searches and algorithms that would allow [historians] to sort through this overwhelming record." For the implications of this abundance on history, both Burton and Sentilles raise the question: "What are the uses of a digital archive or reconstruction of a narrative account?" If we seek digital access to written records, what is revealed by our very query? Just as Google search histories say a lot about the users who ask them, individual users, our archival queries are also accounts embedded in their own contexts—social, political, and economic. To recognize that queries are being made by many more people than traditional scholars, is to also admit that the answers lie in many spaces that historically may not even have been admitted to an academic fold.

One might argue that *cultural practices* define the scope of DH. Hence, DH in India can be decided not only by access to digital tools and resources but also by the recognition of changing cultural priorities and transitions underway—regardless of whether or not we are able to detect these changes in the making. By revisiting where DH has already been—qua computation and literary studies—we can perhaps chart its future course into digital cultures.

Before we may attempt to sketch the contours framing the theoretical considerations that bear on the study of digital cultures in India, we must consider that such acts of translation require attention to an older issue—that of who shall translate, from which source, and to which destination?

## The Allegory of the Digital: A New Textuality

Beyond the idea of the digital as technical, or a solution to a problem, lies the reality of its alchemy. The transition to digital has obviously exacerbated the idea of the divide but the fact is that those with *and without* access have been changed by this "technical" transformation. The point of this now is to study what the digital "does" in cultural terms. Apart from the stellar work done on infrastructures, publics, and platforms by Aswin Punathambekar and Sriram Mohan[11] is the question of a thick description of digital cultures in India, not only from a transnational or diasporic standpoint but also from a local one. To gain a view of this alchemy is to change the perspective of "nation" as an anchoring device. This requires a view extending beyond that of tools and techniques (of what we think of as a DH methodology) to an added attention on cultures birthed and alchemized by the digital. Akin to the ways in which we are trained to read the "literariness" of texts, we now also need to lay focus on the "digitality" of culture. That being said, the digital is not only a rupture with the past but also a mutation which bridges the past and the future.

So, is that focus then on the question of medium, form, messaging, re-mediation, or audience, or all of these together? Is it a question of representation in the digital or the very construction of that representation? Just as literary studies encompass author studies, genre studies, historical studies, and theoretical considerations, the study of digital cultures too entails all aspects named here. Significantly though, these analyses would need to rupture the inherited views of how we study representation in at least two ways in the Indian context: one, in terms of *what* and *how* we close and distant read, and two, in our understanding of representation as allegory. A brief description on the question of allegory follows as this is also about an attention beyond metaphor to the literal questions of who is reading, and from which location.

If the argument was made that the novel in English in India is an allegorical representation of the nation (since Homi K. Bhabha's *Nation and Narration* in 1990 to Aijaz Ahmad's debates with Frederic Jameson, etc.[12]), then the digital clearly cannot be understood in those terms. Not only is the digital not an allegorical form (as a computational site it is, if anything, often very literal), offering a new arena of sociality, but also it is actually a site of public anxiety about incompleteness. In constantly being made and re-made, if the internet is itself a text to be read, then the WhatsApp forwards, Twitter injunctions, and Facebook families are all characters deserving of our collective attention. Even as a temporal contradiction, the differentiation of "online" and "offline," as distinct from each other or as incompatible, hardly even comes close to describing the ground realities of digital access in India. The co-ordinates of digital India have to acknowledge the intersecting paths of the analogue and the digital.

To understand this differently, perhaps we need to return to the site of the computational turn in literary studies. Though Franco Moretti's groundbreaking work, *Atlas of the European Novel* (1998), shifted the field of literary studies in terms of what we read, it was the fixation of literary studies itself that had assumed that the exalted text was always literary. The efforts of postcolonial literary scholars had often been added to the existent canon, as we had seldom questioned why we read what we read. The challenge to the history of what had been placed in the canon was abetted by cultural studies, of course, but also by the push that exposed the arbitrariness of canonical choice. In an interview, Moretti narrates the accidental trajectory of how this came to be in the American academy. In 2005, Moretti published *Graphs, Maps and Trees*, a work which emanated out of experiments at Stanford. The master distant-reader, Franco Moretti, best contests the assumption that literary and computational modalities have distinct stop and start points when he states in the interview that, in the

> 2000s there was interest in these new digital techniques, but not great interest. First graduate seminar that Matthew Jockers and I offered in 2004, it was called "Electronic Data and Literary Theory," had one student. But we insisted and insisted and insisted. And then one day in 2010 I told Matt, "Look, let's take a piece of paper, write "Stanford Literary Lab" on it, put

> it on a door and let's see if this changes things." I went to the chair of the English department, said, "Can we have that room that is always empty?" We were given the room, I printed the paper and we put it there with Scotch tape. . . . One thing that happened was that we found the way for graduate students to count their work at the lab for some credit. Then the Lab received the money from the university for its first two years. It was exactly 20,000 dollars for two years, since we have to buy computers, screens and everything was really nothing. But beside that we did not need a lot of money. What we needed, and this is something we got, was some free time. It is something we need much more than money. Some free time to think, to read, to study, to talk (Hackler and Kirsten 2016).

I cite this chronology of events to draw attention to the fact that, though the resources invested in the digital querying of literature were limited, what was even more essential was the provision of *intellectual* space that allowed for an imagination of questions of technical application. Hardly ten years ago, even in a university nestled in and beloved by Silicon Valley, the interest in computational humanities was miniscule and almost akin to a quirk or hobby. And yet Moretti's achievements were appreciated even by living writers. To quote renowned novelist, Jonathan Franzen,

> to use new technology to look at literature as a whole, which has never really been done before, rather than focusing on complex and singular works, is a good direction for cultural criticism to move in. Paradoxically, it may even liberate the canonical works to be read more in the spirit in which they were written (Schantz 2013).

The idea of uniting the Humanities and computational tools, despite a long history of possibility, had just never received the treatment of first principles thinking.

In the decade since these utterances, the scope of "digital humanities" has moved far beyond the realm of electronic textuality. With what the 2006 *Time* magazine Person of the Year ("You," representing individual content creators on the World Wide Web) foretold, the scale of the digital has only increased. The entanglements of the digital far exceed their utility for only literary studies, as the changed venues of participation are witness to a proliferation of expressions. After all, we now live in an era wherein India is the leading country in the world for Facebook audience size. All told, we are in desperate need of an update to fully assess the meaning and new textuality of these rapid and irrevocable changes.

## Considerations for Digital Futures: Scholarly Engagements

Not only has digital humanities changed the way in which we query textuality and meaning, but it has also pushed into focus multiple new cultural texts that displace the idea of an exalted "literary" text. What has effectively happened since is that the ideas of authorship, translation, and audience have also advanced. We are seeing this manifest in cultures around streaming, mobile-first technologies, and increased social media manipulation.

To examine what is made possible by thinking through these digital forms in context, several descriptions of Digital Humanities as they exist in India raise attention to emergent cultures in a wider frame.[13] The recent story of DH from large archival works to more public facing efforts involved the curation not just of "heritage" projects but also the fact that these applications underlie a new approach to Cultural Studies in India. To now cleave open space for a focus on the work that remains to be done requires a real spotlight on future tasks which in turn require significant collective efforts and a concomitant focus on these emergent forms.

Alongside the lenses of several disciplines, whose quantitative analytical method DH has adopted, there are several questions of qualitative humanistic interest. To take a broad view of what is possible through these new modalities, I offer a short list by way of suggestion (by no means comprehensive) of what could be examined in constituting changes in the public sphere brought on by the impact of the digital:

1. Public history: cultural heritage, societal engagement, and pedagogy[14]
2. Textual and film scholarship: book history, textual study, and digital corpora[15]
3. Digital adaptations in music, film, theatre, and media and visual studies[16]
4. The gamut of digital rights and activism, hate culture, hacktivism, free speech, and net neutrality
5. Ethical challenges around the medium of the digital: privacy, data protection, digital surveillance, cyberbullying, data justice, and issues in digital governance[17]
6. New cultural forms: electronic literature, digital arts, digital identities, spatial humanities, gaming cultures, re-mix culture, FOSS, and open culture[18]

Through the transitions effected by large curatorial interventions and digitalization, a new area of study has emerged—one which encompasses digital fields as cultural symptoms and requires further scholarly attention. The access desired by models of public humanities, as content, intersects with these new forms. The intersection also determines the always-emergent nature of this field. Since uniquely Indian challenges also pertain to public access, *this historical moment also offers unparalleled opportunity*. The diversity of India's digital cultures, alongside the fact that public access can directly address these formats, is only an initial scholarly capture of the disruption of the digital alongside attempts to bridge social divisions. With the wide array of practices that conventional categories would discreetly view as activism, identity politics, public history, oral history, etc. cultural interventions that all fall under the umbrella term DH/dh show the possibilities that lie ahead for what questions are made visible in this burgeoning field. A survey of DH in India began with Puthiya Purayil Sneha's monograph published online (Puthiya Purayil 2016) by the Centre for Internet and Society, which queried the identification of what could be rightfully called "DH" work. Today, the questions that concern us far exceed debates on definition. What now requires deep thought is a priority sequence of how we shall think through and with change, as the digital landscape rapidly accelerates and transforms public cultures.

Posing the challenges of the digital as a function of presentist limitations is to miss the point entirely. At the end of the day, what becomes DH/dh in India will be decided by the capacity of its practitioners. Akin to the historic problem of limited translators across Indian languages,[19] we need to prepare for the challenge of how digital thinking will be apprehended both culturally and in scholarship.

To start off, we need to see how the "maker culture" (Ray Murray and Hand 2015) of DH is a key to decolonizing the Humanities in India and part of these practices, in part, stem from adapting emerging digital cultures developing in India to wider uses. The digitalization of scholarly and expressive practices in India—from Project Madurai to TikTok[20]—constitutes a public sphere of a new kind. It is for this reason that digital cultures span varied initiatives around efforts to expand public access as constituting experiments in the Indian narrative of DH. These instances include public experiments with digital engagement, pedagogical adaptations in the aftermath of the pandemic's disruptions, and, most significantly, the language possibilities of digital media for education and expression.

## Multilingual Digital Cultures: Streaming and Tweeting

To understand how digital cultures in India are shaped by the language question, we have to attend to what affordances businesses are also creating for Indian consumers. In January 2021, when Jeo Baby, the director of *The Great Indian Kitchen*, prepared for the film's release on the Malayalam platform, Neestream, he could hardly have imagined what a landmark event this would be for OTT[21] in India. With a nation still recovering from the hard lockdown experience of the pandemic, the drudgery of the kitchen captured in the film hit a nerve for audiences far beyond the Malayalam speaking world. This was a film that had been rejected by Amazon Prime, Netflix, and several regional channels, turning out to be a sleeper hit of digital media.[22] To not view this "hit" film as a one-off is to attend seriously to the question of language in India. Digital media is re-constituting the idea of audiences by unleashing immense trans-cultural possibilities.

Since the pandemic, OTT has boomed across rural and urban areas in India—a direct result of greater internet access nationwide.[23] It is estimated that nine out of ten users are expected to use Indian languages by the end of 2021 to reach 53 crore users (at an annual growth rate of 18%) compared to the growth of English users (at a 3% rate) which would reach approximately 20 crore persons. All these would make India the sixth largest OTT market in the world by 2024.[24]

While the demographic majority of Hindi speakers tend to crowd the attention of Indian media, the highest internet adoption levels in India come from Tamil speakers.[25] Exactly for this reason, the growth expected from languages besides Hindi and English heralds a tsunami of change for the digital public sphere in India. According to Vishnu Mohta, the co-founder of the Bengali OTT platform,

Hoichoi, a majority of users in the non-metro markets consume internet content in their local/native languages. According to Mohta, "A single-language-focused platform allows the aggregation of different kinds of content within the same language." Hoichoi, with a subscriber base of almost 13 million people, has itself made 75 original shows, and hosts over 650 films spanning more than 60 decades of Bengali cinema. Its parent company is a legacy media house, and it is owned by SVF Entertainment. SVF is the largest production company in East India and is now in its 25th year of operations—having made 160 movies and 10,000 hours of television content.[26]

Interestingly, while Hoichoi was launched in 2017, it is rapidly catching up to its parent company in terms of its subscription base. Today, Hoichoi has a fast-growing userbase of more than 13 million plus subscribers. In comparison, Aha, the Telugu-streaming platform launched on the Google Play Store in March 2020, saw five million app downloads in one year alone. Planet Marathi, launched in May 2017 as an aggregator platform for existing digital entertainment, is now looking at launching Planet Marathi to showcase its own original Marathi-language programming. Aiming to launch in May 2021 with 15 new web series and a ready library of 200 Marathi films, Planet Marathi's goal is to garner subscribers from the 200-million-strong Marathi-speaking population. As a study in contrasts, Pallav Parikh, the co-founder of CityShor.TV, an OTT-streaming platform launched in November 2020, estimates that only 40% of the Gujarati-speaking population in the country accesses digital-streaming platforms. Nevertheless, Parikh's plan for CityShor.TV is also to reach a target audience of 200 million plus Gujarati speakers.

The sheer scale of subscriptions these platforms imagine capturing portends entire language worlds within their ambits. Additionally, language dubbing also takes place, such as when the Telugu OTT platform, Aha, dubbed into Telugu, various Tamil and Malayalam films—including Jallikattu, which was selected as India's official entry to the 2021 Oscars. This realization, of leveraging the power of language, is now recognized by international investors in India also.[27] The fact that digital media are so easily accessed across languages with subtitling and dubbing options that OTT platforms offer is a game changer in imagining audiences for digital content.

In addition to streaming, which constitutes a fundamental shift in how media is produced and consumed, is the radical transformation effected by social media for opinion formation, fact-checking, and the very creation of news.[28] For reasons akin to the American migration to social media platform Parler, the swadeshi reasons to adapt India's answer to Twitter, Koo, come from a vantage point of language. The creators of Vokal, described by the founders as "Quora with audio," weren't unique in the idea of crowdsourcing expertise for answers, but for the fact that they could do it across 11 Indian languages. Though Vokal has yet to turn a profit, the bet is hedged on the future importance of moderation and curation from within a language's strength. Koo, which was launched in March 2020 as India's local language microblogging platform[29] (and crossed four million users within weeks of its launch prompting speculation about the profile of its users) is currently available in eight languages and aspires to include 22 more, with plans to eventually include Sanskrit and Urdu, among others languages.[30]

Koo is currently dominated by Hindi speakers as per a recent study,[31] which calls it a "nationalist Twitter." However, the jury is out on whether Koo signals a proliferation of different breakaways across languages. Not surprisingly, this prompted *WhatsApp* CEO Will Cathcart to say,

> A lot of the decisions we're going to make on the internet, our governments are going to make on the internet over the next 10–20 years, I think will really shape whether this is a global market, or whether each country has its own *mini*-internet with its own mini-apps. And I think the latter would be worse.

Whether Cathcart's prophecy holds true for the fortunes of WhatsApp or the rest of the world remains to be seen, but there is no doubt that what he calls the "splinternet" is most certainly aided by the language fragmentation of what Google calls "the next billion users" will cause. With such trends in play, across films, news, blogging, opinion formation, and sports, there is no doubt the language question will dominate the shape and form of digital cultures in the future.[32]

## The "Splinternet:" Decolonizing Education

Perhaps education is one sphere that will especially be benefitted by the "splinternet." Given that 2020 will be remembered not only for COVID-19 but also in India for the National Education Policy 2020, the move towards digital might also find another rationale in the move towards decolonizing education. Given that higher education in India is almost exclusively conducted in English at the post-college level, this move could radically change the access story for many college aspirants in India. In the spirit of decolonizing our epistemologies alongside our choice of texts, it is important to stress the urgency of building new infrastructures. As yet, even as many of these interventions may seem small and local, in time, the turn to multiple sites for remembering our histories and telling our stories will only fortify the substantiveness of a digital public sphere.[33]

While the digital divide[34] was all-too-real during the pandemic, questions of digital learning exceed the contours of COVID-19's shadow, and higher education does face unique challenges for digital delivery. What we think of as online learning has been in existence for almost a decade with the rise of Coursera, Edx, SWAYAM, and many other public and private platforms that premised the learning experience on a totally virtual experience, much differently than what we practice in brick and mortar classrooms. But in the realm of digital learning, we are severely challenged by the limited understanding of learning as the *delivery of content*. Again, here it is important to mention that the offline classroom experience which preceded the COVID pandemic was itself in need of urgent repair.

So to first take on the challenge of format—if MOOCS and other certifications can essentially enable the equivalent of delivering a college degree—why go to college at all? Coursera offers over 3,000 courses, Edx around the same, and Future Learning is approaching the 1,000 mark. With so much choice already available, it is now apparent to those who lived through schooling in lockdown that "presence" needs to be distinguished from engagement. For genuine participation, the barriers of language must be braced. It is heartening to note that online courses offered on the government platforms, SWAYAM and NPTEL, got a boost during the pandemic's emergency and are being translated into eight Indian languages.[35] While this is far from enough, it is a huge step to breaking the English barrier that has served as a ceiling to regional aspirations. Additionally, the hallowed disciplines of engineering (mechanical, civil, electrical engineering, etc.) will be offered across eight regional languages (Bengali, Gujarati, Hindi, Kannada, Malayalam, Marathi, Tamil, and Telugu) at select sites starting in 2021.[36] What this augurs for the future of college in India is revolutionary, as the creation of these materials online and otherwise allows for new audiences and new spheres of legitimacy for the giant demographic of youth aspiration.

## The Next Billion Tongues

The point about the limits of officially admissible languages is one that oral historians have especially noted. As of now, the fact is that the impact of the digital is accelerating in all spheres in India. From the classroom to the museum, public humanities work has a lot to gain from its digital encounters. What Google has dubbed India's "next billion users"[37] leaves no doubt that the changing nature of the digital will be accompanied by a sea change in languages used on the internet and in maker cultures driven by digital users. If the digital is thought to be an inevitability, it also needs to be understood as possessing potential for social change beyond the familiar cultural registers of currently dominant languages.

The practices of knowledge in a digital world need to evolve to answer the questions of how we create our ways of knowing. The development of decolonial thinking needs a real decolonization of how we will know, and the digital offers this as a unique possibility to enhance access for use and for re-creation. Many other complications with AI/ML, etc. might also mark this future, as, when we query digital cultures, we might not even know the difference between human and machinic creations. When we can replicate and simulate archival data, what will be the locus of authority that underwrites the trust of the "authenticity" of what we find? Already we exist in a complicated knowledge economy, wherein the fundamental questions are being asked about the purpose of our reasoning. Given the rise of predatory journals and an unfair playing field that is focused on metrics as impact—who are the "legitimate" users of scholarship, when new audiences are in play? In the future, we may well see machines reading our digital debris; and then, the focus once again will return to that space of humanistic expertise: interpretation.

Posing the challenges and opportunities of the digital as a function of what we know today is hardly the way forward. Towards contouring what such a field could entail, there is a special potential for the study of new communities that emerge with their own forms of inscription. Just witnessing the growth of community archives in India, a view emerges of the amazing work that has already begun under the aegis of Bhasha Institute,[38] Janastu,[39] Keystone Foundation, Srishti Centre for Public History,[40] QAMRA,[41] and more. On the lines of the Keystone Foundation[42] (1993), the Green Hub Fellowship[43] (2003), and the work of many at the Ambedkar University Centre for Community Knowledge[44] (2012), the digital creation of spaces for self-narration affords self-definitions we have not yet seen in the offline commons.

In the realm of the digital, we are afforded the possibility to conceive of communities whose voices we have yet to hear. Digital cultures need interpretation just as much as the printed texts of yesterday. To study the emergent topographies of digital cultures, much beyond the social web, is to listen to the murmurings of an expanded public sphere. The task that now awaits us is to create a more responsive scholarship for an expanded Indian digital public sphere, across languages and registers.

## Notes

1 For more on what constitutes a platform effect see Lohr, Steve (2011). "*The Power of the Platform at Apple*" [Online]. Available at www.nytimes.com/2011/01/30/business/30unbox.html (Accessed: September 30, 2021).

2 This has a long global history ranging from the first broadcast of the 1939 Summer Olympic in Berlin to the arrival of colour television in India coinciding with the 1982 Asian games from Delhi.

3 The numbers are dynamic and a recent report pegs usage across platforms to keep increasing. See Singh, Manish. (2021). TechCruch [Online]. Available at: https://techcrunch.com/2021/01/11/youtube-and-whatsapp-inch-closer-to-half-a-billion-users-in-india/ (Accessed September 30, 2021). As of August 2021, it is estimated there are 680 active internet users in India at www.statista.com/statistics/1232311/india-number-of-social-media-users-by-platform/ (Accessed September 30, 2021).

4 "Leading countries based on number of WhatsApp users". Statista [Online]. Available at: www.statista.com/statistics/1232311/india-number-of-social-media-users-by-platform/ (Accessed September 30, 2021). As per this statistic noted in February 2021, India is the leading country in terms of WhatsApp usage.

5 Leading countries based on number of Facebook users. Statista (2021) [Online]. Available at: www.statista.com/statistics/268136/top-15-countries-based-on-number-of-facebook-users/#:~:text=There%20are%20over%20290%20million,terms%20of%20largest%20population%20worldwide (Accessed September 30, 2021). Again, see www.statista.com/statistics/304827/number-of-facebook-users-in-india/ to note that India is the largest country as per Facebook subscribers. For more, see (Chakravarti 2021).

6 "Number of social media users across India as of February 2021, by platform". Statista [Online]. Available: www.statista.com/statistics/1232311/india-number-of-social-media-users-by-platform/ (Accessed September 30, 2021). For more, see (Jangid 2021).

7 These numbers keep growing too, especially through the pandemic. See www.indiatvnews.com/technology/news-here-s-how-many-facebook-instagram-twitter-users-are-there-worldwide-673451(Accessed September 30, 2021).

8 See the A1 Around Global DH living document for references from virtually all regions of the world at https://docs.google.com/spreadsheets/d/1_PNv9Jlw_QlUh6SeYJrGYFucoRzlZAfLf7OouWu-qe4/edit#gid=9

9 For a brief history of early Humanities computing, see www.forbes.com/sites/robertobonzio/2011/08/11/father-busa-pioneer-of-computing-in-humanities-dies-at-98/?sh=2df6d28445cc (Bonzio 2011).

10 For more on this, see www.youtube.com/watch?v=GRNT9pf-sWA and refer to the chapter on "The Bengali Writing System: Fonts and OCR" DOI:10.1007/978–3–319–23678–0_3 in Chaudhuri, Sukanta. (2015).Bichitra: The Making of an Online Tagore Variorum. Springer International (pp. 13–20).

11 Punathambekar, A. and Mohan, S. (2019). *Global Digital Cultures*. Ann Arbor: University of Michigan Press.

12 "The nation fills the void left in the uprooting of communities and kin, and turns that loss into the language of metaphor," writes Bhabha (1990, p. 139). Bhabha, H (1987) in *Nation and Narration*, Ed., London: Routledge, 1990. Also, see Ahmad, Aijaz (1987), "Jameson's Rhetoric of Otherness" and the "National Allegory." Social Text 17 to constitute the longer context of this argument.

13 Many are described in my earlier work, *Exploring Digital Humanities in India* (Dodd and Kalra 2020).

14 Sites like www.livehistoryindia.com/, www.notesonindianhistory.com/ and www.sahapedia.org/ to name a few in addition to Instagram handles such as www.instagram.com/project.dastaan or www.instagram.com/theurduproject/ (Anon 2019, 2021a; Project Dastaan n.d.; Sahapedia 2018; The Urdu Project n.d.)

15 Some include www.rarebooksocietyofindia.org/ (Rare Book Society of India n.d.) that, as the title suggests, features downloadable editions of rarer finds and other publicly open sites like https://rmrl.in/ (RMRL 2021) and https://pad.ma (Anon 2021b)

16 For an initial directory see www.indianmemoryproject.com/archivedirectory/ (The Memory Company 2019)

17 For several topical pieces, https://cis-india.org/ (The Centre for Internet and Society 2021) and www.medianama.com/ make useful starting points.

18 See the work of Deshbandhu, Aditya (2020) and Ray Murray, Padmini (2014) and the output of organisations such as https://oleomingus.com/ and https://fieldsofview.in/

19 As Arunava Sinha points out,

> this disparity in Indian languages that are translated may have less to do with hierarchical notions of the language and more with a lack of translators from many of these languages. One of the reasons that Bangla and Malayalam have so many translations is because of the abundance of skilled, well-established translators.
>
> *John, Rachel (2021)*

20 It is important to note that TikTok has been banned in India since June 2020.

21 For more information on over-the-top media services in India, see www.financialexpress.com/brandwagon/2020-rise-of-paid-subscribers/2172942/ (Accessed March 2, 2021).

22 For more see www.republicworld.com/entertainment-news/regional-indian-cinema/where-to-watch-the-great-indian-kitchen-heres-how-to-stream-jeo-directorial-online.html (Accessed March 2, 2021) (Arpa 2021).

23 To read more on this see www.warc.com/newsandopinion/news/internet-usage-in-rural-india-overtakes-urban-areas/43588 (Accessed March 2, 2021).

24 See more in the KPMG report (2021) [online] https://assets.kpmg/content/dam/kpmg/in/pdf/2017/04/Indian-languages-Defining-Indias-Internet.pdf (Accessed March 2, 2021).

25 Ibid.

26 See www.forbesindia.com/article/take-one-big-story-of-the-day/can-singlelanguage-ott-platforms-take-on-the-streaming-giants-in-india/66521/1 Accessed March 2, 2021 (Shekhar 2021).

27 Despite launching in India in 2016, Netflix took 4 years to launch its Hindia user interface. In a similar move, Spotify will be introducing 12 new languages for its app in India, while its competitors JioSaavan, Prime Music, YouTube Music and Apple Music are yet to integrate Indian languages in their products while Gaana has Kannada, Malayalam, Marathi and Bhojpuri etc. amounting to accessibility in 9 Indian languages currently and unsurprisingly dominates the Indian market. See more at https://inc42.com/buzz/spotify-tunes-into-hindi-regional-languages-to-celebrate-two-years-in-india/ (Accessed March 29 2021) (Mixed Bag Media Pvt. Ltd. 2021; Naik 2021).

28 A separate chapter would need to be devoted to shifts in this domain but citizen news and user generated content across regions has created radical transformation in content. Efforts like *khabarlahariya*, a newspaper founded by rural women in 2002 as a print based news service published in dialects of Hindi like Bundeli, Avadhi etc. have also gone digital and populate social media platforms too.

29 Koo lets you follow people, read updates in a reverse-chronological feed, add and track hashtags, post a "Koo" in up to 350 characters, attach media, and respond to and like other people's Koos. It also has features unavailable on Twitter, which are tailored to the Indian market and let people filter out content by their chosen language. See more at: www.businessinsider.in/tech/news/koo-the-free-expression-social-media-app-is-the-indian-governments-latest-weapon-in-its-standoff-with-twitter/articleshow/81278680.cms (Accessed March 29, 2021) (Agarwal 2021; Alawadhi 2021; Chaturvedi 2021).

30 See at https://economictimes.indiatimes.com/tech/startups/koo-to-foray-into-22-indian-languages-this-year/articleshow/81657864.cms (Accessed March 29 2021).

31 Another study conducted by University of Michigan's Arshia Arya, Dibyendu Mishra, Joyojeet Pal in February, called "Koo and the attempt to create a 'nationalist Twitter,'" had examined the political and network effects of the new platform contradicting claims made in www.business-standard.com/article/technology/koo-has-a-stronger-network-than-bigger-rival-twitter-says-study-121032600745_1.html (Accessed March 29, 2021).

32 It is worth noting that the subscription bases for other digital services are also growing across languages. In sports for instance, fantasy sports boasts over 100 million users despite a ban by seven states who consider this activity akin to gambling. See https://get.dream11.help/hc/en-us/articles/360021580291-Can-residents-of-Andhra-Pradesh-Assam-Odisha-Telangana-Tamil-Nadu-Nagaland-and-Sikkim-participate-in-paid-contests-of-Dream11- (Accessed March 29 2021).

33 Already the language question has been high on the agenda of Tribal Welfare Departments, such as this case in Telangana. With about 13 recognised tribal communities, languages including Gondi (already on the UNESCO endangered language list), Koya, Kolami, Kondh and Banjara are seeing their speakers dwindle. have been dwindling. According to the state Ministry of Tribal Affairs, plans are on to introduce a digital database of the tribal languages, which includes literature in audio form. See at www.thenewsminute.com/article/telanganas-tribal-languages-face-risk-extinction-how-they-can-be-preserved-153432 (Accessed October 20, 2021).

34 See Sharma, Samrat. (2020). "*Modi's Digital India.*" [online]. Available at: www.financialexpress.com/economy/modis-digital-india-still-a-far-fetched-dream-for-hinterland-not-even-30-of-rural-india-has-internet/2085452/ (Accessed October 20, 2021).

35 For more see, See Anand, Abhay. (2020). https://news.careers360.com/aicte-translate-swayam-nptel-courses-online-indian-languages (Accessed March 29, 2021).

36 As a point of reference, it is observed that till 2021, the most prestigious entrance exam for engineering school, the IIT-JEE was only offered in English, Hindi and Gujarati. As

per an earlier report, a survey on 83,000 students indicated their willingness to opt for instruction in one's mother tongue and that was nearly 44%. As per this article, around 15–20 per cent students in IITs have also shown willingness to pursue engineering in their mother tongue. See details at https://theprint.in/india/education/how-colleges-will-offer-engineering-in-languages-such-as-tamil-telugu-gujarati-from-2021/623083/ (Accessed March 29, 2021) (Sharma 2021).

37 Cesar Sengupta began leading the Next Billion Users initiative to bring in new users around the world. Between 2015 and 2020, more than 1.5 billion people began using the internet for the first time. Another billion more are set to join them online by 2025, Sengupta wrote in a blogpost. See at https://nz.finance.yahoo.com/news/google-next-billion-users-head-045825967.html (Accessed March 2, 2021) (Choudhury and Lee 2021).

38 www.bhasharesearch.org/introduction.html

39 https://janastu.org/

40 www.srishtimanipalinstitute.in/centers-and-labs/center-for-public-history

41 https://qamra.in/

42 Keystone believes in "small is effective/small is global" and hence, is focused on the Nilgiri Biosphere Reserve, where it is currently working in 135 tribal habitations with an estimated number of 15000 individuals https://keystone-foundation.org/networks/ (Accessed March 2, 2021) (Keystone Foundation 2021).

43 By leveraging the medium of videography and filmmaking through the Green Hub Fellowship, Rita Banerji is training and empowering young people from remote geographies of the North East Region (NER) to take charge of their development narrative. Belonging to underserved and marginalized tribes and communities, these young people are being trained as the next generation of change agents. By critically engaging with the dominant, exploitative development practices in the NER, the Green Hub Fellows are building a movement towards creating ecological security anchored in a sustainable economies and livelihoods approach. (from www.ashoka.org/en-in/fellow/rita-banerji) (Accessed March 2, 2021).

44 https://aud.ac.in/centre-for-community-knowledge

## References

A1 Around Global DH (Digital Humanities) (2019) Global list [Online]. *Google Sheets*. Available at: https://docs.google.com/spreadsheets/d/1_PNv9Jlw_QlUh6SeYJrGYFu-coRzlZAfLf7OouWu-qe4/edit#gid=9 (Accessed: 2 March 2021)

Agarwal, Shubham. (2021) Koo, the 'free expression' social media app, is the Indian government's latest weapon in its standoff with Twitter [Online]. *Business Insider India*. Available at: www.businessinsider.in/tech/news/koo-the-free-expression-social-media-app-is-the-indian-governments-latest-weapon-in-its-standoff-with-twitter/articleshow/81278680.cms (Accessed: 29 March 2021)

Ahmad, Aijaz. (1987) "Jameson's Rhetoric of Otherness and the 'National Allegory'." *Social Text* 17: 3–25.

Alawadhi, Neha. (2021) Koo has a 'stronger network' than its bigger rival Twitter, says study [Online]. *Business Standard*. Available at: www.business-standard.com/article/technology/koo-has-a-stronger-network-than-bigger-rival-twitter-says-study-121032600745_1.html (Accessed: 29 March 2021)

Anand, Abhay. (2020) AICTE to translate SWAYAM, NPTEL courses online into Indian languages. [Online]. *Career360*. Available at: https://news.careers360.com/aicte-translate-swayam-nptel-courses-online-indian-languages (Accessed: 29 March 2021)

Anon. (2019) Live History India [Online]. Available at: www.livehistoryindia.com/ (Accessed: 2 March 2021).

Anon. (2021a) Notes on Indian history [Online]. Available at: www.notesonindianhistory.com/ (Accessed: 2 March 2021).

Anon. (2021b) Public access digital media archive [Online]. Available at: https://pad.ma (Accessed: 2 March 2021).

Arpa, C. (2021) Where to watch 'The Great Indian Kitchen'? Here's how to stream Jeo directorial online [Online]. *Republic World*. Available at: www.republicworld.com/entertainment-news/regional-indian-cinema/where-to-watch-the-great-indian-kitchen-heres-how-to-stream-jeo-directorial-online.html (Accessed: 2 March 2021).

Bhabha, Homi. (1990) *Nation and Narration*. 2nd edn. London: Routledge.

Bonzio, R. (2011) Father Busa, pioneer of computing in humanities with Index Thomisticus, dies at 98 [Online]. *Forbes*. Available at: www.forbes.com/sites/robertobonzio/2011/08/11/father-busa-pioneer-of-computing-in-humanities-dies-at-98/?sh=6860fbd3445c (Accessed: 12 March 2021).

Burton, A. (2003) *Dwelling in the Archive*. New York: Oxford University Press.

Chakravarti, A. (2021) Government reveals stats on social media users, WhatsApp leads which YouTube beats Facebook, Instagram [Online]. *India Today*. Available at: www.indiatoday.in/technology/news/story/government-reveals-stats-on-social-media-users-whatsapp-leads-while-youtube-beats-facebook-instagram-1773021-2021-02-25 (Accessed: 2 March 2021).

Chaturvedi, A. (2021) Koo to foray into 22 Indian languages this year [Online]. *The Economic Times*. Available at: https://economictimes.indiatimes.com/tech/startups/koo-to-foray-into-22-indian-languages-this-year/articleshow/81657864.cms (Accessed: 29 March 2021).

Choudhury, A and Lee, Y. (2021) Google's next billion users head Sengupta to leave in April [Online]. Available at: https://nz.finance.yahoo.com/news/google-next-billion-users-head-045825967.html (Accessed: 29 March 2021).

Dodd, M and Kalra, N. (2020) *Exploring Digital Humanities in India*. New Delhi: Routledge.

Hackler, R and Guido, K. (2016) "Distant Reading, Computational Criticism, and Social Critique: An Interview with Franco Moretti." *Le Foucaldien* 2(1): 7. Available at: http://doi.org/10.16995/lefou.22

Jadavpur University, School of Cultural Texts and Records. (n.d.). The Bichitra Project [Online]. *Bichitra*. Available at: http://bichitra.jdvu.ac.in/about_bichitra_project.php (Accessed: 29 March 2021).

Jangid, K. (2021) "1.75 crore vs 6.6 crore: It's math hour over PM Modi's followers as minister reveals number of Twitter users in India [Online]." *The Free Press Journal*. Available at: www.freepressjournal.in/viral/175-crore-vs-66-crore-its-math-hour-over-pm-modis-followers-as-minister-reveals-number-of-twitter-users-in-india (Accessed: 2 March 2021).

John, R. (2021) The real crisis in Indian literature is the translation pyramid. Bangla sits at the top [Online]. *The Print*. Available at: https://theprint.in/opinion/the-real-crisis-in-indian-literature-is-the-translation-pyramid-bangla-sits-at-the-top/625198/ (Accessed: 2 March 2021).

Keystone Foundation. (2021) Networks—coming together for change [Online]. Available at: https://keystone-foundation.org/networks/ (Accessed: 2 March 2021).

KPMG India and Google. (2017) Indian languages: Defining India's internet [Online]. Available at: https://assets.kpmg/content/dam/kpmg/in/pdf/2017/04/Indian-languages-Defining-Indias-Internet.pdf

Lohr, S. (2011) The power of the platform at Apple [Online]. *New York Times*. Available at: www.nytimes.com/2011/01/30/business/30unbox.html (Accessed: 2 March 2021).

Mixed Bag Media Pvt. Ltd. (2021) Medianama [Online]. Available at: www.medianama.com/ (Accessed: 2 March 2021).

Naik, A. R. (2021) Spotify tunes into Hindi, regional languages to celebrate two years in India. [Online]. *Inc 42*. Available at: https://inc42.com/buzz/spotify-tunes-into-hindi-regional-languages-to-celebrate-two-years-in-india/ (Accessed: 2 March 2021).

Project Dastaan. (@project.dastaan) [Instagram]. (n.d.). Available at: www.instagram.com/project.dastaan/ (Accessed: 30 March 2021).

Punathambekar, A and Mohan, S. (2019) *Global Digital Cultures*. Ann Arbor, MI: Michigan Publishing, University of Michigan Press [Online]. Available at: https://doi.org/10.3998/mpub.9561751

Puthiya Purayil, Sneha. (2016) *Mapping Digital Humanities in India* [online]. Available at https://cis-india.org/papers/mapping-digital-humanities-in-india (Accessed: October 20, 2021).

Rare Book Society of India. (n.d.). Rare book society of India. [Online]. Available at: www.rarebooksocietyofindia.org/ (Accessed: 2 March 2021).

Ray Murray, P and Hand, C. (2015) "Making Culture: Locating the Digital Humanities in India." [Online]. *Journal of Visual Communication Research* 49(3): 140–155.

RMRL. (2021) Roja Muthiah research library [Online]. Available at: https://rmrl.in/ (Accessed: 2 March 2021).

Sahapedia. (2018) Sahapedia. [Online]. Available at: www.sahapedia.org/ (Accessed: 2 March 2021).

Schantz, M. (2013) Franco Moretti, "Post-Bourgeois Critic [Online]." *Verso*. Available at: www.versobooks.com/blogs/1353-franco-moretti-post-bourgeois-critic (Accessed: 12 March 2021).

Sentilles, R. (2005) "Toiling in the Archives of Cyberspace" in Buton, A. Ed. *Archive Stories*. Available at: https://doi.org/10.1215/9780822387046-007. p. 141.

Sharma, K. (2021) How colleges will offer engineering in languages such as Tamil, Telugu, Gujurati from 2021 [Online]. *The Print*. Available at: https://theprint.in/india/education/how-colleges-will-offer-engineering-in-languages-such-as-tamil-telugu-gujarati-from-2021/623083/ (Accessed: 29 March 2021).

Shekhar, D. J. (2021) Can single-language OTT platforms take on streaming giants in India? [Online]. *Forbes India*. Available at: www.forbesindia.com/article/take-one-big-story-of-the-day/can-singlelanguage-ott-platforms-take-on-the-streaming-giants-in-india/66521/1 (Accessed: 2 March 2021).

Singal, N. (2021) India bans TikTok permanently; app evaluates notice [Online]. *Business Today*. Available at: www.businesstoday.in/technology/news/india-bans-tiktok-permanently-app-evaluates-notice/story/429086.html (Accessed: 2 March 2021).

Sneha, P. P. (2016) Mapping digital humanities in India [Online]. *The Centre for Internet and Society*. Available at: https://cis-india.org/papers/mapping-digital-humanities-in-india (Accessed: 2 March 2021).

Statista. (2019) Leading countries based on number of WhatsApp users in 2019. Available at: www.statista.com/statistics/289778/countries-with-the-most-facebook-users/#:~:text=There%20are%20over%20340%20million,most%20popular%20messaging%20service%20worldwide (Accessed: 2 March 2021).

Statista. (2021) Leading countries based on Facebook audience size as of January 2021. Available at: www.statista.com/statistics/268136/top-15-countries-based-on-number-of-facebook-users/#:~:text=There%20are%20over%20290%20million,terms%20of%20largest%20population%20worldwide (accessed: 2 March 2021).

The Centre for Internet and Society. (2021) The Centre for Internet and Society. [Online]. Available at: https://cis-india.org/ (Accessed: 2 March 2021).
The Memory Company. (2019) Directory of archives. *Indian Memory Project* [Online]. Available at: www.indianmemoryproject.com/archivedirectory/ (Accessed: 2 March 2021).
The Urdu Project (@theurduproject) [Instagram]. (n.d.). Available at: www.instagram.com/theurduproject/ (Accessed: 30 March 2021).

# 2

# COMMUNITY ACCOUNTABILITY AND ACTIVIST INTERVENTIONS IN THE DIGITAL HUMANITIES

*Dhanashree Thorat*

Digital Humanities and Literary Studies have shared synergistic interests, especially in digital storytelling, digital archiving, and computational methods for literary research.[1] The scope of what counts as "digital literary studies" is quite broad and includes digital methods to study varied literary topics and sites, new and emergent genres of digital textuality and digital literature, and possibilities for teaching, research, and dissemination of research on literature that rely on digital innovations such as hypertext. In *A Companion to Digital Literary Studies* (2007), an early exploration of this topic, Siemens and Schreibman categorized the volume into explorations of traditional disciplinary periodicity, the shifting notions of "text" in the "manifold possibilities presented by new media" and new methodologies for research on textuality. In more recent work, Amy Earhart (2015, p. 7) identifies four key areas under the ambit of digital literary studies: the digital edition form, the digital archive form, cultural studies approaches, and literary data approaches.

Since the early years of the emergence of the digital humanities, the possibilities that digital methods offered for humanistic inquiry have been particularly rich and varied. Computational text analysis, for example, allows scholars to "read" and "analyse" large textual corpora, whether comprised of 1,000 novels or a 100,000 tweets. This kind of analysis at scale was previously not possible for Humanities researchers without expending substantial time and effort. Aided by computer and code, researchers can further perform different kinds of analyses of such corpora, including network analysis and sentiment analysis. In many regards, DH also offered the democratizing potential of open-access publishing, sharing archival material with broader and new audiences, and destabilizing canonical formations by enabling access to writing by minoritized writers. Although these promises have been hindered by structural issues like funding and the hegemonic entrenchment of the Euro-American canon (which I address later), I revisit these affordances of digital humanities methods and platforms in our present moment.

DOI: 10.4324/9781003354246-4

Situating myself in the diasporic and trans/national contexts of India and the United States and drawing on the tradition of activist-scholarship, I explore how DH practitioners can respond to socio-political emergencies in our local and national communities. As we witness resurgent protests by minoritized groups speaking out against systemic violence in both countries, what interventions can Humanities scholars make ethically within our capacity as teachers and community members?

Despite the clear limitations of Internet access, one of the striking affordances of the digital humanities remains the promise of open access: making texts accessible to broader audiences digitally and sharing of scholarship online without barriers to access. Expensive print editions, and electronic paywalls and library databases are substantial hindrances to scholars, especially in the Global South, from accessing knowledge. By insisting on open-access publications, we have new ways of sharing our scholarship without such limitations. In the Indian context, this is exemplified by digital library projects like the National Digital Library of India and Shodhganga which were not conceived as digital humanities projects but represent the capacity of digital technologies to create new pathways of access. Open-access databases, archives, and projects can enable literary scholars to highlight literary texts and writers that have existed on the margins of the white Euro-American canon and in languages other than English. The Multilingual Literary Research (MLR) Digital Project, spearheaded by Nirmala Menon at IIT Indore, is one such digital humanities project. When it is launched, it will enable the sharing of "research articles, essays, books in Indian languages and literature other than English" (Shanmugapriya T *et al.* 2018). Similarly, digital archives can redress the gaps and erasures of colonial and colonized archives by centring and honouring the experiences of minoritized groups. These developments, and the promise of digital humanities to reframe, unmake, and subvert hegemonic spaces and conversations, are an important reason why many of us work in this field.

Literature scholars who completed their schooling in India are likely quite familiar with the literary canon constructed around white, male writers and the emphasis on English as the linguistic medium for professional and social success. In an earlier session at this conference, Prakruti Maniar mentioned that when someone mentions "literature," the assumption is that we are talking about "English literature" (Maniar 2020). This colonial model of education can be traced back to Thomas Macaulay's Minute on Indian Education (1835), which argued against government funding for native languages and literatures. According to Macaulay's assessment, "the dialects commonly spoken among the natives . . . contain neither literary nor scientific information." Macaulay's sweeping generalization is emblematic of the civilizing mission of colonial authorities and the devaluation of native knowledge corresponds with the dehumanization of native subjects. Ironically, this dismissal of native cultures as inferior did not thwart colonial scholars from turning colonized people into the subjects of anthropological, orientalist scrutiny, and the resultant work of this white colonial gaze would be legitimized as scholarship and remains in circulation in many fields.

Decades after Indian independence, this colonial model of education has not been entirely overturned. During my high school and college experiences in Pune, I recall the tensions over the position of William Shakespeare's work in the curriculum of then University of Pune (now called Savitribai Phule Pune University) when the Shakespeare course became an optional rather than core course. Certainly, there have been shifts and additions of other writers, especially Indian and postcolonial writers to the literary canon taught in Indian schools. But the structuring logic of whiteness undergirding the canon cannot be overturned merely by additions, or what Moya Bailey has called the "add and stir" model of diversity (Bailey 2011). The MA English curriculum at Savitribai Phule Pune University, for example, still centres British Literature while offering *optional* courses in Dalit Literature, Feminist Studies, LGBTQ Literature, and even Indian Writing in English (MA English syllabus, Department of English, SPPU 2021).

It is likely that many English literature teachers today completed their own formal education without any substantial engagement with Dalit, Black, Indigenous, or queer literature and perhaps chose to pursue this reading in optional courses, on their own, or in other spaces outside the classroom. As teachers ourselves now, we have both a responsibility and the capacity to advocate for changes in university curriculums and in our classrooms whenever possible. This is part of the cultural and political milieu in which digital humanities operates in India. And this is also the context in which digital humanities, with its collaborative possibilities, open-access initiatives, digital advocacy, new digitization projects, and transformative digital pedagogy, holds so much liberatory promise. While digital technologies can never solely address these historical and systemic issues, we can use digitally mediated interventions (such as the ones I mentioned earlier) to destabilize canonical formations and normative academic codes.

As we take stock of the digital humanities landscape, we can see where this still remains an incomplete project. Lack of funding, infrastructure, and training opportunities are all major constraints in working towards these possibilities afforded by digital humanities, especially in India. There are very few grant-funded opportunities at the university, state, or national level to pursue digital humanities projects. Indian scholars, like other Global South scholars, also often have to perform the doubled labour of being legible as scholars in a field whose major conferences and publishing houses are located in the Global North while simultaneously building their career in response to local exigencies, university frameworks, and scholarly standards. Short-term training programs, often held in the United States, Canada, or the United Kingdom, are practically inaccessible to most Global South scholars due to the costs associated with fees, travel, and lodging.

Equally troubling is the (re)entrenchment and reproduction of traditional academic hierarchies and power structures in this new field of digital humanities. Digital archives that continue to centre dominant voices (e.g. white writers or savarna knowledge formations) can't live up to the liberatory promise of democratizing access. Unfair labour practices, skewed control over cultural heritage material belonging to minoritized groups, and lack of community input on digital projects about them are also vexing concerns. These issues have been addressed by anti-caste, feminist, postcolonial, and Black Digital Humanities scholars such as Varsha Ayyar, Kim Gallon, Roopika Risam, Élika Ortega, Padmini Ray Murray, Jacqueline Wernimont, Maryemma Graham, Christina Boyles, and Barbara Bordalego.

Thus far, I have mentioned the possibilities offered by digital humanities and how those possibilities are curtailed by structural inequities operating in academic institutions and disciplines. These developments in digital humanities are ongoing against the backdrop of an increasingly resonant political activism challenging systemic injustices on and off campuses. "Activism" has been the keyword, a cultural touchstone, for this decade. In the United States, there have been ongoing Black Lives Matter protests, and the #noDAPL protests, and the #metoo movement, among others. In India, we have witnessed the remarkable anti-CAA protests, and, at the moment, farmers have been protesting for months about the government's farm bills. Given the venue of this conference, I want to note too that Jamia students were part of anti-CAA protests in Delhi and, as we know, faced police violence during these marches. Such stories of youth leadership in protest movements have been repeated many times. In Starkville, Mississippi, where I currently live and teach, young leaders were at the forefront of the massive Black Lives Matter march which took place in the summer of 2020.

These two threads, first, the stalled promises of digital humanities, and second, the incomplete project of multicultural democracies, are not unconnected. The stalled promises of digital humanities are intrinsically linked to the social and political systems that we are situated within, as well as the structuring frameworks and effects of colonialism, cis-hetero patriarchy, and casteist oppression undergirding our educational systems and societies broadly. The infrastructural and funding issues which hinder digital humanities scholarship in India are connected to our circumstances as a postcolonial nation. In much the same way, the internet shutdown in Kashmir (the longest such shutdown in any democratic country, ever) is not simply a political issue separate from the digital humanities or academic scholarship in India. This suppression of dissenting voices in one instance anticipates the government acting similarly again, especially in relation to minoritized activisms.[2] Intervention in this crisis must first prioritize the needs of those immediately affected while working to forestall the slow creep of authoritarianism which already hampers academic freedom. The social and political turmoil unfolding around us cannot be considered separate from our classrooms, and neither can we abstract ourselves from that reality as educators and researchers.

As an educator confronted particularly by student activism, I feel compelled to ask myself: what is our role as educators in this moment when our students are on the streets protesting systemic oppression? Where does digital humanities stand in relation to these social justice activisms, and what are our commitments as digital humanities scholars in the face of systemic injustices? How do we respond as scholars to the rise of anti-immigrant, Islamophobic, and other hate groups in the United States and India? What I am proposing is that DH practitioners can and should respond to socio-political emergencies in our local and national communities. Our advocacy for the Humanities (facing shrinking budgets and axed departments) should be connected to our advocacy on behalf of and in alliance with minoritized groups in society. Black Digital Studies scholar Jessica Marie Johnson (2016) framed this along the lines of *accountability*. She argues that a "justice imperative" grounds the role and relevance of the Humanities in a changing world, and that we must ask whether we are accountable to our students and to the communities our universities are located in (Dinsman interview). We can think about these communities in multiple ways: the local communities we are embedded in; the social, cultural, and dialogic communities we choose to be part of or are located within; the kinship communities we find belonging in; our transnational, diasporic, and global communities; and even our sense of planetary belonging and its ecological dimensions. To be embedded in and work through community is also to attend to the exclusions and erasures within our spaces.

As a faculty member affiliated with a university, community accountability means that I am in a position to create equitable learning spaces, centre the voices and experiences of community members (especially historically marginalized voices), and connect scholarly work to the communities I am embedded in. While we can't solve systemic problems solely through personal interventions, we can acknowledge the importance of individual agency and accountability in working towards change wherever we are located. At the core of it, literature, art, and other forms of cultural expression falling within the realm of the Humanities hold the capacity of transgressive imagination. As Humanities scholars, we are well aware that art can envision new worlds and open up foreclosed possibilities. Alan Liu writes about imagination too in his call to develop a poiesis of digital literary studies. In issuing a call to "imagine how old and new literary media allow us to imagine," Liu (2007) draws out the connection between mediation, subjectivity, and imagination. Liu (2007) notes, " 'We' are always mediated creatures, and as such are fully alive in culture when old and new media—the ancestors and children of our self image—collaborate to allow us to encounter the imagination that we could be other." Liu's words invoke a kind of radical imagination and critical making that is possible at the intersection of old and new media.

Instead of adding to the canon or making a place at the table for minoritized people, we have to consider how to disrupt the canon and re-envision equitable academic structures that are different from the ones that have existed. There are many possible points of intervention—we can act within our scholarly communities, bridge divides between universities and their communities by working on community engaged projects, foster radical collaborations with activist groups, adopt a liberatory praxis to guide our DH projects, and guide policy-making and infrastructure-building initiatives. Against the backdrop of a pandemic unfolding amidst state and systemic violence, DH scholars and teachers can enact transformative practices and pedagogies grounded in feminist, anti-colonial, and anti-caste methodologies.

The model liberatory praxis and pedagogy I am suggesting here are not unknown in India and neither is it new in scholarly circles. One example, from one of my local communities in Pune (in Maharashtra), is that of feminist visionaries Savitribai Phule and Jyotirao Phule, who envisioned access to education for women and oppressed castes. In one of her poems in Kavya Phule (1854), Phule emphasizes a liberatory pedagogy that would enable students to learn together and "smash traditions-liberate" (Phule, translated by Sardar and Paul). This was not a colonial or casteist model of education that sought to co-opt students into a normative social order. Rather, the Phules set up schools grounded by a vision of collaborative learning in order to dismantle oppressive systems. In 1942, this message would be echoed at the All-India Depressed Classes Conference by Dr. B. R. Ambedkar (1942, p. 51) in the slogan "educate, agitate and organize, have faith in yourselves and never lose hope." Ambedkar's words connect education to political activism and collective struggle as interlinked processes that call on and for each other. Indelibly linking the personal and political, Ambedkar's words are a call to action to educators about our role in society.

The traditions of *activist-scholars* and *community-based scholarship* also have a long genealogy and are closely connected to fields such as Ethnic Studies. In the United States, Ethnic Studies (Black Studies, Asian–American Studies, Indigenous Studies, and Latinx Studies) emerged in the 1960s as a result of student demands on university campuses. In 1968, student members of the Third World Liberation Front, comprised of a multiracial coalition including Black, Asian–American, Native American, and Latinx students, began striking in California and demanded the decolonization of the university—this included transforming the curriculum which had rendered invisible marginalized knowledge, and diversifying faculty and student representation on campus. In making these demands, students asked universities how they were accountable to the local communities they existed in and to the national communities they contribute to. This campaign was driven by interethnic and interracial coalitions, acting in transnational solidarity with Third World peoples.

Pre-eminent Black Studies scholar Manning Marable (1988) traced the connection between activism and the academic field of Black Studies by noting that

> the function of black studies scholarship should be more than the celebration of heritage and self-esteem; it must utilize history and culture as tools by which an oppressed people can transform their lives and the entire society. Scholars have an obligation not just to interpret, but to act.
>
> (Marable, *New York Times*)

Marable asks about the interventions that we can make as scholars in public life precisely, because we study history and culture—not only structures of domination and oppression but also movements and cultures of resistance assembled by marginalized groups. One example of this interchange is the newspaper editorial, which allows scholars to share their research with broader public audiences. Other scholars, such as Angela Davis and Cornel West, exemplify the tradition of the activist-scholar, who connects activist movements for racial justice with university communities. In her work on community-based teaching, bell hooks similarly writes about liberatory education as "an insurrection of subjugated knowledge"; an "insurrection," as in, a revolt, a mutiny, an active rejection of normative codes. And what is this subjugated knowledge if not ideas, methods, and practices that have been deemed too transgressive to the status quo, and belief systems and ways of thinking stemming from historically marginalized groups whose knowledge pathways were denigrated as inferior?

In Digital Humanities too, this kind of community-engaged, social-justice-oriented scholarship has been taken up in the last several years by scholars who were part of the #transformDH movement; coming to DH with an Ethnic Studies background; or who have taken up critical digital humanities as their area of intervention. The collaborative, open-access ethic of digital humanities, with the capacity of reaching out to community members and building networks between universities and their communities, can lend itself to transformative action. In the opening section of this chapter, I traced what digital humanities offers to scholars who study literature (or other forms of textuality). In this last section, I want to reframe and take up a new question: What approaches, methods, tools, and skillsets does the Digital Humanities offer when we choose to be activist-scholars? What are the possibilities for intervention, disruption, and transformation that we are uniquely positioned for as digital humanities researchers and teachers? I explore these questions in the context of DH projects, communities, and pedagogy.

## Digital Projects Making Critical Interventions

The first set of examples we can consider are digital projects that not only challenge hegemonic systems of power but also are created as active responses to an ongoing crisis. The "Torn Apart/Separados" digital project, for example, was a rapid response project which visualizes immigration detention centres in the United States. Initially created collaboratively over one summer, the initial project started when the Trump administration allowed the separation of children from their families when immigrants crossed the border seeking asylum. The wide-ranging public criticism of this inhumane policy finds reflection in the project utilizing digital technology to illuminate both the vast scale of detention in America, and funding funnelled to states and contractors to maintain a carceral apparatus. Closer home, Dia Da Costa's digital project, "Kashmir: Memories of Colonial Unknowing," draws on ESRI's ARCGIS platform to explore the complicity of Indian citizens in state violence in Kashmir. Combining self-reflection, family memory, and nationalist historiography, this project shows how savarna Indians are trained in the "colonial unknowing" of Kashmir and come to "have a sense of their nation as a colonial force" while disavowing "Kashmiri struggles for decolonization" (Da Costa). Instead of evacuating Kashmiri subjectivity or speaking on behalf of oppressed people, the project asks savarna Indians to grapple with their own internalized ideas and aspirations of national power.

Both these projects draw on the unique affordances of digital technologies (specifically digital mapping tools) to engage in digital storytelling about an ongoing political crisis in national life that affects minoritized peoples. They draw on research expertise and technical skills of scholars (sometimes working in collaboration) to spark broader conversations about social justice issues, foster critical dialogue, and ultimately call for some kind of action from readers. While traditional academic publications on these same issues certainly exist (and some are likely going through the drawn-out process of peer review in academia), these projects respond to the emergency of the moment. The Nimble Tents Toolkit created by Alex Gil *et al.* (n.d.), for example, allows "Rapid Response Research (RRR) projects [that] are quickly deployed scholarly interventions in pressing political, social, and cultural crises." Scholars interested in building such social-justice-oriented DH projects must particularly consider questions of access, materiality, method, ontology, and epistemology (Risam *et al.* n.d.). Among other concerns, projects should be accessible in low-bandwidth environments, follow equitable labour and collaborative practices, and consider which epistemological frameworks are privileged (or disenfranchised) by the narrative of the project. Ethical practices have to be built into the heart of the projects and inform every aspect of the project-building.

Aside from such rapid response interventions, other digital humanities projects take up historically situated but ongoing forms of violence. Rather than tackling new crises, they focus on long-persisting systemic oppression, the sedimented structures and norms that condition our lives, or what Rob Nixon (2013, p. 2) called "slow violence," which occurs "gradually and out of sight."[3] One area of intervention in this regard is the building of critical digital archives that subvert the colonial model of the archive by centring the experiences of those who were systemically silenced in the archives, defining new equitable protocols and standards. Undoing the legacies of colonialism in the archive can also enable us to address the continuing processes and effects of settler colonialism and neocolonialism and other forms of violence and attend to their impact on people today. Taking up the charge of redressing historical erasures, such archives can work towards being more accessible to their communities and rebuilding trust between marginalized communities and universities.

Mukurtu, for example, is a digital platform for Indigenous archiving which centres Indigenous knowledge pathways in the digital archive. Notably, the Mukurtu platform allows Indigenous nations to decide who has access to their cultural heritage and how cultural knowledge is presented. Improved access does not necessarily mean that everyone should have access to the material, as it might contain sensitive or culturally specific knowledge. Metadata is presented along the archival "standards" (such as Dublin Core) but also in alternate schemas, pathways, and protocols oriented around Traditional Knowledge (TK) Labels. TK Labels respect Indigenous epistemologies, outline cultural protocols for access, and act as "social guides for action that help non-Indigenous people better understand and respect different cultural perspectives and concerns about the correct and appropriate ways of listening, viewing, and using traditional knowledge" (Mukurtu-FAQ). Kimberly Christen (2018, p. 410), writing about Mukurtu's practice of collaborative stewardship, observes that building trust with communities is especially important given that these communities have been "historically shut out of these conversations." Moreover, such projects can't operate on a "victim model" on the assumption that these communities need external experts to "come and save them" (410).[4] Community accountability here is about respecting how Indigenous communities want to represent themselves in archives; digital platforms enable them to choose how non-community members access their knowledge.

Another category of timely community-memory projects involves digital projects such as Narmada Bachao Andolan and Baltimore StandUp, documenting protests and resistance movements which national governments might prefer to forget or minimize in public memory. The Documenting the Now project, which archives hashtag activism on Twitter (by collecting tweets from select hashtags), is a similar project which documents social media activism. Given the ephemeral nature of tweets in particular, such projects are necessary, as they preserve material that would otherwise be lost to future generations. These archival projects themselves constitute an act of resistance, as they become holders of community memory and records of collective action against systemic oppression. Instead of relying on institutional memorialization (whether in mainstream media, textbooks, memorial sites, etc.), these projects are grassroots or community based and particularly attentive to the sensitivities of documenting resistance. Part of community accountability in this case involves ensuring that protesters and activists will not be harmed by the collection of protest-related material (for instance, police could use photos or tweets to identify activists).

## Fostering Digital Publics and Community-Oriented Work

The second area where scholars are positioned to make an impact concerns not the building of projects but the building of communities. The emergence of digital publics and their relationship to civic life has been explored at length from various disciplinary perspectives. In the context of Digital Humanities, Pressner (2015, p. 61) argues that "by conceiving of scholarship in ways that foundationally involve community partners, cultural institutions, the private sector, nonprofits, government agencies, and slices of the general public, digital humanities expands both the notion of scholarship and *the public sphere* (emphasis mine)." Digital publics present new opportunities for activist communities to gather members together and collaborate transnationally. Such digital publics predate the rise of Digital Humanities, and notable examples include the Afrofuturism online community founded by Alondra Nelson (1998) and the Crunk Feminists Collective. In India, digital advocacy groups such as Point of View, Velivada, Dalit Camera, and Orindam are an important reminder that academics should acknowledge the activist work already being spearheaded by non-profit and community groups as we consider bridging universities with their broader communities. Part of the mission of these groups is leveraging digital spaces to foster conversations about minoritized groups that have been marginalized in mainstream media.

Working with community-based groups requires a fundamental shift in the traditional academic approach. Instead of looking to this work as a means of building CV lines for tenure and promotion, we prioritize community needs and goals and consider the stakes involved in any form of digital advocacy. And while traditional academic structures have operated on the model of the sole scholar working in isolation and building knowledge by citing other scholars (generally white, male, or established scholars), community-oriented work values the knowledge held by people without academic degrees and requires collaborative and coalition building. As scholars entering an already-existing conversation, we might have to take direction from community groups and activists rather than assuming leadership of a project by virtue of academic rank or role.

## Liberatory Digital Pedagogy

The last area where digital humanities scholars have the capacity to intervene is through our teaching. Liberatory digital pedagogy is predicated on seeing students as active participants in learning and collaboration who can use digital technology to reflect, critique, and transform as needed in relation to violence in their community. Adam Banks (2006, p. 45) notes that transformative access to computers and digital technologies is premised upon attempts to change the very nature of an oppressive system (Banks notes this in the context of the Black liberation struggle) rather than merely being able to operate digital technologies. Digital humanities pedagogy presents us with an array of digital approaches to pursue this kind of reflective and engaged learning. A few semesters ago, I taught a class called "Digital Literary Studies" during which students curated a digital exhibit on race and immigration through Caribbean Literature and Art. Conceptualizing the classroom as a critical and brave space, we took up the immigration crises that were ongoing in America and used digital tools to create an exhibit where broader publics could engage with the histories of cultural exchanges between the United States and Haiti particularly.

To prepare for the project, students visited a local museum, which had an exhibit on Caribbean Art, and then wrote short essays taking up a literary text and an artistic text to examine the representation of Haiti. By the end of the class, we had 13 short essays exploring colonialism, revolution, gender, and spirituality in the Caribbean context through literary and artistic texts. These multimodal essays were then uploaded to our digital exhibit in Omeka. The goal of this assignment was not only aesthetic appreciation of literary and artistic works, but for students to discover how literature speaks to social and political events and how we could speak through literature to current crises unfolding around us. Because my students were aware from the start that their assignment was both digital and public, they were careful about the impact of their writing on a Haitian and Caribbean audience. Could their writing help educate the American public about the joined history and cultural exchanges between Haiti and America? As they worked on the project, we spoke about the colonial histories of academic disciplines that produced knowledge which harmed minoritized peoples, and of the capacity of digital writing to speak critically and inform audiences.

Undergirding the project was the pedagogical idea that digital technologies can facilitate transformation and change in a society *if* they are used thoughtfully and critically, and that the literature classroom can teach aesthetic appreciation even as we enable our students to see themselves as political agents who have the capacity to work for social justice. We acted with the understanding that our classroom existed in a social and cultural community rather than seeing the classroom as alienated from the events unfolding around out. Earhart and Taylor (2016), who have written about their critical digital pedagogy in the digital humanities classroom, note that they taught "digital humanities skills such as data collection, metadata application, and analysis . . . as a means of disrupting . . . erasures, using carefully constructed technological projects to spread digital cultural empowerment through both universities and student bodies." The projects their classes worked on documented Black and women's histories that had been historically minimized in institutional archives. This example also illustrates that critical DH pedagogy can enable students to do transformative work in their own local communities.

## Conclusion

In closing, I want to briefly point out some broader ethical considerations for digital humanities scholars interested in working on social justice-oriented digital projects and digital pedagogy. First, it is crucial to acknowledge the risks of such activist approaches to digital humanities for scholars, especially minoritized scholars who often already face gatekeeping, resistance, harassment, and violence in academic contexts.[5] Academics in precarious or contingent positions (graduate students, adjuncts, pre-tenure and untenured teachers, librarians, and staff) face the brunt of these risks. Speaking out about oppression or resisting the normative order of being often leads to the minoritized person being labelled as the problem. Sara Ahmed (2010), in her germinal piece on the feminist killjoy, writes that "you become the problem you create" when you raise the existence of a problem to public scrutiny. Going against the social order implies a willingness not only to cause unhappiness to others but also to dwell in unhappiness (Ahmed). Aside from concerns like retaliation in professional settings, we must be conscious of the emotional labour and mental health expectations placed on us when we take on social justice work.

Second, as scholars invested in this transformative work, we must be self-reflexive and aware of our position in relation to the issues we take up. In our desire to rectify historically situated violence or intervene in an ongoing crises, we may end up occupying space or centring privileged voices in relation to minority activisms. In India, Ravinder Singh (2018), who is a DHARTI Executive Board member, has spoken about the issue of representation in Indian DH, and namely the over-representation of savarna voices in our circles. Varsha Ayyar's (2020) work on Dalit Panther archives addresses the ethics of savarna scholars taking on digital projects about DBA communities and the extractivist politics that can undergird these projects. While there is much work to be done on conceptualizing a praxis of Dalit-Bahujan-Adivasi Digital Humanities, we have to develop institutional frameworks to support and advocate for emerging and current DBA scholars who are interested in doing this. Community accountability also involves acknowledging how privilege operates in academic circles and understanding what kind of roles we can take on ethically in a collaborative project.

Third, we must consider the issue or urgency: digital humanities projects and other publicly engaged scholarship can allow rapid responses to community crises that are generally not possible with the slower pace of the academic publication process. However, we have to be wary about treating the pain and grief of marginalized communities in crises as an opportunity for scholarship or a byline for the tenure and promotion packet. I am not suggesting that we rush to build digital scholarship or projects about Kashmir, the CAA Bill, the farmer protests, or the experiences of migrant labourers during COVID-19. Some community-based projects require long-term collaboration and trust building, others call for input from community members at different stages of the planning process. Such additional steps can slow down the pace of the project but are necessary for accountability and ethics. Slow scholarship has its own merits even in moments of crisis.

The long arc of liberation and resistance movements serves as a reminder that systemic change does not happen overnight. Choosing to work deliberately with careful consideration and community feedback should be our primary guiding concerns. Today we are in a remarkable moment of convergent and parallel political activisms reminiscent of the 1960s and other historical eras—we have people marching in the streets and raising their voice online. We have borne witness to the anger, frustration, and grief of disenfranchised people within our communities, and we cannot be neutral or silent. As digital humanities scholars and educators, our ethical imperative of the moment must be to intervene where we are located and with the tools and skills at our disposal as we collectively build towards an equitable future.

## Notes

1 This paper is an amended version of a valedictory address delivered at the "Confronting the 'Global', Exploring the 'Local': Digital Apprehensions of Poetics and Indian Literature(s)" conference organized by Jamia Millia Islamia and Michigan State University in December 2020.

2 See Nishant Shah's *South Asian Review* article (2019) on post-access digital humanities in this regard.

3 For Nixon, this was particularly exemplified by environmental disasters that unfold incrementally rather than spectacularly, and the effects of which are accretive rather than instantaneous (2).

4 Christen's overall article defines an ETHICS (Engage, Talk, Help, Invest, Create, Support) model for this kind of collaborative stewardship.

5 The risks of digital activism and advocacy (doxxing, targeted trolling, and cyberattacks) also add to these concerns.

## References


Ahmed, Sara. (2010) 'Feminist Killjoys (And Other Willful Subjects)', *The Scholar and Feminist Online*. 8.3.

Ambedkar, B. R. (1942) *Reply to the Address. Report of the Proceedings of the Third Session of the All India Depressed Classes Conference*. Delhi: Gautam Book Center.

Ayyar, Varsha. (2020) Panel Remarks. *Digital Archives in South Asian Studies: Towards Decolonisation*. Oxford: University of Oxford and University of Pennsylvania.

Banks, Adam. (2006) *Race, Rhetoric, and Technology Searching for Higher Ground*. Mahwah, NJ: Lawrence Erlbaum.

Bailey, Moya Z. (2011) 'All the Digital Humanities Are White, All the Nerds Are Men, but Some of Us Are Brave', *Journal of Digital Humanities*. 1.1.

Christen Kimberly. (2018) 'Relationships, Not Records: Digital Heritage and the Ethics of Sharing Indigenous Knowledge Online', In *Routledge Companion to Media Studies and Digital Humanities*, edited by Jentery Sayers. New York: Routledge, Taylor and Francis. pp. 403–412.

Dinsman, Melissa. (2016) 'The Digital in the Humanities: An Interview with Jessica Marie Johnson', *LA Review of Books*. 23 July 2016.

Earhart, A. E. (2015) *Traces of the Old, Uses of the New: The Emergence of Digital Literary Studies*. Ann Arbor, MI: University of Michigan Press.

Earhart, Amy, and Toniesha Taylor. (2016) 'Pedagogies of Race: Digital Humanities in the Age of Ferguson', In *Debates in the Digital Humanities*, edited by Matt Gold and Lauren Klein. Minneapolis, MN: U. Minn. Press.

Gil, Alex et al. (n.d.) The Nimble Tents toolkit. https://nimbletents.github.io/people/ (Accessed: 10 Jan 2021)

hooks, bell. (n.d.) *Teaching Community* [Place of Publication Not Identified]. Maniar: DEV Publishers & DISTRIBU.

Liu, Alan. (2007) 'Imagining the New Media Encounter,' In *Introduction to a Companion to Digital Literary Studies*, edited by Ray Siemens and Susan Schreibman. Malden, MA: Blackwell. pp. 3–25.

Macaulay, Thomas. (1835) 'Minute on Indian Education. Bureau of Education', In *Selections from Educational Records, Part I (1781–1839)*, edited by H. Sharp. Calcutta: Superintendent, Government Printing, 1920 [Reprint. Delhi: National Archives of India, 1965]. pp. 107–117.

Maniar, Prakruti. (2020, December 20) 'Presenting Purple Pencil Project as a Case Study of Digital Humanities Project in Practice in the Field of Indian Literatures,' In *Confronting the 'Global', Exploring the 'Local': Digital Apprehensions of Poetics in Indian Literature(s)*, New Delhi: Department of English, Jamia Millia Islamia.

Marable, Manning. (1988) 'A Debate on Activism in Black Studies; A Plea That Scholars Act Upon, Not Just Interpret, Events', *The New York Times*. 4 April.

Nixon, Rob. (2013) *Slow Violence and the Environmentalism of the Poor*. Cambridge, MA: Harvard UP.

Pressner, Todd (2015) 'Critical Theory and the Mangle of Digital Humanities', In *Between Humanities and the Digital*, edited by Patrik Svensson and David Theo Goldberg. Boston, MA: MIT Press.

Phule, Savitribai (2012) *Kavya Phule*. Translated by Ujjwala Mhatre, edited by Lalitha Dhara. Mumbai: Dr. Ambedkar College of Commerce & Economics.

Risam, Roopika et al. (n.d.) Social justice and the digital humanities [Online]. http://criticaldh.roopikarisam.com/ (Accessed: 10 May 2022)

Savitribai Phule Pune University—Department of English. (2021) MA syllabus [Online]. www.unipune.ac.in/dept/fine_arts/english/english_webfiles/syllabus.htm (Accessed: 10 January 2022)

Singh, Ravinder. (2018) 'Digital humanities in India? A few preliminary notes towards an argument', In *DHAI Conference*. IIT Indore, Indore.

Shanmugapriya T. et al. (2018) 'Developing A Database for Scholarship in Indian Languages and Literatures: The Multilingual Literary Research (MLR) Digital Project', *Asian Quarterly*. 15.4.

Siemens, R. G. and Schreibman, S (2007) *A Companion to Digital Literary Studies*. Malden, MA: Blackwell Pub.

# 3

# THREE MODELS OF WORLD LITERATURE

*Michael Falk*

## Making Worlds and Making Models

South Asian literatures present some of the most important frontiers in world literary research. South Asia is home to an extreme variety of different literary, linguistic, and cultural traditions. These traditions present a severe challenge to conventional understandings of literary modernity, as scholars such as Sheldon Pollock and Nirmala Menon have demonstrated (Pollock 2005, 2006; Menon 2016). They also present a severe practical challenge for digital literary scholarship. While scholars have made considerable progress in digitizing Indic- and Dravidian-language texts, and the Digital Humanities community is growing rapidly in India in particular, the sheer multilingualism of South Asian literature makes digital analysis difficult. It is only recently that literary scholars have begun to grapple with the challenges of multilingual digital analysis, and the tools required for South Asian languages—OCR and HTR engines, part-of-speech taggers, reference corpora, stopword lists, and practical know-how—are just starting to appear.

In this chapter, I sketch out a vision for a planetary digital scholarship that can accommodate South Asian literatures in all their complexity. As we develop new archives and new techniques, what should our guiding principles be? Twenty years ago, Franco Moretti famously called for a new kind of "distant reading," which would make the whole "slaughterhouse" of world literature visible for the first time (Moretti 2000). But he and his followers have largely failed to incorporate non-Western literatures into their models of world literature. In what follows, I consider why this is, and suggest that a reformulated version of Moretti's approach could provide a way forward. I contrast Moretti's *archival* approach to modelling world literature with two other approaches: the *canonical* approach of David Damrosch, and the *cosmopolis* approach of Sheldon Pollock. I then consider how these different approaches can be instantiated digitally. To conclude, I consider the powerful

DOI: 10.4324/9781003354246-5

materialist critiques of Kath Bode and Roopika Risam, and propose *orthogonality* as a methodological ideal for digital scholars of world literature.

The concept of "world literature" can never be settled, because both the "world" and "literature" are constructed, contingent, and contained. We humans don't simply inhabit the world, or read or write literature. We make a world, and make literature. This is the sphere of activity Hannah Arendt calls "work." We work, argues Arendt, to make "things," which "have the function of stabilizing human life" (Arendt 1958, p. 137). "[T]he most important task of human artifice," she continues, "is to offer mortals a dwelling place more permanent and more stable than themselves" (1958, p. 152). Such a meaningful "dwelling place" is a "world."

For scholars of world literature, there is a double making at stake:

> The first making: Storytellers, poets, listeners and readers create literature in order to make sense of the world, or in other words, to make worlds.
>
> The second making: Scholars unite the these diverse literary worlds into a single world—world literature—which they describe in their research.

A "world" literature is not necessarily universal. The worlds we inhabit are generally small: the household, the nation, the garden, the coterie, the neighbourhood, the desk, and the earth. Writers generally invoke one or more of these small worlds in their works. Has any writer ever succeeded in addressing everyone simultaneously? Meanwhile scholars generally aspire to encompass the widest possible world in their constructions of *world literature*.

There are various proposals for the widest possible world, the most influential of which in recent years has been Gayatri Spivak's "planet." Her proposal is persuasive, because it accepts that no "world" we make can ever fully encompass reality: "When I invoke the planet, I think of the effort required to figure the (im) possibility of this underived intuition" (Spivak 2003, p. 72). The planet is the limit of our world-making, at least until our fantasies of interstellar travel are realized. Everything we make *is* the planet. Each thing we make is an attempt to "figure" the planet, but the planet always exceeds our figuration. The ideal, "(im)possible" world literature would be a planetary literature—all actually existing world literatures fall within this limit.

Spivak's proposal meshes nicely with theories of "modelling" that guide research in Digital Humanities. Spivak argues that when a scholar sets out to describe world literature, they merely "figure" the ideal planetary literature. Likewise, Willard McCarty argues that when digital scholars set out to analyse literature on the computer, they merely "model" the ideal literature that lies beyond the computer's grasp.[1] This does not doom digital scholarship. In fact, "the misfit between model and target not only points a way forward but is the point of the exercise" (McCarty 2005, p. 179). By trying to model literature computationally, the scholar is forced to formalize their assumptions about literature, and test these assumptions against the available data. When the model inevitably fails to encompass reality, the scholar realizes the inadequacy of their assumptions, tries to improve their model, and triggers an "interactive, heuristic process" of criticism and re-modelling (McCarty 2005, p. 81).

A figure is not precisely the same thing as a model. But Spivak's notion of *figure* is broad enough to include McCarty's notion of *model*. A model is just an especially precise figure for something, which can be manipulated computationally. If we accept this synthesis of Spivak and McCarty's views, then questions arise: How can scholars model planetary literature? Or, how can scholars make planetary models of literature? In this chapter, I answer these questions by considering three different kinds of model:

1 *Canons*: Selections of texts that transcend their local context because of their supreme literary qualities, cosmopolitan character, or global reach. Writers make world literature by writing translatable works; scholars make world literature by translating them.
2 *Cosmopolises*: Communities of writers and readers who look beyond their local context, and address a cosmopolitan audience in a cosmopolitan language. Writers make world literature by making a cosmopolitan language; scholars make the cosmopolis by describing the institutionalization of that language.
3 *Archives*: Maximally inclusive or non-selective collections of texts. The ideal archive of world literature is simply the set of all texts ever written. Writers make world literature by writing; scholars make world literature by accounting for what is written.

All these approaches to world literature predate Digital Humanities and the rise of literary "modelling." As I hope to show, however, modelling has the potential to fundamentally alter how *canons*, *cosmopolises*, and *archives* are made in next three sections. Moretti and the distant readers have generally striven to make digital *archives* of world literature, though as we will see, digital *canons* and digital *cosmopolises* are also of great value in contemporary literary scholarship. Of all these kinds of model, it is the *archive* that seems most likely to embody Spivak's ideal of planetarity, and indeed in *Death of a Discipline* she cautiously concurs with Moretti's archival approach (2003, p. 101 but see also 107n1). Although it is indeed easy to think of all the planet's literature as a single giant archive, materialist scholars such as Kath Bode and Roopika Risam have demonstrated how incomplete and overdetermined any actual archive is bound to be. In the final section of the chapter, I take stock of Bode and Risam's arguments, and propose a new ideal of digital literary scholarship, *orthogonality*.

## Model 1: *Canons*

Let us begin with world literature as a canon of texts. "Canon" is a controversial world and is often rejected by scholars who adopt this approach. David Damrosch is a prominent example. In *What is World Literature?* (2003), he argues that world literature is an ever-changing set of literary works which are absorbed from one "national tradition" to another:

> [W]orks become world literature by being received *into* the space of a foreign culture, a space defined in many ways by the host culture's national tradition and the present needs of its own writers.
>
> *(Damrosch 2003, p. 283)*

He denies that such works form "a set canon of texts":

> [D]ifferent groups within a society, and different individuals within any group, will create distinctive congeries of works, blending canonical and noncanonical works into effective microcanons.
>
> *(Damrosch 2003, p. 298)*

In his view, there are as many world literatures as there are reading communities. In my household, we may particularly prize Shakespeare, Hafez, and Cao Xueqin. In your household, perhaps Germaine de Staël, Ngugi Wa Thio'ngo, and Mir Taqi Mir are the key writers. At this level, Damrosch's theory seems extremely sceptical. There is really no world literature at all, but rather a whole chaotic series of world literatures, spontaneously rising and falling all over the earth as readers' preferences change.

Despite this apparent scepticism, Damrosch does argue that world literature is a particular kind of literature, which can be understood as a single thing. First, he supposes that translation is necessary for world literature to exist, and that therefore only texts that "gain in translation" are capable of becoming part of world literature. If texts are not translated, they cannot move easily between national traditions in the way Damrosch describes. There are many things that can impede translation: lack of interest in foreign texts, lack of skilled translators, and lack of time and money. But the ultimate limit to translation, argues Damrosch, is the translatability of literary works themselves.

> Literary language is . . . language that either gains *or* loses in translation, in contrast to nonliterary language, which typically does neither . . . literature stays within its national or regional tradition when it usually loses in translation, whereas works become world literature when they gain on balance in translation, stylistic losses offset by an expansion in depth as they increase their range.
>
> *(Damrosch 2003, p. 289)*

Is it true that some texts are innately more translatable than others? The statement seems dubious, but is a question for another article (or book! or library!). For our purposes, we can simply note that Damrosch's concept of world literature as the set of "those texts that gain in translation" implies a certain research methodology: Damrosch argues that the study of world literature requires more, and better translations, so that a wider circle of readers has access to a larger set of world-literary texts. There is a latent world of translatable texts, waiting for the touch of the translator's wand. There is a single, potential, planetary canon of translatable texts. Each "microcanon" of translated texts is simply a fragment of this ideal planetary canon.

The digital equivalent of Damrosch's *canon* is the *digital edition*. To make digital editions, scholars select particular authors who are particularly worthy to be edited, and expend enormous scholarly resources representing all the folds and complexities of the writer's *oeuvre* in digital form. Following Damrosch's argument, for a digital edition to form part of the canon of world literature, it should contain the work of a "translatable" writer, and present the translation to the reader. But in fact, this is not what the most interesting and successful digital editions do. Digital editions can be highly dynamic and unstable, and can present a very different kind of "translation" to the one Damrosch describes. Damrosch imagines that world literature is made up of texts that slip easily from one language to another. But the most exciting digital editions often showcase writers whose work is highly resistant to translation. One of the best examples is Frances Pritchett's digital edition of the great Urdu *ghazal*-writer, Mirza Asadullah Khan "Ghalib."

If any writer is "untranslatable," it is surely Ghalib. His poetry is highly culturally specific. Much of it takes place in what Frances Pritchett calls the "ghazal world," a universe of imagery, tropes, and concepts which are highly unique and interdependent (Pritchett 1994, p. 104). Moreover, his poetry is dense and structurally complex. He uses particular features of Urdu grammar to maximize the ambiguity and euphony of his verses, and he delights in puns, which often rely on meanings that are very specific to particular Urdu words. In a traditional book-based translation, where space is limited, and readers and publishers expect the book to be pleasant to read through sequentially, the translator has to make stark choices about what aspects of Ghalib's verse to represent in their translation. But in a digital edition, where space is unlimited, and readers expect a more fragmented reading experience, a very different kind of translation is possible.

Here is the translation of the first *sher* of Ghalib's 32nd ghazal, from Pritchett and Owen Cornwall's paperback translation of 2017:

> When there was nothing, then God existed; if nothing existed, then God would exist.
>
> Existence itself drowned me; if I were not I, then what would I be?
>
> *(Ghalib 2017, p. 57)*

There are no footnotes to this version, and the Urdu is reprinted at the back of the book in Urdu script. Here is the version from Pritchett's online edition of Ghalib's Urdu ghazals:

> nah thā kuchh to ḳhudā thā kuchh nah hotā to ḳhudā hotā
> ḍuboyā mujh ko hone ne nah hotā maiñ to kyā hotā
> 1a) when there was nothing, then God was; if nothing was, then God would be

1b) when I was nothing, then God was; if I were nothing, then God would be
1c) when I was nothing, then I was God; if I were nothing, then I would be God
2a) "being" drowned me; if I were not I, then what would I be?
2b) "being" drowned me; if I were not, then what would I be?
2c) "being" drowned me; if I were not I, then what would be?
2d) "being" drowned me; if I were not, then what would be?
2e) "being" drowned me; if I were not I, then so what?
2f) "being" drowned me; if I were not, then so what?
(Ghalib and Pritchett 2020, v. 32.1)

The reader can swap between four different orthographies: Urdu script, Devanagari, this Roman script with diacritics, or a more basic Roman script. Below the poem, Pritchett provides seven commentaries (six by Urdu writers and one of her own), with numerous hyperlinks that take readers to related parts of the site. In this digital edition, it is actually Ghalib's *untranslatability* which makes him exciting to read. In the book translation, the translators had to make painful choices about how to string the different parts of the *sher* together to make a comprehensible whole. In the online version, different possible translations proliferate on the page. It's an exciting reading experience, as the reader experiments with combining the different possible renderings, and checking them back against Ghalib's original text, which can be read in the reader's script of choice. The commentaries provide a range of other perspectives, sparking further experiments in literary interpretation. In a way, the online translation is a kind of anti-translation. It demonstrates how hard Ghalib is to translate, and makes the English reader confront their inability to understand Urdu. This results in its own kind of pleasure.

For Damrosch, world literature is process of mutual understanding; translators move texts from one language to another. Digital editions allow scholars to make a very different canon of planetary literature, founded on mutual bafflement. Digital editions can baffle the reader more effectively than books because of their hypertextuality. "[T]he hypertext," argues Jerome J McGann, "unlike the book, encourages greater decentralization of design" (McGann 2001, p. 71). The text itself becomes decentred: "One is encouraged not so much to find as to make order—and then to make it again and again, as established orderings expose their limits" (McGann 2001, p. 71). A digital edition can thus embody Emily Apter's ideal of the "Untranslatable." A plural translation like Pritchett's online rendering of *nah thā kuchh to ḳhudā thā* is not a finished, polished translation that allows Ghalib to slip easily into English poetry. It is rather a "linguistic form of creative failure with homeopathic uses" (Apter 2013, p. 20). Pritchett's failure to find a single good translation for Ghalib's poem increases our appreciation of the text, and encourages the reader to read more sceptically and creatively. Pritchett's digital edition undermines Damrosch's conception of the canon of world literature: translatability is no longer the criterion that distinguishes world literature from merely local literature. With the help of digital editing, any text may be lifted into the planetary canon and transported about the globe, regardless of how easily or reluctantly it slips from one language into another.

Damrosch makes a second key argument to support his idea that there is a single implicit canon of world literature: he argues that there is a single world. The earth is divided, he argues, into discrete "cultures," "nations," or "national traditions":

> The modern nation is, of course, a relatively recent development, but even older works were produced in local or ethnic configurations that have been subsumed into the national traditions within which they are now preserved and transmitted.
>
> *(Damrosch 2003, p. 283)*

Since the world is divided up in this way, there can logically be only one world literature. World literature is simply the set of literary works that have transcended these national or cultural boundaries. Certain texts may circulate more widely than other texts, but still we have a clear criterion that separates the set of world-literary texts from the set of merely national texts. It is very difficult to credit this argument. It is of course true that most of the world's states can be described as "modern nations," but Damrosch's description overlooks internal divisions within states and transnational institutions that cut across states. The English language, for example, is the "national language" of a dozen or so countries, an everyday medium of communication in several dozen more, and a useful *lingua franca* pretty much everywhere. When writers such as R.K. Narayan, Alexis Wright, or Abdulrazak Gurnah choose to write in English, they do not address a merely "national" audience. Likewise, when a Quechua, Arrernte, or Shertukpen writer publishes a work in their own tongue, it cannot be said that their work is simply "subsumed" by the national traditions of Peru, Australia, or India. It seems that even today, the cultural-linguistic world is lumpy, and no clear distinction can be made between local/national and non-local/world literature. Some languages, such as English, Urdu, or Haka, transgress national boundaries. Others, such as Quechua or Arrernte, exist independent of any particular nation, and have affiliations that cut across national groupings. Do Quechua and Arrernte belong to the Hispanophone or Anglophone worlds in the same way Peruvian Spanish and Australian English do? Different languages and traditions seem to bear different relationships to the planet as a whole. Some languages have a regional or global reach. Others are more local. This realization leads to the second kind of model scholars build: the *cosmopolis*, world literature as literature composed in a cosmopolitan language.

## Model 2: The Cosmopolis

Damrosch sees world literature as a canon of translatable texts that transcend national boundaries. Theorists of the cosmopolis define world literature in a very different way. A world literature or "cosmopolis" is a particular literature which is recognized as a world literature by its own writers and readers. The most famous proponent of this model is Sheldon Pollock. In *The Language of the Gods in the World of Men*, Pollock argues that a "Sanskrit cosmopolis" arose in South Asia in the first millennium of the Common Era. In this period, Sanskrit literature was not a literature that belonged to any particular polity or region. It was a "transregional culture-power sphere," a "great tradition over against the local or vernacular as the indigenous, little tradition" (Pollock 2006, pp. 11–12). What is most striking about Pollock's study is the way it allows us to compare and classify different kinds of world literature. The "globalization" of the last two centuries is only one way that literature can become cosmopolitan. Unlike English or French, Sanskrit was not imposed upon anyone through invasion or corporate takeover, but spread throughout South and South-East Asia through a relatively peaceful process of "transculturation" (Pollock 2006, p. 133). Unlike English or French, it was not used as a weapon of religious conversion, but seems indeed to have been an essentially secular language during the period of the Sanskrit cosmopolis (Pollock 2006, p. 98). And unlike English or French, Sanskrit did not have a core and a periphery—it was a truly cosmopolitan language, a language of nowhere and everywhere, rather than a metropolitan language, the dialect of a prestigious city such as London or Paris. Pollock provides a strong antidote to some of the nostrums of world-system theory. In our late phase of globalization, perhaps English itself has escaped its metropolitan roots, and has become a universal currency that exceeds any of its dialects.

*Canons* and *cosmopolises* imply different research methodologies. To make a canon of world literature, the scholar must select and translate a set of special texts. To make a cosmopolis (or a model of a cosmopolis), the scholar must examine the particular writing and reading practices of a particular historical community. If a particular community use a particular language (or languages) as universal languages, addressing a world audience, then they form a cosmopolis. In fact, a cosmopolis is rarely as universal as it seems to its inhabitants. There are probably few scholars today who would accept Sanskrit literature's claim to universality. Other examples are even more extreme. Jennifer Dubrow argues that Urdu literature formed a cosmopolis in the 19th century, even though it was basically confined to British India. This is because Urdu writers and readers formed "a transnational language community that eschewed identities of religion, caste, and even class" (Dubrow 2018, p. 109). Nineteenth-century Urdu was a language confined to a single state. If a language confined to a single state can nonetheless be "transnational," then what exactly is the difference between a "national" and a "transnational" language?

Pollock provides a powerful answer to this question, rooted in classical Sanskrit theories of knowledge:

> In short, when the absolute perspective of science (*pāramārthika sat*) is at odds with the representations produced from within the traditions of language thought (*vyāvahārika sat*), it is to the latter that we must defer if we are to understand the history made by knowledgeable agents.
>
> *(Pollock 2006, p. 66)*

To crudely paraphrase: if the writers and readers of Urdu and Sanskrit *represent* their language as a cosmopolitan or transnational language, then it is one. A cosmopolis is a social institution, like a state or a church, which exists essentially by the consent of its members. It is not an object that is independent of human actors, though of course any individual will encounter the cosmopolis as something larger and less changeable than themselves.

The *cosmopolis* puts the scholar in a less powerful position than the *canon*. Scholars can, in principle, create a planetary canon easily, by progressively selecting texts from around the world and translating or failing to translate them. Such work, however inadequate so far, has begun. But cosmopolises of the past no longer exist, and cosmopolises of the present are shaped by large forces. At best, scholars can probably only ever *describe* the workings of cosmopolises past and present, and hope to raise awareness of them among the public.

Digital Humanities has embraced the cosmopolis model, particularly in the field of quantitative book history. Such approaches qualify Pollock's dictum that only the *vyāvahārika sat* of a cosmopolis can really be known. The *Oceanic Exchanges* project, for example, has developed tools and resources "to examine patterns of information flow across national and linguistic boundaries in nineteenth century newspapers" (Cordell *et al.* 2017). In the 19th century, facts, poems, stories, or articles that appeared in Calcutta or Sydney one month could appear in Cape Town or Boston the next. The project is able to study such information flows in great detail by linking together national newspaper archives and using clever digital methods to locate related articles. In one study, the project team first searched for articles from around the world that mention Nikolay Bobrikov, the Russian Governor-General of Finland who was assassinated in 1904. Then, they used string-alignment techniques to locate instances of text reuse—in other words, they used software similar to anti-plagiarism software to find when an article had been quoted, plagiarized, or reprinted (Oiva *et al.* 2020, pp. 393–394). In this way, they were able to describe the actual workings of a "cosmopolis" in some detail. Pollock relies on close interpretations of scattered inscriptions and manuscript texts to painstakingly reconstruct the Sanskrit cosmopolis. By interpreting these texts, he is able to reconstruct the *vyāvahārika sat*, the way Sanskrit writers understood the cosmopolis of which they formed a part. By contrast, the *Oceanic Exchanges* team use quantitative methods to reconstruct the *pāramārthika sat* of media cosmopolis of the 19th century. They describe how far, how fast, and how much writing travelled around the 19th-century world. For example, they are able to show that in 19th-century Australia, news went "viral" more quickly than in other parts of the world, with a smaller number of news articles spreading further and faster than elsewhere (Oiva *et al.* 2020, p. 401). Really, the two approaches are complementary, and Pollock himself uses some rudimentary quantitative techniques to provide an objective framework for his interpretations (e.g. observing when and where the first and last inscriptions of a particular kind appeared).

There is an aspect of the *Oceanic Exchanges* project that points beyond the idea of the cosmopolis. The information flows that the authors describe are *interlingual*.

Bobrikov was a Russian functionary in Finland, yet the news that was first announced in Finnish newspapers (presumably written in Finnish, Swedish, or Russian) quickly made its way into French, German, English, and Spanish newspapers. In the modern media landscape, facts quickly become detached from words—and words from facts—zipping away along copper wires to the far reaches of the earth. Pollock's model of the "cosmopolis," like Damrosch's model of the "national tradition," more or less assumes that a particular literature must be defined by a particular literary language (though Pollock does also discuss the subordinate roles that Prākrit and Apabhraṃśa played in the Sanskrit cosmopolis). What if world literature transcends language itself? What if texts form part of wider systems, which are tied together by something other than translation or the sharing of a cosmopolitan language?

## Model 3: The Archive

This brings us to the third model of world literature, the *archive*. On this model, world literature is an arbitrary collection of texts, and the ideal planetary literature is simply the collection of all the texts ever written. The scholar's task is to examine this massive archive and try to determine how it fits together. This archive model is essentially Moretti's gambit in those influential articles from the early 2000s. Distant reading may change "how we look at *all* literary history: canonical and noncanonical: together" (Moretti 2000, p. 208). This "*all*," which Moretti himself italicizes, is the key. Moretti proposes a radically inductive form of literary scholarship. First take *all* of literature, and take it "together," in a single archive that stretches over time and space. Second, find the implicit order in the archive, by searching for "*the repeatable element of literature*: what returns fundamentally unchanged over many cases and many years" (Moretti 2000, p. 225). Rather than imposing their own structure on literary history, scholars should let the archive speak to them, as regularities and patterns emerge from the great mass of data.

This is an arresting model, and it has the potential to solve a common problem that bedevils the study of world literature. The problem is that the concepts we use to explain literary history have generally been developed to explain the literary history of Western literatures, and are often unsuitable to describe literature from elsewhere. This problem often places the postcolonial critic in a tight spot, as Nirmala Menon indicates in *Remapping the Indian Postcolonial Canon* (2016):

> The critique of the limitations of "Western" theory (here, deconstruction) is not to elevate a "nativist" theory but [leads to] the very practical conclusion that the multiple ways of narrativizing multiple postcolonial experiences have probably not been factored into the Western theoretical structure.
>
> *(Menon 2016, p. 142)*

Menon walks a tight line between imperialism and nativism, as she draws on Sanskrit *Bhava-Rasa* theory to try and redefine the act of translation for an Indian context. With her tactful, careful argument, Menon largely succeeds in this particular instance, but Moretti's approach may offer an easier way out. By flattening all the world's texts into a homogenous archive, Moretti suggests that we can reset world literature, and temporarily set aside all the conceptual baggage that so often gets in the way. We can then generate fresh, new concepts of literary history by observing the patterns that emerge from the data as we apply different algorithms to it.

This is potentially a democratic, planetary vision of world literature, which erases the distinction between "world" and "local" literatures entirely. Both the *canon* and the *cosmopolis* presuppose that only certain texts are world literature: only the canonical or cosmopolitan texts circulate globally. But if world literature is simply an *archive*, it becomes possible to think of world literature as a planetary commons, where every literary tradition, every act of writing, and every instance of reading is equally present.

The obvious problem is that there is no planetary archive, no database, or no library where a scholar can easily access the entire literary heritage of humanity—or those parts of it that survive. The scholars who have taken up Moretti's call, such as Matthew Jockers, Ted Underwood, and Stanford's Literary Lab, have not had the resources nor the linguistic expertise required to try and sample world literature as a whole, and have devoted their efforts almost exclusively to English literature (Jockers 2013, Underwood 2019).[2] In recent years, the situation has started to improve. There are digitization projects underway across Asia, Africa, and the Americas, and digital humanists in these regions are developing the teams and the tools required to perform the kind of data-rich analysis that has hitherto only really been possible for prestigious European languages. As the practical barriers recede, however, more fundamental barriers to a planetary literary archive emerge.

The first reason is that the archive is uneven. Roopika Risam makes this point forcefully in *New Digital Worlds*. She argues that the digital cultural record is colonialist in two ways: not only as "a function of *what* is there—what gets digitalized and thus represented in the digital cultural record—but also *how* it is there—how those who have created their projects are presenting their subjects" (Risam 2019, p. 17). Moretti himself provides a good example of this *how*, the way an archive can itself be structured to present the subject in a certain way. In *Graphs, Maps, Trees: Abstract Models for Literary History*, he presents a graph of the "Rise of the Novel, 18th to 20th Century" (Moretti 2005, p. 6). It is an arresting graph, placing the history of British, Italian, and Spanish literature alongside that of Japan and Nigeria. Each country appears as a line in the graph, representing the number of novels published in each country in a certain year according to rigorous scholarly bibliographies. It has two axes: the x-axis indicates year of publication and the y-axis indicates the number of novels published that year. The data underlying the graph rely on four key assumptions:

1 The passage of time in literary history is measured in years.
2 The quantity of literature is to be measured by the number of printed books.

3 Texts are to be grouped into national traditions by place of publication.
4 The novel is a (or possibly *the*) crucial genre of modern literature.

While each assumption may be justifiable, the graph as a whole resolves every assumption according to traditional Western models of literary modernity. Books published per year is a unit that only makes sense for a large country with an extensive printing industry—Luxembourg and Samoa are simply unplottable on the graph. Grouping texts according to place of publication only makes sense if the published literature is national in character—but the texts that Moretti groups under "Britain" include Irish, Scottish, and colonial texts. Most problematic of all is the focus on the novel. Moretti's vision in "Slaughterhouse" was to search the archive for the "repeatable elements" in literature, and to allow a pattern to emerge from the data. But here the "repeatable element" is assumed *a priori*—any literature that falls outside the definition of "novel" simply cannot be included. This makes Moretti's argument in the piece somewhat circular. He wants to prove that world literature is convergent in the modern world, and cites the "rise of the novel" as a key piece of evidence. All literatures are becoming similar, because they are all becoming "novelized." But by setting up the graph this way, it could *only ever* provide evidence for such convergence. It's true that such a graph can display the *absence* of the novel in a particular time and place, but if there is a process at work in any of these places that is *not* the "rise of the novel," the graph simply will not show it.

This is what Risam is targeting when she argues that it matters "*how* [the data] is there" in the digital cultural record. The very structure of the archive can predetermine what kinds of question we are able to ask, and what kinds of answer we are able to give. If your archive is an archive of novels, grouped into nation states, with the year of publication recorded, then the only real question you can ask is the old question of the "rise of the novel." How can digital scholars ever discover other patterns in planetary literary history with archives like these?

There is a second, deeper problem with approaches like Moretti's—they are too idealistic, too inattentive to the grubby material reality of things. Moretti hopes that if an archive is large enough, then the selection of texts within it will be essentially random, and therefore free from prior interpretation. This is what allows him to clear the deck and generate new concepts for world literary history. But as Kath Bode shows through her close study of Australia's *Trove* database, one of the largest and most comprehensive newspaper databases in the world, even the largest and most comprehensive archives have been edited and shaped by human hands—first the hands of the editors who edited the newspapers, then the hands of the librarians who preserved and catalogued them, then the hands of the computer scientists who wrote the software that digitized them, then the hands of the readers who correct them, and so on (Bode 2018). All archives have such a grubby, material history, that if Bode is correct, then the time will never come when we can flatten the world's literature and start afresh in the way Moretti describes. Every archive will always be lumpy, encoding not only the "raw data" of literature but also the inadvertent data of the people who made the archive. What has been preserved? By whom? Why? There are gaps in the data—what is their shape? Even a postcolonial archive, such as Risam advocates, will have this same lumpiness and incompleteness.

There is actually nothing wrong with Moretti's novel graph in and of itself. It is a masterful piece of literary-historical storytelling. But the constraints of this particular graph have become the blind spots of digital literary scholarship. And this undermines the whole enterprise. For ultimately, *canons* and *cosmopolises* rely on *archives*. All our models of world literature lie strung between the *planet* and the *archive*. The planet is the unattainable target of our aspiration. The archive is the inescapable source of all our evidence. If Risam and Bode are right, and even the best archives are radically incomplete, then what is the future for digital literary history?

## Between Worlds, Orthogonality

I would like to conclude by indicating how I think a version of Moretti's vision may still be possible. Where Moretti goes wrong is in his hope to grasp world literature as a whole—"*all* literary history . . . together." As Risam and Bode so convincingly argue, this whole is simply not present in the archive, and may never be present. Indeed, arguably there is no whole, no single literary history into which every act of writing can be integrated. Where Moretti goes right is in his hope for a more inductive literary history—searching for the "repeatable elements," the waves, and fluctuations in the flow of words that spark comparisons and analysis. I propose *orthogonality* as the methodological ideal that can guide this search for "repeatable elements." In its most homely meaning, *orthogonal* is roughly synonymous with *perpendicular*. More abstractly, it refers to the separation of different features of a system. In practical terms for digital literary scholars, *orthogonality* means the *search for axes*. In Moretti's graph, the three axes were time in years (x-axis), novels published (y-axis), and country of publication (grouping variable). What other axes of comparison can we find to compare and contrast traditions, texts, tropes, words, or characters in the disparate literatures of the planet? In Moretti's graph, the selection of axes was more or less determined by the data itself: he derived the graph from a set of bibliographies that listed novels by year of publication divided by country. But as full-text databases proliferate for more and more languages, digital literary scholars will have more and more "unstructured" textual data at their disposal. What are the measurable quantities of a mass of text? What measurements can we make that apply with equal validity to texts in languages A, B, and C? Will the same measurements still be valid if applied to texts in languages B, C, and D? If I compare the distribution of personal pronouns in English and Hindi texts, to reveal something about the literary representation of subjectivity, how can I then include Italian or Swahili texts in my analysis, when they use personal pronouns so rarely? We are just now approaching the time when such questions can really be asked.

*Orthogonality* presupposes that there isn't a single world with a single literature. It sets aside the goal of creating a single unified model for all of literary history, and sets a humbler goal in its place. If there is no single map of world literature, then there is no single latitude and longitude by which to plot the literary history of the world. We should aspire for a profusion of maps, each revealing the particular gridlines that demarcate that little pocket of literary reality. We may never know the whole, but we can systematize our bafflement. In this way, digital scholars can help to figure the (im)possibility of a truly planetary literature.

## Notes

1 In fact, he is making a broader argument about modelling *anything*, but his arguments can be applied to literature in this way.
2 The Stanford Literary Lab's series of pamphlets are available at https://litlab.stanford.edu/pamphlets/.

## References


Apter, E. (2013) *Against World Literature: On the Politics of Untranslatability*. London and New York: Verso.

Arendt, H. (1958) *The Human Condition*. Chicago, IL: University of Chicago Press.

Bode, K. (2018) *A World of Fiction: Digital Collections and the Future of Literary History*. Ann Arbor, MI: University of Michigan Press.

Cordell, R., Beals, M.H., Russell, I.G., Nyhan, J., Priani, E., Priewe, M., Salmi, H., Verheul, J., Alegre, R., and Hauswedell, T. (2017) *Oceanic Exchanges*. DOI: 10.17605/OSF.IO/WA94S. Available from: osf.io/wa94s.

Damrosch, D. (2003) *What is World Literature?* Princeton, NJ: Princeton University Press.

Dubrow, J. (2018) *Cosmopolitan Dreams: The Making of Modern Urdu Literary Culture in Colonial South Asia*. Honolulu, HI: University of Hawaii Press.

Ghalib, M.A. (2017) *Ghalib: Selected Poems and Letters*. Bilingual edition. New York: Columbia University Press.

Ghalib, M.A., and Pritchett, F. (2020) A Desertful of Roses: the Urdu Ghazals of Mirza Asadullah Khan Ghalib [online]. Available from: www.columbia.edu/itc/mealac/pritchett/00ghalib/index.html#index [Accessed 18 Dec 2020].

Jockers, M. (2013) *Macroanalysis: Digital Methods and Literary History*. Urbana, Chicago and Springfield, IL: University of Illinois Press.

McCarty, W. (2005) *Humanities Computing*. Houndmills: Palgrave.

McGann, J.J. (2001) *Radiant Textuality: Literature After the World Wide Web*. Houndmills: Palgrave.

Menon, N. (2016) *Remapping the Indian Postcolonial Canon*. London: Palgrave Macmillan UK.

Moretti, F. (2000) The Slaughterhouse of Literature. *Modern Language Quarterly*, 61 (1), 207–228.

Moretti, F. (2005) *Graphs, Maps, Trees*. London and New York: Verso.

Oiva, M., Nivala, A., Salmi, H., Latva, O., Jalava, M., Keck, J., Domínguez, L.M., and Parker, J. (2020) Spreading News in 1904. *Media History*, 26 (4), 391–407.

Pollock, S.I. (2005) *The Ends of Man at the End of Premodernity*. Amsterdam: Royal Netherlands Academy of Arts and Sciences.

Pollock, S.I. (2006) *The Language of the Gods in the World of Men: Sanskrit, Culture, and Power in Premodern India*. Berkeley, CA: University of California Press.

Pritchett, F.W. (1994) *Nets of Awareness : Urdu Poetry and Its Critics*. Berkeley, CA: University of California Press.
Risam, R. (2019) *New Digital Worlds*. Evanston, IL: Northwestern University Press.
Spivak, G. (2003) *Death of a Discipline*. New York: Columbia University Press.
Underwood, T. (2019) *Distant Horizons: Digital Evidence and Literary Change*. Chicago, IL: Chicago University Press.

# PART II

# Archives, Ethics, and Praxis

# 4

# DIGITAL ARCHIVES FOR INDIAN LITERATURES AND CULTURES

## Challenges and Prospects

*Parthasarathi Bhaumik*

## I

The relationship between humanities and archiving is historical and dates back to classical antiquity, both in Europe and in India. The preservation of manuscripts and books in religious institutions, like churches and temples, or in ancient universities, continued to illumine the practice of humanities for ages. The etymology of the word "archive" shows its close connection with institutions such as government and state in Europe; however, in India, manuscripts, or *punthis*, were preserved largely by families as their sacred inheritance from their ancestors, and their access was limited within the family. The exclusive access to such archives enabled the family members to be privileged owners of specialized knowledge, and this may have some relations with the profession that the family practiced through generations. Thus, the tradition of the preservation of knowledge in India, in the forms of both memory and scriptures, happened to be, to some extent, familial, communitarian, and local. The interventions of colonial education and knowledge systems undeniably played a role in reshaping concepts of knowledge and its propagation and retention, bringing epistemology to a larger arena of mass participation and exchanges. However, it should also be mentioned that placing knowledge in a global network started in pre-colonial times, especially with Buddhism. The patterns of systemic and large-scale preservation, archiving, and curation of knowledge in India and their legacies thereafter need to be perceived from the perspectives of both global participation and Indigenous traits. The introduction of digital technology in India in 1980s, and launch of the internet in 1995, initiated readjustments of knowledge architectures to a great extent, as it happened in other cultural sites as well. The ever-increasing interventions of digital technology and its popularity not only bred euphoria and excitement but also brought forth anxiety for Indian archives to equip themselves to meet demands of a new generation

DOI: 10.4324/9781003354246-7

of scholars, particularly of humanities, who wanted quick discovery and access to cultural resources in suitable formats. On the other hand, scholars of humanities need to understand rapidly changing contours of archives, particularly in the digital era. Preparing Indian literary and cultural resources for digital curation entails challenges and continuing negotiations. The concept of the archive, for a number of thinkers, was an endeavour against the grain of life and time: something "unnatural." Wolfgang Ernst (2013), a German media theorist, described it as a desire which is anti-"entropic," a term from thermodynamics meaning resisting gradual changes/degradation towards stability. In other words, an archive can be described as a frozen frame photograph, looking at the natural flux of life with disdain. Michel Foucault (2002) found that the "archive deprives us of our continuities; . . . it breaks the thread of transcendental teleologies." Of course, Foucault's idea of the archive goes beyond the archive that this chapter endeavours to address and signifies an *a priori* system that governs discursive practices. Nevertheless, the existence of the archive within continuous cultural processes may precipitate certain unease, some discontent among their participants, while also inciting some desires continuously. Working with and curating an archive of humanities in a multicultural and multilingual country like India invites certain challenges, provokes expectations, and breeds anxieties which are not easy to negotiate.

## *Physical Archives for Humanities in India: Survival Questions*

The general perceptions about "archive" as a place for storing materials from a dead past is a great hindrance to the growth and development of the archive. The more an archive boasts of itself as a storehouse of rare resources from "time immemorial," the more detached it becomes from its contemporary time. Accentuating temporal difference and harping on an exotic past may attract a few curious glances to an existing archive, but this strategy ultimately fails to establish any effective and long-lasting bond between the archive and present time. The purpose of an archive is not to stand as a wonderful denial of time, holding and carefully guarding materials from natural ravages that come with age, but to act as an integral part of the living world, an unavoidable accessory to everyday ubiquitous life. If archives fail to contemporize themselves and are unable to reach people other than researchers and scholars, there is little possibility for the archives in India to survive the ever-dwindling public attention. Apart from theoretical questions about the very concept of the archive in temporal contexts, Indian archives face more mundane challenges like funding. A centralized archive is an expensive affair, and unless the archive itself raises sufficient money for and from its everyday operations, it has to depend on government grants for its survival. However, surviving only on government grants is not an easy option for Indian archives, as evident from the following table:

Apart from centralized grants, there may be other sources of financial support for libraries and archives, but understandably, they are far from being adequate for such institutions. This scenario may be compared, albeit ambitiously, with that of the British Library in London. The British Library alone has an annual budget in the range

**TABLE 4.1** Details of libraries/archives in urban/rural areas and the budget allocated for such purposes

| | |
|---|---|
| Number of libraries/archives in rural areas: | 70,817 |
| Number of libraries/archives in urban areas: | 4,583 |
| Total number of libraries/archives in India: | 75,400 |
| *Source*: Census of India 2011 | |
| Money allocated for public libraries and archives 2020–21 | Rs. 103.51 crore |
| Average money allocated for establishment expenditure for each library/archive per month: | Rs. 1,144 |

*Source*: Union Budget (2020)

of £98 million (Rs. 724 Crore), approximately seven times the total budgetary allotment for all the libraries and archives in India. The UK Government provides 73% of it in the form of grant-in-aid from the Department of Culture, Media & Sport (DCM), and, most importantly, an independent survey recently concluded that for every £1 in subsidy, the British Library generates £4 for the economy. Archives and libraries are never perceived as a money-making institution; they are regarded as passive repositories of source materials for researchers to retrieve and use in their research. Literary researchers may, for instance, try to locate rare books and documents which are impossible to procure in market or contemporary circulations. It effectively pushes archives off the realm of living literary traditions and practices and limits it to the role of a passive caretaker of dusty records and vintage texts.

Apart from financial uncertainties, Indian archives face challenges of physical space to accommodate their ever-burgeoning quantum of materials. Physical space is, of course, a necessity for any good archive to update its collections regularly. Moreover, the proliferation of types of resources and their various forms—from paper to digital—demand new policies for the physical archives to ensure their proper curation and dissemination, which need continuous advancement in adopting technologies and their proper understanding. Since changing epistemological practices are gradually leaning towards digital technologies and an exponential growth of both digitized and born-digital materials, it appears that the digital archive is going to be an answer to a plethora of problems that Indian archives encounter for their survival. This begs the question: how far would the digital archive come as a much-needed panacea for ailing Indian physical archives, and how can the interventions of digital technologies as a supposed enhancer of repositories of cultural materials facilitate its preservation and accesses in India?

## II

Representing Indian literatures and cultures has always been a difficult job, particularly for academia, in their efforts to accommodate them in respective disciplines for the convenience of study. The tradition of "literature" in India has never been one-dimensional and homogeneous: it cannot be circumscribed within a singular genre, much to the disadvantage of academic study and research. There have always been juxtapositions, shared areas, lively transactions, and dissolutions of generic boundaries in Indian literary traditions: the term "sāhitya" (togetherness) seems to be a more apt expression than "literature" (something written) in this context. Apart from generic interrelations, close proximity and coexistence of different languages enabled Indian literatures to flow into each other, and in consequence, has rendered the complacent study of literature produced in single Indian language or Indian literature as a unified entity redundant. The study of Indian literatures needs interfaces which would accommodate its complex pattern, interwovenness, and transactions for holistic studies. Besides, the coexistence of analogue and digital formats of the present time needs new parameters for critical studies, researches, methodologies, and workflows which the traditional studies of literature finds wanting in their approaches. This is where, probably, the role of the digital archive and curation in the contexts of preservation, access, and visualization may play a vital role.

There is a general euphoria in our country around the idea that India is progressing rapidly towards a digital future, with undeniable increase in internet users in recent years. According to a report published by the Government of India (2019), there are 636.73 million internet users in 2019, a majority of who use wireless/mobile internet. There is also a huge difference between urban and rural users: the percentage of people who access the internet in urban areas is 97.94, while the figure for rural areas is 25.36 (*Telecom Statistics India-2019*). Moreover, the lower costs of accessing internet in India compared to other countries may drive us to be optimistic of the future of digital archiving and dissemination of its digital resources. However, there have been no enquiries in India about any correlation between easy availability of internet and use of digital archive. The patterns of usage of digital archives among the people may help us conceptualize and plan archives and curatorial strategies more effectively.

A survey conducted by the Department of Digital, Culture, Media & Sports, The Government of UK in 2018, shows a dwindling figure of footfalls in archives in the UK, despite their user-friendly infrastructure and continuous updating of collections, but there is a relative increase in visits to online archives over the recent years in the UK. Such visits shot up significantly during 2012–2013 because of the London Summer Olympics (Table 4.2). The latter development shows a trend of increasing general, public participation in accessing digital archives when an occasion incites general interest in various facts, and archives were successful in bringing them to their own collections. The mass participation of people in digital archives depends on various primary factors such as computer literacy and internet access. It also depends on the availability of culture-specific materials on digital platforms, and their visibility and user-friendliness. This is where Indian literary and cultural texts need more attention: the texts need to be digitized as per international standards, visualized according to people's interests, easily discoverable, and accessible. In short, the digital curation environment for Indian literary and cultural resources should ensure mass participation of people beyond academic domains.

The ecosystem in the digital curation environment was emphasized by Applehans *et al.* (1999) and later expanded by Arjun Sabharwal (2015) in his book *Digital*

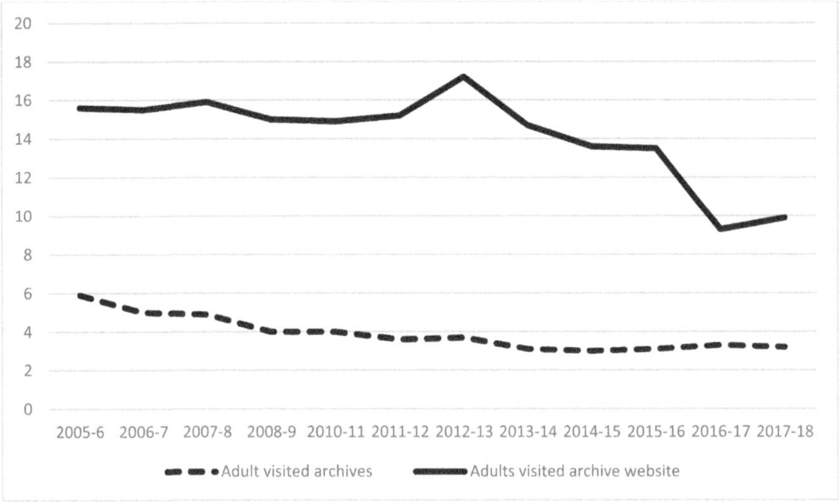


**TABLE 4.2** Graphs showing percentage of adults who had visited (i) an archive or record office in the last 12 months and (ii) an archive or record office website

*Source*: National Statistics, Department of Digital, Culture, Media & Sports, The Government of UK 2018

*Curation in the Digital Humanities*. The ecosystem integrates people, resources or contents, and technologies into meaningful relations. Needless to say, such a structure cannot be an objective one, as it is determined by institutional policies, finances, staff profiles, and politics. The much-accepted standard for the digital curation lifecycle model, as provided by the Digital Curation Center at the University of Edinburgh, shows various curatorial activity levels around digital objects. The primary level of activity around the digital content is creation/receiving resources, appraisement, and selection, which would constitute the ingest process of the archive (Sabharwal 2015). The appraisement and selection of resources for the digital archive is a complex and intriguing process, and this alone could create curatorial dilemma particularly in India, where funding is limited and a majority of resources are endangered. Selecting less privileged literatures and histories, which are at greater risk, could have been a choice, and digital technology may contribute to their retention as opposed to their quick extinction. For instance, subaltern texts may be prioritized in this regard, but there remains some suspicion lurking around in allowing the transformation of subaltern texts into digital objects in particular, and subaltern digital archive in general. Radhika Gajjala (2019), for instance, wrote,

> The project of producing, maintaining, and curating (even sometimes gatekeeping) archives of digital subalternity poses many issues. The text/image work and code work we do in the digital humanities are very important indeed, but these efforts must be supplemented and enhanced with dialogic, collaborative, and ethnographic immersion. Such immersion would entail

> actual travel to subaltern spaces for extended periods of time. . . . Frictions and contradictions must be worked with—not simplified and flattened. In building archives of subalternity, we need the strong presence of countertexts and counterarguments to prevent those archives from being engulfed by the market logic that aspires to mobilize the "bottom of the pyramid" as consumers.
>
> *(432)*

Radhika's concerns show the necessity of bringing together curatorial procedures and digital humanities, where curators and archivists must work collaboratively to anticipate and assess implications of digital objects, as she fears that various digital representations on virtual interfaces may replace the reality in favour of creating some feel-good environment much in contradiction to real and actual situations.

In 2009, the British Library undertook the Endangered Archives Programme (EAP) to facilitate the "digitisation of archives around the world that are in danger of destruction, neglect or physical deterioration" (EAP Website). Lisbet Rausing, the co-founder of the Endangered Archives Programme, described this project in the following words: "The Endangered Archives Programme captures forgotten and still not written histories, often suppressed or marginalised. It gives voice to the voiceless: it opens a dialogue with global humanity's multiple pasts. It is a library of history still waiting to be written" (The British Library Endangered Archives Programme n.d.). The digital version of the endangered texts would be freely available online, while the physical material would remain in the possession of the grantee who undertakes the programme. The School of Cultural Texts and Records, Jadavpur University, decided to participate in this programme for the preservation of Bangla market books, popularly known as *bāzāri boi*, which are sold by hawkers and vendors to train and bus commuters or in less fancied places. These books are widely read, yet their status remains ephemeral, and they may vanish suddenly. However, when the project was completed, their digitized versions could not be uploaded on unresolved copyright issues. Most such Bangla books emerge without much information about their publishers or authors. The notion of anonymity in the Indian book tradition comes into conflict with international copyright laws when they are selected for digitization. As a result, the entire digitized collection of Bangla market books becomes an exclusive property, which can only be accessed on-site. The stringent copyright laws on intellectual property, in effect, bring discriminations in favour of big and affluent archives, effectively disadvantaging small and non-profit archives in countries such as ours. It also paves way for exclusive commercial digital archives, a tradition which has already taken roots in India.

## *Data Visualization and Working in Isolation*

The relationship between the digital archive and digital humanities (DH) probably becomes significant once the need for appropriate data visualization is felt. The representations of digital objects in formats and ways convenient for their analyses, interpretations, and further outreach for various interest groups need strategies that necessitate active collaboration with DH. The use of digital artefacts such as interface, software, and digital objects should be integrated in such ways that they would contextualize data and provoke intersubjective reading. Ramsey and Rockwell (2012) argue that digital artefacts are, in fact, hermeneutic tools and visualization tools. The ubiquitous tone of such general assessments of DH in the contexts of literature and cultures, however, often conceals the fact that all these tools and DH in general have leanings towards English corpora. Franco Moretti in one of his interviews commented:

> It has had, in my opinion, an enormous and unfortunate consequence for comparative literature, which is that digital humanities has basically developed within literary studies focusing almost exclusively on English corpora, English in America. So you have the completely paradoxical coexistence of a very new—some people might even say revolutionary tool, and an enormous provincialism in its field of application. . . . I would not claim that a digital humanities is a conceptual breakthrough. I think it's basically more of a development in terms of the archive and the tools than the concepts. It's very strong in its archive and very strong on tools.
>
> *(Moretti 2017, 273)*

It is precisely for this reason that the visualization of digital objects becomes a challenge, especially for smaller archives in India, notwithstanding the promises of DH. The available and often default tools, which facilitate data visualization, fall short when they need to process non-English languages.

The School of Cultural Texts and Records of Jadavpur University embarked on creating the "world's largest integrated literary database" (Chaudhuri 2015): *Bichitra*, a variorum of Tagore's literary works. It was the biggest of all the variorums on a single author, covering 140,000 pages of primary material, of which majority are in Bangla. Since it involved Tagore's original manuscripts and multiple printed versions of his works, powerful OCR software was required to turn such a mammoth quantum of primary materials into digital objects, as no good OCR for Bangla script is available to date. Despite the fact that 3% of the world population speaks Bangla, its digital presence is negligible, and almost invisible. According to a web technology survey by W$^3$Techs (n.d.), approximately 0.019% websites use Bangla in December 2020, where English tops the list with 60.5% share followed by Russian with 8.5% share of all the websites, though Bangla is the fifth most spoken language in the world while Russian ranks eighth in this list.

This digital divide entails the ready availability of relevant software such as language-specific OCRs, and in Bangla, the best OCR offered 98% accuracy. This mere 2% inaccuracy may be a huge burden for a project of such magnitude as *Bichitra*. Besides, there was no collation software which could detect variations of

**TABLE 4.3** Languages: digital presence and percentage of native speakers

| *Rank* | *Language/Percentage of native speakers* | *Percentage of websites using the language* |
|---|---|---|
| 1 | English 4.9 | 60.7 |
| 2 | Russian 2 | 8.3 |
| 3 | Turkish 0.1 | 3.9 |
| 4 | Spanish 0.6 | 3.8 |
| 5 | Persian 0.07 | 3.3 |
| 6 | French 0.1 | 2.7 |
| 7 | German 0.09 | 2.3 |
| – | Hindi 4.4 | 0.1 |
| – | Bengali 3 | 0.019 |

*Source*: W³Techs (n.d.) and Wikipedia (n.d.) (list of languages by number of native speakers)

scripts written in Bangla and its non-Roman alphabet. It has been a major factor in promoting DH projects for Indian *bhāsā* literatures, and Professor Sukanta Choudhuri, the coordinator of *Bichitra* project, writes,

> Metaphorically speaking, we had to start even before zero, as we were working with a non-Latin font. Those who do not can have no idea of the additional challenges this poses. . . . Also, the English or Roman alphabet has the benefit of many analytic tools, developed over the years and available on the Internet. With Bengali, as with almost all non-Latin alphabets, if there are any such tools at all, they are hard to find and often imperfect.
>
> (99)

The *Bichitra* Project thus had to invest much of its time and resources to develop collation tools, besides its regular job of digitization and transcription. This resulted in the in-house production of *Prabhed*, the first text processing software ever created for a non-Latin font; its use was later extended to Roman fonts, too. But arriving at *Prabhed*, it went through two more stages of its development in *Tafat* and *Pathantar*.

Finding necessary digital tools for underpinning visualization of cultural data, making algorithms of those codices, which are almost non-entities in global digital networks, and negotiating a technology which has comprehensive bias towards the epistemologies of the Global North are the recurrent challenges for building digital archives in India. Despite the fact that such endeavours make it almost imperative for the builders of Indian digital archives to make their own tools (as Choudhuri mentioned), it is quite unlikely that one could start it from scratch. Building it in isolation is an idea that has become obsolete, and nearly absurd, in the present systems of coding, wherein cutting, pasting, and modifying codes are essential features of programming. Even when building digital tools for Indian cultural contents, one needs to rely on existing codes and programmes and follow the strictures of the international standardization. The norms for standardization, though claimed universal, are often not conducive for all kinds of cultural materials. This coding is a high-skilled job, often facilitated and financed by the corporate bodies of the Global North in general, and often the USA in particular. Miriam Posner (2012), in one of her interviews, opined that coding, as a process, is never neutral, and is largely dominated by white men. On the other hand, the tools which facilitate visualization and build interfaces are also engaged in the production of knowledge out of the repositories of accumulated data. In other words, tools are very often used to give answers, or answers are the outcome of the building of tools. When codes are made in a culture-specific environment, they exhibit tendencies of a particular epistemology. The exercise of DH and building digital archives in India become acts of addressing the silences and invisibles, what Risam (2018) called, "uncovering the colonial biases that subtend knowledge production in digital humanities" (52).

The availability of ready tools and templates is directly proportional to their marketing potential, and it is never unusual that the sellers would always want to maximize the catchment area of their products. This can be done in two ways: first, making the product inclusive and multipurpose in nature, which alone can meet various demands of diverse cultural contexts. Second, if the diversity of cultural demands can be minimized, some particular form can be passed on as a "standard," and then the obligation of accommodating all the demands may be set aside only to make others compromise their demands in a desperation to fit their projects in the "standard" format. Though these two methods run simultaneously, the latter one seems more cost-effective, as it involves ideologies only, and no costly innovations or regular update of technology. On the other hand, the fear of not being "standard" and thus not acceptable to the international community remains at the core of every attempt for the building and visualization of Indian cultural resources on digital platforms. The dilemma between the opportunity for global participation by compromising some uniqueness of culture-specific data or languishing in isolation by refusing to give away cultural specificities remains.

In the Digital Humanities Manifesto 2.0, published in 2009–2010, Jeffrey Schnapp and Todd Presner *et al.* set up a brief, no-nonsense "Instruction Manual," which starts with "don't whine." The call is loud and clear: that in spite of all the impediments, DH must move on, and one needs to carve out one's own path and tread on untrodden territories. The Manifesto rightly stands against all kinds of strictures and calls for "the university/museum/archive/library *without walls*" (Schnapp *et al.* n.d.) The feasibility of open archive and library is still a distant dream to achieve specifically for the countries like India, where the digital environment for archive is limited by non-availability/restrictive nature of tools. There is no imminent solution to this problem unless free tools are made for this purpose. A regular awareness about digital archive projects of other countries having similar infrastructural and financial restrictions may be a necessary step towards recognizing and negotiating inherent problems. Risam (2018), talking about Early Caribbean Digital Archive, indicates the gradual simplification of emerging technology, which enables even little-trained persons to use the tools effectively. Therefore, the directors of the project depended on a close collaboration between "a digital knowledge commons" and "laboratory for scholarly textual analysis." This creates a digital space where the user community may contribute by using easily the tools for "annotations, notebooks, bookmarks, personal folders." This would create personal collections within the corpus of the Archive (55). This model, with little changes, may be relevant for Indian contexts as well. The rise of a young generation with ample digital skills and increasing internet penetration in the country may facilitate such model, though at the same time, it should be mentioned that there exist gaps in the overall picture of computer literacy in India. The digital divide between rural and urban, male and female, is conspicuous, and may have its impact on any such models.

## *Metadata and Search*

The digital collection, apart from being a database of retrievable fragments, may also constitute an uninterrupted seamless narrative once associations among those fragments can be made and visualized subsequently. This association may be made in predetermined ways, but when they are subjected to the user's query, there may emerge possibilities of creating endless narratives. The metadata and search engines may work in close coordination to bring out relevant data for visualization, often in a list form, arranged in multifarious ways according to the wish of the user. Chronology, theme or scope, geopolitical location, linguistic feature, etc. are the chosen parameters to constitute multiple narratives, and every such narrative may provide the contextual knowledge to the data. Creation of metadata is significant not only for the search engine, but it is also necessary for contextualization of the database, and this contextualization also brings much-needed provenance of the archive. Sternfeld (2011) argues,

> Archival theory provides the conceptual framework with which to assess how an interface prioritizes data or records, to suggest topics of inquiry, or to guide the user towards historical conclusions. A well-structured system for search and retrieval can tear down the barriers separating what Thomas Kirchhoff *et al.* call "digitization islands." . . . Evaluation of a digital historical presentation should include an assessment of how the search interface facilitates the construction of contextual bonds among its content.
>
> *(558)*

People are often sceptical about the digital archive due to questions of its authenticity, which is further enhanced by the very nature of digital technology. Digital technology facilitating easy editing, uploading, and quick dissemination stands in the way of the authenticity of a digital archive, though the same features of the technology have been utilized for building such archives. There exist unmentioned rules in academia to trust physical archives more than their digital counterparts. The digital archives associated with big institutions like the British Library or the Library of Congress are held trustworthy, but the small digital libraries or archives, privately owned or having no association with an institution of such stature, may not enjoy that privileges of being a trustworthy archive. A majority of the digital libraries and archives of the developing world are of this nature, and India is no exception. Therefore, it is imperative that Indian digital archives build extended metadata and robust search options for the user as necessary steps for the provenance of its resources.

In Indian contexts, the problem is not merely of "digitization islands." The archives themselves often exist in isolation with their own resources and metadata. The isolated existence of small digital archives in terms of their catalogues, metadata, and repositories may not facilitate their provenance, visibility, and sustainability. They need to join with each other, especially in terms of their metadata and catalogues. An integrated online catalogue, where all the archives in India would harvest their metadata, would enable a researcher to search her item across archives on a single interface. This integrated catalogue not only would bring all the archives in the country closer irrespective of their size and prominence, but also would put the resources in context for their provenance as well. The National Archive of the UK follows similar model as a nodal agency through its "Discovery" online catalogue (https://discovery.nationalarchives.gov.uk/), which holds more than 32 million descriptions of records held by the National Archives and more than 2,500 archives in the UK.

One of the major problems for building an integrated catalogue in India is its multilingualism, where the metadata description would include words from various Indian languages. However, the keyword schema for search invariably would use Roman letters, as all available technologies in this regard are functional on this script. Thus, it becomes imperative for the archivists to transcribe words from Indian language into Roman script. Unfortunately, there is no standard rule for such transcription, and a word in an Indian language could be transcribed in a number of ways. The use of diacritical marks would complicate the process both for the user and for the technology. A close coordination among archives of various linguistic backgrounds may come together to decide on the standardization of the Roman transcription of Indian names.

## Personal Digital Archives, Social Networking, and Web 2.0 Tools

The big archives supported by the state or institutions have their relevant importance in preserving and disseminating collective memory. The sharp rise in state documents after the World Wars in Europe resulted in the building of state archives, where the focus was on the documentation of social, cultural, and economic activities of the state, with citizens as the recipients of such state policies. The people, with their everyday activities, featured in such archives as members of the families or/and communities, workers in factories, institutions, and farms. The huge colonial archives on India, like that of the British Library (e.g. India Office Records & Private Collections), focus on community, everyday people as state subjects, and public memory on the basis of its high-volume records. Prioritizing such an archive on digital platforms may not be a good option for India, for reasons discussed earlier; in addition to them, the contour of digital archiving is changing worldwide—the big-data state archives are giving way to (not replaced by) personal and private archives. This latter development is enhanced by the proliferation of social networks in the Web 2.0 phase. Web 2.0 signifies the shift from the earlier use of internet (Web 1.0), and not to any specific technical upgrade to the internet. This phase ensures active participation of the users who could also contribute, unlike the users of the Web 1.0 where the control of internet contents was in the hands of few programmers and code makers, and users largely remained passive. In the Web 2.0 phase, with the proliferation of social media, the idea of a centralized archive has gone through fragmentation as each person, institution, and community already started to build their own archives, putting on resources pertaining to micro-level lived experiences and histories. It is an immersive, and subjective exercise which has started to redefine earlier notions of archive. Besides digitized data, born-digital data are rapidly gaining significance as archival resources. The proliferation of such data on network sites and Web 2.0 platforms is quite astonishing; its growth is exponential.

In the face of the explosion of data and personalized resources, the physical archives or digital archives of digitized materials seem struggle to find out right strategies to deal with the world of exponential growth of cultural materials. Cook (2013) rightly points out,

> There is simply too much evidence, too much memory, too much identity, to acquire more than a mere fragment of it in our established archives. Furthermore, removing such archives, such memory, such evidence, from the originating communities to our archives may be problematic and undesirable for several reasons.
>
> *(p. 13)*

The generation of the extra-ordinary quantum of data on Web 2.0 platforms, and especially on social media, has brought new challenges and opportunities for Indian digital archives. With an ever-increasing Indian population and traffic on social networks, personal archiving has found new venue for their preservation and visualization. Though it also to be admitted that the tools used for social networks do not follow standard norms for archiving, but they may serve the purpose of outreach quite well. Moreover, in India, when a centralized archive may precipitate controversy and ethical dilemma regarding identities of different identity groups and is always at risk of offending some sentiment of a community, individual and personal archives, in spite of the lack of proper archival protocol, may come as an excellent option. For instance, the British Library earlier launched an outreach programme for the Indians to know their ancestry online which would be provided from their collections of the India Office Records. Majority of such information came from military service records where the particulars of the Indian soldiers working under the East India Company or the British Government were preserved. Such an outreach programme may be proved disturbing for some Indian families who may find any information regarding their forefathers being British soldiers unpalatable. Small, personal, and communitarian archives could take a closer view of the local histories and aspirations of even small communities.

The role of social network sites and Web 2.0 platforms is generally thought to be that of outreach and networking. But this role has been further extended in the curation map, and that creates opportunities for cross-curation. This can be understood with the help of an example: *People's Archive of Rural India* (PARI) (https://ruralindiaonline.org/en/), which uses Facebook, Twitter, Instagram, and YouTube. The information space here does not focus on a single domain or the website; it involves multiple interlinked domains in the form of social networks. These sites, namely, Facebook, Twitter, and Instagram provide links to the website and thereby reinforce the centrality of the website. YouTube also has link to the PARI website, but in addition the website also feeds it. Thus, the relationship of the website with YouTube is that of both "link" and "feed." YouTube thus here allows cross-curation. This model may be convenient for Indian digital online archives where big data (here videos) could be co-archived. The social networking sites, on the other hand, have their own interconnectedness; a tweet generated in its Twitter account will be reflected in other social networking sites, Facebook for instance. This map can be represented in the following manner:

The use of social network, notwithstanding reinforcing the mother website, has decentralized the curation, and brings in hypertextual environment in the entire dynamics. In India, when a centralized curation is difficult in terms of resources, infrastructure, and ethical issues, such model of social ecosystem may be advantageous for Indian digital archives.

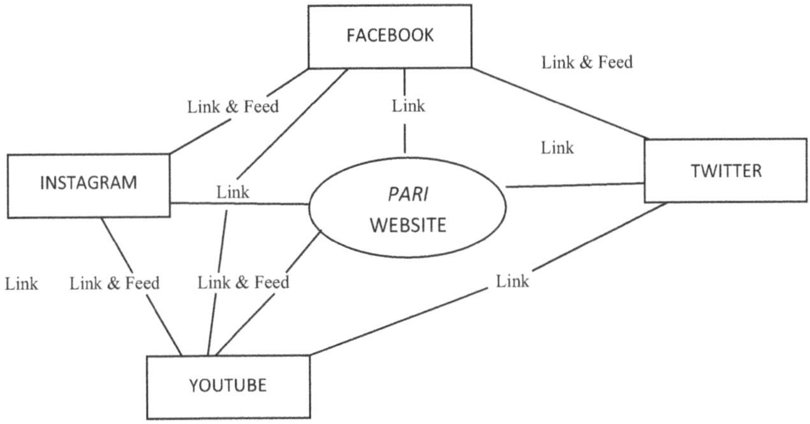


**FIGURE 4.1** Node–link relationships in the social network used by *PARI*

*Source*: People's Archive of Rural India (PARI)

This experience of working for the digital archives in India has taught the need for close coordination among different institutions engaged in creating digital repositories of Indian resources and their visualizations, developing tools for Indian languages and cultures. The mutual communications and sharing of expertise and findings would save a lot of our limited means that we spend in working in isolation. Creating a common platform for all Indian digital archives, strengthening mutual networks, and investing more on collaborative projects may be the only available option for Indian archives. The questions still remain about the standardization, whether all the archives located at multifarious cultural contexts would follow a single standard for their resources captured from diverse and heterogeneous data environments, or they should evolve their in-house methods. How would they negotiate the call for the global standardization without affecting their uniqueness? Will the scholars, historians, researchers all over the world be able to use Indian archives to answer their questions? Probably, it is too early, and we have too little to answer these questions, and could leave them in the care of the future developments.

## References


Applehans, W., Globe, A., & Laugero, G. (1999) *Managing Knowledge: A Practical Web-Based Approach.* Boston, MA: Addison-Wesley Professional.

Chaudhuri, S. (Ed.). (2015) *Bichitra: The Making of an Online Tagore Variorum.* New York: Springer.

The British Library Endangered Archives Programme. n.d. Retrieved from https://eap.bl.uk/. Accessed on 12 December 2020

Cook, T. (2013) Evidence, memory, identity, and community: four shifting archival paradigms. *Archival Science, 13,* 95–120. http://dx.doi.org/10.1007/s10502-012-9180-7

Ernst, W. (2013) *Digital Memory and Archive.* Minneapolis, MN: University of Minnesota.

Foucault, M. (2002) *The Archaeology of Knowledge and the Discourse on Language.* A. M. Sheridan Smith (Trans.). London: Tavistock.

Gajjala, R. (2019) Caring archives of subalternity. In *Debates in the Digital Humanities.* Matthew K. Gold and Lauren F. Klein (Ed.). Minneapolis, MN: University of Minnesota Press.

Moretti, F. (2017) Comparative literature and computational criticism: A conversation of Franco Moretti. In *Futures of Comparative Literature: ACLA State of the Discipline Report Pari: People's Archive of Rural India.* Ursula K. Heise (Ed.). Retrieved from https://ruralindiaonline.org/en/. Accessed on 3 March 2021.

National Statistics, Department of Digital, Culture, Media & Sports, The Government of UK, (2018) Retrieved from https://assets.publishing.service.gov.uk/government/uploads/system/uploads/attachment_data/file/740242/180911_Taking_Part_Adult_Annual_Report_-_Revised.pdf. Accessed on 28 April 2022.

Posner, M. (2012) Some things to think about before you exhort everyone to code. *Miriam Posner's Blog.* Retrieved from https://miriamposner.com/blog/some-things-to-think-about-before-you-exhort-everyone-to-code/. Accessed on 2 February 2021.

Ramsey, S., & Rockwell, G. (2012) Developing things: Notes towards epistemology of building in the digital humanities. In *Debates in the Digital Humanities.* M. K. Gold (Ed.). Minneapolis, MN: University of Minnesota Press.

Risam, R. (2018) *New Digital Worlds: Postcolonial Digital Humanities in Theory, Praxis, and Pedagogy*. Minneapolis, MN: North Western University Press.

Sabharwal, A. (2015) *Digital Curation in the Digital Humanities: Preserving and Promoting Archival and Special Collections*. Kingston: Chandos Publishing.

Schnapp, J et al. n.d. The digital humanities Manifesto 2.0. Retrieved from www.humanitiesblast.com/manifesto/Manifesto_V2.pdf. Accessed on 2 February 2021.

Sternfeld, J. (2011) Archival theory and digital historiography: Selection, search, and metadata as archival processes for assessing historical contextualization, *The American Archivist*, 74(2): 544–577

Telecom Statistics-India. (2019) *Economics Research Unit Department of Telecommunications Ministry of Communications Government of India*. New Delhi: Telecom Statistics-India.

Union Budget. (2020) Expenditure for ministry of culture. Retrieved from www.indiabudget.gov.in/doc/eb/sbe17.pdf. Accessed on 11 December 2020.

Wikipedia. n.d. List of languages by number of native speakers. Retrieved from https://en.wikipedia.org/wiki/List_of_languages_by_number_of_native_speakers. Accessed on 2 February 2021.

W$^3$Techs. n.d. Web technology survey. Retrieved from https://w3techs.com/technologies/overview/content_language. Accessed on 12 December 2020

# 5

# BICHITRA

## The Online Tagore Variorum Project

*Spandana Bhowmik*

In the autumn of 1910, a poet was enjoying the puja holidays in Shilaidaha, beside the river Padma. He was tired and unwell, but at the request of the teachers and students from the school he had set up a few years ago in Santiniketan, he started writing a play. In his letter to Santoshchandra Majumdar dated 19 October 1910 (Bengali 2 Kartik, 1317), Rabindranath Tagore writes that he has started working on it (*Rabindra Bhabana* 1987, p. 12). In another letter to Charuchandra Bandyopadhyay on 11 November (25 Kartik), he mentions that he has finished the first draft, but is yet to revise it (Tagore 2000, pp. 27–28).

Thus began the story of the play *Raja* (Tagore 1911), *The King of the Dark Chamber* in its English avatar (Tagore 1914). Born from a story of the *Jataka* (Mitra 1882, pp. 110–111 and 142–144), written in approximately 22 days, this is a theme that would draw Tagore again and again over the next 30 years and give birth to three different titles in two forms and two languages (either partially translated and/or partially edited by Tagore himself) over 30 versions that can be traced. The narrative of this transmission is intricately linked to Tagore's personal journey as a playwright and philosopher, and critical in understanding the evolution of the style and method of his editing and revision of texts.

Before *Bichitra: The Online Tagore Variorum* (n.d.) existed, this is where an interested reader/researcher would take a pause, wondering about the sheer volume of research it would involve in retrieving all the versions and the time one would require to compare them side-by-side for a deep textual analysis.

This is exactly the space where *Bichitra* stakes its claim to be useful. As the researcher who actually asked the same questions during her own research and did indeed retrieve and compare all available versions manually and through *Bichitra*, I can testify that the difference in the time taken was astonishing. A mere half-an-hour could be enough to browse through the site and figure out the various versions as well as access the ready collation of all those versions. A researcher

DOI: 10.4324/9781003354246-8

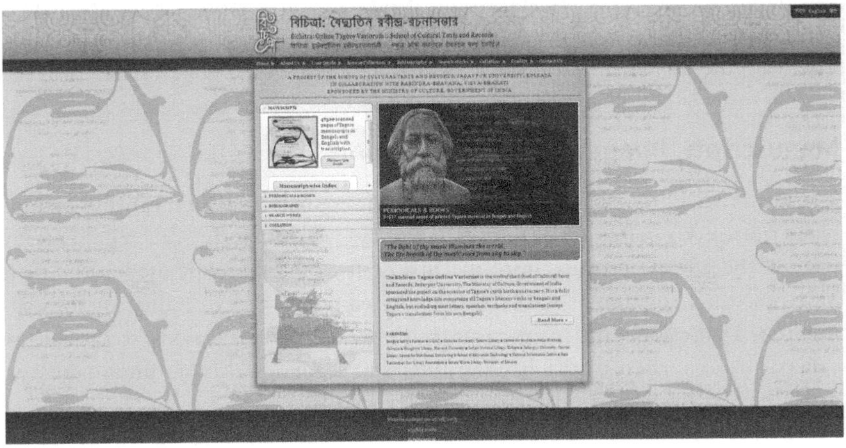

**FIGURE 5.1** The Bichitra homepage

can then use the tools that *Bichitra* provides to take her analysis forward. Let us see what these tools are and how they work towards this end.

*Bichitra: The Online Tagore Variorum*, or just *Bichitra* in short, is a virtual archive that contains almost all the works by Rabindranath Tagore, the first Nobel laureate from Asia. It was a project of the School of Cultural Texts and Records (SCTR), Jadavpur University, Kolkata, supported by the Ministry of Culture, Government of India to commemorate the 150th anniversary of the author's birthday (see Figure 5.1).

Tagore's genius is reflected through multiple facets—poems, songs, short stories, novels, essays, travelogues, plays, and more. He was not only a writer but also a composer, painter, educator, and a visionary. Anyone who worked with his texts would also know that Tagore was almost obsessively critical about his works, which made him edit them multiple times. The aforementioned example is one instance but such stories are available in varying degree for almost every title. He turned his novels into plays or vice versa, plays and poems into dance dramas, incorporated his songs or poems into other writings, translated some of his own works, wrote about a topic in both Bengali and English. The complex creative process and the textual transmission of his works can only be understood by looking at the textual evidence from each stage of the work, if available. *Bichitra* makes it available.

A variorum edition means an edition that contains all the variant readings of the text from the manuscripts and printed versions. *Bichitra* contains images and transcriptions of all textually important versions of most of Tagore's works, amounting to approximately 140,000 pages. I say "most," because 40 out of the 450 rare books and 300 out of 3,200 journal items could not be obtained by the *Bichitra* team. Additionally, *Bichitra* contains a hyperbibliography that interconnects the various versions of a work. *Bichitra* also provides a detailed result collating (comparing) the various versions of a work, broken down at three levels—chapters/cantos/scenes, paragraphs/stanzas/speeches, and words. It also contains a search engine and hyper-concordance tool that enables a user to find the specific works they are looking for. These are the three major tools that *Bichitra* provides for a user-researcher.

## Manuscripts, Images, and Transcription

The term manuscript usually signifies handwritten material. But it can also include typescripts, even computer printouts nowadays. A manuscript can represent any stage of the writing process, from the first draft to the fair copy used at the press for typesetting. Sometimes a printed previous edition can serve as the base for revision too. Transcribing the manuscripts was essential for two reasons: to provide an easier-to-read version of the handwriting, and second and more importantly, to make the text machine-readable for further processing.

The manuscripts of Tagore present every possible complication and challenge that one can think of with regard to manuscript transcription. Let me draw from our previous example of *Raja* here. Of the two available manuscripts of *Raja* at Rabindra Bhavana archive, Santiniketan, ms.143 is most probably the first draft (Tagore 1910a). Handwritten in a foolscap exercise book, the complexity of the textual changes in this version is such that at places one can find four to five different layers of deletion and insertion. But that is not all. While it is clear that the revised text in ms.143 gave birth to ms.148 (Tagore 1910b), a fair copy or a press copy that was used for typesetting the first edition of the play published in 1910, close reading of ms.143 also shows the author marking sections that were omitted in ms.148 but brought back in the next edition of the play, published as part of the *Kabyagrantha* collection in 1916. One can imagine the difficulty of the transcriber in representing the text here. There are other kinds of complications too. Tagore's handwriting had changed over the years. Sometimes he used dictation as a method; sometimes his followers, assistants, or secretaries made fair copies of the manuscripts. Determining authorship also becomes a challenge in such cases. A manuscript may also contain writings by multiple individuals of whom the author is one. Sometimes the manuscript is just a collection of stray sheets, containing writings from different times.

The *Bichitra* team received most of the manuscripts as low-resolution images from the Rabindra Bhavana Archive, Visva-Bharati, and Santiniketan. Copies of the English manuscripts of Tagore were given to the team by the Houghton Library, Harvard University. The low-resolution files made it difficult to understand the layers of revision. The way the text had been laid out on the pages was another challenge to reproduce in flat left-to-right linear transcriptions.

To represent these layers, the team had to figure out a strategy. Decisions had to be made on issues such as whether to correct apparent miss-outs in "dotting the i's and crossing the t's" by the author while writing in a hurry, and whether to keep to his habit of spelling some of the words differently, especially since towards the later part of his life he was backing a spelling reform movement. Considering all these, the work of transcribing a text also became an exchange between the author and the transcriber, where the transcriber had to peek into the mind of the author through the window of the text.

*Bichitra* tries to provide a full transcription of each manuscript page by page, incorporating all deletions, insertions, transpositions, and comments. It determines the structure of the manuscripts, identifies the titles or items. It was also required to filter out a "final version" of the text, so to say, created after all revisions, to be used for collation. Finally, the team created two types of transcriptions—one pagewise, the other separately for each Individual Item. As a manuscript might contain various poems, songs, parts of a novel, or perhaps a speech, scattered through its pages, if the user wants to check the transcription side-by-side with the original, she has to match the two pagewise. At the same time, the item-wise transcription is needed to link the text with the full bibliographical table, and extract the manuscript reading of a particular item.

Using an XML markup or TEI encoding proved to be time-taking, resource-heavy, and cumbersome to deal with for a large corpus of Bengali texts. With the kind of layers of complexities I have just discussed, it would need experts in TEI to find the right ways to represent the details, and the average end-user could not make sense of the output. The transcriptions had to be in plain text format to give it the flexibility to be used in any system of visualization or text processing: this also precluded detailed mark-up. Eventually, the team went ahead with an innovative markdown system, marking the additions, deletions, insertions and transpositions with simple symbols (see Figure 5.2). The symbols, however, as well as the intricate layers of revisions had to be filtered out by a software to prepare a cleaner version of the text, presenting the final text emerging from that particular manuscript. Bhupati Ray, a graduate student from the Computer Science Department of Jadavpur University, created such a software for the team. The filter would read the transcriptional markers and remove the deleted texts, place the transposed texts in their final positions, and follow other instructions as indicated by the symbols. The

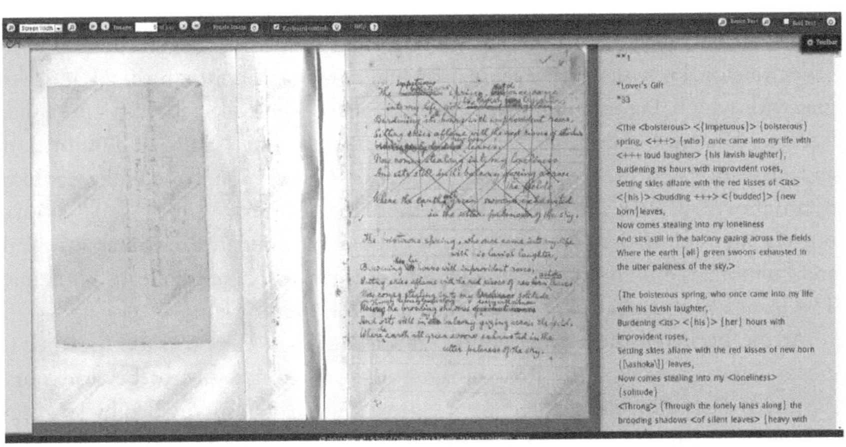


**FIGURE 5.2** Pagewise transcription with manuscript image

team did not attempt to analyse the reasons behind the revisions: its primary task was to generate a research tool providing data, not decisions.

## The Hyperbibliography

*Bichitra* presents 139,157 pages of primary material, of which 47,520 pages are manuscripts and 91,637 are printed. There are 711 manuscript volumes. The printed Bengali texts comprise 361 books and 2,426 journal items containing 4,441 poems and songs, 84 dramatic pieces, 165 novels and stories, 1,191 essays, and other non-fictional texts. Printed texts in English, on the other hand, comprise 51 books and 433 journal items covering 1,035 poems and songs, 17 dramatic texts, 5 short stories, 338 essays, and other non-fictional writings. Both Bengali and English corpora also contain hundreds of very short poems and songs. The sheer number of the individual items was obviously a challenge. They had to be classified and ordered to make sense to both humans and computers, in their different ways. The bibliography had to be an index and the pathway to the contents of the website. Each entry had to be linked to its images, text, and collation files, accessible through the search engine and also through the Timeline, turning it into a hyperbibliography. This makes *Bichitra* an integrated website, where the primary content and the related data can be accessed through any of the tools or paths across the board.

At the most basic level, the items were organized by language, and then by genre—Poems and Songs, Drama, Fiction, and Non-Fictional Prose. At the next level, *Bichitra* decided to include only the textually significant versions of the items. For example, there could have been hundreds of imprints of a poem from *Gitanjali*, but *Bichitra* has only included the versions that are known for revisions, or given the provenance, were possibly revised. So the bibliography includes all manuscript versions, all early versions printed in journals, the first print version in volume form or included in a book-length publication, the first edition published by the Santiniketan Press or Visva-Bharati Publication Division (presumed to carry special textual authority, as the institution founded and headed by Tagore himself), any other version known to have textual or bibliographical importance, all anthologies with which Tagore might have been associated, the collected works published by Visva-Bharati Publication Division (*Rabindra-rachanabali* 1939-) and translations and adaptations by Tagore of his own work. For each version, basic bibliographical data is provided. While much of the details for Bengali texts were available in various resources created by Sankha Ghosh, Swapan Majumdar, Prashantakumar Pal, and Pulinbihari Sen, most of them did not cover the whole of his creative timeline. The team had to gather data and do fact checks at every level.

At the backend, there were control sheets and masterlists meshed together to create a framework for the texts, images, and collation results to be stored and retrieved. The items were stored as types (text and image), subdivided by language (Bengali and English), genre (anthology, drama, fiction, non-fiction, poems, and songs, and collected works for Bengali; drama, fiction, non-fiction, poems, and

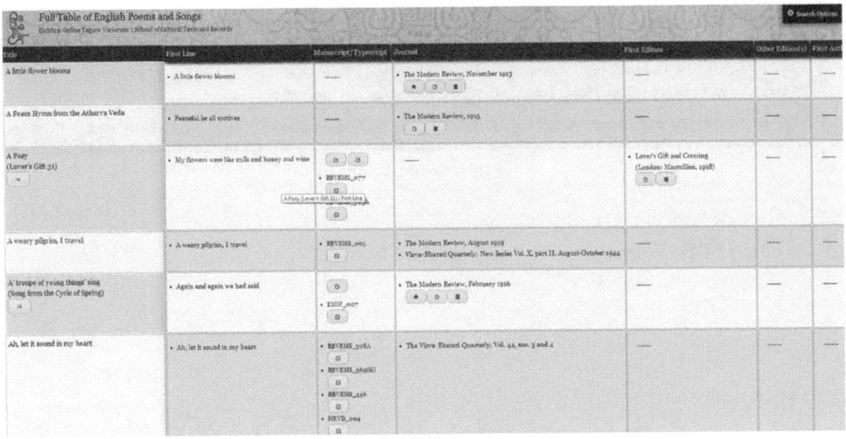


**FIGURE 5.3** Full table of English poems and songs

songs for English), title, edition, and then image files for that particular edition of the title. Each genre had its separate spreadsheet linking it to the masterlist of texts and images. In the genre-wise lists, each item was linked to its manuscript, collation files, journal publication and various other editions, translations and recasting (for Bengali works) and originals (for English works). These assimilated spreadsheets served as integrated checklists of Bengali and English works under the head "Bibliography," where each entry under each genre provided a descriptive bibliography, a list of alternative and associated titles, and a separate manuscript index, thus creating the most detailed bibliography perhaps ever existed for all of Tagore's works. The user can use the alphabetical index of works, or the full table of all works in a particular form or genre (see Figure 5.3), each entry containing links to the images of manuscripts and printed works, clear reading text and special information along with a link to the collation result.

While the masterlist for English writings is similar to the lists described earlier, it additionally contains the exact image reference and cites the opening words of every variant version. Comments in square brackets provide editorial notes, if any. Every poem has been entered twice in this list, under the first line as well as the title, to help access and cross-referencing.

The other feature of the hyperbibliography in *Bichitra* is the Timeline. It provides a year-wise list of volume-form publications and a month-wise list of journal items. There are separate spreadsheets among the backend files for these two types of publications.

## Search Engine and Hyperconcordance

A simple search engine would show the user the names of the files in which the search term appears. But for *Bichitra*, the need was to provide a result with a link to the actual work, and some context for the search term. In literary scholarship,

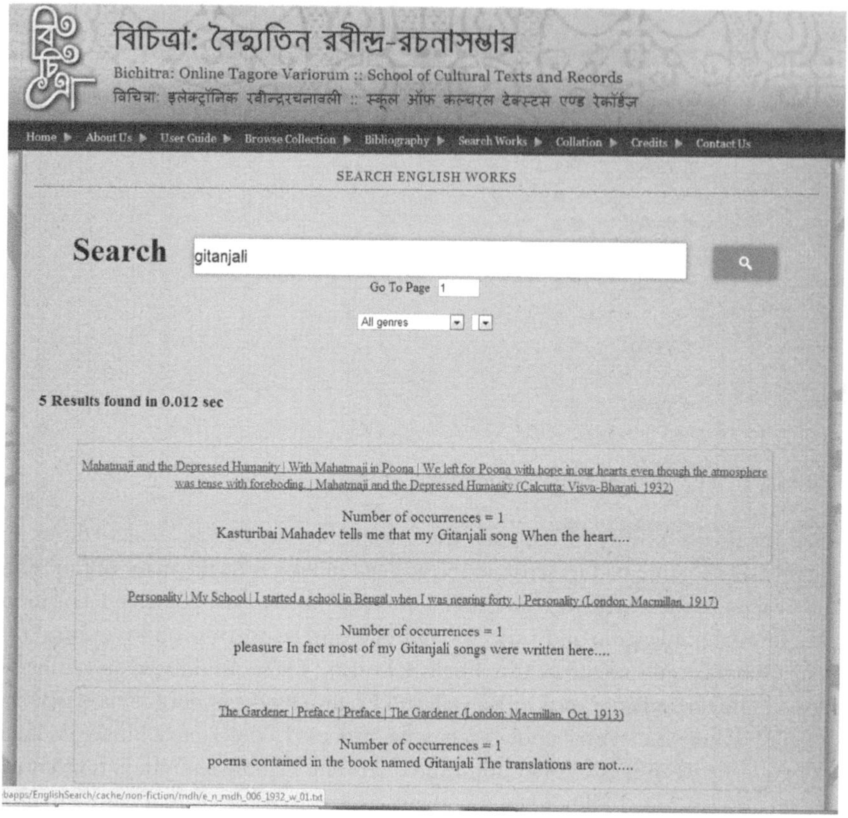


**FIGURE 5.4** Search results

a list of all words found in an author's works, with their immediate textual context, is called a concordance. The search result in *Bichitra* constitutes a hyperconcordance, as it provides hyperlinks to the actual works. Drawing on the metadata sheets, it also cites the genre and title of the text, brief bibliographical details, the chapter or act/scene number for a novel or play, collection name for a poem or song, as well as the number of occurrences of the word(s) within the piece (see Figure 5.4). To incorporate these features, a customized search engine had to be created for *Bichitra*: we could not simply use the tools available on the web. To avoid repetition of the same results over and over from various versions, it works only on the texts of a single version, usually the Collected Works (Rachanabali) in Bengali brought out by Tagore's own university, Visva-Bharati. For the English works, the first extant printed edition was used. The engine works with a precreated index to reduce processing time. It is created by two graduate students of the Computer Science Department of Jadavpur University, Prakash Koli Moi and Arabinda Moni.

## The Collation Tool in *Bichitra*: Prabhed

Perhaps the most important tool provided by *Bichitra* for a textual scholar is the collation engine. As explained at the beginning, it is an invaluable boon for a researcher to get all the textually significant versions together, already interlinked after crosschecking facts and data. *Bichitra* provides such a textual comparison, computationally executed, so that the researcher does not have to do it manually. Unlike the other tools in *Bichitra*, which were generated for this project, the collation tool was something that a group of researchers at the School of Cultural Texts and Records had been working on for a few years. It was also by far the most complex of all the programs developed for the *Bichitra* project. It was written primarily for a non-Latin font and later extended to other languages, which was unique. This complicated the task, as many of the text-processing softwares available for Roman script did not perform well with Bengali.

I was a member of this Digital Development team. The challenge was to figure out how to explain and analyse the subtle variations in literary texts through a machine which can only read instructions in clear and conclusive terms of a programming language. There are tools available for textual computation using the English or Roman alphabet, developed over the years. But in Bengali, or almost any non-Latin alphabet, other than the small projects that the SCTR had conducted over the years, not much had happened. By the time of the *Bichitra* project, the Unicode had come into use. The *Bichitra* team created all text files using the Unicode version UTF-8, so all the computational tools had to work with UTF-8 too. The Tagore corpus is mostly in two languages, Bengali and English. The beauty of following Unicode/UTF-8 is that it works with code points for characters, and each character across thousands of languages has a unique code point. The team wanted to keep the software open for processing other possible languages.

The experiments at SCTR began in 2005 with Tafat. "Tafat" means difference. It could handle Unicode texts in three alphabets, Bengali, Devanagari, and Roman, saving the results as plain-text or linked-HTML files marking additions and deletions; words replacements; and transpositions or changes in position. But it was unable to handle transpositions over a certain span. Another problem was that it could only present results for two versions at a time.

The next step towards achieving a better result was Pathantar, the second software the School developed for collation. "Pathantar" literally means Textual Variants. It could do all that Tafat could, comparing texts at the word level; additionally, by choosing the sentence delimiter (punctuations or newline marker), one could instruct the software to identify prose or verse. It was also better at handling transpositions. Arunashis Acharya, a young instructor at the School of Education Technology at Jadavpur University who later became an important member of the digital development team, prepared a four-window display to showcase the results generated by Pathantar. But we soon realized that the processing a text containing both prose and verse, distant transpositions, and the logic of handling sentence-matches by word-sequencing would need significant human intervention, and it would be impossible to complete processing the whole bulk of Tagore's corpus through Pathantar on time.

The digital development team started thinking whether it is possible to do two types of matching within texts—one in broad sections or segments, to roughly identify matching chunks of texts, and the other to collate those matching chunks word by word. We called these two stages gross collation and fine collation. A gross collator would generate structural matches between the various versions of the work, effectively resolving the issue of distant transpositions (where sections of texts had been moved from one point of the text to another across some distance—as it may be, from one chapter to another), while the fine collation would only work on the already-matched sections.

The team started working on creating such a gross collator to work in tandem with the word-level collation already available in Pathantar. Sunanda (Neel) Bose, a freelance programmer who just joined the team, and I closely worked on this with guidance from Arunashis and Prof. Sukanta Chaudhuri, Professor Emeritus, Jadavpur University. The experiments that started as an add-on feature finally generated a completely new software, Prabhed.

## *Prabhed*

Prabhed (difference) is actually a package of two softwares, Chhatrobhango and Tafat 2.0, that run at the backend of an integrated user input interface. The gross collation, processed via Chhatrobhango, works at two levels, sections and segments, while Tafat, the fine collation processor, works at the word level. The three levels are defined as follows:

- **Sections:** the chapters of a novel, the scenes of a play, or the cantos of a long poem
- **Segments:** the paragraphs within a prose chapter, speeches within a scene, stanzas within a canto; or a short poem, story, or essay in its entirety
- **Words**

We are not aware of any other collation program that can process text in as many levels. The complexities of Tagore's writing and editing practice that I already described before gave the team a chance to dig deep into the problem of translating the same nuances to a computer.

The Collation icon in the Full Bibliography page takes the user to the first or section-level result where different versions are represented with colourful bands spread across the page. Each colour indicates the full text of one version, and the blocks within the band indicate the sections (chapters, scenes, cantos, etc.) within it. If one selects any section in any version as the base text, the matching sections in the other versions are highlighted (see Figure 5.5). As soon as one clicks on a base section, the selection panel at the bottom shows matches with percentage of

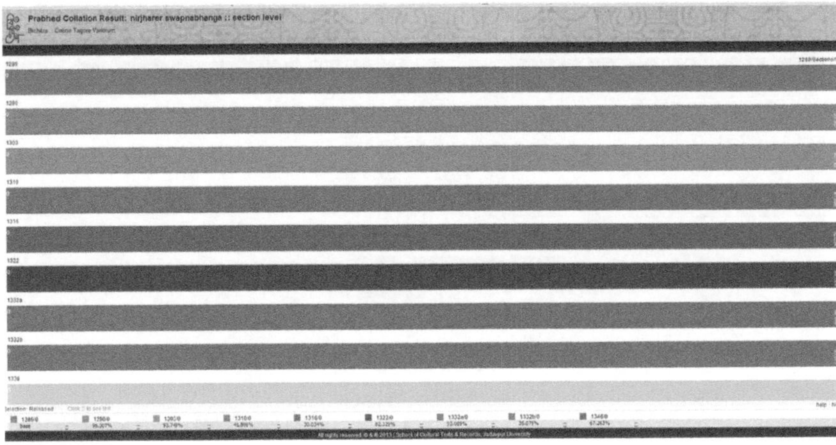


FIGURE 5.5 Section-level collation result

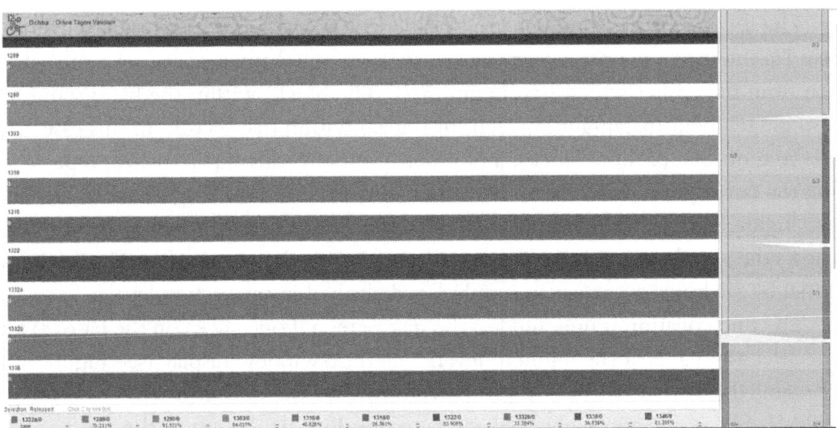

FIGURE 5.6 Section-level collation: one-to-one sidebar

correspondence (match-percentage) placing the base text as the first entry to the left and the others following. The tiny hollow square icon beside each section in the selection panel is the link to the plain text file of the corresponding section. If one clicks on any of the other versions at the selection panel, a vertical panel opens to the right of the screen, showing a segment-by-segment comparison (paragraphs, speeches, stanzas) between the base text and that version (see Figure 5.6). Within the panel, the base segments are represented on the left while the reference segments are on the right, grey lines connecting the corresponding ones. This is a 1:1 collation. But the major purpose of Prabhed is to provide results of *n*:*n* collation—that is, comparing all the versions against one another—though displayed on a 1:*n* basis.

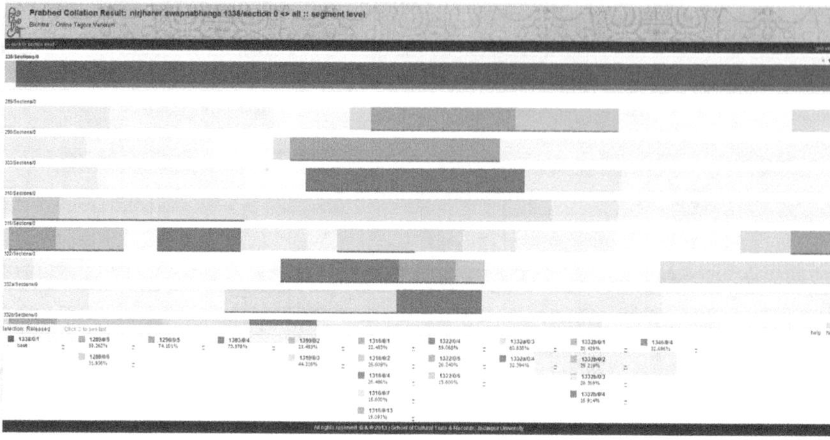


FIGURE 5.7 Segment-level collation result

The second or the segment-level result repeats the same pattern with a single band at the top of the page, representing the section (chapter, scene, or canto) chosen from the earlier screen (see Figure 5.7). The blocks within the band stand for a single segment (paragraph, speech, or stanza) within that section in this case. On clicking on one of these blocks, a number of other bands appear below, representing the corresponding blocks in the other versions: the matching segments in each are highlighted and underlined in red. Again, the selection panel at the bottom shows the match-percentage, and one can open the relevant text from the selection panel by clicking on the square symbol as described in the section level.

The fine collation is presented in the next screen if one clicks on the base text at the selection panel at the segment level. The four-window display (see Figure 5.8) contains the base text in the top-left window, and the collation result as a linked HTML file in the top right. On clicking any link in the latter, the lower right window displays the variant readings in the other versions: each version separately colour-coded. The lower left window is reserved for displaying any one of the other versions as chosen by the user from a drop-down list. The collation result on top right window uses colour codes to mark words that are the same in all versions (black), missing in one or more compared versions (red), and missing from the base text but present elsewhere (green). This four-window interface is actually adopted from the one that Arunashis created for Pathantar.

## *The Working Principle of Prabhed*

Prabhed parses the texts, after being instructed whether to treat it as prose or verse, and to demarcate the lines accordingly (at a full stop, marking a sentence-break for prose, and the Return/Enter command marking the end of a line for verse. The chapters/scenes/cantos and paragraphs/speeches/stanzas are identified using this technique, before going to the word level.

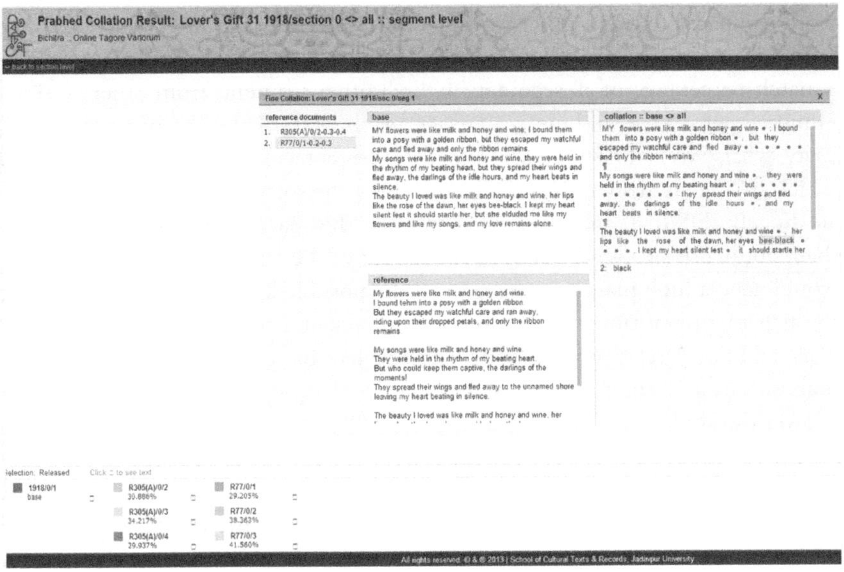


**FIGURE 5.8** Fine collation result: the four-window display

The software then literally compares everything with everything. Our previous experiments using a heuristic logic did not work for a complex language and script like Bengali. So it starts by comparing a single base text against a number of different versions, one by one, and combines the results in a single file. This gives a 1:*n* collation. It then takes each of the other versions in turn as the base text, and repeats the process. By combining all the results at the end, we get an *n:n* collation. Match-percentages can only be calculated with reference to a single base text taken as 100. Using the same logic, when proceeding from one level to the next—section, segment, and word—the software takes a single version as the base, and measure the others against that. A true *n:n* collation engine which can collate all versions in a single instance is yet to be created, as the computational logic is too complicated for such a process.

How does Prabhed determine whether two words are the same? For a synthetic language like Bengali, where a much higher proportion of words are inflected, it creates difficulties. A slight difference in the ending might reflect as two completely different words to the software. But on the other hand, the same situation might also mean two entirely separate words. The general principles of word comparison that the team could finally define which would work for majority of the differences are as follows:

- In a word of four or fewer characters, all of them must match
- In a word of more than four characters, the program would allow one difference for every four subsequent characters. Thus, a word of 5–8 characters could differ by one character; a word of 9–12 characters by two; and so on.

The software compares the texts from bottom up, that is, starting with single word compared to every other word in every other version. As I observed earlier, it literally compares everything with everything. It then calculates and produces a match-percentage of all segments with all other segments from other versions. Hundred per cent would mean an exact match, and 0% the absence of any similarity whatsoever. The user can choose a percentage, a threshold value, above which two segments will be called a match by the software. Where two versions are hugely different, one may need to keep the margin low. To some extent, the margin also needs adjusting to the nature of the language. A text in English would need a high margin, as because of the possible high matches found due to the articles, prepositions, and conjunctions in a sentence such as *of, on, in, and, or, a, an,* and *the.* A relatively synthetic language like Bengali, where the articles and prepositions are represented by suffixes rather than separate words, may require a lower threshold.

Once all segment-level results are calculated, a review of gross match-percentages of sections versus other sections from other versions is taken into account to figure out the section-level match. Prabhed uses a **weighted mean.** That is to say, it considers not only the match-percentage between compared text-units but also the relative size of those units, or their proportionate space within the larger unit (the section) of which they are a part. In cases of **split and merge:** that is, a segment is split into multiple segments in one of the versions when viewed from one direction but merged (in case of other versions) when viewed from the other, Prabhed checks for match-percentage values from both ends, and if the value is considerably high, it identifies the segments or sections as a split-and-merge.

At this point, the first two levels of collation are done.

- The result provides the degree of similarity between sections and segments, and stores and extracts the corresponding percentage values as needed
- The result stores plain text files of the sections and segments
- The result traces the addition, deletion, or transposition of a text-block at section or segment level.

All these results are organized within an appropriate directory structure, so that the program and in turn the *Bichitra* server can easily fetch the required files from the huge corpus.

The distant transposition as discussed earlier is not a problem for Prabhed, because it compares every section, segment, and line with every other such blocks of every version, and then, depending on the margin set for the match-percentage, identifies similar passages irrespective of their locations. It can therefore identify if a section is from one position to another, as well as the split sections, anywhere between the beginning and the end of the work. It can also spot multiple occurrences in Version B to match a single occurrence in Version A. We believe this to be a function unique to Prabhed.

### *Gross to Fine Collation*

Once the similar text-blocks have been identified, and appropriate filtering of the results carried out, the software creates a list of "comparable sets." These comparable sets are sent to the character-level collator or fine collator. For this purpose, we used a second version of Tafat (**Tafat 2.0**) that had been created by this time. It produced HTML results which we displayed through the user-friendly four-window interface that we used before. This involved some adaptation of the original Tafat 2.0 code, as the original form of the HTML output was not geared to the four-window display. The basic collation program, however, was left untouched.

With the expanded 64-bit version of the total program up and running, Prabhed could successfully collate five files together, each of approximately 100,000 words, without any glitch. It took a lot of time, but that was understandable and acceptable considering the thoroughness of its process.

The software is not available at the *Bichitra* site. Only the collated results are provided. To run such a resource-heavy software, the response time of the website would vary widely—sometimes unacceptably with long texts. Furthermore, multiple collation requests at the same time, many or all of them involving complicated text sets might turn the server unresponsive or crash the system. As running live collation would be dependent on the server load capacity, network speed, or type and number of requests at a given time, the website performance will become unpredictable and difficult to access by the users with basic computers and slow Internet connections. The team therefore chose to collate the files offline, and upload the results on the website. All the images of manuscripts and printed books are with low resolution too, keeping this in mind. At the end, coming back to the personal experience of someone who dealt with manual collation and also been part of the development team for Prabhed, it was wonderful to see that the software actually matched all the manually identified changes in the texts I was working with.

Tagore's works are a very important resource not only for their textual richness and complexity but also for understanding a certain period of time in colonial India. The textual changes in his writing over time also reflect the changing mental landscape of one of the most influential figures of late-19th- and early-20th-century Bengal and India. *Bichitra* becomes a tool to trace all these crucial historical phenomena. Its well-researched and verified resources provide a base for any literary, cultural, or historical analysis involving Tagore's works. Given the opportunity, the team looks forward to creating more such tools for processing texts in future, in Bengali or indeed in other languages.

## References

*Bichitra: The Online Tagore Variorum.* (launched on 5th May 2013.) Available at: http://bichitra.jdvu.ac.in (Accessed: 18 October 2021).

Chaudhuri, S. (eds.) (2015) *Bichitra: The Making of an Online Tagore Variorum.* In Quantitative Methods in Humanities and Social Sciences Series. New York: Springer Verlag.

Ghosh, S. (comp.) (2001) Granthaparichay. In *Rabindra Rachanabali*. Vol. 16. Kolkata: Government of West Bengal.

Majumdar, S. (1988) *Rabindra Ghranthasuchi*. Vol. 1. pt. 1. Kolkata: National Library.

Mitra, R. (1882) *The Sanskrit Buddhist Literature of Nepal*. Kolkata: Asiatic Society. pp. 110–11 (Kuśa Játaka) and pp. 142–44 (Story of Kuśa, Mahávastu Avadána) [Tagore's personal copy with handwritten notes on the margin shows his familiarity with the stories].

Pal, P. (1982) *Rabijibani*. Vol. 1. Kolkata: Papyrus. 1984–2003. Kolkata: Ananda Publishers.

Sen, P. (2009) *Pulinbihari: Janmashatabarshik Shraddharghya*. Kolkata: Visva-Bharati Publishing Division.

Tagore, R. (1910a) *Ms. 143* [Rabindra Bhavana Archive]. Santiniketan: Visva-Bharati.

Tagore, R. (1910b) *Ms. 148* [Rabindra Bhavana Archive]. Santiniketan: Visva-Bharati.

Tagore, R. (1911) *Raja*. 1st Edn. Kolkata: Indian Publishing House.

Tagore, R. (1914) *The King of the Dark Chamber*. 1st Edn. London: Macmillan.

Tagore, R. (1916) 'Raja' in *Kabyagrantha*. Vol. 9. Sen, Mohitchandra (eds.). Allahabad: Indian Press.

Tagore, R. (1939) *Rabindra-Rachanabali*. 32 + 2 Vols. published so far. Kolkata: Visva-Bharati Publication Division.

Tagore, R. (1987) 'Letter to Santoshchandra Majumdar'. *Rabindra Bhabana*. Santoshchandra Majumdar issue. Kolkata: Tagore Research Institute.

Tagore, R. (2000) *Chithipatra*. Vol. 14. Kolkata: Visva-Bharati.

# 6

# DIGITAL HUMANITIES IN PRACTICE

## A Case Study[1]

*Prakruti Maniar*

### A Brief Introduction to Language, Literature, and Politics in Post-Independence India

> A newspaper editor calls on the character of Mario Lawrence, a crossword solver, to create a crossword puzzle based on Bombay rather than importing it from an award-winning crossword maker in London. "We want indigenous crosswords. . . . I want Sridevi, Shiv Sena, vada pav in my crossword. I need someone to dig out the names of things, places, and people from the gullies of Bombay and fit them into these square grids. It should be our culture, people and food, yaar, not about the Big Ben and the Queen, or that English Breakfast. Forty years since independence and we are still not decolonized, you know what I mean?" he says.
>
> *(Borges 2019, p. 147)*

This little scene is from a work of fiction, but the situation it illustrates is both real and relatable. The crossword is just one of the cultural products in a whole consignment that has been imported to India from largely the United States of America and England in not just 1979, when the scene takes place, but even in 2020. This import process, recognized as "cultural imperialism" (Parmeswaran 1989), has been made more ubiquitous with the digital turn in cultural consumption, as access to all avenues of human expression—movies, songs, clothes, design, and books—has become easier and cheaper for the average urban Indian consumer. It is to the general trend in the last industry—that of books—that this project is framed by.

After gaining independence in 1947, language has played a key role in Indian cultural and political life. On the one hand, India adopted English increasingly as a tool for economic progress and used it to educate children to be ready for the global job market. On the other hand, English helped find common linguistic ground in a country with 14 official languages (before the 1990s). In 2021, the

DOI: 10.4324/9781003354246-9

number is 23, and over 1,000 mother tongues "classified under 105 languages" (Ananthamurthy 2015), coming from four different language families. While the new nation's constitutional plan was to adopt Hindi as the only official language by 1965, there were protests across the country (Haque 2021) that saw Hindi as an imposition of the ruling class in India and especially exclusionary to the Southern and North-eastern states. According to the Department of Linguistics at University of Illinois Urbana-Campaign (2021), this led to *The Official Language Act, 1963*, which cemented English's permanent position in the socio-cultural milieu of the nation, wielding hegemony even as it empowered its people.

In 1981, Salman Rushdie's *Midnight's Children* won the Booker prize. This was followed by the global success of other Indian writers who wrote in English, including Arundhati Roy, Vikram Seth, and Jhumpa Lahiri (Singh and Iyer 2016). *Bhasha* (Hindi for "language," in this paper, to mean any Indian language besides English) became unimportant to the reading public outside individual and institutional literary circles. So a Marathi writer was just that, a Marathi writer. His identity as an Indian writer was erased in this push for English.

The global publishing industry too started making forays into India. With it came an influx of global literature in the urban Indian markets. It is not surprising that while I grew up speaking four languages, "literature" always meant Anglo-American works written in English. Whether it was the school library or used-book stores in the neighbourhood, it was easy to find everything from authors like Enid Blyton and Roald Dahl for children to Sydney Sheldon, Jeffery Archer, Dan Brown, and Nicolas Sparks for the older reading public, and books like *Harry Potter, Tintin, Nancy Drew, Famous Five, The Hardy Boys*, and *Princess Diaries*, but hardly any books in *bhashas*. This association has only strengthened, as literacy rates in India have gone up.

This introduction does not mean to invalidate the use of English, or make a call to replace it with the *bhashas*. This is to lay the foundation of how *bhashas* have been erased by leisurely reading habits of the urban elite at least—in a metropolis like Mumbai where people come from all over India, one would be hard pressed to find a non-English book in almost all bookstores.

Several works cited in this chapter most prominently (Ananthamurthy 2015; Singh and Iyer 2016) spell out this phenomenon—of erasure of *bhashas* and the struggles of the *bhasha* writer to find a place in cultural discussions on the national and global scale—much more eloquently.

Eventually, the number of writers writing in English grew—a strategic move on the part of writers to shrug off their regional (related to language and state) identities—and the situation has come to be that to be recognized nationally, or globally, an Indian writer must write or be translated into English (Gupta 2012).

## On the Digital

When I ran a search for "Indian authors" on Google, which is a "prevailing tool for searching for information, has the power to shape as well as diminish understanding of subjects like Indian Literature" (Stella 2021), the panels showed the following authors, on 17 April 2021, 1:00 AM CST:

1 Arundhati Roy
2 Salman Rushdie
3 Jhumpa Lahiri
4 Aravind Adiga
5 Ruskin Bond
6 Vikram Seth
7 Shashi Tharoor
8 Khushwant Singh
9 Chitra Banerjee Devakurni
10 R. K. Narayan
11 Kiran Desai
12 Amitav Ghosh
13 Chetan Bhagat
14 Anita Desai
15 Rabindranath Tagore
16 Mahatma Gandhi
17 Rohington Mistry
18 Amish Tripathi
19 Preeti Shenoy
20 Mulk Raj Anand
21 Devdutt Patnaik
22 Ravinder Singh
23 V. S. Naipaul
24 Sudha Murty
25 Anuja Chauhan
26 Ashwin Sanghi
27 Ramchandra Guha
28 Satyajit Ray
29 Jerry Pinto
30 Premchand
31 Jeet Thayil
32 Jawaharlal Nehru
33 Durjoy Dutta
34 Twinkle Khanna
35 B.R. Ambedkar
36 Anand Neelkantan
37 Indu Sundaresan
38 Vikram Chandra
39 Suketu Mehta
40 Upamanyu Chatterjee
41 A. P. J. Abdul Kalam
42 Chanakya
43 Amrita Pritam
44 Sadhguru
45 Manu Joseph

46 Sarat Chandra Chattupadhyay
47 Anita Nair
48 Kamala Markandaya
49 Kiran Nagarkar
50 Swami Vivekananda
51 Raja Rao

All but five of these authors write originally in English, and others represent only three other languages.

The internet is an important site for reading culture at large today. I conducted a survey about reading habits for readers within and outside India in January 2021. Of the 108 global respondents, 50 voted that they discover books through "Booklists" online, 34 via "Instagram," 45 via "Bookstores," and 20 answered "Goodreads" (as part of the "Other" option). A similar survey was conducted for Indian readers, and for the same question, 69 of the 161 Indian respondents chose "Booklists online," 48 chose "Instagram," "56" chose Bookstores, and 48 answered to "What's in the news in general."

When I conducted the survey of Indian readers, I included questions at the intersection of reading and languages. One hundred ten respondents read for leisure at least once a week. One hundred twenty-three respondents speak two or more Indian languages (with 17 speaking more than four Indian languages), but only 28 of them read in a language besides English within a week. When asked the main reason for not reading more often in their mother tongues, 50 of them opted for the option "I see only English online, don't really come across it in daily browsing." The second-most picked answer was "I am much slower in reading in anything besides English," picked by 54 respondents. Some answers in the "Other" box talked about how non-English stories were not easily available outside their home state, or online.

So while readers are using Internet, the internet itself does not reflect the diversity of the languages that these readers represent.

Let's head to Goodreads—where under the "Explore section" for Indian literature, two images—Figures 6.1 and 6.2—are the first encounters:

Again, the same story. The first impression is that when one looks for Indian writing, one only sees writing in English. If you look into the "Indian Literature" shelf on Goodreads (2021), there are 26,000+ books included. On the first three pages, there are four non-English books, and they are in Hindi. While subsequent pages do have a select few titles in Kannada, Malayalam, Odia, and Marathi, their percentage is miniscule.

The *de facto* association of Indian writer as Indian writer in English is shown even in the language of Wikipedia entries on *bhasha* authors. An Indian writer writing in Marathi is described as a "Marathi writer" (Jaywant Dalvi 2021), but an Indian writer writing in English is described simply as an "Indian writer."

According to a survey (Gupta 2012),

> of the [333 million] literate youth [in India] . . . the internet is accessed by only 3.7% of youth, of which a mere 4% use it for reading books online

**FIGURE 6.1** Screenshot taken on website on 10 April 2021 shows the arbitrary subject-wise categorization

> and a tiny 1.2% use it to search for book titles. We can assume that the great majority of those with access to the internet have some level of proficiency in the English language.

It would not be a stretch to say that on the web, it is the English-speaking, English-reading public which creates the *image* of what Indian literature is, which then becomes a standard for those looking outside in. Someone who is not Indian, and may not be aware of the complexities and range of languages, would get 1/20th of the picture.

It mirrors the situation off the web, or reproduces the social world of literature in India (and perhaps literary discourse across many parts of the world), where "difference is underlined and corroborated by the fact that both writers and readers

**FIGURE 6.2** Screenshot taken on website on 10 April 2021

of a particular and individual literature are overwhelmingly concerned with their own literature and own literature only" and masks the nature of the literary system which is best described as "not an entity but an inter-literary condition" (Dev 2000). It also masks the nuances of the social world of India, where multilingualism is second nature to a majority of the population, in a situation where "copyrighted algorithms and protocols manipulate and control languages" (Fiormonte 2016).

So, for a reader, *bhasha* literatures can only be discovered one at a time. Someone intentionally looking for a representative body of Indian works would have to search for that language, making language a genre in itself, thus "othering" the work in mainstream literary discussion. This leads to a "culture of proxy" (Roy 2021)—"an Indian writer's responsibility [is to] represent their nation, and the marginalized writer's responsibility [within India] to represent their local culture."

The overall situation is this: when looking for inclusivity and diversity in Indian literature, using a search engine, which wields enormous power in a "society that is searching" (Noble 2018), is to look at a very disorganized library, and looking at a specific library is to restrict search to their collections and their arbitrary category making (e.g. see Figure 6.1). The problem is one of classification. It is because *bhasha* books are not categorized at the same "site" as the English books, that languages become a genre in itself, not an attribute of a work.

Good information design "should provide access to information at multiple granularities" (Murray 2011). In literature, these multiple granularities would be subjects, languages, authors, year of publication, genres like fiction, non-fiction, poetry, plays, and other such categories of classification. But Indian *bhasha* literatures, as I have shown, cannot be accessed with ease at that level of granularity in existing interfaces. For example, the title *Kunvan*, on Chicago Public Library's website, is listed under the subject and genre "Gosvami, Asokapuri, 1947—Translations into Urdu" (Chicago Public Library 2021).

This arbitrary categorization emerged as a pattern in my research—Indian books even in English, especially in non-English languages, were in the digital equivalent of a hidden section in a library. Unless someone knows exactly what they were looking for, it is difficult to get these books in the consciousness of the reading public.

The ideal system would be one, where each individual Indian reader has a many-to-many relationship with the stories of another Indian language. They would search for say, romance novels, and be confronted with novels in Assamese, Bengali, Marathi, and Hindi. This brings the regional work out of its sphere, into a more common ground, in a way that encourages readers to engage with these works. Such a dynamic representation has two roles to play; one, as pointed out earlier, as an unifying element; second, to put a more holistic, inclusive literary system on map of world literature (and Digital Humanities at large), and break the image of India as a homogenous mass of land, bringing balance to the "language-knowledge-power equation" (Sadana 2012, p. 31) and "address the geopolitical unbalance and the economic interests that operate at the heart of the DH system" (Fiormonte 2016).

## Purple Pencil Project and Digital Humanities in Practice

Purple Pencil Project began in January 2019, as a result of wondering why it was difficult to discover Indian authors outside the mainstream, outside the English-writing canon alone. It is built using the WordPress CMS, and co-owned by Prakruti Maniar and Saurabh Garg.

From the very beginning, we have focused on bringing *bhasha* literatures to the spotlight by featuring translations more frequently and conducting interviews with *bhasha* writers. We have also made sure that there was a sense of action in our approach. There is a wealth of information out there; long-form features or encyclopaedia-style entries on authors, on the literary history of a region, of seminal moments. This form of archiving is nothing more than dry documentation, more digitization alone, than Digital Humanities *in Practice*. But I wanted to take the book out of the passive past and into the active present.

**FIGURE 6.3** Screenshot of the landing page of Purple Pencil Project

*Source*: Purple Pen Project (2021)

For this reason, we have the sections *Book Reviews* and *Q&A*, which helps connect readers to other readers (we don't have professional reviews), and readers to authors who may otherwise have been just names on a cover. Both the *Reviews* and the *Q&A* have gradually approached bilingualism, although not consistently. So while a bilingual interview includes a translation of the questions and answers, a bilingual review is a review of a Hindi or Bengali book, written in English. This is a nuance I am trying to solve, but the point is to make *bhashas* visible, which these approaches do. Posts as part of the *Book Reviews* category also have an author wiki on the sidebar—so a reader is introduced to the author and their other works, as they read the book review. This is difficult to maintain, as we have to re-enter data for every book of an author.

In 2020, we launched and completed one season of a podcast, *India Booked*, that "leans into the idea of India, through the lens of its literature." This was centred around non-fiction books, to draw Indians at large in, whether they read fiction or not. We launched the *Folktales* section in 2020 too, to deliver one folk story to the audience each Friday. Once again, with a focus on active engagement. Each of these posts are amplified on our Facebook, Twitter, and Instagram channels to draw the community in, and into the sometimes glamorous, sometimes dusty-looking *chauraha* of literature.

The *Book Review* posts are tagged with [author name][genre][language][format], and often use [themes][publishers][Awards awarded], etc. This was the first iteration to try and achieve the "granular" level of data access, and to start making connections between these. So if a reader searches for "murder mystery," it should murder mysteries written in English, those translated from other languages, or (ideally) those written in other languages.

Even as we were doing these things, as an editor, I found that I always "stumbled" upon more books than could be reviewed or shared on Instagram stories or as Facebook posts. And these places I stumbled upon new books were due to an intensive research process of going through academic papers, just following the web of hyperlinks and finding something mentioned.

Over the course of the Spring 2021 semester, I also realized that I was also falling prey to the same trap; English was the default in our taxonomy too, and language was becoming a genre in our system too. Plus, tags, without controlled vocabularies, can quickly get out of control and become arbitrary, which then erodes their power.

Two new questions emerged. First: how could I "display" more books in a permanent manner, and at scale? Second: how could books be consistently tagged, what were the parameters I should use to relate books to their authors, to the other books they have been translated into, to the translators, to its language?

Through my first year of the MA, I was introduced to the critical infrastructure of databases, more specifically, the relational database that structured data to then later be able to retrieve it. This is what I need, I thought! A way to enter data once, and then establish its relationship to another object, and to categorize and tag better so that I could indicate that the book was in Marathi, without isolating that as a genre/theme of the book. This became the research project for my DIGH 201 Capstone class at Loyola University Chicago.

## Same Problem and New Approach

The Capstone project was simple design of a multilingual database of Indian literature using MySQL (used by WordPress). I kept a key principle of good information and good database design in mind: to find information with ease and flexibility, labels must be attached with appropriate levels of granularity, and the design should make this happen (Murray 2011).

I also borrowed from case studies such as *Wampum, Sequoyan, and Story: Decolonizing the Digital Archive* (Cushman 2013) to be mindful of the idea of decolonizing the database, so that it would:

1 Preserve the "context of collection"
2 Recognize how an "artefact," in this case the book and the story, works in "mediating knowledge for the user or onlooker . . . and an object becomes 'dead' and no longer used"
3 "Preserve the language"
4 Give a contextual "sense of time and tradition"

To ensure that, I started with the most common denominators of any literary history; "succession in time, distribution in space, and likeness and difference in character" (Mukherjee 1977). This translated to year, place of publication, formats

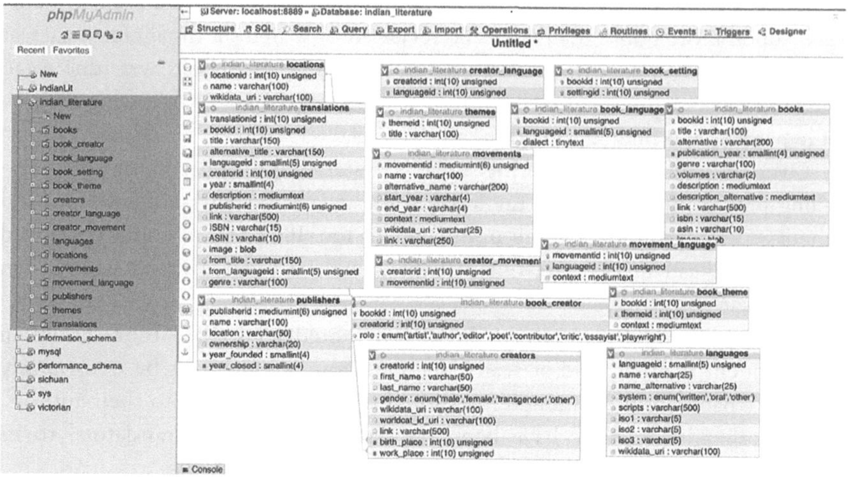


**FIGURE 6.4** Screenshot of the final database design

of the books (fiction, non-fiction, poetry, and drama), and the themes they fell under, and built up from it.

Bit by bit the design built up. The final design looks as shown in Figure 6.4.

Just having a MySQL database solved my first problem—that of display at scale. Even at its most basic, it has 200 titles, a number we achieved in reviews after only a year of Purple Pencil Project.

The second, that of inconsistent and inadequate tagging on WordPress, was solved by the design. Like I mentioned earlier, we used [author] [name] [genre] [language] [format] [themes/subjects][publishers] [Award awarded] as the standard tags. I could now use the power of MySQL to turn mere tags into rich metadata and most of the design process was spent figuring out what should go as a separate table, and what should go as a column within a table.

*Books*, *creators* (because authors are just one category of artists associated with a book), *languages*, *publishers*, and *themes* were the obvious table choices.

It was not all straightforward. How do genres and themes work? A book could be a fiction *and* horror, talking about feminism, psychology, science, anthropology, and more. What was the theme and what was the genre? When using the tags, everything was a tag, which meant that there was much we could not capture, as tags should ideally not be more than five. For the database, I split it. In the *books* table, I added a *genre* column. Which would use a combination of the following set: Fiction, Novel, Novella, Chapbook, Non-fiction, Graphic, Essay, Poetry, Play, and Collection. Now we have powerful granularity. Then, things like "historical" or "Mughal" or "modernist" could be individual entries in the themes table and the *book_theme* table establishes a many-to-many relationship between the two. So now a historical work could be anything—comic, fiction, non-fiction, poetry or play, or essay. Again, it allows for granular search and eventually, granular representation online—one that encourages exploration.

My second major problem was dealing with translations. I mentioned how we at Purple Pencil Project focused on translations for representation. In the capstone, this question went one step further. How could one flatten the hierarchy and establish a network? The database had an answer. So the original book went to the *books* table, and then the translated book went to the *translations* table. The *translations* table had a *bookid* column, which was a foreign key referencing the books table. A *languageid* column, indexed as a foreign key, was referencing the *languages* table. So now I could retrieve data efficiently. For example, here is a Gujarati novel, translated into Marathi.

The *locations* table was the latest entry. In India, states are linguistically divided for the most part, and language and state have a strong association. I want to be able to say that the setting or the book is in Delhi or Mumbai, without adding that association of language. So there is a *book_location* table, but not a *language_location* table. This way, I will not need to create a list for "Top 10 books set in Shimla" by Google for the topic and then rehashing those books which have been spoken about. I can take data critically gathered for the purpose of retrieval in this manner.

This final design emerged partly as a course-correction for Purple Pencil Project, and partly from the data-gathered. For the purpose of building this database, I chose to access the archives of Sahitya Akademi's journal *Indian Literature* between the years 1965 and 1985. I went through the "annual lists" published for each language, and then picked the novels and short story collections from them to add to the database.

However, this database design can be used to add any new book; contemporary or ancient, whether poetry or play. The. sql file can be found. It is a private repository at the moment.

Over the next few months, a new tab will be created on the Purple Pencil Project website, called *The Library* which will allow users to discover books as they would be in a bookstore or a library. You can access the wireframes for this at: https://uvov9u.axshare.com. A data entry interface will also be built so that data can be crowdsourced, like Goodreads does.

A note follows on how some key web interface design decisions and how they are influenced by the arguments made in the chapter:

1 On the landing page, under the "Select Criteria" drop down, I deliberately did not allow languages. This rests on part research and part assumption. As I mentioned earlier, 40% of Indian readers taking the survey replied that they did not read more in their mother tongues, because "they did not see it enough." I wanted to "make visible" the diversity of languages from the get go. The assumption is that if readers are given a choice at the very beginning, confirmation bias may kick in and they may then choose just the language they know.
2 However, there is an option to select languages when choosing the "View Random" book, because if a user is just landing at one particular book, it makes more sense to allow them the option of choosing their language.

## Back to Purple Pencil Project

Purple Pencil Project began as an independent platform, using a hybrid model that defines a lot of public-facing, community-driven Digital Humanities projects; "part research, part startup" (Jenkins 2020), and borrows from the successes of frameworks in social entrepreneurship which focuses on a path of both public good and financial sustainability (Martin and Osberg 2015).

What such a site can do is bridge the gap between material archives and digital collections, between mere digitization and robust data structuring, the literary archives and the reading public, and the gaps between the many publics as is the case for multilingual countries. The database structure allows critical and ongoing data gathering that can then reach the public across the world. As part of Purple Pencil Project, we would get catalogues each quarter from independent publishers across India, and no way to feature even a fraction of these books. Now, we can just enter it in the database and there you have it—on the same platform where someone finds an Arundhati Roy or a Salman Rushdie, they will also find a Volga, or a NS Madhavan. Where it is not the social media prowess of a publishing house that gives them the upper hand, but the curiosity of the reader.

The work has begun in earnest; even though all the pieces are not quite technically fitted together yet. But some key challenges remain:

- **Financial Sustainability**
  - Towards that end, it will turn to merchandising and publishing for sustaining. The decision to merchandise is driven by this notion of active engagement that has driven the project. How does a story become part of a collective memory or a book enter public consciousness? Many ways, but one of the most common ones today is cultural merchandising. Daak, Khwaab Tanha Collective are examples of ventures that are using stories, transforming them into products. Purple Pencil Project plans to do something similar.
- **Human resources**
  - A work of this scale is not possible without collaboration, not only because of the quantity but also because of the diversity. I speak only four languages, and can call myself a literary scholar of just one. The next step is to establish partnerships with language departments to hire staff or interns to help in building the database. A technical resource is required to build the front-facing *Library* and to build the MySQL database on the live server. The prototype used here was built on the local server
- **The constraints of print and language**
  - Reading is not the most preferred form of content, and requires literacy. There are plans (delayed by the pandemic), to use these stories for film adaptations, to take them to a wider public.

This project began with a personal curiosity, and I think its work will have ended when this new literary system manifests in every-day life of any Indian, or any literary consumer, or both. I want to see a list of "Which character are you more like" which include not just characters from English and American literature; I want to see Buzzfeed quizzes about "Which Bengali detective are you most like?" or "The perfect Anuja Chauhan boyfriend based on your personality"! I want kids to grow up knowing about life in New York as much as in Mysore, or of reimaginations of Bath's social life as much as that of Porbandar or Alleppy in the 1800s. This "dual consciousness" already exists within us in our social lives; I am just hoping that it reaches our literary lives as well.

## Note

1 I realized that literary discourse in India was centred around English language and Anglo-American works in 2017. It was the first time the need to have a more democratic system of representation presented itself. But without the two years at Loyola University Chicago, with support from the Center for Textual Studies and the course design and cohort of the MA in Digital Humanities, I would not have been able to envision it, or build the structure that will continue long after this paper. I want to thank Dr. Elizabeth Hopwood, Dr. Catherine Nichols, Dr. Marta Werner, Dr. Nicoletta Montana, Seth Green, Elliot Post, and Brian Abrams for being such wonderful professors, and creating classroom environments that were fun, engaging, and tremendously enriching. To the Class of 2020 and the Class of 2021, who have been such a smart, supportive cohort, and whose projects, ideas, and discussions continually inspire me. To Srijon Sil, Akshay Lakhi, Regina Hong, Abha Nadkarni, and Zachary Stella, for making the time to talk with me at various stages of my simultaneous project, help clear technical and theoretical doubts, and give critical feedback. To Niamh Mcguigan, Margaret Heller, and Ashley Howedshell for helping me understand how library catalogues classify books, how to use existing standards of Authority Control, and how to use the Dublin Core Metadata Set, respectively. To Troy Bassett, director of the *At the Circulating Library* database of Victorian Fiction, for sharing his. sql file and allowing me to see and borrow from the backend, and for sharing his process of building the database over five years. To the Digital Humanities Alliance for Research and Teaching Innovations (DHARTI) India, for providing the resources and the network that helped me contextualize DH work in the Indian context. And to Saurabh Garg, my partner at Purple Pencil Project.

## References

Ananthamurthy, U. R. (2015) Towards the Concept of a New Nationhood: Languages and Literatures in India. in Espoito, A. A et al. (ed.) *In Her Right Hand She Held a Silver Knife with Small Bells*. Germany: Harrassowitz Verlag.

Borges, J. (2019) *Bombay Balchão*, Mumbai: Tranquebar.

Center for Textual Studies and Digital Humanities (2020) *The Fashion and Race Database* [Facebook], 12 November. Available at: www.facebook.com/LUCCTSDH/videos/371525360929774. (Accessed: 1 March 2021).

Chicago Public Library. (2021) *Kunvan*. Available at: https://chipublib.bibliocommons.com/v2/record/S126C1729020 (Accessed: 10 April 2021).

Cushman, E. (2013) Wampum, Sequoyan, and Story: Decolonizing the Digital Archive, *College English, 76(2), pp. 115–133*. www.jstor.org/stable/24238145. (Accessed: 20 April 2021).

Department of Linguistics at University of Illinois Urbana-Campaign: (2021) *About Hindi*. Available at: https://linguistics.illinois.edu/hindi/about-hindi (Accessed: 16 April 2021)

Dev, A. (2000) Comparative Literature in India, *Comparative Literature and Culture, 2(4)*. https://doi.org/10.7771/1481-4374.1093. (Accessed: 15 April 2021).

Fiormonte, D. (2016) Toward a Cultural Critique of Digital Humanities, *Debates in the Digital Humanities 2016*. Available at: https://dhdebates.gc.cuny.edu/read/untitled/section/5cac8409-e521-4349-ab03-f341a5359a34 (Accessed 20 April 2021).

Goodreads Community Shelf: (2021) *Indian Literature Books*. Available at: www.goodreads.com/shelf/show/indian-literature (Accessed: 17 April 2021).

Gupta, S. (2012) Indian 'Commercial Fiction' in English, the Publishing Industry and Youth Culture, *Economic & Political Weekly 2012*, (February). Available at: www.epw.in/journal/2012/05/special-articles/indian-commercial-fiction-english-publishing-industry-and-youth (Accessed: 4 April 2021).

Haque, M. (2021) The Language Movement of India, *The Business Standard*, 21 February. Available at: www.tbsnews.net/bangladesh/amar-ekushey/language-movement-india-205015 (Accessed: 27 April 2021).

Jaywant Dalvi (2021) Wikipedia. Available at: https://en.wikipedia.org/w/index.php?title=Jaywant_Dalvi&oldid=1016372993 (Access: 6 April 2021).

Jenkins, Kimberley, Lunchtime Lecture at Center for Textual Studies and Digital Humanities (2020), The Fashion and Race Database [Facebook], 12 November. Available at: www.facebook.com/LUCCTSDH/videos/371525360929774. (Accessed: 1 March 2021).

Martin, R. L. and Osberg, S. R. (2015) *Getting Beyond Better: How Social Entrepreneurship works*, Boston: Harvard Business Review Press.

Mukherjee, S. (1977) Towards a Literary History of India, *New Literary History, 8(2), p. 225*. https://doi.org/10.2307/468519 (Accessed: 5 April 2021).

Murray, J. H. (2011) *Inventing the Medium: Principles of Interaction Design as a Cultural Practice*. Cambridge, MA: MIT Press.

Noble, S. U. (2018) *Algorithms of Oppression: How Search Engines Reinforce Racism*, New York: New York University Press.

Parameswaran, U. (1989) Towards an Aesthetic of Opposition: Essays on Literature, Criticism and Cultural Imperialism by Arun Mukherjee," *World Literature Today, 63(4)*.

Purple Pen Project (2021) Available at: https://www.purplepencilproject.com/ (Accessed: 29 April 2021).

Roy, S. (2021) Beyond the Guilt Tax, *The Point 2021* (January). Available at: https://thepointmag.com/criticism/beyond-the-guilt-tax/ (Accessed: 30 March 2021).

Sadana, R. (2012) *English Heart, Hindi Heartland: The Political Life of Literature in India*. Berkeley: University of California Press.

Singh, A. and Iyer, N. (2016) Introduction: Beyond the Anglophone—Comparative South Asian Literatures, *Comparative Literature Studies, 53(2), p. 209*, https://doi.org/10.5325/complitstudies.53.2.0209 (Accessed: 3 April 2021).

Stella, Z. (2021) Email to Prakruti Maniar, 23 April.

# 7

# ARCHIVING "COMMUNITY'S VOICES" IN KARBI ANGLONG

## Collective Memory and Digital Apprehensions

*Debashree Dattaray*

### Introduction

The chapter aims to describe and evaluate the significant interdisciplinary work done to textualize and preserve oral traditions by the Centre for Karbi Studies and the Karbi Lammet Amei in Karbi Anglong, Assam. Karbis are the largest hill community in Assam, India, and have struggled over the years for the retention of their cultural identity and sovereignty. Cultural activists and organizations, such as Dharamsing Teron and Sikari Tisso, the Karbi Lammet Amei and the Centre for Karbi Studies, have worked extensively for the preservation of the rich Karbi oral heritage, which both celebrates and laments life. These institutions have contributed to the documentation and preservation of oral traditions, which in turn are embedded in the cumulative experiences and teachings of Indigenous peoples. The focus has been on the creation and development of Indigenous value systems through constant engagement with Indigenous literature, art, and cultural practices as part of lived experiences. Roopika Risam writes of "the need for the creation of new methods, tools, projects, and platforms to undo the epistemic violence of colonialism and fully realize a decolonized digital humanities" (Risam 2018). Given the history of discrimination and negation of Indigenous communities in the Northeast, the process of archiving and documentation has been a slow and tenuous process. The chapter discusses the opportunities and challenges of the long-term preservation of, and access to, Karbi oral traditions. It also explores issues of research integrity and curriculum plans in the context of the "archive" in North East India in the context of taking the first step: the articulation of voices from the community and the necessity of Indigenous agency. The chapter discusses certain recent instances of the ways in which Indigenous agency has been established in the digital space within the Karbi community. It is now possible, albeit in extremely adverse circumstances, to think of the "promise of the digital humanities"—an

DOI: 10.4324/9781003354246-10

"opportunity to intervene in the digital cultural record—to tell new stories, shed light on counter histories, and create spaces for communities to produce and share their own knowledge, should they wish" (Risam 2019, p. 5).

The chapter is divided into three sections. The first section explores transcultural narrative reconstructions of Indigenous identity through a long and tenuous linguistic conflict involving processes of institutional archiving in Karbi Anglong. The second section expands the documentation of popular cultural memory of/in the North East and highlights nationhood in cinematic representations of/from the Northeast of India. As a geopolitical space, the Northeast has been associated with insurgency and economic and political negligence by the Indian state. Situating the role of memory within local, national, transnational contexts and temporalities, this chapter would finally focus on recent articulations of digital assertion and resistance by Indigenous communities with particular reference to the Karbi community.

Indigenous scholars have often resisted the Digital Humanities, since the question of appropriation of stories/data has been abiding concerns for Indigenous communities. According to Mohawk artist, Skawennati and Cherokee scholar, Jason Lewis,

> If Aboriginal peoples learned one thing from contact, it is the danger of seeing any place as terra nullius, even cyberspace. Its foundations were designed with a specific logic, built on a specific form of technology, and first used for specific purposes (allowing military units to remain in contact after a nuclear attack). The ghosts of these designers, builders, and prime users continue to haunt the blank spaces.
>
> *(Lewis and Skawennati 2005)*

The basic premise of memory is to articulate resistance to inaccurate and fabricated central narratives of control called "history." Memory acts as a safeguard against attempts to silence voices of transgression and dissidence, and, in turn, memory is often implicated in that silencing. Situating the role of memory within local, national, transnational contexts and temporalities, this chapter focuses on the turbulent history of conflict and fragmented selfhood in the Northeast of India.

## Section I

Oral traditions have constituted a growing field of enquiry in India, particularly in terms of educational innovation and ecological sustainability. Epistemologically and ontologically, oral traditions offer possibilities of creating shared capacities that can challenge conventions of practice and counter market norms.

Since its inception in 1966, the Karbi Lammet Amei as an apex literary body of Karbi Anglong has been instrumental in the preservation of Karbi language. In a project funded by the National Science Foundation involving the Karbi Lammet Amei and Linda Konnerth, the following were archived online that would promulgate the language of the Hills Karbi:

The online collection comprised a total of 2 hours (approximately 12,500 words) of the following types of texts:

- 9 folk stories
- 2 personal narratives and one other narrative
- 1 stimuli-based narrative (pear story)
- 4 procedural texts
- 1 conversation/interview

*(Linda Konnerth and Chikari Tisso 2019)*

This is an important collaboration of the Karbi Lammet Amei which was established for the promotion of the Karbi language in schools and institutions across Karbi Anglong. With its headquarters at Diphu, the KLA has had branches across Karbi Anglong in villages and towns as well. It has been an integral to the history of Karbi letters.

The marginality of Indigenous languages has been a defining trope, which contests universalist assumptions of literary traditions and also factors into unique ethnic and cultural experiences which demand critical evaluation. Language has been a powerful tool for Indigenous people across the world, used to overcome the injuries of imposed change, political exclusion, and loss of identity. Within the constraints of state legal systems and the plethora of public ideas and expectations, Indigenous people have been involved in seeking cultural justice, while rearticulating and redignifying the collective self. From the perspective of India's Northeast, "The common man in the Northeast is painfully caught in the mayhem of violence produced by unending militancy, inter-ethnic feuds and the oppressive measures of the state" (Baral 2013, p. 10). Karbi Anglong in Assam has been part of such a history since the 1950s. When the first "State Reorganization Commission" was formed in 1954, it did not recommend statehood for the tribal districts in Northeast India. Consequently, the "Hill State Movement" intensified its demands and by the time of the elections in 1957, all of the six Autonomous District Councils of Assam were under pressure to form independent Hill states. However, ruling Karbi leaders were in opposition to the formation of Hill States. In reaction, in 1959, the Karbi Students' Association (KSA) was formed—the first of its kind. Meanwhile, the Diphu Government Boys' High School was established in 1958, while the first and only government-run college, Diphu Government College, was founded in 1964. Discussions on language rights and cultural activism centred around these urban locations in and around Diphu in East Karbi Anglong. The Assam Official Language Act (1960) led to widespread agitation, and the KSA became active participants of the newly formed All Party Hills Leaders' Conference (APHLC). They propagated the cause of the APHLC and also advocated the use of the Roman script for Karbi language amidst the staunch opposition of ruling Karbi leaders who were part of the then Mikir Hills Autonomous District Council. By Article 244 A in the Constitution of India as per the Assam Reorganization (Meghalaya) Act of 1969, the Autonomous state of Meghalaya was created in 1970. Karbis were given the opportunity to join the state of Meghalaya, to have new autonomous state of their own, or to remain in Assam. Ruling Karbi leaders opted to be part of Assam, which was seen as a betrayal of the Karbi people by the KSA, which then continued the statehood campaign from time to time. In 1973, the "Roman Script" movement resurfaced, and KSA demonstrated in Diphu in December of the same year. They were subjected to brutal assaults by the state police, and many KSA leaders were arrested and jailed. Inside prison, the idea of the Karbi Youth Festival was developed in order to create cultural awareness and protect and promote dying traditions from Karbi Anglong. In 1974, Karbi Youth Festival (KYF) was first held in Karbi Club, Diphu, in January coinciding with New Year celebrations. It was a small affair, lasting for three days, and drew only a limited attendance. But it had a huge impact on the youth and students. Since then, the organizers made the KYF into an annual event. An apex cultural body called the "Karbi Cultural Society" (KCS) was formed in 1977, which directly started supervising the KYF. Under the guidance of KCS, annual KYF began to be held in rural areas in all parts of Karbi Anglong. KYF grew in strength and prestige as rural youth and students rallied solidly behind it, in spite of the state government's apathy and refusal to give any financial assistance. But the KYF continued without any lapse and flourished to become the Karbi national cultural platform. In the cartographic imaginary, Karbi Anglong, as reiterated by the annual Karbi Youth Festival, has existed and survived over centuries through its myths, legends, songs, dances, artistic traditions, and through its conflicting history and moribund politics. Most importantly, the Karbi Youth Festival takes cognizance of differentiation rather than assimilation, whereby language plays a mobilizing force in identity formation.

In 1994, KYF began a new experiment, when it decided to hold a five day event at Taralangso, a sprawling and serene venue in Diphu, with an aim to build up a Cultural Complex called "Karbi Peoples' Hall" (KPH). Since then, the KPH continues to be the venue of annual KYF. The KYF draws more than 2,000 young rural artists, folk singers, and dancers in their colourful traditional dresses. They perform folk dances such as Chomkan, Chong-kedam, Banjar (related to death ritual), Lingpum-Sokchon, Haccha, and Ritnong-Chingdi (farming related) in accompaniment with traditional drum (cheng) and related folk songs. Participants come from the 21 zonal committees of the KCS, with each zone organizing its own fund for 100 members or more and taking part in competitions for folk and modern singing, folk and modern dancing, dress-shows, and traditional sports, etc., which draw a crowd of thousands. At present, Taralangso has developed an ethnic amphitheatre and huge three open air stages where hundreds of dancers/singers can perform at a time. Besides, there are Westernsong competitions, drawing in new talents experimenting with new-age fusion music, which may incorporate themes of youth frustration, unity, change, and assertion of identity. The five-day event is almost trouble-free, without the presence of a single police officer, as it is manned by hundreds of KCS volunteers. The festival begins with a traditional procession called "Rongketong," or the "Hundred-Drum Ensemble," presented by artistes of the Department of Art & Culture, Karbi Anglong Autonomous Council (KAAC). Dances as varied as Ritong Chingdi/Hen'up Ahi Kekan, Lingpum Sokchon,

Nimso Kerung, Hacha Kekan, Chong Kedam, and Banjar Kekan are performed by young men and women from the 26 KCS zones along with other invited groups across the region. Karbi creation songs, such as *Mosera Khir* or the *Bong'oi*, and contemporary Karbi songs and dances such as *Luncheto* and *Lunchethak* are part of the repertoire at KYF. Traditional musical instruments such as Muri Tongpo, Krongchui, and Kum Li'eng reiterate the virtuosity and skills from the region as do the active participation in traditional sports such as HambiKepathu, Kengdongdang Kekat, and Bathili Ke'ap.

In the course of the events at the Karbi Youth Festival, the community redefines itself in the light of the emergence of a new discourse of Karbi identity and ethnic presence in the hills. The festival is a site of resistance, celebration, and reaffirmation of Karbi cultural heritage. Lamenting on the gradual transformation of the Karbi "rong" or village to a Kuwehonchi (Guwahati), or concrete jungle, the festival narrates tales of exclusion, inclusion, and survival amidst all adversities. The Karbi Youth Festival blog gives a clarion call to all with the following lines:

*Today, the land that we call ours is encroached upon and there are more strangers than kinsmen where have they all gone? We are still looking for them, in the hills and plains and valleys!* (Karbi Youth Fest 2020).

The blog has now been converted as a dynamic website: http://karbiyouthfestival.com/ which provides a detailed history of the youth festival along with an interface linked to Facebook groups on the Youth Festival. Furthermore, the website provides information on Karbi cuisine and a traveller's guide to the Festival. The interface has created a global impact in relation to the enriching history of the festival. The website also highlights the structure of the Nothengpi, a silver earpiece unique to the attire of elderly Karbi women. The website foregrounds Karbi cultures as a living and thriving tradition. This is in contradistinction to much of the cultural policy vis-à-vis the Northeast in post—Independence India that emphasized categories of the "folk," implying that Indigenous cultures from the region were to be seen as archaic and stagnant, and needed to be preserved as such in their pristine purity. Furthermore, such an approach fed upon nationalist perceptions of Indigenous cultures as backward and often at odds with rhetorical notions of Indian nationalism. On the other hand, given government policies granting political privileges on the bases of ethnic identity in the Northeast, the Indigenous elite strove to uphold the "tribal identity" before the nation setting the stage for a unique political and cultural identity. According to Daisy Hasan, "By being alternately denigrated and romanticized, the indigenous cultures of North—East India lost much of their dynamism and political potential" (Hasan 2010, p. 32).

With the perpetuation of reductive stereotypical categories of "backward," "violent," and "underdeveloped" in national media and films, the loss has been aggravated. Consequently, there has been an acute sense of cultural distance between the Northeast and mainland India. Prasun Sonwalker writes:

> Below the normative discourses of democracy, multiculturalism and nationalism, lies a discursive web of relations reified in the binary of "us" and

> "them". It is based on material as well as psychological factors. The binary can be a key tool to explore and identify group perceptions and consciousness, and, in turn, help unravel banal journalism and explain the coverage and non-coverage of a society's "other".
>
> *(Sonwalkar 2005, p. 271)*

Mainstream Indian cinema, popular media, and news posit the Northeast as the "other," more than often, from patronizing, or limited perspectives. More than often, the cultural vision of the Northeast is jeopardized in its fractured relations with the rest of India. This relationship, which dictates the visual regime of popular mainstream culture, has often been described as "a cultural gap, an economic gap, a psychological gap and an emotional gap" (Baruah 2005, p. 166). Bollywood films on the Northeast, which are far and apart, exemplify the imagined space of the region as articulated by the "rest of India." The political and cultural agency of the Northeast itself is denied in the process. On the other hand, cinema from the Northeast foregrounds discursive gaps between lived Indigenous practices and non-Indigenous reception of the same, and directs our attention to the growth and development of new ways of understanding the world from the perspective of Indigenous discourses. In the following section, the cinematic presence of the Northeast may be studied as a crucial moment of transition as one moves towards the digital presence of Indigenous communities in Northeast India.

## Section II

Jyotiprasad Aggarwala's *Joymoti*, the story of the Ahom princess who sacrifices her life for democracy, was released in 1935. Combating the neo-imperial presence of institutionalized studios in Bombay and Kolkata, Aggarwala wrote:

> In India, Indian films must be made . . . otherwise it would be impossible to put an end to the suction of money by foreign films. . . . For sometime, the Assamese people, instead of comparing an Assamese production with Bengali, Hindi or American films, must take an Assamese film eagerly and endearingly as one belonging to the first grade despite its lack of quality if there be any.
>
> *(cited in Mazid 2007, pp. 37–38)*

Aggarwala would return to Assam after training in Germany's UFA studios to establish the Chitralekha Moviestone Company at Bholaguri Tea Estate in Assam. People involved in the movie's production belonged to village communities in the region. However, despite the long and complex multilingual history of cinema from the Northeast, one seems to remember only a Pramathesh Barua, S.D. Burman, Bhupen Hazarika, or a Seema Biswas, all as but scattered names from the Northeast pantheon. What is forgotten is the conscious, continual process of "de-territorialising diversities," closely connected to the concept of bringing to the centre the fluid cultural borders and boundaries and "closed" spaces (Srivastava *et al.* 2014, p. 21). Mishing, Karbi, Kokborok, Bodo, Manipuri, and Assamese are just some of the languages in which Northeast cinema has been made. Complex cinematic texts connect the political and the public, moving beyond the mainstream media discourse on insurgency and military intervention.

For instance, *AFSPA, 1958*, written and directed by HaobamPebam Kumar in 2006, is a documentary movie which focuses on the plight of women from Manipur in the aftermath of the Manorama Devi AFSPA episode. On 10 July 2004, Th. Manorama had been picked up from her home in Bamon Kampu Village in Imphal East District by the 17th Assam Rifles on the basis of her alleged connections with the People's Liberation Army. The next morning, her bullet-ridden corpse was found along with semen marks on her skirt suggesting rape and murder. It led to widespread protests, and a group of women belonging to the "Meira Paibi," or "Torchbearers," demonstrated in front of the 17th Assam Rifles by stripping naked and calling on the army to rape them as Manorama had been raped. *AFSPA, 1958* offers a sustained and poignant diary of the events of 10 July 2004 and its consequences which highlight failure of justice and the controversies around AFSPA.

The deprivation of land, forced migration, and the eradication of Indigenous ways of life have been integral to narratives from the region. Joseph Pulinthanath, with his origins in Kerala, has spent much of his time in the Northeast. In 2008, he made his second feature film in the Kokborok language titled *Yarwng* or *Roots*. Located in the idyllic banks of the Raima and the Saima, the movie revolves around a Hydel Project in Tripura in the 1970s which led to a large-scale displacement of Indigenous peoples.

Manju Borah has directed eight movies in Assamese, Mishing, and Bodo, and has also received several international and national awards. However, for her last film, titled *Dau Huduni Methai (Song of the Horned Owl, 2015)*, which is based on the Bodo insurgencies' effects on villagers, Borah expressed her apprehensions:

> I don't think it will ever have a theatrical release. With most theatres favouring mainstream cinema and even audiences, it's impossible for films from other languages to make it to cinemas. . . . It's really sad that only Hindi and English films manage to enjoy theatrical release. What about other language films? We produce films in so many languages but why the focus is always on Bollywood?
>
> *(The Indian Express 2015)*

Borah's 2012 film *Ko: Yad (A Silent Way)*, in Mishing, revolves around the life of Pokkam from the Mishing community. Based on Anil Panging's novel *Ko: Yad*, which was published in instalments in the weekly Assamese daily *Xadin*, the movie won the Best Assamese Mishing Film Award along with the Best Cinematographer award for Sudheer Palsane at the 60th National Film Festival in 2012. The story of a driftwood collector and the betrayal she faces from his family, creditors, and the river itself are emblematic of the human condition.

*Orong*, directed by Suraj Kumar Duwarah, won the Best Feature Film Award in Rabha at the 62nd National Film Festival. The story of the teenager Rasong and his struggle to live life in his own terms may be juxtaposed with that of the elderly Apu, a former "head-hunter," and his travails in the dense forests of Nagaland, in Nilanjan Dutta's *The Head Hunter* (2015) in the Wancho language.

"Returning home" is a significant trope in many contemporary films from the Northeast, given pains of alienation, exile, and a diminishing sense of "homeland." It becomes crucial to be able to return to the geographical space of the homeland before one can enter the process of reclaiming identities and attempt a completion of performance. *Crossing Bridges* (2013), directed by Sange Dorjee Thondok, is the first feature film in Shertukpen, one of the languages of Arunachal Pradesh. The movie tells the story of middle-aged Tashi, who returns to his village after losing his job as a web designer in Mumbai. In the long wait for new openings in the city, Tashi experiences the world views of his people which change his perception of life and his aspirations. In an interview, Thondok, a graduate from the Satyajit Ray Film and Television Institute, Kolkata, asserts that to make a film in Shertukpen was a conscious decision. He also divulges that

> I didn't have the fear of it not reaching the audience as the basic idea of making the film in my language was to preserve it in whatever small way and at the same time show rest of the world, which knows very little about our culture and way of living.
>
> *(montymajeed 2014)*

Tashi, the protagonist, would like to "get out" of home, which he feels does not have anything to offer. Yet, through his days of unemployment, he connects, albeit unwillingly, with his ageing parents, friends, and children in a school he decides to teach in for a while. He realizes that, for them, Mumbai is "foreign land," while for him, his village and its people have become "foreign." Yet, he is haunted by remarks and questions like, "You seemed to have lost our taste for butter tea," or "Why don't the outside world know about us?" The movie is a beautiful kaleidoscope of little surprises in the pristine valleys of Arunachal Pradesh, yet remain rooted in real questions on how important it is to "stay back."

Films from the Northeast involve going back in history and also engage in a continuous negotiation with contemporary forces, such as globalization, neo-imperialism, and the power politics within Indigenous communities. Directors from the Northeast are establishing a new path of Indian film production. Through a lyrical use of nature and locations, and a discussion of hard-hitting issues pertinent to the region, they weave tales of wonder and woe, producing profound art which "returns" the gaze. In "Volumetric Cinema," Ferguson argues:

> Is there not a way to rediscover a new kind of space in cinema, a digital humanities that can look past the flat screen and explore moving image texts as dimensional objects? In doing so, can we outline an experimental stance

> more broadly for the digital humanities, which would both position cinema and media studies more firmly within the field and generate new strategies for other DH practices to visualize collections of images as three-dimensional objects?
>
> *(Ferguson 2019, p. 336)*

Cinema from the Northeast interrogates transcultural narrative reconstructions of victimhood in Northeast India and attempts a reading of categories of alienation/belonging. Lived realities in/of the Northeast underscore the significance of narrative as a discursive mode, with the potential to destabilize the symbolic foundation of nations and collective identities thereby offering a transforming aesthetic of contingency, unknowability, and the deferment of resolution.

Cinema from the Northeast can provide a technological realm through which one can trace an alternative genealogy anchored by digital representations that may foreground the strengths and vulnerabilities of Indigenous communities.

## Section III

The world is now witnessing the emergence of a digital resistance to all forms of colonial and imperial violence that enable the development of creative methods of acknowledging Indigenous ways of life across online networks. In "Drumbeats to Drumbytes," Ahasiw Maskegon-Iskwew writes that the digital world has transformed into a veritable platform for Indigenous presence in the midst of the colonial apocalypse.

> To govern ourselves means to govern our stories and our ways of telling stories. It means that the rhythm of the drumbeat, the language of smoke signals and our moccasin telegraph can be transformed to the airwaves and modems of our times. We can determine our use of the new technologies to support, strengthen and enrich our cultural communities.
>
> *(Ahasiw Maskegon-Iskwew 2015)*

The protest against Dakota Access Pipeline's construction on sacred Lakota Sioux lands found more than one million supporters who used Facebook to "check into" Standing Rock in solidarity with water protectors. In Australia, the vast survivors of "Stolen Generations" organized networks of social support, as they tried to relocate families across ancestral lands. In May 2021, the Tk'emlups te Secwepemc nation announced that it had located 315 unmarked graves of children at the site of a former residential school in Kamloops. Canada. The news led global initiatives of solidarity among Indigenous communities across the digital platform and redefined the meaning of the National Day of Truth and Reconciliation in Canada.

In recent times, digital affirmation and resistance through Facebook check-ins, Twitter hashtags, Instagram stories, YouTube channels, blogs, vlogs, zines, and listservs have functioned as some of the most crucially publicly accessible place-making platforms that (re)centre and (re)circulate Indigenous issues into the public consciousness. For instance, the Centre for Karbi Studies promulgates Karbi history and traditions through its page including information of academic and cultural achievements within the Karbi Community. According to Dharamsing Teron, the Founder of the Centre for Karbi Studies and one of the administrators of their Facebook page, "Digital Presence for Karbi culture is definitely very important because of its easy and affordable accessibility" (Teron 2021). However, Teron cautions us on the fact that "the presence is not vibrant; to the contrary—it is becoming more anarchic due to the so-called freedom of expression that digital platforms offer which is doing more harm than good" (Teron 2021). Teron's concerns should be read in the larger context of archiving of Karbi material culture and narratives and the dangers of appropriation. The Centre for Karbi Studies was established in 2015 as an independent research organization of Karbi scholars, activists, and academics. The logo for the Centre is inspired by the traditional red–black–white colour and represents the "mi-ring-rang," a Karbi equivalent of the universal symbol of a labyrinth that stands as the "doorway to life and death and rebirth." The logo also has the numerical "9" embedded in each of the three squares as the numerical holds special significance in Karbi worldview. Through the Facebook page, the logo has become synonymous to the assertion of Karbi identity and belief systems.

The digital platform has provided networks for the presenting instances of Karbi cuisine, language, and textiles. For instance, a funding from the Firebird Foundation for Anthropological Research enabled a collaboration between the Centre for Karbi Studies and the Kohima Institute to facilitate a full transcription, translation, and musical annotation of the Kecharhe Alun funeral epic in Karbi Anglong, recorded by a team led by Michael Heneise and Dharamsing Teron in 2017. Performed from memory, the Kecharhe Alun is one of the most significant and longest (several days) single piece of chanted poetry in the Karbi oral literature repertoire, and the project enabled its recording and transcription and archiving for the first time.

In the essay on "The Archive after Theory," Ward and Wisnicki write:

> We cannot have a future archive without the realization of the digital archive's haunting by the imperial archive, an acceptance of the impossibility of ever being free of that ghost, and a bedrock reliance on critically mediated digital building to accommodate that dual position. It is this very sense of after-ness that affords the digital archive a future orientation that is not utopian and a past orientation that never stagnates.
>
> *(Ward and Wisnicki 2019, p. 203)*

A Fulbright Alumni Project in 2019 led by Debashree Dattaray and in collaboration with the Centre for Karbi Studies brought together three generations of Karbi women—weavers, professionals, and students together for an intensive workshop that would archive songs related to weaving in the region. Indigenous story tellers and weavers such as Kasang Teronpi Kajek Tokbipi and Bina Rongpipi were involved in the process of recording and archiving of Oral Karbi narratives related to weaving. The project initiated conversation between Karbi women weavers, urban Karbi women, and experts in Indigenous studies and gender studies to develop a collective of women groups working for the community and beyond through the platform of the Centre for Karbi Studies and its fast-growing digital presence in social media. Serdihun is known as the first woman who introduced weaving to the Karbis. Songs from the region narrate how the first jir-ik (a dark blue/black cover for the upper part of a woman's body) and then the first pe-seleng (a dhoti worn by men and boys) are woven by her with the help of her intricate tools—therang (Karbi backstrap loom), uvek (bamboo sticks for drawing patterns), and ser-langvet (a water container necessary for smoothening of the woven cloth). According to the myth, the tools are still found on the top of the Punja hill near Vothatlangso. Till this day, weavers pray to Serdihun at the onset such that they may be relieved of any physical pain during the act of weaving. Seleng, choi-ang, and poho—the three-piece set for men—and pini, pekok, and vamkok for women are designed according to the social status and the role played by the individual in the community and the environment. A YouTube channel titled "Pini, Pekok, Vamkok" has been dexterously archiving Karbi weaves, and the platform is often shared by social media. The Centre for Karbi Studies has also tried to archive material by master storyteller Longsing Bey, one of the most iconic Karbi oral storytellers in contemporary times. In 2020, the Centre for Karbi Studies also organized a month-long tenuous process of digitization of Karbi language, language teaching, literature, and culture and the representation of Karbis through an Orientation Programme organized by young Karbi scholars. Sabeen Rongpipi, one of the organizers of the event, explains further on the digital presence:

> It is important to first understand what kind of digital representation is being carried out, by whom, and for whom. Minority communities that rely heavily on orality walk on cultural fragility when it comes to digital representation. Orality carries variations, versions, and it is on these variants that the cultural richness of the communities depends on. Digitalisation is in a way similar to written word; once something is digitalised, and accessed by public, it becomes the representative of let's say a folklore tradition. That effectively erases the multidimensionality of it. What then will be represented, or forced to become a representative, is one-dimensional that cannot reflect the actual depth of a culture.

> However, with the encroachment of dominant communities, minorities face the threat of the erasure of their culture. In that scenario, preservation of a culture becomes important. This is where digital representation comes in.
> *(Rongpipi 2021)*

The digital space offered the young Karbi community with a creative agency emblematic of a reclaimed self-determination in terms of a relationship to both a sense of space and place. The media became a virtual space of autonomous control whereby the virtual world transformed as a methodology of creative production. For the young Karbi community, their desire to explore possibilities that would promote, renew, and enrich Indigenous worldviews is being articulated through digital technologies that enable the creation of a platform for virtual sovereignty. As members of Indigenous communities, these youngsters participated in what Cherokee sociologist Eva Marie Garroutte terms "indigenism"—the communal influence one another towards substantial decolonization efforts (Garroutte 2003). The disruption and dismantling of exploitative non-Indigenous epistemic structures that threaten community lifeways are crucial goals. Cheryl L'Hirondelle writes:

> As we move forward into virtual domains we too are sneaking up and setting up camp—making this virtual and technologically mediated domain our own. However, we stake a claim here too as being an intrinsic part of this place—the very roots, or more appropriately routes. So, let's use our collective Indigenous unconscious to remember our contributions and the physical beginnings that were pivotal in how this virtual reality was constructed.
> *(L'Hirondelle 2016, p. 160)*

Indigenous communities must in fact be strategic in the ways in which they choose to share, analyse, and learn from each other. In order to celebrate World Tourism Day 2021, Government Model College, Deithor, organized a photography competition on the natural and cultural heritage of Karbi Anglong. The fact that competitors would be eligible to submit their work via WhatsApp generated great public interest among young members of the community as they tried to create an archive of the material culture of Karbi Anglong. The project in collaboration with World Tourism Organization, an UN agency that promotes Tourism and Sustainability, offered possibilities of articulating Karbi culture despite limited connectivity in the region. A more recent project that would commence in November 2021 and that would involve the Karbi community is part of Sutradhaar and is called "Indigenous Pathways." The project is informed by Indigenous networks that are moving towards each other across the digital and real spaces. "Indigenous Pathways" entails a "Return to Roots" with an exploration through Indigenous elders and would embark on a revitalization of Indigenous connections to earth and ecology. Planned as three month-long intensive learning programme in alignment with Northeast India's Indigenous Communities, it is based on the premise of sharing of different knowledge systems through the "sutradhaar" or the storyteller. Sabeen Rongpipi, a team member for the project, informs:

> I have already been a part of quite a few projects directly or indirectly. They were a mix of indigenous and non-indigenous populace. I did realise that almost all these projects did not have far-reaching effects. As soon as they were over or completed, only the person who organised benefited from them. The community either did not have any benefit or was given a compensation that did not really help them beyond the project. It is high time that the digital representations and the projects associated to them think of long-term goals that keep the indigenous communities at forefront and treat them as equal and not a project. I believe that an indigenous community should contribute directly, have an authority over what should be added or removed, and have the last word. This is one of the few ways where the genuine participation of a community is reflected.
>
> *(Rongpipi 2021)*

"Indigenous Pathways" plans to archive the Chomangkan, also known as "Thikarhi," the funeral song that is sung by the Charhepi or the dirge singer. Karbi songs are rooted in the Tibeto-Burmese language family. Karbis use the Roman script. Mosera or the creation song is an integral part of the Karbi Keplang. Rongkim a-lun is the song (alun) of how the first Karbi village (Rong) was built (Kim) by a village elder or Kasen. The songs are sung by trained singers/performers who are specialists in their chosen narrative repertoire. The "Karhi" performed as a celebration of death is as much a celebration of life in Karbi tradition. This funerary ritual that embodies the philosophy of death and rebirth, eroticism and fertility, the art of music and dance, and a communal cultural activity is also the essence of the cultural edifice of the Karbis. But the tragedy now is that the "chomangkan" or "Karhi" is well becoming only a celebration of death and decay, reflecting the crude realities within the Karbi society which itself is gasping for survival between tradition and modernity. Karbi belief system has been variously defined as a "worship of demons" from one extreme to another, which categorizes it as a "crude form of Hinduism." The categorization (or assimilation to be specific) of the Karbis into the "official" religion has wider implication as the same old colonial ideology continues to dominate the thought process of a good number of mainstream intellectuals and the census operation. The *Mi-ring-rang* songs attempt to locate specific colonial situations in the contexts of imperialism and modernity and draw attention to sexuality as a central site for the production and negotiation of so-called colonial modernities. A censorious, "civilized," "modernist" gaze has rendered the "*Mi-ring-rang*" songs almost extinct in contemporary times. Perhaps, the gradual disappearance of the ancient ritual performance is subject to a hierarchical, neo-imperialist, "modernist" gaze. The songs had not only reflected the last vestiges of crucial fertility-rites prevalent among the Karbis, but had also been an ideal platform for young men and women to express their sexual desires within the precincts of sanctioned community traditions. The songs, a part and parcel of Karbi tradition, engage in conceptual issues at the cutting edge of research on sexuality as an interpretative category. In the context of a liberal democracy such as India, one recognizes in the Karbi tradition a history of colonized peoples of the globe The songs are explicit validation of preexisting sexual traditions with their own vocabularies of desire and difference—which neither colonizer nor colonized may imagine as the "erotic margin"—a primordial blank space waiting for the pen "from above" to come doodle in it. In the context of an Indigenous, eclectic domain, the songs exhibited a quality of the erotic created in subjective experience and affective reflections, extending the limits of intellectual understanding. The oral tradition negotiated involvement of men and women in a communal aesthetic activity, thereby uniting the past and the present in memory in an otherwise mundane existence. This further highlights the deconstructive intimacies and gendered memory invoked by this powerful erotic culture through the string of narratives. The Centre for Karbi Studies has been instrumental in the recording of these songs across the regional variations available through East and West Karbi Anglong. Through the Facebook page and through the presence community members in social media, the impact of the continuous work being done by Centre through Indigenous agency and collaboration has had far-reaching impact for the community in terms of identity and self-determination.

Indigenism promulgates the meeting of ideological positions within a framework of responsible and ethical modes of assertion. The digital platform provides an evolving site of knowledge systems that impact both large-scale global social transformations and microcosmic initiatives of change and movement in response to deeply entrenched histories of social injustices and exploitation. Arundhati Roy writes, "The only thing worth globalizing is dissent" (Roy 2016, p. 193). Therefore, it is imperative to work towards the possibility of a digital platform that would recognize Indigenous practices, vocabularies, and rhetorical concepts in relation to Indigenous representation and ethics.

## References


Baral, Kailash C. (2013) Articulatıng Marginality: Emerging Literatures from Northeast India. In Margaret Ch. Zama (Ed.), *Emerging Literatures from Northeast India: The Dynamics of Culture, Society and Identity*. New Delhi: SAGE Publications India Pvt. Ltd.

Sanjib Baruah. (2005) A New Politics of Race: India and Its North East. In *IIC Quarterly* (Vol. 32 (2& 3) Winter, pp. 165–76). New Delhi: India International Centre.

Daisy, Hasan. (2010) Talking back to 'Bollywood': Hindi Commercial Cinema in North-East India. In Shakuntala Banaji (Ed.), *South Asian Media Cultures: Audiences, Representations, Contexts* (pp. 29–50). London: Anthem Press.

Kevin L. Ferguson. (2019) Volumetric Cinema. In M. K. Gold & L. F. Klein (Eds.), *Debates in the Digital Humanities 2019* (pp. 335–349). Minneapolis, MN: University of Minnesota P ress. https://doi.org/10.5749/j.ctvg251hk.31

Eva Marie Garroutte. (2003) *Real Indians: Identity and the Survival of Native America*. Berkeley: University of California Press.

*The Hindu*. (n.d.). *Archive News*. [online] Available a t: www.thehindu.com/fr/2005/04/01/stories/2005040102180200.htm. Accessed on 14 October, 2020.

IndiaGlitz.com. (n.d.). *Bollywood News*. [online] Available at: www.indiaglitz.com/tango-charlie-banned-in-assam-hindi-news-14152.html. Accessed on 14 October, 2020.

*The Indian Express*. (2015) *Don't Think My Film Will Make It to Theatres: Manju Borah*. [online] Available at: https://indianexpress.com/article/entertainment/regionIont-think-my-film-will-make-it-to-theatres-manju-borah/. Accessed on 22 October, 2020.

Karbi Youth Fest's Blog. (2020) *Karbi Youth Fest's Blog*. [online] Available at: https://karbi-youthfest.wordpress.com/. Accessed on 27 October, 2020.

Konnerth, Linda and Chikari Tisso. (2019) *Karbi Texts: Original recordings of a corpus of different genres*. Endangered Languages Archive. Handle: http://hdl.handle.net/2196/00-0000-0000-0013-DB0B-2. Accessed on 3 November, 2021.

Lewis, Jason and Skawennati Tricia Fragnito. (2005) Aboriginal Territories in Cyberspace. *Cultural Survival Quarterly Magazine* (online). Available at: www.culturalsurvival.org/publications/cultural-survival-quarterly/aboriginal-territories-cyberspace. Accessed on 20 January, 2021.

Cheryl L'Hirondelle. (2016) Codetalkers Recounting Signals of Survival. In Steven Loft and Kerry Swanson (Eds.), *Coded Territories: Tracing Indigenous Pathways in New Media Art*. Calgary: Calgary University Press.

Ahasiw Maskegon-Iskwew. (2015) *Drumbeats to Drumbytes: Origins—1994* [online]. Available at: http://drumbytes.org/about/origins-1994.php. Accessed on 30 October, 2021.

A. Mazid. (2007) Jyotiprasad and Joymoti: The Pioneer and the First Assamese Film. In M. Barpujari and G. Kalita (Eds.), *Perspectives on Cinema of Assam* (pp. 29–50). Guwahati: Gauhati Cine Club.

Montymajeed. (2014) *Interview: Sange Dorjee Thongdok*. [online] Portfolio. Available at: https://montymajeed2.wordpress.com/2014/09/30/121-interview-sange-dorjee-thongdok/. Accessed on 22 October, 2020.

R. Risam. (2018) *Decolonizing Digital Humanities in Theory and Practice*. [online] Available a t: https://digitalcommons.salemstate.edu/cgi/viewcontent.cgi?article=1006&context=english_facpub. Accessed on 3 November 2021.

Roopika Risam. (2019) *New Digital Worlds: Postcolonial Digital Humanities in Theory, Praxis, and Pedagogy*. Evanston: Northwestern University Press.

Sabeen Rongpipi. Interview by Debashree Dattaray via email, 30 October 2021.

Arundhati Roy. (2016) *The End of Imagination*. Chicago: Haymarket Books.

Prasun Sonwalkar. (2005) Banal Journalism. In S. Allan (Ed.), *Journalism: Critical Issues* (pp. 261–273). Maidenhead: Open University Press.

Prem Kumari Srivastava and Gitanjali Chawla. Eds. (2014) *De-territorialising Diversities: Literatures of the Indigenous and Marginalised*. New Delhi: Authorspress.

Dharamsing Teron. Interview by Debashree Dattaray via email, 29 October 2021.

M. Ward and A.S. Wisnicki. (2019) The Archive after Theory. In M. K. Gold & L. F. Klein (Eds.), *Debates in the Digital Humanities 2019* (pp. 200–206). Minneapolis, MN: University of Minnesota P ress. https://doi.org/10.5749/j.ctvg251hk.21

www.rediff.com. (n.d.). *Dansh: Unusual Film, Usual Flaws*. [online] Availab le at: www.rediff.com/movies/2005/sep/02dansh.htm. Accessed on October 14, 2020.

www.youtube.com. (n.d.). *Pini Pekok Vamkok—YouTube*. [online] Availabl e at: www.youtube.com/channel/UC4GYQeCMcA8kAQj5mMv0T4A. Accessed on 3 November, 2021.

# 8

# FROM REKHTA TO REKHTA.ORG

## Digital Remappings of Urdu Literary Culture and Public Sphere

*Nishat Zaidi and Mohd Aqib*

### Introduction

The tradition of Urdu language extends over nearly 1,000 years during which it originated, and spread across the Indian subcontinent. During this course, it has produced literature of several kinds adapting ancient and foreign genres and also developing many of its own. Similarly, it has also varied in its nomenclature, orthography, and phonetics across regions and times which make its history vivid and controversial. Conventional approaches to literary history which treat languages as finished products assume a retrospective position disregarding the temporality of the texts and of the language in which they are created. Sheldon Pollock (2003, pp. 12–16) has suggested an alternative approach which focuses instead on the fluidity of languages and literatures replacing the notion of literary history with that of the history of literary cultures. Tracing literary cultures in history entails a study of the idea of literariness observing how it has been defined and redefined in the course of its history. It is observed that this idea is constantly influenced by both the producers and the consumers of literature, while also by the means and agencies of its production, and circulation. It is also affected by languages which while enabling literature themselves undergo processes of change. Their vocabularies, functions, and modes go through transition such that their essential identity is found to be contained only in the continuum of changes that occur along an identifiable trajectory which yields to a language the elusive element of its historicity. While a literary culture is chiefly recognized by the prevailing idea of literariness, literary public sphere is where this idea is collectively practiced through production, circulation, and interpretation of texts. In the last 10 to 15 years during which literature has been increasingly consumed in the digital medium, there have occurred several noticeable transformations in the Urdu literary and public sphere. Situating these transformations in the history of its literary culture, this chapter closely observes

DOI: 10.4324/9781003354246-11

the digitization project of Rekhta Foundation, analysing the ways in which digital technology has transformed literary practices in Urdu. To analyse the readership of Rekhta, a survey was conducted which was participated in by 451 participants. The questionnaire was circulated through social media, and the participants were majorly the social media followers of the young poets who have performed at Rekhta or have been published on its website or books.

## Evolution of Urdu Literary/Public Sphere

### *Oral to Manuscript: Urban Cosmopolitan Moorings of Urdu Literary/Public Sphere in 17th–19th Centuries*

A new literary culture stabilized in Delhi in the late 18th century when Rekhta rose to domination (Farooqi 2003a, p. 849). Poetry mainly circulated at that time in the oral form through *mushairas* as did prose through *dastangoi*. At its centre, Rekhta had the poets who had inherited the legacy of *sabk-i-hindi* poetry (Indian style of Persian poetry) (Farooqi 2003b, p. 7) and who were now turning to Rekhta's literary potential which had recently started gaining royal patronage (Farooqi 2003a, p. 807). The young poets who hitherto sought to emulate Persians masters now wanted to learn this "new" language and its poetic craft that its earliest masters had been perfecting over nearly a century. There emerged, because of this aspiration, the peculiar "institution" of *ustad* (master) and *shagird* (disciple) (Farooqi 2003a, p. 849) and expanded the horizons of Rekhta's literary sphere. In it, poetry was regarded as an *ilm* (science) and a *fan* (pronounced like the English "fun"), that is, a craft or skill which the young disciples learnt from their *ustads*. The number of disciples and their success at poetry was a matter of prestige for the masters. Rivalries about poetic excellence and correct usage of the language played out between different masters and their disciples. *Mushairas* were the assemblies of the poets which convened at the house of a poet, noble, or patron, and the attendees (who were mostly all poets) read out (*tahtal- lafz*) or sang (*tarannum*) their *ghazals* with the host beginning first for the pleasure of his guests. Where the poet was placed in the reading order was a serious matter, because it represented poet's reputation. Also, in these gatherings, humorous poetry was read out first and *ghazals*, considered a higher form of poetry, were read later. Usually an all-male affair, *mushaira*, was also the site where literary rivalries played out. This was most prominent in the case of *tarhi mushaira* in which a *misra-e-tarah* (a poetic line with a fixed metre, rhyme and refrain—elements which together make the *zamiin* of a *ghazal*) was given well in advance and each poet participating in the *mushaira* was supposed to write a *ghazal* in that *zamiin* and using that *misra*. *Mushairas* were also at the same time the launch-pads for young poets who apprenticed under a master. The *ustads* used to help the disciples with their *ghazals* in correcting or improving them, because any error by the *shagird* would ultimately bear on *ustad's* prestige. There were also held similar but smaller gatherings called *nashists* or *mahfils* (Naim 2004, pp. 109–111). Rekhta poetry rose to this position of prominence in Delhi not without the contribution of *Dakan* (Deccan) in the South. Quli Qutub Shah, a *Dakani* poet of late 16th century, is famously known as the first poet to have compiled and published a *divan* (a collection of *ghazals* which has at least one ghazal ending in each of the letters of the Urdu alphabet). Vali Dakni is another major figure from *Dakan* who came to Delhi in the 18th century and left people in awe, showing them that "Rekhtah/Hindi was capable of great poetry, just as Gujri/Hindi and Dakani/Hindi were. He also showed that Rekhtah/Hindi could rival, if not surpass, Indo-Persian poetry in sophistication of imagery, complexity, and abstractness of metaphor, and the 'creation of themes' (*mazmun-afrini*)" (Farooqi 2003a, p. 848).

Since its origin and to a considerable extent even after the arrival of print in the 19th century, Rekhta's literary culture remained largely oral—first in the form of the devotional and didactic teachings of the Sufi saints (Farooqi 2003a, p. 822) which their disciples used to note down to prepare manuscripts (*malfuzaat*) of them—and later in the form of *mushairas* which still enjoys an overwhelming popularity. The interplay of repetitive sounds in *qaafiyas* (rhyme) and *radiif* (refrain), rhythms in the patterns of sound (*bahr* or *vazn*) which ascertains the necessary musicality of a *ghazal*, the extensive use of *iihaam* (punning), and quotability as a creative pursuit while writing *shers* which would then enter conversations to prove a point or defend an argument, etc. are all signifiers of this orature. Until late 19th century, Urdu's literary sphere was restricted to the nobles and aristocrats who would be present at the *mushairas* as guests or hosts, and who had access to the illustrated manuscripts. The name "Urdu" gradually replaced "Rekhta" during the course of the 19th century (Farooqi 2003a, pp. 806–819).

## Print Technology and Urdu

Literacy influenced the public sphere of Urdu literature majorly with the foundation of Fort William College, and this "rupture" (Pollock 2003, p. 21) in the oral tradition was brought about by the print technology. With the arrival of print in India, there occurred massive changes which became more and more visible towards the end of the 19th century. The translation projects which commenced at the Fort William College introduced the literary public sphere of India to western texts. Similarly, Indian texts were also translated for the western readers. Texts, like Mir Amman's *Bagh-o-Bahar*, were commissioned (Farooqi 2003a, pp. 811–812) for the purpose of educating the British civil servants in regional languages. "New" (western) genres of literature emerged and gained popularity (Stark 2007, p. 32). Realistic novels were written in place of fantasy *dastans, nazms* in place of *ghazals*. *Ghazals* began to veer from their high-intellectual and imaginative realm of the *sabk-i-hindi* poetics and incline towards realism; foregrounding themes of socio-political reformation. However, the orature of the language continued to prevail alongside these transformations. In fact, these changes were only visible in Delhi at first. Lucknow, for instance, remained unaffected by these trends with the traditional literary practices and public spheres flourishing as before. This was despite the fact that the headquarter of the Munshi Naval Kishor Press, founded in 1858, was in Lucknow!

*Mahfils* were regularly convened. Traditional forms of *Qissa-goi, Qissa-khwani* and *Dastan-navisi* continued unabated. Lucknowites criticized Sir Syed Ahmed Khan and others who wanted a literary revolution and educational reforms. They also questioned the language of their Delhi counterparts calling it incorrect. *Inder Sabha* was still staged as in the days of Wajid Ali Shah. *Dastan-e-Amir Hamza* and *Tilism-e-Hoshruba* were narrated as usual. There were no Realistic novels in Lucknow like those of Deputy Nazeer Ahmed in Delhi. Instead, it was prose works like *Fasana-e-Azad* (more *dastan*, less novel) that were popular in Lucknow. By the end of the 19th century, however, these conventional literary practices in Lucknow also succumbed to the colonial duress and revolutionary thoughts gained currency.

*(Bari 2004, pp. 59–64) (Translated)*

## Politicization of Urdu Public Sphere in Early 20th Century

Replacement of Persian by Urdu as the official language in the 1830s represents a crucial significance of the "rupture" that print technology caused. There arose voices that sought to emphasize the twoness of Urdu-Hindi and demand their recognition as distinct languages. From this contestation emerged the Hindi/Nagri movement, and in the following years, the divide between Hindi and Urdu became noticeable. It was further broadened by the failed uprising of 1857, after which both Hindu and Muslim communities sought to negotiate with its experience in diverse ways and with it the antithetical positions of Urdu and Hindi intellectuals became more and more prominent (Rai 2000, pp. 5–6). Communities like Nagri Pracharini Sabha and Hindi Sahitya Sammelan emerged to further the cause of Hindi/Nagri in an attempt to dismantle Urdu from position of power. This communalization of languages was the result not only of the indigenous disputes and power tussles but also of colonial interventions in local literary cultures (Farooqi 2003a, pp. 808–810; Rai 2000, pp. 1–2; Stark 2007, pp. 38–45). The colonial grammarians and lexicographers had understood "Hindustani"—with a rich Indo-Persian content in diction and themes—to be the language of Muslims while Hindi to be the language of Hindus. As the Nationalist Movement gained further momentum in the 20th century, the question of a common language resonated throughout the nationalist struggle and many leaders including Gandhi saw Hindustani/Hindi as the only language that could claim the status of national language. By Hindustani/Hindi was meant the language which was commonly understood over a large part of India—neither Persianized Urdu nor Sanskritized Hindi. It could be written either in Nagri or in Nastaliq depending on the choice of the speaker (Rai 2000, pp. 11–13). Some political leaders, writers, and scholars also sought to dispel the "confusion" of distinction between Urdu and Hindi, but to no avail (Farooqi 2003a, pp. 816–819).

In terms of the changes in the idea of what would be considered literary and what not, the literature prescribed by the Progressive Writers Movement (1935) gained authority. Flourishes of imaginative writing *(khayal bandi)* and fantasy literature were discouraged in favour of literature that corresponded to concrete reality.

Progressive *(taraqqi pasand) ghazal* dominated the public sphere. Country/nation became the muse in place of the beloved or God. At the same time, there was a counter movement of *Halqa-i-Arbab-i-Zauq* (beginning in 1939) in which there could be witnessed the reminiscences of *sabk-i-hindi* poetics: aspiring to a complexity of thought and language and high imagination of the classical Rekhta poetry. Yet, that too occurred in a different literary form, that is, *nazm*, composed in *avant garde* style, and often outside the reach of the common masses among whom progressive poetry was far more popular.

## Post-Partition Ghettoization of Urdu in Late 20th Century

Since Pakistan adopted Urdu as its national language, the Muslim–Urdu connection became more concrete in the immediate aftermath of Partition. The bifurcation of Urdu-Hindi into disparate languages finally led to Urdu losing the official language status to Hindi in the debate on national language (Pai 2002, pp. 2705–2706). Central government's three-language policy was interpreted in controversial ways and Urdu stopped receiving state patronage which could have salvaged its situation (Russell 1999, p. 44). With emphasis on modern scientific education which was mostly to be provided in English, Urdu received another blow. Already tagged as a Muslim language, it was confined to Urdu-medium schools which were few in number and *madarsas* which were the centres of religious education. Centrality of English in educational and legal spheres and propagation of the "new Hindi" that was forged by Sanskritization made Urdu struggle for a space of its expression. Owing to a diminishing role of Urdu in non-literary sphere, its neglect at the hands of governments, and its literature reducing to the margins, it was commonly apprehended towards the end of the 20th century that Urdu was declining in India.

Progressive Writers Movement in Urdu majorly migrated to Pakistan. Poets of *Halqa-i-Arbaab-i-Zauq* who privileged high literariness remained on the margins and did not garner any popular influence. *Mushaira*, however, remained as popular as ever, though it too was not unaffected by the changes that came with technological advancements and language politics. With the involvement of common masses, poets participating in the *mushaira (mushaire ke shair)* tended to use patriotic or Islamic themes to appeal to the audiences which unlike the niche audiences in the previous centuries could now be larger because of the availability of microphones (Naim 2004, pp. 114–119). Others who privileged literary over popular distanced themselves from *mushairas* and sought to seek their audience through print media. Many poets and writers turned to Hindi Film Industry to find work. As opposed to the prestige among the elite circles of poetry connoisseurs, in whom there persisted the concept of high literariness of the classical age, it was popularity among these larger audiences that came to dictate the literary merit of a poet. This had the effect of de-Persianization of Ghazal's diction, approximation of the spoken language, poetizing simpler themes, and portrayal of the common man in place of the stock lover modelled after *Majnun* (in *Laila-Majnun).*

### *Digital Apprehensions of Urdu Literary Sphere*

Contrary to the apprehensions about Urdu's extinction, the intervention of the digital technology is providing reasons to speculate that this could be the moment of another "rupture" in its literary sphere. Since the digital medium has become popular, the general perception about Urdu's decline seems to be changing. In the recent times, many digitization projects have been started across languages and literary cultures producing significant changes in their respective traditions. Million Book Project of the National Science Foundation, USA at Carnegie University and the Indian Institute of Science, Bangalore, digitization of the Parliament Library, National Digital Library of India, National Mission for Manuscripts, newspapers and journals in several languages like Aajkaal and Anandabazar Patrika in Bengali, Urdu Adab in Urdu, the Nuqoosh Research Centre in Pakistan, British Council Library, Bichitra: Online Tagore Variorum, and rekhta.org are some of the examples. Nuqoosh Research Centre's digitization project was launched in 2009 to "provide researchers easy access while preserving the original documents" (Qutab *et al.* 2017, p. 88). It is a repository of the correspondences of literary figures in Urdu language which also include Dagh Dehlvi's handwritten *ghazals*. The digitization is said to be running with 4,700 out of the 14,000 letters in the Nuqoosh Museum already digitized. Tagore Variorum is making preservative and scholarly use of digitization. Tagore's original scripts and print materials have not only been scanned but also converted into transcript to make it readable for online tools and also help the researchers guide through illegible manuscripts as well as making them searchable. "[The Bichitra Project] is the biggest integrated knowledge site devoted to any author in any language to date (Jadavpur University, no date)." In 2020, British Council Library's Hyderabad branch became "fully online offer, supplemented with programming and partnership activities relevant to [our] audience" (Murthy 2020). Its online library allows downloading the digital copies of the books and keeping them for up to two weeks. A membership is mandatory and unlimited journals can be read online or downloaded.

Digitization is rigorously at work at Rekhta Foundation, and in the course of last few years, its website rekhta.org has gained immense popularity and social significance. Its focus on providing authentic Urdu literature in digital form has helped it establish a certain prestige which its consumers even regard as authority. Most of the readers of rekhta.org comprise an audience that Urdu literature has been able to reach through digital technology. It seems to be offering ways to circumvent the factors that have limited it in its post-Partition history. Consequently, it has served to revive the unsettled and ignored issues about Urdu's fate in India, giving them contemporary socio-political and literary relevance.

## Digital Revolution of rekhta.org

### *Genealogy*

Rekhta was conceived in 2012 when Sanjiv Saraf, who owns Polyplex (one of the largest manufacturers of PET films in the world), revisited his childhood fondness for Urdu poetry. He looked online for the poetry of Ghalib and noticed that there was no credible source of it on the internet. He felt the need for a digital repository of Urdu poetry. Before rekhta.org, there were very few websites on the internet where Urdu poetry could be read. Even where it was available, it was replete with textual errors. In its beginning, rekhta.org was intended to be an authentic online source for classical Urdu poetry. Talking about rekhta.org, Saraf says,

> Later, when business got established and was growing well, I stepped back from business to focus on learning Urdu. In the process, I realised there wasn't enough content or resources available on the Internet and what was available was incomplete, non-credible and mostly in Urdu script. The younger generation, attracted to the eloquence, beauty and versatility of the language had no easy recourse.
>
> (*Jamal 2020*)

Saraf soon acquired command over Urdu language and its script by learning it from a professional Urdu teacher. With rekhta.org in his mind, he formed a team which included six members, each having a firm grasp over classical Urdu poetry. The first few tasks that this team had at hand included collecting print sources of classical Urdu poetry, composing digital texts with greatest care such that the resultant text was authoritative, and making it available online for lovers of Urdu poetry like Saraf himself. The website was launched in 2013 at the India Habitat Centre in New Delhi. Within a year of its launch, it was being seen in more than 140 countries and had had around 250,000 online visitors.

In its initial years, rekhta.org got patronage from lovers of Urdu all over the world. This initiative was also supported by the leading poets, fiction writers, and scholars. Following the unanticipated response that the website generated, Rekhta soon began to grow as a Foundation starting many other projects related to the preservation and popularization of Urdu literature. In the year 2015, it launched *Jashn-e-Rekhta* which is now the largest Urdu festival in the world. Two years later, in 2017, Rekhta released a new website—aamozish.com—to help Urdu lovers learn the language and its script. Again, in 2019, it released sufinama.org—a collection of Sufi-Bhakti literature and in 2020, hindwi.org—a website for building the largest online repository of Hindi literature and its promotion. Aside from publishing content in the digital form on its website, Rekhta also has a print publication wing called Rekhta Books which published its first book in 2016 and whose website rekhtabooks.com was started in 2020. A digital Rekhta Dictionary also came out in 2020.

Rekhta Foundation currently has more than 120 employees working on its several projects. It is a non-profit organization which survives on the donations it receives from its patrons. However, the donations are very small compared to what Saraf has to pay from his own pocket for running it. The organization has recently been seeking means to self-reliance so that it doesn't have to depend on Saraf.

## *The Digital Network of Rekhta—Portals and Functions*

### *rekhta.org*

rekhta.org is the largest online repository of Urdu literature. It has a collection of more than 40,000 *ghazals* and around 8,000 *nazms* in the form of searchable digital texts. This repository is constantly expanding with new content being added every day. It also has a huge repository of audio-visual content in the form of poetry recitations, literary discussions, qawwali performances, etc. Digital text on the website is available in three different scripts: Roman, Nagri, and Nastaliq which includes all of Ghalib's *ghazals*—published and unpublished, major works of the 18th-century poet Mir Taqi Mir, his contemporaries and successors like Mirza Rafi Sauda, Vali Dakni, Khwaja Mir Dard, and Momin Khan Momin among others. There are also available short stories of writers such as Sadat Hasan Manto, Krishna Chandar, Surendra Prakash, and Intizar Husain. While reading the content on the website in any of the three scripts, the reader can access meanings of unfamiliar Urdu words by clicking on the word.

By presenting Urdu content in Roman and Devanagri, Rekhta Foundation has been able to reach thousands of new readers who couldn't access it earlier because of the Nastaliq script in which Urdu is traditionally written. Rekhta has developed a standard key to replicate Urdu phonetics in Roman script which is used on its website as also in its various publications. However, it is the Devanagri script which is most popular with its non-conventional Urdu readers. Most of them access the website in Devanagri.

From beginning with classical Urdu poets, rekhta.org has come a long way and it now hosts a collection of poetry ranging from the earliest poets of the 16th century to postmodern poets and further including the contemporary ones. In addition to poetry, it also has collections of prose—stories as well as scholarly articles comprising of the works of Urdu scholars such as Shamsur Rahman Farooqi, Shamim Hanafi, Gopi Chand Narang, Shahid Ahmed Dehlvi, Mirza Fathulla Beg, Sir Syed Ahmed Khan, and Shibli Nomani. There are also biographies of several thousand poets and writers, literary jokes, and the satirical pieces of writers such as Mushtaq Ahmed Yousufi, Patras Bukhari, Ahmed Jamal Pasha, and Khwaja Hasan Nizami, which have been compiled together in easy to access digital collections. The website has dedicated sections for several genres and presents assorted collections of *ghazal*, *geet*, children's poetry, *doha*, *rubai*, *rekhti*, *masnavi*, *nazm*, *marsiya*, and *qita*. It also features a blog in which many young contemporary poets and writers regularly contribute with their articles. rekhta.org also has a lecture series on Urdu prosody and syllabi of various universities and other material useful for research scholars.

### • *eBooks*

One of the major projects that Rekhta has undertaken is that of digitization of printed books, all of which are available on rekhta.org for free access. It has

30 high-end machines installed in different libraries across India which add 2,500 books to Rekhta's eBook section every month. More than 120,000 books have been digitized so far and around 85,000 of them are currently available on the website. The digitization project was started in Rekhta's earliest phases when the Foundation's objective was focused on the preservation of Urdu literature, that is, before making the serendipitous discovery that has been interpreted by many commentators as "revival."

These eBooks have been categorized into sections of Fiction, Short-story, Poetry, Humour/Satire, History, Biographies and Auto-biographies, Children's books, Linguistics, Law, Geography, Prosody, Science, Philosophy, Medicine, Banned Books, etc. and there are also magazines, journals, and periodicals in the collection alongside. This collection includes all of the 46 volumes of the *Dastan-e-Amir Hamza* which remains the most popular *dastan* to this day. It also includes a collection of books published by the Munshi Naval Kishor's revolutionary Naval Kishor Press. There are several libraries listed as the partners in this project: Anjuman Taraqqi Urdu (Hind), Delhi; Darul Musannifeen Shibli Academy, Azamgarh; Delhi public Library, Delhi; Ghalib Academy, Delhi; Ghalib Institute, New Delhi; Government Urdu Library, Patna; Idaara-e-Adabiyat-e-Urdu, Hyderabad; Khuda Bakhsh Library, Patna; Madhya Pradesh Urdu Academy, Bhopal; Pratham Books, New Delhi; Rampur Raza Library, Rampur; Shahrah, Delhi; Sundarayya Vignana Kendram, Hyderabad; and Urdu Arts College, Hyderabad.

Digitization of the print material at Rekhta Foundation occurs in three stages as discussed here:

i) Tool: The first task is the segregation of "fresh" and "duplicate" copies of physical books collected from different libraries or individual contributors. "Duplicate" copies—as opposed to those "fresh"—are the ones of which a digital version is already available on Rekhta's website. Since there are 30 scanners in 18 libraries across 17 cities in the country, there is a high possibility of repeated digitization which will of course be wastage of resources. In order to avoid this, Rekhta's IT department has created a tool to enable this segregation at the initial stage. Before a copy is put on the scanner, some of its basic details—its metadata—like author, language, script, and publisher are entered into the tool to check for duplication. Having confirmed its "freshness," the date and time of the beginning of its digitization are entered and stored in the tool. Along with this, the name of the machine operator is also stored to keep a track. Each scanning machine has two cameras focused on the lateral pages of a book illuminated by an inbuilt lighting system which are both scanned in one go and are at once visible on an attached computer with a suitable software. Once they are scanned, the operator lifts the pressing glass and turns over the leaf to scan the next pages. All of Rekhta's machines are manually operated, although Atiz (a company based in Thailand from which Rekhta has purchased all of its machines each of which cost INR 1,100,000) also sells automatic machines which do not require an operator. One of the merits of the scanners that Rekhta uses is that they ensure that the physical copies, even those with feeble spines, are not destroyed in the process. The libraries where these machines have been installed provide with space, electricity, and furniture for the scanning to be done. On an average, the output of each scanner is approximately 1,500 digitized pages per day. All of these data are saved on a hard disk and once it is full, the size of its data is recorded at the respective location and then this disk is couriered to the head-office of Rekhta in Sector 1, Noida. When the hard disk arrives at the head-office, its data size is read on a computer and cross-checked with the sending location to confirm that no data has been damaged in the process of transportation. Having obtained this confirmation, the stored data are saved on the server and hard disk is cleared to free memory. From the server, the data are accessed by a team of editors for the next stage.

ii) Editing: An editor copies the data from its main location on the server to another location for editing which includes the use of Photoshop software to adjust its visual appearance—brightness, contrast, etc.—such that the resulting pages provide a smooth reading experience. This also includes removing the library stamps from its title page and inner pages which can distract the reader. Usually, the partnering libraries do not mind this erasure of their stamps. For every three scanners, there is one editor. Thus, an editor produces an output of around 4,500–5,000 edited pages per day. Currently, the editing team comprises of 12 members which brings the total output per day to approximately 55,000–60,000 digitized and edited pages. Once editing is finished, the digital copy is forwarded for the final stage.

iii) Tagging: Tagging is the process of filling in all the available details of the digital copy on the tool read from its cover, title, and index pages. The metadata filled in the first stage by the operator contains only essential details to prevent duplication. Detailed entries are filled in at this final stage. The tool that tagger uses displays first 10–15 pages of the book and has spaces for entries like: category (poet, writer, college/school, publisher), editor (in case of anthologies, journals or periodicals), translator (wherever applicable), language (mostly Urdu, but sometimes also Hindi and English), book type (poetry, fiction, novel, history, etc.), title, title in transliteration (as it is displayed in all three scripts—Nastaliq, Devanagri and Roman—depending on user's settings), sub-title, edition, price, discount, date/year of publishing, and index page number. The entries like publisher, author, poet, writer, institutions, colleges, printing presses are termed in the tool as "entities," which are eventually visible to the user of the website. Since most of these eBooks are in Urdu, the tagger is required to know the Urdu language as well as its script. Once all of these details are entered and saved on the tool, a publish command within the tool is generated by the tagger, which takes effect at midnight when the server restarts and the digitized copy begins to show in the eBook section and made available to the search engine of the website. There are six taggers in Rekhta at present.

eBooks is just one section on rekhta.org which provides its users with other varieties of digital content too. On the top of its homepage are displayed the other sections: Poets, Sher, Dictionary, and More which open up sections of Prose, Blog, and Qaafiya among others. A user who comes looking for a particular *ghazal*, *sher*, or story can enter related keywords in its search engine and find from the results what he/she is looking for. These data are separate from eBooks, available on the website after a process called composition. For instance, majority of Mirza Ghalib's works can be read on the website itself, without having to go to the eBook section; that too, in any of the three scripts mentioned earlier. The transliteration of *ghazals*, stories, *shers*, *qitas*, *marsiyas*, *masnavis*, jokes, and *qissas* involving popular literary personalities, and brief biographical sketches called *khaake*, etc. is done by the tool itself once the content is entered in any of the three scripts in the composition process. The content need not be typed separately in all these scripts. However, it is still prone to errors and requires expertise of a composer or editor (this editor belongs to the Editorial Department of Rekhta Foundation and is separate from the editors engaged in the second stage of digitization) to select correct transliteration of a word and at times to manually type it.

- *sufinama.org*

Sufinama is another website run by Rekhta Foundation. It has a collection of literature on mysticism, composed and propagated by Sufi and Bhakti saints, or written on them. It also has a vast variety of content which captures the cultural practices celebrating Sufi-Bhakti spirituality across the country. It brings together the works of mystic saints of India and Iranian Sufism to present a historical picture of what has been varyingly understood as the inclusive nature of Indian culture and society. It is a compilation of the works of poets such as Amir Khusro, Rumi, Hafiz, Saadi, Bulle Shah, Baba Farid, Mirabai, and Kabir. It has "Sant Vani" and "Sufi Kalam" collected alongside. In all, there is a collection of the works of around 1,200 saints available, again in three scripts, and features 634 *dohas*, 909 *pads*, and 625 *kalaams*. There are also around 3,200 eBooks and 793 videos on the website.

- *aamozish.com*

As mentioned earlier, *aamozish* was launched for helping the readers of Rekhta learn Urdu script and language in the year 2017 after numerous requests from rekhta.org's visitors to start a course on Urdu script. On its homepage, aamozish.com currently boasts of a "family of 116,000 Urdu learners." Almost all of the digitized books on rekhta.org, and also the less popular stories, poetry, articles, etc. on the website, are still available only in Nastaliq. *Rasm-ul-Khat*—an Urdu learning course featuring on aamozish—aims to enable Rekhta's users to access the Urdu texts. Combined with audio technology, the course takes only seven hours in all to learn the Urdu script. In 2019, Rekhta also published a *Rekhta Urdu Learning Guide* transforming this into print content. It was quickly followed by a Devanagri version of the book. Other than this, Rekhta also organized physical classrooms for a certificate course in Urdu language and script and more than 1,000 students—from kids to elderly—have benefitted from these classes. Aamozish has another course called *Alfaaz* which is a collection of 100 most common words or phrases in *ghazal* poetry, demystifying for the users their metaphors and enabling the "new" Urdu readers to make sense of *ghazal* poetry. Along with it, there are examples of their usages in *shers*, the translations of these *shers* and their interpretations in English and colloquial Urdu-Hindi (Hindustani). *Alfaaz* attracted hundreds of subscribers within hours of its launch.

## • *hindwi.org*

Hindwi.org is among the latest projects of Rekhta Foundation and aims to replicate the success of its exalted precedent rekhta.org. It has the same objectives of preserving and promoting Hindi literature, just as rekhta.org does it for Urdu. Launched in 2020, this website now has a collection of the works of over 750 poets—a total of more than 10,000 verses including 8,659 *kavita*s, 1,098 *pada*s, 1,604 *doha*s, and 389 folksongs. More content is being constantly added. It also has collections of prose literature of Hindi. Once again, the emphasis is on authenticity and ease of access.

There emerged a controversy when Rekhta Foundation released the poster of its flagship event *Jashn-e-Rekhta* in 2019, subtitled "celebrating Hindustani language" while earlier it used to be "celebrating Urdu." Many from within the Urdu-speaking community opposed this move and speculated political pressure, even questioning Rekhta's role and alleging a betrayal. The controversy soon died down when the subtitle was rephrased to: "a festival of Urdu language celebrating Hindustani culture" which indicates the openness of contemporary Urdu literary culture which seeks to detach itself from religious or community underpinnings and push for the ancient inclusive tradition of India. The echo of identities like Hindustani culture or Hindustani language in the popular discourse is crucial from a scholarly point of view, as it signifies a number of different possibilities:

i) unification of Urdu and Hindi into a more colloquial contemporary language
ii) diminished roles of both Urdu and Hindi as literary languages
iii) emphasis on the inclusive tradition of India in contemporary literary sensibilities

From this perspective, hindwi.org is a highly significant initiative, as together with rekhta.org and sufinama.org, it presents a compendium of literature that can ultimately be traced back to a unified history. While rekhta.org brings non-Urdu speakers to Urdu literature, it can be expected that hindwi.org will bring Urdu speakers to Hindi literature. In fact, most of the subscribers of hindwi.org are indeed the existing rekhta.org users.

## *Jashn-e-Rekhta*

*Jashn-e-Rekhta* is a three-day literary festival that Rekhta organizes every year in New Delhi. It was first held in 2015, and this flagship event of Rekhta Foundation has been gaining popularity ever since, with recorded footfall of over a million in its latest editions. It features four different stages catering to varying literary interests of different audiences. Spread over three days, it hosts events like musical performances—*qawwali*, folk, Sufi-Bhakti songs, literary discussions among leading scholars, poets, and writers, *daastaangoi*, *soz*, renditions of Indian epics like Ramayana and Mahabharata, lectures, interactions with film personalities who talk about the tradition of Urdu in Bollywood and its most popular and annual feature: the Grand Mushaira. Judging from the conscious array of events that have been organized under the banner of *Jashn-e-Rekhta* so far, the idea seems to be to showcase every avenue from where one can gather the evidences of an alive and vivid tradition.

Over the years, it was thought that *Mushaira* was losing its literary value with the interest of the poets shifting from poetry to performance. This made several poets distance themselves from *mushaira* stages which were earlier considered to be the launch-pads of their new *ghazals*. Because some major poets like Mohd. Alvi and Zubair Rizvi chose not to go to *mushairas*, this tradition was feared among the intellectuals to be dying. It was against this backdrop that Rekhta introduced its "Grand Mushaira" in which the emphasis was brought back to poetry from performance. It has its basis in the notion that all performance is contained within the poem (*ghazal*) and is not needed to be provided from outside the text. It is to be noted that Grand Mushaira has quickly escalated to the position of one of the most prestigious *mushairas* in India which are regularly held under different banners such as Jashn-e-Bahaar Mushaira and Shankar-Shaad Mushaira.

Other than the "Grand Mushaira," *Jashn-e-Rekhta* also hosts a "Young Poets Mushaira" which features young Urdu poets from across the country. Just as the "Grand Mushaira," "Young Poets Mushaira" also attracts a huge audience and many of the young poets who have featured in it have already established a strong fanbase. That the sixth (latest) edition of *Jashn-e-Rekhta* also held a series of "Poetry Masterclasses" shows that there is indeed some curiosity about it. Rekhta also organizes smaller gatherings; or smaller *mushairas* with limited audience, called "*Shaam-e-Sher*." It is a travelling *mushaira* which has also been organized in cities like Chandigarh and Hyderabad other than Delhi.

*Jashn-e-Rekhta* also holds within its premises a book fair. The fair includes a Rekhta stall selling Rekhta books and merchandise, a food bazaar selling ethnic dishes, calligraphy workshops where many visitors ask the calligraphers to write their names in Urdu script, and a handicraft bazaar alongside. *Jashn-e-Rekhta* has its own website jashnerekhta.org and a separate team at Rekhta Foundation looks after its affairs. During the pandemic, Rekhta hosted an online festival which was called "Rekhta Live."

## Qaafiya Dictionary

*Qaafiya* is one of the fundamental elements of *ghazal* poetry along with *vazn* (metre). In a *ghazal*, a word (or a group of words) (*radiif* or refrain) is generally repeated at the end of the second line called *misra-e-saanii* (or just *saanii*) in each couplet of a *ghazal*. In the first couplet however, called *matla*, it occurs at the end of the first line as well which is called *misra-e-oolaa*, or simply *oola*. *Qaafiya* occurs just before *radiif* and is governed by the specific pattern of sounds in a particular *ghazal*. These intricacies are further complicated in long words where one might have to check not just the penultimate sound, but also the last but third, or last but fourth and so on in order to choose the correct rhyming words. Non-conventional readers of Urdu poetry who are unfamiliar with them and who have been seeking to learn Urdu poetry in the recent years face difficulties, because there is no easy way for it. The *ustad-shagird* institution is fast diasappearing and the texts from which it could be learnt are not accessible to the new readers because of the Nastaliq script and Arabic nomenclature. Taking a step in this direction, Rekhta has launched a *qaafiya* dictionary which helps young poets overcome one of these challenges while learning to write *ghazals*. This online dictionary asks the users if they have already written the *matla* or not, and based on their answer, it enlists all of the *qaafiyas* that they can use while writing a *ghazal*, along with examples of the existing usages of those *qaafiyas* by the master poets. There is also given the *vazn* of the *qaafiya* in the Qaafiya Dictionary.

## Rekhta Dictionary

rekhtadictionary.com came out in 2020. It is an online dictionary which provides meanings of words in Urdu, Hindi, and English and also the pronunciation of the word in an audio file. The word being sought can be entered in the search box in any of the three scripts: Nagri, Nastaliq, or Roman. In addition to the meanings, there are also given examples of their usages in *ghazal* poetry. This dictionary also features segments such as "word of the day," "proverb of the day," and "trending words." It also provides an array of homophones and singular and plural forms of different words. In addition to this, there is another dictionary embedded in rekhta.org which provides trilingual meanings, and the meanings in the Platts dictionary, and also links to physical (scanned) dictionaries such as *Farhang-e-Asifiya, Noor-ul-Lughat, Farhang-e-Amira*, and *Lughaat-e-Kishori*.

## Rekhta Books

Starting with some sporadic publications initially, Rekhta's publication wing has now grown into a full-fledged rekhtabooks.com which was launched in 2020. It publishes a wide range of books from classical to contemporary Urdu and Hindi poetry and prose. One of its notable publications is *Ghazal Usne Chheri* in six volumes. It is a collection of *ghazals* that begins with the *ghazal* of Amir Khusro in medieval period and ends with that of Faza Ibn-e-Faizi Faizul Hasan who breathed his last in the year 2009. This collection, proudly declaring to have captured the essence of an 800-year-old poetry tradition, has been put together by Farhat Ehsas, Rekhta's Editor-in-Chief. It is interesting to note that this collection has been dedicated "to the creative soul of the Hindustani culture which gave birth to Urdu language and poetry" (Translated). *Ghazal Usne Chheri* coheres with the points about the historiographical perspective that aims at secularizing and democratizing Urdu language and literature and undoing partition politics in the process of freeing it from its reduction to one community.

Rekhta Books has also published several modern and contemporary poets such as Farhat Ehsas himself, Zafar Iqbal, Shariq Kaifi, Zulfiqar Adil, Mohd. Alvi, Noman Shauq, Anwar Shaoor, Jamal Ehsani, Irfan Siddiqi, Sarvat Hussain, and Bharat Bhushan Pant and young poets such as Ameer Imam, Salim Saleem, Kashif Hussain Ghayar, Mahendra Kumar Sani, Manish Shukla, and Tarkash Pradeep and an anthology called *Qaafila-e-Nau- Bahaar* comprising of the works of 11 young poets. While most of these books are in Devanagri script, some have their Nastaliq versions as well. In the Devanagri script, the meanings of the words which can be unfamiliar to non-Urdu speakers are given right below the *sher* in which they occur to help the reader understand them. Rekhta has also published some select stories of Munshi Premchand and essays of humourist Patras Bukhari. Recently, it released a collection of select *ghazals* of major Urdu poet of the late-19th-century poet Dagh Dehelvi. Rekhtabooks.com has recently collaborated with Raj Kamal Prakashan.

## Literature and Technology

Rekhta, Hindwi, Sufinama, Jashn-e-Rekhta, and Rekhta Books—all have their dedicated pages on social media platforms such as Facebook, Instagram, and Twitter. Some of these websites are also available in the forms of mobile applications. Adapting to the contemporary trend, Rekhta has also started recently audio podcasts providing its audience with audio versions of stories, poetry, and essays. Rekhta's office in Sector 1, Noida, also houses a Rekhta Studio which regularly releases videos commemorating the birth or death anniversaries of major literary figures, and also the videos of poetry readings and interviews with contemporary poets, writers, and scholars. Recently, Rekhta started an interview series called "*Guftugu*" which is hosted by Syed Mohd Irfan who used to host a program on Rajya Sabha TV by the same name. In the latest version of *Jashn-e-Rekhta*, Rekhta also distributed a *Jashn-e-Rekhta* magazine each of whose printed pages could be scanned using mobile camera and read as a digital copy. In its videos, Rekhta is seeking to employ the technology of virtual reality giving its audience a chance to re-live the 3D experience of the festival.

Rekhta's Facebook page is followed by around 1.5 million people, which is largest among all of its official pages on social media. *Jashn-e-Rekhta* and Sufinama pages also have considerable followings and Hindwi is beginning to get momentum. On these social media pages, *shers*, poems, pieces of prose, videos of performances or recitations, clips from Guftugu, words with their meanings, idioms and proverbs with their usages, grammatical rules, common errors in the use of words or their pronunciation, and their corrections are regularly shared under different kinds of social media campaigns. The followers are often asked to compose their own poems and comment on these posts.

## The Worldwide Reach and Readership

rekhta.org has readers in more than 150 countries of the world. The website is mostly accessed for reading Urdu poetry, but there has also been seen a rise in prose readership lately. Rekhta's social media pages which earlier used to share only *shers* can now be seen sharing prose pieces also. On the website, there is now a separate section "Prose" which was missing earlier. In 2020, the website had a total of 16 million visitors of which 10% traffic was directed at the eBook section. Within India, most users of Rekhta belong to metro and tier-2 cities. It has been expressed time and again and with great enthusiasm that most of the readers of rekhta.org and visitors to the Jashn-e-Rekhta festival are young people who are tech-savvy. When Rekhta celebrated its first anniversary in 2014, its founder gave an estimate of around 10,000 young boys and girls across the country writing Urdu *ghazals*. It was one of the major factors in making the website's content available in Nagri and Roman, since most of them were unfamiliar with the Perso-Arabic script.

In spite of the overwhelming popularity that Rekhta has garnered in a decade, there are critics who actively voice their concerns over the future of Urdu which, according to them, remains mired in the whirl of extinction and they do seem to have a point. The concern is chiefly because of the decreasing employment opportunities and lack of formal education in Urdu and its reduced legal role, such as after the Delhi High Court order of 2019 which demanded minimal use of Urdu and Persian words in FIRs. According to these critics, Rekhta's popularity must not be confused with Urdu's revival. It is the aesthetic ambience of Jashn-e-Rekhta—a show of lost artefacts, not the signs of animation—which attracts the youth. Also, popularizing Urdu as the language of love, romance, or *tehzeeb* cannot serve the purpose until it is recognized as a language capable of expressing both the literary and the mundane.

## The Halfway Digital: Gaps and Drawbacks

Even with the rigorous commitment that Rekhta has shown in a decade, its digitization project is far from complete; and that which is said to be accomplished may be only partial. Printed books have indeed been scanned, but they are not available in transcript forms unlike in the case of the Bichitra Project. Content available on the website can be divided into three categories: scanned, curated, and created. Scanned content constitutes the scanned manuscripts and print materials which are available in the eBook section. Curated content is that material which appears in a digitally constructed form. While some of it is drawn from the scanned copies, other is collected from diverse sources, sometimes even recorded from memory and tagged with an anonymous category. Curation includes a range of activities: transliteration of Nastaliq text into Nagri and Roman while also the transcription of scanned texts in Nastaliq; conversion of texts into audio forms such as *ghazal* and *nazm* recitations; attaching images with *shers* and circulating them on social media; indexing *shers* and *nazms* as per themes, subjects, poets in categories called "tags"; taking data from Rekhta's own repository and presenting it in different ways to suit forms and contexts; or videos which through animation or human agent convey Urdu writings to those who can't read the texts because of lack of availability or interest. Created content is the original content like blogs, stories (for audio podcast), and videos. Scanned content which is mostly in the Nastaliq script is not accessible to the search engine. OCR tools can't read through these scanned copies which poses a major difficulty in retrieving that material from Urdu books which could relate to the contemporary trends in reading and writing practices. Such an absence is a major roadblock in gaining traction to the website. It also restricts scholars and research activities.

Large texts like novels are available only in the form of scanned content. Making large texts available in non-Urdu scripts requires overcoming several challenges, such as:

i) Devanagri is the only option, Roman is not considered readable
ii) Composing large texts in digitally available versions requires separate infrastructural investment
iii) rekhta.org's audience majorly consumes poetry, that too, *ghazal* poetry and in non-Urdu script

There are no filters in the search box. In order to search (say) a particular *sher* of Ghalib, one would have to type in whatever portion of the *sher* one remembers or knows about and then scroll through results looking for Ghalib's *shers* in them, until spotting the one being searched. Also, to search a particular text, *sher*, *ghazal*, word, poet, etc., one needs to key in only those alternative spellings which are pre-saved in the metadata and make it searchable. Sometimes the word can be spelt in so many wrong ways which the taggers or editors can't pre-think. This limits the visibility of that content. Digitization for preservation requires financial investment for which Rekhta needs to be able to generate revenue. Sources of revenue are minorly Rekhta books, paid courses like *Rasm-ul-Khat* and *Alfaaz*, and majorly sponsorships, advertisements, and donations.

## Digital Transformation of Urdu Literary Culture and Public Sphere

### *Globalizing Urdu Literary Sphere*

With digitization, Urdu literature is opened for free and easy public access and thus opens a gateway for those who can't find literary books in their vicinities, because those books simply don't sell there, nor are there any libraries nearby. Such readers who contended themselves with other stuff such as periodicals and newspapers get the choice of going beyond the limited number of Urdu texts which circulate in those regions in printed form. Presenting Urdu literature in digital transliterated forms attracts and sustains those who recognize spoken Urdu but are unfamiliar with the Nastaliq script. Audios and videos further help in promoting and popularizing Urdu literature. Urdu literary sphere is thus accommodating new consumers of Urdu literature who constitute popular demand and necessitate the production of content which keeps the website visible. To make this possible, *shers* are interpreted in multiple ways and related to trending universal themes. Poetry, with the scope of multiple meanings, proves especially useful for this purpose and takes Urdu literature to newer audiences who are then introduced to the other strands of Urdu literary culture. Although the majority of viewership is limited to India, rekhta.org is also viewed in other countries, including Australia, Germany, Netherlands, Pakistan, Qatar, USA, and UK. In India, rekhta.org has its consumers mostly in urban spaces of Delhi, Punjab, Bihar, Uttar Pradesh, Madhya Pradesh, Maharashtra, Haryana, Rajasthan, Karnataka, and Jammu-Kashmir (survey responses).

## De-Communalizing Urdu and Redefining Identity

In order to free Urdu from the margins and re-situate it in open space, the Urdu-Muslim myth needs to be busted. Rekhta.org seems to be offering an antithesis to the communal politics that brands Urdu as Islamic. Of the 451 people who participated in the survey, 35% stated their religion as Islam while only 26.6% people call their mother tongue "Urdu" (Figures 8.1 and 8.2). The audiences have their own stories of connecting with Urdu. Rekhta Project seems to be structured around a cosmopolitan ethos. Related projects of Sufinama, Hindwi, *Ghazal Usne Chheri*, Publishing Urdu in Nagri, and offering educational courses are all indicators of pushing for

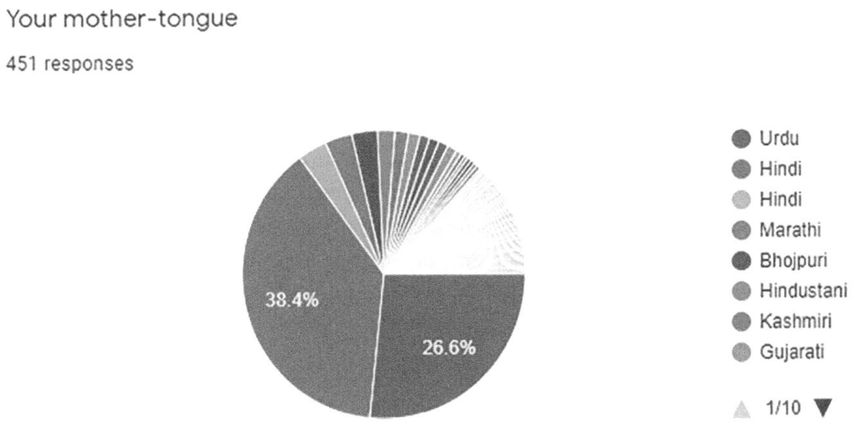


**FIGURE 8.1** Mother tongue of the participants (others include Awadhi, Bangla, Bhojpuri, Dogri, Gujarati, Haryanvi, Hindi, Kashmiri, Marathi, Maithili, Marwadi, Mewati, Nepali, Punjabi, Rajasthani, Sindhi, and Tamil)

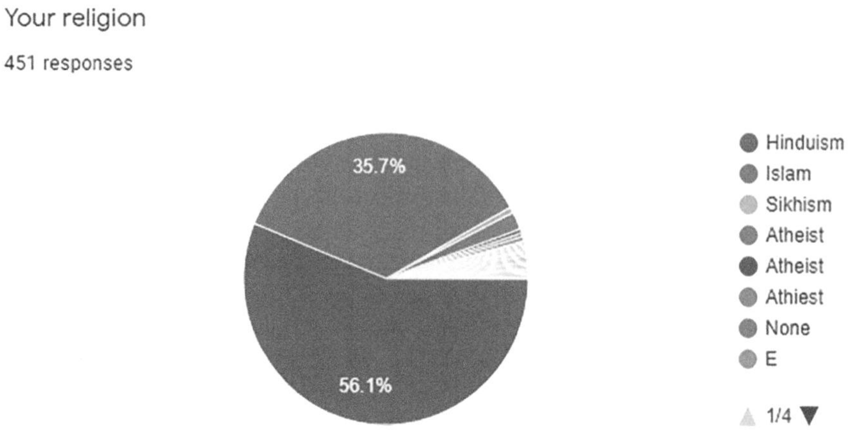


**FIGURE 8.2** Religion of the participants

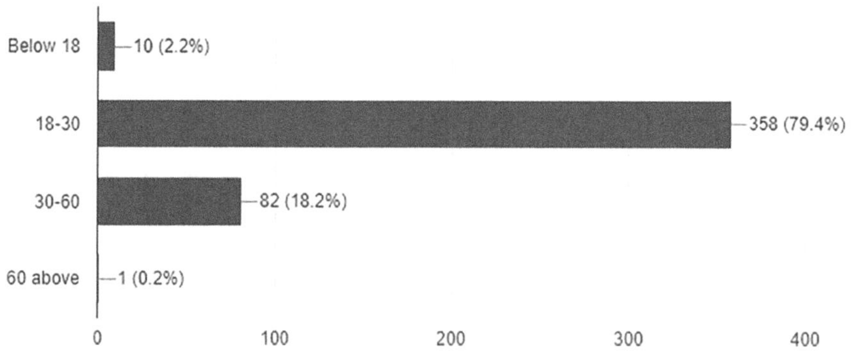


**FIGURE 8.3** Age of the participants

the de-marginalization of Urdu literary culture. In the courses like *Rasm-ul-khat* and *Alfaaz*, people from different communities join to learn Urdu script and the diction of *ghazals*. At *Jashn-e-Rekhta*, the largest audience is that of the youth. Most of the audience of rekhta.org also falls within an age group of 18–39. Nearly 79.4% participants in the survey marked their age as between 18 and 30 (Figure 8.3). These are indications of a renewed interest in the literary culture of Urdu which seems to be open to re-assimilating all that was purged of it in a fit of linguistic chauvinism and a wave of communal politics. The aim is to exemplify an inclusive Urdu which has both potential of intellectual thought and commonness of day-to-day language.

## *Reinvigorating Script*

It appears from the survey results that one person uses more than one script to read or write Urdu, but the use of Nastaliq is superseded by the use of Nagri. Almost all of Rekhta's print publications of poetry and prose are in Nagri script. Yet, it is contrasted by a visible interest in learning Urdu script and recent inclusion of Urdu script in "Image shayari" that is circulated by Rekhta as part of its daily social media campaign. Nagri and Roman help in taking Urdu literature to non-Nastaliq readers, but the readership that is gained from promotion has no option but to learn the script to further their reading interests realizing that a lot of content is still in Nastaliq. This need for learning the script erodes the political cast around it, dissociating it from identity of faith, and asserting its functional importance. In such a context, Nagri, Nastaliq, and Roman play complementary roles in foregrounding Urdu literature. On the other hand, they also compete for closer intimacy with the spoken language when it comes to removing the need of learning a new script. While some sounds in Urdu cannot be conveniently differentiated in Nagri and Roman, words of English which frequently occur in prose writings are often unreadable in diacritic-less Urdu script in which short-vowel sounds are usually not represented. In books, these words or terms are often written in their English-Roman forms. Urdu seems to be in a dynamic orthographic mode where script is seen as either functional, that is, for reaching a particular audience or accessing a particular work, or simply a matter of choice.

## *De-Escalating Perso-Arabic Influence and Retrieving Hindwi*

In the curated and created content, a tendency is observed towards simple language by which is meant that it avoids Perso-Arabic words and incorporates those words from Hindi which don't skew its phonetic continuum. In videos and social media posts, the English meanings of these words are provided alongside; while in print publications, not only are Hindi meanings placed just below the *sher* in which they occur, but also Hindi words are frequently used in the main text of introductions. The diminishing use of Perso-Arabic words and techniques like *izaafat* for creating compound words is indicative of a transformation in the contemporary vocabulary of Urdu which seems to be veering away from the Persian approximation of late 18th century and inching closer to a version which is more like Hindwi than Rekhta. The size of audiences in the *mushairas* had already grown significantly in the 20th century. The reach of digital technology is increasing it further forcing the poets to use only those words which are commonly understood. The Persian legacy is therefore pushed into the background, and creative energies are harnessed in quest of new themes and metaphors which can be conveyed in the language of common parlance or in rendering the Persian-ness into non-Persian constructs. The increased use of Nagri in place of Nastaliq is another symptom of diminishing Perso-Arabic influence.

## *Reclaiming the Marginalized Genres Such as Rekhti and Safarnamas*

Digitization at Rekhta has carved out a space for marginalized genres in two ways. First, in the preservation project, there is no hierarchy of genres. Whatever has had anything to do with Urdu literary culture, at the periphery or its core, is to be converted into digital form. Second, what is digitized for the purpose of preservation also provides content for promotion in showcasing the holistic culture of Urdu. Therefore, those genres which submerged under the popularity of *ghazal* get reflectivity. There is also a third way that reinforces this. In the annual festival of *Jashn-e-Rekhta*, there are organized discussions and talks on these genres which are then circulated in the form of videos on social media. It helps in contextualizing these genres for the new reader of the digital era. They also serve to provide the readers with alternate texts to get over the monotony of the popular genres. Similarly, the viewers are introduced to other genres such as *marsiya*, *mukhammas*, *masnavi*; *qissas*, and *latifas*, which are now considered obsolete. Currently, rekhta.org has Rekhti poetry of the 18th- and 19th-century poets Insha Allah Khan Insha, Meer Yaar Ali Jaan, Rangin Saadat Yaar Khan, etc. It also has 34 *marsiyas*, 8 *qasiidas*, 15 *manqabats* of Mir and 3 *masnavis*, 1 *mukhammas*, 1 *salaam*, 3 *sehras*, 34 *rubaaiis*, and 28 *qitaas* of Ghalib. However, even in the case of Mir and Ghalib, most of this content is only in the Urdu script which shows that most of these genres are still not accessed by a common reader.

## *Transforming Readership*

Current readership of Rekhta comprises those earlier readers who participated in the Urdu literary sphere of pre-Rekhta times and who have now either shifted from printed texts to digital ones or use both. There are also those readers who were reading Urdu texts on smartphones or computers before Rekhta. Around 29% of participants had read an Urdu book in print or digital form before Rekhta was founded while nearly 28% have never read any Urdu book at all (Figure 8.4). It is quite possible that at least some of them equated "Urdu books" with those written in Nastaliq. Yet, 44.3% were those who read an "Urdu book in print or digital form" after Rekhta was founded with majority—32.2%—of those who read it after 2015, that is, the year when the first *Jashn-e-Rekhta* happened. *Jashn-e-Rekhta* and

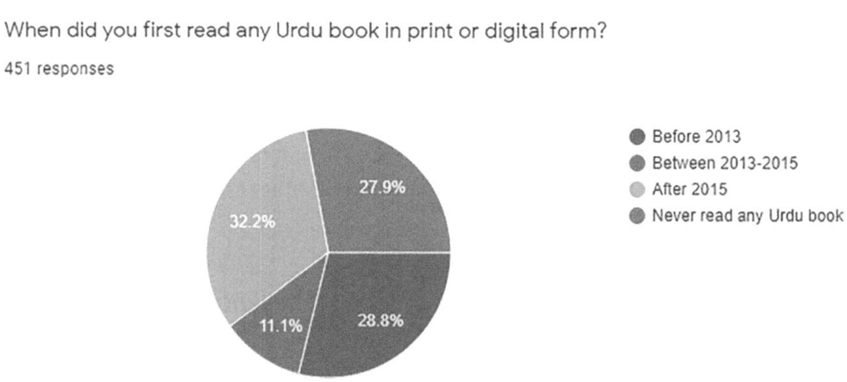


**FIGURE 8.4** When did you read first Urdu book?

other events like *Shaam-e-Sher, Rang-e-Rekhta* that Rekhta frequently organizes provide rekhta.org visibility in popular media while digitization project also draws scholarly attention. Rekhta has added many of those readers to the Urdu literary sphere who were and are still unfamiliar with its script, literary traditions, metaphors, and allusions. In spite of these obstructions, there are only about 2.9% of them who "do not use rekhta.org" (Figure 8.5). Still, 70.3% of the participants read less than one Urdu book every month (Figure 8.6) although 57.9% of them are regular readers who read at least one book in a month's time (Figure 8.7). This shows that most of the new readership of Urdu engages with the digital transcript rather than books. eBook section, as mentioned earlier, draws only 10% of the total traffic that website gets and its printed books also have limited readerships. Among the participants, only 12.9% (Figure 8.8) participants read/see the eBook section. However, 93.3% participants do read/see Ghazal/Sher on rekhta.org (Figure 8.8). Considering these data, it becomes clear that majority of this literary interaction at Rekhta happens in non-Nastaliq form (in digital or print production of texts). It suggests that there has been an expansion in Urdu's readership since 2013, that is, after rekhta.org was launched, and this readership is different from the traditional

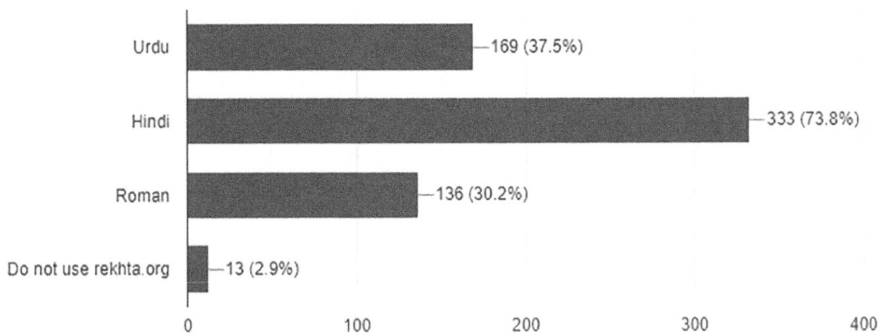


**FIGURE 8.5** In which script do you use rekhta.org?

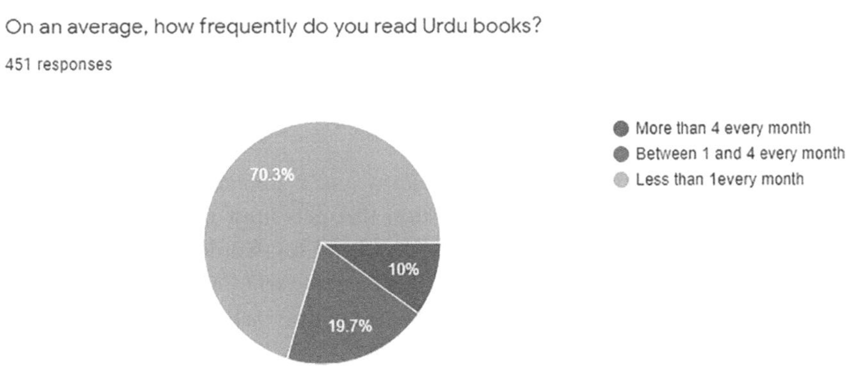


**FIGURE 8.6** How many Urdu books do you read every month?

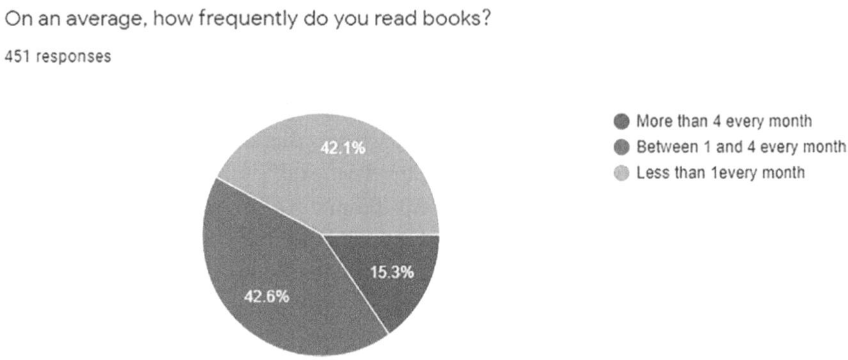


**FIGURE 8.7** How many books do you read every month?

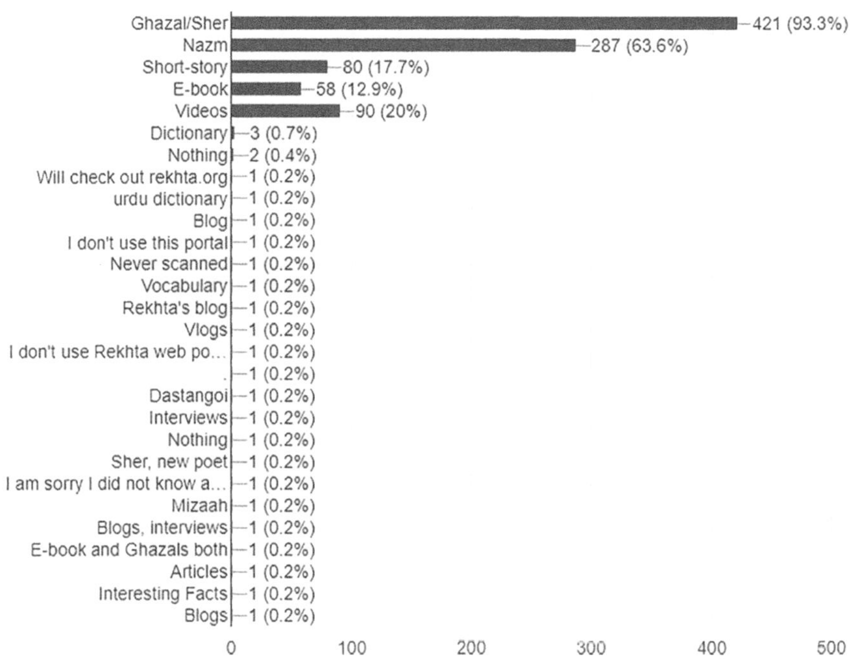


**FIGURE 8.8** What do you mostly read or see on Rekhta?

readership of print. It meets Urdu halfway: in a non-strictly Nastaliq, not-too-dense-Perso-Arabic mode. The section that gets most number of views on the website is "Tags" where content is arranged and key-worded in an explicit sort of way: "Famous shayari," "Sad shayari," "Visaal shayari," "Motivational shayari," "Filmi shayari," etc. There are also collections such as "Top 20 Visaal Shayari." In these sections, not only is the content most viewed or read but also the one that is most digitized. It is consistently available in all three scripts with meanings, links to the root *ghazals*, a critique box, and social media link attached. This content is repackaging of what is already available on the website in other sections, as part of a different whole, collected from scanned pages or other places. Yet, it plays a significant role in catering to contemporary literary needs. They also dictate the norms of what is considered marketable Urdu literature in the content industry. Poets respond by composing in a simple language and style-creating contemporary metaphors. The use of *izaafat* in their *shers* diminishes. In print, those poets are published who are easy to understand. In this, there is a departure from the tradition of *sabk-i-hindi* poetics which leans towards complexity.

## Conclusion

The name Rekhta recalls the glorious past of a literary tradition which was at its peak just before its fall. It has been known by many different names and has changed several forms. In its history of "ruptures," it has both adapted to contemporary trends and retained a continuity of aesthetics. It has had a fluid character which cuts across geographical spaces, and which also reflects in its foundational poetics of movement (theory of *ravani*) (Farooqi 2003a, p. 826). Over the course of last 10 years, the general perception about it seems to be changing. The speculations about its extinction seem to be replaced with wonder and conviction that it is not the state of affairs anymore. However, there are still major concerns which need to be addressed. There are practical issues of capital required for materializing this transformation. The digital medium is still not consistent with Indian languages and scripts which therefore must be indigenized to be able to actually harness its benefits. Nevertheless, digitization at rekhta.org has offered many insights into the interaction of Urdu with the digital medium. It has caused noticeable changes in the Urdu literary/public sphere which include expansion in readership, transformation of literary preferences, re-interpretation of past, variations in phonetic and orthographic systems, and also the mode of literary consumption. Out of the two major forms, poetry has reached much higher stage of digitization on rekhta.org than Prose. Although it is limited majorly by the constraint of OCR and capital, Rekhta has taken steps in the direction of digitizing prose as well. Excerpts have begun to be shared on social media. The *Rekhta Rauzan* magazine was recently launched. Prose collections have also been published in paperback forms. Rekhta Blogs has also become more active encouraging prose writing. One of the major tasks it has before it right now is to cater to the huge demand of learning Urdu language and prosody among the youth.

## References

Bari, S.A. (2004) 'Munshi Naval Kishor Ka Ahd Apne Adabi, Tahzibi Aur Muashrati Tanazur Mein' in *Naval Kishor Aur Unka Ahd*, New Delhi: Maktaba Jamia Limited, pp. 56–67. *Rekhta e-book collection* [online]. Available at: www.rekhta.org/ebooks/munshi-naval-kishor-aur-unka-ahd-ebooks# (Accessed: 3 November 2021)

Farooqi, S.R. (2003a) 'A Long History of Urdu Literary Culture, Part 1- Naming and Placing a Literary Culture' in Pollock, S. (ed.) *Literary Cultures in History-Reconstructions from South Asia*, Berkeley, CA: University of California Press, pp. 805–863.

Farooqi, S.R. (2003b) 'A Stranger in the City: The Poetics of Sabk-i-Hindi', *A Desertful of Roses: The Urdu Ghazals of Mirza Asadullah Khan "GHALIB"* [online]. Available at: www.columbia.edu/itc/mealac/pritchett/00fwp/srf/sabkihindi/srf_sabk_i_hindi.pdf (Accessed: 10 November 2021)

Jadavpur University, *the Bichitra Project* [online]. Available at: http://bichitra.jdvu.ac.in/about_bichitra_project.php (Accessed: 10 November 2021)

Jamal, A. (2020) 'Rekhta: From Amir Khusro to Mirza Ghalib, Sanjiv Saraf's Initiative is saving India's Urdu heritage, one book at a time', *Hindustan Times*, 26 August [online]. Available at: www.hindustantimes.com/art-and-culture/rekhta-from-amir-khusrau-to-mirza-ghalib-sanjiv-saraf-s-initiative-is-saving-india-s-urdu-heritage-one-book-at-a-time/story-5pYJ3iX1NgcveAkw5wTCmI.html (Accessed: 10 November 2021)

Murthy, N. (2020) 'Hyderabad's British Council Library dons an e-avatar', *The Hindu*, 22 June [online]. Available at: www.thehindu.com/society/hyderabads-british-council-library-dons-an-e-avatar-and-plans-to-open-a-mobile-app-version-of-the-digital-library-by-june-end/article31876117.ece (Accessed: 10 November 2021)

Naim, C.M. (2004) 'Poet Audience Interaction at Urdu Mushai'rahs' in *Urdu Texts and Contexts*, Delhi: Permanent Black, pp. 108–119.

Pai, S. (2002) 'Politics of Language: Decline of Urdu in Uttar Pradesh', *Economic and Political Weekly*, 37(27), pp. 2705–2708. [online] Available at: www.jstor.org/stable/4412322?read-now=1&refreqid=excelsior%3Ac7f0f2dbf064710e5d3b118fbc76047c&seq=2#page_scan_tab_contents (Accessed: 3 November 2021)

Pollock, S. (2003) 'Introduction' in Pollock, S. (ed.) *Literary Cultures in History-Reconstructions from South Asia*, Berkeley, CA: University of California Press, pp. 1–36.

Qutab, S., Saqib, F., and Shafi Ullah, F. (2017) 'Antiquity into Digital: A Case Study of Urdu Literary Magazine 'Nuqoosh' Research Centre (NRC) and Digitization Project', *Trends in Information Management*, 11(1) [online]. Available at: www.researchgate.net/publication/319088118_Antiquity_into_Digital_A_case_study_of_Urdu_literary_magazine_'Nuqoosh'_Research_Center_NRC_and_Digitization_Project (Accessed: 10 November 2021)

Rai, A. (2000) *Hindi Nationalism: Tracts for the Times*. Delhi: Orient Blackswan Private Limited.

Russell, R. (1999) 'Urdu in India since Independence', *Economic and Political Weekly*, 34(1/2), pp. 44–48 [online]. Available at: www.jstor.org/stable/4407548?Search=yes&resultItemClick=true&searchText=Ralph%20Russell%20Urdu%20in%20India&searchUri=%2Faction%2FdoBasicSearch%3FQuery%3DRalph%2BRussell%2BUrdu%2Bin%2BIndia%26so%3Drel&ab_segments=0%2Fbasic_search_gsv2%2Fcontrol&refreqid=fastly-default%3Ae0b4e8bba30541a2e59e97ad7569461e (Accessed: 3 November 2021)

Stark, U. (2007) *An Empire of Books: The Naval Kishore Press and the Diffusion of the Printed Word in Colonial India*. Delhi: Permanent Black.

# PART III

# Forms in Flux I

## Trajectories of Digital Cultures in Indian Literatures

# 9

# "DIGITIZING DEROZIO: EXPLORING INTERTEXTS TO ENGLISH ROMANTICISM IN *COLLECTED POEMS OF HENRY DEROZIO*"

*Amardeep Singh*

## Introduction: The Archive Gap

Since Henry Derozio is a writer strongly associated with the Romantic period, it seems appropriate to begin with two bits of explanatory context for the digital edition of Derozio's works that is the present occasion for this chapter.[1] The first is an ongoing engagement in a phenomenon I have called the *Archive Gap*,[2] by which I mean the disparity between the extent and quality of digital archives for white, Euro-American, and Canonical writers, and those in the colonial and postcolonial world. The causes of the Archive Gap are many and begin with decisions about which sorts of primary texts were preserved and which were discarded, especially under colonialism. The Gap in preservation means that there is a much better British record of key historical events like the 1857 Indian uprising against the British Raj than there is of the Indian side. One sees a similar discrepancy when it comes to the preservation of materials in South Asian languages, especially 19th-century newspapers. Nearly perfect records exist of many English-language newspapers published in places like Calcutta, Lucknow, Allahabad, and Lahore throughout much of the 19th century; by contrast, the preservation of newspapers printed in Bengali, Urdu, or Punjabi was much more uneven. A second phase in the Archive Gap relates to how materials that were preserved were later acquired by research libraries, and which of those collections were catalogued and made accessible to users. In many collections, important documents and manuscripts remain uncatalogued and therefore essentially off the grid. For literary critics working on South Asian literary history in particular, important periodicals might be lying in boxes in dusty rooms, known essentially only to librarians with deep knowledge of the holdings. These materials are not being digitized, and in many cases are not even really being protected from the elements.

DOI: 10.4324/9781003354246-13

The final phase in the Archive Gap involves digital archives. There are impressive digital archives, often developed with significant grant funding and sizeable staff and technical support, for British and American writers such as Walt Whitman, William Blake, and Emily Dickinson. These archives have not only digitized published texts but also often different versions and editions, manuscript materials, and personal correspondence; they are tagged and marked up with TEI; they might use advanced tools like GIS maps or topic modelling to explore their corpora. It is much harder to find work of this kind with South Asian writers. Many writers who are clearly important—like Henry Derozio, or Krupabai Satthianadhan (an early Indian woman novelist and one of India's first women doctors)—have until now not had any digital archives dedicated to their work. To be clear, I am not suggesting that their work has not been *digitized*; page-images of the works of Krupabai Satthianadhan can be found on Google Books and HathiTrust. Rather, the issue is that these works are not accessible as *texts*, with contextual information, editorial commentary, and annotations, or metadata that might help readers find and situate the materials. This problem is so well-documented in the digital humanities that Roopika Risam has described the field as essentially "digital *canonical* humanities."[3] Sites like the William Blake Archive, the Rosetti Archive, and the Walt Whitman Archive have been key to the development of Digital Archives as a field, and projects like NINES, which aggregate 19th-century digital collections, are overwhelmingly dominated by Anglo-American authors and texts.

## Rectifying the Archive Gap

While European and American digital humanities communities have been slow to respond to this problem, in recent years, we have seen some progress, with projects like Livingstone Online (which takes a self-reflexive approach to the European encounter with cultural otherness in Africa), the "One More Voice" project, and The Early Caribbean Digital Archive.[4] In the South Asian context, one is impressed by the richness of the Tagore Variorum,[5] but there remains much more room to work, especially when it comes to writers other than Tagore. There are many important South Asian authors whose works remain underrepresented in digital collections, especially early writers and writers who worked in South Asian languages.

The desire to rectify the Archive Gap led the author of this study to embark on a project that is in a way the immediate precursor to the digital edition of Henry Derozio's poems that is the subject of this chapter. That is the Literature of Colonial South Asia text corpus.[6] This open-access corpus brings together writings by British and South Asian writers, which are known to be out of copyright in the U.S., into a simple collection of plain text files. One goal of this project is to enable and encourage people who use quantitative methods to consider applying them to South Asian Anglophone materials, and, for this, clean plain-text files are considered an essential starting point. And while one can find corpora of various sorts online to use as a basis for text analysis, most of these aim for massive scale rather than thematic specificity. But another central goal is to increase the accessibility of these texts, especially for teachers and students.

This project in turn emerged out of a digital collection I initiated in 2015, centred around the Kipling family—especially Rudyard, his sister Alice Fleming, and his father, John Lockwood Kipling.[7] As that project continued to develop, it became apparent that for many 21st-century readers, the Kipling family might be less interesting than their various Indian interlocutors. In the present project, alongside expected figures like Toru Dutt, Michael Madhusudan Dutt, Rabindranath Tagore, Bankim Chandra Chatterji, Dhan Gopal Mukerji, and Cornelia Sorabji, there's scope to create accessible digital editions of somewhat lesser-known figures like S.B. Banerjea and Krupabai Satthianadhan. And on the British side, the corpus includes obvious mainstays like the Kiplings, Maud Diver, Flora Annie Steel, and Sara Jeannette Duncan, but also some lesser-known figures like the American writer G.A. Henty and the Irish romance novelist B.M. Croker.

And, of course, one is interested in the *dialogue* between the British and the South Asian writers mentioned earlier. What influence did British writers have on emerging South Asian literature in English? Conversely, what influence, if any, did South Asian writers have on British colonial writers? People who read Rudyard Kipling or Flora Annie Steel know well that their prose is rich with Hindustani terms, sometimes used a little imprecisely. How dense, exactly, is their engagement with South Asian languages? When and how do we see engagement with South Asian languages in their works? What does the geographical representation look like? To some extent, the idea of creating an open-access corpus entails bringing these texts together to make them readily accessible to human researchers. But some of these questions might also be addressed through computational methods, including natural language processing queries that might be used to discover geographical representations and proper names.

By and large, with respect to materials in the Literature of Colonial South Asia text corpus, the goal is not to produce full digital editions. With some of the more obscure writers mentioned earlier, it's not likely that very many people will need fully functional versions of their texts, which could potentially be assigned in a 21st-century university classroom; at least with some of these figures, distant reading might be more important than close reading.

One exception to that might be with Henry Derozio, who has special importance, because he appears to be the first Indian poet to write in English. And because of his education and his family background, he appears not to have been self-translating from an Indian language, but rather writing first and foremost in English. Though Derozio died when he was quite young, and some of his poems have a juvenile quality, many of his best poems are formally sophisticated and likely to be accessible to students. Finally, because of the work of scholars like Rosinka Chaudhuri, Mary Ellis Gibson, and Manu Samriti Chander, his works have, in the past ten years, begun to gain more visibility for scholars and teachers of Romantic poetry, especially those influenced by the growing movement to bring greater diversity and inclusion to studies of the Romantic period, a movement sometimes referred to as "Bigger 6" Romanticism.[8]

In effect, while specialist scholars of global Romanticism might know Derozio, and many Indians will know his name (as he is taught in some English-medium colleges and universities), he could potentially be better-known than he is, especially in the U.K. and the U.S. (The Open Syllabus project, which uses web crawlers to find college syllabi published on the web, only shows three "hits" for Derozio's name. By contrast, one sees 4,150 hits for Percy Bysshe Shelley and 2,180 hits for Byron.[9] As a person of mixed Portuguese, British, and Indian heritage who wrote not long after the advent of English-medium education in India, Derozio's position seems structurally connected to that of the Anglo-Indian community. Mary Ellis Gibson sums him up nicely when she writes: "It is ironic—but absolutely right—that a poet of complex political views and of complex ethnic, religious, and familial identifications should be thought of as the paterfamilias of Indian English poetry" (Gibson 2011, p. 2). Derozio wrote exclusively in English at a time when few other Indians did so. When he wrote about the conflict between Greeks and Turks,[10] he sympathized with the Greeks over the Turks, in part because of his *religious* background as a Christian. But Derozio taught at Hindoo College in Calcutta (later Presidency College, and now Presidency University)—a school exclusively for Indian students, and his actual poetry is enthusiastically and patriotically Indian.

For those various reasons, it seemed appropriate to assemble a simple digital edition of Derozio's poetry, containing the poems from his two published collections; this work was completed in the summer of 2020. One of those two books, *The Fakeer of Jungheera and Other Poems* (1828), could already be found as a page-image scan on HathiTrust; Derozio's first book was available in print via a British library reprint, so digitizing it required a bit more work.

The Scalar platform was chosen for this project for several reasons. First, it is a free platform developed by university-affiliated librarians and digital humanists,[11] rather than a for-profit company; this reduces the need for external funding to support the project (which may be especially problematic five or ten years down the line). It also has a helpful "Paths" structure that is well-suited to the presentation of materials in sequence. Scalar also has a built-in visualization engine that can be helpful for giving users a visual point of entry into their collections. It also helps that the university where I teach has been able to install an "instance" of Scalar, which should remain permanently accessible even if the platform ceases to be updated at some point in the future. Many digital projects also use the version of Scalar hosted by the University of Southern California.

The central principle here is flexibility. People come to digital collections for different reasons and with different amounts of expertise; it's not terribly effective to construct sites that are too narrowly framed, and only focused on highly experienced users; such users are few and far between, especially with less well-known writers. Some users will know what they're looking for, while others will simply be browsing and curious to find something engaging, perhaps something that might be accessible to students. With that multiplicity in mind, *The Collected Poems of Henry Derozio* is a site with multiple ways "in."

## Some Features of the Collection

Reading Derozio's major poems, one cannot help but notice the remarkable frequency of the author's engagement with British and Irish Romantic poets. Sometimes, he explicitly tags the poem he is borrowing from with an epigraph, making the task of detecting the borrowing much easier. In the present digital edition, tags have been included that link to the original British or Irish poem referenced to make tracking references easier for the reader. In Derozio's poetry, there are 17 such poems, and users interested in this particular side of Derozio's poetry can see those links collected on a single page.[12]

Derozio's descriptions of Indian locales in his poetry are also notable. Though he was born and raised in Calcutta (Kolkata), Derozio spent some time as a teenager working in his uncle's indigo factory in Bhagalpur, Bihar, and as a result had at least some exposure to rural India and the broader Indian landscape. Many of these geographical reference points show up in his long poem, *The Fakeer of Jungheera*, but another strong poem along these lines might be "The Ruins of Rajmahal," describing Shah Shuja's palace in what is today Jharkand. These poems have all been tagged and collected on a single page, "South Asian Locales."[13]

A third feature to highlight is the "Resource for Teachers."[14] This is a collection of ten poems that might be effective in a college classroom for a one-day unit on Derozio. This includes some obvious choices, such as Derozio's "The Harp of India," some poems that seem important because of their thematization of British Romanticism (Derozio's "Heaven"), and some that engage with South Asian locales (the aforementioned poem "The Ruins of Rajmahal").

As mentioned earlier, there has been a wave of recent criticism, which has had a significant impact on how scholars understand Derozio. Chief among them is Manu Samriti Chander's book, *Brown Romantics: Poetry and Nationalism in the Global Nineteenth Century* (2017). There, Chander argues that writers like Derozio, and the Guyanese writer Egbert Martin and the Australian writer Henry Lawson, were engaged in close dialogue with canonical British Romanticism. Their output could be described as imitative, but still reflective of a marginalized positionality. And the fact that these figures were largely overlooked as the Romantic canon came to be organized suggests a hidden racialized agenda in the process of Canon-formation:

> To put it another way, "Brown Romantics" are not marginalized because they are brown; on the contrary, they are brown because they are marginalized. Their capacity to participate as poets in the cultural field is restricted by their relationship to the colonizer prior to their participation in it, which in turn exposes the racial dimension of "the world republic of letters."
>
> *(Chander, 3)*

What Chander is alluding to here seems like an important point when reading Derozio. While Derozio does identify, strongly and exclusively, as an Indian poet—with a strong Indian *national* identity—he does not identify necessarily as *racially other* to the poets with whom he is in dialogue. To some extent, this reflects the unique moment in time of the early 19th century, where Derozio was educated at schools that included British, mixed-race Eurasian, and Indian young men (women were not admitted to these schools). Chander builds on a reading of Derozio by Makarand Paranjape, who wrote, "it is not possible to explain or understand a poet like Derozio merely by speaking of influence and imitation. In fact, whatever he borrowed, he superimposed in his local, Indian material, creating a new idiom in English poetry" (cited in Chander [2017] 22–23). For Chander, this suggests that we can understand Derozio's complex positioning as a "transcultural assemblage," "by means of which the poet retains his position of authority in a field that places supreme value on originality and situates himself in relation to fellow bards" (Chander 2017, p. 23).

Chander goes on to explore, in some depth, Derozio's dialogue with Lord Byron in Derozio's poem "Heaven." Here are a few lines from the first stanza of Byron's "The Bride of Abydos":

> Know ye the land where the cypress and myrtle
> Are emblems of deeds that are done in their clime?
> Where the rage of the vulture, the love of the turtle,
> Now melt into sorrow, now madden to crime?
> Know ye the land of the cedar and vine,
> Where the flowers ever blossom, the beams ever shine;
> Where the light wings of Zephyr, oppressed with perfume,
> Wax faint o'er the gardens of Gúl in her bloom;
> Where the citron and olive are fairest of fruit,
> And the voice of the nightingale never is mute;
> Where the tints of the earth, and the hues of the sky,
> In colour though varied, in beauty may vie,
> And the purple of Ocean is deepest in dye;
> Where the virgins are soft as the roses they twine,
> And all, save the spirit of man, is divine—
> Tis the clime of the East—'tis the land of the Sun—
> Can he smile on such deeds as his children have done?
> Oh! wild as the accents of lovers' farewell
> Are the hearts which they bear, and the tales which they tell.[15]

What is the Orient in Byron's poem? It's a place of exotic foliage ("crypress and myrtle") and various forms of sin and crime ("deeds that are done in their clime" where "clime" rhymes with "crime" two lines later). The word "deeds" is repeated twice in the short excerpt here, as is the word "clime"; and there's a strong and repeated emphasis on the revelation of secret truths of those sinful deeds. This is classic Orientalism, in effect, where the properties of the East are seen as at once immutable and beyond human agency—and inherently sinful and unspeakable. It is Orientalism as a form of projection—the East as the West's unseemly underbelly rather than a cultural context in its own right. And while Derozio would not have had access to Edward Said's critique when he read this in the 1820s as a teenager, his homage to Byron in "Heaven" aims to tell a decidedly different story:

Know ye the land where the fountain is springing,
Whose waters give life, and whose flow never ends;
Where cherub and seraph, in concert, are singing
The hymn that in odour and incense ascends?
Know ye the land where the sun cannot shine,
Where his light would be darken'd by glory divine;
Where the fields are all fair, and the flowret's young bloom
Never fades, while with sweetness each breath they perfume;
Where sighs are ne'er heard, and where tears are ne'er shed
From hearts that might elsewhere have broken, and bled;
Where grief is unfelt, where its name is unknown,
Where the music of gladness is heard in each tone;
Where melody vibrates from harps of pure gold,
Far brighter than mortal's weak eye can behold;
Where the harpers are robed in a mantle of light,
More dazzling than diamonds, than silver more white;
Where rays from a rainbow of emerald beam,
Where truth is no name, and where bliss is no dream?—
Tis the seat of our God! 'tis the land of the blest—
The kingdom of glory—the region of rest—
The boon that to man shall hereafter be given—
'Tis Love's hallowed empire—'tis Heaven! 'tis Heaven![16]

It is striking that Derozio does not mark the East here as "other"; indeed, within the text of the poem, it appears that he is not naming the "east" at all in "Heaven." Rather than a space of sin, Derozio has decided to use the exotic framing to describe a holy place, the "seat of our God." While the poem itself might suggest that the place he's describing is literally intended to be understood as heaven (not a terrestrial location), because of the intertext—the homage to Byron's very well-known poem—this is an unmistakable recasting of an exotic locale from a space of sin and degraded otherness to a kind of sublime and sacred otherness. This is a powerful gesture for an emergent Indian writer to make in 1826.

One surprise for non-specialists in reading Derozio's poems is the way the Romantic Canon looked a little different to him than it does to us today. There are several poems in Derozio's corpus inspired by Lord Byron and Percy Shelley, to be sure, but there are also almost as many inspired by writers like Thomas Campbell, Letitia Elizabeth Landon, and the Irish poet Thomas Moore. Several of Derozio's poems drawing from Byron focused specifically on the idea of a valiant and noble people, of ancient pedigree, resisting foreign domination. While Byron usually figured the plight of the noble resistance as Greeks resisting Ottoman occupation, in Derozio's adaptive transplanting to the Indian context there emerges a strong potential for a subversive reading, as the posture of nationalist resistance could be interpreted by Indian readers as a challenge to British colonialism.

Thomas Moore, as an Irish poet and an exponent of "Bardic nationalism," is particularly salient. While Derozio seemed to repurpose Byron in "Heaven" for his own purposes, here his poem aligns with Moore's sentiments much more affirmatively—though it resituates the poem in India rather than Ireland. We should begin with Moore's "Dear Harp of my Country":

Dear Harp of my Country! in darkness I found thee,
The cold chain of silence had hung o'er thee long;
When proudly, my own Island Harp! I unbound thee
And gave all thy chords to light, freedom and song!
The warm lay of love and the light tone of gladness
Have waken'd thy fondest, thy liveliest thrill;
But so oft hast thou echo'd the deep sigh of sadness,
That e'en in thy mirth it will steal from thee still.
Dear Harp of my Country! farewell to thy numbers
This sweet wreath of song is the last we shall twine,
Go, sleep with the sunshine of Fame on thy slumbers,
Till touch'd by some hand less unworthy than mine.
If the pulse of the patriot, soldier, or lover,
Have throbb'd at our lay'tis thy glory alone;
I was but as the wind, passing heedlessly over,
And all the wild sweetness I waked was thy own![17]

Here, Moore takes on the posture of the national bard—the person who has, by chance, been given the opportunity to play the "Harp of my Country." The poet disavows any special capacity ("some hand less unworthy than mine" needs to emerge to truly play the Harp as it should be played), but clearly the disavowal is a kind of theatrical gesture rather than a serious part of the argument. From this point on, after I play it, the poet suggests that the "wild sweetness" of the Island will be given life through "sweet wreath of song."

Let us compare Moore's bardic nationalism to Derozio's take on the same gesture, in his poem "Harp of India" (1827):

Why hang'st thou lonely on yon withered bough?
Unstrung for ever, must thou there remain;
Thy music once was sweet—-who hears it now?
Why doth the breeze sigh over thee in vain?
Silence hath bound thee with her fatal chain;
Neglected, mute, and desolate art thou,

Like ruined monument on desert plain:
O! many a hand more worthy far than mine
Once thy harmonious chords to sweetness gave,
And many a wreath for them did Fame entwine
Of flowers still blooming on the minstrel's grave:
Those hands are cold—but if thy notes divine
May be by mortal wakened once again,
Harp of my country, let me strike the strain![18]

Mary Ellis Gibson has a persuasive reading of this poem; she describes Derozio's gesture as a "poetics of cancellation," noting the somewhat confusing hint of a silenced Indian music. If and when that music were to be awakened, what exactly would it sound like? Gibson notes that "Harp of India" reflects

> the complexity of the poet's situation as a person of multiple identities and identifications, from the impossibility of writing a national poetry for a nation that can only be imagined in some futurity, and from the extreme tensions already visible in the biblical progenitor of the bardic trope.
>
> *(Gibson 2011, p. 78)*

Manu Chander echoes that reading when he writes:

> What qualifies Derozio to stand as a representative of India? Is it the fact that, unlike earlier Anglophone poets living in India, he was born there? Or is it the trace of native ancestry in the "Eurasian" poet of primarily English and Portuguese descent? Indeed, is it even possible to speak of a national poet of India in the 1820s, decades before the rise of coherent nationalist movements in the region?
>
> *(Chander 2014, p. 21)*

Assessing the similarity between the two poems, one sees slight rhetorical differences that perhaps help to alleviate the concern that Derozio's attempt to claim a kind of bardic nationalism might be premature. Where Moore's disavowal of his status as bard-presumptive is framed in the past tense ("I was but as the wind"), Derozio's is anticipatory—proleptic. The national song, in his version, is yet to be sung.

A final example offers a slightly different resonance on the subversive possibilities of Derozio's engagement with English Romanticism. This is in Derozio's poem "Freedom to the Slave," which contains an epigraph from Thomas Campbell's "Pleasures of Hope" (1799). Campbell's poem is a celebration of Enlightenment optimism about human nature and progress, including a clear ambition to free enslaved peoples around the world. Here is a portion of Campbell's poem:

Come, bright Improvement! on the car of Time,
And rule the spacious world from clime to clime:
Thy handmaid arts shall every wild explore,

Trace every wave, and culture every shore.
On Erie's banks, where tygers steal along,
And the dread Indian chaunts a dismal song,
Where human fiends on midnight errands walk,
And bathe in brains the murd'rous tomahawk;
There shall the flocks on thymy pasture stray,
And shepherds dance at Summer's op'ning day,
Each wand'ring genius of the lonely glen
Shall start to view the glittering haunts of men;
And silence watch, on woodland heights around,
The village curfew as it tolls profound.
In Libyan groves, where damned rites are done,
That bathe the rocks in blood, and veil the sun,
Truth shall arrest the murd'rous arm profane;
Wild Obi flies—the veil is rent in twain.
Where barb'rous hordes on Scythian mountains roam,
Truth, Mercy, Freedom, yet shall find a home;
Where'er degraded Nature bleeds and pines,
From Guinea's coast to Sibir's dreary mines,
Truth shall pervade th' unfathom'd darkness there,
And light the dreadful features of despair:—
Hark! the stern captive spurns his heavy load,
And asks the image back that Heav'n bestow'd.
Fierce in his eye the fire of valour burns,
And, as the slave departs, the man returns!
(Thomas Campbell, "The Pleasures of Hope")[19]

Here, we see Campbell enumerating many sites around the world where an Enlightenment-driven concept of personal liberty has not yet found a place. These are mostly spaces where various cultural others exist—the "Dread Indian" on the banks of the Erie River, who threatens with "murd'rous tomahawk"; Libyans who engage in "damned rites"; "barbarous hordes" of Scythians in western Asia. All of these societies have yet to be penetrated by the light of "Truth," though Campbell's expectation is that they will be: "Truth shall pervade th' unfathom'd darkness there." With that move towards Enlightenment comes the reassertion of fundamental human rights. Notably, Campbell nowhere mentions the transatlantic slave trade, or the denial of liberty that followed British colonial subjugation in Asia, or the Western Hemisphere. The "slavery" he depicts is entirely one perpetrated by unenlightened black and brown cultural others: not by subjects of the Enlightenment themselves: western colonists, traders, and plantation owners. Reading 200 years later, the omission seems like a blind spot: a 21st-century reader encountering the word "slavery" cannot help but think of that compromising legacy.

Derozio's response to Campbell does not entirely rectify this, though it does leave open the possibility of an anti-colonial reading in line with other anti-colonial gestures we have seen earlier. The line Derozio will borrow and deploy to set his own poem in motion is the final one in the excerpt from Campbell quoted earlier: "And as the slave departs, the man returns!" Here then is Derozio's "Freedom to the Slave":

How felt he when he first was told
A slave he ceased to be;
How proudly beat his heart, when first
He knew that he was free!—-
The noblest feelings of the soul
To glow at once began;
He knelt no more; his thoughts were raised;
He felt himself a man.
He looked above—the breath of heaven
Around him freshly blew;
He smiled exultingly to see
The wild birds as they flew,
He looked upon the running stream
That 'neath him rolled away;
Then thought on winds, and birds, and floods,
And cried, "I'm free as they!"
Oh Freedom! there is something dear
E'en in thy very name,
That lights the altar of the soul
With everlasting flame.
Success attend the patriot sword,
That is unsheathed for thee!
And glory to the breast that bleeds,
Bleeds nobly to be free!
Blest be the generous hand that breaks
The chain a tyrant gave,
And, feeling for degraded man,
Gives freedom to the slave.[20]

Derozio's poem echoes many of the core themes and ideas of Campbell's famous poem, including the passionate belief in personal liberty. However, Derozio's poem is curiously devoid of reference to specific geographic or political frameworks in which enslavement is enacted. The Libyans, Obi-worshippers, and "murderous tomahawks" are all missing, and instead the poet engages in a reflection on the experience of freedom that is as at once much more abstract and much more personal. What Derozio is describing is the slave's personal experience of *discovering* freedom after having been denied it: "Then thought on winds, and birds, and floods,/And cried, 'I'm free as they!'" Is it possible Derozio, writing with a strong identification as an Indian, might be understanding his own status as a "brown" poet as producing the experience of unfreedom he describes here? In other words, does his response to Campbell contain a critique of the racialized capitalism embedded in the colonial project?

## Conclusion: Next Steps

As indicated earlier, the South Asian digital humanities community has made some very impressive strides in the past five years alone, but there is much more that could be done. With respect to Derozio in particular, there are apparent questions that could be explored in further work, possibly in collaboration with other scholars. First, in the poems discussed earlier, we have here marked particularly important keywords where Derozio borrows language directly from British and Irish poets. Would it be possible to use natural language processing to find a quantitative way of measuring the influence of one poet on another? A similarity index—or better yet, an Influence Index—not so unlike what Plagiarism detection tools use? The goal of course is not to diminish a poet who borrows as Derozio does, but rather to indicate the broad prevalence of this practice in literary history. Second, just as Derozio was influenced by British and Irish poets, he also left quite a legacy in Calcutta in the years following his death, with the rise of the Young Bengal Movement, which featured a formidable group of intellectuals and writers, most of whom published on social and historical topics (Peary Chand Mitter did publish at least one novel). Is there a hidden line of influence between Derozio and subsequent Indian English poetry? Third, how and where is Derozio being taught? Earlier it was argued that Derozio is not being widely taught in the U.K. or the U.S. It appears that he is taught more often in India; one gathers that he continues to be celebrated at Presidency University in particular. But how widely is he being taught? Can that presence be quantified—perhaps by doing a version of the Open Syllabus project that would focus on South Asian writers taught within South Asian universities? To what extent have English departments at Indian universities effectively moved to decentre the English Canon, specifically with reference to early Indian writing in English and the shape and scope of the British Romantic tradition?

Beyond Derozio, one returns again and again to the Archive Gap mentioned at the start; rectifying it will be a broad and collective effort. In addition to simply building out useable digital collections that are accessible to a broad range of readers, there's considerable work to be done with respect to quantitative text analysis. A collection like the Literature of Colonial South Asia corpus could be a start in moving in that direction, but much remains to be done.

## Notes

1 See https://scalar.lehigh.edu/derozio/
2 Singh, Amardeep. "Beyond the Archive Gap: the Kiplings and the Famines of British India." *South Asian Review* 40.3 (2019): 237–252.

3 Roopika Risam, New Digital Worlds: Postcolonial Digital Humanities in Theory and Praxis. Chicago: Northwestern University Press, 2019, p. 16.
4 Http://https://livingstoneonline.org/; http://onemorevoice.org;
5 http://bichitra.jdvu.ac.in/index.php
6 www.electrostani.com/2020/08/text-corpus-colonial-south-asian.html
7 https://scalar.lehigh.edu/kiplings/
8 See https://bigger6romantix.squarespace.com/
9 http://opensyllabus.org
10 See for instance Derozio's poem, "Greece" along these lines: https://scalar.lehigh.edu/derozio/greece-1?path=poems-1827
11 https://scalar.me/anvc/
12 https://scalar.lehigh.edu/derozio/intertexts-english-romanticism
13 https://scalar.lehigh.edu/derozio/south-asian-locales
14 https://scalar.lehigh.edu/derozio/resource-for-teachers
15 Text of poem accessed online here: https://genius.com/Lord-byron-the-bride-of-abydos-annotated
16 Text of poem can be found at Singh, *The Collected Poems of Henry Derozio*. https://scalar.lehigh.edu/derozio/heaven?path=poems-1827
17 Text of poem accessed online here: www.bartleby.com/337/1010.html
18 Text of poem can be found at Singh, *The Collected Poetry of Henry Derozio*. https://scalar.lehigh.edu/derozio/the-harp-of-india?path=poems-1827
19 Text of poem found at David Hall Radcliffe's digital collection, "Spencer and the Tradition: English Poetry 1579–1830." http://spenserians.cath.vt.edu/TextRecord.php?textsid=37917
20 Text of poem can be found at Singh, *Collected Poems of Henry Derozio*. https://scalar.lehigh.edu/derozio/freedom-to-the-slave?path=poems-1827

## References


Chander, M.S. (2014) "The First Indian Poet in English: Henry Louis Vivian Derozio" in Rosinka Chaudhuri, Ed. *A History of Indian Poetry in English*. Cambridge: Cambridge University Press.

Chander, M.S. (2017) *Brown Romantics: Poetry and Nationalism in the Global Nineteenth Century*. Lewisburg, PA: Bucknell University Press.

Chaudhuri, R., ed. (2008) *Derozio, Poet of India: The Definitive Edition*. New Delhi: Oxford University Press.

Gibson, M.E. (2011) *Indian Angles: English Verse in Colonial India from Jones to Tagore* Athens: Ohio University Press.

Open Syllabus Project. Available at: https://opensyllabus.org (Accessed: 10 October, 2021)

Paranjape, M.R. (2011) "'East Indian' Cosmopolitanism", *Interventions: International Journal of Postcolonial Studies* 13.4, 550–569.

Radcliffe, David Hall: "Spencer and the Tradition: English Poetry 1579–1830". Available at: http://spenserians.cath.vt.edu/ (Accessed 10 October, 2021).

Risam, R. (2019) *New Digital Worlds: Postcolonial Digital Humanities in Theory and Praxis*. Chicago: Northwestern University Press.

Singh, Amardeep: (2019) "Beyond the Archive Gap: The Kiplings and the Famines of British India," *South Asian Review* 40:3, 237–251.

Singh, Amardeep, ed. (2020) *Collected Poems of Henry Derozio*. Available at: *https://scalar.lehigh.edu/derozio/index* (Accessed 10 October, 2021).

# 10

# THE INTERNET IN THE CONTEXT OF INDIAN WOMEN'S POETRY IN ENGLISH

*Shruti Sareen*

The primary focus of this chapter is how the internet and our digital electronic devices are connecting us at so many levels and creating flux, hybridity, and a process of becoming, thereby deconstructing several binary oppositions around us. Our internet connections, which literally provide us "connectivity" in the age of Internet 2.0, that is, the age of social media, are connecting us through forming gift economies and discourse communities.

Hypertext and hypermedia, with their hyperlinks, connect text to text and to audio-visual elements, just as the internet connects people to people. In this process, several binaries are broken down, most importantly, the binaries between reader and writer, between text and visual, and between written and oral. I examine how hypertext and hypermedia are changing the production and consumption of poetry. The internet is the age of "secondary orality" coming back to literature, according to Walter J Ong. In this process, humans are in flux, humans are becoming cyborgs, and the binary between the human and the machine too is broken down. Humans are in flux, in the process of becoming, just as a text, for example, a poem put on social media may be subject to collaborative authorship and might undergo several revisions and edits as a result of feedback by other people. Thus, both the human and the texts are in flux, and binary oppositions are being broken down.

The chapter looks at these concepts in the context of Indian women's poetry in English: its realities and its potential and possibilities. The chapter is divided into three parts: first, I discuss how the internet is forming gift economies and discourse communities, then I discuss hypertext and hypermedia, and finally I examine the concept of cyborgs, which may have darker undertones as opposed to the utopian ideal of the gift economy. The internet seems to be leading us into a post-structuralist universe where binary oppositions are broken. The gift economy and discourse communities break the binary between writers and readers, hypertext

DOI: 10.4324/9781003354246-14

and hypermedia break boundaries between, text, audio, and visual, and the concept of cyborgs attempts to break the binary between human and machine. Fluidity also seems to be a hallmark of the age, whether in terms of texts or humans.

## I

The term "gift economy," first used by Marcel Mauss and Emile Durkheim, seems to refer to a form of living which is closer to communism, where each gets according to their need, and not necessarily according to their place in the wage hierarchy. Mauss, as quoted by Daniel Weinbren (2006, pp. 319–336) in "The Good Samaritan, friendly societies and the gift economy," argues that, although gifts in theory may seem voluntary and selfless, they in fact form a cycle of mutual obligation. This cycle of exchange may replace other forms of capitalistic exchange. These gifts could be material in terms of economic capital, or symbolic in terms of social or cultural capital, recognition, and so on, or services rendered such as holding office, attending funerals, and comforting the bereaved. At the same time, people do not help another, only looking for personal gain, but out of goodwill, as the other person may never really help them directly. It is a community of gift-giving where people know that someone will help them in their hour of need, just as they help others. It may be seen as a sort of personification of the parable that good comes to those who do good. Thus, self-interest and goodwill become interlinked and mutually dependent. Weinbren points out that such societies may be seen, for example, in church groups, in the idea of the Good Samaritan, and in Sunday schools. He also points out several historic instances in medieval to early modern England where the poor often lived in such communities of gift economies. This can easily be seen even in poor people's communities in India today, wherein people help each other out, take credit, give loans, and so on, on the basis of need, knowing that their neighbours and community will similarly help them out if they need it someday. The concepts of charity, donations, and pensions are also associated with the idea of a gift economy and somehow doing good without immediately expecting good in return—yet, while knowing that good usually does come round to the doer in some shape or form. As Weinbren points out, these societies can be seen as enacting a critique of capitalist forms of societies, and as such, are better for times of risk than depending on the salary savings of capitalism. He also points out that, in the context of the friendly societies that he discusses, however friendly these societies, and however much they operated on principles of goodwill and the Good Samaritan, this exchange was always limited to men. Women were never on the scene of exchange of any kinds of gifts and services in these societies. These gift economies end up forming communities of their own within which this goodwill happens and is returned.

In this chapter, I attempt to see whether the world of poetry communities can be seen as replicating something like a gift economy. The world of poetry, unlike that of fiction, does not operate by books being financially viable and becoming bestsellers. Poets, as well as poetry publishers and poetry journals, hardly make any money due to the fact that it is not a very popular genre in the mainstream—thus, poetry becomes a labour of love, which is often sustained as a gift economy by people, often out of their own pockets. It is the small, tiny poetry presses that have been responsible for keeping poetry alive, as the bigger names in the publishing industry only publish the "big names" from which they may profit, if they profit at all. The same situation is seen with respect to other Indian languages which is even worse than the situation in English. Mainstream multinational publishers do not publish in Indian languages at all. Literature in these languages is forced to depend upon small presses and bilingual journals. There are a few small, independent publishers who keep the momentum going through blogs, and bilingual or multilingual publishing houses. Each state would have small presses for publications in their language. We also see this phenomena happening worldwide. It is small independent presses and journals which keep the genre of poetry alive. Publishers subsist on pennies, incur losses, and require separate day-jobs. It is rare for mainstream publishers to publish individual collections of poetry, as it is not profitable for them. On rare occasions, they might publish a well-known poet or a poetry anthology. Thus, it ends up being a labour of love, surviving because of the gift economy.

The internet has been a boon in this regard and has helped the proliferation of poetry. The short length of the genre is particularly suited to the space of the internet, and people's short attention spans, although—as I discuss using Katherine Hayles in the next section—this is also ironical, as reading poetry is a much more labour-intensive task than much of the flippant, skim-surface-reading which happens on the internet these days. The growth of a wide range of open-access poetry journals on the internet also shows that this is a labour of love; these journals are managed mostly without any monetary rewards or gains. Contributors are usually not paid and readers do not have to pay to access the poetry, either. There are poets who see this as exploitation, and who demand that poetry should be seen as worthy of remuneration just as any other profession. However, it must be said that the world of poetry seems to oppose, or, rather, to function despite the world of capitalism to an extent. There are also a few journals online which require paid access, and which also pay their contributors. Print journals, of course, require payment and usually try to pay their contributors, although they often struggle with lack of funds themselves. Poetry journals and presses are usually not based on any profit-making motive, but out of sheer love for the art form. It seems to perhaps function like a gift economy in that poets offer their poems for free, and mostly get recognition from readers in turn. Readers get to read poetry for free or at a small cost, and, in turn, offer symbolic tribute and appreciation. Poetry journals and publishers do subsist and survive with minimal expenditures, and do not profit monetarily, but rather in terms of social and cultural recognition. However, this community of the gift economy is no longer a polarized community where readers are separate from writers and so on.

This community of the gift economy forms a discourse community. A discourse community is a community with a common knowledge base and repertoire—in this case, of poetry. Distinctions between writers and readers have been destroyed in the age of the internet, where everyone can turn a poet on social media, in an age where spoken-word-poetry rages on street corners. Here is an age where everybody can read, and everybody can write, and hierarchical divisions have to some extent been broken. Poetry is a niche art, and thus, its discourse is limited to within the community. Only people within the discourse community read poetry, whereas the outer public does not really care for it. Poetry journals, anthologies, reviews, awards, spoken word poetry, and, very importantly, social media help in creating a discourse community. Social media platforms, discussion groups, and so on also help greatly in forming this discourse community, and also form a gift economy. As hierarchies are obliterated to some extent, readers become writers and vice versa, and a community spirit of sharing and solidarity is formed, which perhaps is the most important facet of the mutual sense of obligation which forms the basis of a gift economy.

A "discourse community" has also been seen as a closed community of like-minded individuals, where there is a "niche audience for everyone." Cass R. Sunstein has also called these "information cocoons" Kevin Robins (2000, p. 91), whom David Bell and Kennedy (2000, p. 105) cite characterizes virtual communities as "a domain of order, refuge, withdrawal," a community that is elective and selective, contingent and transitory. However, Howard Rheingold believes in the power of these online communities to form active, participatory audience instead of passive ones so as to lead to a greater and more involved form of democracy. David Bell in An Introduction to Cybercultures (2001) examines the nature of these virtual communities. Bell looks at traditional village communities where everyone knows everyone and at huge urban conglomerations where there is a heterogeneity of anonymous people. He observes three processes, namely those of detraditionalization, disembedding, and globalization. Due to globalization, we are able to access global flows of ideas and information and are thus getting disembedded from local communities. At the same time, globalization and an influx of new ideas are leading to detraditionalization. In the face of all this uprooting, people need to find a way to belong, and the internet offers exactly that, although it is not clear whether the internet is part of the problem or the solution. Thus, people are beginning to imagine new forms of community. Communities are ultimately imagined, writes Bell, referring to Benedict Anderson's description of the nation as an "imagined community" where people who may not know each other come together and share a common feeling of belonging to a group. Ferdinand Tönnies (1957) in Community and Association outlined two types of community: the gemeinschaft which is like the traditional community where everyone knows everyone, helps everyone and bonds are tight and multiple, and the gesellschaft which is the urban community where there are heterogeneous anonymous multitudes, uprooted from the traditional community life, and people are so busy that the bonds they form are shallow and instrumental. According to Bell, the virtual community seems to be more like the gemeinschaft. However, gemeinschaft's strong ties are matched by their small minds, community spirit with oppressive regulation, and safety with surveillance. Moreover, everyone is part of a gemeinschaft since birth merely by virtue of being born there. In contrast to this, Bell prefers to use the term "bund" for virtual communities suggested by Kevin Hetherington in Expressions of Identity. A Bund is an elective grouping, bonded by affective and emotional solidarity, sharing a strong sense of belonging.

Howard Rheingold (2000) in *Virtual Community: Homesteading on the Electronic Frontier* terms this as a "gift economy" where people lookout for each other, share information, and help each other out without necessarily expecting it in return, yet knowing that they might be helped similarly by someone else in the community. Richard Lanham (1993, pp. 29–52) writes in *The Economics of Attention* as quoted by Andrea A. Lunsford and Lisa Ede (2009) in "Among the Audience: On Audience in the Age of New Literacies" that we have moved from a "stuff economy," one based on material goods, to a "fluff economy" based on immaterial information. Material economics is governed by scarcity, whereas in a fluff economy, there is simply too much information. Information, unlike material goods, can be kept and given away at the same time.

These gift economies and discourse communities may not necessarily be ideal spaces. There are critiques of these discourse communities, in that they may become "echo chambers." There certainly are differences, but the dangers of devolving into echo chambers also exist. Moreover, these communities may also have a certain incestuous nature, which may also be known as the culture of "back-patting" where coteries take centre stage, as opposed to genuine quality and merit. Thus, although the concepts of gift economy and discourse community sound ideal, we must strive to guard ourselves against the pitfalls they pose.

However, there is a sinister and darker reality to communities on the internet as Rheingold reminds us, which need not always be as utopian as bunds and gift economies. These virtual communities functioning as gift economies are a form of globalization from below. However, there is a totalitarian, hierarchical globalization that is happening from above, one which turns individuals into data, one which tracks their online activities and messages in order to send them customized advertisements and RSS feeds, one which wants complete surveillance over the internet in a manner strangely akin to Foucault's Panopticon. Facebook administrators remove content from people's timelines according to their discretion. Mark Zuckerberg, CEO of Facebook, has apparently discouraged the sharing of informative links and has encouraged the use of more photographs of family and friends instead. Job employers keep surveillance over the social media accounts of their employees, and governments are also known to take action against people for some seemingly objectionable content that they posted on social media. Rheingold describes an even more sinister scenario where there is "paid democracy," where there are watchdogs or paid agents of the powers that be who are specifically paid in order to mould public opinion on social media. This can ironically lead to complete censorship of expression and suppression of dissenting opinions, the very antithesis of a democracy. The internet may also be privatized which will imply that there is no gift economy or free sharing of information. Private companies such as Facebook attempt to privatize the internet, although Tim Berners-Lee, the founder of the internet, is against it. India too saw a debate over the privatization of the internet in recent times, where ultimately TRAI, the Telecom Regulatory Authority of India, a government body, passed a resolution in favour of net neutrality and against privatization. Even apart from questions of surveillance, the gift economy can be abused and misused by people. It is true that virtual communities give us freedom and an element of playfulness with regard to the representation and expression of our identities. However, there is a difference between anonymity and pseudonymity. Anonymity gives us freedom to construct alternative identities and to role-play, without deceiving others. Pseudonymity, however, enables people to completely misrepresent themselves and to mislead people, often leading to shocking deception. Although many critics see this as empowerment, I do not think that power is necessarily always good, nor that empowerment is always beneficial. In the last section of this chapter, I discuss the implications that disembodiment poses before us in these virtual communities.

## II

The second section of this chapter discusses hypertext and hypermedia. Hypertext and hypermedia form interlinked pathways and connect text and media of various kinds to each other, just as our discourse communities and gift economies connect us human beings. This section also shows how hypertext and hypermedia are breaking binary oppositions between writers and readers, between text and visual, and between written and oral. It is also producing new forms of reading.

In this section, I discuss how the concept of hypertext and hypermedia has changed the way we produce and consume poetry on the internet. A noteworthy point worth mentioning about hypertext is its non-linear, non-hierarchical, interwoven, and interlinked natures. This brings clear boundaries of beginnings and endings into question. It gives agency to the reader in terms of creating their own path through the text, the freedom to annotate, write marginalia, or give comments through other means, and the concept of individual authorship giving way to group or collaborative authorship. Hypermedia basically blurs the boundaries between the dichotomies of the textual, the audio, and the visual, and challenges the primacy that we have given to the textual all along. Hypertext and hypermedia essentially help blur the difference between the author and the reader by affording interaction between them and by making the text more interactive. I apply these concepts and explore the difference these have made to Indian (women's) poetry in English, as well as potentialities that could be exploited but which have remained unexplored so far.

George Landow (1992) in *Hypertext* substantiates and historicizes the concept of hypertext and explains it in great depth and detail. The term hypertext actually predates the history of the internet and was coined by Ted Nelson in the 1960s to mean "nonsequential writing—text that branches and allows choices to the reader, best read at an interactive screen. As popularly conceived, this is a series of text chunks connected by links which offer the reader different pathways." Even before this, in 1945, Vannevar Bush envisioned the idea of a memex, a sort of literary machine where one could make links through associative indexing and add marginalia. This was thought of as a "poetic machine," as poetry works through analogy and association. These ideas seemed to gain concrete materiality in the form of the internet created by Tim Berners-Lee.

The concept of hypertext can actually be linked to modernist texts and Roland Barthes's concept of writerly texts. Modernist texts, such as those by Virginia Woolf and James Joyce, employ the stream of consciousness technique, move by association instead of by chronological linearity, and offer us multiple viewpoints as seen through the consciousness of various characters. It is common for 20th-century texts not to give a concretized ending to the reader. According to Barthes, writerly texts are those which require active participation on the part of the reader to make meaning. Modernist texts, as well as hypertexts, can be seen as such writerly texts.

In order to explain the concept of hypertext, I must clarify a few terms. A website is also called a domain or a database. This domain has many hyperlinks in it, each of which lead to a separate page, which is technically called a node. Links can be intranodal; that is linking two lexias or blocks of text on the same node, internodal; that is linking two different nodes on the same domain, or extranodal; that is linking text with a node on a different domain. Text on a single node, although connected to other lexias and nodes through hyperlinks, is itself a fragmented, isolated, and yet complete piece of text. The hypertext on a single node needs to be such that it can be comprehended in and of itself, without needing to follow other hyperlinks. This is because the structure of hypertext is not linear and text on one node does not follow or come after text on any other node.

Hypertext is often compared to Deleuze and Guattari's concept of the rhizome: "It has no clear beginning and no end, it is not linear like a taproot, nor is it a circle where all spokes are attached to one centre." According to Deleuze and Guattari (1988), in their introduction to *A Thousand Plateaus*, the linear mode is a hierarchical mode, a mode followed by capitalism and patriarchy. In a rhizome, however, any point can, and must, freely flow and connect with any other point, as there are no fixed or rigid pathways. This is the principle of connectivity. Flows can happen in any direction. Linearity is like a tree with a taproot, whereas a rhizome is like grass. A rhizome is what bulbs and tubers form under the earth's surface, a mesh of interconnected roots with no clear beginnings or ends. The two things that the rhizome connects must be completely different from each other. This is the principle of heterogeneity, which means the multiple in the one, which is to say that what we consider singular is in fact plural. An orchid and a wasp are mutually interdependent, and thus there is multiplicity even within the one. Deleuze and Guattari see the book not as a unitary thing, but as a machinic assemblage, consisting of many different narratives and many different subjects, digressions, and flows. They see music as a rhizome where different lines at different levels of pitch are flows moving in different directions. A rhizome can move freely in any direction.

If its growth is stopped, it will flow and move in a different direction. This feature is called an asignifying rupture.

A burrow of ants is like an animal rhizome. Our brains, according to Deleuze and Guattari, are like a rhizome; they make associations and connections and flows in any direction. Sexuality is a rhizome, as is desire. History is a rhizome, but the writing of history—like that of linguistics and psychoanalysis—has been linear and unidirectional. Short-term memory, with its lapses, is like a rhizome, whereas long-term memory is like a tree. Neurons are connected, they argue, not through dendrites, but through lapses and ruptures known as synapses between cells. Viruses carry the genes of one host to another and form an animal rhizome; for example, a virus infecting a human may carry the genes of a baboon and a cat. This is aparallel evolution. However, they are in favour of multiplicities and against any kind of monolithic or binary structure. For this reason, they do not make a binary opposition between trees and rhizomes. The roots of a tree can branch out into a rhizome, while a rhizome may also form tree-like structures within itself. Aerial roots and underground stems which break the binaries are the most beautiful and political things, they write, and rhizomes.

This brings to mind Nabina Das's (2013, pp. 93–94) "When Kali Speaks For Us," where the clamouring voices of people are shown to be "a mesh of roots with no origin." This seems to be remarkably similar to a rhizome. The voices of people come not from any one source but democratically from multitudes of people. We may perhaps also say that these voices would flow in many directions like a rhizome, desire leading to desire.

However, Alice van der Klei (2002), in "Repeating the Rhizome," points to the fact that Moulthrop and other theorists of cyberspace tend to read and quote secondary texts on rhizomes, and in fact, do not read Deleuze and Guattari's founding text on the rhizome. Klei argues that Deleuze and Guattari do not link the rhizome to hypertext in the original text and that this is a later extrapolated interpretation by certain theorists. She also writes that Deleuze and Guattari have clearly mentioned the rhizome as being an impossible ideal, which is hard to replicate through images and text.

George Landow (2006, pp. 41, 61–62) earlier associated the rhizome with hypertext as certain theorists tend to do, later corrected himself in *Hypertext 3.0 Critical Theory and New Media in an Era of Globalisation*, wherein he clearly writes that hypertexts should not be confused with rhizomes.

According to these theorists, hypertext is not like a rhizome, because the principle of linearity is not completely obliterated in hypertext. Many webpages and websites form dendritic-tree-like structures, rather than rhizomes, where multiple nodes emerge from one origin. Some other hypertext systems may seem to operate more like rhizomes, but linearity cannot be completely obliterated, as even the html code or the url is linearly produced. Moreover, the pathways that readers construct for themselves while following these hyperlinks tend to be linear, and they do not experience it as a rhizome. Also, the principle of connectivity—that each and every point of the rhizome can be connected to any other point of the rhizome—would also not be true for hypertext. The principle of asignifying rupture, which means that, in case a rhizome's growth is stopped, it automatically restarts and grows in a different direction, would also not hold true for hypertext.

However, it may be tempting to liken hypertext to rhizome in that it does try to thwart linearity to some extent, and helps us make links and connections. Alice van der Klei, whom I quoted earlier, also argues in "Repeating the Rhizome" that hypertext does connect heterogeneous points or texts like the rhizome, in that one particular text may have references to writers and theorists from many different countries and continents. The rhizome can perhaps be seen as the ideal that hypertext aspires towards, but can never fully and practically reach.

I think Tennyson's *In Memoriam* can be seen as a hypertext. Although there is a movement in the text from doubt to faith, one can gain any entry point into the text, and still comprehend each individual poem perfectly. Hypertext works well with repetition with a difference, for example, a pattern of poems on the same theme. Hypertext makes for a writerly text, because it calls for active participation from the reader in terms of clicking on links. A collection of letters, by, let us say, Virginia Woolf, is like a hypertext, because one can flip through the letters randomly, without really reading the whole book chronologically. A poetry book is itself like hypertext. Hypertext fiction, such as that by Michael Joyce, offers several different versions of a story through hyperlinks, different narratives with different perspectives, chronologies, and endings. Thus, there is no story anymore, there are only stories, and the reader must create his or her own story by choosing pathways or links on which to click. This has been likened to videogames where one must choose one's own character or avatar, and often create one's own story.

Even ordinary websites such as Wikipedia comprise hypertext which is embedded with hyperlinks which create a wide variety of pathways. Which link to click on, and where to go, requires the active participation of the reader. As a reader is presumably not going to click on each and every hyperlink, each node must have lexia which is itself complete and comprehensible, although fragmented. Hypertext also enables the reader to write marginalia, which is a creative process of the reader's own responses to the text. Readers may often give their comments in online journals and social media sites. These begin to blur the boundary between writers and readers and writing becomes a collaborative project instead of an individual one. Hypertext through its links makes for a lot of intertextuality. A citation may be quoted in a particular context, but the hyperlink takes us to the entire text of the quoted fragment. This is also why hypertext is decentred. Like a rhizome, it has no centre. This quoted text, when opened in a new page or node, is no longer subordinate to the text within which it was cited but instead stands independently on its own. Thus, there is no hierarchy between the texts.

Hypertext is also multivocal. Like Bakhtin's concept of heteroglossia, hypertext contains within it polyphonous voices and comprises of different narratives. Intertextuality too leads to heteroglossia as an article from a women's magazine may be quoted in an academic paper or in Joyce's novel. Hypertext threatens to turn literature into something completely different as hyperlinks connect text to text to form a vast web consisting of all of human cognition. In this interconnectivity, the role of the individual author will almost be annihilated. No wonder, then, that writers, and literature departments, have not welcomed the concept of hypertext very eagerly, as it would completely transform the concept of the book as we know it now.

Academic texts are hypertexts, as they continually link to a range of different texts via citations and footnotes. However, even academic texts could have been written very differently were they have to be written in hypertext. For example, if my PhD thesis was to be written in hypertext, I could have linked to the full text of each and every poem, instead of merely summarizing it or quoting fragments from it. Footnotes can also be expanded into whole, full-length documents in themselves, if written in hypertext. Often, while writing my thesis, I had a problem with linearity. In a chapter on love poetry, I dealt with touch and water, and a lot of poems dealt with both. It was hard to decide which path to follow. Although I tried to follow both simultaneously, hypertext would have allowed me to make intranodal links to link all the water poems or all the touch poems together. Then, a poem would speak of water/liquid and taste, and it was a bigger dilemma whether to keep the water flow or to rupture the touch flow. A greater problem arose when some of these touch-water poems had to be used for another section on the systolic-diastolic movement in love. As I could not use them for both sections, I ended up not talking about the touch-water elements in these poems. Hypertext would have easily circumvented this problem.

Indian poetry in English has mostly not used hypertext as much as it could have. Online journals have the titles of poems in hyperlinks to take one to the separate nodes of the poems, or the names of poets in hyperlinks which link to the poet's profile or bio. However, Indian poetry in English has so far never even attempted to use hyperlinks in the texts of the poems themselves. Carrying forward the water example, one could have the word "water" in hyperlink in Sharanya Manivannan's poems, which, upon being clicked, would lead to a drop down menu or interface with hyperlinks leading to similar water poems by Priya Sarukkai Chabria, Anindita Sengupta, Uddipana Goswami, and/or Rochelle Potkar. All the water poems could then be interconnected into one whole through this system, and there would be no need for me to collate the water poems together in my thesis. Similarly, all the poems on the body, or on any other theme, could easily be linked through hyperlinks, which would perhaps facilitate the process of poems "talking" to one another.

A poetry book, I think, is somewhat like hypertext. There are no beginnings or endings. One can keep flipping and flitting between the pages and choose the order in which one wants to read. Of course, linear reading is not completely eliminated, because even if one does not read the entire book in linear format, one will still have to read each individual poem in a linear way. Poems can also be associatively connected to other poems and may even talk to each other, within a book or even across books.

Hypertext also leads to a different mode of reading. N. Katherine Hayles (2010, pp. 62–79), in "How We Read," differentiates between close, hyper, and machine reading. Close reading, which garners the most currency within English departments, was introduced by New Critics such as I. A. Richards, W. K. Wimsatt, and John Crowe Ransom. This focus on closely looking at words and their interpretations within different contexts, and the literary devices used within, was a revolution in literary studies, because earlier the focuses had been only upon ideologies, author biographies, literary histories, and the etymology of words, and not on the words themselves at all. However, if close reading is what we do with print texts, then what we do with electronic hypertexts can more appropriately be called "hyperreading." Close reading demands deep attention, whereas hyperreading demands hyperattention. Hyperreading happens when the influx of information is too great, as on the internet, and one must skim through it in order to get the gist and to sort out the most relevant material. Research shows that people read print texts and electronic hypertexts very differently, and this is in fact altering their brains. Hyperreading puts a greater cognitive load on the brain as one keeps going back and forth through multiple tabs, deciding which hyperlink to follow, and thus rupturing the continuous flow of reading, giving perhaps greater importance to audio-visuals—which have a greater primacy on the web—and in between checking email or social media sites. Hayles argues that machines "read" in a certain sense, too, although with limited comprehension, as they are programmed to search for keywords, phrases, and to keep a lookout for patterns. She argues that close and hyper reading are not altogether different, as after scanning the contents, one does have to closely read the relevant passage that one picks out. Similarly, machine reading is better at scanning while hyperreading is better at "getting the gist." Thus, she concludes that each kind of reading has its own merits and demerits, and that instead of discouraging hyperreading, as most literary departments seem to do, the effort should be to enhance hyperreading without forgetting the art of close reading. Poetry is short, and thus is ideally suited to the web-based reading, as compared with longer forms like novels and short stories, as it does not require attention for a long duration, and has indeed proliferated extensively with the advent of the internet. However, poetry cannot be skimmed or scanned. It is necessary to pay close and deep attention to a poem, albeit for a short duration. Reading a poem as hypertext then seems to require close reading, but poetry is also well-suited for the electronic medium, because of its shorter length. However, a poem online cannot be read the way anything else might be read online, that is, through skimming or scanning.

In "Performance Stylistics: Deleuze and Guattari, Poetry, and (Corpus) Linguistics," Kieran O'Halloran (2014, pp. 160–188), using Deleuze and Guattari's work on becomings, multiplicities, and rhizomes, illustrates a different way of reading hypertext poetry. This strategy involves an outward movement of searching the web for certain terms in the poem and then returning to the poem with such extraneous information, and then applying it to the poem. In some cases, this can help enhance the meaning of the poem when one has more knowledge about the terms. For example, O'Halloran may figure out from a poem that the subject may be depressed, and then reads on the web about depression, connecting this information with some other aspect of the poem, such as a seeming lack of interest in sex. Having more in-depth knowledge on the subject may help us make a more informed reading of the poem. He also uses the method of "collocation," which involves seeing the frequency in which groups of words occur together. If one googles the web for common occurrences of terms within phrases, and the sort of words with which they generally form syntagmatic relations, one may be able to deduce whether the usage of the word in the poem is typical or in some way atypical, strange, or unusual. However, usually we do not find such intensive analyses of poetry.

Andrea A. Lunsford and Lisa Ede (2009) in "Among the Audience: On Audience in an Age of New Literacies" put forth the concept of a "discourse community" to describe a blurring of the roles of author and reader. The classical triangle of author, reader, and text no longer holds true, just as Aristotelian emphasis on beginning, middle, and end no longer holds true in the context of hypertext. In the age of Web 2.0 and interactive media, readers become writers and vice versa. Writers and their readers interact through social media. Blogs, Twitter, and Facebook allow every one of us to self-publish, and therefore, everyone becomes a writer. Readers write book reviews on Amazon. There is no longer any dichotomy between writers and readers which brings us to the question if there is an audience at all. There is definitely an audience who is reading what we write on social media, for example, but this audience is available to anyone with an internet connection. The nature of this audience also keeps shifting. Readers add comments and may change the shape or nature of a poem which brings us to the question of collaborative writing. Writing is no longer an individual, solitary act. We are, in a sense, going back to the age of orality where songs, epics, and poems were composed together by communities. Walter J. Ong has called this the age of a "secondary orality." A Wikipedia page can be edited by practically anyone with an internet connection. Google Docs can be edited by a group of participating people. Writing is becoming a collaborative activity. A blog allows one to write poetry (or anything else) on which readers can then comment and give feedback. A blogroll has hyperlinks leading to other blogs which act as recommendations of the blog owner. These may also help form a kind of community. A blog owner can moderate comments in order to filter spam and unwanted comments. Posts on Blogger, My Space, Live Journal, Word Press, and so on also allow one to edit and alter the post at any point of time. Thus, a poem no longer remains a fixed entity but can be endlessly altered, played around, and tinkered with. Twitter which allows one to write only 140 characters has trend for haiku-writing which has gone viral. Tumblr has its own brand of poetry, some of which is strongly feminist, but seems to be more amateurish and un-academic. With the possibility of self-publishing anywhere on social media, there is a lot of bad poetry around as well, and one has to learn to differentiate. There are poets who have risen to Tumblr and Instagram fame where they post regularly.

Digital poetry, Christopher T. Funkhouser (2007) writes, is mainly of three kinds: poetry which is produced digitally through algorithms and permutation-combinations of words, concrete or visual poetry, and hypertext poetry. The digital poetry of the first kind is not found in India at all. Neither is kinetic poetry where words are programmed to move and to zoom in and out and so on. Hypertext, as I mentioned earlier, has been utilized by Indian poetry in English to an extent, but a very limited extent when seen in the context of its vast potential. Concrete poetry is also not seen much. However, Meena Kandasamy's (2010) poem about the Dalit girl and the pot of water has been itself shaped in the form of a pot, and thus is an example of concrete poetry. Visual poetry can also be seen in irregular spacing or placing of lines in many poems (Priya Sarukkai Chabria's, 2008, pp. 49–50). "The Husband, the Wife, and the Robber" has three different columns to show the viewpoints and narratives of all three. Other poems may also have some visual aberrations in the typesetting, orthe layout of the poem on the page in terms of spacing and lines. However, Indian poetry in English has not really exploited the potentialities of the visual medium as much as it could have. Although online journals do sometimes put up illustrations with the poems, these seem to be secondary embellishments and do not deeply intertwine with the poems such as Blake's paintings did with his poems. On the internet, however, visuals play a much greater role than they do on the page. In fact, a dichotomy can no longer be created between text and visual, because text itself is becoming a visual. The text is something to be interpreted, but also something to be seen. Richard A. Lanham (1993, pp. 29–52) argues in "Digital Rhetoric and the Digital Arts" that text becomes something just as much to be looked AT as to be looked THROUGH. The computer offers a wide range of fonts and colours that one can use, and these transform the text itself into something visual. Different fonts and colours create different effects of play, seriousness, and so on. The size of the fonts can also be changed and varied, and this contributes toward the creation of meaning. Ekphrasis, a type of poem written for a painting or a photograph, too shows an intimate relationship between text and visual. We see Nitoo Das writing several poems as ekphrasis, which means that these poems are actually written for visual paintings. Long before the advent of the internet, we can see calligraphy as a process which turns text into art; or the lettering on ancient Greek vases which was meant not only to be read but to appear aesthetically pleasing. In an age where huge billboard advertisements show enlarged text, text seems to have become something to be seen, and not just read.

Audio recordings or videos of poets reading their poems can be found here and there on the internet. These audio and visual dimensions of poems also add to the semiotic aspect as opposed to the symbolic. Charles Bernstein (1998), known for his work collapsing the dichotomies between text and audio, suggest that these audio recordings are extremely important. Bernstein argues that the phonetic letter was meant to transcribe a sound. And, with the advent of the internet, poems could just as well be circulated in the audio form, because poetry is ultimately meant to be heard and recited. Even when one reads the text of a poem, argues Bernstein, one is sub-vocalizing the words in one's head and in a sense, hearing the poem. Poems could be circulated as individual digital files just like music, he argues. Audio versions of poems could be prescribed as course material for students instead of texts, in which case sound itself would become a sort of text. Just like close reading, Bernstein argues for close listening which would involve paying attention to tone and timbre of voice, beat, and isochrony and would entirely change the field of prosody, which is at present limited to metre and rhyme. Bernstein argues for the importance of the disembodied voice, where there is no image of the poet at the podium to distract us, but where complete attention can be given to the voice itself.

However, Christopher Grobe (2012), in "The Breath of the Poem: Confessional Print/Performance circa 1959," criticizes Bernstein's idea of a disembodied voice. Grobe emphasizes the importance of reading out loud, in first-person, autobiographical poetry, and argues for the "body presence" of the poet and the reader. Grobe writes of the importance of reading out loud in confessional poetry, and gives us examples of Sylvia Plath, Anne Sexton, and Robert Lowell, for all of whom it was routine to read their poems out loud, to themselves as well as in public. Grobe sees these figures as important influences in slam poetry, which also uses the first-person mode. He notes that "Beat poet" Allen Ginsberg actively used his body while reciting his poems. Ginsberg and the Beat poetry movement were, of course, a major influence on the birth of slam poetry. According to Grobe, the confessional first-person demands that the body have to be brought in, that one should be able to smell Sylvia Plath's perfume and the vodka on Anne Sexton's breath. Grobe criticizes the trend of poets meekly reading at a drab podium with "clothes that aspire to invisibility." It must be noted that Indian women poets, however, do give a lot of emphasis to the body, and certainly do not try to efface the body or wear clothing that aspires to invisibility. On the contrary, they dress up well for such occasions, in their own unique styles, and at times also bring in elements of performance, especially in the case the performing poet is also involved in music or dance—whether it is Sharanya Manivannan sporting a bright red hibiscus, or Tishani Doshi combining elements of dance and yoga with poetry, or Arundhathi Subramaniam, whose body of a dancer reveals itself in every posture. Others too seem to give attention to the way they present themselves and their poetry.

In this section, I have tried to discuss the open-ended, non-hierarchical, rhizomatic nature of hypertext and hypermedia and the implications it has for Indian poetry in English, although this immense potential has hardly been explored till now. I have also attempted to explore the effects of hypertext and hypermedia in their implications for consuming poetry, that is, reading and listening to poetry. Section one showed the breaking of the author–reader binary, while section two has shown the breakage of the binary between text and audio-visual. Section two has also shown the text as fluid, unfixed, forever in the process of changing and becoming.

## III

This section shows yet another sort of binary being broken—that between human and machine. Just as the previous section showed texts as being in flux, this one shows the fluidity among humans themselves.

Donna Haraway (1985), in *A manifesto for cyborgs: Science, technology, and socialist feminism in the 1980s*, writes that the cyborg is a cybernetic organism—part organism and part machine, living in a post-gender world. For Haraway, we are all cyborgs, because we are constantly using machines such as computers, cameras, cars, and phones to extend and enhance our own faculties. Posthumans and cyborgs can use aeroplanes to fly, something that humans, per se, cannot. Haraway dissolves the binary opposition between man and machines, because, she writes, our machines grow more intelligent and cognitive day by day, whereas we ourselves are frighteningly inert. She also destroys the binary opposition between animals and humans. One of the ways in which she does this is by showing that humans are not the only lifeforms possessing agency. Even when animal activists speak out for animals, we do not accord agency to the animal itself. Haraway observes that animals—like humans—have sex for pleasure, and not merely for reproduction. Thus, they do not work through mere programmed instinct, but have their own level of agency. This is just one of the ways by which Haraway seeks to dissolve the opposition between animal and human, as well as human and machine. She also observes that animals are capable of handling tools and machines, just like humans. The cyborg, then, according to Haraway, is a hybrid creature, a monster who bridges the oppositions between human and animal, human and machine, nature and culture, man and god, and physical and non-physical. This makes Haraway a post-structuralist and a post-modernist. Perhaps, the binary between nature and culture is already broken when we see the body as a product of both, instead of either-or. The binary between man and god is obviously broken in an age where man can form babies in test-tubes, alter sexes, and create intelligent machines which can think, and artificial human beings themselves called robots. The binary between physical and the non-physical breaks when we postulate that human beings are part organism and part machine. Machines are no longer seen necessarily as dead, inert, and lifeless things. This hybrid monster of the cyborg, according to Haraway, has the potential to transform the world through writing, the acquisition of which, she writes, is especially important to those marginalized communities which have remained largely oral communities. This hybrid cyborg for her is a monster which causes upheavals. The cyborg is not innocent. The cyborg does not yearn to return to an Edenic holistic unity. Haraway contrasts the cyborg with the goddess, although she has been critiqued for falling into the trap of binary oppositions herself. The goddess is the innocent woman from the Garden of Eden, close to nature and far away from technology. Haraway writes that she would rather be a cyborg than a goddess. Haraway also attempts to change the discourse of ecofeminism as she links humans with animals and with nature, without however succumbing to the charge of essentialism. Nor does she see nature as a "mother," but instead seeks to build solidarities, affinities, and coalitions between the human and the non-human.

Although Haraway sees us all as cyborgs with revolutionary potential, she is criticized by Radhika Gajjala (2000, pp. 117–137) for not paying enough attention to the reality of third-world women. Haraway mentions third-world women being involved in "homework economies," making microchips for computers. Gajjala critiques Haraway for seeing these women as revolutionary cyborgs and for seeing technology as an unmitigated good. The homework economy is one where women can work from home, have no fixed working hours, and nor any fixed wages. In fact, women are often employed in these places as their labour is cheaper than men's. Gajjala argues that these women are as oppressed as others working in factories, and that being involved in the manufacturing of this technology does not actually give them any access to this technology. Gajjala agrees that greater access to technology for women will empower them, and that such access accords revolutionary potential. However, she argues that this technology cannot be imposed upon third-world women, and that it will not necessarily do them any good to gain access to the internet if it is not on their terms, and if the discourse is dominated by first-world White women. Gajjala and Mamidipudi (1999, pp. 8–16) argue that the advent of technology has eroded traditional practices and has led to the loss of livelihood in many arenas, such as the textile weaving and dyeing industries and therefore cannot necessarily be seen in a positive light. Gajjala writes that a village woman may go to the local entertainment show, and that a television will not necessarily improve her life in any way. She also remarks that technology in the third-world is in bad shape, and that the village may be marked by a lack of access to technology even if it is nominally there. Clearly, the materiality of production of technology outsourced to poor women in third-world countries is a very far cry from the utopian vision of gift communities. Even as we talk about gift communities, we cannot afford to lose sight of the material reality they are rooted within.

The question of embodiment takes on a new significance altogether with respect to the posthuman and the cyborg. N. Katherine Hayles (2008), in *How We Became Posthuman*, tells us about disembodied human consciousness that can be downloaded into a computer. According to Hayles, the early modern project of humanism has now given way to posthumanism. Humanism viewed men as having a unified self. Posthumanism, on the other hand, has increasingly shown that the boundaries of our bodies are fluid and even extend to the machines that we use and into cyberspace. The posthuman cyborg is hybrid and in flux. Hayles argues that we are fractured and not unified subjects, pointing to the postcolonial subject as a case in point. She refers to herself as if she has different computer programs working within her, saying that her "sleep agent" is telling her to sleep, whereas her "hunger agent" is telling her to go to the store. This makes us realize that perhaps we have always been posthumans without unified selves, and that the humanist project was false from its inception. The posthuman has a fluid body with shifting boundaries and no unified self, and reminds us of Deleuze and Guattari's rhizomatic body without organs. The humanist project also eliminated differences and set up the White, upper-class male as the universal subject. This has been severely critiqued by feminists and postcolonialists. Humanism stressed the autonomy and agency of the individual, and also prioritized the mind over the body. Posthumanism does not give complete autonomous agency to the individual who is seen in a matrix of other relations. Posthumanism too idealizes a vision of embodiment as illustrated in the example given earlier of downloading human consciousness into a computer. In this sense, both humanism and posthumanism have a fantasy of disembodiment.

This is precisely what Hayles critiques. Hayles critiques the disembodiment and lack of agency seen as a part of posthumanism. She cites the immaterial nature of information, arguing that information needs a material body through which it can be conveyed. She argues, unlike a lot of posthuman theorists, that consciousness can never be enclosed in a machine the way it can be in a human body which has evolved over centuries. It is naïve, she writes, to think that the machine can replace the centuries of historicity and evolution which have gone into adapting the human body to its changing environments and circumstances. She also critiques posthumanists for forgetting material reality and moving completely into an abstract and mathematical realm, as reality does not work like that. Hayles writes that these technologies were born at certain points of time, in certain conditions, and are therefore rooted in those conditions. The contexts of militarism, capitalism, and state-socialism within which such technologies appeared cannot be discounted. She also writes that works of science fiction, which postulate a posthuman future, may be better able to envision embodiment, as literary works are more embedded in a material narrative than abstract theory. Hayles believes neither in technological determinism nor in social constructionism. She believes that technology and social forces mutually shape and in turn are shaped by each other. As seen earlier in this chapter, William Gibson's envisioning of cyberspace played a key role in the development of the internet, as did the visions of Ted Nelson, Vannevar Bush, and Deleuze and Guattari in the development of hypertext. The chapter also showed how hypertext in turn has changed the way in which we read and perceive literature. Thus, society and technology are mutually shaping and shaped by one another. Hayles argues that narrative is a more embodied form of discourse than analytically driven systems theory and by turning technologically determined bodiless information into narratives which arose in specific contexts between specific people, she hopes to restore materiality. Abstract theory can never fit itself into real people's lives and communication patterns the way narratives can. Thus, the abstract and the material are enmeshed within each other. Hayles writes that the posthuman vision can engender fear if we think of humans being wiped off and replaced by machines. However, she writes that one may take a less radical vision of machines taking over unwanted tasks and thus enabling humans to live better lives. Thus, the posthuman vision is not something necessarily to be feared.

Donna Haraway too—coming from a biological-feminist standpoint—insists on materiality. Haraway argues that machines extend the faculties of our bodies and help us see, hear, reach, and speak beyond the physical limits of the body; thus, they can be considered extensions of bodies themselves. This is how we become part human and part machine. Thus, both Hayles and Haraway try to put back the materiality of the body within posthumanist discourse. Whether we have synthetic limbs and artificial pacemakers or not, all of us are cyborgs and posthumans because of our continuous entanglement with machines and technology. And yet, we must not once again fall into the humanist trap of disowning our bodies.

There is an opinion that as we can construct our own identities online, our race, gender, caste, and sexuality no longer matter. However, people still find out these identity markers via speech patterns and direct the same discrimination towards them as they would in "real life." People are still curious about identity markers and even if a white man plays the role of a black one, he will be subject to ridicule. Thus, we do not choose from a mix of equal identities but between identities overlaid by various degrees of power and oppression. Also, the idea of disembodiment as leading to equality does not appeal to me. The challenge is to accept all our various bodies, instead of seeking to do away with the body itself, which in a sense is a rejection of all bodies. However, embodiment is vital and the mind and the body are not separate as discussed in Chapter 1. Hubert L. Dreyfus (2013), in *On the Internet*, shows us the primacy of embodiment, and argues that virtual communities and remote-learning virtual classrooms can never take the place of real ones. Dreyfus writes that a virtual community can never achieve the mood or atmosphere, so integral to a real poetry reading or event, and that there is no "immersion" with all the senses of the body. He also writes that in a virtual environment, one can never see the spontaneous reactions of the audience or the students, and that impromptu questions can never be asked nor answered. A virtual poetry reading is a one-way event, not a two-way interaction, and can never afford us sensory immersion within the poetry itself.

The issue of embodiment is an important one with respect to women's communities and self-representation on the internet. Certain cyber-feminists are of the view that disembodiment on the internet leads to freedom, as women can play around with their identities. Ann Travers (2003) contradicts them arguing that disembodiment has been a project of the Enlightenment and has always served patriarchal interests. She notes that it was the white male who has disembodied mind, whereas women, children, the aged, slaves, and people of colour were always associated with the body and could not afford to ignore it. Travers observes that the choice of putting on an identity does not happen in a neutral, vacuum space but is enmeshed with networks of power. She cites examples of women who have embraced the disembodiment of the internet as freedom, but also women who have sought a reaffirmation of their identity in cyberspace through identitarian support groups. She concludes by saying that feminists should put up a strong resistance towards the vision of cyberspace as a disembodied domain. Claiming equality by disowning the body once again falls into the trap of patriarchy. Jessie Daniels (2009) in "Rethinking Cyberfeminism(s): Race, Gender, and Embodiment" writes that it is only in theory that people switch identities and create alternate ones in cyberspace. Surveys show, she writes, that in actuality, people go online more often to affirm their identity than to escape from it. Daniels gives us the example of anorexic girls and transpeople who go online to support groups in order to reaffirm their identity than to escape it. There are similar communities and support groups for people of all ethnicities where they can find solidarity and even form resistance to desist disembodiment.

The cyborg figure that we are all turning into is perhaps not seen anywhere better than in Nitoo Das's (2017) title poem of her collection, *Cyborg Proverbs*. Das breaks all oppositions between plants, animals, humans, and machines. In "Cyborg Proverbs," she writes that we were always meant to fly like Icarus. This creates the sense of the immense possibility that we as human beings have, in the literal sense of flying with aeroplanes and also metaphorically. She writes that a wire rose smells just as sweet as a real one. While the idea may seem laughable, one must acknowledge the truth of this in today's world. She writes that the woodpecker was never dumb, thus breaking preconceptions about birds and binary oppositions between animals and humans. Perhaps the climax comes when Das writes that the ghost in the machine is a living tree. This makes it seem as if machines have a life of their own. Towards the end of the poem, she writes about the photocopy: "all dreams depend on it." This is certainly true in Walter Benjamin's "Age of Mechanical Reproduction." Das shows how much our world today is dependent upon replication, and this process can only be carried out by machines. She ends the poem with "These eyes are mine. / They will / also be yours." These lines are very apt to begin a poetry collection with, as the reader sees through the poet's lens or worldview while reading. However, this is also literally true in today's world when transplantation of eyes is just another photocopy, just another replication. Proverbs are epigrams, age-old, and tested truths that cannot be questioned. Das seems to suggest that we need new proverbs to describe our lives today and that the old ones are no longer enough.

Poets such as Aditi Machado and Sumana Roy seem to abide by Haraway's linking of humans to animals and machines, and even stretch it to plants. Machado (2017), in *Some Beheadings*, writes of herself as if she were a tree, her own system as botany. She is a root which grows into a trunk, which grows into a branch and gives out stems. She has stamens within her, which bear pollen (p. 80). In fact, she is terrified to be a human. One of the terrors of the bed, she writes, is to wake up to find oneself a man (p. 82). She also sees movement as an animal or a plant with a whip behind it (p. 53). Time, too, is a whip which makes everything move. Thus, all forms of life are linked and connected in movement. In "Letters, Minor," Machado asks "What is an animal/but a human of no consequence to itself." This again shows the inherent similarity between human and non-human life forms. She quotes from Lewis Carroll: "the proper definition of 'man' is 'an animal that writes letters.'" In "A girl is running," Machado shows us the oceans that lie within the girl as she sleeps; her rhythmic breathing resembles oceanic tides.

Sumana Roy, in "How to Draw a Tree," sees the tree as a person. In "I Want to Be a Tree" (30 October 2017), she shows us a tree's sexuality as she imagines birds to be wooing trees. She shows the natural sleeping human body to be branched like a tree. In "Trees and Air," she shows air to be the lover of a tree (11–12). In "Tree Sap" (30 October 2017), she compares babies' drool with the sap of young plants, which oozes from everywhere. As saplings mature into trees, they become dry and restrained, like using hankies. In "Root Vegetables" (August 2016), she compares leaves inside the earth, which cannot move, with the dead. Besides linking humans with trees, Roy also seems to link them with god and with machines, which may seem strangely akin to Haraway. In "God is a Vegetable," she begins by writing everything we imagine God to be: calmness, stillness, nourishment, silence, one-way communication, and lack of rabble. She ends by asking why it is difficult to find god within ginger or peppercorn. In "How to Karaoke Like a Tree," she writes about the totalitarianism of technology and compares the silence of trees and vegetables to silence inside a mike, stretching like a rubber bind. Ironically, she calls this silence "loud," and equally ironically, she chooses to find silence and stillness within a mike.

This chapter has shown the discourses of poetry as operating within certain "discourse communities," which seem akin to the concept of a gift economy in that they are not self-seeking and interested in monetary rewards, but which largely sustain themselves as friendly, co-operative societies, working for and towards a greater cause with passion. I have then explored how the internet, which is a vital component of this discourse community and gift economy, has changed poetry production, and consumption. In this context, I have tried to discuss hypertext and hypermedia's audio-visual elements and the implications they have for Indian poetry in English. I have briefly explored how the internet changes modes of reading as well. I end the chapter by attempting to see how the internet is turning us into cyborgs and posthumans, crossing boundaries between animal, human, and machine. Thus, the internet, in a lot of ways, has been responsible for creating connections between things that seem to be disparate or even opposites, thus breaking down binaries in the process. It has also contributed to fluidity and a state of flux.

## References

D. Bell. (2001) *An Introduction to Cybercultures*, London and New York: Routledge.

D. Bell, and B.M. Kennedy eds. (2000) *The Cybercultures Reader*. New York: Psychology Press, p. 105.

C. Bernstein. Ed. (1998) *Close Listening: Poetry and the Performed Word*. Oxford University Press.

P.S. Chabria. (2008) 'The Husband, the Wife and the Robber', In *Not Springtime Yet*, Noida: Harper Collins, 49–50.

J. Daniels. (2009) 'Rethinking Cyberfeminism (s): Race, Gender, and Embodiment.' *Women's Studies Quarterly* 37.1 and 2 (online) Available at http://muse.jhu.edu/article/266600/pdf. (Accessed 10th Oct 2018).

N. Das (2013) 'When Kali Speaks for Us', In *Into the Migrant City*, Kolkata: Writers Workshop, 93–94.

N. Das (2017) 'Cyborg Proverbs', In *Cyborg Proverbs*, Mumbai: Poetrywala, p. 1.

G. Deleuze, and F. Guattari (1988) 'Introduction', *A thousand plateaus: Capitalism and schizophrenia*. London: Bloomsbury Publishing.

H.L. Dreyfus. (2013) *On the Internet*, New York: Routledge.

C.T. Funkhouser, and S. Baldwin. (2007) *Prehistoric digital poetry: An archaeology of forms, 1959–1995*. Alabama: The University of Alabama Press.

R. Gajjala. (2000) 'Internet Constructs of Identity and Ignorance: "Third-World" Contexts and Cyberfeminism.' *Works and Days* 33.17&18, pp. 117–137.

R. Gajjala, and A. Mamidipudi. (1999) 'Cyberfeminism, Technology, and International Development.' *Gender & Development* 7.2, pp. 8–16.

C. Grobe. (2012) 'The Breath of the Poem: Confessional Print/Performance circa 1959'. *PMLA* 127.2 (online) Available at <www.jstor.org/stable/41616812>. (Accessed 10th Oct 2018).

D. J. Haraway (1985) *A manifesto for cyborgs: Science, technology, and socialist feminism in the 1980s*. San Francisco, CA: Center for Social Research and Education.

N.K. Hayles. (2008) *How We Became Posthuman: Virtual Bodies in Cybernetics, Literature, and Informatics*. Chicago, IL: University of Chicago Press.

N.K. Hayles. (2010) 'How We Read: Close, Hyper, Machine.' *Ade Bulletin* 150.18, pp. 62–79.

M. Kandasamy. (2010) *ONE-Eyed' In Ms Militancy*. Delhi: Navayana.

A. Klei. (2002) 'Repeating the Rhizome.' *SubStance* 31.1, pp. 48–55. Available at <www.jstor.org/stable/3685805.

G. Landow. (1992) *Hypertext: The convergence of contemporary critical theory and technology*. Hoboken, NJ: John Hopkins University Press.

G. Landow. (2006) *Hypertext3.0 critical theory and new media in an era of globalisation*. Hoboken, NJ: John Hopkins University Press, pp. 41, 61–62.

R.A. Lanham. (1993) 'Digital Rhetoric and the Digital Arts,' In *The Electronic Word: Democracy, Technology, and the Arts*. London: University of Chicago Press, pp. 29–52.

A.A. Lunsford, and L. Ede. (2009) 'Among the Audience: On Audience in an Age of New Literacies.' In M.E. Weiser, B.M. Fehler, and A.M. Gonzalez, Eds, *Engaging audience: Writing in an age of new literacies*, Urbana IL: NCTE.

A. Machado. (2017) *Some Beheadings*. Brooklyn, NY: Nightboat Books.

A. Machado. *Letters, minor*.(online) www.thediagram.com/14_6/machado.html. (Accessed 29th September 2018).

A. Machado. *A girl is running*. www.bettermagazine.org/003/aditimachado.html. (Accessed 29th September 2018).

K. O'Halloran. (2014) 'Performance stylistics: Deleuze and guattari, poetry, and (corpus) linguistics.' In D.L. Hoover., K. O'Halloran, and J. Culpeper, Eds, *Digital Literary Studies: Corpus Approaches to Poetry, Prose and Drama*. London: Routledge, pp. 160–188.

H. Rheingold. (2000) *The virtual community: Homesteading on the electronic frontier*. Cambridge, MA: MIT press.

H. Rheingold. (2008) 'Using participatory media and public voice to encourage civic engagement.' In *Civic life online: Learning how digital media can engage youth*, pp. 97–118.

K. Robins. (2000) 'Cyberspace and the world we Live in', In D. Bell, and B.M. Kennedy, Eds. *The cybercultures reader*. London: Psychology Press, p. 91.

S. Roy. 'God is a vegetable'. *Domus*. (online) Available at <www.pressreader.com/india/domus/20170912/283012579918667>. (Accessed 10th Oct 2018).

S. Roy. 'How to karaoke like a tree'. *Domus*. (online) Available at <www.pressreader.com/india/domus/20170912/283012579918667>;. (Accessed 10th Oct 2018).

S. Roy. (2017) 'I want to be a tree'. *The Clearing*, 30th October <www.littletoller.co.uk/the-clearing/poetry/new-poems-sumana-roy/>. (Accessed 10th October 2018).

S. Roy. '(2016) Root Vegetables'. *Berfrois*, August. www.berfrois.com/2016/08/root-vegetables-sumana-roy/. (Accessed 10th October 2018).

S. Roy. 'Trees and air'. *Domus*. (online) <www.pressreader.com/india/domus/20170912/283012579918667>. (Accessed 10th October 2018).

S. Roy. (2017) 'Tree sap'. *The Clearing*, 30th October <www.littletoller.co.uk/the-clearing/poetry/new-poems-sumana-roy/>. (Accessed 10th October 2018).

F. Tönnies. (1957) *Community and Association*. New York: Harper & Row.

A. Travers. (2003) 'Parallel subaltern feminist counterpublics in cyberspace.' *Sociological Perspectives* 46.2. (online) <www.jstor.org/stable/10.1525/sop.2003.46.2.223>. 223–237. (Accessed 10th Oct 2018).

D. Weinbren. (2006) 'The Good Samaritan, friendly societies and the gift economy.' *Social History* 31.3, 319–336.

# 11

# PUTTING THE LOCAL IN THE GLOBAL—INDIAN GRAPHIC NOVELS

## The New Vogue of Indian Writing in English

*Aibhi Biswas*

Suman Gupta says in the article titled "Indian Commercial Fiction in English, The Publishing Industry and Youth Culture" (2012) that Indian literature in English has been successful since 1988. Its success was followed by a diversification of genres and forms. Gupta makes a distinction between Indian literary fiction and Indian commercial fiction, which does not have a respectable face to show abroad. Indian commercial fiction in the English language, which is often a sort of domestic pulp fiction created by Indian writers, is published by India-based publishing houses and before consumption by an Indian readership. Indian publishers take pride in publishing Indian fiction in English, unlike in other countries. Indian literary fiction has more international visibility and is circulated in Anglo-American markets, grabbing critical attention and cultural value. Nowadays, commercial fiction is written in non-academic diction and has both Indian literary and pop-culture, "catchy"-type characters, appearing as fresh and cutting edge. Its popularity with the middle- or higher-class English educated youth gives them power in India's global affluence and local/national identity-making. Since the 2010s, the changes in economic and political policies of India have led to the slackening of market rules and regulations, aiding the boom in India's publishing market with the establishment of many independent domestic publishing houses and the entry of international publishing corporations such as Harper Collins, Penguin, Hachette, and Routledge. The Indian graphic novel's rise, and the revival of the Indian comics, are situated in this nexus.

These changes led to shifts in the socio-cultural environment, which affected Indian commercial fiction writing written in English.

> Many Indian authors—especially younger ones—will tell you that they experience a certain pressure, strengthened by internationally active publishers, to act as cultural ambassadors. . . . But a younger generation of authors

DOI: 10.4324/9781003354246-15

> now appears to have emerged in the English-language literary sector whose common development manifests a kind of caesura. All are between 25 and 35 years [of age]. . . . All came of age in an India where access to the wider world was available via mouse click, and all feel at home within the most divergent cultures—and they play with this intercultural network in their literary work as well. At the same time, nonetheless, they are rooted in India to an astonishing degree, and they write about this sense of connection in new and innovative—and at times surprising—ways. A marked turn toward localism is observable, leaning toward the microcosmos of one's own lived world, to the history of the individual towns where these authors lead their lives.
>
> *(Claudia Kramatschek qtd in Gupta 2012, p. 48)*

Indian graphic novels are primarily written in English, presumably because English has both national and international visibility and accessibility. International interest in India, as a brand, is increasing every day. The international publishing industry, too, has shown its interest by including Indian fiction written in the English language in festivals, book fairs, and exhibitions, and in nominations for prestigious awards such as The International Young Publishing Entrepreneurs Award, which was awarded to S. Anand's publishing house Navayana in 2007. The Navayana publishing house brought to us excellent Indian graphic novels, like Bhimayana: Experiences of Untouchability (2011) by Srividya Natarajan and S. Anand, and art by Durgabai and Subhash Vyam, *A Gardener in The Wasteland: Jotiba Phule's Fight for Liberty* (2011) by Srividya Natarajan, art by Aparajita Ninan, which got received international acclaim. Indian English-language publications, which include Indian graphic novels, have a great international scope. Many popular Indian graphic novels and Indian comic books are created with the help of grants/fellowships from foreign institutions and governments—for example, *Bhimayana, Corridor* and *Priya's Mirror*, and *Priya and the Lost Girls*. These were created for local circulation and consumption, albeit in an international language.

> Graphic narratives represent the relationship between language, national signifiers, and the image that accords understanding at a more universal level. The global memory serves in this tension between the local and the global and the structure of the graphic novels . . . lends itself to the exploration of memory as its already concerned with the production of chronological order.
>
> *(Joanne Pettitt qtd. In Nayar 2019, pp. 146–147)*

The graphic novel *A Gardener in The Wasteland* provides an excellent example of how Indian graphic novels connect local and global histories and memories, removing aspects of distancing and othering; a collective common history or memory emerges, which transgresses the boundaries of time and space. Few instances rather double-page spreads of *A Gardener in the Wasteland* prove this point. The first such instance is on pages 18 and 19 of *A Gardener in the Wasteland*, where Jotiba Phule is reading out Thomas Paine's book *Rights of Man*. We see Paine emerge from the book like a hologram, reciting lines from his own book. Phule, the character, draws a parallel between Hindu Brahmin practices and the king's deposition during French Revolution; he agrees with the ideals of the French Revolution, which broadly proclaim, "the rights of man are liberty, property, security, and resistance to oppression" (Thomas Paine qtd. In Natarajan and Ninan 2011, pp. 18–19). The ideals come alive and connect to the oppressive state of the Untouchables in India. The essence of the French Revolution is thus embodied in the pages of an Indian graphic novel. The French Revolution and its ideals find relevance and are evoked into the life of Jotiba Phule, who envisions revolutionary application in the subcontinent to build a better future. On pages 20 and 21 of the graphic novel, we see that a line of revolutionaries/thinkers is shown. This line seems to be heading towards a fortress—maybe the Bastille—where, at the very end of the line, is the Phule couple. The line comprises of Karl Marx, Guru Nanak, Buddha, Nelson Mandela, Fidel Castro, Martin Luther King, Ambedkar, etc. However, they are not standing chronologically, in order of their lives and deaths; inscribed above them is the slogan of the French Revolution: "liberty, equality and fraternity" are inscribed. The scene is an enactment of the motives, ideals, and histories these personalities share. Academician Pramod K. Nayar suggests that the dialectics of global and local memory are at play here, resulting in the creation of a global landscape without any historical specificity. The line of revolutionaries conveys the fact that traditional boundaries of chronology, linearity, and national history are not rigid, and that historical discourse is progressive in nature. Slavery, casteism, capitalism, patriarchy, and the exploitative nature of totalitarian regimes resemble one another in terms of their attitude(s) towards humanity. In Nayar's article, "Graphic Memory, Collective Histories, and Dalit Trauma: A Gardener in the Wasteland," Debarti Sanyal says that, when we are shown the global-memory landscape, we can recognize the various disguises and forms such exploitative systems may take. Another instance, found on the left-hand side of pages 24 and 25 of the graphic novel, shows a depiction of molten iron being poured into the ears of a Dalit. His crime—listening to the Vedas—were recited. Meanwhile, another Dalit's tongue is being cut off for uttering a word from the Vedas. On the right, we see a depiction of Black people being lynched in America; several bodies are hanging from a tree in the foreground, while, on the side, we see a group of Ku Klux Klan. Further to the side, we see—intriguingly—a Brahman offering fruit to a Klansman, all while a person, presumably a Dalit, witnesses this exchange with a horrified expression. The creators use the spatial rhetoric of the graphic novel to connect two different places and two different regimes of oppression in the same diegetic space. The Brahmin feeding the KKK member indicates that these histories share aspects of the same experiences, oppressions, and exploited peoples' aspirations of being free. Casteism and slavery may be different, but the traumatic memories of oppression bring them together, evoking empathy for each other. Debarati Sanyal says that the effect is the creation of an alternative ethnocultural grounding for collective memory or memories. Graphic novels, then, can bring together cultural and collective memories from people across the world—people who have shared experiences of the structuring of unequal societies, oppressive regimes, and memories of violence. They can relate and recognize the commonalities between them, creating a shared geopolitical space and evoking a global contemporary awareness, all without reducing them into regional identities.

*Priya's Shakti*, the first entry in a trilogy of a comic-book-like graphic novels by documentary filmmakers Ram Devinei and Vikas K. Menon, featuring art by Dan Goldman, explores the issue of gender-based violence. *Priya's Shakti* tells the story of how Priya, a rape survivor, gains the blessings of the goddess Parvati. She gains self-confidence and encourages women to both fight against injustices and live their lives with confidence. The three-part series contains *Priya's Shakti, Priya's Mirror*, and *Priya and The Lost Girls*. The last two speak of the issue of acid attacks on women, and human trafficking—especially that of young girls—respectively. *Priya's Shakti* was an outcome of the strong emotions that the creator felt after seeing protests in response to the 2012, Delhi gang rape. At the time, many government authorities and law enforcement officials were blaming the victim for her assault. Ram Devineni conducted extensive research on this topic of sexual violence, interviewing many rape survivors. He found out that the burden of shame and impurity placed on women, by their families and friends, makes life extremely hard for them. They are constantly under threat, and always discouraged from seeking justice by the authorities. Conversely, the perpetrators often live free, happy lives. Devineni realized that the deep-seated patriarchy in society is the cause of these attitudes; women do not need to change, society does. *Priya's Shakti* is a multimedia project that uses the "Blippar" app to engage its readers with augmented reality technology. The digital incorporation of digital features within the graphic novel results in an enhanced reading experience. *Priya's Shakti* was available online; the partner app was also free. When certain pages of the comic book are scanned with the app, short interviews, animations, and pop-ups, frequently appear, giving more information to the readers. The project has won international acclaim and popularity and has been represented in festivals held in China, the United States, and Italy. It had 500,000+ downloads globally. UN Woman honoured it with the Gender Equality Champion label. It resonated with people all over the world who want to speak out against gender-based violence. The first book managed to gain so much international attention that the World Bank-funded *Priya's Shakti's* developers to create a graphic novel dealing with acid attack victims, to be put under the Wevolve project banner; this resulted in Priya's Mirror in 2014. This entry was also successful in connecting women across the world. It features acid attack survivors from across the world, in places such as New York, Bogota, and New Delhi. It tries to educate youth that gender-based violence and harassment are deeply rooted social issues, reinforced by patriarchy, but that collective effort can change society.

The contemporary Indian graphic novel straddles the line between the literary and the pulp genre, between the local and the global; hence, the English used in them has also changed. Literary diction is no longer used; rather, the English used is Indianized, without exotification. Indian words, idioms, regional enunciations, etc. are used without any connotations, expecting the readers of the work to already know them. This distinct use of English creates a sense of familiarization for the readers making these works successful. For example, the graphic novelist can use onomatopoeia words in Hindi to characterize a situation or character such as dhapp, chapak, and tring. Once the reader reads, and maybe re-reads, the graphic novel, he can relate the words to the object or person, thereby creating an implicit understanding. Though meant for an Indian audience, it has potential for the international. The visual narration presents international readers with easily consumable pictures of Indianness—rather than heavy exoticism—without being too explanatory. This creates a sense of defamiliarization from Indianness, as it simultaneously shows India as a modern nation with westernized education and its own kind of native English. English, after all, is a language which is pan-Indian. "The homogenisation of India under one banner of Indianness, foregoing the regional specificities and languages and its othering from other nations under the gaze of post coloniality has rendered India as a brand globally and within India" (Graham Huggans qtd. in Gupta 2012, p. 48). A survey by ACSDS-KAS in 2009, authored by Peter Ronald de Souza *et al.*, shows that 33% of the population comprises literate youth (13–35 years), of whom 25% read books for leisure, relaxation, knowledge, and of whom 42% prefer to read in English. Only 37% of youth have access to the internet, of which only 4% use the internet to read books online, says a 2010 survey by Rajesh Shukla (NBT-NCAER). Youth who have good proficiency in English is often bilingual, insofar as they speak their regional language/mother-tongue, English in school and college—if, of course, their education was in English medium and may use English in their personal space and time, too. They have internalized English and may even ridicule westernized versions of it. Although English is domesticated, they are aware of the global standard and the political and social implications linked to them. Hence, Indian graphic novels—though they appear satirical, funny, and light—may contain complex structures of critique and subversion, reflecting the attitudes of contemporary Indian youth. These contain discourses of domestic hierarchies, sexual violence, class structures, casteism, gender inequalities, and reflects the perspective of contemporary Indian youth.

Post-liberalization, India has become more domestic-economy-minded, focused on consumption of and by domestic markets, investment in domestic entrepreneurship, and innovation techniques. Liberalization led to the opening of Indian markets and slacking of restrictions. Shifts and innovations in Indian fiction in English gained the attention of foreign publishers. The establishment of multinational publishing houses in India, such as Hachette India, Penguin India, Harper Collins India, and Routledge India led to a greater availability of books at cheaper prices. Various literature festivals are held in India. The first Indian literature festival, the Jaipur Literature Festival, transformed Indian writing into a cultural commodity. Since 2006, the number of literature festivals held annually in India has increased to 90. These festivals impacted the formation of a South Asian literary canon; Indian graphic novels have become an important part of this. The increased technological advancement including the advent of the internet has made connectivity faster, smoother, and more efficient, between authors, readers, publishers, and literary agents. Such enhanced connectivity facilitated the establishment of domestic and small-scale publishing houses, geared towards publishing graphic narratives. Examples of these sorts of domestic and small-scale publishing houses include Poa Collective, Zubaan Books, Tara Books, Rupa Books, Blaft, Manta Ray Publishing, Phantomville, and Liquid Comics.

The graphic novel is an alternative hybrid form of storytelling which combines art and writing. It has become a popular cultural medium associated with cognitive development, language learning, and knowledge acquisition. Contemporary graphic novels have internalized the western influences on them, using such influences to reinvent traditional stories and art forms. They also integrate contemporary Indian influences from popular culture and religious mythology, creating a unique, and original, Indian cultural product. They retain their ethnic identity while fitting into the global socio-economic picture. They are used for educational and socio-cultural awareness, and are appreciated for their art and, details of tradition, culture, and history. They are further, contemporarily relevant, and do not blindly imitate the art of Western comic books, nor their form and, at times, vulgar and violent depictions. Penguin India has published a graphic novel series of Satyajit Ray's *Feluda* stories. Campfire India has also brought out graphic books based on Puffin classics, available for global readership; they have specifically targeted the NRI readership, who want to reconnect to their Indian cultural roots. Campfire's graphic novels target the new generation of readers, offering genres like biography, mythology, classics, and original graphic novels to a global audience. Dipavali Debroy (2011) notes that Indian graphic novels have great potential and profitability in the globalized future. V. K Karthika, editor of Penguin India, recognized this potential and risked publishing *Corridor* (2004) by Sarnath Banerjee, before graphic novels were known to the Indian publishing scene. A decade later every publishing house wants to publish a graphic novel in India, especially if they innovatively use Indian art styles like *Bhimayana*. There is a demand for great stories which can cut across national and international boundaries. Technological evolution has made it possible to access these stories globally, and the graphic novel format makes it easier to understand and relate to them. Indian graphic novels have become crossed the lines between East and the West, without othering alternate kinds of literature or defamiliarizing from its origins. They have also succeeded in deriving their own Indian identity within a globalized world, making Indian graphic novels a success in the world book market. Graphic novels can help learn a classical or regional language text. The visual narration makes comprehension easy, and facilitates longer memory retention. They initiate alternative discussions and thinking processes. The language style is compact, using everyday language and situations, embodying personal beliefs and communities' ways of life. Indian graphic novels can also help in developing vocabulary and promoting traditional Indian values and morals. Readers seem to retain, and reapply, the vocabulary and facts, and even the morals or life lessons that they encountered in graphic novels. These lessons are presented in a relatable and relevant way, linked to contemporary urban society. Unforgettable characters, their behaviours, conversations, perspectives, and ways of life resonates with the readers. Prominent Indian graphic novel characters embodying such characteristics include Jehangir Rangonwalla and Digital Dutta from *Corridor*; V.P. in *Delhi Calm*; *Kari*'s Kari; and Malgu Gayan in *River of Stories*.

Pramod K. Nayar observes that India's graphic novels have, from their inception, represented contemporary Indian society and its serious socio-cultural and often political issues, which were mostly ignored by the mainstream media. *River of Stories* (1994) by Orijit Sen was the first prototype of the Indian graphic novel form. The work, a 64-page-long graphic novel with black and white, sketch-like illustrations, tells the story surrounding an environmental protest happening in the Narmada Valley. It discusses the consequences of development faced by Adivasis during the construction of the Sardar Sarovar Dam. The story asks: what does development mean, and does it even benefit marginal people like displaced Adivasis? It raises further questions about the harm done to the environment, and the impacts on tribal peoples' cultures and lifestyles. Though the plot is about a specific community in a specific region, seeks to connect displaced peoples all around the world, relating to environmental protestors and making readers aware of the environmental damages sometimes inherent to so-called developmental projects carried out by governments. The protest described within the book itself was international, as seen in the book's depiction of a Japanese protestor at the Narmada Bachao Andolan. *A Gardener in the Wasteland*, by Srividya Natrajan and Aparajita Ninan, is a graphic novel which depicts the sufferings and injustices inflicted by the dominant community of the society, that is, the Brahmans of India, on the oppressed social community—the Untouchables. It connects their traumatic memories and injustices to other communities who also faced communal violence and injustices, across both time and space. The graphic novelists have linked Dalit sufferings to acts of racial injustices and violence, as well as the oppressions faced during the French Revolution, etc. Indian graphic novels are able to construct alternative historical narratives, "thereby contributing to the global graphic novel movement of the 21st century" (Basu 2017, p. 27). *Bhimayana*, a graphic novel on Dr. B. R Ambedkar, introduces its readers to the larger social history of segregation based on caste, still prevalent in India. It shows recent news reports of caste-based violence, killings, and injustices. It also shows that casteism exists in India and tries to gain global empathy and support for these victims. *Bhimayana* sold 10,000 copies in English in India, and many more globally. With this book, the publisher wants to mobilize global support for oppressed Dalits in India. Pramod K. Nayar points out that such narratives can spread certain Indian social imageries that can be understood by anyone, thereby spreading alternative readings of Indian history, cultural practices, government systems, lifestyle, and their respective shortcomings. References in Indian graphic novels come from deep-rooted traditional and cultural practices, the varied histories of the subcontinent, and global histories, memories, cultural influences, and mass media, making these narratives complex and multilayered, situating themselves within larger global processes yet retaining distinct socio-cultural identities.

Another "glocal" (global and local) feature of Indian graphic novels is that they deal with socio-political issues that exist in the public domain while simultaneously affecting the personal domain. When this happens, a constant, fluid interaction between the two domains occurs. On the level of the macrocosm, this can also be seen in terms of the association of personal and national histories, memories, and feelings; on a further level, the connecting of national and international histories, memories, and feelings. The individual sufferings related to national, and socio-cultural crisis, finds a new dimension within the contemporary world via multilayered, often nonlinear narratives, which attract and appeal to people from a range of disciplines and fields. Sometimes they garner reactions from people who are working in that certain fields, such as social workers and legislators. These works are expanding globally, expanding past their niche section of readers, and gaining a general audience, thereby creating a space for human connection. *Delhi Calm* (2010) by Vishwajyoti Ghosh is an excellent example of this. The graphic novel depicts the political, turbulent times of the 1975–1977, when the Indian government, under the leadership of Prime Minister Indira Gandhi, declared a national emergency for 21 months. A lot of rules and regulations were imposed, and the civil rights of citizens were suspended; the government had control over everything. The greater implications of the event were emergency directly affected the general public, who worried about their livelihoods and socio-cultural lifestyles. V.P., the protagonist, worries about his monthly salary not coming rather than the emergency imposed. This event can be relatable to any person who has experienced totalitarian government or experienced any government-imposed lockdown. Thereby *Delhi Calm*, therefore, presents an interesting, relevant, and critical work, a glocal social commentary depicted through a mix of fact and fiction. The year 2020's pandemic lockdowns around the globe can be construed as a somewhat mellower version of a similar experience.

Indian graphic novels involve the representation of histories, socio-cultural spaces—especially urban spaces—and cultural stances on social issues such as gender biases, sexual exploitation, social discrimination, and labour exploitation. The dialectic relationship between the visual and the textual is a key point in the critical discussion that a graphic novel initiates, converting the visual literacy present into critical literacy. It gives a critical cultural and literary value to the work. Value, here, is measured based on the relevance, significance, and the relatability that the narration and characters hold for its readers on a global platform. The form is self-analytical and reinvents itself through self-examination and global exploration. The themes it explores are glocal, such as disaster, disease, deprivation, discrimination, and displacement, on which global campaigns can be initiated.

Indian graphic novels are not published according to the Western corporate-conveyor-belt system of production, wherein one comic book is the work of a team of workers, already including colourists, inkers, pencilers, artists, and story writers. It is an individualized and intimate product, which embodies the personal opinions, feelings, and socio-cultural influences the author-artist had experienced in his or her own lived experiences and conceptualizations of economics and politics. The creation is an imaginary, lively, yet critical and complex, a combination of modern narratives and experimental storytelling. It combines traditional storytelling forms with printed media. Tara Books, for instance, published *Sita's Ramayana*, written by Samhita Arni with art by Moyna Chitrkar, and *I See the Promised Land* by Arthur Flowers with art by Moyna Chitrakar, which, while based on the biography of Martin Luther King, combines aspects of King's biography with the Bengali's *Patta Chitra* style of scrolls. *Bhimayana* presents a more impressionistic and inspiring incorporation of traditional Pardhan Gond art from Madhya Pradesh into a contemporary tale-cum-biography of Dr. B R Ambedkar. Duragbai Vyam and Subhash Vyam, the artists of this book, retain their identity in depicting their tribal arts values, while gaining understanding and sympathy from readers all over the world through their intelligent use of their folk, Digna art. The book does not capture the characters within panels, yet shows narrative progressions, expressions, and feelings clearly; for example, the speech bubbles of oppressive characters have a scorpion sting depicting their hurtful words/behaviour, while suppliant characters are shaped like a bird, depicting their urge to be free of these restraints.

Cultural changes in multimedia can be seen in the rise of fan conventions, collectives, and comics events held across the country. Comic conventions held across the country attract a lot of international personalities in the field, like Robert Crumb, who visited Comic-Con Delhi in 2012. Despite the dominance of international and Japanese comics franchises, festivals do encourage local publishing houses and attracts new audiences. Graphic novels are printed, as well as published on online platforms, which can be read on mobile phones easily. Although Indian graphic novels generally tackle deep-rooted, traditional problems within society, they are all set in, or relate to, contemporary times—this relevance is what catches the attention of the youth in the present scenario. Many popular Indian graphic novels are set up exclusively in urban city centres, like Delhi in the case of Corridor and The Harappa Files, Mumbai in the case of Kari, and Hyderabad in Hyderabad: A Graphic Novel, written by Jai Unduriti. These have an urban Indian setting, yet debunk the myth of the comfortable, modern city life, showing the realities of urban centres where lives are alienated, realities are fragmented, and identities are in a flux. The characters are conventionally Indian but follow an urban globalized lifestyle. These comics are written in English while depicting an Indian context; Indian languages (in this case, nativized Indian English) offer these creators prestige on the international market and access to the English-speaking elite of Indians and foreigners. Creators no longer need a multinational publishing house to gain international visibility. They publish a work via a domestic Indian publishing house and may be successful in gaining the attention of international publishing houses. Quite a few Indian graphic novels have gained international acclaim and popularity, such as *Corridor*, *Kari*, *Delhi Calm*, *Bhimayana*, and *The Hotel at the End of the World*. The advent of mass media, especially via the use of social media and digital devices like phones and tablets—all used by middle class youth—have been an advantage for the authors, booksellers, and publishers. These works portray a new urban realism utilizing a highly realistic style, highlighting local details and regional cities. Metropolitan-city-based works depict themes such as discrimination, corruption, violence, fragmentation, urban hypocrisy, and the double standards of people on issues such as caste, religion, and gender. The creators utilize the form of graphic novels to depict relations between the state and the individual, religion, and individual, society, and individual dynamics, and actively question discrimination and marginalization against rural people and impoverished people. The global popularity of these graphic novels is because these global issues are raised in a fun, satirical, non-threatening, and easy-to-digest way. *Kari*, by Amruta Patil, picks up the topic of LGBTQ in the conventional cultures of India, and in an intriguing way. Cotemporary graphic novelists use cultural and global aesthetics to discuss and challenge traditional ideas. They thereby celebrate hybridity, and the intermingling, transformation, and unique combinations of humans, cultures, ideas, politics, aesthetics, and forms within their works. Pramod K. Nayar suggests that those graphic narratives, which are interested in encoding the modernity of India within India's post-millennial production and distribution systems, will need to negotiate and make space for themselves within the literary world. The advantage these graphic narratives have is that they show us a contemporary, lived Indianness, and do not hide the loopholes or the underbelly, presenting readers with an alternative—yet realistic—a picture of India. Written in English, these graphic novels add to the confidence and power of India on the global platform.

According to Supriya Banerjee (2019), Indian graphic novels have an immense impact on their readers' socio-political consciousness and encourage thinking of alternative solutions to contemporary issues. Banerjee further says that they also engage readers by forcing them to question traditional constructs like gender roles and patriarchy. Contemporary Indian comics and graphic novels have transformed many traditional categories and roles, especially that of the self-sacrificing, suffering woman; this has been done through the publication of works such as *Devi*, *Kari*, and *Aranyaka*, *Sita's Ramayana*, *Priya's Shakti*, and *Drawing the Line: Indian Women Fight Back*. They show the picture of the modern, global women who work in, live in, and often manage a superpower. The art, form, and stories of these works may vary, but all of them aim to present and promote the powerful identity of women who do their share by encouraging others around them, including their readers. The readers of these works are generally the elite, literate sections, but can even include semi-literate audiences who relate to the visual narrative/language. The fictional, sometimes fantastical world depicted in these graphic novels is balanced by their depiction of recognizable images of monuments, places, events, objects, etc. Although these graphic novels present traditional tropes of unity, love, acceptance, justice, determination, etc., they do not yearn for mainstream affirmation, but rather present alternative histories, challenging established structures, and remaining open to new ways of thinking.

*Corridor* (2004), by Sarnath Banerjee, is a contemporary Indian graphic novel that centres around the metropolitan city of Delhi. The details and descriptions of the characters, roaming around the circles of Connaught Place, seedy by-lanes of old Delhi, etc. are instantly recognizable in the book. Although there are fewer descriptions of Kolkata in the book, since it is only described when Brighu visits his parents there for some time, the scenes of everyday life in Kolkata nonetheless give readers a sense of the old-world charm of Kolkata. All the characters in the book are urban, educated Indian citizens, yet embody characters and situations that anyone, especially readers from South Asia, can relate to. For instance, Brighu is an intellectual youth searching for a certain book, staying away from his parents, living in a big city alone, and trying to make a livelihood, yet feeling lost in his constant search for a fulfilling relationship. There is also Digital Dutta, full of ambitions and dreams, who values his Marxist philosophy yet is under constant pressure to secure a stable future. Dutta strives to get a foreign visa so that he can work and maybe settle abroad. Such characters are universally relatable yet so deeply rooted in the Indian societal landscape. Then there are unforgettable characters like Jehangir Rangoonwalla, the bookstore owner who supposedly acquired enlightenment at the Nariman Point elevator, and who now continues to share his tea and wisdom with customers who come to his bookstore. Everyone at some point in their lives must have heard or met such an enlightened, almost otherworldly personality. Alongside them, the city of Delhi itself becomes alive. Various facets of Delhi are shown: the modern and the old, via descriptions of the British- built Connaught Place contrasted with the narrow, congested lanes of Old Delhi. The advanced and the traditional are juxtaposed in the depictions of Delhi during the day and at night; the day when Brighu and his friends visit Rangoonwalla's bookstore and at night when Brighu's girlfriend tells him to drop her as she feels unsafe on Delhi's streets. As the story progresses, the nuances of the characters are highlighted alongside the nuances of the city. These nuances are primarily brought out through sketch-like illustrations. A certain panel depicts Old Delhi in the early morning, an urban city awakening, before all the hustle-bustle begins and crowds begin barging in. The readers can compare this peace to the tranquillity of early-morning London, as Wordsworth famously described in his poem *Composed upon Westminster Bridge*. The graphic novel also uses some idioms and expressions which are very local, recognizable, and relatable to Indian readers, like the phrase "doing god knows what," going to a hakim, taking long train journeys, reading *The Statesman* newspaper popular in Kolkata—or wearing a monkey cap. All these are recognizable symbols of a particular region and culture yet are almost forgotten by the present generation. The book provides a perfect entry into the Indian middle-class lifestyle, which is fragmented and in which, identities are multifaceted, with the country's socio-cultural issues constantly interlacing their personal lives.

*The Harappa Files* (2011), by Sarnath Banerjee, is a fictitious story set in an urban locale, where the fictitious "Greater Harappa Rehabilitation, Reclamation and Redevelopment Committee" is based. The committee comprises elderly, high-ranking, and intelligent individuals, who decide to compile a report on the hormonal changes the nation is undergoing. The graphic novel showcases random, everyday objects and instances, like a mother taking her children to school, or a government employee at his table, surrounded by pending files. These images are instantly recognizable and relatable to the Indian readership, and they evoke a variety of feelings and even discussions regarding the greater forces behind them. Banerjee points out the cultural degeneration, the globalization, and the loopholes in the nation's governance in this graphic novel. These themes could easily be applied to any other country. Banerjee's works invokes a postmodern identity by using a psycho-verbal language, significant illustrations, fragmented narration, and authentic portrayals. The narratives offered are multivocal and alternative, demanding the reader's active participation. They present the interplay of a fragmented reality, social thoughts, and social interaction in a space of disillusionment, created by the graphic novelist's imagination.

Scholar Isha Jain (n.d.) notes that Sarnath Banerjee's works are centred around the everyday lives and experiences of urban Indian individuals and can often be anecdotal and autobiographical. Jain observes that Banerjee's works also portray the loss of architecture, history, and cultural values in the country's development and modernization, best shown through vivid illustrations of urban reality. Graphic novels provide an innovative way to talk about contemporary issues, which are so complex that only words or only pictures cannot describe them; only an amalgamation of both can give them a voice. Banerjee's works portray a tension between the individual and society, and between Indian society and the world. His works are situated between local geography and social issues, but this personal tale can transcend boundaries to address larger community concerns and global socio-political issues.

Amruta Patil, who is seen as India's first woman graphic novelist, made an impact with her debut graphic novel, *Kari* (2008), published by Harper Collins India. The work is done in black and white sketches and has a few pages in colour, giving a sudden, momentary burst of colour. Her works have been well received in India, as well as abroad—especially in France, where she temporarily resides, and the U.K. *Kari* was originally written in English and has since been translated into French and Italian due to popular demand. Due to her education in fine arts, she has knowledge of domestic and international art and carefully incorporates an amalgamation of both in her graphic novel. *Kari* is a beautifully drawn graphic novel with a few references to internationally known artists works, which are recognizable to most urban globalized audiences. Along with that, it tackles the issue of homosexuality. Kari, the protagonist of the graphic novel, is a young lesbian woman who faced a breakup, survived a suicide attempt and moved to an urban city to earn a livelihood. At the beginning of the graphic novel, we see two lovers Ruth and Kari sharing one heart—a tribute to Frida Kahlo's painting, "The Two Fridas." The book is mostly in dark and grey shades, along with a few coloured panels, which are themselves mostly a tribute to the works of famous painters such as Paul Gauguin, Frida Kahlo, and Leonardo da Vinci. It describes the alienation one feels in a big city, especially if you are a homosexual in a heteronormative society. It opens the discussion regarding the acceptance of same-sex love, and the pain of separation and dread caused by the abrupt ending of a relationship. The story is based in "Smog City," but the descriptions and illustrations clearly show that this city is inspired by Mumbai, where the media houses and Bollywood reside. Sketches of colonial buildings in the by-lanes of "Smog City," the local buses, and the seafood culture are clearly regional, yet the frustrations Kari feels in her relationships, her search for her own space in the society, the alienation and fragmentation that one feels in an urban city, and the moral policing of a traditional, heterosexual culture, are recognizable and relatable to audiences worldwide. *Kari* links the Indian graphic novel to the significant ongoing debate and exploration of a larger LGBTQ discourse happening around the world. Patil's works have gained global acclamation and international recognition; she was awarded The Nari Shakti Puraskar by the Ministry of Women and Child Development in 2017 for her impressive and socially relevant graphic novels. Gokul Gopalakrishnan (2014) talks about the impressive use of art in her graphic novels. In the case of *Kari*, he approves of the brilliant way she used visual association techniques to connect her domestic and global readers. *Kari* is written in English, and these references are available to all those who can read the language, yet the art itself is iconic, and the globalized, educated audience will be able to recognize them. These colourful artworks are a tribute to great artists such as Gustav Klimt and Frida Kahlo, enhancing the effect of the dark sketches of the city which the protagonist experiences. For example, the suicide attempt is a reference to the work of Andrew Wyett's "Christina's World," which sums up the mental state of her character in a single panel. It has the fear, despair, determination, and struggle to survive in "Smog City" after her failed suicide attempt. The image needs to be iconic, in order for the readers to transpose the original painting's feelings to this page in the book. To some extent, the graphic novelist must have faith in their readers' ability to decipher such references. This affirms the fact that contemporary Indian graphic novelists are trying to expand their readership beyond the niche of traditional comic book readers to a more mature, globally aware, and well-versed audience. These graphic novels demand the attention and involvement of their creators, as well as the audience's participation. Parallel conversations regarding instances, objects, and references are held when the readers are decoding such references. A reader needs to be an active participant in the global visual culture, unrestricted by stereotypes of niche culture. This helps increase Indian graphic novels' relevance and market space, penetrating into the general reading public by expanding the target base. The graphic novelist will also bring his own socio-political understanding and personal perspectives into the graphic novel, which has visual appeal and the potential for social impact, making it a popular cultural product catering to a variety of audiences universally.

The comics industry, of which the graphic novel is a part, is exploding. Digital access has shrunk the world. Graphic novels can now be read online. Some graphic narratives are specially made for online reading. Many works are first previewed online, to see the readers' response, and then published in print; for instance, the Mixtape graphic anthology was initially released by Kokaachi Publications online. It got an incredibly good response from its readers, encouraging Tina Thomas, co-owner of Kokaachi, to bring out a print edition. The technologically advanced world provides many opportunities for intersections between the literacy, education, young adults, graphic novels, and webcomics. This use of technology created new social spaces beyond the panels of the graphic novel. These spaces are open to the creators and the readers. James Bucky Carter observes that the graphic novel explores spaces beyond the written pages and finds a way to bring these spaces into the traditional framing of the printed, new forms, creating new spaces. Web-based technology has enhanced the efficiency and immediacy of interactions and connections between the graphic novelist and its audiences. They can share their work online, not necessarily the final work. The kind of response ascertained from the readers can lead to it turning into a print book. In many cases, independent individual works of graphic novelists shared on their personal blogs became so popular that established publishing houses offer to print them in the form of a graphic novel. Works can also be published online directly, on a weekly or monthly basis, making it easier for the readers to purchase and read the work in instalments. The communicative space opened up on the internet for author–reader interactions can be used by the creators to promote their future works, to gain more readership, and, at times, fundraise money for print publications. These virtual spaces, blogs, and interfaces facilitate a more open and intimate exchange, which helps build a community for the creators and the readers of these graphic novels. Contemporary Indian graphic novels, which tend to target the educated youth, tend to use new and hybrid social spaces, which have an extensive reach, even more so than the traditional print market. The new generation of laptop- and phone-users are being reeled in by interesting exchanges with the publishers, who have now started publishing graphic novels online. Digital comics give the readers a multimodal feel through visual literacy, creating a reading experience which is literary yet multimodal. This encourages reading beyond the pages in the larger production, consumption, and creation processes of the final product. Digital graphic novels, or comics, are sometimes created using technological tools. They may be originally published online, on websites specifically designed for graphic novels and comics reading, like Graphic India. These sites share works and previews of works on social networks such as Facebook and Twitter. They hold the readers' interests, exploring spaces beyond the pages with interactive apps, games, animations, etc. Indian graphic novels' digital turn is representative of globalization in that Indian material is transformed by the latest Western technology, rendering itself easily consumable by an international audience. Though it does not mean fundamentally changing the context of the story, it rather presents it in a cooler way. The services offered by internet devices, like the iPad, laptop computers, and mobile phones, have evolved to such an extent that they provide interactive engagement with a single touch, making the experience of reading online more interesting than reading on a printed page. Publishers agree that devices like the iPad are suited for the comics medium, making the experience of reading more fun. To reach a wider audience, publishing digitally makes sense. Social media forms an important part of the literary; the language structures of the contemporary world, publications of graphic narratives on social media will grab attention and invigorate the imagination by bringing characters out of the page leaving deep impressions on consumers of new fictions (graphic novels).

"The contemporary Indian graphic novel is a hybrid form that balances the elite literary modes and the cultural mass of images" (Biswas 2021, p. 57). It is neither very traditionally native nor an assimilation of foreign influences. It carries an air of sophistication, and it is global in its reach, "does not pretend to be Western, but is cosmopolitan" (Biswas 2021, p. 57) in its links to international networks while remaining indigenously rooted. Although these are originally written in English and have Western connections, they retain an Indian sensibility. This preservation of locality is a distinct feature of Indian graphic novels. Indian graphic novels are thus a powerful medium with which to interact with the larger society, since they have "the advantage of both literary and visual devices" (Biswas 2021, p 57), offering the highest contact zone to the readers. Indian graphic novels are a part of the popular culture, because they engage global citizens, who are interested in stories but do not have time for them. In "oral storytelling traditions, like India's, this new form of storytelling liberates readers from a rigid storyline" (Biswas 2021, p. 57) accelerating cognition through the application of a hybrid textual-visual discourse, making the story fluid and imaginative.

> Diversity in Indian graphic novels is increasing since the 2000s, and it is competing for cultural space and relevance with other dominant mainstream media, like cinema and popular fiction, trying to reach to a general readership. They explore the socio-political concerns prevalent in India, critiquing the contemporary socio-political milieu of India. These works aim to [cultivate, educate, and] make the community vigilant, [and to urge them] to engage in problem-solving.
>
> *(Biswas 2021, p. 57)*

Reciprocally, Indian graphic novelists' creations help them understand the world around them in a better way, understand the dynamics of existence in the larger world, and helps them explore the impact their works can have on the society. It helps them reframe their own worldview and create practical, globally relevant graphic novels.

## References

Anjum, Z. (2014) 'Kitaab Interview: Indian Writing in English Has Got an Exciting Future Ahead of It: E. Dawson Varughese.' *KITAAB*, 16 Mar, (online). Available at: kitaab.org/2014/03/16/kitaab-interview-Indian-writing-in-english-has-got-an-exciting-future-ahead-of-it-e-dawson-varughese/ (Accessed 3 Mar. 2020).

Banerjee, S. (2019) 'The Rise of the Graphic Novel and Linguistic Development in India—An Analysis.' *1Library*, [online]. Available at: 1library.net/document/q51epmwy-rise-graphic-novel-linguistic-development-india-analysis.html (Accessed 19 Jun. 2020).

Basu, A. (2017) 'Representation of History in the Indian Graphic Novel: An Analytical Study of History through the Frame of Graphic Narratives.' *The International Academic Forum (IAFOR) Journal of Arts & Humanities*, 4(2), pp. 25–39 [online]. Available at: https://iafor.org/journal/iafor-journal-of-arts-and-humanities/volume-4-issue-2/article-3/ (Accessed 9 Mar. 2020).

Biswas, A. (2021) 'Indian Graphic Novels: The New Mode of Storytelling', *Research Journal of English Language and Literature (RJELAL)*, [online] 9(3), pp. 52–58. Available at: www.rjelal.com/9.3.21/52-58%20AIBHI%20BISWAS.pdf (Accessed 24 Sep. 2021).

Carter, J. B. (2011) *Graphic Novels, Web Comics, and Creator Blogs: Examining Product and Process*. New York: Taylor & Francis. Available at: www.tandfonline.com/doi/abs/10.1080/00405841.2011.584029 (Accessed 23 Sep. 2021).

Christabel, G. A. (2018) 'Negotiating Identities: A Representation of Contemporary India in the Novels of Sarnath Banerjee', *Language in India*, 3(18), pp. 129–135, [online]. Available at: www.languageinindia.com/march2018/auseminar1/jerushanovelssarnathbanerjee1.pdf (Accessed 15 Jul. 2020).

Creekmur, C. K. (2015) "The Indian Graphic Novel," in Anjaria, Ulka (ed.) *A History of the Indian Novel in English*. Cambridge: Cambridge University Press, pp. 348–358. Doi: 10.1017/CBO9781139942355.024.

Debroy, D. (2011) 'The Graphic Novel in India: East Transforms West', *Bookbird: A Journal of International Children's Literature*, 49(4), pp. 32–39. Doi:10.1353/bkb.2011.0060. [Online]. Available at: www.ibby.org/archive-storage/06_Bookbird_14579/1081435/1081435_PDF_00001.pdf (Accessed 15 Nov. 2019).

DNA India. (2007) '*Global Award to Boost Dalit Cause, Says Publisher.*' 9 May [online]. Available at: www.dnaindia.com/india/report-global-award-to-boost-dalit-cause-says-publisher-1095645 (Accessed 24 Sep. 2021).

Gilon, C. & Somasundaran, J. (2016) Graphic Novels Radically Rooted in Indian Market. *The New Indian Express*. [online]. Available at: www.newindianexpress.com/magazine/2016/dec/03/graphic-novels-radically-rooted-in-indian-market-1544633.html (Accessed Nov. 2020).

Gonsalves, R. (2016) 'We Need to Talk about Caste: Roanna Gonsalves Interviews S Anand', *Cordite Poetry Review*, 1st August, [online]. Available at: http://cordite.org.au/interviews/gonsalves-anand/ (Accessed 24 Sep. 2021).

Gopalakrishnan, G. (2014) 'Art in Comics', *Marg*, 1 December, pp. 40–49 [online]. Available at: www.thefreelibrary.com/Art+in+comics-a0399094261 (Accessed Apr. 2020).

Gravett, P. (2015) 'The Indian Graphic Novel is Here to Stay', *British Council*, 29 October 2015 [online]. Available at: www.britishcouncil.org/voices-magazine/indian-graphic-novel-here-stay (Accessed Apr. 2020).

Gupta, S. (2012) 'Indian "Commercial Fiction" in English, the Publishing Industry and Youth Culture.' *Economic and Political Weekly*, 47(5), pp. 46–53 [online]. Available at: www.epw.in/journal/2012/05/special-articles/indian-commercial-fiction-english-publishing-industry-and-youth (Accessed 24 Sep. 2021).

Gupta, S. A. (2014) 'Introduction: Aniruddha Sen Gupta', *Marg- A Magazine of the Arts*, 66(2), pp. 1–9 [online]. Available at: www.thefreelibrary.com/Introduction%3A+Aniruddha+Sen+Gupta-a0399094257 [Accessed 24 Sep. 2021].

Jain, I. (n.d.). 'Indian Graphic Novel and how it emerged.' *Academia*. [online] Available at: www.academia.edu/30083473/Indian_Graphic_Novel_and_how_it_emerged. (Accessed 24 Sep. 2020).

MIT—Docubase. (2021) *Priya's Shakti*. [online] Available at: https://docubase.mit.edu/project/priyas-shakti/ (Accessed 6 Oct. 2020).

Natarajan, S. & A. Ninan. (2011) *A Gardener in the Wasteland: Jotiba Phule's Fight for Liberty*. New Delhi: Navayana.

Nayar, P.K. (2019) 'Graphic Memory, Connective Histories, and Dalit Trauma', *English Language Notes*, 57(2), p. 143–150 [online]. Available at: www.academia.edu/40975169/_Graphic_Memory_Connective_Histories_and_Dalit_Trauma_A_Gardener_in_the_Wasteland_ (Accessed 4 Sep. 2020).

Parthasarathy, A. (2014) A silent storm. *The Hindu*, 23 March [online]. Available at: www.thehindu.com/features/metroplus/a-silent-storm/article5819230.ece (Accessed 24 Sep. 2021).

Priya's Shakti. (n.d.) *Workshops.* [online] Available at: www.priyashakti.com/workshops/ (Accessed 24 Sep. 2020).
Sarma, I. (2017) 'Negotiations of Home and Belonging in the Indian Graphic Novels Corridor by Sarnath Banerjee and Kari by Amruta Patil', *South Asia Multidisciplinary Academic Journal,* (16). [online]. Available at: https://journals.openedition.org/samaj/4384 (Accessed 12 Aug. 2020).
Singh, A. (2018) 'The Indian Novel in the 21st Century', *Oxford Research Encyclopedia of Literature,* March, [online]. DOI: 10.1093/acrefore/9780190201098.013.414, Available at: www.lehigh.edu/~amsp/The_Indian_Novel_in_the_21st_Century.pdf (Accessed 24 Sep. 2021).
Stoll, J. (2014) 'Telling Stories and Building Community: Making Comics in India', *Marg,* 1 December, pp. 16–25 [online]. Available at: www.thefreelibrary.com/Art+in+comics-a0399094261 (Accessed Apr. 2020).
Stoll, J. (2017) 'Art & Avarice: Tracing Careers in Indian Comics', *International Journal of Comic Art,* 19(2) [online]. Available at: www.academia.edu/36755120/Art_and_Avarice_Tracing_Careers_in_Indian_Comics (Accessed 24 Dec. 2020).
Varughese, E. D. (2017) 'Publishing Indian Graphic Narratives Post Millennium', in *Visuality and Identity in Post-millennial Indian Graphic Narratives.* Cham: Palgrave Macmillan, pp. 1–11. https://doi.org/10.1007/978-3-319-69490-0_1
www.sutrajournal.com. (n.d.) *Priya's Shakti: Addressing Gender Imbalance through Religious Art.* [online] Available at: www.sutrajournal.com/ram-devineni-on-priyas-shakti (Accessed 24 Sep. 2021).

# 12

# QUANTITATIVE STEPWISE ANALYSIS OF THE IMPACT OF TECHNOLOGY IN INDIAN ENGLISH NOVELS 1947–2017

*Shanmugapriya T., Nirmala Menon, and Deborah Sutton*

## Introduction

Technology invariably embodies the attitude, prejudice, resistance, moral, ethical, social, and cultural aspects of the period in which it arises, as it is not always deployed as a neutral factor. Though we have been studying embodied features in literature, we never used technology itself as a tool to measure and interpret the cultural transmission between humans and technology. How does technology influence literature? We rarely ask this question, as we are cognizant of the liaisons between technology and literature, from the codex period to digital. However, this does not mean we should abandon this question, as this field has not really materialized for Indian literature. This project examines the impact of technological devices such as the telephone (1882), television (1959), and computer (1955), on the corpus of post-independence Indian English novels published from 1947 to 2017. We do this by leveraging digital humanities methods and tools. The reason why we particularly focus the post-independence Indian English novels is the growth of Indian English literature and technological devices primarily emerged after the independence due to: (a) the induction of many new publication houses, the increase in the number of authors and literary awards, and the rise in the literacy rate and (b) though few technologies such as radio and telephone are introduced in colonial India, the widespread acceptance of technologies occurred after independence. The selection of novels is also determined and constrained by the availability of the digitized and digital novels even in the payment mode. Together with this, we also limit ourselves to focus only the three the aforementioned modern gadgets as compared to other technologies such as the earlier ones telegram and gramophone; these devices have brought tremendous changes in our everyday lives starting from leisure to work. Their effects apparently echoed in the literary sphere and transformed the literary culture from passive to active and static to dynamic in terms of narrative, publishing, and practice.

DOI: 10.4324/9781003354246-16

We have studied the corpus of 47 novels to analyse the larger trends and patterns of technological artefacts and their discourses in the novels through computational analysis. For this study, we deployed a new method, quantitative stepwise analysis (QSA), for studying literary works in a systematic way. We used R-software for text-mining tools such as Keyword-in-Context (KWIC) and topic modelling. The questions we ask in this chapter are: are there any significant changes in the presence of technological devices in the novels over the period of 70 years? Do they suggest any substantial discourses and overall patterns in the novels published over these years? Does a quantitative study through algorithmic computing propose a new insight into our argument? Before exploring such questions of text mining and analysis, we briefly discuss the gap in existing quantitative methods and introduce the new method, quantitative stepwise analysis.

## Existing Methods and New Method

The quantified approach in literary studies is mainly attributed to Moretti's distant reading, Stephen Ramsay's algorithmic criticism, and Jockers' macroanalysis, which are designed to function optimally within the larger corpus of texts. Of these methods, distant reading has a long history of intense debate, especially regarding its application in the literary studies, and concerning issues such as resisting normative method, the treatment of text as data, abstract results, and lack of methodology. Heather Love (2010, pp. 374–375) argues that disengagement with close reading "is not the only way to get traction on these institutional and ethical questions." John Frow (2008, p. 142) contends that Moretti's notion, of treating the literary objects as patterns and trends, falls short by "ignor[ing] the crucial point that these morphological categories he takes as his base units are not pre-given but are constituted in an interpretive encounter by means of an interpretive decision." Apart from these criticisms, the problems of an empirical approach in distant reading and macroanalysis are, in effect, the lack of methodology and scholarly infrastructure. Andrew Goldstone (2015) comments on methodological issues in distant reading method, raising questions as to how we can understand the individual agent (micro) within large-scale structures (macro), and how we can explain the cultural-historical patterns we see in the results.

As Bode (2017, p. 79) notes, despite the distant reading and macroanalysis methods' immense contributions to literary computing and research practice, Moretti and Jockers offer little information for processing data to glean results. A few questions remain unaddressed by methods: How did Moretti and Jockers complete their experiment by using quantitative methods? What kind of methodology exactly do they follow in their research? What and how many steps are involved during the experiment? Øyvind Eide proposes a new, divergent text analysis method known as critical stepwise formalization, a conceptual modelling process that has distinct strategic techniques for processing the data. These strategic techniques can assist in creating, curating, and analysing data. Eide employs this modelling for converting text into maps through computational method. He says, "[c]ritical stepwise formalisation consists of studying a media expression through the process of adapting it into a new expression in another qualified medium" (Eide 2015, p. 41). However, in short, this method does not deal with the larger corpus of texts, as quantitative analysis does, but instead focuses on the larger material which cannot be easily handled by a human mind, "but [is] smaller than what is usually used for statistical analysis" (Eide 2015, p. 74).

Hence, it is clear that quantitative analysis such as distant reading and macroanalysis lack the methodology for processing the corpus. At the same time, the critical stepwise formalization has a proper methodology, but deals with a smaller unit of text. Hence, we coalesce both quantitative and critical stepwise formalization methods to form a new method, "quantitative stepwise analysis" for our literary research. It will have to deal with the particular portion of a larger corpus of texts. This method will also have a clear organizational structure which will be borrowed from the critical stepwise formalization. We provide a rationale for the need of a new method of empirical research before explicating the method. Our empirical method has an organizational structure which incorporates questionnaires, a specific portion of the text, stepwise formation, graphical expressions, and analysis. In such an exercise, as we mentioned earlier, we combine the quantitative analysis and critical stepwise method to form a new method, quantitative stepwise analysis (QSA). This new method is mainly inspired by the existing methods of Moretti, Jockers, Bode, and Eide, and discourses on the quantitative methods of Underwood and Goldstone.

QSA is a method for studying literary works in a systematic way. This method is applied to study specific portions of the texts from an entire corpus. It is deployed to study event-based features, places, objects, and their influences in the novels which can be derived from the specific part of texts. These strands of studies require step-by-step analysis. Needless to say, "quantitative" refers to a larger corpus of text—but what is stepwise analysis? The term is inspired by the method of Eide's critical stepwise formalization. Eide (2015, p. 71) explains that "stepwise formalisation in computer science [is] a process of making unstructured data more and more structured in a stepwise manner." Hence, the extracted, unstructured data turn into structured data by applying a number of stepwise formalizations. Also, the collected, structured data, after pre-processing, transform into a number of different data modelling in order to understand the data more in a better way. Unlike in Eide's critical stepwise formalization, the subsequent step may or may not rely on the previous step, but both are equally analysed for the same argument. The recognition of each step is important, because they add crucial value to the research questions. The QSA can optimize for the stepwise analysis of the data through algorithmic computing. Eide segregates the aggregation of many steps into four stages. He says,

> Each stage is the result of a number of steps from the previous stage. Each step is the process in which one statement in the modeling system is changed from one form to another. The whole state of the modeling system at a

> certain point in the stepwise formalisation is called a stage. So while a step will always be local to one statement, a stage will always represent all statements found at a certain level of formalisation. The stages are arbitrary and could in principle have been chosen differently, but in an implementation applied to a certain research project a stage will typically represent a level of understanding which is meaningful to the modeller.
>
> *(Eide 2015, p. 72)*

As he says, the QSA also carries a number of steps for transforming text into visual objects in order to make a specific room for our study. Hence, we reconfigure here his four stages for QSA: 1. source text, 2. primary model, 3. secondary model, and 4. target product.

## Methodology

1 **Source text**: In this first stage, we identify novels with distinct characteristics representative of different time periods, places, and situations. We do this by ensuring that our selections include: 1. novels from each decade; 2. canonical and non-canonical authors' novels; 3. novels from all sorts of settings such as urban, rural, and varied locales. Also, we focus on three technological devices: the telephone, television, and computer, and we include their substitutes and acronym during extraction.

2 **Primary model**: The primary model is an important stage in the experiment. The following stages are built upon the primary model. It isolates the desired data from the text for the further experiment. This model subsumes (1) aggregating the digital files and pre-processing the text and (2) studying the entire corpus would limit the results as the technological devices may/may not have primary roles in the narrative. Hence, we will extract the keywords of technological objects and their neighbours by using Keyword-in-Context (KWIC).

3 **Secondary model**: In this stage, we deploy the topic modelling tool Mallet for analysing the discourse of modern gadgets in the novels.

4 **Target product**: We create the visualizations of the results for further study.

## Topic Models' Results and Discussion

The text mining tool topic modelling is widely applied to study literary works in order to find the hidden thematic structure. For instance, Jockers and David Mimno (2013) apply topic modelling to uncover the relevant themes in the larger corpus of 19th-century English novels. In his seminal book, *Macroanalyis*, Jockers (2013) derives thematic information in Irish American novels by applying topic modelling. We deploy topic modelling not to identify the theme of the novels but to study the substantial discourses of each of technological objects and the overall patterns of all the modern objects in the novels published after independence.

The topic modelling tool, Machine Learning for LanguagE Toolkit (MALLET) software package, was developed by David Mimno under the direction of Andrew McCallum at the University of Massachusetts in 2002 (Jockers 2013, p. 124). Many parameters and strategies of pre-processing involved in reaching the specific results such as stopword list, chunk size (number of words from the text), number of topics and terms, hyperparameter, and optimization. Mallet comes with inbuilt pre-processing codes for the text: stopword list and codes for removing regular expressions. But we can prepare a customized stopword list to remove the particular words which we do not want to affect our results. Hence, we prepared the stopword lists to eliminate the names of technological devices during the modelling processes. Also, deciding the number of units or chunks of words will influence identifying the constellation of terms which occur together. The document should be neither too large nor too small. Hence, we segmented the documents of each device into 1,000 words. After this preprocessing of the corpus, another important parameter for topic modelling is that the user has to determine the number of topics and the number of words for each topic. Jockers (2013, p. 7) says that there is no fixed rule for determining the topics other than "a firm understanding" of the dataset. Hence, to avoid the issues in determining the number of topics and the hyperparameter optimization, we executed the code multiple times, and after many trials and errors that drove us to finally settle on the 15 topics and 30 terms of each technological gadget and 200 hyperparameter optimization. After this processing, we exported all topics of each device and along with its weights in an excel sheet for the data visualization. Then, we used RAWGraphs (Mauri *et al.* 2017) the data visualization tool to investigate the topic terms in semantic graphical expressions.

## Discourses of the Telephone Artefact

From the results of the telephone artefact, we can locate prominent terms, which are mostly characters-oriented and place names. It depicts that the telephone functioned as an agency for interconnecting the characters from different places which one way or the other stimulates tension in the story. An inspection of some of the topics with their top terms reveals various abstract discourses of the telephone artefact, which we categorize as a discourse of gendered facets. We will discuss these discourses in greater detail with examples in the following section. Besides these recognized discourses, there are some incoherent patterns of topics, such as 4 and 14, which do not propose any clear or certain discourses. Scholars like Jockers (2013) and Schöch (2017) have discussed these issues of generic and vague topics. Jockers (2013, p. 129) says that this is an active area of research for computer scientists and linguists, and thus not a problem for us to delve into the analysis of interpretable topics. He goes on to say that the uninterruptible topic "does not undermine the usefulness of the topics that are interpretable [and] focus our attention on others, say only the most interpretable, we do no disservice to the overall model, and we in no way compromise our analysis" (Jockers 2013, p. 129). As he says, we will then focus on interpretable topics which signify some interesting and relevant discourses of the telephone artefact in the novels over the periods.

## Discourses of Gendered Facets

The top terms of topics 2, 5, 6, 7, 8, 9, and 13 are related to gender in terms of their social relations in the novels. The constellations of terms lead to classify the discourses into female and male facets. The close observation of topic terms of 7 and 8 such as *she, her, day, house, night, left, father, home, wanted, mother, long, picked, face, head, minutes, hand, woman, evening, years, knew, place, happened, glass, end, pick, herself, speak, ten, wait,* and *black* appeared in the novels advocates the discourse of domestic sphere. However, the high-weighted terms *she, her, jamun, house, home, night, day, night, mother, woman, dial,* and *herself* are associated with female facets, except for one male character's name, *Shyamanand* (see Figure 12.1). These terms show us that most of the discourses of female characters are allied with the

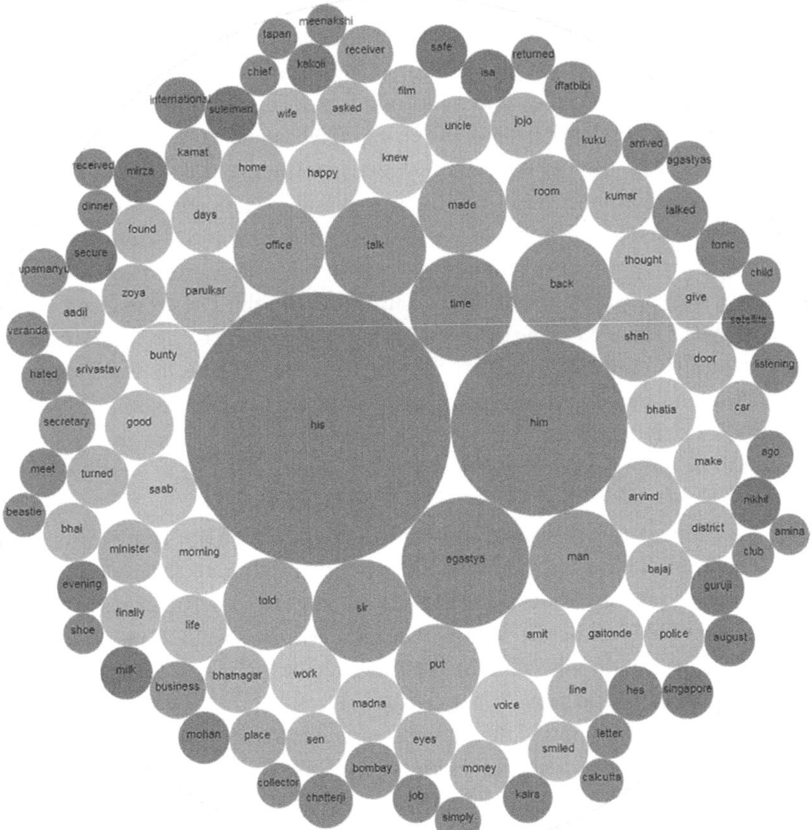


**FIGURE 12.1** Topic terms: female characters' facets of the telephone artefacts

domestic sphere. In her book, *The Women in Indian Fiction 1950–1980*, Shantha Krishnaswamy (1984, p. 351) discusses the realistic portrayal of women characters in the novels of R. K. Narayan, Kamala Markandaya, Anita Desai, and R. P. Jhabvala. She remarks that equality and liberation are "hard to reconcile" for women characters and each female protagonist encounters "harsh reality" and "creating new patterns of revolt against established exploitative system." Similarly, Meenakshi Mukherjee (1971, p. 29) says,

> One might argue that the classical ideals no longer obtain in the Indian context. But in actual literary practice, numerous characters are found to be adhere to classic prototypes—especially the women of fiction who persistently re-enact the suffering, sacrificing, role of Sita or Savithri.

Indeed, in the early period of writing, the novels of R.K. Narayan, Mulk Raj Anand, Rajo Rao, and Kamala Markandaya portray the predicament of women in domesticity. The woman protagonist in their novels mostly has a passive role (Agarwal and Sinha 2003, pp. 30–50). Such conditions of women in the fictions had marginally changed in the writings of Anita Desai, Shashi Deshpande, and Nayanthara Sehgal. The women protagonists of these writers fight for their emancipation and revolt against inequalities and injustices. Though both male and female writers after independence project the changing phase of women's lives in India, in most of the novels, the fights for their rights, identities, and equalities have always been confined within domesticity. In such a milieu, the algorithm conjures up the pattern of telephone topics with domestic-related words for female facets as they frequently appeared together. To examine this observation more deeply, we will study some examples from the corpus of the novels. The woman protagonist Uma in Anita Desai's *Fasting, Feasting* (1999) is restricted to have education and employment, as Ludmila Volná (2005, p. 2) claims that Uma is fasting (hunger) for "education and free development of personality" as they belong only to the male society. Not only education and identity are prohibited to her but also technology which can be embraced only by the male community.

> She stops at a three-legged table on which the telephone stands. She lifts the ear phone, taps at it, humming. Then her fingers fit into the openings for the numbers and she is dialling. The phone rings in some other dark, shadowy house. She bites her lip at her own audacity and stealth. This is not something she can do when Mama Papa are present: their avid curiosity and their disapproval would prevent her.
>
> At last the ringing of the phone is answered. Uma's face falls: it is the servant who has answered. "O' Henry memsahib, is she in?" Uma finds herself enquiring. She fears Papa might spring out of the shadows and grasp her by the shoulder and demand an explanation for her deceit, or payment for the call.
>
> *(Desai 1999, pp. 44–45)*

In the aforementioned quotations, Desai beautifully narrates how Uma makes a phone call when her parents are not around in the house as she perpetrates a transgression. The development in the telecommunication technologies in the later periods of 20th century had slightly changed the access of mobile communication regardless of any gender. The Indian English novels resonate this significant transformation in the social and cultural spheres where the phone becomes a part of everyday life and an inevitable entity of what makes it to appear often in the novels which published after 1995s. For instance, the phone artefact is exercised as a highly primary source and occurred in the novels *Fury* (2001), *Fireproof* (2008) *and She will Build Him City (2015)*.

Subsequently, the top terms of topics 2, 5, 6, 9, and 13 have more male characters' names and their associated terms. Unlike the topics pertaining to female facets, the topics of male facets attribute to both social and domestic spectrums. According to the clusters of top words of these male character topics, we can segregate them into two types such as (1) social, public, and working realm (topics 2, 5, 9, and 13) and (2) domestic sphere (topic 6). The top words of 2, 5, 9, and 13, which are the male characters' names, such as *agastya, madna, parulkar, Arvind,* and *amit, and their associated words place, international, job, meet, happy, saab, collector, uncle, district, talk, sir, knew, film, bombay, business, talked, satellite, singapore, secure, listening, minister, office, secretary, club, dinner, chief, time, man, made, room, work, police, money, wife, talk, car,* etc., present the picture of the discourse of male characters which signify the working and public realm that invariably assumed as it belongs to the male community. Also, we find just one topic which contains male characters' names and some terms such as *raghu, pocket, beach, badal, latika, johnny, boy, gouri, family, tea, minute, drivers, scooter, stall, toppo, ramchand, suraj, babu, ladle, gupta,* and *master* associated with domestic sphere. This depicts that the telephone is conceived as a "masculine technology"—men have more legitimacy and leverage to avail technology in both domestic and social places than women.

> I had to go there for my telephone call to Geneva. My conversation with Charlie was made from a special box fitted with earphones for the convenience of the Censors: censorship had recently been introduced by Ek Nambur over all international communications. On the whole, the new arrangements were satisfactory: the boxes looked like huge glass bowls and you felt like a fish watched from all sides, and I could see for myself the faces the censors made when I had my international phone call. I was told that there were mechanical devices for recording every word one uttered.
>
> *(Ghose 1955, p. 271)*

The aforementionedquote is extracted from the mid-20th-century novel *The Flame of the Forest* (1955) by Sudhin N. Ghose. The male protagonist, who is educated and works part-time as an assistant to a local politician, is a symbol of modernization as he makes a number of telephone calls internationally and nationally. Meanwhile, the female protagonist represents traditionalism as a devotee of lord Krishna. This instance presents the telephone as an important device for men whose identities are always allied with social, political, science, technology, and economic organization. Derné (2000, p. 244) points out that "Indian identity made room for nationalist men [not women] to embrace Western science, technology and economic organization." In such patriarchal setup, women's identity is ended up within certain territories of family and some limited social places, and possesses "an inferior position relative to men economically, socially, and politically" (Calman 1992, p. 942).

## Discourses of the Television Artefact

Quite a large number of topic models of the television artefact convey that television functions as a bridge between inside and outside domestic spaces. This modern apparatus has the ability to shape/control the behaviour of the characters. I identified that topic 7 is uninterruptible; however, the close probing of the remaining topic offers a clue to label them discourse of character.

## Discourses of Characters

The top-ranked terms in topics 1, 4, 5, 6, 9, 12, and 13 have a number of female characters' names, such as *Jojo, Mrs., Jamun, Urmila, Kochu, Maria*, and *Madna*, and a few male characters' names, such as *Solanka, Agastya, Arun*, and *Biju Shankar*. The topic terms aligned with character names, such as *sense, addict, coming, actress, rich, community, felt, Calcutta, mind, sees, mind, thought, mind, producer*, and *government*, offer a hint to the influence of television in both domestic and social spaces (see Figure 12.2). One of the main objectives of television is to "act as a catalyst for social change"; television also has the effect of homogenizing the community by providing a wide range of experience to the individuals (Chayanika 2014, p. 55). The writers of the 20th and 21st centuries employed such parallel concepts in their writings—the characters underwent many changes by experiencing the different versions of the external world that television brings into their homes. Indeed, TV technology has been influencing the Indian public and private spheres since its introduction. It was introduced in India by the end of 1959 as an experimental form of transmission in Delhi. Like radio, this medium also had an aim "to promote economic growth and social justice . . . under the supervision of government" (Sen 2016, p. 135). It was started as part of AIR, and the first public channel named was Doordarshan. It was governed by Prasar Bharathi, a board formed by the government of India, and was established in 1975 with the launch of the Satellite Instructional Television Experiment (SITE). The network initially covered six states and was expanded to other states as well. Subsequently, commercial programmes were introduced in 1975. The most remarkable period of television began after the 1980s with the launch of colour TV. During and after this period, many national programmes included and/or focused upon topics as varied as education, entertainment, and information. It also saw the telecast of the first serial, and other

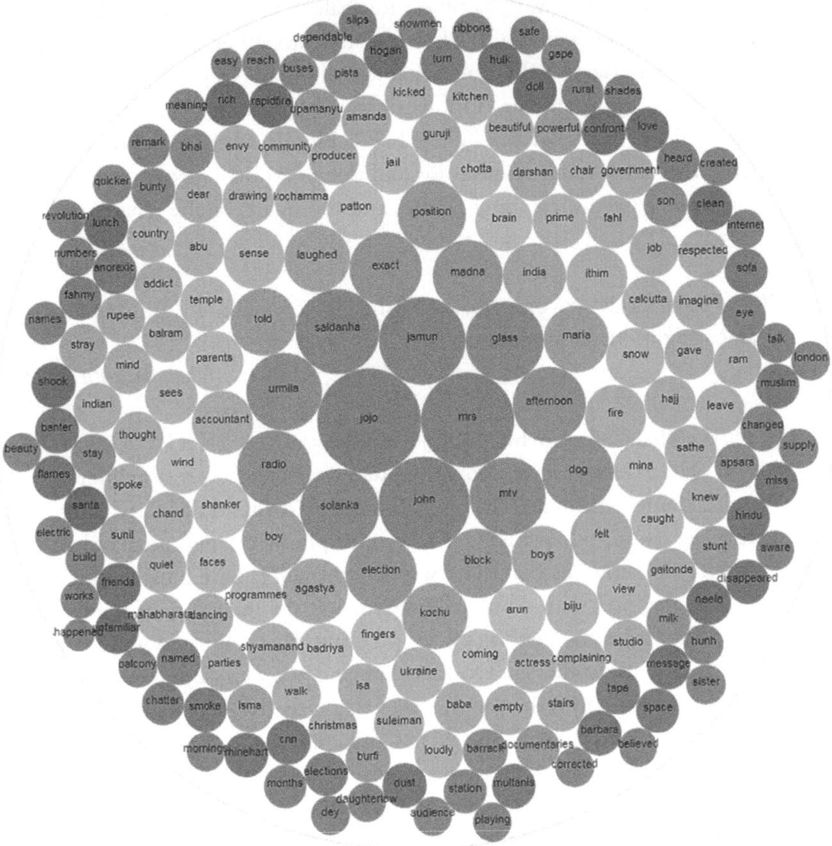


**FIGURE 12.2** Topic terms: discourse of characters of the television artefacts

milestones, too. Following this, India's moves towards economic liberalization in 1991 encouraged many private channels to beginning streaming content in India. Thus, it has become an indispensable entity in the Indian domestic spectrum.

The characteristic features of TV blur the boundaries between the inside and outside domestic realms (Goody 2011, p. 72). This, in turn, offers a plethora of experiences for Indian English writers to incorporate this modern technology as a literary element in their works. In addition to this, we will delve into some key passages for this topic to understand the imprint of this modern technology in the novels. The following passages explicate the discourse of female characters oriented.

> Baby Kochamma had installed a dish antenna on the roof of the Ayemenem house. She presided over the world in her drawing room on satellite TV. The impossible excitement that this engendered in Baby Kochamma wasn't hard

> to understand. It wasn't something that happened gradually. It happened overnight. Blondes, wars, famines, football, sex, music, coups d'etat—they all arrived on the same train. They unpacked together. . . . Baby Kochamma followed American NBA league games, one-day cricket and all the Grand Slam tennis tournaments. On weekdays she watched The Bold and the Beautiful and Santa Barbara, where brittle blondes with lipstick and hairstyles rigid with spray seduced androids and defended their sexual empires. Baby Kochamma loved their shiny clothes and the smart, bitchy repartee.
>
> *(Roy 1997, p. 30)*

> Jojo was a model co-ordinator, and she also owned a TV production company, she produced programmes.
>
> *(Chandra 2006, p. 131)*

The female characters Kochu and Jojo from the novels *The God of Small Things* (1997), and *Sacred Games* (2006) show that each character possesses a different connection with the television artefact. For example, Kochu and Mrs. Chatterjee are addicted to television, while Jojo is a television producer. The portrayal of these women characters shows us that these women characters have a more special relationship with television than do men. If we look at the trajectory of the television in India, we can find many historic television events that resonated with women in society. In "Imagining audience: Doordarshan and Women's Programming" Jayasree Kalathil (1999) discusses the programmes that targeted female audiences by the national channel Doordarshan. She writes that, since its inception in 1959, TV programmes only promoted social and scientific education for the development of the country. This did not change until the report of the Working Group on Software for Indian Television was released, which said that the women are neglected in the programmes. As a consequence of this report, many programmes such as health, food, beauty tips, and home management were targeted to women audiences, meant to encourage them "to adopt modern behaviour and attitude towards life which constantly keeps on changing with the times" (Kalathil 1997, p. 89). Kalathil (1997, p. 90) highlights,

> The targeted audience is mainly women [and many] programmes on housekeeping, cooking, beauty tips, first aid, home decoration, and serials. A quick look at the contents of these programmes showed that most of them centered around the "home" and aimed at educating women to be better home keepers.

Indeed, most contemporary writers find this transformation phase as a raw material for their writings. They portray women characters as always indulging themselves, watching television programmes, and discussing serials and other programmes with other women. On the contrary, novelists illustrate men as socially responsible people who critique women's relationship with television. The following excerpts from the novels *Narcopolis* (2012), *Sacred Games* (2006), and *Last Man in the Tower* (2011) illustrate how television brings conflict between female and male characters, as male characters invariably suggest that female characters spend too much time in front of the TV, and even learn words from programmes. The following scenes portray women as they become "addicted" to TV serials and other potentially manipulative programs, which are suggested as having been produced particularly for women. For example:

> He walked in the door and the television was blaring in the bedroom. His wife wouldn't get up and say hello. She was always tired, so tired she woke up exhausted, which wasn't surprising, since she spent most of her time watching Doordarshan.
>
> *(Thayil 141)*

> "I have nothing to say." He was sure she had heard the line in some TV serial.
>
> *(Chandra 2006, p. 487)*

> Whole of India is full of idiots like her. Bad influence of films and television.' That made Jojo laugh, and for a few seconds she left off from her bhashan and laughed with me.
>
> *(Chandra 2006, p. 534)*

> My wife of thirty-one years. Without TV, what is a home?
>
> *(Adiga 2011, pp. 31–294)*

In opposite to this, male characters use television for learning purposes through watching news, sports, business, and other programmes. For instance, we can observe this in the following quote: "[h]er husband was watching a replay of a classic India versus Australia cricket match on TV. . . . He subscribed to the Economic Times; watched CNBC TV" (Adiga 2011, pp. 32–80). In parallel to this, we can also find a few male characters' names and associated terms such as *country, election*, and *business*. Like the result of telephone, the male characters' names and its associated terms tend to have social and political connotations. For instance, in *Fury* (2001), the protagonist Solanka withdraws from his career as an academician and joins a television station to pursue his dream. Concurrently, terms such as *election* and *business* convey that television has special programmes which target adult men with programmes on business, economics, sports, and political affairs. The terms *producer* and *actress* in the selected novels reveal that television also provides a career realm for the women community after the advent of many national and international private channels that paraded into India. Hence, television is not merely "infotainment media" but also "an institution" capable of building the nation and transforming the sociocultural milieu.

## Discourses of the Computer Artefact

From the results of the computer artefact, we identified incoherent topics 3, 4, 10, and 12—the close investigation of them showed that the computer has multiple roles in novels which resulted in its presentation in many different settings and topics. For instance, computers are harnessed for communication, entertainment, transportation, sources of information, profession/business, and so on. The remaining topics signify a topic of discourse of male characters.

## Discourses of Male Characters

The prominent keywords are the names of male characters such as *Solanka, Saxel, Girish, Rohit, Reddy, Jayojit, Rijk, Ashok, Parukalr*, and *Srnivas*, in conjunction with other words such as *square, window, webcam, sign, city, street, cybercafé, talking, guruji, entire, make, thought, email, travelled, terminal, classes, hundred, machine, America mother, professor, bright, bonny*, and *Bangalore* (see Figure 12.3). These words confirm that

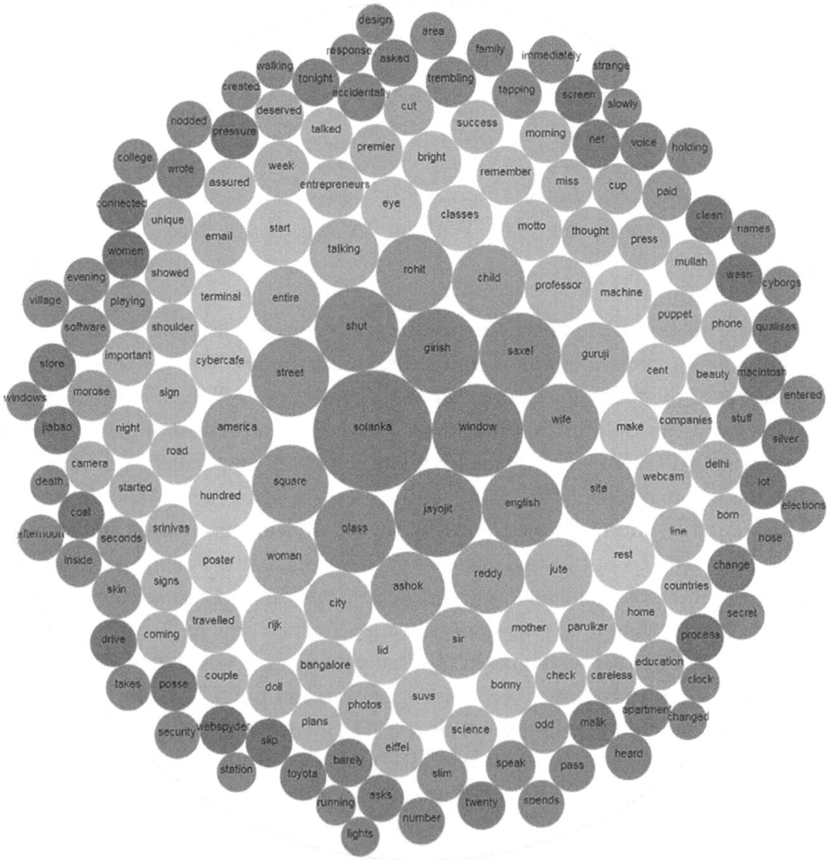


**FIGURE 12.3** Topic terms: male characters for the computer artefact

male characters deploy the computer artefact as a way to explore the external world, in terms of profession/business/communication/information and so on, which create a network in the plot. In parallel to the gendered topics of telephone, novelists portrayed that computer and Internet technologies "predominantly belong to men" (Moghaddam 2010, p. 722). We can see a few terms related to the female gender, such as *girls, wife, women* and *woman*, and one woman-character's name. The algorithm did not pick up many women characters' names, as they did not frequently appear along with the computer artefact and its related technologies. Hence, it corroborates the supposition that novelists tend to portray only male characters when deploying the computer artefact. For further study, we shall discuss the trajectory of computer technology in India before beginning the discussion on the imprint of the computer artefact in the selected novels. The computer and internet revolution had brought a paradigm shift "in the development of a new look and scientific culture" in India (Sen 2016, p. 69). The period from 1955 to 1970, in India, laid a strong foundation for computer technologies through the manufacture of Indigenous computers. Following this, from 1970 to 1978, the formation of the Department of Electronics and the Electronics Commission promoted self-sufficiency in the computer industry, which allowed the public-sector Electronics Corporation of India Ltd. (ECIL) (which had been established under the Department of Atomic Energy) to "market a totally indigenous system [and] indigenous in design" (Subramanian 2006, p. 179).

The same period also witnessed the realization of computer science as a discipline in Indian educational institutions. The pre-liberalization period between 1978 and 1990 saw liberalized policymaking on the manufacture of minicomputers, and led to the emergence of many technical entrepreneurs. In the ensuing years, liberalization, the inception of the internet, and a boom in the Information Technology (IT) field brought many further changes, in areas ranging from education to entertainment. This spectrum opened up a plethora of opportunities in fields such as business and information technology. Since then, India produces millions of software engineers every year. Another important factor that we should take note of, in light of this growth in the computer and IT realms, is that gender disparity is pervasive in a patriarchal society like India, wherein gender parity in science and technology has yet to be fulfilled. A few recent studies demonstrate the waning of gender disparities in the field of computer science education; it has become a "woman-friendly field" (Varma and Kapur 2015, p. 1). In her article "Why I Chose Computer Science? Women in India," Roli Varma (2009, p. 2) says that "there has been a significant increase in the number of women pursuing a bachelor's degree in CS. This is despite the prevalence of patriarchy in India." However, many studies explicate the gender disparity in the computer science field in India, owing to various factors such as "opposition to women's access to technology education, lack of income to use public Internet facilities, inconvenient location of such facilities along with security concerns about frequenting them at night, and little leisure time" (Etzkowitz *et al.* 2010, p. 91). Together with these factors, historically, computers and the internet have been conceived as a male-dominated realm. Such attitudes might be embodied in the narrative of the novels. For instance, computer technology could be employed as a source of occupation for male characters. It could be used to signify their skill in using computers.

> I called in Arjun Reddy, my computer-wallah, and he sent out my commands through secure e-mail. He assured me, as he did every week, that we were using the most advanced encryption technology, that we changed our cipher every week, that even if the CIA and the entire American government spent a billion dollars and their entire computer force on one of our e-mails, it would take them two hundred years to break the code. But e-mail still made me nervous. No matter how much Reddy assured me of steel-clad protection, I couldn't get rid of the image of my words swimming through the stomachs of the planet's computers, alone and vulnerable.
>
> *(Chandra 2006, p. 543)*

> Serious and geeky, he turned out to be, sure enough, a computer graphic designer. He was doing this work from a sense of apamaan (of having been insulted).
>
> *(Chaudhuri 2013)*

> But for now, they're both wearing bright yellow, still in their first flush of marriage—one to a computer engineer, the other to a music producer in Bollywood.
>
> *(Doshi 2010, p. 198)*

> Your husband is so good with computers and wires.
>
> *(Adiga 2011, p. 175)*

These passages are extracted from novels such as *Calcutta: Two Years in the City* (2013), *Sacred Games* (2006), The *Pleasure Seekers* (2010), and *Last Man in Tower* (2011) in which the algorithm has collected the frequent appearance of male characters' names. In these novels, either major or non-major characters are allied with computers in many ways. They are either computer engineers or possessing skills in harnessing it. They use it for their entertainment, for example, playing games, watching porn movies, and chatting with other characters. The publications of these novels mainly occurred after the establishment of Information Communication Technology (ICT) and the internet which brought a major shift in social and economic development. This new "knowledge society" and modern urban India unleash new experiences for the novelists to dwell on themes which are primarily integrated by the modern gadgets of computer, internet, and mobile phone. In such conditions, these modern technologies become ubiquitous in some novels published in the late 20th and beginning of the 21st century.

## Conclusion: Overall Pattern of the Technological Devices

The results and discussion bring our attention to the considerable lacuna in the novels: the relationships between male and female characters with technological devices. First of all, male characters' names appeared more frequently than the names of female characters. This gender gap unambiguously exemplifies the gender disparity in the first place. Many scholars like Ritu Menon, Nivedita Menon, Rajeshwari Sundar Rajan, and Shantha Krishnaswamy have discussed the struggles of women for their identities, rights, recognition, and equalities in society and literary novels. However, gender inequality in the science and technology realms, especially in discourses about occupation and access, are less discussed topics in India. Consequently, they have been overlooked by Indian literary scholarship.

Gender disparity is a common phenomenon in India, in terms of access to education, economic conditions and opportunities, science careers and literacy, and the technological fields. Not surprisingly, the technological gender gap in the novels suggest similar such disparities for women characters, especially regarding the possession and accessibility of modern gadgets. The conventional literary interpretation of women and their role and status in society has been questioned since the 1960s. Many writers like Ismat Chughtai, Amrita Pritam, Mahasweta Devi, Krishna Sobti, Kamala Das, and Kamala Markandaya have couched and explored concepts and conceptualizations of bodies, identities, and sexualities. Nevertheless, R. K. Gupta (1993, p. 157) says that the "oppression and exploitation of women" have been an "ever-present theme in Indian literature." He rightly points out that "many modern Indian writers have continued to project and sustain traditional values and to extol old roles and models in their presentation of women" (Gupta 1993, p. 157).

In such a milieu of women characters in the history of Indian English novels, the topic terms of women characters for telephone and computer technologies reinforce the traditional notion that women are barred from harnessing technologies, which are presumed to be part of a male-dominated technological realm, or are otherwise treated as predominately "men's" objects. Novelists did not intentionally portray such settings for women characters, but in order to set up the context for their narrative, they reflected the social imperatives. Overall, these technologies are exercised to reinforce the traditional ideologies of prejudice and create new conventional ideologies for women and men. Such representations of disparity are naturalized and integrated in the narratives and formulated as normative modes of gendered categories. Women have been invariably marginalized/hidden throughout the history of technology, which explicitly and implicitly resonates in the novels. Our topic modelling results, likewise, correspond to such stereotypical gender inequalities. Digital Humanities theory and technologies locate this new insight of gender divide in the novels, which may have been gone unnoticed otherwise.

Goody (2011, p. 1) astutely remarks on the key connection between humankind and technology, in the 20th and 21st centuries, in the following quote:

> [w]hat the twentieth century reveals about technology [primarily communication and network technologies] is its profound fusion with the human; as the century progressed it became impossible to maintain an absolute distinction between the organic expressions of human nature and the technological process, forms and devices which recorded and communicated those expressions as culture.

Such a kind of enmeshed ripple effect, of the technological and the human, offers an alternative trend to Indian novelists, who may incorporate such ideas as a literary artefact in their novels. Agrawal and Sinha (2003, p. v) have observed that, "Indian English novelists of the post-Independence era use not only the thought, imagery and consciousness of their own country milieu but also a familiar rhythm in order to project the growing major trends in Indian milieu." This familiar rhythm encompasses all the transformations of social, political, and cultural states, which also comprise the ripple effects of technological devices that occurred after Independence. For instance, television literary artefact is manipulated as dovetails of social and domestic settings. Television heralds the domestic sphere, and even the sound of the name *television* brings the notion of "home" into our minds. It is not merely employed to deliver news or to entertain its customers, but it also has a personal attachment and emotional connection as it conveys and constructs cultural entities within the living room.

Indeed, the writers of the 20th and 21st centuries insert cultural objects into narrative so as to signify transformation, and such perpetuated actions and transformations affect the group and create dense networks between the characters. For example, the computer and internet create numerous networks to share the information among both individuals and groups. It is important to note that the modern computer and smartphone have the potential to enact the roles of traditional technological institutions such as television. Overall, if we remove these technological artefacts in the novels, the plot would be distorted. The quotidian presence of these cultural apparatuses in society turns out to be unavoidable literary artefacts of 20th- and 21st-century Indian English writers.

Acknowledgement: This chapter is part of the project "A Digital Narratology of Technology as Literary Actors and Artefacts of Settings in Indian English Novels" sponsored by Scheme for Promotion of Academic and Research Collaboration (SPARC). It is a collaborative project between Indian Institute of Technology (IIT) Indore and Lancaster University. The national PI is Dr. Nirmala Menon, IIT Indore, and the international PI is Dr. Deborah Sutton. Experimentation has been completed during the first author's visit to Digital Humanities Hub, Department of History, Lancaster University, through SPARC Visiting Researcher award. The analysis of the experiment completed in the Digital Humanities and Publishing Studies Group, School of Humanities and Social Sciences, Indian Institute of Technology Indore, during the PhD tenure of the first author.

## Bibliography

Agarwal, B.R. and Sinha, M.P. (2003) *Major Trends in the Post-Independence Indian English Fiction*. Chennai: Atlantic Publishers and Distributors.

Adiga, A. (2011) *Last Man in the Tower*. London: Atlantic.

Bathrick, D. (1997) "Making a National Family with the Radio: The Nazi Wunschkonzert." *Modernism/Modernity*, 4(1), pp. 115–127. Available at:10.1353/mod.1997.0001.

Batra, R and Thomas G. Reio Jr. (2016) "Gender Inequality Issues in India." *Advances in Developing Human Resources*, 18(1), pp. 88–101. Available at: 10.1177/1523422316630651.

Bode, K. (2017) "The Equivalence of 'Close' and 'Distant' Reading; or, Toward a New Object for Data-Rich Literary History." *Modern Language Quarterly*, 78(1), pp. 77–106. Available at: 10.1215/00267929–3699787.

Bode, K and Dixon, R. (2009) "Resourceful Reading: A New Empiricism in the Digital Age." In Katherine B and Robert D (ed.) *Resourceful Reading: The New Empiricism*, Sydney: Sydney University Press, pp. 1–27.

Bode, K and Tara M. (2014) "Methods and Canons." In Paul, L. A and Katherine, B (ed.) *Advancing Digital Humanities*, Hampshire: Palgrave Macmillan, pp. 175–193.

Calman, L. J. (1992) *Toward Empowerment: Women and Movement Politics in India*. Colorado: Westview Press.

Chandra, V. (2006) *Sacred Games*. New York: HarperCollins.

Chaudhuri, A. (2013) *Calcutta: Two Years in the City*. New York: Knopf Doubleday Publishing Group.

Chayanika, S. (2014) *Electronic Media and its Impact on the Youths*, PhD thesis, Gauhati University, Available at: shodhganga.inflibnet.ac.in/handle/10603/66154.

Derné, S. (2000) "Men's Sexuality and Women's Subordination in Indian Nationalisms." In Mayer, T. (ed.) *Gender Ironies of Nationalism Sexing the Nation*, London: Routledge, pp. 237–258.

Desai, A. (1999) *Fasting, Feasting*. London: Chatto & Windus.

Doshi, T. (2010) *The Pleasure Seekers*. London: Bloomsbury.

Eide, Ø. (2015) *Media Boundaries and Conceptual Modelling: Between Texts and Maps*. Hampshire: Palgrave Macmillan.

Etzkowitz, H., Namrata, G., and Carol K. (2010) "The Gender Revolution In Science And Technology." *Journal of International Affairs*, 64(1), Available at: sites.asiasociety.org/womenleaders/wpcontent/uploads/2010/05/gender-revolution-in-science-andtechnology.pdf

Frow, J. (2008) "Thinking the Novel". *New Left Review*, 49, pp. 137–145.

Ghose, S. (1955) *The Flame of the Forest*. London: Michael Joseph Ltd.

Goldstone, A. (2015) "Distant Reading: More Work to be Done", *Andrew Goldstone*, 8 August[Online]. Available at: andrewgoldstone.com/blog/2015/08/08/distant/

Goldstone, A. and Underwood, T. (2014) "The Quiet Transformations of Literary Studies: What Thirteen Thousand Scholars Could Tell Us." *New Literary History*, 45(3), p. 359–384. Available at:10.1353/nlh.2014.0025.

Goody, A. (2011) *Technology, Literature and Culture: Themes in 20th and 21st Century Literature: Themes in 20th and 21st Century Literature and Culture*. Cambridge: Polity Press.

Gupta, R.K. (1993) "Feminism And Modern Indian Literature." *Indian Literature*, 36(5), pp. 179–189. Available at: jstor.org/stable/23339720.

Jha, R.K. (2008) *Fireproof*. London: Pan Macmillan.

Jha, R.K. (2015) *She Will Build Him a City*. Londres: Bloomsbury.

Jhabvala, R.P. (1985) *To Whom She Will*. London: Penguin Books.

Jockers, M.L. (2013) *Macroanalysis Digital Methods and Literary History*. Urbana: University of Illinois Press.

Jockers, M.L. (2014) *Text Analysis with R for Students of Literature*. Cham: Springer.
Jockers, M.L. and David, M. (2013) "Significant Themes in 19th-Century Literature." *Poetics*, 41(6), pp. 750–769. Available at: 10.1016/j.poetic.2013.08.005.
Jockers, M.L. and Underwood, T. (2015) "Text-Mining the Humanities." In Susan S. et al., (ed.) *A New Companion to Digital Humanities*, Malden: John Wiley & Sons Ltd., pp. 291–306.
Kalathil, J. (1999) "Imagining audience Doordarshan: Doordarshan and Women's Programming." *Journal of Arts and Ideas*, pp. 87–93. Available at: dsal.uchicago.edu/books/artsandideas/pager.html?objectid=HN681.S597_ 32–33_089.gif.
Khandelwal, D. (2019) "Bridging the Gap for Women in Science and Technology." *ET Rise, Economics Times*, 8 March[Online]. Available at: economictimes.indiatimes.com/small-biz/startups/newsbuzz/bridging-thegap-for-women-in-science-andtechnology/articleshow/68315670.cms?from=mdr
Krishnaswamy, S. (1984) *The Woman in Indian Fiction in English 1950–1980*. New Delhi: Ashish Publishing House.
Love, H. (2010) "Close but not Deep: Literary Ethics and the Descriptive Turn." *New Literary History*, 41(2), pp. 371–391. Available at:10.1353/nlh.2010.0007.
Mauri, M., Elli, T., Caviglia, G., Uboldi, G., and Azzi, M. (2017) "RAWGraphs: A Visualisation Platform to Create Open Outputs." In *Proceedings of the 12th Biannual Conference on Italian SIGCHI Chapter*, pp. 28:1–28:5. New York: ACM. Available at: 10.1145/3125571.3125585.
Moghaddam, G.G. (2010) "Information Technology and Gender Gap: toward a Global View—Semantic Scholar." *The Electronic Library*, 28(5), pp. 722–733. Available at: 10.1108/02640471011081997.
Mukherjee, M. (1971) *The Twice Born Fiction; Themes and Techniques of the Indian Novel in English*. Delhi: Pencraft international.
Roy, A. (1997) *The God of Small Things*. Leicestershire: Clipper Audiobooks.
Rushdie, S. (2001) *Fury*. London: Jonathan Cape.
Sen, B. (2016) *Digital Politics and Culture in Contemporary India: The Making of an Info-Nation*. New York: Routledge.
Schöch, C. (2017) "Topic Modeling Genre: An Exploration of French Classical and Enlightenment Drama." *Digital Humanities Quarterly*, 11(2). Available at: www.digitalhumanities.org/dhq/vol/11/2/000291/000291.html
Subramanian, R. (2006) "India and Information Technology: A Historical & Critical Perspective." *Journal of Global Information Technology Management*, 9(4), pp. 28–46. Available at: 10.1080/1097198x.2006.10856431.
Thayil, J. (2012) *Narcopolis*. London: Penguin Books.
Varma, R. (2009) "Why I Chose Computer Science? Women in India." *AMCIS 2009 Proceedings. 413*. Available at: https://aisel.aisnet.org/amcis2009/413
Varma, R., and Deepak K. (2015) "Decoding Femininity in Computer Science in India." *Communications Of The ACM*, 58(5). Available at: 10.1145/2663339.
Volná, L. (2005) "Anita Desai's Fasting, Feasting and the Condition of Women." *CLCWeb: Comparative Literature and Culture*, 7(3) Available at:10.7771/1481–4374.1272

# 13

# (UN)SCRIPTING HINDUSTANI

## The Special Case of Hindi-Urdu Audiobook

*Abiral Kumar*

Audio media, such as podcasts and song streams, are specifically composed for the audio format and are usually not grounded in any pre-existent form, such as a text. An audio book, however, works as a translation between mediums. The material already exists in another format, that is, the text, which then is converted into an audio recording and is meant to be consumed as an aural experience. Once converted, the text is rendered free from its dependence on the script. Often uploaded on free streaming websites, they can be accessed any time on the global scale. Centred around this liberating notion, this chapter looks at audiobooks as a crucial subset in digital humanities. I argue in favour of the inclusiveness that audiobooks emulate in a postcolonial context. The chapter raises the following question in the process: What does a Hindu-Urdu[1] audiobook mean for the two languages that are believed to be distinct from each other? Hindi and Urdu share the same grammatical structure but are written in different scripts. They are the two claimants to a single linguistic and literary tradition (Faruqi 2003, p. 806). Since an audio book disregards the script, what does it mean for the two languages? Have Hindi and Urdu diverged to the extent that they have become unintelligible to the speaker/listener of the other language? And does the commonality between the two leave any ground for the old ghost of Hindustani to be resurrected?

The chapter is divided into three sections: the first section briefly traces the history of Hindustani in literary discourse and print culture of late 19th century through its defense in Devakinandan Khatri's works; the second section takes up the argument and looks at Hindustani in the aural medium; the third and final section makes use of reader/listener response criticism to closely analyse Hindi-Urdu audiobooks based on the works of Nayier Masud, Intizar Husain, and Kamleshwar. The linguistic and spatial positioning of these writers across two nations and literary cultures serves to make visible the connecting thread—the common literary idiom—that runs between them but is all too often obfuscated by borders of

DOI: 10.4324/9781003354246-17

scripts, cultures and nations. All audiobooks considered in this chapter have been narrated by Tasneef Haidar and his team; they can be accessed from their YouTube channel *Adbi Duniya*.

## Appropriating the Common Tongue

Literary histories of single languages primarily base themselves on archives that support the claims of historical superiority of that particular language while simultaneously excluding the presence of other languages, or scripts, that may challenge their authority.[2] The archive itself is inert; however, meaning is attributed to it through its interaction with agents that seek to define or build a narrative on its basis. Thus, while the actual record, the archive, assumes a secondary position of inert data, the group that writes and therefore controls the narrative gives meaning to the archives. In this way, very different histories, based on different principles and aimed at sometimes even opposite ends, can be written using the same archive. Such discrepancies mostly occur through principles of exclusion and silences.

In this section, I will briefly discuss the history of Hindustani, the possibilities it highlighted, and its gradual dissection into Hindi and Urdu. Instead of focussing upon the separate histories of Hindi and Urdu, I will illustrate the disavowal of Hindustani through the works of Devakinandan Khatri, a writer from the late 19th century who claimed to be writing in the language of the masses, Hindustani.

The debate around the Hindi-Urdu divide, since the late 19th century, has primarily operated between three parties. One holds that Hindi was a pristine language that existed as a derivative of Sanskrit and Prakrit. With the Muslim invasions of the 12th century AD and subsequent patronization of Persian in the Mughal court, the local language gradually lost its pristine quality and borrowed words from Persian and Arabic. The literary history of "early Hindi" is then traced up to Amir Khusro, who, they claim, wrote verses in *Hindavi* in the 13th century AD.[3] This group privileges Hindi over Urdu as the primary language that contained Urdu within itself as a *saili*, a style (Trivedi 2003, p. 960).

The second group argues that no such separate language as Hindi ever existed until the advent of the 19th century. Alternatively, several regional dialects prevalent in parts of North India existed, such as *Khari boli*, *Avadhi*, and *Brajbhasa*. These North Indian dialects can be seen as claimants to the position, which Hindi tries to usurp through a fantastical fabrication of being the native language of the Awadh region. What is now known as Hindi, *Hindavi*, *Gujri*, *Dihlavi*, *Dakhni* or *Rekhta*, were but different names for what is today known as Urdu (Faruqi 2003, p. 806).

As can be inferred from the two approaches, one ingenious strategy adopted by the supporters of both Hindi and Urdu has been to assume that the rival language did not exist at all, and that it is only a modern phenomenon, or at best a dilution of the original (or pure) language by the influx of foreign vocabulary.

The third group, which consists mostly of English philologists along with local agents like Raja Shivprasad, Devakinandan Khatri, and later, Gandhi, Premchand,[4] and Tarachand, believed that the common language of the masses has been neither

Hindi nor Urdu. In fact, both these languages, as they were presented and disseminated into the 19th-century public sphere, in their sanskritized and persianized forms, respectively, were not even close to the language that the people generally spoke in their day-to-day lives. Instead, Hindustani comes across as a more suitable term that could be used to describe a common tongue used by and among the people. Hindustani was spoken equally by all, irrespective of their caste, class, or religion (barring official purpose), but was nonetheless taught to them, and was written in two different scripts, *Nagari* and *Nastaliq*,[5] respectively.

Others point out that Hindustani was simply a label given by the colonizers, understood as "a jargon associated with Muslims and useful for giving orders to soldiers and servants" (Lelyveld 1993, p. 669). Later, Gilchrist—an English trader and subsequently associated with the Fort William college, Calcutta—would prepare a dictionary of Hindustani based on his discovery that Hindustani was not a jargon at all, but "the grand and popular military language of all India" (Lelyveld 1993, p. 670). This erroneous homogenisation of the linguistic variety, that of the "whole of India," ensured that Hindustani remained nothing else apart from a label, and a false one at that. Its existence remained confined between two dictionaries, one prepared by Gilchrist at the beginning of the 19th century, and another prepared by S. H. Vatsyayan "Agyeya" and Chaudhuri Hassan Hasrat in 1945 as the official lexicon for Hindustani news broadcast over All India Radio. In both these cases, the dictionaries did not amount to much, and Hindustani became a language confined to the periphery of the linguistic history of India. The debate surrounding Hindi, Urdu, and Hindustani is very much alive even today, with all three camps holding onto their own arguments. But perhaps it would be better to reconsider the question itself.

Rather than asking what Hindustani was/is, it is perhaps more important to ask what ideological and practical purposes it stood for. In this sense, an answer can be attempted; it reveals the changing definitions of Hindustani over time. For Gilchrist, Hindustani was the language of Hindustan. For Mir Amman and Lallu Lal—the first self-reflexive practitioners of Urdu and Hindi, respectively—the ornate, classically dominant language served as the ideal they wanted to set for Hindustani. For Raja Shivprasad, Hindustani became the language that is spoken by the masses but is not reflected in the literature meant for them. For instance, school books featured two different scripts for pupils who spoke the same tongue. Harishchandra and his followers saw Hindustani as closer to Urdu—in fact, they often referred to the synonymity of the two, thereby rejecting it in the favour of sanskritized Hindi. Khatri sought a slightly different route from both Raja Shivprasad and Bharatendu Harishchandra. For him, language served an undeniably practical purpose, that of dissemination of information and entertainment. He saw Hindustani as the local market language, one that sells and has a larger audience than any other literary language in India. By now, the literary tradition had already been divided into the two separate camps of Hindi and Urdu. Khatri's main achievement lay in his attempt to align these two opposing camps. It is in this effort that popular literature, such as *Chandrakanta*, caused Hindustani to resurface as the literary language for the masses.[6]

By the time Khatri was writing the sixth and last part of the series *Chandrakanta Santati*, the debate had moved on from being about the recognition of Hindustani to the choice between Hindi and Urdu. For Khatri, the crux of the debate was about the usage of "foreign words," particularly those of Persian import, while using the *Devnagri* script.[7] Critics like Hazari Prasad Dwiwedi and Ramchandra Shukl accused him of maligning the traditions of Drona and Bhisma, both of them being guiding personages from the *Mahabharata*, by importing Persian words into pristine constitutions of Hindi, written in the script of the gods, *Devnagri*.

In the 24th part of *Chandrakanta Santati*, Khatri makes a case for the inclusion of the vernacular and Persian vocabulary in his writing and for Hindustani in general. He claims to be using Hindustani, and not Hindi, as the medium for his novels. He refers to the contribution made in the field of Hindi by reputed writers such as the poet Pratap Narayan Mishra, Ambikadutt Vyas, Raja Shivprasad, and Raja Lakshman Singh but also criticizes them. He says,

> Although their modus operandi differed from writer to writer, their final goal was to develop the monopoly of the mother tongue [Hindi] on the soil of Bharat. And it is not to be believed that they could not commit any mistakes, albeit the only mistake they did commit was their lack of attention towards the popular/colloquial words in general parlance.
>
> *(2002b, p. 256)*[8]

This statement in and of itself points to at least three different things. First, Khatri acknowledges the contribution made by his predecessors in his chosen field. He thus displays his familiarity with the prevalent discourses and the direction they are headed towards. Second, he subtly refers to the contribution his work has made by creating a market for Hindi literature where there existed none. Finally, he draws attention to what he finds lacking in the approach of his peers—the complete exclusion of the vernaculars and Persian vocabulary—which he promptly remedies in his own literature, *Chandrakanta*, *Santati*, and *Bhootnath*, among others.

This move towards Hindi could only be achieved if the masses were in possession of an extensive Hindi vocabulary which could define Sanskrit words within the proper contexts, enabling them to use this language in literature and even in their daily lives. Khatri's ingenious manoeuvre lay in first familiarizing them with the Perso-Arabic words, as they occurred in general parlance, and then, eventually, replacing them with Sanskrit-Prakrit derived vocabulary. This allowed the reader to get acclimatized to the linguistic change, and enabled a better understanding of modern Hindi. The popularity of the novel, on the other hand, allowed for its quick proliferation through the Hindustani-speaking population. However, the change, embodied in the removal of "800 years of superstition and foreign custom" [referring to the Mughal rule and Muslim presence in the region] within numbered days, had to be brought in gradually without going against what Khatri (2002a, p. 259) calls the "natural flow" of things. He argues,

> If a philosophical text or letter calls for the effort of combing through a dictionary, then it can be excused, but if a text dealing with standard subjects requires the same treatment then it calls for criticism. My Hindi falls in which of these categories of Hindi I cannot be the judge of, but I do know that one does not need a dictionary to read my work.
>
> *(2002a, p. 258)*

In this regard, Khatri appears to be the first modern writer in India who considered language as a platform for practical usage and experimentation. However, he uses its dynamic multilingual nature to push it towards monolingual standardization. A gradual development in his use of Hindustani can be observed; he steadily moves from simple colloquial speech towards a refined literary complexity. The lexical diversity found in *Chandrakanta*, for instance, is different from that in *Santati* or *Bhootnath*.

These two pages are almost 20 years apart in their publication but belong to the same body of work by Devakinandan Khatri. By comparing the two, one can clearly observe the linguistic shift that occurs through the course of the series' publication history. For instance, on the left panel, an excerpt from *Chandrakanta*,

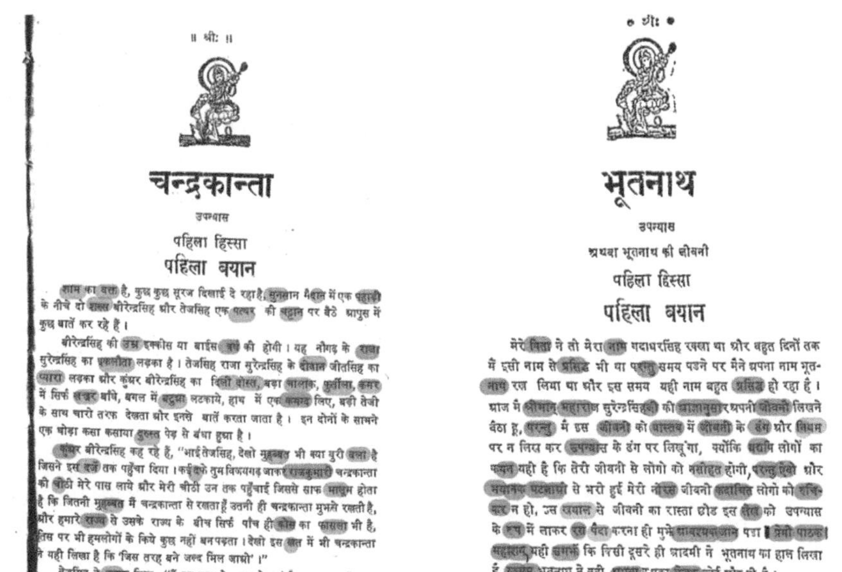

॥ श्रीः ॥

चन्द्रकान्ता

उपन्यास

पहिला हिस्सा

पहिला बयान

शाम का वक्त है, कुछ कुछ सूरज दिखाई दे रहा है, सुनसान मैदान में एक पहाड़ी के नीचे दो शख्स वीरेन्द्रसिंह और तेजसिंह एक पत्थर की चट्टान पर बैठे आपुस में कुछ बातें कर रहे हैं।

वीरेन्द्रसिंह की उम्र इक्कीस या बाईस वर्ष की होगी। यह नौगढ़ के राजा सुरेन्द्रसिंह का इकलौता लड़का है। तेजसिंह राजा सुरेन्द्रसिंह के दीवान जीतसिंह का प्यारा लड़का और कुंअर वीरेन्द्रसिंह का दिली दोस्त, बड़ा चालाक, फुर्तीला, कमर में सिर्फ खंजर बांधे, बगल में बटुआ लटकाये, हाथ में एक कमन्द लिए, बड़ी तेजी के साथ चारो तरफ देखता और इनसे बातें करता जाता है। इन दोनों के सामने एक घोड़ा कसा कसाया दुरुस्त पेड़ से बंधा हुआ है।

कुंअर वीरेन्द्रसिंह कह रहे हैं, "भाई तेजसिंह, देखो मुहब्बत भी क्या बुरी बला है जिसने इस दर्जे तक पहुँचा दिया। कई दफे तुम विजयगढ़ जाकर राजकुमारी चन्द्रकान्ता की चीठी मेरे पास लाये और मेरी चीठी उन तक पहुँचाई जिससे साफ मालूम होता है कि जितनी मुहब्बत मैं चन्द्रकान्ता से रखता हूँ उतनी ही चन्द्रकान्ता मुझसे रखती है, और हमारे राज्य से उसके राज्य के बीच सिर्फ पाँच ही कोस का फासला भी है, तिस पर भी हमलोगों के किये कुछ नहीं बन पड़ता। देखो इस खत में भी चन्द्रकान्ता ने यही लिखा है कि 'जिस तरह बने जल्द मिल जाओ'।"

तेजसिंह ने जवाब दिया, "मैं हर तरह से आपको वहाँ ले जा सकता हूँ मगर

श्रीः

भूतनाथ

उपन्यास

अथवा भूतनाथ की जीवनी

पहिला हिस्सा

पहिला बयान

मेरे पिता ने तो मेरा नाम गदाधरसिंह रक्खा था और बहुत दिनों तक मैं इसी नाम से प्रसिद्ध भी था परन्तु समय पड़ने पर मैंने अपना नाम भूतनाथ रख लिया था और इस समय यही नाम बहुत प्रसिद्ध हो रहा है। आज मैं श्रीमान् महाराज सुरेन्द्रसिंहजी की आज्ञानुसार अपनी जीवनी लिखने बैठा हूं, परन्तु मैं इस जीवनी को वास्तव में जीवनी के ढंग और नियम पर न लिख कर उपन्यास के ढंग पर लिखूंगा, क्योंकि यद्यपि लोगों का कथन यही है कि तेरी जीवनी से लोगों को नसीहत होगी, परन्तु ऐसी और भयानक घटनाओं से भरी हुई मेरी नीरस जीवनी कदाचित लोगों को रुचिकर न हो, इस खयाल से जीवनी का रास्ता छोड़ इस लेख को उपन्यास के रूप में लाकर रस पैदा करना ही मुझे आवश्यक जान पड़ा। प्रेमी पाठक! महाशय, यही समझें कि किसी दूसरे ही आदमी ने भूतनाथ का हाल लिखा है, स्वयम् भूतनाथ ने नहीं, अथवा इसका लेखक कोई और ही है।

**FIGURE 13.1** First page of Khatri's *Chandrakanta* (1888)

*Source*: Left panel—Khatri (2002a)

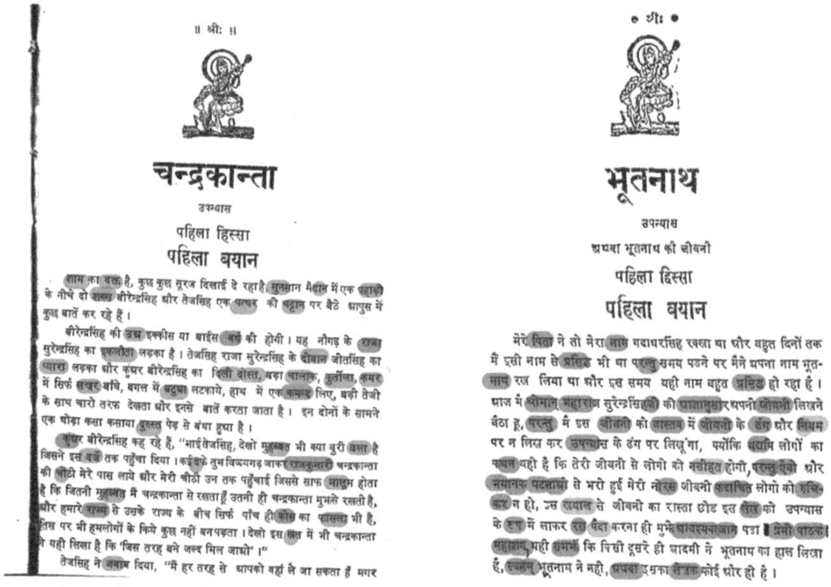


**FIGURE 13.2** First page of Khatri's *Bhootnath* (1907)

*Source:* Right Panel—Khatri (2002b)

the first part in the series, has been used. The words marked with a dark highlight denote the Perso-Arabic words in common use. The words highlighted lightly denote Sanskrit-derived words. The drastic change between the first novel and its later sequel can be observed from the increase in the number of Sanskrit-derived words for the Perso-Arabic ones. The dialectic influences also make their presence felt through inflections within the words, such as *sabhon* instead of *sabhi*, or *sabke saath* or *taine* instead of *Tu ne* or *Tum ne* and colloquial words such as *paji* and *muue*.

Also, the spoken registers of the characters differ from one to another, giving one of the first instances of polyglossia within a modern novel. Nazim Ali and Ahmed Khan's speech is heavily persianized. Krur Singh depends on similar vocabulary only slightly less than that of the Muslim *aaiyars*. Interestingly, all of them together form the antagonistic core of the novel. Tez Singh and Chapla, a pair of *aaiyar* and *aaiyara* who support the protagonist, use a mixed vocabulary but restrict themselves to colloquial and easily understandable words. Birendra Singh and Chandrakanta, along with King Shivdutt and others, who belong to the royal families, primarily rely on sanskritized speech.

In this way, as the reader engages with each text, s/he develops a context-based understanding of the language, which makes use of a mixed vocabulary borrowing from Persian, Arabic, and Sanskrit while sustaining several other dialectic influences. This observation stands in agreement with Khatri's stated intentions in using such a style. He asserts,

> [O]ne will not be able to point when and where the language of *Chandrakanta* and *Santati* diverged, yet on close examination one is sure to find the difference between the beginning and its end; it is similar to the difference between a child and an old man. Had I made use of an extensive vocabulary, it wouldn't have been possible to get the illiterate villagers to remember the Sanskrit words. The result of my efforts is so surprising that even they, who opposed my use of language, have begun to include Urdu words in their *pure Hindi*.[9]
>
> *(Maduresh 2002, p. 59)*

This is evident again in the first two chapters of *Bhootnath*. One cursory glance reveals that the influx of Sanskrit vocabulary has increased many folds, and yet the change has been so gradual that it does not compromise the flow of the narrative. An example can be found in this selection of words, *bhayanak, ratri, vyarth, asthah, tathapi, prashat, pakshapati, dharmatma, vichitra, pralapavastha, aashchaya, kadachit, dukhant, punah, kratagya, parichya, nisandeh, kadapi, yadyapi*, etc. Therefore, by the time the reader arrives at *Bhootnath*, the register has completely changed. Even the Muslim characters, such as Sher Ali Khan, make use of *tatsam* words—derived from Sanskrit sources—such as *vilamb* and *uchit* in their sentences.

How is this deliberate transformation of language to be understood? And more importantly, what does it signify? Primarily, it reveals the common ground that existed between Hindi and Urdu, in the name of Hindustani, before they diverged into two distinct languages. But more importantly, Khatri's Hindustani stands as a substantial proof of not only the existence of Hindustani as a viable language but also his move towards standardization of the language into purified Hindi, thereby silencing the very language he claimed to be writing in. The ambiguity surrounding Hindustani becomes its greatest strength in Khatri's hands. Emphasizing his service to Hindi and Sanskrit, Khatri writes,

> Whether one is Hindu, Jain, Buddhist, a follower of Arya Samaj or Dharma Samaj, for those whose ancestors have adorned and blessed this land, why would they not want the dedicated propagation of the pure and sweet Sanskrit.
>
> *(2002, p. 257)*

It is to be noted that he entirely excludes Muslims from having any presence in history and ancestry of "this land," India, while the Jains and the Buddhists are seen as belonging to one family tree, one ancestry, and most importantly, one script. Urdu, Arabic, Persian, and in association with it, its practitioners—the Muslims—are projected as foreign elements that did not belong in the Indian culture, thereby emphasizing the autochthonous and historical superiority of Hindi/Hindu which supposedly flowers naturally from the Indian custom.[10]

Khatri concludes, "In any case my views on language remain that it be simple and in *Nagri*, for the characters of the language exercise a pull towards the root languages from which they spring" (2002, p. 259). Therefore, writing in *Devnagri* assumes more importance in Khatri's point of view, rather than the usage of words, whose etymological roots can be traced back to Sanskrit alone. While the vernaculars, such as *Kaithi* and *Brahmi*, that also existed as rival scripts but shared a common identity in terms of religious affiliation and cultural synonymity, could either be ignored for their low status in the literary sphere and fewer speakers or were incorporated into the fold of Hindi by the logic that they sprang from the same fountainhead of a root language—Sanskrit, or even by citing that they are broken forms of the same language, Prakrit; the real challenge came from an erstwhile court language that used a different script.

In his 1868 memorandum titled *Court Characters in the Upper Provinces of India*, Raja Shivprasad pointed out that the alphabets in the *Nastaliq* script required repeated interpretation. Their phonemes were easily alterable, thus making an easy matter of forgery and error in official documents. Minor changes in strokes could make for a different alphabet and a different word, giving it a very unstable dispensation. The alphabets of *Devnagri* script, however, were more starkly defined and thus could provide for a more efficient use in official work.[11]

Following the example of Raja Shivprasad's memorandum, another memorandum titled, *Court Characters and Primary Education in the N-W Provinces and Oudh*, was compiled in 1897. No authorship was attributed to it, although Dalmia believes that Madan Mohan Malviya played a prominent role in its construction (1997, p. 176). It features a detailed review of arguments presented by Raja Shivprasad, and goes on to quote him extensively on the topic. It argues that the British made a mistake by replacing Persian with Urdu as the language of the court of Law in 1837, since the language of the masses had clearly been Hindi from the time of Muslim invasion.[12] It went on to claim that on a practical level, owing to inherent defects in Urdu's Persian-derived script and a vocabulary composed largely of Persian and Arabic loan words, Urdu is incomprehensible to most. The official use of *Nagri*,[13] on the other hand, would lead to the rise in literacy levels and primary education in India (Ahmed 2008, p. 1168).

Simultaneously, once the supremacy of the script has been established over all its rivals, the ascendency of the culture follows, and a composite Hindu nationality can be asserted, free of all challenges from competing scripts, vernaculars, or cultures.[14]

This argument finds support in a prominent discussion between Alok Rai and Shahid Amin. When prompted to speak upon Khatri's Hindustani as an alternative to Hindi, Rai argues that Khatri's claim for Nagri as a common script was a non-starter to begin with. He asserts that,

> Khatri completely missed the point that the whole impulse of the script movement was precisely to create a demand, which would be acceptable to only a few people. The script demand was of its essence, of its intrinsic and necessary nature, a divisive demand; it was a demand for a claim against some people.
>
> *(2005, p. 202)*

While Rai's larger argument itself is precise, its first part stands to be challenged. The impact *Chandrakanta* had in creating a public familiar with modern Hindi, in line with Khatri's own stated intentions, shows that he was keenly aware of the contemporary language politics and was, in fact, an active participant in it. Not only did he make a case for the use of *Nagri*, he also employed it in his work of immense popularity, thereby creating a demand that extended from being acceptable to only a few people to being the requirement for producing any literature of consequence. Simultaneously, the demand for the script—a divisive demand, as Rai calls it—much aggravated by *Chandrakanta*'s popularity, worked as the first crack between two communities, one which ultimately resulted into the partition of India.

*Chandrakanta*, despite its claim to have been composed in Hindustani, and following Khatri's passionate defense of its language, is now firmly claimed by the archivists of Hindi literary tradition as its own. It is regarded as one of the first novels in Hindi and is credited with establishing the base for Hindi as a language and the novel in India, in general. The question of the script finds emphasis here as well. As Rai argues, the demand for separate scripts was essentially a divisive demand. The respective scripts came to identify Hindi and Urdu and with it carried the associations of Hindu and Muslim identity.[15] Hindustani, as a language and identity, appeared to have no place in this binary division, at least until Gandhi made it into a nationalist agenda and invoked it as the repository of a pan-Indian identity. The move was entirely political and could not maintain its promise in the long run. The two scripts had carved out their channels and guarded their literary and intellectual history exclusively. Few writers, such as Premchand, who wrote and published in both the scripts, also found it practical to choose to write in one script over the other. Although their books appeared in both scripts in a varying number of editions, they are claimed by one side or the other and are denied a common existence in a common literary history of the one language, in two scripts.

## Hindustani in the Aural Culture

The Hindi-Urdu audiobook comes as a crucial intervention in this highly fraught/contested history of the two languages. Its uniqueness derives from the fact that an audiobook, by its very nature, must disregard the script in its final production. As has been mentioned in the Introduction, one of the key features of an audiobook is its independence from the script. The listener's experience of the narrative is solely based on the oral aspect of the text and performance of the language by the narrator. The text is rendered free of the script, and with it the reader too is not dependent on it. One is not actively involved in the process of deciphering symbols off the page. Instead, it is being done for them by the narrator of the text. This characteristic of the audiobook is exploited particularly well in the case of Hindi-Urdu audiobooks. The two languages, independent of their respective scripts, are brought back into the spoken domain. Here, the similarity between the two languages—their common heritage—expresses itself, thereby making it intelligible to speakers of both these languages.

However, this is not the first instance where the language freed from the script has been produced for the auditory medium. In 1947, the Muslim League was adamant that Urdu alone was the language of the masses—both Hindus and Muslims in North India—and that any imposition of Hindi, even under the pseudonym of "Hindustani," was no less than a conspiracy to omit a collective history which has been shaped by Hindus and Muslims alike. However, they did concede to the use of a simplified Urdu which permitted the use of words from Hindi and Sanskrit (Lelyveld 1993, pp. 677–678). A weak compromise was worked out whereby, depending on the station and the population density of Hindus and Muslims in an area, the newscast was read out in Hindi, Urdu, or Hindustani. The three languages primarily differed in the relative mix of Sanskrit, Persian, Arabic, and other dialectic words determined by the advisory committees for each language.

It is interesting to note here that while scientific reasoning was enlisted to enumerate the flaws of one script and validate the other, half a century later, the debate seemed to have shifted to the issue of vocabulary. Yet, even within the spoken medium, script played a large role in further division of the two languages. The broadcast had to be prepared in English, then translated into specific Indian languages, depending upon the chosen language of the broadcast, before it was read out live on air from Delhi. This ensured that the languages maintained a small-but standard, and permitted, linguistic variation. Radio plays and other cultural productions were also either broadcast in specific locations, on the basis of the relative population density of Hindus and Muslims, or they were claimed by one side or the other as their own, thereby rejecting the possibility of a shared culture.

A final attempt to revive this shared culture was made in the name of Hindustani. In 1940, S. H Vatsyayan "Agyeya" and Chaudhuri Hassan Hasrat were tasked by Bukhari to compile a dictionary for Hindustani by listing words from the vernacular translation of news broadcasts and working out "a compromise based on what they considered [the] most common, precise and, if possible neutral" words between the two languages (Lelyveld 1993, p. 679). Their efforts took five years to reach completion, by which time the demand for a separate language, culture, and identity had long since snowballed into demand for a new nation. The project was abandoned, and, with it, Hindustani. Given this history of Hindustani and its run in the auditory medium, what has the Hindi-Urdu audiobook got to offer?

On the surface, audiobooks appear to hark back to an age of orality that predated the writing practice. The experience of "listening" to a story, as opposed to reading it, recalls a pre-modern era of storytelling and community listening. This already configures writing as a technology that reshapes the practice of storytelling. With the advent of writing, the characteristics of a tale told in the telling was permanently altered. In the storytelling format, for instance, the now-ness of narration is most prominent; with the active participation of listeners, the cadence of narrator and the contouring of the story adjust according to the audience. The tradition of *dastan-goi* is a recently revived example of this practice.

A *dastan* can only exist orally; in the written format, it becomes the ghost of the oral word. While the written version dictates, by its very nature, that the tale be confined between the two covers of the book, in its oral domain, the *dastan* can stretch on infinitely. Episodes from the tale are picked up and elaborated upon by the narrator according to the needs and requirements of the gathering. The *dastan* narrator is akin to a virtuoso performer. S/he improvises on the outline of the story and delivers a tale that is new in every iteration. Thus, the same tale does not wear out no matter how many times it is repeated, for, in each of its repetitions, something extra is added to it. This extra quality may be defined by the context in which the tale is narrated.

The audiobook, although it exists in the aural domain, is different from modes of oral storytelling such as the *dastangoi* tradition. The audiobook takes the written text as its basis, and doubles upon its narrative. The narrative, thus, exists in both mediums, the printed and the auditory. Unlike other forms of auditory media, such as television and radio, or earlier forms of storytelling that relied entirely on oral dissemination, the initial form is not consumed in the production of the newer form. The text is not a means to an end, which is produced in the form of a finished audio cassette or a television program. Instead, the text and the audiobook exist simultaneously, one seemingly independent of the other, and yet sharing a deeper umbilical connection with each other.

Moreover, the narrator of the text also acts as its performer. The listener's experience of the text relies on their compatibility with the narrator's style, accent, speed, and voice. The narrator works to embody the text, filling it with their personality. This makes the audiobook a personal dialogue between the narrator and the listener. The immediacy of the listening experience remains intact while also lending to it the permanence of the written text. The audiobook appears to embody the best of both worlds, the oral and the written, while maintaining its own individual contribution as a literary medium. A further examination of the Hindi-Urdu audiobook as a literary medium, through specific examples, will help us delineate its impact upon the idea(l) of literature and the possibility of reviving a shared cultural history.

## The Hindi-Urdu Audiobook

Let me begin with a personal contradiction: some of my favourite short stories and novels come from the Urdu literary sphere, yet I have not had the chance, or the ability, to read any of them. I am not familiar with the Urdu script in which most of these stories exist. Some stories, by writers such as Intizar Husain, I had the good luck to encounter in *Devnagri* script, so I could enjoy them. Gradually, as my interest grew, I scoured all places—the bookstores, the libraries, the online digital archives for his stories—but all of these sources were ultimately exhausted. At this point, the YouTube algorithm recommended the channel *Adbi Duniya*. Here, Tasneef Haidar and his team curate some of the best stories from the domain of Urdu and Hindi literature. They narrate these stories in a simple, lucid, and straight-forward manner, without modifying the original script, so as to make it more appealing and without imposing unnecessary explanations on the text.

This was not my first foray into the domain of audiobooks. I had used them extensively till now to listen to contemporary literature, primarily science fiction and fantasy. Much of the audiobook industry works out of studios and employs professionals to narrate the text. Accomplished actors and personalities often narrate the texts in a dramatic manner to achieve the spoken effect of the written text. However, a large part of it is also produced by individuals and volunteer groups for open-source platforms where the content is not hidden behind a paywall and is made accessible to all. *Abdi Duniya* is one such channel that makes use of YouTube as a platform to create and archive stories from Hindi and Urdu literature.

Apart from professionally produced audiobooks by platforms such as Audible and Storytel, the audiobook market for Hindi and Urdu literature is untapped. The vast amount of literature locked in the two scripts prefigures a market of its own with tremendous possibilities. Online platforms, such as Audible and Storytel, are trying to fill in this gap. Their choices, however, are driven by economic impetus. A quick survey of their catalogue of the Hindi-Urdu audiobooks yields most titles of popular classics, folk-tales, and fewer theory and literary works. This gap is expertly filled in by volunteer organizations that curate, archive, and present literary texts and even translated works from other foreign languages on their website/channels. All of them follow their own specific criteria for the selection of texts they wish to upload in the audio format. Haidar relates that he prefers to adapt only those texts into audio format that provide the listener with a sense of freshness, and which alter their perspective on life and times (Adbi Duniya 2019c). The uniqueness inherent in the experience of listening to a text, a literary work, can sometimes afford a fresh perspective on the work that had hitherto not been so obvious in the text. The growing world-wide popularity of audiobooks testifies to its ability to satisfy the listeners and allow them to engage with literature in their busy lives. In the realm of digital humanities, audiobooks are beginning to carve a space for themselves. Professors, at times, have assigned audiobooks to students as a part of the curriculum (Bednar 2010, p. 79). In the domains of research, and analysis, audiobooks provide unique angles of interpretation, whereby not only the words on the page but also their aural characteristics, especially in the case of poetry, are fully realized.

However, it must be noted that the digitally accessible audiobook is not entirely independent of the written text. While the narrative is delivered aurally to the listener, the paratext associated with the content—such as the title of the story, the brief description that introduces the uploaded file, the credits for narration, editing, and management bring the written text back into prominence, and with it, emphasize the choice of script as well. For instance, the titles of audiobooks uploaded on *Adbi Duniya* generally follow the pattern of mentioning the name of the story/book in three separate scripts—Roman, *Nastaliq*, and *Nagri*—followed by the name of the author in Roman script. The "About" section of the channel appears entirely in Roman script. Whereas most of its publicity material shared on Social media platforms is written out in *Nagri* and less frequently in *Nastaliq*. The choice between Nastaliq and Nagri depends upon the writer whose quote is being shared. For the authors of Urdu literature, the quotes feature in *Nastaliq* script.

Similarly, those posts featuring Hindi writers appear in *Nagri* script. English, on the other hand, is employed only in general informational posts intended for a larger and inclusive audience.

Thus, in the written domain, where it becomes increasingly difficult to negotiate between the two rival scripts, Roman alphabets function as the middle ground. To maintain the original aural commonality that exists between Urdu and Hindi, the title of the story, and the name of the author is transliterated into the Roman script that is accessible to both sides. However, the credits, file description, and further recommendations appear in English and, by its virtue, not only attract the users of the two scripts—*Nastaliq* and *Nagari*—but also invite the new listeners to who may share an interest in the combined Hindi-Urdu literary heritage.

A closer analysis of three audiobooks uploaded on *Adbi Duniya* will help clarify the argument further. Haidar narrates Intizar Husain on his channel, *Adbi Duniya*. In his rendition of *Basti*, the audiobook begins simply with the announcement of the title followed by the text of the novel. No other prefatory material or publication details are read out. It does away with the dedication of the book to "Askari Saheb" and the epigraph, "मै क़सम खाता हूँ इस शहर की" ("I swear in the name of this city") from the Quran (Husain 2019, pp. 5–7). In the Hindi print version of the novel, both of these are given the space of one full page each before the beginning of the first chapter. The weight these words carry is effaced in the audiobook. Moreover, there is no mention of the script or the language, or the author in the narration itself. The title of the video, uploaded on YouTube reads, "Basti l بستی l बस्ती l Intizar Husain l Part 1/10" (Adbi Duniya 2019a). Novels and longer short stories are usually uploaded in parts, so as to allow the reader to toggle between them. The mention of the title in all three scripts invites the readers of all three domains. The writer is further introduced in the description section of the upload. This part can be expanded by the listener by clicking on the "read more" tab, but is usually kept out of the view. The description section also carries the name of the narrator and the financial domain of the channels for the redirection of funds, commissions, and financial support.

The narration begins in line with the text, and we hear Zakir reminiscing about his childhood. Since the text is narrated, it appears as if Zakir himself is telling us the small details and wonders of his life in the village in pre-partition India. In the first few minutes of the narration, very few words come up that can be identified exclusively as Hindi or Urdu. The lexical difference exerts itself in the speech patterns of various characters. Bi Amma peppers her mostly colloquial dialogues with words such as "*lahim-sahim*" (fat and well built) (Adbi Duniya 2020a), whereas the dialogue between more literate and literary personalities such as Hakim Bande Ali, Museeb Hussain, and Abbajan abounds with words that can be identified with Urdu vocabulary. At the other extreme of this is Bhagat-ji, who also employs colloquial dialogue peppered with a few exclusively Hindi words, such as "*shesh*," that can only be culturally defined, since it doubles as the primordial multiheaded serpent, *shesh-naga*, as well as contains the meaning, "remainder"; both of these words, and their definitions, are co-dependent.

Intizar Husain's writing abounds in its lexical variety. In another short story, *Shanti Shanti Shanti*, narrated by Fatima Khan on *Adbi Duniya*, the vocabulary is almost entirely a mix of colloquial and Hindi words (Adbi Duniya 2020b). The story centres around the theme of reincarnations and takes its cultural context from Hinduism. On the other hand, a story such as *Aakhri Aadmi*, narrated by Tasneef Haidar on *Adbi Duniya*, is mainly composed with Perso-arabic words that comprise another spectrum of the Urdu vocabulary. The influence of oral traditions, from the Hindu, Buddhist, and Islamic cultures, can clearly be seen in Intizar Husain's writing. Their presence in the textual form is observable, but when rendered into the audiobook, they become much more pronounced. His works come into their own in the audiobook format.

The same is not entirely true for other writers, such as Naiyer Masud. Masud, a careful writer and craftsman of the short story format, weighs his words carefully. The precision of each word carries with it the context of the narrative and takes it to its extreme ends. For instance, his story *Jaan—e Aalam* makes use of a Perso-Arabic vocabulary to emphasize its contextual theme of the *dastan* in the Awadhi court culture (Adbi Duniya 2016). On the other hand, *Taoos Chaman ki Maina* takes a commoner from the Lucknow of 1850s, who works in the garden of Wajid Ali Shah's palace, as its narrator (Adbi Duniya 2019d). Here, once again, Masud employs words alone to create the atmosphere of Awadh from the mid-19th century from a non-elite, layperson's point of view.

Kamleshwar's *Kitne Pakistan*, narrated by Pooja Bhatia on *Adbi Duniya*, paints a slightly different picture (Adbi Duniya 2019b). Much like Intizar Husain's *Shanti Shanti Shanti*, the narrator employed in the novel is male, but the reading is performed by a female. While one would expect a slight dissonance in the audiobook narration with this gender switch, such is not the case. The narration flows smoothly, and the dialectical plurality of the novel is brought to the fore. The novel makes copious use of court language and thus retains a formal aspect to it. One listener goes on to state, "उपन्यास नही रपोिरताज लगता है" ("Feels more like a reportage than a novel") (Adbi Duniya 2019b). But, to me, this does not take away the experience of the book, rather it adds to it. The language of law and order in India retains the use of Urdu vocabulary, alongside Hindi words and expressions, and employs it for its day-to-day proceedings. The novel reflects this aspect beautifully and the scenes that describe the historical personages from the mixed cultural history of the subcontinent and beyond uses an equally diverse lexicon to give space to their voices. Another listener, Shyam Yadav, praises the audiobook in these words,

> बहुत सुना था इस किताब के बारे में, जितना सुना उससे भी बेहतर।
>
> कीमतों को लेकर खरीदने में असमर्थ होकर फ्री पढ़ने की सोच रहा था पर यूट्यूब पर ऑडियो में सुनकर बहुत खुश हुआ, बहुत बहुत धन्यवाद।
>
> *(Adbi Duniya 2019b).*

I had heard so much about this book; it has still managed to surpass my expectations. Since I could not afford the book I thought of reading it for

> free, but listening to the audio [version] on YouTube has made me happy. Many thanks.
>
> *(Adbi Duniya 2019b)*

This highlights another crucial aspect of the audiobook. Uploaded and accessed on free platforms, these audiobooks provide one with the opportunity of engaging with good literary works free of cost and at their ease. One can access these archives at any time they please, be it during an arduous commute or while doing the household chores. Unlike its printed counterparts, which require greater exclusive attention, the audiobook frees one from overly pedantic and ritualized engagement with literature and brings it back to its flexible and approachable form.

The analysis of these short stories suggests that it is difficult to separate one language from the other. The density of Hindi, or Urdu word clusters depends upon the narrative context. While Intizar Husain's story may well be considered Hindi, plain and spoken, Nayier Masud's Urdu explores a greater degree of literariness, and Kamleshwar's Hindi also stands on the line between Hindi and Urdu. It appears from the statistical analysis of the words that the difference between the two languages, if one discounts the difference of the scripts, remains one that can be explained in a range only, and in no absolute terms. Thus, the language adopts a tenor that suits the context. The diverse traffic of listeners, pouring from both sides of the linguistic divide, reinstates the cultural and literary fluidity across the borders of script, culture, and nation. Nor are these the only examples that illustrate this continuity which serves to deconstruct the binaries of ideology and identity such as the Hindi-Hindu-Hindustan; and Muslim–Urdu–Pakistan analogy. As Nishat Zaidi aptly points out, in the realm of entertainment media, these analogies are challenged on a daily basis (Zaidi 2015, p. 169). Rahi Masoom Raza's genius in the script and dialogue production of the popular serial *Mahabharat* and Ramanand Sagar's screenplay and production of another popular serial *Alif Laila* are a few examples of the same.

## Conclusion

Marshall McLuhan's question on the impact of media enumerates four important questions that can determine the effect a medium has on the content. He asks,

> What does the medium enhance? What does the medium make obsolete? What does the medium retrieve from what was previously deemed obsolete? What does the medium become when pushed to its limits?
>
> *("Old Messengers, New Media")*

These questions can be answered, in the context of Hindu-Urdu audiobooks, by considering whether they enhance the commonality between two languages that have been deemed separate and exclusive to each other while making obsolete the very difference and distance that has been deliberately cultivated over a century and a half. It retrieves the shared cultural and literary heritage of a single community that was divided on the basis of script, language, and identity.

Moreover, it is interesting to note that while Khatri recognized the market potential for Hindustani and at the same time sought to "correct" it and transform it into a purified Hindi, the Hindi-Urdu audiobook does the opposite. As opposed to attempts to "purify" and standardize language in the late 19th century by the practice of exclusion, the Hindi-Urdu audiobook appears to build bridges between the two languages by encouraging inclusion of words from the vocabulary of both languages. This practice is not free from confusion and obstacles either. A listener of Masud's *Jaan—e Aalam* enquires "Sir galib ka kya kya mtlb hota hain?" (Sir, what are the various meanings of *galib*?) (Adbi Duniya 2016), just as another may not understand a difficult Hindi word, like "अनुकंठा". Haidar responds to this issue in *Kuch Zaroori Baatein*. He is of the opinion that the story creates its own context and the words used in the story should be able to signify their meaning within that context. Any external list of word-meanings used in the text not only works to undermine the writer's ability to convey the meaning but also reduces the enjoyment of the story to a pedantic exercise.

Unlike commercial audiobook platforms such as Audible and Storytel that allow for reviews of a certain novel or story, the listeners on YouTube prefer to address the narrator directly. They complement the narrator's craft and leave their suggestions to include the stories they would like to hear. Some praise the narrator's voice through comments like Ravi Bhasin who writes, "क्या बात है तसनीफ भाई! जो मज़ा आ रहा है इस को सुनने का वो लफ्ज़ों मे बयान करना मुशकल है। आपको ढेरों दुआएँ! ❤❤❤" ("Such a pleasure Tasneef *Bhai!* The joy of listening to this [audiobook] cannot be expressed in words. May God bless you! ❤❤❤") (Adbi Duniya 2020a). Another complains, "Tasneef sir kbhe kbhe aap bahot zada boring stories upload karte h.. Manto ya Ismat ma'am ki stories upload Kare plzz" (Tasneef sir, sometimes you upload the most boring stories . . . please upload Manto's or Ismat [Chugtai] ma'am's stories) (Adbi Duniya 2020c).

Haidar addresses these concerns in special uploads where he thanks his listeners, responds to their queries, and tells them about his plan to incorporate their demands. This connection, and responsibility towards the audience/subscribers, is a core aspect of YouTube culture. By facilitating and maintaining the discussions, the stories, and the endeavour are kept alive and thriving, adapting constantly with the changes of the times.

Finally, to answer McLuhan's last question, when pushed to its limits, the future of the Hindi-Urdu audiobook holds a lot of promise as a ground for assimilation of the two languages. It makes it possible for Hindi and Urdu, as Hindustani, to be recognized as a world language. This can only be achieved by the process of inclusion, not exclusion, and inculcating lexical and grammatical flexibility, not rigidity. The Hindi-Urdu audiobook is a welcome step in this direction. By familiarizing the listeners to a diverse vocabulary that includes words from the two languages and various other dialects, it strives towards a literature that can be accessed and claimed by both sides as their own as an inclusive, shared heritage, as it ought to be.

## Notes

1 Throughout the paper, I have used the appellation of Hindi-Urdu audiobooks, instead of Hindi and Urdu audiobooks. While the latter expresses the difference of the two languages, the former emphasizes their commonality in the spoken format. Yet I have not used *Hindustani* to refer to this commonality, given the historical context and the fraught linguistic battle concerning Hindustani in particular. However, it remains a possibility in the future of the Hindi-Urdu audiobook.

2 *Archive*, here, is to be understood as a body of information collected in material form (through the creation of canon, compendiums or court documentations) that later writers draw upon and use for referential purposes.

3 The credibility of Khusro's verses in *Hindavi* is considered dubious since any mention of these verses does not reach back any further than the 17th century. His Persian verses, on the other hand, have a documented history of 500 years. Also, the language used for *Hindavi* verses are very similar to modern Hindi, as it came to develop in the 19th century. Therefore, they appear as attributions to Khusro rather than being his own writing. However, a counter argument can be made in the favour of Khusro's verses in *Hindavi*. Since these verses were composed in the vernacular, they could not receive the canonization that his Persian verses attained. In this regard, while they do not find a place in the authorized anthologies amongst Khusro's Persian verses, the *Hindavi* verses were much more disseminated amongst the folk—the ones who spoke the language and perhaps were its primary audience as well. Thus, it is amongst the folk traditions, such as the *pahelis, doha,* and *geet,* that the *Hindavi* verses of Khusro are celebrated. Cf. Losensky, Paul E.; Sharma, S. (2011) *In the Bazaar of Love: The Selected Poetry of Amir Khusrau;* Saeed, Y. (2003) *Khusrau's Hindvi Poetry, An Academic Riddle?*

4 Premchand's argument, published in *Kuch Vichar*, illustrates his idea of Hindustani. He argues that

> [both Hindi and Urdu] lay claim to the status of India's national language. But they could not fulfill the nation's need in their own independent ways and so their collective collaboration and intermingling naturally began. Their combined constitution resulted into what we rightfully call the Hindustani tongue.
>
> *(103–105)*

5 While the script associated with Persian, Arabic or Urdu has been referred to, respectively, as the Persian, Arabic, or Urdu script in various sources, I find the use of *Nastaliq* as one which describes them best, since it belongs to the calligraphic traditions in Persian, Arabic, and Urdu literature.

6 Taj concludes on a similar note:

> The distinction between Hindi and Urdu was chiefly a question of style. A poet could draw upon Urdu's lexical richness to create an aura of elegant sophistication, or could use the simple rustic vocabulary of dialect Hindi to evoke the folk life of the village. Somewhere in the middle lay the day to day language spoken by the great majority of people. This day to day language was often referred to by the all-encompassing term *Hindustani*.
>
> *(Taj, A., 1997)* Urdu through Hindi: Nastaliq with the help of Devanagari. *Rangmahal Press.*

7 All translations have been done by the author of this paper unless stated otherwise.

8 All translations have been done by the author of this paper unless stated otherwise.

9 Emphasis has been added by the author of this chapter.

10 The roots of such a conjunction of language, script, geographical ethnicity, and religious identity can be seen to develop from here which expresses itself much more clearly in Savarkar's *Hindutva*. Here he lays down the two criteria that determines a Hindu and by extension, a native of Hindustan. First, they must consider Hindustan as their "holy land" and second, it must be the land of their forefathers, "fatherland" (Savarkar 1969,

pp. 4–5). In this regard, geographical ethnicities such as Chinese, Japanese, and Tibet that saw India as their "Holy land" were taken as obvious examples of non-native and in the same line the religious ethnicities such the Muslims, Christians, Jews and Parsees were also excluded as foreign elements to India. Cf. Savarkar, V. D. (1969) *Hindutva: Who is a Hindu?* Bombay: S. S. Savarkar.

11 Along with this document, Raja Shivprasad also compiled a "Unified Hindi-Urdu Grammar" and Khatri refers to as "Raja Shivprasad Hindi" that according to Khatri, "helped bring the light of Hindi into government schools" (2002, p. 257).

12 Not only is the statement false—since the first instance of Hindi as a recognised language appears much later in late 18th—early 19th century itself, and also because the Muslim presence in India can be traced back to the invasion of Sindh led by Muhammad bin Qasim in 712 AD—the logic goes to show that the superiority of the script, *Devnagri*, is traced back to the ancient Hindu past untainted by the Muslim presence altogether, thus making it the only script and by extension the language and Hindu culture that "originally" belongs to India.

13 *Nagri* is often used as a diminutive word for *Devnagri*.

14 However, such was not the case entirely. In 1900, the British government issued a decree granting symbolic equal status to both Hindi and Urdu. Urdu had to share its supremacy with the newly fashioned Hindi. In order to unite the populace and present a united front against the British, Gandhi sought to merge this divide. He proposed the use of either *Devnagri* or *Nastaliq* script to write in the language of, what he called, *Hindustani. Hindustani,* argued for by Raja Shivprasad, brought into literature by Devakinandan Khatri and made the language of Indian unity by Gandhi, remained and prospered to a point where it could be picked up and be used to narrate the stories of Hindus and Muslims alike in the literature of Premchand and others of the era of independence struggle.

15 Although *Chandrakanta* was published, both in *Devnagri* script and later in *Nastaliq*, it was originally written, without accident, in the *Devnagri* script. However, it took as its target audience both the practitioners of *Devnagri* script as well as the *Nastaliq* script.

## References


Adbi Duniya (2016) *Jaan E Aalam By Naiyyar Masood*. Narrated by Tasneef Haidar. YouTube.

Adbi Duniya (2019a) *Aakhri Aadmi | آخری آدمی | आख़री आदमी | Intizar Husain*. Narrated by Tasneef Haidar. YouTube.

Adbi Duniya (2019b) *Kitne Pakistan | कितने पाकिस्तान | کتنے پاکستان | Kamleshwar | Part 1/3*. Narrated by Pooja Bhatia. YouTube.

Adbi Duniya (2019c) *Kuchh Zaroori Baatein | کچھ ضروری باتیں | कुछ ज़रूरी बाते | Tasneef Haidar*. Narrated by Tasneef Haidar. YouTube.

Adbi Duniya (2019d) *Taaoos Chaman Ki Maina | طائوس چمن کی مینا | ताऊस चमन की मैना | Naiyer Masud | Part 1/2*. Narrated by Tasneet Haidar, YouTube.

Adbi Duniya (2020a) *Basti | بستی | बस्ती | Intizar Husain | Part 1/10*. Narrated by Tasneef Haidar. YouTube.

Adbi Duniya (2020b) *Shanti Shanti Shanti* | *Intizaar Husain*. Narrated by Fatima Khan. YouTube.

Adbi Duniya (2020c) *Nudba* || *Short Story* || *Naiyer Masud*. Narrated by Tasneef Haidar. YouTube.

Ahmed, Rizwan (2008) 'Scripting a new identity: The battle for Devanagari in Nineteenth Century India,' *Journal of Pragmatics*, 40.7, pp. 1163–1183.

Amin, S., and Rai, A. (2005) 'A Debate between Shahid Amin and Alok Rai regarding Hindi', *Annual of Urdu Studies*, 20, pp. 181–202.

Bednar, L. (2010) 'Audiobooks and the Reassertion of Orality: Walter J. Ong and Others Revisited', *CEA Critic* 73.1, pp. 74–85.

Dalmia, V. (1997) *The Nationalization of Hindu Traditions: Bhāratendu Hariśchandra and nineteenth-century Banaras*. Oxford University Press.

Faruqi, S. R. (2003) 'A Long History of Urdu Literary Culture, Part 1,' in Pollock, S. (ed.) *Literary Cultures in History: Reconstructions from South Asia*. University of California Press, pp. 806.

Husain, I. (2019) *Basti*. Translated into Hindi by N. Barman and A. Mughni. Radhakrishna Paperbacks.

Lelyveld, D. (1993) 'Colonial knowledge and the fate of Hindustani', *Comparative Studies in Society and History*, pp. 665–682.

Khatri, D. (2002a) *Bhootnath*. New Delhi: Bharatiya Granth Prakashan.

Khatri, D. (2002b) *Chandrakanta Santati 1–6*. Bharatiya Granth Prakashan.

Khusrau, A. (2011) *In the Bazaar of Love: The Selected Poetry of Amir Khusrau*, Trans. P. Losensky and S. Sharma. Penguin Books India.

Madhuresh, (2002) *Devakinandan Khatri*. New Delhi: Sahitya Akademi.

'Old Messengers, New Media: The Legacy of Innis and McLuhan', Library and Archives of Canada.

Savarkar, V. D. (1969) *Hindutva; Who is a Hindu?* Veer Savarkar Prakashan.

Taj, A. (1997) *Urdu through Hindi: Nastaliq with the help of Devanagari*. Rangmahal Press.

Trivedi, H. (2003) 'The Progress of Hindi, Part 2: Hindi and the Nation', in Pollock, S. (ed.). *Literary Cultures in History: Reconstructions from South Asia*. University of California Press, pp. 958–1022.

Zaidi, N. (2015) 'Flows, Counter-flows Across the Artificial Divides: The Case of English-Hindi-Urdu', *Indian Literature*, 59.2, pp. 158–178.

# PART IV

# Forms in Flux II

## Born Digital

14

# JOURNEYING AGAINST THE HEROES

## Subaltern Poetics in Indian Videogames

*Souvik Mukherjee*

### Introduction: Revisiting the Problem of Videogame Poetics

In *Homo Ludens*, his groundbreaking book on play culture, Johan Huizinga writes that "poiesis is in fact a play-function" (Huizinga 1949, p. 119). This is an important comment for Game Studies (or rather, the study of videogames, in particular), where the very outset of the still-relatively new discipline was marked by a rift between those who considered games a storytelling medium and those who did not. Markku Eskelinen, belonging to the latter group of "ludologists," famously commented that,

> If I throw a ball at you I don't expect you to drop it and wait until it starts telling stories. On the other hand, if and when games and especially computer games are studied and theorised they are almost without exception colonised from the fields of literary, theatre, drama and film studies.
>
> *(Eskelinen 2001)*

Even Eskelinen, however, is convinced of the relevance of poetics within Game Studies: quoting literary theorist Tzvetan Todorov, Eskelinen describes poetics as "a sum of possible forms: what literature can be rather than what it is" (Eskelinen 2012, p. 4). Needless to say, those in favour of videogames being storytelling media, such as Janet Murray and Marie-Laure Ryan, are obviously interested in the poetics, and attribute a key role to it. Questions of poetics remain important even today, as the so-called "ludology-narratology debate" has been relegated to the pages of Games Studies history.

It must be made clear that the notion of poetics being considered for Game Studies discussions by both the ludologists and the narrativists is essentially a Western

DOI: 10.4324/9781003354246-19

theorization of poetics, mainly based off Aristotle's Poetics, which concerns itself with a certain kind of theatre. Other conceptions of poetics, such as the Indian *Natyashastra*, "which is not as narratively driven as Western drama" (Schechner 1997, p. 154), are not considered in Aristotle's *Poetics*. As commentators agree, the Poetics was "an analysis of tragedy by an intelligent and well-informed observer who was much closer, chronologically and culturally, to the plays than we are" (Aristotle 1996, p. viii). Aristotle focuses on Greek tragedy, with a very short section on epics and a passing mention of comedy. There is, of course, some speculation regarding a lost part or sequel of Poetics, where Aristotle discusses comedy—but such a text has not been unearthed. Malcolm Heath's very concise but focused comment will be useful in recollecting the basic schema of Aristotelian poetics:

> Tragedy, like all poetry, is an imitation. Specifically, it is an imitation of a certain kind of action. So one constituent part of tragedy is plot, the ordered sequence of events which make up the action being imitated. An action is performed by agents, and agents necessarily have moral and intellectual characteristics, expressed in what they do and say. From this we can deduce that character and reasoning will also be constituent parts of tragedy.
>
> *(Aristotle 1996, p. xviii)*

It must be noted that the pan-European importance of the *Poetics*, as it is known today, dates back to the middle of the 16th century or the later part of the Renaissance (see Tigerstedt 1968, Brazeau 2020). In this relatively long time that the Poetics took to be recognized as the key text for narrative theory, one element emerged as its prime contribution to theories of drama and later, to conceptions of narrative, *per se*. This is the primacy of action. The chief constituent of the narrative was deemed to be the plot, or "the ordered sequence of events which make up the action being imitated." The following section, on the early analyses of the storytelling capabilities of videogames, will clearly illustrate the Aristotelian antecedents of the current theses on videogame poetics.

The focus of this chapter, however, involves a questioning of the "one-size-fits-all" application of the Aristotelian poetics to all videogame narratives. Having addressed how the Aristotelian insistence on the poetics of action is pervasive in Games Studies, it is important to point out that such a framework is not only not inclusive but also quite limiting, wherein videogames are seen as a medium conveying the ideas and messages regarding a diversity of cultures. Furthermore, it aims to analyse the position of the subaltern, the oppressed, and the non-heroic within an alternative poetics of videogames.

## Aristotle in the Videogame

In 1991, Brenda Laurel published *Computers as Theatre* and started the conversation regarding the poetics of digital narratives. Thirty years later, the key issues in the book remain relevant and are much discussed in Game Studies. As she says, Laurel was writing at a time when there was no World Wide Web, no social networks, and no Massively Multiplayer Roleplaying Games—but many of her examples are still relevant today. Twenty years later, in her revised second edition, the original emphasis on Aristotelian drama remains. Laurel comments,

> The idea of enabling humans to take action in representational worlds is the powerful component of the programming-by-rehearsal approach. . . . A central goal of this book is to suggest ways in which we can use a notion of theatre, not simply as a metaphor but as a way to conceptualize human-computer interaction itself.
>
> *(Laurel 2013)*

She gives the following reasons for using Aristotle:

> I present Aristotle's model here for two reasons. First, I am continually amazed by the elegance and robustness of the categories and their causal relations. Following the causal relations through as one creates or analyses a drama seems to automatically reveal ways in which things should work or exactly how they have gone awry. Second, Aristotle's model creates a disciplined way of thinking about the design of a play in both constructing and debugging activities. Because of its fundamental similarities to drama, human-computer activity can be described with a similar model.
>
> *(Laurel 2013, p. 49)*

Laurel notes the six key elements of Aristotelian drama: action (plot), character, thought, language (diction), pattern, and enactment (spectacle).[1] Aristotle's theory reiterates the primacy of the plot and the *Poetics* devotes much more space to discussing this over the other elements. In this action and causality-based framework, Aristotle is clear that the plot must be "necessary and probable" meaning that the tragedy should imitate the action, such that would be likely to happen under a given set of circumstances. Laurel interprets Aristotelian poetics as moving from the material cause, that is, the perception of the spectacle, through the pattern of the characters' actions, thought processes and the use of language, towards comprehending the chain of causation (Laurel refers to this as the formal cause). Michael Mateas elaborates on this:

> When the plot is understood, there should be an "ah-ha" experience in which the audience is now able to understand how the characters relate to the plot (and why they must be the characters they are), why those types of characters think they way do, why they took the actions they did and said what they did, how their speech and actions created patterns of activity, and how those patterns of activity resulted in the spectacle that the audience saw.
>
> *(Mateas 2001, p. 143)*

Mateas points out how the interactivity of the videogame alters the Aristotelian framework somewhat. The chief difference here is that players are able to influence the plot through their own actions. Therefore, the user action that is experienced through the aforementioned "material cause," such as the visual experience that can be mediated and interacted with, is actually the "formal cause" of narrative action. Mateas describes it as "[b]y reasoning about the other characters' thoughts, the player can take actions to influence these characters, either to change their thoughts or to actively help or hinder them in their goals and plans" (Mateas 2001, p. 144). This may be a modification of the Aristotelian framework, in that the action is performed not by an author solely but by the player who is both reader and author; however, that does not change a fundamental point about the poetics of action that this framework also heavily relies on.

Mateas sets up this reading of Aristotle quite carefully, in order to address a major point in reading videogames: the issue of agency, or the determining of the ludic action based on the player's choices. As he says: "the audience's sense of having agency within the story is a genuinely new experience enabled by interactivity. For these reasons, agency will be the category integrated with Aristotle" (Mateas 2001, p. 143).

## Agency and Poetics

Janet Murray's foundational book on Games Studies, *Hamlet on the Holodeck*, spells out the primacy of agency in no uncertain words:

> The more realized the immersive environment, the more active we want to be within it. When the things we do bring tangible results, we experience the second characteristic delight of electronic environments—the sense of agency. Agency is the *satisfying power* to take *meaningful action* and see the results of our decisions and choices.
>
> *(Murray 1998, p. 126; italics mine)*

The questions of power and meaningful action need to be thought through. One could ask who has the power (and over what or whom) and whom does such a power satisfy. Also, for whom is the action meaningful. Marie-Laure Ryan, writing a decade later, also sees the need for agency as the important driving force of the videogame narrative:

> For intensity of user participation, freedom of choice, and depth of immersion, nothing can beat the imaginary Holodeck of the TV series Star Trek, which Janet Murray, in her 1997 classic Hamlet on the Holodeck, proposes as the model of the new kind of narrative experience that digital technology will make possible.
>
> *(Ryan 2009, p. 47)*

Ryan is canny enough to dismiss the Holodeck as a "castle in the air," but she does not question "the validity of its individual features" (Ibid.). She concedes that a game with a spoken dialogue may not be holodeck-like and afford much agency, but that in plots that invest in physical actions, the actions are the key movers of the story. Ryan then goes on to use this to justify the common use of Vladimir Propp and Joseph Campbell as prime influences in the shaping of modern-day videogame plots. Campbell's notion of the Hero's Journey, or the monomyth, is very popular in game design today and will be discussed in the following section.

It must be noted that, challenging the narrativist position, Espen Aarseth and other so-called ludologists have argued against narrative agency, saying that "it is typically the simulation that, on its own, allows actions that the story prohibits, or which make the story break down" and that "players exploit this to invent strategies that make a mockery of the author's intentions" (Aarseth 2004a). In doing so, however, the primacy of agency remains intact. In fact, reading Aarseth's essay, "A Narrative Theory of Games," Conor McKeown infers that

> Aarseth implies that agency is a quality that correlates in various ways to the construction of the game world, objects in that world, characters and the extent to which events in the game are either scripted or open to change. . . . Aarseth's formulation of agency is not so different to Murray's.
>
> *(Mckeown 2019)*

Consider again, the use of the word "ergodic" (originating from *ergos*: work and *hodos*: path) where non-trivial action is the key requirement. In a sense, here too meaningful action is being sought as a means of making choices. Whichever be the position from where the game's poetics is judged, agency as meaningful choice-making emerges as a key requirement. Consequently, the player-protagonist (and also the simulation or the software) also occupies, at least conceptually, a role of privilege and power.

## Just Questing? The Quest and the Hero's Journey in Videogame Poetics

In the wake of the ludology-narratology, scholars had identified the quest-concept in videogames as providing the middle ground. Jesper Juul observes that

> As an attempt at bridge-building between the open structure of games and the closed structure of stories, the concept of quests has been proposed by Ragnhild Tronstad (2001), Espen Aarseth (2004b), and Susan Tosca (2003). Quests in games can actually provide an interesting type of bridge between game rules and game fiction in that the games can contain predefined sequences of events that the player then has to actualize or effect.
>
> *(Howard 2007)*

Juul comments on the non-trivial nature of the quest as being different from other forms of narrative and, just as Ryan says, the quest is composed of physical-action events. As Aarseth states, "the playeravatar [*sic*] must move through a landscape in order to fulfil a goal while mastering a series of challenges. This phenomenon is called a quest" (Aarseth 2004b, p. 368). Jeff Howard points out that, despite differences wherein Aarseth fails to address the content of the quest, especially the meaning of the events, "Joseph Campbell's three-part description of the Hero's Journey is closer to Aarseth's definition than it might at first seem" (Howard 2007), because its narrative associations in Campbell's Hero's Journey or the monomyth complement, the ludological focus on ludic action. Both Ryan and Aarseth's positions can be viewed in comparison to the monomyth.

Campbell's monomyth is characterized by the protagonist moving through the spatial and temporal levels of a narrative following a pattern that can be applied to most stories and myths across cultures:

> A hero ventures forth from the world of common day into a region of supernatural wonder: fabulous forces are there encountered and a decisive victory is won: the hero comes back from this mysterious adventure with the power to bestow boons on his fellow man.
>
> *(Campbell 2008, p. 23)*

The monomyth is a ubiquitous narrative structure that exists in all cultures across all times, according to Campbell and his adherents. The suggestion is based on a theory of archetypes, where Campbell and Moyers conclude that this is backed up by psychological research and "the monomyth is built of the deeper cognitive structure of the brain" (Campbell and Moyers 1991, p. 26). The scientific basis of this statement needs to be further questioned and that is not the objective of this chapter.

Nevertheless, there is an appeal of the monomyth to the authors, scriptwriters, and critics. For example, there is the popular image on the internet that shows the *Harry Potter* and *Star Wars* stories as based on the same template of the monomyth. So, instead of "Luke Skywalker is an orphan living with his uncle and aunt in the remote wilderness of Tatooine," one could replace the proper nouns with "Harry Potter" and "Suburbia" and get the story of Harry Potter. The monomyth is a favourite of game designers as well—and, as an instructional designer comments, "we hold that the monomyth is a structure that is both reliable and flexible [and] well-suited for the nonlinear activity within today's interactive learning environments" (Hokanson and Fraher 2008). Compare this with Jenova Chen's comment on his abstract and visually superb game, *Journey*[2]:

> Journey is more like a story broken apart. There are two stories: There's the ancient civilization's story and the story of the player's own journey. The civilization's story is more broken apart and spread throughout the world for the player to discover. But what is more important is the arc of the

> player's journey itself, which is based upon the Hero's Journey, part of the monomyth.
>
> *(Ohannessian 2012)*

Even an indie game made with a very different focus than most triple-A (blockbuster or mid-size) games uses the monomyth as its model. Chen says that he grew up in China but, on moving to the United States, was deeply influenced by Campbell's book.

However different the look, feel, context, and play experience of these videogames may be, there is one common element among these games, and that is the preference for a narrative of agency. The Hero's Journey, as can be inferred from its name, involves a heroic protagonist and a concern with agency as action or making "meaningful choices." The Aristotelian schema of an action-based dramaturgy is the accepted poetics of the videogame game narrative or play experience.

## Thinking Aloud in Silence: A Poetics Without Agency?

Consider, however, what the scenario would be where the protagonist is in the position of the oppressed; where she cannot exert her choice (or express it, even sometimes). Would videogames fail to represent such a subject? There is no place for those who do not have agency in the aforementioned poetic schema that is so popular in videogames. The default videogame protagonist is expected to be a hero—and indeed, the protagonists of games such as *Fable*, *Skyrim*, *Fallout 3*, and *The Witcher 3* are all such heroes. In fact, the protagonist of *Fable* is even called the Hero of Oakvale. I have elsewhere written about videogames that address issues such as slavery and oppression. *Fallout 3*—and more directly, *Assassin's Creed: Freedom Cry*—both deal with slavery. Adewale, the protagonist of *Freedom Cry*, is a muscular former slave, pirate captain, and member of the secret group of Assassins; throughout the game, he is seen to be freeing slaves. Evan Narcisse of Kotaku.com comments on how the game has tackled the problem of White hegemony head-on; he also goes on to say how the game mechanics support the "collecting [of] freed slaves like coins in Mario" (Narcisse 2013). Narcisse goes on to elaborate that the "game's mechanics essentially has the player treating freed slaves like a resource to purchase stuff. That mechanic is uncomfortably close to the way that slaves were used in the bondage that players are supposed to be freeing them from" (Ibid.). Another point regarding the game that has been overlooked in the analyses is that the slaves never speak when they are freed. There is a marked contrast between Adewale's fully clothed, weapon-wielding macho persona and the helpless and almost naked bodies of the slaves. The slaves don't stay to talk to their liberator but start running; what happens to them thereafter is unknown. Adewale has the agency to go wherever he wishes, free whomever he wishes. It is the slaves among the non-player characters (NPCs) who do not have any meaning except as currency (or not even that after their escape is effected). Another example, unsurprisingly again from a colonial/empire context, is that of the worker NPCs in *Age of*

*Empires*. The NPCs have no voice with which to express themselves and function as extensions or tools of the system of colonization and empire. What happens, therefore, to the poetics of the videogame(s) when the focus is shifted from the protagonist invested with power to those who do not wield power over others? An even more problematic question is whether the videogame narrative is, necessarily, biased towards protagonists who occupy or are expected to occupy a position of power or a majoritarian heroic role.

## Revisiting the "Videogames of the Oppressed"

When faced with the question of whether videogames can be made to represent those who do not occupy positions of power and entitlement, Gonzalo Frasca's comments might be helpful in further understanding how an alternative poetics can be envisaged. Frasca has a different and non-Aristotelian model for videogames:

> [Y]ou could build a non-immersive—and therefore non-Aristotelian—environment where players would not "be themselves" but rather encouraged to become aware of their own performances while trying to perform coherently to their character's personality, as some professional RPG players do. I personally see the potential of the computer not as something that can extend representation and narrative but rather as a laboratory where players could experiment while building and deconstructing the rules of simulated systems. The twentieth century produced interesting alternatives to Aristotelian drama that are built around agency and therefore do not need major modifications to be applied to software design. Non-Aristotelian dramatists such as Augusto Boal provide a much robust theoretical and practical environment for creating interactive pieces.
>
> *(Frasca 2004)*

Frasca's point is that instead of situating the game in the personal agency of the player or in a unified theory of action, the videogame could devolve the agency to a multiplicity of player-character roles wherefrom players could explore other characters and perspectives.[3] In his brilliant masters' thesis (Frasca 2001), Frasca invokes the "Theatre of the Oppressed" by Brazilian playwright Augusto Boal as an alternative model of poetics for videogames. Frasca modifies The Sims game, and also the Space Invaders game, to illustrate his position.

For Frasca, Boal's Forum Theatre is a key entry-point. In brief, Forum Theatre may be described as follows:

> A play or scene, usually indicating some kind of oppression, is shown twice. During the replay, any member of the audience ("spect-actor") is allowed to shout "Stop!", step forward and take the place of one of the oppressed characters, showing how they could change the situation to enable a different outcome. Several alternatives may be explored by different spect-actors. The

> other actors remain in character, improvising their responses. A facilitator (Joker) is necessary to enable communication between the players and the audience.
>
> *(ActionAid 2021)*

Frasca sees the player-character as the spectator; the multiple distribution of agency is one way of experiencing the game-space from the perspective of others. To enable this multiplicity of agency, and perhaps work towards emulating the spectatorship in the videogame, Frasca introduces modified downloadable characters who can be introduced into The Sims game. He goes on to unpack how this is experienced in his "Sims for the Oppressed" mod:

> The household is integrated by a couple, three children and a cat. After the download, the mother is replaced by "Dave's Alcoholic Mother version 0.9". The character is interesting. After playing with it for a while, she realized that when she reaches a certain degree of fatigue, she would start drinking. The more she drinks the less she will care about her family. She would remain calm unless her husband insists on cuddling or giving her a back rub. While Agnes thinks that the character is pretty well depicted, there are details that she does not agree with. So, she goes back to the "Character Exchange" and looks for another alcoholic mother. She finds one that seems promising "Dorothy's Alcoholic Methodist Mother version 3.2."
>
> *(Frasca 2001, p. 82–83)*

Even so, Frasca is well aware that this is not even close to what Forum Theatre achieves by way of creating a multiplicity of experiences, but he argues that "both the multiplicity of behaviours and the fact that amateur designers create most of the experience would foster a critical attitude even in those players who do not create behaviors" (Frasca 2001, p. 85). The Boalian poetics that Frasca points towards holds out significant promise as an "other" (and "othered") poetics that can accommodate the scenarios that Aristotelian poetics, invested as it is in individual agency, cannot fit in.

## The Subaltern and Poetics of the Oppressed

What happens to those who are unable to make themselves heard, let alone participate in any choice-making for a meaningful action? Boal's theatre is aimed at bringing out these voices from their silent corners. In a performance where prisoners and prison guards were involved, Boal writes how, at the end of the performance, it was finally possible for the audience and the prison-guards themselves to hear the voices of the prisoners that they had never before heard:

> With tenderness, we embraced these prisoners, male and female, and their guards and support staff—people who had made us laugh and cry, as they

> performed their stories, their hopes, that day. The time for goodbyes. In the ample auditorium of the Memorial, seven armed soldiers went on stage, and each prisoner gave his arm to his guard, and they set off for the bus that would take them back to their cells. As they set off, one of the guards still had time to say: "Do you know something? As far as human rights go, I haven't learnt a thing—I still don't know what they are. But there's one thing I have understood today—that these guys are not our enemies. They are people."
>
> *(Boal 2002, p. 7)*

Following the historian Ranajit Guha and postcolonial theorist Gayatri Chakravorty Spivak, I refer to these people who have been rendered voiceless by the system and the context within which they are put as "Subaltern." The term was originally used by Antonio Gramsci in his Prison Notebooks and has been used by scholars from the Indian subcontinent and Latin America to refer to those who did not possess an archive and, therefore, had often been written out of the text-based colonial system.

A very poignant example of subalternity is provided by Spivak in her example from Mahasweta Devi's (1995) short story "The Pterodactyl, Pirtha and Puran Sahay." In the story, a pterodactyl is reportedly seen in a tribal village in India. The narrative of the Pterodactyl cannot be articulated within the existing structures of language and civilization. It can only be conveyed through a silent symbol as Alison Shelton comments:

> The young, illiterate Bikhia is also a silent storyteller who creates his own narrative voice by chiseling the image of the pterodactyl on a stone, setting in motion a series of interpretive dilemmas. Upon making this inscription, he falls mute, becoming the pterodactyl's silent guardian. The text reveals, "[Puran] knows Bikhia can hear him. He has only stopped speaking after he drew the picture." . . . A paradoxical, wordless interpreter, Bikhia's muteness and illiteracy suggest that what he is protecting cannot be verbalised or written down.
>
> *(Shelton 2013)*

The story of the pterodactyl is quite distinctly different from Hollywood productions such as *Jurassic Park*. Spivak rightly states that the pterodactyl is neither science fiction nor a symbol and, for modern India, it is an empirical impossibility; conversely, for the modern tribal Indian, it is the soul of his ancestors. She goes on to say that "[t]he fiction does not judge between the registers of truth and exactitude, simply stages them in separate spaces" (Spivak 2003). Indeed, when truth and exactitude are supposedly held in archival forms that have been inaccessible to many communities and cultures, these latter are rendered mute when it comes to expressing their history. How does one represent their stories and what is the poetics at play (literally, in the case of videogames) for such scenarios?

Boal's original description and practice of Forum Theatre is quite ludic, as we see in his Games for Actors and Non-Actors. In describing FT, Adrian Jackson illustrates how the game-like nature of the theatre enables the oppressed and those whose voices could not be heard otherwise to express themselves from the perspectives of both oppressor and oppressed:

> The game is a form of contest between spect-actors trying to bring the play to a different end (in which the cycle of oppression is broken) and actors ostensibly making every possible effort to bring it to its original end (in which the oppressed is beaten and the oppressors are triumphant). The proceedings are presided over by a figure called the "Joker" . . . whose function is to ensure the smooth running of the game and teach the audience the rules; however, like all the participants in Forum Theatre, the Joker can be replaced.
>
> *(Boal 2002, p. xxvi)*

One could argue then that Boal's spect-actors could also attempt to represent subaltern voices. It is now necessary to see how a move away from an agency-based poetics needs to be thought through for videogames.

## Subaltern Poetics: Two Videogames From India

Two videogames from India have been helpful in thinking about the move away from agency-based Aristotelian poetics. Needless to say, there are many games that come to mind, but these two have been chosen, because it was possible to interview the developers and discuss the issues of agency and poetics. Set in a postcolonial milieu of a Global South country with a history of poverty, deprivation, and oppression, it is no surprise that these games do not employ the standard monomyth structure or a poetics that centres on agency. The games in question are *Missing—Game for a Cause*, designed by Flying Robots Studio, and by Studio Oleomingus's *Somewhere*.

Missing, a game based on the "Missing Girls" project started by Leena Kejriwal, is set in Kolkata's Sonagachi neighbourhood, Asia's third largest red-light area. The story is that of a girl, Champa, who has been trafficked into prostitution, and her subsequent attempt to escape. The game is hard to play, both in terms of the gameplay and in terms of the experience of playing as a trafficked girl, for whom rape and exploitation are quotidian events. Rather than empowerment and agency through the making of meaningful choices, even despite the game's linear structure and the ultimate outcome of being rescued, the player rarely feels comfortable and in control of her destiny. An analysis of the game reviews on the Google Playstore will be indicative. A study conducted by Marcus Toftedahl, Henrik Engstrom, and Per Backlund concluded the following:

> One observation is that the tone in the reviews are tied to the star ratings given; i.e. a 5 star rating is generally accompanied by a positive review, and a 1 star rating is generally accompanied by a negative review regarding tone

> and content. There are reviews deviating somewhat from this pattern; mostly reviews that relates to the theme in some way, but are (deliberately?) misinterpreted regarding the context.
>
> *(Toftedahl* et al. *2018, p. 16)*

The reviews revealed the level of discomfort of the players, who are usually accustomed to a game experience that allows them to be in control and engage in narratives that fit in comfortably with the Hero's Journey, thereby granting a sense of agency to the player. For Missing, however, the problems are manifold. A few comments from the PlayStore will put this point in perspective. One reviewer comments, "Very heart touching. I always wonder why streets in Kolkata has #1098?? But now its clear whic [sic] really made me sad and i completed this game within 1 hour with all my curiosity," whereas another who has given the game a low-rating comments:

> When I first started I didn't have to pay much but now I have to pay like 500 and 600 everytime and it gets frustrating because I never get enough because the people with most cash they don't pay that much but people with more lust and less case have a better chance of payin less. I uninstalled.

A third reviewer states: "The controls suck but.. I don't mind. I didn't feel comfortable playing this game but that's the point. I got chills all over. Horrifying. 5 stars. Wow." The star rating is mentioned in this review. Finally, another negative review says that "This game tell us story about human trafficking. It made me feel angry and also sad. Not all girl are willing to do that." What was looking like a sensitive comment suddenly changes its tone in the last sentence implying that being trafficked into prostitution involves agency. The third review comment given earlier is telling: the glitchiness and the difficulty in negotiating the game's space (both the ludic and the emotional space) are felt again and again. There is a feeling of helplessness. Also, while comments such as "people with more lust and less case [cash?] have a better chance of payin [sic] less" not only reveal a lot about the person who is making the comment, but they also provide the sense that, for all kinds of people, the difficulty is perceived in the lack of being in control. Of course, the sadness of the first comment is only to be expected.

A multiplicity of issues and experiences are entwined in the commentary on the game. Not least is the social construction of the stigma of prostitution under the colonial regime, where the Contagious Diseases Act 1864 and other government protocols made it difficult for prostitutes and courtesans to have any social acceptance whatsoever. The case of the courtesan Hira Bulbul, whose son was expelled from the Hindu College (now Presidency University) in Calcutta (now Kolkata) in 1853, illustrates the class privilege and discrimination that existed in colonial times (See Banerjee 1998 for a detailed exposition). In post-Independence India, prostitution is illegal and trafficking is a rampant problem (see Ghosh 2009, Nagraj 2017). *Missing* addresses an extremely difficult social issue and it does so by placing the player in the role of a protagonist who might be described as "the oppressed" in the Boalian schema of theatre described earlier. In a way, the experience, repeated in multiple different contexts (as seen in the reviews), is like Forum Theatre, where even the most staunchly opposed individuals, and even the oppressors, too, struggle to experience agency—and even if they can make choices within the game, these are made within the overarching structure of a denial of choice and representation. Satyajit Chakraborty admits that there is more to be done with game's scenario and more in-depth exploration of the stories of the characters is needed. Perhaps, though, the missing elements in the game will remain untold—possibly because they can never be fully narrated or experienced.

Moving on to *Somewhere*, an interview with the designer, Dhruv Jani, reveals a perspective on design and narrative that differs from the Aristotelian norm:

> I do like to think that even the simplest dislocation of text in interactive fiction requires a slightly altered form of reading and criticism that takes into account *not just a reader's agency but also a reader's labour in assembling the narrative together*. And the intricate ways in which you can arrange and entangle stories not just in most video games but in most forms of hypertext containers like websites—might eventually make it very easy to build other kinds of fictions better suited to such chaotic ideas and incomplete records.
>
> *(Dhruv Jani, personal communication, my italics)*

The shift away from an agency-based poetics involves the reader's labour in assembling the narrative together. Jani's game, however, becomes a Sisyphean experience in that the labour of assembling the narrative is one that is intricate and entangled, because ultimately it concerns itself with incompleteness and chaos.

Somewhere is set in the fictitious locale called Kayamgadh. This excerpt from the fictitious journal of a British colonial official, Charles Henry Conington, reveals a lot about the game:

> The people of Kayamgadh do not speak.
>
> They are afraid that their words might penetrate the layers under which their bodies are hidden. Afraid that some phrase or name might, through woolen caps and cotton plugs and balled bits of torn rags, enter their buried ears and insert itself into their thoughts, prompting them to think of Kayamgadh not as they see it but as it is being described to them by the person speaking these words.
>
> It is a fear so deeply entrenched, that people now see the city with unwilling eyes, shaded behind their hands, lest they be tempted into a sudden burst of verbiage whilst looking upon the wonders of Kayamgadh. A temptation that might resist the doctrine of their self imposed silence.
>
> For Kayamgadh is a wonderful city, where the craftsmen strive hard to put into form all that they cannot give words to, and where the work of

> the craftsman is left undisturbed, for it is only looked upon and but never described by the people, who never speak.
>
> *(Joho 2014)*

The fear that their words will corrupt their bodies and their image of Kayamgadh has rendered the population mute. Their records will not be accessible even via the mediating influence of the Western scholar-intermediary. As a commentator observes,

> People in the story, reducing into single entities because they collide with each other on a map and amalgamate or characters splitting apart in a mitotic act of generating replicas with errors in their recollection of their narratives. This is how the fissures of views and stories now manifest themselves in the game.
>
> *(Warr 2018)*

A true history, so coveted by Western archaeologists and historian, is never made available, because the narratives of different entities keep coalescing and splitting apart. The story of *Somewhere* lies in the fissures of meaning-making. Jani comments that the game

> *Somewhere*, like the city of Kayamgadh, does not exist. . . . You are right, it is always meant to be seen through the occluded lens of our other work. In that it is a little like R.K. Narayan's town of Malgudi or E.M. Forster's Marabar caves. A trope of postcolonial fiction stretched to the extreme, and applied to the very form of telling these stories.
>
> *(Warr 2018)*

The Marabar Caves in Forster's *Passage to India* have always intrigued scholars, and the echoes heard in the caves have eluded any meaning-making process. It is important to note that Jani uses them as a comparison. *Somewhere* keeps pointing out how not all history is available in archives or as written records. The player may be overwhelmed by the artistic beauty of the game, but the play experience is not easy:

> But to go back to what players have been making of Oleomingus's work so far, "There is also often absolute bewilderment as to what the game is 'supposed to do' or why it exists," says Jani. "The literary threads that bind it together seem to many players too loose and too irrelevant to merit the sort of engagement with the fiction that the game requires."
>
> *(Ibid.)*

The sense of bewilderment and the difficulty in making sense of the narrative are intentional and aimed not to grant the player the sense of agency. The difficulty in accessing the narrative of the subaltern (Jani has noted his postcolonial intention in his comment) is reflected in experience of the players losing their way in the loose literary threads of the game.

## In Conclusion: A Journey Against the Heroes

*Somewhere* and *Missing* are not the only examples of games based on a different and non-Aristotelian poetics. *Thralled*, says Portuguese designer Miguel Oliveira, "came from the necessity to talk about slavery and the crimes of my ancestors" (FictiveTruism 2014) is "a surreal game that aims to show the sacrifices and struggles Isaura [a runaway slave] must endure in order to find safety for her and her son" (Ibid.). Other games such as Brenda Romero's boardgame, Síochán Leat or the "Irish Game," also convey an utter lack of freedom within the gameplay experience, because the player is playing Oliver Cromwell's invasion of Ireland as a result of which many thousands of Irish people were left homeless and sold as slaves. All of these examples are about experiencing situations of a lack of meaningful choice or agency and just as Romero's "Mechanics is the Message" series of analogue games suggests a game mechanic that "captures and expresses difficult experiences through the medium of a game" (Romero), Boal's Theatre of the Oppressed can be usefully applied in terms of videogame experiences as Frasca has suggested. The poetics, of course, need to be rethought. Boal's own critique of Aristotelian poetics needs to be invoked here:

> Aristotle constructs the first extremely powerful poetic-political system for intimidation of the spectator, for elimination of the "bad" or "illegal" tendencies of the audience. This system is to this day fully utilized not only in conventional theatre, but in the TV soap operas and in Western films as well . . . united through a common basis in Aristotelian poetics for repression of the people. But obviously, the Aristotelian theatre is not the only form of theatre.
> *(Boal 1993)*

He suggests that Aristotelian poetics is imbued with the politics of power and oppression through its assumption of an agency wherein the bad or illegal tendencies of the audience can be eliminated. In the context of this chapter, Aristotelian poetics and the assumption of agency-based meaningful action invested in the player are challenged in Boal's formulation. Multiple perspectives are necessary to be able to tell the stories of those who do not have the power to choose their own destiny or from whom that choice has been taken away by some process of oppression and exploitation.

Finally, even Boal's poetics of the oppressed, or the representation of the experiences of oppression and the lack of choice in videogames that try to make players engage with the "othered" lives, also needs to acknowledge that ultimately the scenario is that of subalternity and silence. The poetics of the subaltern has to be about acknowledging the absence or the displacement of choice or meaning contra the heroic assumptions of agency in the monomyth; videogames are rapidly emerging as a mature medium that does need to constrain itself to narratives of heroism using a one-size-fits-all notion of poetics but can also represent the stories of the othered and the oppressed drawing on non-Aristotelian models that address questions of multiplicity and subalternity.

## Notes

1 Other interpretations of Aristotle differ slightly. For example, Heath notes the following six component parts of tragedy: "So tragedy as a whole necessarily has six component parts, which determine the tragedy's quality: i.e. plot, character, diction, reasoning, spectacle and lyric poetry" (Heath 11). Note that Laurel has used "pattern" instead of "lyric poetry."

2 I am indebted to Poonam Chowdhury's talk in the Games Studies India Adda series for bringing this to my attention.

3 Frasca draws attention to how Aarseth's notion of agency moves it away from the player-centred notion of agency to the system's agency. This has already been pointed out earlier in this essay. Despite his aligning himself with Aarseth's position, I see Frasca as moving in a somewhat different direction in that instead of the faceless and all-powerful system, his agency devolves in the multiple and the "other."

## References

Aarseth, E. (2004a) 'Espen Aarseth responds', *Electronic Book Review* [Preprint]. Available at: www.electronicbookreview.com/thread/firstperson/cornucopia (Accessed: 10 February 2015).

Aarseth, E. (2004b) 'Quest Games as Post-Narrative Discourse', in Ryan, M.-L. (ed) *Narrative across Media. The Languages of Storytelling*. Lincoln/London: Nebraska UP, pp. 361–376.

Aarseth, E. (2006) 'Genre Trouble', in Wardrip-fruin, N. and Harrigan, P. (eds) *First Person—New Media as Story, Performance and Game*. Cambridge, MA: MIT Press, p. 45.

ActionAid (2021) *Forum theatre—Reflection Action, Reflection Action*. Available at: www.reflectionaction.org/tools_and_methods/14/?from=ov (Accessed: 19 January 2021).

Aristotle (1996) *Poetics*. Translated by Malcolm Heath. London: Penguin Books.

Banerjee, S. (1998) *Dangerous Outcast the Prostitute in Nineteenth Century Calcutta*. Edition. Calcutta: Seagull Books.

Boal, A. (1993) *Theatre of the Oppressed*. Tcg ed. Edition. Translated by C.A. McBride. New York: Theatre Communications Group Inc., U.S.

Boal, A. (2002) *Games for Actors and Non-Actors*. 2nd ed. Translated by A. Jackson. New York: Routledge.

Brazeau, D.B. (ed.) (2020) *The Reception of Aristotle's Poetics in the Italian Renaissance and Beyond: New Directions in Criticism*. London : New York: Bloomsbury Academic.

Campbell, J. (2008) *The Hero with a Thousand Faces*. Novato, CA: New World Library.

Campbell, J. and Moyers, B. (1991) *The Power of Myth*. Anchor Books ed edition. New York: RHUS.

Eskelinen, M. (2001) 'The Gaming Situation', *Game Studies*, 1(1). Available at: www.gamestudies.org/0101/eskelinen/.

Eskelinen, M. (2012) *Cybertext Poetics: The Critical Landscape of New Media Literary Theory*. 1st edition. New York: Continuum.

FictiveTruism. (2014) Exclusive Interview with Miguel Oliveira, Creative Director of Thralled. *Indie Game Reviewer*. Available at: https://indiegamereviewer.com/exclsive-interview-miguel-oliveira-creative-director-thralled/ (Accessed: 9 September 2022).

Frasca, G. (2001) *Videogames of the Oppressed: Videogames as a Means for Critical Thinking and Debate*. Master's Thesis. Georgia Institute of Technology. Available at: https://ludology.typepad.com/weblog/articles/thesis/FrascaThesisVideogames.pdf (Accessed: 19 January 2021).

Frasca, G. (2004) 'Videogames of the Oppressed', *Electronic Book Review* [Preprint]. Available at: www.electronicbookreview.com/thread/firstperson/Boalian (Accessed: 20 February 2015).

Ghosh, B. (2009) 'Trafficking in Women and Children in India: Nature, Dimensions and Strategies for Prevention', *The International Journal of Human Rights* 13(5), pp. 716–738.

Hokanson, B. and Fraher, R. (2008) 'Narrative Structure, Myth, and Cognition for Instructional Design', *Educational Technology*, 48(1), pp. 27–32.

Howard, J. (2007) 'Interpretative Quests in Theory and Pedagogy', *Digital Humanities Quarterly*, 001(1).

Huizinga, J. (1949) *Homo Ludens: A Study of the Play-Element in Culture*. London: Routledge and Kegan Paul.

Joho, J. (2014) 'Rituals presents the surreal fragmentation of narrative in a post-colonial India', *Kill Screen*, 11 September. Available at: https://killscreen.com/articles/ritual-presents-surreal-fragmentation-narrative-post-colonial-india/ (Accessed: 23 November 2016).

Laurel, B. (2013) *Computers as Theatre*. 2nd edition. Upper Saddle River, NJ: Addison Wesley.

Mateas, M. (2001) 'A preliminary poetics for interactive drama and games', *Digital Creativity*, 12(3), pp. 140–152. Doi:10.1076/digc.12.3.140.3224.

Mckeown, C. (2019) "You bastards may take exactly what I give you": Intra-Action and Agency in Return of the Obra Dinn "G|A|M|E", *Game: The Italian Journal of Game Studies* [Preprint]. Available at: www.gamejournal.it/you-bastards-may-take-exactly-what-i-give-you-intra-action-and-agency-in-return-of-the-obra-dinn/ (Accessed: 18 January 2021).

Murray, J.H. (1998) *Hamlet on The Holodeck*. Cambridge, MA: MIT Press.

Nagaraj, A. (2017) 'Rescued Child Sex Workers in India Reveal Hidden Cells in Brothels,' *Reuters* 13 Dec. 2017. www.reuters.com. <www.reuters.com/article/us-india-trafficking brothels-idUSKBN1E71R1>. (Accessed: 19 Jan. 2021).

Narcisse, E. (2013) *A Game That Showed Me My Own Black History, Kotaku*. Available at: https://kotaku.com/a-game-that-showed-me-my-own-black-history-1486643518 (Accessed: 18 January 2021).

Ohannessian, K. (2012) 'Game Designer Jenova Chen On The Art Behind His "Journey"', *Fast Company*. Available at: www.fastcompany.com/1680062/game-designer-jenova-chen-on-the-art-behind-his-journey (Accessed: 18 January 2021).

Ryan, M.-L. (2009) 'From Narrative Games to Playable Stories: Toward a Poetics of Interactive Narrative', *Storyworlds: A Journal of Narrative Studies*, 1, pp. 43–59.

Schechner, R. (1997) 'Review of Dramatic Concepts Greek and Indian: A Study of "Poetics" and "Natyasastra"', *TDR (1988–)*, 41(2), pp. 153–156. Doi:10.2307/1146630.

Shelton, A. (2013) 'Narrative Distancing and the Space for Compassion in Mahasweta Devi's "Pterodactyl, Puran Sahay, and Pirtha"', in Rohse, M. (ed.) *The Many Facets of Storytelling: Global Reflections on Narrative Complexity*. Amsterdam: Brill, pp. 233–241. Available at: https://brill.com/view/book/edcoll/9781848881662/BP000022.xml (Accessed: 19 January 2021).

Spivak, G. (2003) *Death of a Discipline*. New York: Columbia University Press.

Symonds, S. (2013) *Brenda Romero: "The Mechanic is the Message", The Strong National Museum of Play*. Available at: www.museumofplay.org/blog/chegheads/2013/06/brenda-romero-%E2%80%9Cthe-mechanic-is-the-message%E2%80%9D (Accessed: 2 October 2021).

Tigerstedt, E.N. (1968) 'Observations on the Reception of the Aristotelian Poetics in the Latin West', *Studies in the Renaissance*, 15, pp. 7–24. Doi:10.2307/2857002.

Toftedahl, M., Backlund, P. and Engström, H. (2018) 'Missing: Understanding the Reception of a Serious Game by Analyzing App Store Data', *International Journal of Serious Games*, 5, pp. 3–22. Doi:10.17083/ijsg.v5i4.251.

Warr, P. (2018) 'The story of Somewhere, a game that might not exist', *PC Gamer*, 5 June. Available at: www.pcgamer.com/the-story-of-somewhere-a-game-that-might-not-exist/ (Accessed: 19 January 2021).

## Ludography

Flying Robot Studios. 2016. *Missing: Game for a Cause*, Kolkata: Flying Robot Studios [Android, iOS, PC]

Lionhead Studios. 2004. *Fable: The Lost Chapters*, Redmond: Xbox Games Studios [PC, Xbox 360]

Maxis. 2000. *The Sims*, San Mateo, CA: Electronic Arts [PC]

Oliveira, Miguel. 2013 [under development]. *Thralled*, n.p.: Tiffany Mang [Ouya, PC, iOS]

Romero, Brenda. 2009. *Síochán Leat (aka The Irish Game)*, n.p.: Brenda Romero [non-digital installation]

Studio Oleomingus. 2014 [under development]. *Somewhere*, Chala: Studio Oleomingus [PC]

Ubisoft Montreal. 2013. *Assassin's Creed: Black Flag—Freedom Cry*. Montreal: Ubisoft [PC, PS3]

# 15

# NARRATIVE AND PLAY

## Some Reflections on Videogames Based on Bollywood

*Nishat Haider*

Foregrounding the crucial role of games in digital culture studies and digital humanities, this chapter delineates the aesthetic connections between Bollywood films and video games in order to critically engage with issues of interactivity in consumer culture, narrative (Mactavish 2002), film aesthetics (Grieb 2002), and spectatorship (Howells 2002). India is the emerging "digital cinema laboratory" of the world (Gopal 2011, p. 131). Although a 2007 study by market researcher Icube revealed that only 5% of India's 42 million Internet users are active gamers, the report of Ernst and Young reveals that India is seen as a major player in the video game industry with an estimated growth at a CAGR (compound annual growth rate) of 49% by 2012 (Wolf 2012, p. 313). One of the most significant recent developments in the Indian film industry is the collaboration between Hollywood (DreamWorks) and Bollywood (Reliance Big Entertainment, owned by Anil Ambani) that has resulted in a cross-flow in crafts, music, art, and games, which has been far more pervasive than in movies (Pieterse 2009, p. 62). Although videogames and Bollywood have a synergistic relationship with licensing tie-ins, in which videogames are designed based on mainstream movies (a huge variety, including films such as *Krrish* series, *Ghajani*, and *Ra.One*), video games remain understudied and applications of critical theory to the study of digital gaming are still in the preliminary stages. Delineating the aesthetic connections between Bollywood films and video games, this chapter critically engages with the interactivity in consumer culture, the issues related to film aesthetics (Grieb 2002), spectatorship (Howells 2002), and narrative (Mactavish 2002) to understand the place of economic, political, legal, social, and cultural institutions in mediating and partly shaping technological change (Krzywinska and Lowood 2006; Mortensen 2006). This chapter will also extrapolate the process of transformation when a story moves from a film text to a gaming text. Since video games can be adequately explained neither by a narratological approach (Murray 1998; Ryan 2001) nor by a ludological approach (Frasca

DOI: 10.4324/9781003354246-20

1999; Juul 2005; Mäyrä 2008; Newman 2004), this chapter argues that a hermeneutics of digital signs that can be put to use by humanists and technologists alike requires a diversity of approaches to the computer game. While a survey of all the theoretical positions that scholars have brought to the understanding of the texts of games/gaming is beyond the scope of this chapter, this chapter tries to review some of the approaches—from aesthetic criticism to critical cultural theory—which offer important analytical tools to engage with the complex, interactive worlds of gaming that inform my discussion of video games on Bollywood movies. Although Herz (1997), Poole (2000, p. 35), and Wolf (2001, p. 17) refer to games on arcade machines, consoles, and PCs as "video games," Cornford *et al.* (2000) prefer to distinguish between computer and video games, and Haddon (1993) uses the broad term "interactive games." This chapter, despite the definitional differences, uses the terms like "video games," "computer games," and "digital games" interchangeably, to refer to the entire field and to embrace arcade, computer, console, and mobile games in all their diversity.

The chapter is divided into two parts. The first part of the chapter will frame the key concepts, approaches, and disciplinary tools of Game Studies (Walther 2003), the evaluation of games as designed artefacts and emergent culture (Juul 2003; Steinkuehler 2006), the game design process (Salen and Zimmerman 2003), narrative and its role in games and game play (Fuller and Jenkins 1995; Herz 1997; Juul 1998, 2001; Murray 1998; Poole 2000), the ideological implications of the medium as a whole (Salen and Zimmerman 2003; Magnet 2006), and the relationship between players and designers, and the actual industry practices (Sotamaa 2007). From this conceptual core, the second part of the chapter will limn out an understanding of the digital games of Bollywood movies, and gaming within wider social, cultural, and global forces. In this chapter, the video games of Bollywood movies will be examined through the lens of Ian Bogost's notion of procedural rhetoric, a practice/technique of using processes persuasively for making arguments with computational systems and for unpacking computational arguments others have created. To elucidate the intricate conventions of the game industry and the ways in which players are woven into its fabric, I will examine the movie simulations and games of a few mainstream Bollywood movies for outlining some of the current industry practices and for considering the issues and/tensions attached to them. I am particularly interested in the production, circulation, and reception of this form of "public culture" in postcolonial India (Appadurai and Breckenridge 1988, p. 5), a zone of cultural debate, which negotiates the tensions between national sites and transnational/globalizing processes. Furthermore, extrapolating the process of transformation when a story moves from a film text to a gaming text, the chapter aims to examine not only the intermediality of media and convergence culture but also the ways in which games construct conceptions of spatiality, political systems, ethics, and society. Instead of presenting a mere status report on Bollywood and the Indian gaming culture, I will map out the trajectory of the fast-changing entertainment landscape of India. Hence, I have intentionally avoided statistical data, charts, and figures, unless extremely crucial and verifiable.

## Part 1

### *Understanding Games: Theories and Approaches*

Games are a "mangle" (Pickering 1995) of social and material world, and consumption of human intentions and designed experiences, material constraints, and affordances, and evolving sociocultural practices (Steinkuehler 2006, p. 97). Though video games have been defined variously by Johan Huizinga in *Homo Ludens: A Study of the Play- Element in Culture* (1950), Roger Caillois in *Man, Play, and Games* (1961), Elliott M. Avedon and Brian Sutton-Smith in *The Study of Games* (1971), and Gonzalo Frasca (1999) in recent works, but a few overlapping elements in all these approaches that have been taken in delineating the video game are: an algorithm, player activity, interface, and graphics. As Alexander R. Galloway puts it, if photographs are images, and films are moving images, then

> video games are actions. . . . Without the active participation of players and machines, video games exist only as static computer code. Video games come into being when the machine is powered up and the software is executed; they exist when enacted.
>
> *(2006, p. 2)*

Since these actions or enactments are undertaken across and between multiple actors—creators, developers, and gamers (in the case of online games often with a cast of thousands)—this makes computer games extremely challenging to study, because it is difficult to identify and recreate "recollections of how they were inspired and of the myriad collective and negotiated decisions that gave them their final form, as well as explanations of how and in what contexts they are eventually to be experienced" (McAllister 2004, p. viii). Inspired by Henry Jenkins (2006), this chapter aims to engage with this issue of media convergence "as a process instead of a static termination" (Thorburn 2003, p. 3), that is, "the flow of content across multiple media platforms, the cooperation between multiple media industries, . . . [and] the search for new structures of media financing that fall at the interstices between old and new media" (Jenkins 2006, p. 640). Hence, at the convergence of technology, cinema, and new media, there is intense experimentation with, and research of video games, which apply film-narratives, cinematic strategies, and aesthetics to the creation of interactive environments.

Feature films and videogames are industries closely related to the traditional electronic media that vie for the attention of the mass electronic media audience, and sometimes videogames even surpass them in terms of their popularity and revenues (Veugen 2012, p. 48), so much so that large media corporations now regularly release films with an accompanying computer game. In videogames, the three-dimensional landscape, virtual reality, is an "interactive, immersive experience generated by a computer" (Pimentel and Teixeira 1993, p. 11). The point of departure in an analysis of games is "a closer look at interactivity as the link that connects the media presentation with the experience of usage, thus constituting it as the minimal requirement for bidirectionality of immersion" (Härig 2012, p. 211). The quality of attention, which these kinds of interactive processes produce, is often described as "immersive." The immersive nature of computer games and the invisibility or transparency of the medium that Moulthrop suggests this produces work both to empower the user and to simultaneously serve the interests of the oligopolies that produce them (2004, p. 66). The "text," if we are to use that term at all for computer games, "becomes the complex interaction between player and game—or what is described as gameplay" (Liestol 2004, p. 400). The immersion of the computer game player "is less the submersion in virtual reality as the quality of intense concentration produced by having to attend to the combination of activities—understanding control systems, guessing out the gameplay, puzzle cracking, enemy killing and strategic planning" (Dovey and Kennedy 2006, p. 8). Additionally, Ermi and Mäyrä mention that the players do not just involve themselves in ready-made gameplay but also keenly engage "in the construction of these experiences: they bring their desires, anticipations and previous experiences with them, and interpret and reflect the experience in that light" (2005, no page). Computer games appeal to people, because "they are configurative, offering the chance to manipulate complex systems within continuous loops of intervention, observation, and response," which enables an avowal of player agency and indicates the difference between gameplay and other types of cultural consumption (Moulthrop 2004, p. 64).

Games simultaneously function as both culture and cultural objects (Nasir 2005, p. 5)—as microcosms for studying the emergence, maintenance, and transformation of both designed object and emergent culture, caught up in broader conversation with politics, contemporary life and academics. Some of the outstanding research on different aspects of the games studies has been done by, for example: Diane Carr (2002, 2005) and Helen Kennedy (2002, 2006) on preferences and pleasure, Jennifer Jenson and Suzanne de Castell (2005, 2008) and Mary Flanagan (2009) on critical play and alternative game design, Lisa Nakamura (2008) on race and ethnicity, Nick Taylor (2011) and Taylor *et al.* (2009) on gender and gaming cultures, and T.L. Taylor on gender and embodiment in online games (2003a, 2003b, 2006). If we map the terrain of the emerging field of video game theory, the different trends in research and theorizing, we will find that it is a site of convergence of an expansive diversity of approaches, which encompass film and television theory, semiotics, performance theory, game studies, literary theory, computer science, theories of hypertext, cybertext, interactivity, identity, postmodernism, ludology, media theory, narratology, aesthetics and art theory, psychology, theories of simulacra, among others. The next section of this chapter delineates some of these disciplinary paradigms/frameworks to map out the changes in Bollywood digital culture and Bollywood-based video games from the two positions of technologically and socially determined view of game production and representation. Bollywood games are analysed from an industrial/institutional perspective that considers the extent to which their qualities are shaped by the business strategies. Examining Bollywood video games is extraordinarily difficult, since

> they are so socially complex; recollections of how they were inspired and of the myriad collective and negotiated decisions that gave them their final form, as well as explanations of how and in what contexts they are eventually to be experienced, are difficult to identify and reconstruct.
>
> *(McAllister 2004, p. viii)*

To analyse Bollywood video games, two interrelated concerns—those of (a) gaming and culture and (b) the textual/narrative universe of games, that is, paratexts to the game (e.g. game reviews) and reference texts (like films)—will be addressed in the next section.

## Part II

### *Getting Into the Game: Bollywood and Videogames*

Bollywood has an extensive global reach, which is evident by the fact that, in many countries, a significant amount of bandwidth carries cultural content in the form of Bollywood movies and networked video games (Howard 2010, p. 163). The term "Bollywood,"[1] which is a popular name for Hindi commercial cinema produced in the city of Bombay, came into being in the 1990s subsequent to the transnational popularity of Bombay cinema (two films entered the top 10 of British cinema charts in 1998) and its replication of the Hollywood genre. At present, with nearly 800 releases in a year, India holds the distinction of making more films than all the countries of Europe combined, and at roughly four times the rate of the U.S. (Bose 2006, p. 18). The revenues of Indian entertainment industry have grown at an incredible rate of 360% in the period 1998–2005 and 58% in the 2001–2005 phase. Since the entertainment industry in India has outperformed the economy and is one of the fastest growing sectors in India, the Indian government gave it industry status in 2001.[2] This not only allows the industry to access institutional finance and clean credit for new projects but also facilitates *foreign investment by corporatized entertainment companies.* As the media and entertainment landscape in India transformed during the 1990s and early 2000s under the impact of the Indian state's decision to deregulate many sectors of the economy, the production and circulation of paratexts for Hindi-language films became a far more complex affair. Promoting and marketing a Bollywood film acquired new dimensions: authoring promotional ideas, tailoring promotional videos for various television channels, crafting innovative making-of features, negotiating for film stars on spots for film stars on different television programs, designing websites for each film, coordinating online chat sessions involving transnational fan communities, contests and games for various mobile phone platforms, and so on. In the past few years, Disney, Viacom, News Corporation, and Sony Pictures have all done deals with Bollywood companies.

With 27% share of India's total entertainment industry revenues, Bollywood enormously impacts not only the video, music, television, and live entertainment sectors but also gaming and the videogames industry (FICCI-KPMG 2007). However, due to media convergence, film is no longer a single medium, and its commercial dominance is challenged by new media platforms.

Gaming is an inextricable part of the contemporary postcolonial sensibility, defined by a strong reliance on post-reflexivity and centred on performativity (Kavoori 2006, p. 14). The feature films and videogames industries are so intimately linked to traditional electronic media that film entertainment in India is a key driver for content on television, videogames, music, animation, and advertising. Bollywood incorporated gaming with the release of several film-themed titles, such as *Ghajini*, *Ra.One Genesis*, *Agneepath*, *Singham*, and *Don 2*, across multiple platforms. Though localized gaming content faces stiff competition from international content, which tends to have better quality, but given the success of games such as *Ra.One Genesis* have seen in the past, the Indian gamer appears to be open to content that is on par with international standards. The numerous new social gaming platforms incorporating micropayments, like Games 2 Win's "Appuccino" and Nazara Technologies' "G-City," have been designed to cater to the Indian context. The Indian gaming industry can be divided into three separate segments: Mobile Gaming, Console Gaming, and PC & Online Gaming. Though the Indian gaming industry is still at an embryonic stage and, in terms of a global presence, lags far behind the U.S., China, Canada, Australia, and Japan, the Indian animation, gaming, and VFX industries nonetheless saw a growth of 24% in 2007 over 2006 (FICCI-KPMG 2012 Report). Today, more and more movies are marketed with an official game, usually on mobile phones. With the growing reach of mobile phones penetrating even rural areas, mobile service providers are fledging the market with new movie-based applications, games, videos, and news alerts. With this backdrop in mind, it is no surprise that movies releasing these days come with their own mobile and web games. According to the FICCI-KPMG Report (2012), the Indian gaming sector achieved revenues of INR 13 billion, in line with last year's forecasts (p. 90). Although the wireless gaming market (14%) draws its strength from the Asia-Pacific region, particularly Japan and South Korea, analysts say that, going by the explosive growth in the mobile phone users' base in India, the generation of gaming content may well become "the next big thing" to happen in the country after IT outsourcing. India is the world's fastest-growing cellular market, and has the second largest consumer base after China. According to the Telecom Regulatory Authority of India, there were 752.2 million mobile phone subscribers as of 31 December 2010. The research company Gartner Inc. last year predicted that 82% of India's 1.2 billion populations would have a mobile phone by 2014. There is also the Nasscom-McKinsey study of 2005, which states that leisure spending in India will be stimulated largely by the IT-enabled industry (Bose 2006, p. 16). Bollywood is fast discovering the magic of mobile telephony, everything from running pre-release publicity teasers as text messages to selling ring tones, ring tones and other forms of film music.

The games resembling popular Bollywood movies are getting popular in mobile app stores. Blockbuster movies like *Krrish 3, Dhoom 3, Chennai Express, and Race 2,* have smartphone games with their respective names and characters. Among the most popular India-made games are *Bhagat Singh,* by Mitashi Edutainment Pvt. Ltd; a mobile game based on *Dhoom 2*; and *Orampo,* an auto-racing game based on a Tamil film of the same name. Hungama and Game Shastra have developed state-of-the art games around the iconic 1975 Bollywood film *Sholay,* and Rajinikanth's Tamil movie *Kochadaiiyaanin,* which has been released in Tamil and five additional languages, including Hindi, Telugu, Bengali, Marathi, and Punjabi. The *Krrish 3* game, launched a few months ago, has over 2 million downloads globally, between the Android and Apple app stores. These games are free but still generating revenues through the "freemium" model, where the game is free but in-app purchases are charged. The filmmakers license their titles and characters to game developers on a revenue-sharing basis. Indeed, there are not only Indian companies vying to acquire the franchisee rights of Bollywood stars like Amitabh Bachchan and Shahrukh Khan for their mobile games but also Chinese giants, who have been trying to enter this field with plans to release a dozen new gaming products featuring only Hindi film actors (Bose 2006, p. 111). In terms of capital, star-quality, and technology, Bollywood cinema is competing in the international market today.

While the examination of production practices and marketing strategies of the Indian games industry mostly falls beyond the scope of this chapter, I nevertheless will now examine the movie simulations and games of some mainstream Bollywood movies for the purpose of outlining some current industry practices. Since there is a chasm in research within gaming literature that traces the transmediated stories and the manner in which transmediation impacts gamers, the next section of the chapter addresses this *aporia* of the aesthetic to examine the entire complex process in which the negotiated cinematic image blends with an adapted, transmediated text (videogame) to construct imaginable story-world trajectories for players to visualize. Also, there is less literature on how Bollywood gaming worlds draw on discourses, rhetoric, and emotions to create storied worlds. Identifying the linkages between cinema and video games, Angela Ndalianis (2004) observes that in these contemporary entertainment forms "media merge with media, genres unite to produce new hybrid forms, [and] narratives open up and extend into new spatial and serial configurations" (p. 2–3). Through the engagement with an immersive, computer-generated visual syntax and multilevel "digital" narrative in Bollywood videogames, the next section of the chapter maps out how these diverse yet interconnected issues coalesce to imply the likelihood of new modes of spectatorial identification that may be possible as the cinema and video games become increasingly cross-fertilized and hybridized. My discussion will function in all the registers—theoretical, literary, and cinematic—leveraging a comparative procedural criticism to motivate an analysis of the following two videogames: *Krrish 3: The Game* and *Dhoom: 3 Jet Speed.* If at any point I seem to dwell on only one of these registers, it is for a purely strategic purpose.

## *Bollywood Gaming*

### *Krrish 3: The Game*

*Krrish 3: The Game*, the official game based on the superhero-science fiction film *Krrish 3* (2013), is a free, fast-paced, multiplayer runner-type game made for the fans of superhero and action-adventure games. The game, based on the character of Krrish, intends to provide the players with a chance to relive the superhero's life, perform breath-taking stunts, and use state of the art gadgets and weapons to take down the enemies. It is based on a particular gamer subculture, which is focused on the practice of "speed runs," that is, high-speed rushing through either a single level or the entire game. In accordance with both representational and gameplay focus, the player's attention is typically centred more on the main character. However, the players have an option to choose between four characters to play with, Krrish, Kaaya (a shape shifting female mutant), Kaal (a handicapped evil genius who possesses telekinetic powers), and Frogman. The gameplay of *Krrish 3: The Game* presents the player with the clear and simple challenge of surviving while shooting everything that moves. The level design of *Krrish 3: The Game*, which shows the first-person view in a realistically modelled and textured 3D environment, is a vital constituent of immersion that is not only useful in introducing the multidimensional nature of immersion experiences but also central to our understanding gameplay experiences. When playing this game, the player gets a strong sense of being there himself/herself. The quality of the identification and immersion in *Krrish 3: The Game* is distinct, as it is not only the player who is jumping, climbing, and seldom falling, but also the player is also guiding Krrish, the player character, to do the combat and the acrobatics. This duality of game player's role within the game as both a subject and an object has an effect on the gameplay experience, as there is manipulation and/performance of identity and identification involved. The powerful quality of the interactive moving images and sounds provide the overpowering embodied kinaesthesia and strong sensory immersion for the player. Throughout the game, the players are always trying to outrun and trap each other using gadgets and their relevant skills. On the swipe of a finger, the player enacts the superhero life by performing awe-inspiring stunts, scaling obstacles, jumping and sliding from building to building for an aerial thrill, using state of the art gadgets and sophisticated weapons, outrunning opponents, and defeating enemies. The gamer has the choice to select his weapon from a wide selection of gadgets and upgrades customized to his/her style, attacks, and skills. When the *Krrish 3* gameplay is combined with the distinctive way it is executed, the consequent heart-stopping action, in totality, provides abundant player immersion and gaming bliss, which is one of the central concepts for analysing gameplay experience.

While the movie *Krrish 3* activates a "disembodied" gaze that corresponds with the camera "eye" to represent the subjective viewpoint of a character, the videogame incorporates an immersive, embodied experience, which encompasses the self-referential analysis of the character's body not only as the medium of his viewpoint but also as the instrument of the player's perspective. The players ally with Krrish to see and experience the game space as he does. The game players "reload ammunition, change weapons, and examine clues from the perspective of an embodied gaze, not a disembodied one, an alignment which heightens the player's sense of immediacy and presence within a given game space" (McMahan 2003, p. 71). Second, the freedom of movement—one of the most significant elements in the gameplay experience—amazing and intense free runs with cutting-edge graphics and a breath-taking view of Bombay's skyline, crazy stunts in a real-world scenario, the speed and immediacy with which the game environment reacts to one's actions, and the hectic tempo of the game are likely to induce another kind of immersion, as the player becomes immersed in actions of play. Finally, though the game has a visceral appeal, it is emotionally gripping too. As the player runs through the streets of Bombay, in an environment teeming with action, threatening snarls coming from somewhere close by, and sometimes also the sudden loss of light and attacks from the dark, he discovers random missions, collectibles, and gradually unlocks secrets. In this powerful experience, "in this intensity, this absorption, this power of maddening, lies the very essence, the primordial quality of play" (Huizinga 1950, p. 2). The multiple dimensions of gameplay experience facilitate procedural literacy. Since, to role-play, gamers must choose a role, interpret elements, choose sides, and know one's environment, videogames compel players to engage in cognitive processing. The game enables the player to appreciate and understand the complexity and multidimensionality of human nature. The game has powerful symbolic undertones, available for analysis at the level of its core gameplay, where the focus is on conquering powerful enemies while navigating spaces. At the representational level, *Krrish 3: The Game* utilizes science fictional imagery, which contributes to the powerful gameplay experience it has been reported providing.

The chief goal of the game is winning the race by reaching the target destination in the least possible time. This running game is designed to be closer to reality, so as best to provide players with a chance to re-enact the life Hrithik Roshan, the actor in the original movie, lives as Krrish, and to experience the resulting adrenaline rush. The game consists of the players racing through the rooftops of Mumbai, dodging obstacles, leaping between buildings, and deploying gadgets to entrap each other. The 3D environments of the game are made up of a variety of settings, which include the four distinctive districts (New, Old, Industrial, and Dockyard) of the city of Mumbai. Some critics of videogames compare this virtual game world with Baudrillard's portrayals of Disneyland as "hyperreality," or simulation that is offered to consumers as "better than the real thing" (Kellner 1989, p. 82). Though some may reject such critique as overstated disquiet about something that is basically just amusement and games, but cultural critics like Pobłocki (2002) claim that objects of amusement are all the more "dangerous" in their seemingly neutral and simplistic manner of presenting their microworlds. As J. C. Herz puts it in her book *Joystick Nation*, "you can build something that looks like Detroit without building in racial tension. . . . [I]f you are going to play these games—it is a good idea to know who's making up the rules" (1997, p. 223). However, since gamers and gaming are enmeshed in the macrocosm of the larger social and cultural milieu, it can be asserted, "videogames are computational artefacts that have cultural meaning" (Bogost 2007, p. ix). Actually, this cultural meaning does not lie in the content of videogames, as the serious games community claims. Rather, it is ingrained in the very way videogames mount claims through "procedural rhetoric," a practice/technique of using processes persuasively through rule-based representations and interactions rather than the spoken word, writing, images, or moving picture (Bogost 2007, p. 46). In fact, *Krrish 3: The Game* employs procedural rhetoric, for making arguments with computational systems effectively. Another important question that arises is whether videogames do, at least on occasion, prompt morally creditable perspectives on their indisputably unsettling death and violent content? It is my contention that *Krrish 3: The Game* does succeed on both these counts. Alluding to Grant Tavinor, here I want to strike a balance between the two kinds of positions: "game activities are not immune to criticism, as some gamers seem to assume, but neither are they wholly wicked" (2009, p. 153). Furthermore, the ubiquity of violence and shooting is not a particularly distinctive feature of videogames. According to Steven Pinker, more than 80% of fiction and drama are

> defined by adversaries (often murderous), by tragedies of kinship and love, or both. In the real world, our life stories are largely stories of conflict: the hurts, guilts, and rivalries inflicted by parents, siblings, children, spouses, lovers, friends, and competitors.
>
> *(1997, p. 427)*

Our enduring interests in violence in the arts and media may be natural, yet this is not to ethically validate those interests. Gaming and gamers are a lot more reflective than they are often given credit for, because they understand the ethical paradigms of the interactive text of the game. My contention is that, in fighting the evildoers, aliens, and mutants in *Krrish 3: The Game*, the protagonist Krrish actively engages with malevolence and seeks to redress moral difficulties and ambiguities.

When modes shift from a cinema image to a video game, modal properties and limitations change. In the cinematic narrative, the author can integrate Krrish's superhuman powers into the plot as he or she sees fit, but in the ludo-narrative world of the video game, Krrish's invincible capabilities makes for problematic game development. Embedded within a worldview that matches actions to consequences (Wolf 2001, p. 109) and one that rewards audacious and frequently hazardous action based on an alert analytical examination of one's surroundings, this video game narrative articulates the type of far-reaching cultural ambivalence and indeterminacy that Bukatman (1998) summarizes while exploring cyberspace and virtual environments. If the game developers remain true to the character in the film *Krrish*, then players who control Krrish are essentially unstoppable and unassailable. Furthermore, if the accomplishment of the player's goal becomes inevitable, then the players would not require stratagems, incisiveness, talent, or creative thinking to achieve their goal and enjoy the game as victory is ensured even before the game begins. Thus in order to transmediate and speculate on the distinctive nature of possible gamers, the game developers and designers had to work hard to retain the core ideas, boundaries of *Krrish 3* movie, to design a world shaped around the movie based on gaming logic, shaping it all around possible imagined story worlds. Through bricolage, the designers construct characters and backdrops that are remixed and converged versions of the cinematic text.

## *Dhoom: 3 Jet Speed*

*Dhoom: 3 Jet Speed* is the first game in the *Dhoom* series based on the Bollywood movie *Dhoom 3*. It was released alongside its theatrical release on 20 December 2013. In fact, Yash Raj Films' licensing and merchandising division Yash Raj Films Licensing signed a multiyear, multititle licensing agreement with Robosoft's mobile games subsidiary 99Games to develop and publish mobile games based on the *Dhoom* film franchise. Yash Raj Films' *Dhoom: 2* is one of the very first films to develop a console game. After a thrilling high-speed bike race through the streets of Chicago in *Dhoom: 3 The Game*, which saw over 12 million downloads worldwide, the chase continues on the Chicago River in *Dhoom: 3 Jet Speed*, the second game in the series for fans of the *Dhoom* franchise. The game has players donning the role of *Dhoom: 3* movie protagonist Sahir—played by superstar Aamir Khan—as he rides a supercharged Aqua Jet through the congested Chicago River. There are obstacles to avoid, and the police are at their very best with ACP Jai Dixit (Abhishek Bachchan) and Ali (Uday Chopra) leading them in the chase. The digital narrative encourages an immersive mode of "video" pleasure as the spectator moves vicariously via the protagonist through multiple levels of action, encountering various rewards and punishments that serve as feedback loops while *en route* to an ultimate destination or goal. And increasingly, it seems that the game evokes our sympathy with the characters; this emotional response both wires us to their digital worlds and drives the gameplay and narrative forward. The player can use a variety of power-ups to help evade and get the best score, but they must watch out for the health of the Aqua Jet. The game features realistic water animation and graphics for a great gaming experience. The game aims to maintain continual engagement with users, with the likelihood of refreshes to game play (through the addition of new levels and/or characters). According to Aarseth, though video games are formed by game play (the player's performance, stratagems and motivations), game structure (the guidelines of the game, incorporating simulation rubrics), and the game world (fictional content, topology/level design), but an adapted video-game world has also undertaken an extra procedure of transforming a previous textual universe requiring a fusion of the existing fictional content with game play (2007). As Wolf (2001) asserts, since contemporary video game narratives have long since moved beyond simple tests of hand-eye co-ordination or puzzle-solving skill to draw on select principles of cause-and-effect-driven cinematic narrative, players have become decidedly more vested in their outcome (p. 101) and the imagined story world, that is, the meaning negotiation and/transaction that happens between the story and the player's agency and subjectivities. The multiple immersive dimensions of gameplay experiences foster what Ian Bogost calls "procedural literacy," that is, "a capacity to restructure and reconfigure knowledge to look at problems from multiple vantage points, and through this process to develop a greater systemic understanding of the rules and procedures that shape our everyday experiences" (Jenkins *et al.* 2009, p. 45). Since experimenting with new combinations of familiar elements is a vital characteristic of video games, "we become procedurally literate through play" (p. 35), as it "encourages active experimentation with basic building blocks in new combinations" (Bogost 2005, p. 36). Through their game play, the players learn to appreciate and understand the complexity and multidimensionality of human nature.

## Conclusion

While there is no single structure or stylistic convention that would encompass game studies, this chapter acknowledges that games are cultural texts and concedes that the study of processes involved in their production and consumption underscore the implications for Bollywood digitalization and gaming. If the media are "systems for the production, distribution and consumption of symbolic forms" (Garnham 2000, p. 39), then the Bollywood digital games industry can be situated within the wider media system and regarded as an emergent and dynamic set of institutions, forms, and practices. While the socio-techno-economic analysis of Bollywood games, their proposed thematics, and ideological implications are vitally important for any analysis, for a comprehensive study, it is imperative to consider gameplay, interactivity, and immersion as constitutive elements of games, especially in the analysis of games as sociocultural texts. The power of videogames to engage our personal/social emotions, and to use these emotions to supply our gaming actions with added import, will be promising in the future creative design/production/consumption of Bollywood videogames. Instead of confining ourselves solely to its textual features, design, production, and marketing, we have to pay particular attention to the instant of its enactment as it is played. The game becomes the site at which the complex interaction between player and game—or what is described as gameplay—takes place. Bollywood games and gamers, through the entire gamut of gameplay and gaming, enable the understanding of the participatory nature of computer games and the manipulability of the software, which facilitate new forms of creative consumption. Bollywood video games establish not only just how "global" and "new" these digital games really are but also the fact that gaming is an immersive, playful form of spectatorial address, which mounts procedural literacy through procedural rhetoric. Since the meaning in videogames is not fixed but is created by the transitory production of users' interactions with the medium, understanding Bollywood games in terms of both social construction and textual practices can "help us tackle the problem of describing, or rematerializing the object of our study," which, due to digitalization, can be seen to dematerialize the text and textuality (Cubitt 2000, p. 87). Although Game Studies is a nascent field in which there are many unknowns, but as we gaze into the future, given the rapid strides made by Bollywood cinema in the last decade, it is not possible to imagine the future possibilities and trajectories, other than that this is just a beginning and Shahrukh Khan's line from the movie *Om Shanti Om*, "*picture abhi baaqi hai mere dost* [the film is yet to continue, my friend]," serves as an apt coda.

## Notes

1 For further discussion regarding the term Bollywood, see Rajadhyaksha 2003; Prasad 2003.

2 For further information on the Bombay film industry and the granting of industry status to it, see *Indian Express* (9th, 11th and 12th May, 1998).

## References


Aarseth, Espen. (2007) 'Playing research: Methodological approaches to game analysis', *Artnodes*, 7 [online]. DOI: 10.7238/a.v0i7.763 (Accessed: 17 Oct. 2020).

Appadurai, A. and C. A. Breckenridge. (1988) 'Why public culture?', *Public Culture*, 1(1), pp. 5–9.

Avedon, Elliott M. and Brian Sutton-Smith. (1971) *The study of games*. New York: John Wiley & Sons.

Bogost, Ian. (2005) 'Procedural literacy: problem solving with programming, systems, & play procedural literacy: Problem solving with programming, systems, & play', *Telemedium*, (Winter/Spring), pp. 32–36.

Bogost, Ian. (2007) *Persuasive games: The expressive power of videogames*. Cambridge, London: MIT Press.

Bose, Derek. (2006) *Brand Bollywood: A new global entertainment order*. New Delhi & London: Sage Publications.

Breuer, J. (2009) 'Mittendrin—statt nur dabei' in Mosel, M. (ed.) *Gefangen im flow? Äasthetik und dispositive atrukturen von computerspielen*. Boizenburg: Verlag Werner Hülsbusch, pp. 181–213.

Bukatman, Scott. (1998) 'Zooming Out: The End of Offscreen Space', in Lewis, J. (ed.) *The new American cinema*. Durham, NC: Duke UP, pp. 248–72.

Caillois, R. (1961) *Man, play, and games*. New York: Free Press.

Carr, Diane. (2002) 'Playing with Lara', in King, G. and Kryzwinska, T. (eds.) *Screenplay: cinema/videogames/inter-faces*. London: Wallflower Press, pp. 171–80.

Carr, Diane. (2005) 'Contexts, Gaming Pleasures, and Gendered Preferences', *Simulation & Gaming*, 36(4), pp. 464–482.

Cornford, J., R. Naylor and Driver, S. (2000) 'New Media and Regional Development: the case of the UK computer and video games industry', in Giunta, A., Lagendijk, A., and Pike, A. (eds.) *Restructuring industry and territory: The experience of Europe's regions*. London: Stationery Office, pp. 83–108.

Cubitt, Sean. (Spring 2000) 'The distinctiveness of digital criticism', *Screen*, 41(1), pp. 186–92.

Dovey, Jon and Kennedy, Helen W. (2006) *Game cultures: Computer games as new media*. Berkshire (England): Open University Press.

Ermi, Laura and Mäyrä, Frans. (2005) 'Fundamental components of the gameplay experience: analysing immersion', in de Castell, Suzanne and Jenson, Jennifer (eds.) *Proceedings of chancing views: Worlds in play (digital games research association's second international conference).*

Vancouver: DiGRA and Simon Fraser University. [Online]. Available at: www.digra.org/dl/db/06276.41516.pdf (Accessed: 2 August 2021)

FICCI-KPMG Indian Media and Entertainment Industry Report 2012.

FICCI-KPMG Indian Media and Entertainment Industry Report 2007.

Flanagan, Mary. (2009) *Critical play: Radical game design*. Cambridge, MA: MIT Press.

Frasca, Gonzalo. (1999) 'Ludology meets narratology: Similitude and differences between (video) games and narrative', *Parnasso*, 3, pp. 365–371. [Online]. Available at: www.ludology.org/articles/ludology.htm (Accessed: 25 August 2020).

Fuller, Mary and Jenkins, Henry. (1995) 'Nintendo® and new world travel writing: A dialogue', in Jones, S.G. (ed.) *Cybersociety. Computer-mediated communication and community*. Thousand Oaks, CA: Sage, pp. 57–72.

Galloway, Alexander R. (2006) *Gaming: Essays on algorithmic culture*. Minneapolis, MN: University of Minnesota Press.

Garnham, Nicholas. (2000) *Emancipation, the media and modernity*. Oxford: Oxford University Press.

Gopal, Sangita. (2011) *Conjugations: Marriage and form in new Bollywood cinema*. London: University of Chicago Press Ltd.

Grieb, M. (2002) 'Run Lara run', in King, G. and Krzywinska, T. (eds.) *Screenplay: cinema/videogames/. Interfaces*. London: Wallflower Press, pp. 157–170.

Haddon, L. (1993) 'Interactive games', in Hayward, Philip and Wollens, Tana (eds.) *Future visions: New technologies of the screen*. London: British Film Institute, pp. 123–147.

Härig, Dominik. (2012) 'Inside and outside the game', in Fromme, J. and Unger, A. (eds.) *Computer games and new media cultures: A handbook of digital games Studies*. Dordrecht Heidelberg, New York, London: Springer, pp. 209–18.

Herz, J. C. (1997) *Joystick nation: How video games gobbled our money, won our hearts, and rewired our minds*. London: Abacus.

Howard, Philip N. (2010) *The digital origins of dictatorship and democracy*. Oxford and New York: Oxford University Press.

Howells, S. (2002) 'Watching a game, playing a movie: When media collide', in King, G. and Krzywinska, T. (eds.) *Screenplay: Cinema/videogames/interfaces*. London: Wallflower, pp. 110–121.

Huizinga, Johan. (1950) *Homo ludens: A study of the play-element in culture*. Boston: Beacon Press.

Indian Express. (1998a) 'Bollywood's Woes to Get a Hearing Finally', *Indian Express*, 9 May [online]. Available at: www.expressindia.comie/daily/19980509/12950624.html (Accessed: 24 September 2020).

Indian Express. (1998b) 'Finally an Industry', *Indian Express*, 12 May [online]. Available at: www.expressindia.comie/daily/19980512/13250064.html (Accessed: 21 September 2020).

Indian Express. (1998c) 'Industry Status for Film World', *Indian Express*, 11 May [online]. Available at: www.expressindia.com/daily/19980511/13150654.html (Accessed: 24 August 2020).

Jenkins, Henry. (2006) *Convergence culture: where old and new media collide*. New York: New York University Press.

Jenkins, Henry, Purushotma, R., Weigel, M., Clinton, K., and Robison, Alice J. (eds.) (2009) *Confronting the challenges of participatory culture: Media education for the 21st century*. Cambridge, MA: MIT Press.

Jenson, Jennifer and de Castell, Suzanne. (2005) 'Her Own Boss: Gender and the Pursuit of Incompetent Play', *Proceedings of DiGRA 2005 Conference: Changing Views—Worlds in Play* (Vol. 3) [online]. Available at: www.digra.org/wp-content/uploads/digital-library/06278.27455.pdf (Accessed: 1 August 2020).

Jenson, Jennifer and de Castell, Suzanne. (2008) 'Theorizing gender and digital gameplay: oversights, accidents and surprises', *Eludamos: Journal for Computer Game Culture*, 2 (1), pp. 15–25.

Juul, Jesper. (1998) 'A clash between game and narrative', Paper presented at the *Digital arts and culture conference*, Bergen, Norway [online]. Available at: www.jesperjuul.net/text/clash_between_game_and_narrative.html (Accessed: 1 August 2020).

Juul, Jesper. (2000) 'What computer games can and can't Do', Paper presented at *DAC Conference*, Bergen [online]. Available at: www.jesperjuul.net/text/wcgcacd.html (Accessed: 12 August 2020)

Juul, Jesper. (2001) Games telling stories?—A brief note on games and narratives', *Game Studies* 1(1) [online]. Available at: http://gamestudies.org/0101/juul-gts/#1 (Accessed: 1 August 2020).

Juul, Jesper. (2003) 'The game, the player, the world: Looking for a heart of gameness', in Copier, Marinka and Raessens, Joost (eds.) *Level up: digital games research conference*. Utrecht: Faculty of Arts, Utrecht University Press.

Juul, Jesper. (2005) *Half-real: Video games Between real rules and fictional worlds*. Cambridge, Mass.: MIT Press.

Kavoori, Anandam. (2006) *The logics of globalization: Studies in international communication*. Lanham, Plymouth: Lexington Books.

Kellner, Douglas. (1989) *Jean Baudrillard: From Marxism to postmodernism and beyond*. Stanford: Stanford University Press.

Kennedy, Helen W. (2002) 'Lara Croft: Feminist icon or cyber bimbo? On the limits of textual analysis', *Game Studies* 2 (2) [online]. Available at: www.gamestudies.org/0202/kennedy/ (Accessed: 10 August 2020).

Kennedy, Helen W. (2006) 'Illegitimate, monstrous and out there: Female "quake" players and inappropriate pleasures', in Hollows, J., and Moseley, R. (eds.) *Feminism in popular culture*. Oxford: Berg, pp. 183–202.

Kirkpatrick, Graeme. (2007) 'Between art and gameness: Critical theory and computer game aesthetics.' *Thesis Eleven*, 89, pp. 74–93.

Krzywinska, T. and Lowood, H. (2006) 'Guest editors' introduction', *Games and Culture*, 1(4), pp. 279–280. DOI: 10.1177/1555412006293515 (Accessed 12 Oct. 2020).

Liestol, Gunnar. (2004) ' "Gameplay": from synthesis to analysis (and vice versa)', in Liestol, G., Morrison, A., and Rasmussen, T. (eds.) *Digital media revisited: Theoretical and conceptual innovations in digital domains*. Cambridge, MA and London: MIT Press, pp. 389–414.

Mactavish, A. (2002) 'Technological pleasure: The performance and narrative of technology in Half-Life and other high-tech computer games', in King, G. and Krzywinska, T. (eds.) *Screen play: Cinema/videogames/interfaces*. London: Wallflower Press, pp. 33–49.

Magnet, Shoshana. (2006) 'Playing at colonization: Interpreting imaginary landscapes in the video game *Tropico*', *Journal of Communication Inquiry*, 30 (2), pp. 142–162.

Mäyrä, Frans. (2006) 'Welcome to mapping the global game cultures: Issues for a Sociocultural Study of Games and Players', Paper presented at the Gaming Realities Conference Proceedings, Greece.

Mäyrä, Frans. (2008) *An introduction to game studies: Games in culture*. Thousand Oaks, CA: Sage.

Mäyrä, Frans. (2008) 'Open invitation: Mapping global game cultures. Issues for a sociocultural study of games and players', *European Journal of Cultural Studies*, 11(2), pp. 249–257. DOI: 10.1177/1367549407088337 (Accessed: 18 August 2020).

McAllister, K. (2004) *Game work: Language, power and computer game culture.* Tuscaloosa: University of Alabama Press.

McMahan, Alison. (2003) 'Immersion, engagement, and presence: A method for analyzing 3-D video games', in Wolf, Mark J. P. and Perron, B. (eds.) *The video game theory reader.* New York: Routledge, pp. 67–86.

Mortensen, Torill Elvira. (2006) 'WoW is the new MUD: Social gaming from text to video', *Games and Culture,* 1(4), pp. 397–413 [online]. DOI:10.1177/1555412006292622. (Accessed: 1 Aug. 2020).

Moulthrop, Stuart. (2004) 'From work to play: Molecular culture in the time of deadly games', in Wardrip-Fruin, N. and Harrigan, P. (eds.) *First person: New media as story, performance and game.* Cambridge, MA and London: MIT Press, pp. 56–70.

Murray, J. H. (1998) *Hamlet on The Holodeck.* Cambridge, MA: MIT Press.

Nakamura, Lisa. (2008) *Digitizing race: Visual cultures of the internet.* Minneapolis: University of Minnesota Press.

Nasir, N. S. (2005) 'Individual cognitive structuring and the sociocultural context: Strategy shifts in the game of dominoes.' *The Journal of the Learning Sciences* 14 (1), pp. 5–34.

Newman, James. (2004) *Videogames.* New York: Routledge.

Ndalianis, Angela. (2004) *Neo-baroque aesthetics and contemporary entertainment.* Cambridge, MA: MIT Press.

Pickering, Andrew. (1995) *The mangle of practice: Time, agency, and science.* Chicago: University of Chicago Press.

Pieterse, Jan Nederveen. (2009) *Globalization and culture: Global mélange.* New York: Rowman & Littlefield Publishers, Inc.

Pimentel, Ken, and Kevin Teixeira. (1993) *Virtual reality: Through the new looking glass.* New York: Intel/Windcrest McGraw Hill.

Pinker, Steven. (1997) *How the mind works.* London: Penguin Books.

Poblocki, Kacper. (2002) 'Becoming-state: The bio-cultural imperialism of Sid Meier's civilization,' *Focaal—European Journal of Anthropology,* 39 (1), pp. 163–77.

Poole, Steven. (2000) *Trigger happy: the inner life of video games.* London: Fourth Estate.

Prasad, Madhava. (2003) 'This Thing Called Bollywood', Seminar, 525, [online]. Available at: www.india-seminar.com (Accessed: 14 August 2020).

Rajadhyaksha, Ashish. (2003) 'The "Bollywoodisation" of the Indian cinema: Cultural nationalism in a global arena', *Inter-Asia Cultural Studies,* 4 (1), pp. 25–39.

Ryan, M. L. (2001) 'Beyond myth and metaphor: The case of narrative in digital media', *The International Journal of Computer Game Research,* 1(1) [online]. Available at: www.gamestudies.org/0101/ryan/ (Accessed: 9 August 2020).

Salen, Katie and Eric Zimmerman. (2003) *The rules of play: Game design fundamentals.* Cambridge, MA: MIT Pres.

Sotamaa, Olli. (2007). 'Perceptions of player in game design literature', in Akira, B. (ed.) *Proceedings of the 2007 DiGRA International Conference: Situated Play, DiGRA 2007.* Tokyo. Available at: www.digra.org/wp-content/uploads/digital-library/07311.59383.pdf (Accessed: 19th Aug. 2020).

Steinkuehler, Constance A. (2006) 'Why game (culture) studies now?' *Games and Culture,* 1(1), pp. 97–102.

Tavinor, Grant. (2009) *The Art of Videogames.* Oxford: Wiley-Blackwell.

Taylor, Nicholas, Jen Jenson and Suzanne de Castell. (2009) 'Cheerleader/booth babes/halo hoes: Pro-gaming, gender and jobs for the boys.' *Digital Creativity,* 20(4), pp. 239–252.

Taylor, Nick. (2008) 'Periscopic play: Re-positioning 'the field' in MMO studies', *Loading,* 2(3). Availableat: http://journals.sfu.ca/loading/index.php/loading/article/viewArticle/43 (Accessed: 15 August 2020).

Taylor, Nick. (2011) 'Play globally, act locally: The standardization of pro *Halo 3* gaming', *International Journal of Gender, Science and Technology*, 3(1), pp. 228–242. Available at: http://genderandset.open.ac.uk/index.php/genderandset/article/view/130/260 (Accessed 16 August 2020).

Taylor, T. L. (2003a) 'Multiple pleasures: women and online gaming', *Convergence*, 9(1), pp. 21–46. DOI: 10.1177/135485650300900103 (Accessed: 15 August 2020).

Taylor, T. L. (2003b) 'Intentional bodies: Virtual environments and the designers who shape them', *International Journal of Engineering Education*, 19 (1), pp. 25–34. Available at: https://citeseerx.ist.psu.edu/viewdoc/download?doi=10.1.1.400.9258&rep=rep1&type=pdf (Accessed: 15 August 2020).

Taylor, T. L. (2006) *Play between worlds: Exploring online game culture*. Cambridge, MA: MIT Press.

Thorburn, David and Henry Jenkins. (2003) 'Toward an aesthetics of transition', in Thorburn, D. and Jenkins, H. (eds.) *Rethinking media change*. Cambridge, MA: MIT Press, pp. 1–18.

Veugen, Connie. (2012) 'Computer games as a comparative medium: a few cautionary remarks', in Fromme, J. and Unger, Alexander (eds.) *Computer games and new media cultures: A handbook of digital games studies*. Dordrecht, Heidelberg, New York, London: Springer, pp. 47–60.

Walther, Bo Kampmann. (2003) 'Playing and gaming: Reflections and classifications.' *Game Studies* 3(1), [online]. Available at: www.gamestudies.org/0301/walther/ (Accessed: 12 August 2020)

Wolf, Mark J.P., (ed.). (2012) *Encyclopedia of video games: The culture, technology, and art of gaming*. Santa Barbara, CA: Greenwood.

Wolf, Mark, J.P. (ed.). (2001) *The medium of the video game*. Austin, TX: University of Texas Press.

# 16

# *HITMAN 2* AND ITS SPECTRE OF MUMBAI

## A City Lost in Translation

*Samya Brata Roy*

We are all aware of the different stereotypes of India that are propagated through literary texts, movies, and other media. But the aspect which still remains to be brought into regular limelight is the aspect of video games. If games can tell stories and be an active site for engagement, why can they not be a place to study as a site of meaning making and ideology? Considering that idea, I want to proceed in this chapter and discuss the (mis)representation of India in one particular game of a massively popular game franchise. By the title of the chapter, it is obviously clear that the game I have chosen to discuss is *Hitman 2* (IO Interactive 2018), and, more particularly, a mission in the game which deals with Mumbai. My proposition here is that the Mumbai of *Hitman 2* looks absolutely like any other collection of stereotypes. Not only that, the gamic space reads like a poorly translated novel. The essentialist gaze of the makers becomes very apparent in how they appropriate the culture of one of the most vibrant cities in the world, reducing it to just another commodity of the West. The discourse propagated thus reinforces the idea of India or the Orient as a literal plaything of the West. Before going into the central analysis and discussion, I find it imperative to layout a few certain things to make clear. I have tried, at first, to give a very brief overview of the methodology that I have adapted, that is, the overarching lens via which I will be approaching this kind of a study. As my method, I will be using the CTDA method of Andre Brock, which I will elaborate upon immediately. After having discussed my method, I will move on to talk about the literature I have studied, in order to contextualize my study within the scope of other studies that have been done in this area. For this chapter, I have chosen to review and draw from the works of Soraya Murray, Lisa Nakamura, Souvik Mukherjee, and Phillip Penix-Tadsen. Murray's extensive research on ideas of race and gender in the gamic space provided me with a crucial understanding of these topics, from which I could build my own idea. Murray extensively uses the work of Stuart Hall, among others, which helped me use the postulates while

DOI: 10.4324/9781003354246-21

drawing my own conclusions. Nakamura's exploration of racial behaviour in online spaces has been applied here to show how the character, and the things done by the character, conform her idea of identity tourism. Last but not the least, I draw from the extensive study on postcolonialism in video games by Mukherjee to understand the history of representations of India in the gamic space. Penix-Tadsen's deep dive into game semiotics, especially in the context of Brazilian favelas, helped me make a case better for the slums of Mumbai via juxtaposition.

## I

Andre Brock in his article on Critical Technocultural Discourse Analysis (CTDA) advocates for a new method of analysing the discourse, one which emanates through the internet and new media. While my area is not strictly that which Brock dealt with in his chapter, that is, the Black experience on Twitter, his method can very well be applied, as it falls under new media.

> This critical cultural approach, which I am calling "Critical Technocultural Discourse Analysis" (CTDA), combines analyses of information technology material and virtual design with an inquiry into the production of meaning through information technology practice and the articulations of information technology users in situ.
>
> *(Brock 2018, p. 1,013)*

This mode of looking into the game actually examines the mode—in this case, the game—in which ideology is situated; and how the interplay of signifiers and signifieds create new meanings exclusive to this particular mode. Ian Bogost, in his seminal work on procedural rhetoric, comments that:

> Procedural media like videogames get to the heart of things by mounting arguments about the processes inherent in them. When we create videogames, we are making claims about these processes, which ones we celebrate, which ones we ignore, which ones we want to question.
>
> *(Bogost 2007, p. 339)*

For example, in a text, the meaning-making is determined by the textual mode and the arrangement of words employed by the author. For a film, the dynamic changes to the visual context, where one frame or shot can signify 100 different things at the same time; something which Christian Metz (1990) talks about in much detail in his work. But, when we come to the domain of video games, the dynamics once again take a new turn with the change of mode. Here, the interactive aspect and the notion of playability come into picture. The way a person interacts with the environment is how they make the meaning out of it as the signifiers, to borrow from Hayles (2010), become "flickering" ones. That should logically mean that there are no bounds for the meaning-making process, right? Not really, because the way a person can interact with the gamic space is actually limited, and the meaning that is produced boils down to a particular set of messages, no matter how open the world might be. Thus, one can conclude that the style of showing and playing a game becomes more the play-site of the author or maker than for the player. It seems as if the gamic space, and the player him or herself, become a literal play site for the author or the developer. But is it so simple? Does the game become a site for the passive consumption of media? Definitely not, as we have come to know from our understanding of Hall. Therefore, like the text or the film, the game also becomes an artifact which can be studied to understand what ideology or relations of power the creator(s) is trying to propagate. It is to be noted that, like any other form of media, not everything might be intentional or deliberate, but the way things are presented can tell a deeper story than what meets the eye. Therefore, like Brock, this chapter also does adopt a critical cultural approach to read the essentialist projection of a culture in a gamic space.

> This conceptual framework is then applied twice: once to the material, practical, and discursive properties of blogs, web-sites, and video games, and a second time to examine the cultural practices that take place in these digital spaces.
>
> *(Brock 2018, p. 1,013)*

The first application of the framework, as Brock points out, is to be used on the properties of the media and then to the practices that take place there. Extending his argument for my case, I would say that the first application of the framework would be to read how the gamic space operates on its own without the intervention of the player, or when the player is not playing, via cut scenes, etc. Next, I would go forward to look into the feedback mechanism and the haptics involved. That is, to see how the gamic space, along with its micro-spaces, react to the very essential act of play. In spite of decades of game-studies research, the act of analysing games and considering them to be a subject worthy of serious discussion is still found lacking in many so-called elite non-game studies spaces. The attitude towards game studies still seems to be like the general attitude of a parent who thinks that gaming is nothing more than a waste of time. Like Brock and many other game studies scholars, I am also trying to reinforce the point that a mere instrumentalist approach is not enough. Technology or e-artefacts, like games, must be seen as intrinsic to a person's being. Therefore, just like in films or texts, games can also provide a peep into the psyche of the makers or author. Here, by reading the essentialist and reductivist portrayal of Mumbai in *Hitman 2*, we can uncover that the now-residual and neo-imperialist fetish of the West, to other-ise the Orient, is still very much existent. Before I go into a detailed analysis, it is imperative that I mention that I will not be dealing with representation in the online multiplayer space. The online mode throws up totally different modalities, and all set notions otherwise go for a toss in that arena, which has to be a separate area of discussion. When virtual identities collaborate in a space, then the meaning-making process is totally turned on its head. Therefore, I have consciously decided to limit my reading to the single-player story mode, and not the online multiplayer experience which I believe requires a separate space to be dealt with.

## II

Games are very complex forms of visual culture and operate as site to unearth ideology, like any other cultural artefact. Soraya Murray, in her seminal work *On Video Games: The Visual of Politics of Race, Gender and Space*, takes the help of cultural studies theorists like Hall to talk about how people do not just consume games. The relation, here, is very similar to what Hall charts in his famous work on encoding and decoding. Here, the developers or the author(s) are trying, consciously or not, to package a culture in accordance with their whims. But the players are not necessarily embracing such packaging with open arms.

> It would be a mistake to reduce modern-day video games to military simulations, and players of games to passive receptors of mass media. The origins of games do not necessarily define the limits of their potential. However, they do play a powerful role in the capacity to imagine what might be possible, and how we understand the world and our relations within it.
>
> *(Murray 2017, p. 5)*

Hall (1973), in his famous work, talks about the layered complexity of communication via mass culture. He was of the opinion that the viewers of these images did not necessarily conform to the meaning that the author tried to fix for them. According to Murray, the origins of games do not necessarily define their origins. I think, by origins, she is talking about what Hall understands to be the feature of encoding. Via the design of the gamic space or its interactive mechanics, it is clear that the makers are trying to propagate a certain kind of play. But it is not necessarily true that the player will conform to the makers' vision of play.

Lisa Nakamura (2001), in her work about identity in the online space, comments that the aspect of being able to pass off, in the online space, as any identity, without having to go through the lived experience of such an identity, can be very interesting to the point of fetish. In this game, for example, if we extend Nakamura's concept a little bit, it can be seen that the stoic and almost non-masculine masculinity of Agent 47 becomes a site of entry and unmitigated play into what they understand to be something like Mumbai. The ability for a White person to intervene and make things right, as a neo-colonial desire, can be studied very promptly from this case. Here, one might suppose that, if you start looking at everything like this, then all representations become bad or improper representations. It is true that no one can reproduce something extrinsic to them with absolute authenticity, but they can at least try. While *Far Cry 4* (Ubisoft 2014)'s depiction of an Indian-Nepali hybrid, called Kyrat, was problematic, it was evident from the experience that the makers had tried to bring some kind of authenticity to the experience.

Like the Mise en scène in cinema, one can also read this space as something purposefully constructed for the purpose of show and nothing else. Aarseth echoes this notion of the massive of the gamic space where he comments that

> The defining element in computer games is spatiality. Computer games are essentially concerned with spatial representation and negotiation, and therefore a classification of computer games can be based on how they represent—or, perhaps, implement—space.
>
> *(Aarseth 2001, p. 154)*

Even Murray acknowledges the importance of the aspect of spatiality, and that is what I meant by comparing the gamic space with the cinematic Mise en Scène. The space, which apparently looks like the real, is actually not so. It is a fictional place, with its own history; only the names are the same. This can be equated with Baudrillard's notion of the "Hyperreal," where he suggests that the signifier takes on a meaning of its own without any relation to the actual signified (1994). In this case, what happens is that the image of Mumbai shown in a popular game like Hitman becomes itself massively popular; and people who have not been to Mumbai fall under the illusion that Mumbai actually looks how it is portrayed in Hitman. Needless to say, Mumbai's portrayal in Hitman bears no resemblance to real life. Therefore, the created signifier of Mumbai takes on a life of its own, with no apparent relation to its signified in the real world. Carrying this argument to its logical extension, Murray here mentions Nezar AlSayyad's work titled *Cinematic Urbanism: A History of the Modern from Reel to Real*:

> urban historian Nezar AlSayyad describes a challenge he set forth to his students: Imagine if there was no real New York or real Los Angeles or no trace left of them and the only thing we have are films that depict them or use them as a backdrop for their cinematic story. What kind of history would we write? . . . Like AlSayyad, I ask: if all we had were gamic representations of the global city, how would those cities be described, and what would those simulated places tell us?
>
> *(Murray 2017, pp. 183–184)*

This is to say that, if Mumbai ceases to exist one day and all the memory we have of the place is this mission from *Hitman 2*, then what kind of a representation would we have left? Will it not be a misleading and a very essentialist representation? Yes, it absolutely will. But is there then an authentic representation at all? Perhaps we can never know if something is authentic, but we can always know if something is not. One thing that we can definitely say, for sure, is that the image which, as Said says, was "created" (Said 2001, p. 5) here is absolutely based in the neo-colonial or neo-imperialist gaze, which engages in a fetish to reduce the so-called Orient to certain, basic stereotypes. This reductionist approach reduces a culture to be nothing more than a techno-orientalist commodity which reinforces the hegemonic relationship between the Occident and the Orient. In order to situate Said in the context of games studies, Murray goes on to draw a connection between Said's scholarship and the work Vit Šisler. Šisler's work, *Digital Arabs: Representation in Video Games*, takes on the stereotypical representation of Arabs and Islamic societies in games. Like Russia, I believe that the Middle East has become a favourite setting for the act of Other-ising. The famous *Call of Duty: Modern Warfare 2*'s mission, "No Russians" (INFINITY WARD 2009), comes to mind as the best on-the-face depiction of othering, where the players can mercilessly slaughter through an airport filled with Russians. The warning before the mission seems almost comical, as the instructions say that players can choose to skip the mission if they feel uncomfortable with it. Šisler's work also draws on the same tropes; he argues that Arabs or Muslims are presented in such a way as to signify a certain type of dress, skin colour, and, obviously, terrorism. The same thing happens here in Hitman, where Mumbaikars are doused in frames of light yellow and crow skulls and mysticism.

Be it Russia, the Middle-East, Brazil, or India, there seems to be an omnipresent Western, Anglophonic Whiteness which tries to control the discourse. This becomes even more important for the Hitman games, as exploring exotic locales seem to be an intrinsic feature of the new instalments (apart from innovative methods of killing). Therefore, the pretext of creating an exotic locale lies in the root that it has to be destroyed in one way or the other—and it has to be done by the White man. Here, if we look at the origin of Agent 47, the dynamics become even more layered. Agent 47 was given powers in a lab. He was an experiment and had his memory wiped away. He was a product like no other, which can be identified by the iconic barcode behind his head. He is an assassin for hire who can mould into any shape of form to the extent of it being comical. It thus raises the question: who is Agent 47, and does he have any agency at all? My answer is no! Agent 47 has no agency, as he has to obey the orders of his superiors. Thus, when he commits violent acts, he only does so because he is ordered. Agent 47 thus becomes a metonymic representation of the neo-imperialist empire, just like the soldiers of the British Raj who themselves had no agency and were bound to follow orders. Similarly, however, as we proceed with the Hitman story, we see Agent 47 questioning his laboratory consciousness. This journey can also be equated as a sort of meta-allegory of the Orwellian colonial soldier who realizes that they are a plaything in the hands of a greater power.

Therefore, when he visits exotic locales to kill, it is not he who is doing it, but the overarching powers. This almost meta-violence, which serves to create a space for the sole purpose of destroying, reveals how hegemony works in gamic spaces. Things become even more interesting when an Indian gamer has to kill supposed Indians inhabiting the space. It is to be noted that representation of India in games has not been as widespread as the representation of some other countries. Thus, Indian gamers are still new to the idea of seeing their country as a playable environment. So, when an Indian plays the game—without having seen a lot of games take place in their own country—how do they actually play it? Is there a detachment involved? Or something else?

## III

Needless to say, the treatment of colonialism in video games—apart from a few exceptions—is riddled with a very Western bias. In order to understand this fact, it is crucial to recognize the brief history of representation of India in video games. To refer to brief standpoints in the history of representation, I will draw from Souvik Mukhejee's paper *Playing Subaltern: Video Games and Postcolonialism*:

> One of the earliest video games to feature an Indian character is *Streetfighter 2* (Capcom 1991). Here Dhalsim is portrayed as kicking out in "yogic" posture and as wearing a torn saffron shorts and necklace of skulls so as to emphasize his oriental Indian mystique. He can spew fireballs, levitate and likes curry, and meditation. To add to his image of the oriental, he is very protective of his son Datta and his wife, who rather strangely is named Sari (after the dress worn by Indian women)! Another classic set of stereotypes is to be seen in the empire building games that feature India. Besides the points already made in connection with the inaccuracies in Empire: Total War, there are far greater problems that emerge in the stereotypes created by Age of Empires 3: The Asian Dynasties (2007), for example. Here, there are gross mistakes in that sepoys (as the Indian soldiers in colonial armies were called) are thought of as an ethnic community in themselves and that Brahmin priests are shown as warriors riding elephants. When cities such as London and Los Angeles are depicted so carefully in video games, the "Temple City Ambush" level in Hitman: Silent Assassin (2002) can only manage to show the protagonist moving from warehouse to warehouse and ultimately meeting an auto-rickshaw driver. Even more bizarre is Call of Duty: Modern Warfare 3's (2011) mission "Persona Non Grata" that is set in Himachal Pradesh. The ubiquitous Indian auto-rickshaw is to be seen but strangely, in a shootout between the British commandos and Russian terrorists, the Indian army or any Indians, for that matter, seem to have decided to stay away!
>
> *(Mukherjee 2017, p. 1)*

This paragraph provides an excellent overview of the representations of India in games. From the blatant stereotyping of Streetfighter to the startling nonchalance of Call of Duty, the thread of othering remains common throughout. Adding to this, Mukherjee, in his book *Video Games and Postcolonialism: Empire Plays Back* (2017), says about *Age of Empires 3* (Ensemble Studios 2005), states that, while they correctly show Hindus to not consume beef, but they nonetheless conflate "Indian" with "Hindu." What happens is thus a misappropriation of culture, which leaves out the layered truth. Mukherjee further adds that, in *Civilization V* (Firaxis Games 2010), Gandhi becomes famous for dropping nukes very contrary to his actual image.

While playing with stereotypes can be fun and games, such blatant denials of cultural pluralism can be rather hurtful. Another notable example, something which I have already mentioned, is the hybrid India-Nepal-like nation called Kyrat in *Far Cry 4*(Ubisoft Montreal 2014). I call this a hybrid, because it is situated at the weird meeting point between India and Nepal. The terrain is shown to be that of Nepal, yet the language they choose is Hindi! While *Far Cry 4* fares much better in the department of aesthetics and creating a likeness, it still falls prey to a very essentialist trap of language for the sake of commerce, or whatever other purpose there might be. Another element of comparison with the icon of the Indian slum would definitely be the Brazilian favela! Phillip Penix-Tadsen, in his *Cultural Code: Video Games and Latin America* (2016), talks about the icon of the Brazilian favela while discussing game semiotics. He first acknowledges that game developers insert these signifiers to fall back on the notion of familiarity, or to bring in a sense of diversity. This means that, if we think of the Middle East, there has to be a desert or camel; similarly, a favela for Brazil, and slums or other mystic elements for India. The AAA game developers obviously are looking to simulate the experience of a particular country, and the more "exotic" locations that they might bring, the more it will sell. That is why these signifiers are repeated on and on and it thus reinforces the hegemonic oriental notions of a specific culture.

> Brazilian gamespace is readily characterized by certain signifiers of brasilidade that have been utilized once and again by game designers: soccer, an ethnically diverse population, bossa nova music, a tropical landscape replete with vibrant colors, and, to return to an earlier example, the Christ the Redeemer statue. But the center of this semiotic domain today is the ultimate twenty-first-century sign of Brazil for the outside world—and arguably for Brazilians as well: the favela. The representation of the favela within entertainment is certainly nothing new.
>
> *(Penix-Tadsen 2016, p. 162)*

Thus, following Penix-Tadsen's idea, one could make a similar comment about India and its representation: how certain signifiers such as crows, slums, and mystic elements, such as skulls, are necessary and also used by Indians as well. Yes, it can be used by Indians, but what is the intention behind when it is used by an international game developer? Penix-Tadsen was actually talking about *Max Payne 3* in relation to Brasil and in that game he elaborates that

> Max quips, "This was the kind of reality Americans paid top dollar to see. Slums had become tourist attractions, places where yuppies could gawk at the endless spirit of the poor from the inside of their bulletproof buses." *Max Payne 3* offers the player an armchair opportunity to inhabit the favela, but Max's antiheroic experiences offer painful reminders of the importance of maintaining awareness of the cultural cues in the surrounding environment rather than acting like a naïve tourist.
>
> *(Penix-Tadsen 2016, p. 166)*

Therefore, is *Hitman 2* trying to do a similar thing by providing an armchair peep in the lives of the dirty Indians? In order to deduce the same, it is imperative to look at the mission closely.

*Hitman 2* is a predominantly stealth video game developed by IO Interactive and published by Warner Brothers Interactive Entertainment by 2018. It is the seventh major instalment overall but also the sequel to a new series which started in 2016. The player controls Agent 47, an assassin for hire working for the ICA, or International Contract Agency. This rather crudely named agency sends him to various, often exotic locales around the globe to eliminate high profile targets. But there is more to what meets the eye in the story of Agent 47. Via the earlier games and the storyline, we come to know that he was experimented on as a child, giving him the skills needed to become an assassin. Also, the same experimentation took away his memory. So, some of the journeys of Agent 47 also collide with the journey of finding his own sense self. Coming to the point, the mission that I am specifically looking at in this chapter is set in Mumbai. It is the fourth mission in the game and is named "Chasing a Ghost." The objective is to eliminate a mysterious gang leader, known as The Maelstrom, while also eliminating two other pieces of the broad criminal puzzle: Dawood Rangan and Vanya Shah. It is important to note that this is not the first time Agent 47 is visiting India! He did so more than a decade ago, when he apparently visited the Golden Temple in Punjab. One must say that the choice of Punjab was rather interesting, and I would have preferred that, despite setting the mission in a very stereotypical slum. I am not saying that it would have been better. But, given the technological advancements, it would have been good to see if they can actually show a religious place. But I believe that it is more due to advancement and the full-blown e-globalization that it becomes even more risqué. Nevermind—returning to Mumbai, then.

It is good to mention that, at first, and going to Brock, I will be looking at the properties, which are apparent first, and then, I will delve into the act of play. While the mission is not very elaborate, it is incredibly dense because of the slum, the stacked high-rise of Dawood, and a compact bunch of shops, laundry stations, etc. Having all of these together makes an interesting journey, both horizontally and vertically. Starting with the self-proclaimed Queen of Slums, Vanya Shah is shown as an inverted Disney princess with some weird Oriental fashion sense. She is literally seen with Peacocks models adoring her presence. Even her maids are dressed to fit her billing. Her character and setting seem like an inverted dream sequence stolen from a cheap rip-off of *A Mid-Summer Night's Dream*. I am not denying the presence of a seedy underbelly of a society; I am sure that Mumbai has its gang lords and ladies, but it is the quasi-mystic representation which bothers me.

Next up is Dawood Rangan: the shady Bollywood producer—and the most shameless nod to the crime lord Dawood Ibrahim the world has ever seen. I have no problems with a nod to the past of Mumbai, which was embroiled in criminality—it's just that it is shown two to three decades too late. The setting screams of the 1980s and 1990s of India, whereas the other locations, like Miami or Italy, seem to have perfectly caught up with the present day. Also, Dawood is supposed to meet with a celebrity Broadway actor called Gregory Arthur. He can be spotted in the slums, having bowel malfunctions after tasting the local cuisine (a location where, coincidentally, he can be easily eliminated). This fits right to the typical image of a lack of hygiene. Last but not the least comes the Maelstrom, who can be found lurking around his gang, The Crows. Before talking about Maelstrom, it is imperative to talk a little bit about The Crows. This gang has chosen the skulls of crows to be the symbol for their gang, and as such, skulls and dead crows can be seen hanging from balconies and whatnot. This signifier takes up a meaning which is beyond the mission or the game. It shows how Indian society is still caught up with the whole mystic dynamics of skulls and snake charmers. In a sense, it is no different from the yogi in *Streetfighter 2*.

The Maelstrom can be found lurking in and around the slums, looking for a shave. Here, Agent 47 can dress up as a barber and give him a really close shave. Now, does a gang leader and such an important figure in the international crime scene really need a shave from the slums? I do not think so. It is done so that Agent 47 can deliberately take up the role of a barber. He does something similar when he is given the choice to dress up as a tailor to measure Vanya Shah. Be it the laundry man, the tailor, the barber, and the hygiene issue—what is actually seen here is the act of a white man, who by no means resembles Indians, slipping ever-so-easily in these roles; what Nakamura calls the act of "identity tourism." It is almost like a fetish or a performative act done by the game, which seems to be trying to tick certain boxes to qualify for "Indianness" without having to go through the complexities of the lived experience. Going back to Brock's method of dual implication, I have looked at the game's constituent parts or the properties just as they are presented by the makers. The second step in the method would be thus to go inside the gamic space as a player and look at the interactive mechanics and the even finer representations of macro space which can only be seen in the act of play to see how the macro properties and these finer aspects come together to form a totality.

Once the actual act of play begins, a lot of other and seemingly hidden elements come to the fore, which influence the experience massively. Starting off with the initial aesthetics of the roads and surroundings, the first things which automatically catch the eye are the store boards where upon names are written. The shops are hilariously named as "bartano ki dukaan" (shop of utensils), "fulo ka guldusta" (a bouquet of flowers), "chicken bhajan" (chicken meal), etc. These names read like direct translations from English. No shops are ever named like that.

This might sound minor, but it shows how the research team did not really care to keep the cultural authenticity intact. Of many shops present throughout the map in a rather repetitive manner, a particular one caught my eye. It happens to be a cybercafé. It is no ordinary cybercafé as it features a bunch of arcade game machines. It is also important to note that the cybercafé is very curiously named "aarkshan" (reservation). One might wonder: why is that so? It is so because, in India, people use cybercafes mostly for booking train and flight tickets. The signifier thus is borrowed from that context, which apparently seems meaningless. It can, however, be read in two ways. It is either a mark of genius, by which the maker is trying to give a nod to Indian culture, or (which is more likely) it just shows detachment from a culture. Judging by the names that they have used for the other shops, I am inclined to think the latter is true here.

I used to frequent such cafés when I was a kid, to play games, and have never seen a sub-urban shop that features so many arcade machines. That is how game parlours work in the West, with a lot of expensive equipment, but that is not the case in our country, as shop owners cannot afford to buy such expensive machines. Speaking of naming, I would also like to bring attention to the names of films that have been chosen for the production company of Dawood Rangan. "Mumbai Hero," which is known to everyone at the outset, is finishing production, and if one closely listens to the NPCs, they will get to hear names of other productions. The movies are hilariously named as "The Snake and Mongoose" and "Blundering Frights." The names sound more apt for kids and not a shady film producer from the underworld. What is important to note here is that the makers of the game actually decided to encode these little details, which shows that they are trying to propagate a particular kind of impression. The NPCs can also be overheard saying that Agent 47 is wearing a very strange outfit. I wonder what is so strange about a waist jacket and trousers! If anything at all, it is now perhaps more Indian than anything else. But, as I said—quite clearly—the Indians in this gamic space have not caught up with civilization as the other places have, so it is not their fault, really. Sarcasm aside, I would like to emphasize that lines like these try to show how backward Indians are. I am not saying Indians are not backward, or they do not say things like this. Of course, we are not a very rich country. But, at the same time, the situation is not so hilariously off the track as it is shown here. Mumbaikars are very familiar, and have been, with trends because of the influence of Bollywood. What is even more funny is Dawood wears almost the same dress as Agent 47, yet people find Agent 47's attire to be strange and out of place. Now, be it the names of shops or the expensive cybercafes or the ignorance of the NPCs, these macro spaces reinforce the ideology of the Orient being stuck in some kind of a time loop. This is not what society is, but how they want society to be perceived by others. This is the case for the most non-anglophonic spaces, as they tend to be tied up in one stereotype or the other. Brazil and favelas, India and slums, Middle-East and desert . . . the list goes on and on. Yes, Brazil does have favelas and India does have slums, but these spaces have a lot of other things going on as well. Therefore, the representation should not be this myopic in nature, especially when the technical capabilities for design have become so advanced.

Therefore, the micro-interaction with the space churns up what can be called a "generic whiteness," by which this space has also been looked at. The prosperous Mumbai skyline seems like a distant background from the top of Dawood's unfinished tower, which can be called a metonymic representation of the mission in itself: impressive but unfinished!

## IV

No matter what you try to represent or adapt, there will be problematic elements in it. Then, how should it take place? I believe that there should be a constant critic and dialogue, via academics and otherwise, to point out the flaws and just be critical about things without accepting it for face value. The attitude towards engaging with games must be similar to what it is for films, which I believe would arise at one point of time like it did for films after it started to veer away from the mainstream. Now that we have indie games and new creators being more and more inventive, it opens up the normal player to juxtapose the normal AAA titles with these and see the difference, if any, for themselves, just like what happens for big studio films and indie makers. This passage from Mukherjee and Hammar *Introduction to the Special Issue on Postcolonial Perspectives in Games Studies* sums it up

> Scholars within game studies (and not only those concerned with postcolonial analysis) should ask themselves what exactly game studies as a field hope to achieve. Will game studies continue to be subsumed under the neoliberalisation of academia, in which the only telos is profit, and which churns out workers for the factory that is mainstream game development? Or will game studies reflect on and question the ways that games are embedded in the (historical) global power structure? Will game studies adapt and question the ways the postcolonial is reproduced in academia, as well as in games?
>
> *(Mukherjee and Hammar 2018)*

If a game like Grand Theft Auto is showing a particular city, then I would expect all the stereotypical elements to be there, as it very consciously is a parody. But a serious entry like Hitman is supposed to deal with the elements with some more nuance as the aesthetics and ideology propagated by the game is not very parodic in nature. To sum up, I've tried to take a critical approach, and the method of close reading, akin to that prevalent in Literary Studies. Via analyses, the conclusion that emerges is that representation is always a slippery slope and will be criticized no matter what. More so in games, because the relationship of the signifiers and its signifieds is constantly altering in the act of play. But certain aspects can seem very on-the-face and borderline racist as compared to others. What the authors and makers should do, however, is to try and understand the culture better, in order to create a virtual version of it. What they end up creating most of the time is another techno-orientalist commodity driven by the White and Anglophonic gaze. While game developers, including the developer of Hitman, claim that their team is composed of people of various backgrounds, the inclusivity is not really reflected in the gamic space they are building. Being an Indian gamer, I have to admit that I am happy seeing my country featured in such mainstream titles—but what makes me sad is how they choose to do it even if done in a sarcastic vein. It is a start, and

I hope steps are taken towards the right direction, which properly show the notion of inclusivity most developers claim to aspire to these days.

## Acknowledgements

Finally, I would like to express my gratitude towards the people at Jamia and Michigan, especially Dr. Nishat Zaidi, who made this possible; Dr. Thomas Apperley for his suggestions to my reading list, Dr. Dibyadyuti Roy and Dr. Souvik Mukherjee for their amazing insights, Dr. Prakash Kona for his generosity with my then institutional time, and last but not the least my friends and family who are subjected to whim on a daily basis.

## Bibliography

Aarseth, E. (2001) 'Allegories of Space. The Question of Spatiality in Computer Games', *University of Jyväskylä. Department of Arts and Culture Studies*, pp. 152–171.

Baudrillard, J. (1994) *Simulacra and Simulation*. Translated by S.F. Glaser. Ann Anbor, MI: University of Michigan Press.

Bogost, I. (2007) *Persuasive Games: The Expressive Power of Videogames*. Cambridge, MA: MIT Press.

Brock, A. (2018) 'Critical Technocultural Discourse Analysis', *New Media and Society*, 20(3), pp. 1012–1030.

FIRAXIS GAMES (2010) *Sid Meier's Civilization 5*. [CD] PC. USA: Aspyr, 2k Games.

Hall, S. (1973) *Encoding and Decoding in the Television Discourse*. Birmingham: Centre for Cultural Studies, University of Birmingham.

Hayles, N.K. (2010) *How We Became Posthuman: Virtual Bodies in Cybernetics, Literature and Informatics*. Reprint. Chicago: Univ. of Chicago Press.

INFINITY WARD (2009) *Call of Duty: Modern Warfare 2*. [CD]. PC. USA: Activision.

IO INTERACTIVE (2018) *Hitman 2*. [Online]. PC. EU: Warner Bros. Interactive Entertainment.

Metz, C. (1990) *Film Language: A Semiotics of the Cinema*. Univ of Chicago edition. Translated by M. Taylor. Chicago: University of Chicago Press.

MICROSOFT GAME STUDIOS (2005) *Age of Empires 3*. [CD]. PC. USA: Microsoft Corporation.

Mukherjee, S. (2017) *Videogames and Postcolonialism: Empire Plays Back*. New York: Palgrave Macmillan. Doi:10.1007/978-3-319-54822-7.

Mukherjee, S. (2018) 'Playing Subaltern: Video Games and Postcolonialism', *Games and Culture*, 13(5), pp. 504–520. Doi:10.1177/1555412015627258.

Mukherjee, S. and Hammar, E.L. (2018) 'Introduction to the Special Issue on Postcolonial Perspectives in Game Studies', *Open Library of Humanities*, 4(2). Doi:*10.16995/olh.309.*

Murray, S. (2017) *On Video Games: The Visual Politics of Race, Gender and Space*. London: I.B. Tauris.

Nakamura, L. (2001) 'Head Hunting in Cyberspace: Identity Tourism, Asian Avatars and Racial Passing on the Web', *The Women's Review of Books*, 18(5), pp. 10–11. Doi:*10.2307/4023600.*

Nakamura, L. (2002) 'Alllooksame? Mediating Visual Cultures of Race on the Web', *Iowa Journal of Cultural Studies*, 2(1). Doi:10.17077/2168-569X.1019.

Penix-Tadsen, P. (2016) *Cultural Code: Video Games and Latin America*. Cambridge, MA: MIT Press.

ROCKSTAR NORTH (2013) *Grand Theft Auto V*. [Online]. PC. USA: Rockstar Games.

ROCKSTAR STUDIOS (2012) *Max Payne 3*. [Online]. PC. USA: Rockstar Games.

Said, E.W. (2001) *Orientalism*. Gurgaon: Penguin India.

Shakespeare, W. (2017) *A Midsummer Night's Dream: Third Series*. Illustrated edition. Edited by P.S. Chaudhuri. New York: The Arden Shakespeare.

Šisler, V. (2008) 'Digital Arabs: Representation in video games', *European Journal of Cultural Studies*, 11(2), pp. 203–220. Doi:*10.1177/1367549407088333*.

UBISOFT MONTREAL (2014) *Far Cry 4*. [Online]. PC. USA: Ubisoft.

# 17

# ELECTRONIC LITERATURE IN INDIA

## Where Is It? Does It Even Exist?

*Justy Joseph and Nirmala Menon*

### Introduction

Electronic Literature Organisation (ELO) defines electronic literature as a term that refers to "works with an important literary aspect that takes advantages of the capabilities and contexts provided by the stand-alone or network computer" (Electronic Literature Organization 2015). As Katherine Hayles (2010) points out, this definition directs attention not only to the changing nature of computers but also to the new, different ways in which the literary community mobilizes these capabilities. There have always been contested definitions for digital literature. Esko Lius presupposes an artefact to fulfil three distinctive criteria to be called as digital literature:

1. The main forms of delivery and consumption must be digital (new media)
2. Object of research may use various languages (sign systems), but the verbal language must be an essential meaning carrier
3. Central focus of the artefact and the reader's experience should be aesthetic.

Contrasting this criterion, Raine Koskimaa (2000) divides digital literature into four categories:

1. Digitization of print literature
2. The digital publication of original text
3. Literature using the new technologies made possible by the digital format.
4. Networked literature.

Electronic literature in India often falls into the first two points of Koskimaa's categorization. It is not mostly "born digital but are digital versions of the text"

DOI: 10.4324/9781003354246-22

(Mukherjee 2017). Indian electronic literature often fails to explore the diverse capabilities of the web to create interactive fiction, flash literature, generative fiction, location narratives, or computer art installations. Publishing houses and authors in India initially regarded electronic literature either as an extension of the print or as a yardstick to test the market before launching the print version. But the COVID-19-induced lockdown, which saw books being classified as non-essential goods, has brought out a colossal shift in Indian literature, its publishing system, and reading; unfettering the incessant potential of digital/electronic literature.

The primary objective of this chapter is to trace the current trends in Indian electronic literature by locating the digital literature and publishing platforms in English as and in regional languages across India. This research also attempts to study the responses to the "digital first approach," through a survey sampling the publishing houses, small-scale digital publishing platforms, and authors who have brought out their works in 2020, and also a diverse readers' community.

The chapter is divided into two main sections. The first section traces the current digital literature in English and regional languages. The second session summarizes the results and discussions from the survey to study the responses of authors, readers, publishing houses, and digital publishing platforms towards the current digital first approach. The chapter concludes by highlighting the future of post-COVID Indian digital literature.

## Tracing Current Electronic Literature Trends in India

A recent book consumption survey (16 October 2020) in India confirms that over 71% of the year's reading was on digital platforms. According to the latest Nielsen India report, audio book consumption went up by seven hours per week during this period. The report observes that 20% of respondents were reading more books in the print format, while more than 50% of readers had started consuming books online. Publishers are reconsidering their practices, as many customers go online to consume books. The recent Google-KPMG report suggests that internet access by Indian users in regional languages will reach 536 million by 2021. Amazon's exponential sale of regional eBooks and the rise of small-scale platforms such as Kahaniya, Pratilipi, and Free Tamil Ebooks (FTE), especially after the pandemic, foreground this shift in digital reading from being done only in English to being done in regional languages, too. There are also user-generated multilingual content-sharing platforms, like Momspresso and Maturbharati, which saw more page views for regional languages than for English. Across the board, consumption and publication of digital literature have resulted in the empowerment of independent authors and small regional publishing houses by taking their works to a larger audience, putting forth an affordable option, preserving rich literature in regional languages, and making the literary sphere more inclusive. Though it is evident that existing digital literature in India is mostly a reproduction of print text in digital form, there are millions of non-English digital readers in India who prefer to read books in regional languages, be it the translated version of an international best seller, or an original work by a regional author. In order to reach this audience, there is now a gradual inclusion of regional language works in e-book platforms, e-readers, and apps that can publish content in more than 25 Indian languages, out of which Tamil, Malayalam, Hindi, Guajarati, and Marathi are predominant. The current Indian electronic literature exists in five forms:

1. Texts converted from print format to electronic format and then disseminated on the internet
2. Published digital texts (self-existing or launched before the print version)
3. Texts that utilize the multiple capabilities of the web (multimedia technology)
4. International best sellers that are translated to Indian regional languages in a digital format
5. Literary games
6. Social media writings.

This section attempts to trace the electronic literature published from India in English and other Indian languages locating it across these five forms.

### *Digital Versions of the Print Text*

While the theory and practice of Western electronic literature suggest the usage of machines for the creation of literature, Indian digital literature is using digital and multimedia technology for preserving and disseminating its diverse literature. There are digitization projects across languages that aim to make literature available free of cost for public search and analysis. There are two approaches to digitization in India:

1. Translate and digitize
2. Software/keyboard mapping

Projects like the National Digital Library of India, National Mission for Manuscripts, epustakalay.com (a collection of Hindi PDF books), Two Centuries of Indian Print (Bengali), the Ulloor Archive (Malayalam), Tamil ebooks (Tamil), Project Madurai (Tamil), Grandashala (Malayalam), Khudsa Baksh (Medieval Arabic and Persian literature), and The Mukthabodha Project (Ancient Texts) attempt to convert texts from print format to disseminate it on the internet. There are also university- and library-level initiatives to digitize existing literature such as Bichitra (Jadavpur University), the Tunchath Ezuthachan University digitization project (Malayalam), Million Books Project (IISC Bangalore), Kalasampada (Indira Gandhi National Centre for Arts), and initiatives from IIT Kanpur, Allahabad University, the Central Institute of Higher Tibetan Studies, and National Institute of Advanced Studies, Bangalore. Such digitization efforts not only archive and preserve the rich literature but also empower the individual authors of regional languages and small-scale publishers. It facilitates inclusive publishing wherein the works are made available to the print disabled including individuals with inability to read printed materials due to cognitive or physical disability. It also makes the content analyzable and searchable. But the major challenges in the digitization of Indian literature are the unavailability of cost-effective technological advancement, lack of multiple Indian language OCR, lack of a standard data description and transmission characteristics, lack of a proper digitization policy, rigidity of publisher's policies, and inadequate property rights policies.

## *Digitally Published Texts*

The second form of electronic literature available in India is the digitally published literature that almost resembles the format of the print literature. As the writer K.R Meera said in one of her interviews to The Indian Express,

> There is a generation of people who love to read the stories in printed format. It only caters to a specific group of readers now. However, as a new medium and online being the future, I think, it will cater to a wider audience in the near future.
>
> *(Gopika 2018)*

The year 2020 saw a huge rise of literature written in English, published digitally from India, including Tanweer Fazal's *The Minority Conundrum: Living in Majoritarian Times* (Vintage books), Devdutt Pattnaik's *Pilgrim Nation: The Making of Bharatvarsh* (Aleph Book Company), Sonali Gupta's *Anxiety: Overcome it and Live without Fear* (Harper Collins), and self- published digital books, such as Aparna Das Sadhukan's collection of short stories, "Escape Routes" a book about the inherent human desire to escape troubled situations, and Deepika Priya's work "Being A Mother: It's A Different Hormone Altogether" published on Amazon Kindle Direct Publishing (KDP).

Despite the low technological infrastructure when compared to English, there is an increase also in the regional language literature published digitally. A group of contemporary Tamil writers is trying to break the shackles that the local publishing industry has created about electronic publishing by releasing their works for free in smart device-friendly formats like ePUB and mobi, through the website www.freetamilebooks.com. This platform has published 650+ free e-books under creative commons license including the works of renowned writers such as N. Chokkan, Payon, and Pa. Raghavan. Another important initiative in Tamil digital literature is by New Horizon Media, one of the few publishers to have an app, NHM Reader, on leading mobile phone platforms. Writers in Tamil are also publishing through platforms like Amazon Kindle Direct Publishing (KDP). Senthil Balan, a doctor, who practises in Muscat, was picked as one of the winners of KDP's Pen to Publish contest for his self-published book, *Parangi Malai Irayil Nilaiyam* (St Thomas Mount Railway Station), part of a series of books based on the character he created, Detective Karthick Aldo. Writer Sundari Venkatraman has an inspiring success story too, with about 41 self-published titles to her name. Vignesh Selvaraj has also written the short-form writing, *Article About Isai's Poetry*, on KDP. Writer Payon (pseudonym) says a lot more needs to be done to increase the availability of Tamil literature on digital platforms. In an email interview to *The Hindu*, he points out: "I'm sure we'll see more sites like freetamilebooks.com. Using services like Instamojo, authors can directly sell their e-books online. I know some publishers have plans to make some or most of their books available as ebooks" (Subramaniam 2018). While Kindle introduced Hindi e-books on its platform a few years ago, it nonetheless failed to attract new readers. But lately, after the pandemic, there has been a reversal in the trend, whereafter readership has shifted online. In Hindi, self-publishing through KDP happens with increasing frequency, with examples such as Nandini Kumar's introspective book on a woman whose relationship with her fiancé ends abruptly, and Dev Singla's book *Aatman*, a compilation of thoughts and perceptions shown through poetry. Slowly but steadily in the pandemic period, alternate mediums are giving new dimensions to the Hindi book world and transforming it. Malayalam literature is thriving across digital platforms, too, with innovations taking place in form and narratives, as well as in the way Malayalam Literature reaches out to new readers. Valmeeki.com, Indhuleka.com, Pusthakakada, Saikatham Online, Kelkaam, and True Copy are all recent start-up projects that publishes stories, poems, novellas, movie scripts, graphic novels, or student theses in digital format. Malayalam literature online is mostly short stories; they are plenty in various sites, such as Valmeeki, Kelkaam, Pratilipi, Nallezuthu, DC online, and Wattpad Malayalam. They have a surprising number of reads when contrasted with the actual penetration of online writing platforms in the state. DC Books, the leading Malayalam language publisher, made news when it, in a stroke of brilliance, partnered with the food delivery app, Swiggy, to home-deliver books in the midst of a pandemic. DC also extended their e-book store transforming most of their content into the digital by utilizing the interactive qualities of the web and also providing by writers a platform to publish digitally. Kalpabiswa *by Dip Gosh is a* portal devoted to digital publication of sci-fi and fantasy in Bengali. An important initiative in Goan literature is "Goa,1556," which publishes books under Creative Commons licenses and works through crowd funding. Amazon's Kindle has recently enabled the sale of Hindi, Tamil, Marathi, Gujarati, and Malayalam editions. It is expected by the readers that the Introduction of KDP will facilitate a huge rise of digital literature in other regional languages too.

## Born Digital Works

Despite the general criticism that electronic literatures in India are digital versions of the print, there are new works and authoring platforms emerging which utilize the varied capabilities of the stand-alone computer and the web. They exist in varied forms, like multimedia fiction, interactive fiction, flash fiction, generative poetry, slam literature, and social media writings. The rise in electronic literature has altered the patterns of the Indian literary system with regard to creation, distribution, circulation, and participation of users. Artist's identity is no longer the most important aspect of creativity and the constructing factors are humans and machine, with imagination having digital elements added to it. There also is a larger, more engaged user community that is not silent, which often acquires protagonist-type roles. It has made literature public and has led to the development of creative artistic literature and the cultural industries.

Audio books with embedded multimedia effects, such as graphics, texts, and hyperlinks, have emerged as a prominent form in case of regional languages, and are picking up, with Storytel and Audible changing the scene. Storytel hosts over one lakh titles in English, Hindi, Marathi, Tamil, Kannada, Telugu, Malayalam, and Bengali. The app titled "Kelkaam" (Let's hear) in Malayalam has a compilation of short stories and poems. The recently released Onam (annual harvest festival of Kerala) special audio anthology by the app features stories in Malayalam and Tamil by Shihabuddin Poythumkadavu, Ashitha, P F Mathews, Priya AS, Damodaran Radhakrishnan and Sreebala K Menon.

Other widely accepted forms of digital literature across India are flash fiction and micro-fiction, which are popular across social media. Terribly Tiny Tales (TTT), Scribbled Stories and Commas, and Half Stories are widely acclaimed among the new generation readers. There is also slam poetry mostly popularized on YouTube, and also through projects like the First Post Poetry Project by Ankitha Shah, Kommune-a collective of story slams and city chapters and Airplane poetry movement. In an attempt to bring about bit-sized immersive fiction, Anushka and Vineet, graduates from IIM-Bangalore, have developed an app named Plop as part of the Golden Startup programme. Plop incorporates multiple media—text, video, audio, simulations, and role-playing to offer an interactive content experience. Another important initiative is eFiction India, which attempts to bring together stories across the country by providing a 4D reading experience.

Auria Kathi is the first Artificial Intelligence bot-artist, from India developed by Fabin Rasheed (a designer based in Bengaluru) and Sleeba Paul (an engineer from Kochi). Rasheed and Paul explain that their AI artist-poet was named "Auria kathi" based on an anagram for AI Haiku Art.

> We started off trying to create a bot which continuously produced Haikus (to us this meant short poems). We wanted Auria to create poems which does not make complete sense in the beginning but has some meaning to it eventually.
>
> *(Arakal 2019)*

Auria's first poem is as follows:

> I Was a little
> catastrophic, I was
> just a little kid.
> This is nothing you

look like your son has ever
Been done with the game.
It worked like a month.
I wasn't a fan.
(Kathi 2019)

Another noteworthy E-literature platform is *We Are Angry*, which evolved after the upsettingly brutal 16 December 2012 gang-rape in New Delhi. *We Are Angry* is an effort to keep anger and conversations about the brutality of rape alive by fusing traditional storytelling with other media, bolstered by real news content and annotations and showcasing a range of art and expression from a team of people who want to harness their anger to work creatively for change.

Social media is used in multiple ways in Indian digital literature: first, as a platform for publication, and second, as a medium to mobilize published works, especially after COVID-19. Authors are trying to communicate and attract audiences to their works through social media involvements and micro-writings. Sahitya Academy Award winning writers Vinod Kumar Shukla, Ramesh Chandra Shah, and veteran writer Ashok Vajpeyi regularly host Facebook live streams, while Ajit Anjum operates YouTube channels. Rajpal and Sons (publisher) launched an online series titled Karona Charcha, meant to engage their readers on social media, programming digital session for their books since the month of April, this engagement has had a positive impact on their online discoverability. The Asmita Theatre Group, headed by Arvind Gaur, ran an online Nukkad Natak series during the lockdown, called the Quarantine Theatre Festival, which recently completed its 120th day. Other online programmes were launched too, such as the e-Sahitya Aaj Tak by India Today Group; Jagran's online discussion forum; the Prabha Khaitan Foundation's Author's Afternoon; and Ek Mulaqat, the People's Hindi Festival, all of which have kept the momentum going. Leading Hindi publisher Rajkamal Prakashan is sending daily WhatsApp list of reading to their readers (they call it the WhatsApp book). Ashok Maheshawari, managing director of Rajkamal Prakashan, says that these lists reach more than 25,000 readers daily. Recently, jankipul.com has created an account on the Telegram instant messaging app to provide free PDFs of copyright free books to readers. In a way they are creating new readerships and trying to grow a phone-based readership base.

## Literary Games

The concept of text-driven digital games is still at a nascent stage in India. Traditional Indian academia is yet in its path to accept games as literature. An important outbreak in literary games in India is Oleomingus, a game design studio co-founded by Dhruv Jani and Sushant Chakraborty who brought out an anthology called *Somewhere*. Works like *The Pause between the Ringing* and *A Museum of Dubious Splendors* are widely approved for their literariness. *The Pause Between the Ringing* is a set of stories nestling within one another; being an interplay of text and multimedia environments, they fall within the intersection of literary fiction and gaming. They act as links between postcolonial literature, speculative architecture, and games. There are other community creation and sales platforms like Steam and Itch.io that has begun publishing para text based socially relevant games.

## Responses Towards the Digital First Trend in Indian Literature

It is important to look into responses from authors, readers, and publishers towards the current digital first attitude, as to foreground possible developments in Indian digital literature. The initial response towards digital literature was that of academic inadequacy, and a reluctance to accept it as a serious form of writing. Later, the stigma shifted to the lack of literature produced digitally, especially in regional languages, and the quality of the available literature. Indian digital literature then gained momentum, as the publishers and writers started regarding digital publications as both an extension of the print literature and a yardstick with which they could test the market. The current pandemic has brought out a huge shift in publisher's approach to digital publications and also to their readers, and writers. This section through a survey studies perceptions of digital literature, and the reasons for choosing and not choosing digital publications.

### *Reader's Response Towards Digital Literature*

Since the mid-1990s, digital reading has been an object of devout scholarly and literary debates. Oftentimes, digital reading has been associated solely with what may happen between readers and screens. In dominant approaches, digital reading devices have been seen to be producing radically different readers when compared to printed book readers (Koepnick 2020).

Most of the digital literature available in India is conventional literature disguised as "digital literature" or "digital publishing," as Raine Koskimaa names the production and marketing of literature with the aid of digital technology. Indian readers mainly regard digital literature as an extension of the print. However, in the literary academies, literature published in interactive digital platforms is not considered serious reading.

The survey for this study was conducted among readers who read English, Tamil, Hindi, Malyalam, Punjabi, Bengali, Urudu, Gujarati, Odiya, and Marathi. Among the surveyed readers, 5% read only in print, 7% read literature only through digital mediums, and the rest read in both mediums. The following graph shows the readers' response to the question about the availability of content in their respective regional languages. When asked to rate the accessibility of digital literature on a scale of 0 to 5, the languages were rated as follows by the readers: Tamil, 4; Malayalam, 3; Bengali, 2; Odiya, 5; Marathi, 4; Hindi, 3; Telugu, 4.5; and Gujarati, 2.

The main reasons listed by the readers to choose digital publications over print are: availability, accessibility, lower cost, portability, content analysis possibilities,

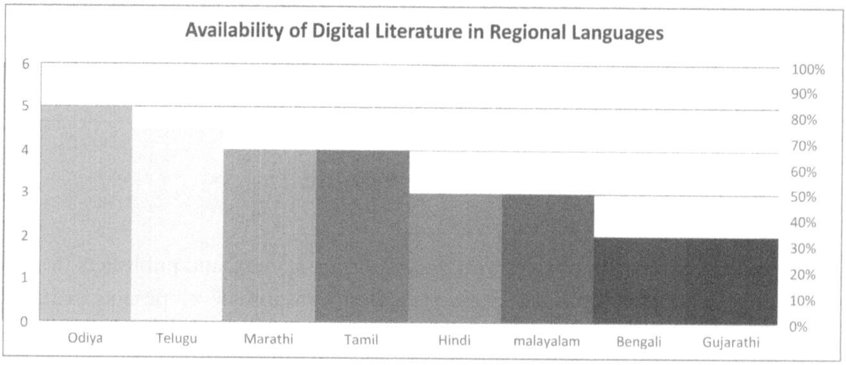


**FIGURE 17.1** Availability of digital literature in regional languages

*Source*: Author's own survey

**TABLE 17.1** Reasons for choosing digital publications by the readers

| *Reason* | *Agree (%)* | *Disagree (%)* | *Neutral (%)* |
|---|---|---|---|
| **Accessibility to all readers (including print disabled)** | 83 | 8 | 10 |
| **Interactive reading possibilities** | 71 | 15 | 16.6 |
| **Availability** | 90 | 6.6 | 5 |
| **Lower cost** | 81.6 | 6.6 | 13 |
| **Easy content analysis** | 71.6 | 16.6 | 13 |
| **Better engagement (readability)** | 56.6 | 33 | 13 |
| **Portability** | 86 | 8 | 8 |
| **Eco-friendly nature** | 85 | 8 | 8 |

and interactive nature of the digital medium. Readers have slight disagreements about the readability and engagement offered by the digital medium when compared to the print. When compared to foreign digital literature, readers believe that although Indian literature is less expensive than foreign digital literature, foreign digital literature is nonetheless more easily available. Furthermore, they believe that foreign literature better utilizes the possibilities of the web when compared to Indian literature. Following table summarizes the readers' reasons for choosing digital literature.

The most-observed criticism about digital literature is that it does not facilitate serious reading and does not provide the contentment of reading the print. Most of the readers who participated in this survey do not find accessibility, availability of quality content and internet connectivity, loss of content over time, and legal and copyright issues as reasons to stop them from choosing digital literature. Table 17.2 summarizes the readers' responses for the reasons of not choosing digital literature.

**TABLE 17.2** Reasons for not choosing digital literature by readers

| *Reason* | *Agree (%)* | *Disagree (%)* | *Neutral (%)* |
|---|---|---|---|
| **Accessibility (internet)** | 35 | 45 | 21.6 |
| **Technical issues** | 40 | 38 | 23 |
| **Doesn't facilitate serious reading** | 55 | 38 | 6.6 |
| **Loss of content over time** | 30 | 45 | 25 |
| **Lack of quality content** | 26.6 | 56.6 | 16.6 |
| **Contentment of having a print version** | 58 | 30 | 11.6 |
| **Health Concerns** | 46.6 | 35 | 18 |
| **Legal issues** | 23 | 45 | 33 |

Reader has a superior role in majority of digital literature than in conventional literary works, as they are participants in the narration, and in some cases, the choices of the reader even decide the course of events in the plot of the narrative. The role of the reader thus transforms from a recipient to a participant, because of the paradoxical contamination between the world of the telling and the world of the told what Genette calls as "metaleptic discourse" (Genette 2009). It is not that the role of the reader has completely changed; it is that the reader is allowed to establish their self in profoundly diverse platforms.

## *Writers' Response*

Except for a very few recent works in online digital platforms like flash fiction, generative poetry, and graphic animated narratives "Electronic literature, as it is understood in Europe and the USA, does not have a presence in Indian literary and cultural traditions yet" (Mukherjee 2017). Digital literary writers in India mainly focus on publishing digital versions of their print books, or the digital version first. They are yet to explore the numerous interactive capabilities of the web. Simon Murray's argument is that the author is far from dead in the digital age; instead, authors are held to a performance of identity and intimacy with reading publics online (Murray 2018). This is true when considering Indian literature of this age. Influences of retailers like Amazon, and the concomitant innovations in the process of writing, publishing, and literary marketing, are apparent in the current literary practices and media involvements of the writers.

This survey was conducted among 60 literary writers in India of whom 47.8% writes only on digital platforms whereas 52.2% writes and publishes on both print and digital platforms. Though the surveyed authors are from different parts of India, most of their writings are in English, Tamil, and Malayalam. Figure 17.2 represents their perception of digital literature.

A total of 36.5% of the surveyed writers use digital literature as an extension of print and another 36.5% believes that it is a first-hand publication medium. A key

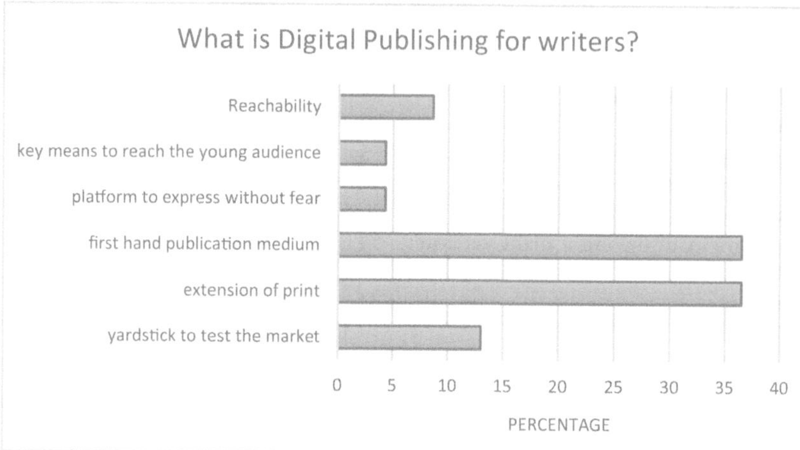


**FIGURE 17.2** What is digital publishing for writers?

**TABLE 17.3** Reasons for choosing digital publishing by authors

| *Reason* | *Agree (%)* | *Disagree (%)* | *Neutral (%)* |
|---|---|---|---|
| **Higher acceptance from readers** | 78 | 4 | 17 |
| **Chances of self-publication** | 86.9 | 4 | 13 |
| **Covering a larger base of audience** | 78 | 8.6 | 21.7 |
| **Accessibility to all readers (including print disabled)** | 69 | 8.6 | 26 |
| **Interactive possibilities for narration** | 86.9 | 0 | 13 |
| **Higher revenue** | 34.7 | 34.7 | 39 |
| **Easy content updating and creation of newer editions** | 86.9 | 0 | 13 |

factor highlighted by small-scale writers is the freedom of expression that digital platforms offered them. The writers who advocated for traditional, non-digital writing are still ready to use digital publishing as an option to test the market; furthermore, 8.3% of the traditional writers agrees that digital literature can be used to reach younger readers. A total of 56.5% of the writers agree that social media interactions have contributed positively to their writings and have influenced them in publishing digitally. Whereas 8.7% of the participants disagreed and 34.8% has neutral opinions towards the influence of social media. Tables 17.3 and 17.4 summarize the reasons suggested by the writers for choosing and not choosing digital publications.

Though it is commonly observed that Indian digital literature rarely makes use of the interactive capabilities of the web, most of the writers cite the possibility of

**TABLE 17.4** Reasons for not choosing digital publications by writers

| *Reason* | *Agree (%)* | *Disagree (%)* | *Neutral (%)* |
|---|---|---|---|
| **Legal and copyright issues** | 43 | 21 | 34.7 |
| **Accessibility (Internet)** | 26 | 52 | 21.7 |
| **Lack of support from Govt. (archaic policies)** | 43 | 30 | 26 |
| **Technical issues** | 34.7 | 30 | 34.7 |
| **Lack of awareness of users and publishing houses** | 47.8 | 34.7 | 17 |
| **Being regarded inferior to print** | 52 | 34.7 | 13 |
| **Demands social media involvement of the writer** | 52 | 30 | 17 |

creating interactive narratives as a key reason to choose digital platforms. Other reasons that greatly attracts writers towards publishing digital are the chances of self-publication, easy content revision and less troublesome ways for creation of newer editions. Though there is a slight difference of opinion when it comes to acceptance from readers and revenue, most of the writers are nuetral about the issue of accessibility.

The inferior regard to print in literary and academic spheres, and its higher demand of a writer's social media presence, are the two commonly cited reasons for writers' dislike towards digital publishing. Most of the writers disagree towards the inaccessibility and inhibition of the publishing houses to start publishing digital and they have neutral opinions when it comes to legal, copyright and technical issues with regard to digital publications.

The new digital media has finally allowed for the "death of the author" and the birth of the "writing reader." Looking into Indian digital literature, the author has been greatly revived by the new media and continues to thrive within it. The author mostly takes up the role of the content creator and publisher. Though current authors rarely explore the interactive and collaborative possibilities of digital literature, authorship is being redefined by the higher acceptance of digital publications especially after the COVID-19-induced lockdown, as agreed by the 69.6% participants of the survey.

## *Publishers' Response*

India has historically been one of the major publishing centres. In addition to English, India also publishes in 24 regional languages. There are almost 15,000 publishers registered in India, publishing between 70,000 titles annually, in 24 languages, 18 of which are prominent, highly developed, and used by millions of people (India First Foundation 2020). However, though the registered number of publishers is high, the majority of them are inactive and not currently publishing at all; some of them are publishing just their own institutional titles, so the average number of

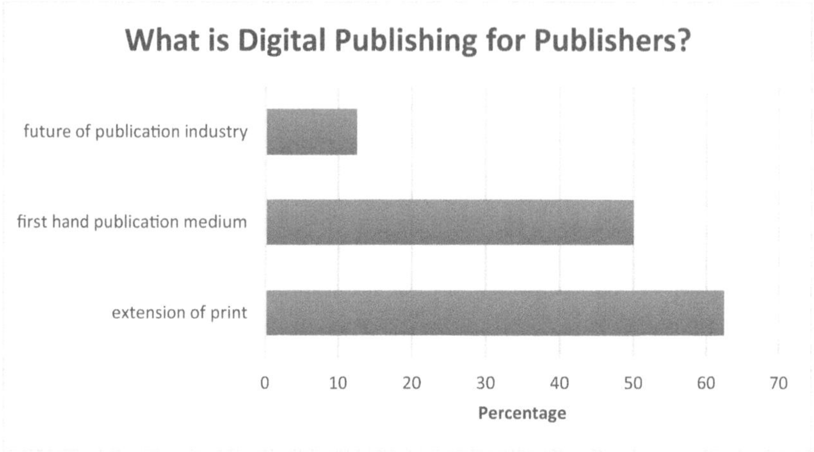


**FIGURE 17.3** What is digital publishing for publishers?

publications produced by such publishers is very low. In each state, the output of local publishers is mostly in the language of its own people. Following the IT boom in India, many publishing companies started publishing electronically. There are also a number of e-publishing service providers such as Tata Infomedia, Mumbai; Dx Technologies, Pune; eMacmillan, Bangalore; Creative Graphics, New Delhi; Mizpaz Publishing Services Pvt Ltd., Chennai, that are involved in the production of e-publications and offer e-publishing-related services.

The survey for this study was conducted among the publishers from India delivering content in languages such as English, Malayalam, Bengali, Tamil, and Hindi. A total of 12.5% of the total respondents published only in print, 37.5% of the publishers deliver their content digitally, and 50% of the publishers who responded to the survey publish in both print and digital. Among the respondents, 62.5% do their sales online, and 12.5% using traditional mediums; 25% of respondents utilize both. Figure 17.3 represents their perception of digital publishing.

While none of the publishers use digital publishing as a yardstick to test the market, 62.5% of them sees it as an extension of print. Fifty per cent of the publishers use it as a first-hand print medium whereas 12.5% regard it as the future of the publishing industry. While 12.5% of the participant publishers began digital publishing in 2010–2011, the rest of them begun publishing digitally in 2019—20.50% of the participants acknowledge that social media has a positive impact of digital publications, 37.5% remarks on the negative impact of social media, and 12.5% of the participants are neutral about the social media impact. Figure 17.4 suggests the revenue generation methods in digital publishing.

While 12.5% depends on subscription and advertising for revenue generation, most publishers depend on pay-asper-use, licensing, or outright purchase. Donations and trust funds are also sources of income. It is important to note that there

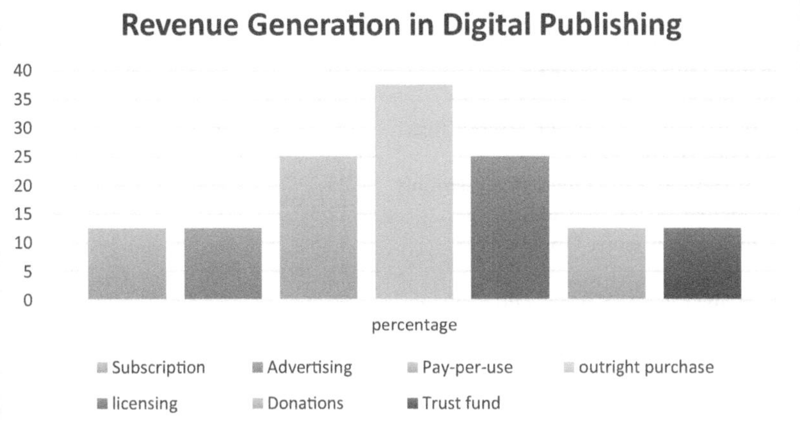


**FIGURE 17.4** Revenue generation in digital publishing

**TABLE 17.5** Publisher's reasons for choosing digital publishing

| *Reason* | *Agree (%)* | *Disagree (%)* | *Neutral (%)* |
|---|---|---|---|
| **Higher acceptance from readers** | 50 | 25 | 25 |
| **Lower production cost** | 87 | 0 | 12.5 |
| **Covering a larger base of readers** | 87 | 0 | 12.5 |
| **Easy global mobilization and marketing** | 100 | 0 | 0 |
| **Accessibility to all readers** | 87 | 0 | 12.5 |
| **Easy content updating and creation of newer editions** | 100 | 0 | 0 |

are no Government subsidies available for digital publishing in India. Tables 17.5 and 17.6 summarize the reasons suggested by the publishers for choosing or not choosing digital publications.

Though most of the publishers do not accept digital medium to the same extent as readers, they list lower production costs, easy mobilization, accessibility, and the flexibility in the creation of new editions as the key reasons for venturing into digital publishing.

Most of the publishers do not regard legal and copyright issues, internet access, marketing, and lack of defined marketing strategies as reasons for not venturing into digital publishing. Rather, their major concerns are archaic governmental policies, technical aspects of digital publications, and lack of interest from the authors and readers. Seventy-five per cent of the publishers who participated in the survey agree that their perception of digital publishing is positively influenced by the COVID-19-induced lockdown.

The important challenge in digital publishing is associated with regional language publishing. The regional language digital publishing industry has not yet

**TABLE 17.6** Publisher's reasons for not choosing digital publishing

| *Reason* | *Agree (%)* | *Disagree (%)* | *Neutral (%)* |
|---|---|---|---|
| **Legal and copyright issues** | 25 | 62.5 | 12.5 |
| **Accessibility** | 25 | 62.5 | 12.5 |
| **Lack of defined publishing, marketing, and sales strategies** | 12.5 | 62.5 | 25 |
| **Lack of trained and skilled professionals** | 25 | 25 | 25 |
| **Maintenance of the platform** | 12.5 | 25 | 37.5 |
| **Lack of support from Govt.** | 37.5 | 37.5 | 25 |
| **Technical issues** | 25 | 25 | 25 |
| **Lack of awareness in users and authors** | 50 | 37.5 | 12.5 |
| **Lack of quality content** | 12.5 | 25 | 37.5 |

found a solution to the glaring technological gaps in the production of e-books. Except for Tamil and Malayalam, current software like Adobe, InDesign, or Corel are still not compatible with traditional fonts, that are identifying only Unicode fonts that have been rejected by readers and authors due to their low aesthetic appeal. As only text files produced in Unicode are suitable, regional-language content creators are still struggling to plug these two-pronged gaps that have considerably slowed down the production of digital literature. Another important challenge is reaching out to the rural areas. As Ravi DeeCee, CEO of DC books (a leading publisher) writes

> Digital is a big thing in India, but it will still take some time to find roots in rural areas. Here, rural libraries have a strong role to play. If every Panchayat can have local libraries, it will give a big boost to increase readership.

Electronic literature in India is gaining momentum alongside the call for preservation of India's vast literature, the need to become a digital economy, the cultivation of a knowledge-based society, and the discovery of alternative platforms and strategies for publication and reading. The literary community is no more circumspect in experimenting on the multiple capabilities of the computer and the web. The rise of small-scale publishing platforms, interactive content creation software, support from the large-scale publishing houses, migration of the reading community from the traditional approach to reading, and the availability of quality digital content has accelerated the growth of digital literature. The born-digital and digital-first approaches are thus widely acclaimed by the readers, writers, and publishers as concluded from the survey, especially after the pandemic, though there is still a lack of effective publishing strategies and government policies.

## References

Anderson, P. (2020) *Book Publishing Market Report*. Delhi: Nielsen Book India.

Arakal, R.A. (2019) 'Auria Kathi, an AI bot generates Haiku poems and art to go with it', *The Indian Express*, 2 August [online]. Available at: https://indianexpress.com/

article/cities/bangalore/auria-kathi-an-ai-bot-generates-haiku-poems-and-art-to-go-with-it-5871866/ (Accessed: 5 November 2020).

Electronic Literature Organization. (2015) *Electronic Literature Organization* [online]. Available at: https://eliterature.org/ (Accessed: 20 November 2020).

Genette, Gérard. (2009) *Métalepse de la figure à la fiction*. Paris: Éditions du Seuil.

Gopika, I.S. (2018) 'Online Platforms Welcome Amateur Malayalam Writers'. *The New Indian Express*, 4 November [online]. Available at: www.newindianexpress.com/states/kerala/2018/oct/29/online-platforms-welcome-amateur-malayalam-writers-1891342.html (Accessed: 18 November 2020).

Hayles, N.K. (2010) *Electronic literature new horizons for the literary*. Notre Dame: University of Notre Dame Press.

India First Foundation. (2020) *Publishing Industry Growing by Over 12% in India* [online]. www.indiafirstfoundation.org/archives/news/03/september/b&enews_m.htm#b&e57/ (Accessed: 15 November 2020).

Kathi, Auria. (2019) *Auria Kathi* [online]. Available at: https://auriakathi.com/ (Accessed: 10 November 2020).

Koepnick, L. (2020) 'Reading in the Digital Era', *Oxford Research Encyclopedia of Literature* [online]. Available at: https://oxfordre.com/literature/view/10.1093/acrefore/9780190201098.001.0001/acrefore-9780190201098-e-2. (Accessed: 29 September 2020).

Koskimaa, R. (2000) *Digital Literature: From Text to Hypertext and Beyond*. Jyväskylä: University of Jyväskylä.

KPMG. (2016) *Digital classifieds In India 2020* [online]. Available at: https://home.kpmg/in/en/home/insights/2016/09/digital-classifieds-india.html (Accessed: 28 September 2020).

Lius, E. (2003) *Digital Narrative Literature and the Changing Role of the Reader* [online]. Available at: www.academia.edu/1885725/Digital_Narrative_Literature_and_the_changing_Role_of_the_Reader (Accessed: 28 November 2020).

Mukherjee, S. (2017) *'No country for E-Lit?'—India and electronic literature*. Hyperrhiz: New Media Cultures.

Murray, S. (2018) *The Digital Literary Sphere: Reading, Writing, and Selling Books in the Internet era*. Baltimore, MD: Johns Hopkins University Press.

Subramaniam, K. (2018) 'Tamil Writers Try Out E-publishing'. *The Hindu*, 19 May [online]. Available at: www.thehindu.com/news/cities/chennai/tamil-writers-try-out-epublishing/article5840772.ece (Accessed: 18 November 2020).

# PART V
# Digital Atmospheres

# 18

# THE CULT OF YOUTUBE MUSHAIRAS IN INDIA'S SMALL TOWNS

*Yousuf Saeed*

While mushairas or Urdu poetry symposia are an age-old and popular cultural practice, attracting thousands of attendees in rural and small-town India irrespective of religious affiliation, the internet and social media have lately provided new platforms for this tradition to flourish. All over Urdu-knowing India, especially in the qasbas of Uttar Pradesh, Madhya Pradesh, Haryana, Punjab, Maharashtra, Telangana, Karnataka, etc., real mushairas are video-recorded and uploaded to social media platforms such as YouTube and Facebook, where they are watched and shared by the millions of fans of young and local poets like Nikhat Moradabadi, Danish Ghazal, Shabana Shabnam, Saba Balrampuri, Lata Haya, and many more. One needs to explore if the mushaira fan clubs on YouTube are giving a new dimension to Urdu poetics and performance.

Although this chapter is about the popular culture of Urdu language and the impact of digital media on its poetics, it is important to start with a brief about the historical and socio-cultural role played by Urdu mushairas in South Asia. The fact that, on an average, some video recordings of mushaira performances are being watched 40 lakh times or more in a year on youtube.com requires a serious study of the phenomenon. One possibly cannot understand why mushaira videos are a craze on social media without exploring why a mushaira, or Urdu poetry in general, continues to attract the masses in India.

The word mushaira comes from the Arabic *masha'ira* meaning to compete or excel in poetry (although Arabic *masha'ir* means feelings or emotions). In Persian, it also meant a competition between two individuals or teams, who recite verses starting with a letter with which the previous team's verse ended—something that has been known in South Asia as *bayt bazi* (or *antakshari* in Hindi). But today's mushaira in South Asia is a stage symposium where poets are invited to recite their poetry, although it could have an element of competition too. Private or public soirees (and sometimes competitions) of poetry were patronized by almost

DOI: 10.4324/9781003354246-24

all Indo-Muslim rulers, starting from the Delhi Sultanate in 12th century, and resulting in a vibrant tradition that has continued till today. These sorts of recitations are largely responsible not only for the popularity of Urdu poetry but also in inculcating a culture of *adab* and *sukhan shanasi* (connoisseurship) among the masses (Naim 1989). Besides poetry of high literary calibre, the mushairas also feature popular verses, especially humourous or mazahiya shayeri—often, entire evenings are devoted to humour. Mushairas were very popular in the middle of 18th century, being regularly organized at night in the open, upon the rooftops of homes, in Sufi shrines, and in the royal courts (Baig 2010). Many mushairas were attended by the elite or "high-class." A culture and etiquette of praising (*daad dena*) and encouraging the poet by the audience was a common and essential part of the symposia, although strict rules were to be followed to avoid indecency. Even the attendees would often be poets, and it would be difficult to differentiate between the poets and the listeners. The host used to be (and still is) the *sadr* (president) or *muntazim* (organizer/convener) of the event, inviting other poets after reciting a few of his own couplets. The youngest poets are usually invited first, and the senior-most, at the end. In the past, a *shama* (lamp or candle) used to be placed before each poet at his/her term to recite. Needless to say, that with the non-sectarian identity of Urdu in the past, the mushairas were attended by Hindus, Muslims, and all others. The pre-modern mushairas comprised mostly of male poets on stage, and predominantly male audiences, although some women could be seated in secluded sections of the audience. Women poets may have started appearing on the stage from the start of 20th century, probably with the influence of cinema where women qawwals and singers started appearing on the screen.

It is interesting to note that the popularity of mushairas continued or probably increased in modern India, despite a parallel political debate about the identity of Urdu language in India after 1947. After the Partition of India, it was largely assumed that Urdu belongs to the Muslims who left for Pakistan, and, hence, it has no place in India. Urdu was removed from most of the schools and colleges in North India as a medium of learning, and also as a subject itself (Pai 2002). Thus, an entire generation of Indians grew up without an essential language and the ethos with which their ancestors easily identified. Naturally, then, the first thing to be affected was Urdu's connection with mainstream media, industry, politics, and professional lives of people. By the end of 20th century, far fewer people were learning Urdu, even among the Muslim community. However, the continued popularity of mushairas in these regions, even among audiences who could not read or write Urdu, meant that the language and its cultural nuances were not lost. And even now, a large number of non-Muslims participate as audience as well as poets. At many occasions, the poetry events are a mix of mushaira and *kavi sammelan* (Hindi poetry soiree) and see diverse forms of participation and expression. The funny or humorous poetry is often the biggest attraction of mushairas, besides poets reciting in *tarannum* (singing), although these qualities may disrupt the serious kinds of verses which many poets bring.

Throughout the 20th century, mushairas have been organized along with local and rural festivals and events such as annual *melas* (fetes) for agriculture and livestock, and for religious purposes, too. These include, for instance, Rampur's industrial *numaish*, or exhibition, and Meerut's Nauchandi mela, which have continued for last 130 years or so. At Chandausi in Sambhal District, Uttar Pradesh (UP), a mushaira is held during the Hindu festival of Ganesh Chaturthi. Similarly, mushairas are held in Shimla (Himachal Pradesh) at the annual summer festival, along with folk dances and flower shows. A mushaira and kavi sammelan is held at Nainital (Uttarakhand) during the Sharad-utsav, while Ludhiana in Punjab holds a memorial mushaira for the famous poet Sahir Ludhyanvi every year. Mushairas are also held during most *urs* festivals of Sufi saints. Many great poets of India started and evolved their poetic careers from these local mushairas. Besides these, many smaller mushairas and *nashist*s (gatherings) are organized in *qasba*s (small towns), *muhalla*s, and bazaars by local *anjuman*s (committees) every month or fortnight, where young and old poets alike bring their new compositions. Even though these local mushairas have less chances of earning money or fame, as compared to the national- or international-level events, they are still the most important carriers of a rich performative tradition. Being part of agricultural or seasonal festival means that people of all economic or professional backgrounds, including farmers, landowners, craftspeople, businessmen, politicians, students, and even housewives, attend and appreciate mushairas. The events usually continue the entire night with people of all religions and communities participating and praising the recitations enthusiastically, suggesting that they follow the nuances of language and poetry even if they don't read or write Urdu.

From the start of 20th century, new media forms such as cinema, sound amplification (loudspeakers), radio, gramophone, printing press, photography, and, later, television, affected everything in South Asia's popular culture, especially the performative traditions connected with languages and literatures. Popular stage traditions such as musical *nautanki*, Parsi theatre, and various kinds of religious *katha*s (storytelling) transformed in various ways into cinema, especially after the coming of sound in the movies in 1930s. Poetry was always an integral part of the staged performative art, and Urdu or Hindustani was, for centuries, the South Asian *lingua franca* for such traditions. Thus, mushaira is a performative rather than strictly literary tradition. After the introduction of loudspeakers and lights at night, most performative arts could serve much larger crowds as compared to the past, when they were restricted to the elite in restricted spaces. This shift of a tradition, from elite to mass audiences, demanded very different modes of performance and poetics, from the poets as well as organizers. Even though there was a larger risk of the mass audience not adhering to the formal etiquettes of listening—or receiving the poetry more or less the way they watch popular movies and other staged or street performances—the bigger crowds also brought more popularity, fame, and a larger appreciation of poetry. The poets had to compose poetry that would appeal to the masses and the classes. Even their mode of recitation changed with the presence of a microphone and loudspeaker. The "mass mushairas" could also be commercialized through sponsors, who could fund the event by paying the poets their fees, travel costs, etc. Thus, the mass media of 20th century not only helped evolve a robust, mass culture of mushairas all over South Asia but also changed the way poetry is recited and audience appreciation (*daad*) is sought.

The moment one mentions mushaira and its popularity, a debate about *me'yar* (standards) or *me'yari shayeri* is bound to follow. Most scholars and critics of Urdu feel that it is important to maintain the high literary standards and that "the standards of poetry and its appreciation are falling in mushairas gradually." They feel that fame and money are allowing poets to do *ghair-me'yari* (below-standard) poetry, thus turning the mushairas into an institution of *tamasha* (spectacle) (Bhopali 2014).

> Mushairas are now a *mandi* (market) of literature. And in the mandi only that item comes to sells which is in demand. At one time, the *she'r* (verse) used to carry a weight. Now, only the *shayir* (poet) carries a weight.
>
> *Safdar Hamdani (Rizvi 2014)*

Critics usually refer to the mushairas in local and rural areas (even though some of them may have originally hailed from the same places). One must point out that the decline of standards, or what the critics often call *chhichhora-pan* (vulgarity), does not necessarily come from the small towns. Many qasbas of South Asia, such as Rampur, Tonk, Amroha, Azamgarh, Behraich, and Bilgram, have been centres of great literature, refined culture, and civility. In fact, most great poets of South Asia have had their roots in these qasbas as one can see from the place-related suffix they add with their names. The poetry composed and recited at these towns does not lack in any "standards." Furthermore, the grand mushairas of national and international levels are not devoid of either vulgarity or commercialization. Mehtab Qadar writes:

> Mushairas have become an expression of uncivility. The worth of a great or lesser poet is not measured by their poetry's stature, but by the expertness of their theatrics and shrieking on the microphone.
>
> *(Qadr 2012)*

In any scholarly discussion about mushairas, there is always an effort to measure each mehfil through the supposed "standards" of literature (Islahi 2014). The organizers of the large mushairas are, especially, held responsible for maintaining the decorum and standards. There is also a great emphasis on maintaining the correct *talaffuz* (pronunciation) of words in poetry recitation, suggesting that anyone who cannot pronounce Urdu letters (such as *sheen*, *qaaf*, and *ze*) correctly is not an Urdu-wallah (Qadr 2013). This raises the question of whether Urdu is, or should be, the language of only a certain community or religious affiliation, or can also be practiced and appreciated by those who have not formally studied it. While Delhi, Lucknow, Hyderabad, etc. may historically be considered the literary, canonical centres of Urdu, wherein the me'yar is upheld, the reality is that practiced Urdu and its talent is thriving more in smaller towns, each having their own local linguistic or dialectical differences that make their poetic production unique. Many qasbas have given rise to child artists or young poets who acquired world fame. For instance, Sufyan Pratapgarhi, a 12-year-old poet from Raniganj, Pratapgarh (UP), has been reciting at mushairas since the age of 9. Similarly, Iram Gulzar of Mundyar, Azamgarh, and Iram Sultanpuri from Jaganpur, Faizabad, have been performing as child artists at Mushairas.

One of the biggest attractions for the masses in mushaira and Urdu poetry is its image as a powerful language of love and beauty. For them, the mushairas evoke the popular culture of ghazals, qawwalis, movie songs, romantic slogans inscribed behind vehicles, even the images of wine, Mughal architecture, Mughlai food, *saqi*, the *tawaif*s kotha (courtesan's quarters), and other symbols that have somehow traditionally been associated with Urdu/Farsi poetics. Apparently the late author Khushwant Singh once said "*Agar aap Urdu seekhna hai to ishq kar lijiy, ishq karna chahte hain to Urdu seekh lijiye*" (If you wish to learn Urdu, fall in love, and if you wish to fall in love, learn Urdu.) (Rekhta 2018). Thus, a large number of people, especially the youth, are attracted to mushaira and its related culture because of its expressions of love. In fact, remembering Urdu *shers* (verses) and spontaneously quoting them during conversations has been part of daily life in South Asia—although, once again, such references are acquired not necessarily through reading. In the past, the audience of mushairas would often remember couplets and entire ghazals simply by listening to them being recited. People used to return from mushairas and recall before others the entire verses of famous poets that they had heard. Great mushairas and recitation of great poets were remembered by participants for decades. Oral memory, as opposed to the textual one (i.e. remembering by reading), was more important for such a recall.

The question is thus: what does the new hobby of mushaira video-sharing on YouTube mean for the younger generation? What does internet do to the tradition of mushaira, and poetry itself, which wasn't possible or imaginable earlier? The production and instant sharing of videos worldwide, by anyone, are a revolutionary ability, something that could not be imagined a decade or so ago. Among the various kinds of videos of literary and performative arts that one finds online are performances of music, stage drama, speeches, stand-up comedies, and others, whether filmed in a controlled environment (and edited/polished later) or performed live for a spontaneous audience. The most revolutionary change that digital and online media has brought in our lives is to allow us to virtually "own" a little piece of live culture and share it further as a meme. In the pre-digital era, one could share pieces of poetry in conversations or through written letters or books. Technology in 20th century allowed us to own and share sound recordings on vinyl or tape and then videos on VCDs and DVDs. But recordings of mushairas were still out of the ambit of commercially produced units like a DVD. It is only the online video-sharing platforms like youtube.com which made it possible to upload an unlimited amount of recordings and even live streaming of events allowing enthusiasts to watch a live mushaira sitting at home, keep its recording and share it further. Many recordings are also short videos of particular poets and not the full hours-long events, so that only a specific poet could be watched or shared. One should also note that the sharing of large video recordings became easier and more affordable in India around 2013–2014, when mobile-driven internet data suddenly became free or very inexpensive via certain service providers like Reliance Jio.

Recorded mushairas are a unique, multidimensional medium where, in addition to the poet's recital, the audience reaction and the interventions of the organizers/conveners become equally important to make the experience richer. Most mushairas are recorded now by a multicamera set-up which is either edited or mixed live or sometimes even later. This ensures that the video watcher catches all sides of the action—the poet's recital, the audience reaction and the convener's interventions. The microphone's position and volume are equally important—very often, the convener's voice is heard louder than the actual poet's. The convener not only makes short comments and praising sounds (such as *wah wah, aah*, and *kya baat hai*) in the middle of a recital, but he/she can also ask the audience to be more or less enthusiastic about praising, clapping, etc. Most poets (especially the women) are invited on stage with statements like "*zordar taaliyon ki goonj ke saath inka isteqbal kijiye*" (welcome her/him with a thunderous applause). Sometimes, the convener's interjections can be very irritating, as in the case of the popular Hindi poet Kumar Vishwas, who is often invited to large mushairas. Usually, the poet himself/herself reminds the audience about their poor response, if required. Most often, the women poets talk about the fact that they have come all the way from such and such place to perform here, but are not getting an enthusiastic feedback. In some ways, large mushairas sound like political gatherings, wherein politicians make fiery speeches accompanied by slogan-shouting and active audience participation.

Important themes in today's mushairas, especially those that are frequently watched online, are the identity of Indian Muslims and Hindu–Muslim communalism. There is hardly any poet, young or old, who doesn't compose poetry on such socio-political themes. In a way, mushairas have emerged as a medium for the expression of the Muslim community's fears, insecurities, and social ostracization, besides sarcastic criticism of the ruling class. One even finds non-Muslim poets speaking for the rights of the minorities, or at least composing poetry for upholding Hindu–Muslim harmony. Mumbai's poetess, Lata Haya, cannot easily be recognized as a Hindu Brahmin due to her unique voice in Urdu poetry (Mushaira Media 2015). In places like Mumbra (Thane), the name of the poetry event is *All India Yak-jehti* (unity) *mushaira* where poets such as Lata Haya, Imran Pratapgarhi, Altaf Ziya, Heena Anjum, Ghayal Kanpuri, and Anjum Dehlvi not only celebrate Urdu as a symbol of Hindu–Muslim unity but also make efforts to separate Islam from terrorism, etc. Almost all mushairas taunt the ill-practices of the current government, and make fun of the corrupt and hypocritical politicians through both veiled and clear expressions. But if the criticism or taunting of a particular phenomenon crosses certain limits, it can get problematic as well. Recently, when Aligarh's Rehana Shaheen tried to make fun of yoga through her poetry in a mushaira, even though the audience loved it, the mushaira's president almost scolded her for attacking a particular community's practices. Similarly, in a recent mushaira in Moradabad, when a poet recited verses glorifying terror convicts Afzal

Guru and Ajmal Qasab, questioning their death sentence, etc., it led to an uproar, with the local police taking action against the organizers (Bhaskar 2016). In fact, some local mushairas take an effort to show the ultra-patriotism of their patrons and organizers, too. One of Bihar All India Mushaira's events is called *Ek Shaam Pulwama ke Shaheedon ke naam* (an evening dedicated to the martyrs of Pulwama attack of 2014), where the poetess Shabina Adeeb was requested by the convener on stage to especially salute the police officers present as guest (Gomtiagencies 2019a). This video, with over 16 lakh views in one year, was uploaded by the Mushaira Gomti Agencies, which has over eight lakh subscribers on YouTube.

Local mushairas, especially at small towns and villages, are not disconnected from local politics and protocols; for instance, of giving importance to certain local personalities, politicians, etc. Mushairas are generally organized by local "committees" comprising several members, who manage tasks like the installing of the *pandal* (tented venue), stage design, electric wiring, loudspeakers, hospitality of the guests, publicity, and everything else. Every few minutes, the names of the convener, the president, the local organizers, and even some sponsors pop up on the video, with Urdu terms such as *zere sadarat* (under the presidentship of), *zere nigrani* (under the supervision of), and *zere qayadat* (under the leadership of). Almost every poet, especially the younger ones, make it a point to praise and thank the organizers and conveners in the middle of their recital for having invited them and organizing the event. At least a few of these local mushairas, such as *Aaj ki sham betiyon ke naam* (an evening devoted to daughters) mushaira in Meerut, are organized and managed by a few women, led by Shaheen Parveen. A recording of the poetess Shaista Sana from this Meerut event has had 12 lakh views in two years (Mushayra Media 2018).

The constant expression of gratitude from the stage is probably a ritual that has continued from the pre-modern period in South Asia, where a person was obliged to graciously thank their patrons, superiors, or the ruling class, especially in the royal courts. They also seek the attention of special guests seated among the audience, such as government officials and local politicians or business tycoons. Very often, they read out the names and official positions of eminent guests such as the district collector, commanding officer, *tehsildar* (chief of a district block), and magistrate, as one may notice in a recording of a mushaira in Kadipur-Sultanpur (UP), organized by the Bar Association (of lawyers), with Vijay Bahadur Singh being the main organizer (Gomtiagencies 2019b). Somehow, speaking from the stage on a loudspeaker becomes a special privilege which gives the speaker the power to make announcements and statements, even the most mundane ones, that sound profound enough for the audience make an uproar.

Some of companies or agencies that are in the forefront of recording and uploading mushaira videos are *Waqt Media Mushaira, Andaze Bayan Aur* (covering mostly Dubai-based events), *Mushayra Media, A1 Mushaira media*, and *Mushaira Gomti Agencies*, etc. many of which send recording teams all over India to cover them. Most of them have a very large subscriber base (numbering in lakhs) and qualify for YouTube's monetizing programme, which means that they may be making substantial amounts of money through the advertisements running on their videos. Besides youtube.com, many of these producers have pages or groups on other social media platforms, such as Facebook.com, Instagram, and WhatsApp, which help spread their videos to more viewers. One can say that the local mushaira committees and video producers are doing an enormous service for the popularization of the Urdu language, which even a large number of well-funded institutions meant to promote Urdu are not able to do. Of course, one can argue about the "quality" and standard of poetry being promoted in these local mushairas (as discussed earlier). The mushaira committees, organizers, and the video producers have also realized that the most widely watched videos happen to be those of attractive women poets, who sing their poetry with tarannum, tease their audiences with witty comments, *adayen* (postures), and coquetry. Thus, many of them encourage and invite young women poets who are known for such crowd-pulling tactics, even though they may be too "junior" in their careers. Very often, people learn about such poetesses on YouTube and then send a *farmaish* (request) to the organizers to especially invite them to the local mushairas.

Hina Anjum is a young poetess from Allahabad who travels all over the country to attend mushairas—her YouTube recording of recital at the mushaira of *Tahriqe Urdu Adab* (sic), Madhubani, Bihar, has been watched 13 lakh times in the past year (Mushayra Media 2019). Similarly, national-level mushaira star Rukhsar Balrampuri's recordings have been watched, on an average, 50 lakh times in the past several years. In the middle of one recital, Rukhsar has a *nok jhonk* (impish argument) with the convener, Nadeem Furrukhi, which basically ends up cracking the audience into laughter (Mushaira Media 2016). For instance, when Rukhsar comes to hold the microphone, she is slightly awkward, and the convener says "*Yeh current maar raha hai na*?" (Isn't the mic giving an electric current?) The poetess says "yes there seems to be some current." And some voices from the audience immediately retort: "*jab Rukhsar stage par aati hain to current to lagta hi hai*" (When Rukhsar Balrampuri comes on stage, one is bound to get an electric shock). Usually, more time is spent in conversations and crowd-pleasing than the actual verse recital in the case of most women poets. Compared to male poets, the women are almost always better-dressed and often look as if they came straight from the beauty parlour. But in most cases, their demeanor is modest, usually wearing a headscarf or dupatta and starting with a salam or aadab to the audience, which is always replied by the crowd enthusiastically.

When present in the crowd or watching a recording, one can only see the loud and crude feedback of the audience. But it is the comments section on YouTube recordings where one gets a more subtle and often honest opinion of the listeners. When poetess Saima Ahmed (in a recording of *Mahfil e Tehzeeb o Adab*) recites a free-verse nazm (poem) about the men's beards, she is not wearing a headscarf or dupatta (Mahfil e Tahzeeb o Adab 2019). One doesn't hear any voice from the audience in the recording, but the YouTube comments section definitely has a few men telling her "*Sister, apne sir pe dupatta kyun nahi rakha. Jitna dhakogi, itna achhi lagogi. Barabar mein buzurg baithe hain, zara bhi haya nahi?*" (Sister, why didn't you cover your head with a scarf. The more you cover yourself, the better you'll look. There are elders sitting nearby—you don't have any shame?") But beyond such moralistic comments, what is more important for us are comments about her *aazad* or free-verse style of poem. So one viewer comments: "Is this aazad poetry? Nice thoughts, but you need to learn more about poetry," suggesting that her non-rhyming lines are a sign of immaturity in poesy. Nevertheless, Saima's video has had 21 lakh views in the past one year.

In many cases, the uploader of the video disables the comments, probably to avoid many adverse or lewd comments. While most comments are short praises such as "Great," "Wow," "*Bahot khoob,*" or "Excellent," some can also be rather judgemental. For example, in a recording of a Tamseeli mushaira (where actors act as famous poets, reading the original poetry in their style), when Sadia Fatima reads out a nazm of the famous Pakistani poet Parveen Shakir (and the title and description mentions clearly that it's not the real Parveen Shakir), many viewers make negative comments, such as "Fake video. This can't be Parveen Shakir" or "*Yeh to Parveen Shakir ki jooti bhi nahi hai*" (this one is not even close to the shoe of Parveen Shakir) (Yousuf Saeed 2018). In some cases, the actual poet or someone on her behalf also replies to the comments, often thanking the commentators. The audience's urge to be a part of a mass event process and maybe even become a little famous comes true when they are able to make a comment online. Of course, today's generation also uses digital reactions such as emojis and emoticons in the comments section to express their praise. There are even comments like "*taaliyon ki awaz naqli lag rahi hai*" (the sound of clapping in the recording seems fake). Thus, social media provides an additional and long-term medium for dialogue and feedback about the poetry and performance of mushairas. Subscribers and viewers of mushaira videos are not only watching the local events—but they are also equally fascinated by international mushairas held in Dubai, Qatar, and elsewhere in Gulf—or, even, Pakistan. In their minds, they form a universe of poets who are successful and great, and always look out for them. It is the local audiences who request the organizers to invite a particular poet who they may have heard online.

There is no dearth of good poets and poetry. But the question is this: are the best really invited, or given the deserved space at the mushairas? One definitely has to market oneself by not only writing appealing poetry but also evolving a style and form of elocution which may make one popular among the masses. Besides the *daad* and appreciation one gets in a live mushaira, the entire mushaira industry is also looking to feedback on social media to see who is doing well or being appreciated online. The number of subscribers, viewers, and those "liking," "disliking," or writing comments on each video are being seriously studied to gauge the worth of a poet. Mushairas promote a lot of young talent when they see their potential. So, despite the fact that only the more established ones manage to reach Dubai, one often finds young surprises there. Ankita Singh is a young computer professional from Bangalore who was invited to a Dubai mushaira, *Andaz-e Bayan Aur*, convened by Kumar Vishwas and presided by Munawwar Rana. Her poetry is not immature, and manages to impresses the audience. Interestingly, a lot of poets are writing even to appeal to the young generation hooked on to their smartphones and social media. One finds at least one example of what one may call intermediality, that is, a connection between different media. Thus, in one of the couplets recited by Ankita, there is a reference to the social media itself in relation to love (Ankita Singh 2020).

> *Teri baaton ke phoolon se ghazal makhdoom karti hoon.*
> *Mein chupke se teri* DP *ko jab bhi* zoom *karti hoon.*
> I offer a ghazal with the flowers of your talk, when I secretly zoom into your DP.
> *(display picture, as used on social media platforms)*

This popular, or mass culture, of mushaira videos on the internet is a large phenomenon, especially giving mass popularity to Urdu language and poetics. But unfortunately, it is totally ignored or evaded by mainstream Urdu scholarship, because they believe them to be too kitsch or vulgar. Many scholars believe that such mushairas do not add any value to Urdu literature, and are, in fact, damaging the cause of language. The question really is whether a language and poetry with a classical image should remain secluded within its elite world and allowed to decay, or should it be left free among the people through newer media to thrive and be more popular, even if with some dilution of its *me'yar*? The truth is that even if the formal scholars of Urdu literature resent about the new trends, the popular culture of local mushairas will continue to thrive on its own without any efforts from the institutions that are supposed to uphold it. What Urdu poetics needs today is wider and multidisciplinary approach to the various phenomena that are taking it forward, rather than worry about the erosion of its "pure" and classical standards.

## Bibliography

Ankita Singh (2020) *Teri DP ko zoom karti hoon, Viral Poetry of Ankita Singh, Dubai Mushaira, Kavi Sammelan*, Apr 1, 2020 [Online video] www.youtube.com/watch?v=GPo4oAzWYQM, accessed 18 Oct. 2021.

Baig, Farḥatullah (2010) *The last musha'irah of Delhi, Translated from the Urdu by Akhtar Qamber*, New Delhi: Orient BlackSwan.

Bhaskar (2016) 'Mushaire mein shayar ne padhe aatanki Afzal-Kasab ki shan mein qaside, shrota'on ke hangama'. *Dainik Bhaskar* [Hindi newspaper]. www.bhaskar.com/news/up-meer-poet-praise-terrorist-afzal-guru-and-kasab-in-mushaira-5021593-pho.html, accessed 18 Oct. 2021.

Bhopali, Manzar (2014) 'Ab mushaire nahi muzahire hote hain'. *Urdu Khabrein* [Online blog]. http://urdukhabrein.blogspot.com/2014/06/blog-post_3065.html, accessed 18 Oct. 2021.

Gomtiagencies (2019a) *Shabina Adeeb, Bihar All India Mushaira, -Ek Shaam Pulwama Shaheedon Ke Naam*, March 20, 2019 [Online video] www.youtube.com/watch?v=7RVwpZt1k_U, accessed 18 Oct. 2021.

Gomtiagencies (2019b) *Sultan Jahan, Kadipur Kavi Sammelan & Mushaira*, Dec. 11, 2019 [Online video] www.youtube.com/watch?v=b2z0cP0RVfA, accessed 18 Oct. 2021.

Islahi, Ziaurrahman (2014) 'Aajkal ke mushaire kya adab ke liye mufeed hain?' *Hausla.net.* http://hausla.net/view.php?article=63, accessed 18 Oct. 2021.

Mahfil e Tahzeeb o Adab (2019) *Saima Ahmed—Mahfil-E-Tahzeeb-O-Adab Mushaira & Kavi Sammelan*, April 25, 2019 [Online video] www.youtube.com/watch?v=IsOtEt8WDik, accessed 18 Oct. 2021.

Mushaira Media (2015) *Lata Haya, All India Mushaira, Sameer Faizi's 100th Mushaira, Mumbra*, 09 Feb 2014 [Online video] www.youtube.com/watch?v=YFiSCbOaCBI, accessed 18 Oct. 2021.

Mushaira media (2016) *Rukhsar Balrampuri, Maudaha Hamirpur Mushaira*, 15/11/2016. [Online video] www.youtube.com/watch?v=HAlds5CWjJY, accessed 18 Oct. 2021.

Mushayra media (2018) *Shaista sana, Gazal, Geet, Meerut, All India Mushaira, Con-shaheen Parveen*, ON 27 APRIL 2018 [Online video] www.youtube.com/watch?v=lslqD5zJfYY, accessed 18 Oct. 2021.

Mushayra media (2019) *Tumhari aankhon se neend chura bhi sakti hoon, Hina Anjum, Bihar, Tahriq e Urdu Adab, Mushaira*, Oct. 01, 2019 [Online video] www.youtube.com/watch?v=uZMbLc6HH6A, accessed 18 Oct. 2021.

Naim, C.M. (1989) 'Poet-audience interaction at Urdu musha'iras', in Christopher Shackle (ed.), *Urdu and Muslim South Asia, Studies in Honour of Ralph Russell*, New Delhi: Oxford University Press, pp. 167–73.

Pai, Sudha (2002) 'Politics of Language: Decline of Urdu in Uttar Pradesh', *Economic and Political Weekly*, Vol. 37, No. 27, pp. 2705–08.

Qadr, Mahtab (2012) 'Commercial shu'ra aur aalami mushaire'. *Urdufalak.* [Online Urdu newspaper] www.urdufalak.net/urdu/2012/09/22/35248, accessed 18 Oct. 2021.

Qadr, Mahtab (2013) 'Ab mushaire yoon hone lage'. *Mahtabiyan* [Online blog]. http://mahtabiyan.blogspot.com/2013/08/blog-post_2649.html, accessed 18 Oct. 2021.

Rekhta (2018) *Khushwant Singh #5YearsofRekhta* [Online post] Jan 11, 2018. https://twitter.com/rekhta/status/951455468781580288, accessed 18 Oct. 2021.

Rizvi, Farkhanda (2014) 'Mushaire, talluqat-e aamma aur dostiyon ki bhaint', *Saach* (Pakistani Lifestyle magazine), www.saach.tv/urdu/15236/, accessed 10 Dec. 2020.

Yousuf Saeed (2018) *Sadia Wahidi as Parveen Shakir in tamsili mushaira, Delhi*, Feb. 20, 2018 [Online video] www.youtube.com/watch?v=rrE3eonItNQ accessed 18 Oct. 2021.

# 19

# PERFORMATIVE POLITICS IN DIGITAL SPACES

## An Analysis of *Lokshahiri* (People's Poetry) on YouTube

*Avanti Chhatre*

### Introduction

Sometime before midnight on 14 August 2020, performers belonging to Mumbai-based *Yalgaar Sanskrutik Manch* (Yalgaar Cultural Troupe) began a live performance on their YouTube channel. The cultural troupe, which brings together artists, performers, and *Lokshahirs* (literally, people's poets), or activist-singers who utilize folk idioms, has been at the forefront of Dalit cultural resistance in Maharashtra since 2015. They begin their performance, titled *Aman Ke Rang*, an Independence Day special, with "Dosti Zindabad," a motto that opens all their performances.[1] What follows is a concert, constituting songs and poems which cross borders of every kind: social, political, and cultural. Interestingly, the performance includes *Main Toh Dekhoonga* (I Will See It) by Pakistani pop band *Strings*, envisioning an egalitarian social order, and times marked by convergences, as "banners of different colours will merge into one flag, and roads moving towards different directions will meet at the crossroads."[2] After a series of songs, interspersed with commentary highlighting realities of caste, class, and gender inequalities, the concert culminates at midnight, with the members calling for the need to celebrate every colour and reject divisive rhetoric, as only then can the grounds be made for "sachhi azaadi," or freedom in the truest sense, to take root. Alongside the video, comments by viewers pour in, cheering the performers.

In another video, Charan Jadhav, a young Mumbai-based Dalit activist and Lokshahir, along with singer Pravin Done, presents a song titled "Bol" (Speak Up).[3] Images of the Una flogging incident, along with those of other atrocities against Dalits across the country, form the background of the video. Holding Brahmanism to be anti-national, Jadhav and Done urge their audiences to speak up against injustice and embrace *Jai Bhim* (victory to Ambedkar), a slogan which they say belongs to the entire country. The song calls for unity of the oppressed within the

DOI: 10.4324/9781003354246-25

all-encompassing space of resistance indexed by Jai Bhim. This video is like several others on Jadhav's YouTube channel, constituting songs, sung to the tune of a *duff* or drum, protesting against upper-caste hegemony, patriarchy, capitalism, and the plight of farmers.

The aforementioned performances express the essence of Yalgaar's and Jadhav's music, the poetics and politics of which are at the centre of this chapter. Yalgaar, a 15-member troupe, was brought together by Dhammarakshit Randive in an attempt to form an alternative space of resistance for the marginalized, and to facilitate youth-led cultural movements. While most members are Dalits, the group includes several Muslim and upper-caste members. They travel with their songs across the country, singing against caste and patriarchy, in addition to a host of socio-political issues. Likewise, Charan Jadhav, hailing from Paithan, Maharashtra, came to Mumbai in 2013, after studying theatre at Dr. Babasaheb Ambedkar Marathwada University, and immersed himself in the sounds of anti-caste resistance.

These singers are entrenched within the broader landscape of Dalit cultural mobilization in Maharashtra and beyond, wherein music has played a pivotal role as a site for critiquing caste inequalities, challenging Brahmanical religious practices, and engendering a strong political consciousness (Junghare 1983, pp. 271–295; Zelliot 1995, pp. 63–85).[4] A case in point is *Lokshahiri*, a performative/musical tradition which has been utilized by Dalits to understand, articulate, and assert their anti-caste agency since pre-Independence times, and has evolved in dialogue with changing socio-historical forces (Maitreya 2019, p. 71). *Shahirs* (poet-composers) perform *powadas* (ballads) and songs about Ambedkar's thought and personal/political struggles, known as *Bhim Geete*, in addition to songs on historical Dalit struggles for social justice and contemporary socio-political realities affecting the marginalized across the subcontinent. Songs address key concerns such as violence against women, increasing curbs on the freedom of expression, and privatization of education. Lokshahirs perform in rural and urban contexts, during cultural programmes in colleges, *Vidrohi Shahir Jalsas* (gatherings of Ambedkarite counterpublics), events such as Ambedkar Jayanti and demonstrations, and in spaces such as *bastis* in Dalit dominated localities.

More recently, digitally enabled spaces such as YouTube have developed as crucial sites for performance, as several Shahirs present new videos of their songs, renditions of popular songs by earlier generations of Shahirs, poetry recitations, short films shot on smartphones, poetry recitations, conversations with scholars, and recordings of live performances. Channels by Yalgaar (started in 2016) and Jadhav (started in 2018) draw 5,230 and 13, 600 subscribers, respectively. Through this chapter, with specific focus on these channels, I wish to explore the changing landscape of Ambedkarite music in Maharashtra, in the wake of inroads made by digital media technologies. I take cue from Nick Prior (2018, pp. 3–10), who calls for an exploration of intersections between the sonic and the digital, given how the internet is deeply embedded in musical worlds, from shaping structures of cultural production, to informing our musical tastes. Digital media technologies take music production to new sites, beyond the high walls of high-end studios, offering amateur artists new avenues for expressing subjectivities through good quality content. Styling their music for digital spaces, singers create variegated protest repertoires, drawing upon diverse musical styles such as rock, pop, and mashups.

Moreover, understanding the content and contexts of these Lokshahirs' performances on YouTube, I seek to probe the ways in which sonic articulations of Dalitness in digital spaces posit Dalitness as a united identity of protest. This unifying potential of music becomes especially important when viewed alongside the fragmented domain of Dalit politics in Maharashtra (Wankhede 2019, p. 10). In the region, much like in other parts of the country, caste divisions and rivalries within Dalits run deep, deterring the formation and maintenance of unified anti-caste struggles. Lokshahirs straddle caste divides within the Dalits in Maharashtra, enabling the creation of solidarities across social divides of caste, class, and gender. This chapter shall attempt to understand the same, focusing, in particular, on ways in which Jadhav and Yalgaar appropriate YouTube in their activism. In addition to analyses of select videos on these two channels, I draw upon semi-structured interviews with Jadhav and Yalgaar's founding member, Randive.

## Lokshahiri: Brief Overview

Explicating the history of Lokshahiri, Bhagwan Thakur (2004, pp. 10–22) suggests that Shahiri has roots in the *Tamasha* tradition, stigmatized as "obscene entertainment" by the upper castes and sections among the lower castes. By the late-19th century, the Tamasha came to be radically re-invented as the Satyashodhak Jalsa, as the Satyashodhak Samaj deployed the tradition to spread Phule's thought. Lokshahirs performing during Jalsas sought to inculcate among Bahujan masses a sense of *asmita* (pride), cement solidarity, contest superstition, and challenge the exploitation of lower-castes, peasants, and workers. The Satyashodhak Jalsa prefigured the *Ambedkari Jalsa*, through which Lokshahirs, from the 1930s forward, communicated Ambedkar's message. Subsequently, the tradition grew increasingly prominent, as new generations of Lokshahirs—such as Wamandada Kardak, Annabhau Sathe, and Vitthal Umap—began performing in or from the 1950s, creating new genres of Bhim Geete and Buddha Geete (Rege 2012).[5] Throughout the succeeding decades, Lokshahiri has continued to register its critique through groups such as *Avahan Natya Manch*, and, more recently, the Pune-based troupe, Kabir Kala Manch (KKM), in addition to the Shahirs I examine in this chapter.

Throughout, Lokshahirs' emphasis has been on united resistance. For instance, noted *Ambedkari jalsakar* Keshav Aher posited "jalsa," belonging to all the oppressed, as "jal sa," analogous to water and the equality it exemplifies (Thakur 2004, p. 97). Present-day gatherings at Ambedkarite events are rooted in this longstanding Jalsa tradition. Deborah Matzner (2014, p. 131), focusing on the music performed at these rallies in urban spaces, states that the sonic component of these gatherings—because of their ability to reach far and wide, traversing obstructions and barriers—is perhaps more efficacious than the visual component in announcing Dalit presence to those outside the Dalit community, and claiming belongingness to the city. Arguably, the sonic creates transient aural spaces, enabling coalescence, causing music to cross social divides, just as it crosses physical barriers. Central to these aural spaces, the Lokshahir, as Shahir Nandesh Umap implies in an interview to a news channel, protests against injustice, oppression, and discrimination of any kind, thereby building bridges.[6] The Lokshahir *joins*.

Since the late-2000s, with several singers—particularly those belonging to KKM—facing arrest due to alleged Maoist links, Lokshahirs face an increasingly hostile environment. While these singers are currently out on bail, and repression is a perpetually looming threat, Shahirs continue to perform their radical critique, increasingly turning to digital spaces. Their songs, as ringtones, audio files circulated over WhatsApp, and, most notably, as YouTube videos with views running into thousands, become part of everyday soundscapes. At this juncture, I shall highlight the multiple possibilities created by digital media technologies for Ambedkarite music in Maharashtra.

## Lokshahiri on YouTube: Changing Styles and New Spaces

Scholars (Burgess and Green 2009; Kumar 2016; Prior 2018) writing on digital media technologies vis-à-vis vernacular cultural expressions emphasize the role of users, in addition to that of developers, in shaping the socio-cultural trajectories of technologies. Technological artefacts acquire meaning, as they become part of users' everyday lives, facilitating their interactions with the world. In other words, technologies come to life, as users appropriate them in localized practices, in settings such as basements, living rooms, and studios.[7] Different users approach YouTube with various purposes, and it is mainly through localized appropriations that the platform assumes significance as a participatory culture for its users, getting embedded in their quotidian worlds.

YouTube's importance as a "top-down" platform for disseminating popular culture is apparent in the dominant presence of mainstream cultural institutions, such as Bollywood, on the site. Bollywood has largely produced songs that are escapist in tenor, divorced from contemporary socio-political issues (Kvetko 2009, p. 112). However, concurrently, YouTube is pivotal as a "bottom-up" platform for vernacular creativity, engendering avenues for user-created content which can collectively throw up challenges to hegemonic cultural production as YouTube users express their concerns to distributed audiences. Moreover, with digital technologies becoming accessible, boundaries around cultural expertise grow increasingly permeable, creating ground for the rise of self-sufficient amateur musicians with negligible access to mainstream institutions. Complex machines and spaces that previously imposed financial barriers to production are no longer prerequisites for good quality, with laptops and smartphones increasingly becoming cultural devices capable of generating high-quality content. Music technologies, no longer confined to high-end studios, migrate into the bedrooms of amateur artists, resulting in a proliferation of digital folk cultures. This proliferation is the most apparent on YouTube, where variegated user-generated content circulates through rapidly expanding networks of communication, and ordinary people produce culture with unprecedented energy.

The channels opened by Yalgaar and Charan Jadhav, like those of other singers, can be viewed in this context. While access to mainstream media remains limited, YouTube enables Ambedkarite singers to perform their sonic politics, taking music production to new spaces. To begin with, several videos indicate the ways in which the production of this radical music has become a part of the quotidian. Most of Jadhav's videos are recorded in his room, as he sings to the camera, playing the duff, often looking into his cell-phone to confirm the lyrics he has recently composed. Conveying his process to me in an interview, he said that he composes songs spontaneously. Chaityabhoomi, where he often goes to write his thoughts, is a major source of inspiration, with its immense social-symbolic significance and calm surroundings. Additionally, being an avid consumer of music videos, he mentions that he derives motivation from YouTube videos by other singers/activists, for instance, the popular Warli Revolt song which fuses rap and folk styles. YouTube, embedded in Jadhav's everyday world, enables instantaneous production, circulation, and feedback which comes through comments.

Similarly, numerous videos by Yalgaar are recorded in artists' rooms. Some music videos bring together singers collaborating on the song from geographically dispersed locations. Randive tells me how YouTube became especially significant during the COVID-19 lockdown, as members were able to collaborate on songs and upload their productions, organize conversations with scholars, and stream key cultural programmes taking place in the interiors of Maharashtra on their channel. For instance, the group celebrated "Digital Bhim Jayanti 2020" by presenting a song wherein singers across dispersed locations collaborated on a classic by Wamandada Kardak, *Udharali Koti Kule* (The Community Rises).[8] The video, with 1,573 views, punctuated by images of Wamandada, Ambedkar, and the Buddha, brought together members, who sang parts of the song, placing emphasis on Babasaheb's ideals, from their homes. Images of the song being mixed and mastered digitally, using a digital audio workstation software, are interspersed into the video, giving an insight into the process of production.

These spaces can be considered as part of what William Straw (2004, p. 413) calls a "music scene," facilitated by amateurs through media technologies. Taking shape at the fringes of cultural institutions which cannot absorb clusters of creative energy that permeate urban life, scenes mobilize local energies, bringing together these clusters of social-cultural activities into a space with permeable boundaries. Moreover, while top-down forms of training continue to exist, the cultural wherewithal required for a career in the artistic fields is increasingly accumulated by individuals in the process of moving from the margins to the centre of the music scene. Scenes thereby grow horizontally, and the movement of individuals into and within the scene is assisted by technologies such as YouTube, through which amateurs can express themselves, find like-minded individuals, and expand their social/entrepreneurial activities. Eventually, scenes are defined by a broad coalescence of cultural energies, which generate cultural resources and enable the creation of collective identities.

The Ambedkarite music scene is bolstered, as singers make their way through this scene with the help of digital media technologies. In addition to aiding production, facilitating dissemination, and permitting collaboration, a major motivation underlying the singers' deployment of YouTube is the possibility to widen their reach. While these singers aim to reach all age groups, the youth is a crucial section of the audience. Randive communicated to me that the group's ongoing efforts are oriented primarily towards making content that appeals to the young, as these are sections where divisive political rhetoric has not created rifts yet. In order to connect to wider audiences, especially the youth, concomitant to the rise of digital assertions of Lokshahiri has been the rise of music that infuses Lokshahiri's folk idioms with various styles, such as pop, rock, and rap.

In a recent music video titled *Blue Nation*, Lokshahir Sambhaji Bhagat represents himself as a "Rockshahir." The song, calling for all the oppressed to speak up, fuses elements of pop-rock and Marathi folk, utilizing instruments such as drums, keyboard, guitar, and saxophone, in addition to the *sambhal, dholki*, and *shehnai*.[9] Talking about the need to tailor musical styles to rapidly changing times, Bhagat, in a documentary, says that the Shahir must hold the duff in one hand and the laptop in another.[10] This drive to experiment with modes of expression is implicit in the interviews I conducted with the Shahirs. Jadhav maintains that music exists for experimentation, and folk mediums cannot be held as reified objects of the past to be kept intact in the present. In an interview to *Vice*, Yalgaar members talk about their openness to exploring new ways of presenting their songs, asserting that they do not wish to preserve Lokshahiri by keeping it in museums, and therefore incorporate wide-ranging elements in their music such as qawwali, Western musical styles, guitars, and African instruments.[11] As noted earlier, in the case of Yalgaar's rendition of *Udharali Koti Kule*, the digital audio workstation is indispensable to cultural production at large.

Elaborating on the need to constantly find ways of broadening Lokshahiri's reach, Randive tells me about the group's engagement with aspects such as mashups. To cite an instance, in a video titled *Imagine plus Main Toh Dekhunga Mashup*, group members combine John Lennon's *Imagine* with String's *Main Toh Dekhunga*.[12] Like the Digital Bhim Jayanti, this video too is a collaboration of singers from dispersed locations in the country and beyond. In the description below the video, the group presents the mash-up as their interpretation of these two anthems of hope, and their tribute to dreams of emancipation, freedom, and equality, that hold people together across the globe. They envision the world as a place where boundaries and wars take a backseat and love, peace, and solidarity are prioritized.

Addressing the infusion of Western-inspired styles into radical folk cultural forms, and the role played by "hybrid" performative traditions in reaching wider cross-border audiences, Nadeem Karkabi (2018, p. 174) examines the synthesization of the *Dabke*, a tradition appropriated widely in Palestinian national struggles. She writes that the synthesized "electro-dabke," combining rooted authenticity with cosmopolitan aesthetics, and performing localized and universal sentiments, appeals stylistically to various audiences across the globe, generating international solidarities to the Palestinian struggle. Though coming from a markedly different socio-political context, this illustrates the possibilities of vernacular musical traditions to draw upon diverse stylistic sources and engender synergies that cross social, cultural, and political borders. As mentioned earlier, at the core of Lokshahirs' politics is the need to unite people beyond borders, constructing collective identities of protest.

## Music, Media, and Solidarity

Reflecting on the role played by music in constituting identities, Simon Frith (1966, p. 108–115) argues that the act of composing/performing/listening to music creates an aesthetic experience which requires people to experience themselves in different ways, offering them ways of being in the world and making sense of it. Identities are constructed in the act of participating in the musical experience, as performers (or listeners) become aware of themselves as members of a collective force. Through music, social relationships, collective identities, and solidarities are worked out. Surmising the unifying import of music, Frith holds it to be a space without boundaries, a cultural form best able to cross physical and social borders (Frith 1966, p. 125). Along a similar vein, writing about "black music," Christopher Small (1987, p. 87) argues that African slaves in the United States developed musical performances that affirmed a sense of solidarity, welding experiences of sorrow, despair, and hope into a higher unity.

Music therefore constitutes an ideal domain for creating solidarities. Lokshahirs' music can be seen in this light, as a rallying point for the oppressed across the social divides and political differences that characterize the Dalit community in Maharashtra. Interviews revealed that a key motivation driving the increasing usage of YouTube is the need to cross caste, class, and gender divides, and to create "alternative online worlds of resistance." Noting the centrality of media technologies to solidarities, Manuel Castells (2015, pp. 7–10) and Kaarina Nikunen (2019, p. 26) imply that the media can reinforce a sense of togetherness in struggles against social injustice. Castells argues that digital media, as politically potent mediums of sharing hope and despair across endless networks of interactive communication, are capable of uniting people from diverse socio-cultural, ideological, and political locations. While power hinges on shaping meaning in people's minds through communication, counterpower relies on the same, and can strengthen itself in the digital age. At a societal level, the production of meaning in people's minds, with digitized communication technologies, is effected through mass-self-expression. These technologies allow individuals to express themselves to endless networks of users, creating immense possibilities for dissenting narratives to travel along networks of interactive communication, hence building horizontal solidarities of ordinary people resisting mainstream hegemonic narratives. More importantly, the horizontal networks along which mass self-communication takes place can easily bypass government control, offering participants autonomy vis-à-vis societal institutions (Castells 2015, p. 7).

Nikunen (2019, p. 16) writes on how the media can represent, enhance, and impede a sense of belongingness to communities, as well as a sense of shared commitment to struggles against oppression. YouTube music channels, news, etc. potentially generate and keep alive feelings of solidarity through everyday social media feeds. Also, media events such as concerts and streamed live on YouTube constitute spaces in which participants from diverse social positions build connections to social worlds of other people, and express and reinforce radical collective imaginings of how society should be, and build inclusive imaginaries of the community/nation.[13]

Significantly, Nikunen highlights the polarizing role media can play in constructing exclusionary solidarities, wherein groups exhibit forceful antagonism to "other" groups. A case in point are aggressive ethno-nationalist movements, hinging on nationally bound solidarity and a reified "we" against "them." The democratizing and exclusionary potential of social media is discernible in the intersections between online abuse or *gaali* cultures and political discourse (Udupa 2018, pp. 1514). While abuse opens new lines of political participation, lowering barriers to political debates, also deployed as a gendered political tactic, it seeks to silence dissenting voices, as can be seen in troll attacks on politically vocal women. It is therefore important to view digital media environment as a contested terrain, in which solidarities are enabled, even as they are constrained by aspects such as divisive rhetoric, in addition to commercialization, individualization and fragmented audiences.

## Lokshahiri: Engendering Solidarities

Notwithstanding the aforementioned challenges to solidarities in digital spaces, the inclusionary potential of the internet with regard to Dalit resistance, as a medium that allows Dalits to generate their narratives, constitute the self and the community, build collective memory, contest the silences of mainstream media, circumvent political repression, and make an entry into national discourse, has been well-established by scholars (Nayar 2014, pp. 1–6; Thakur 2019, pp. 360–375; Thirumal and Tartakov 2011, pp. 20–40), Similarly, focusing on digital citizen journalism through the YouTube channel *Dalit Camera*, Paul and Dowling (2018, pp. 1–16) argue that the medium allows ordinary citizens to contribute videos of incidents of caste atrocities, discrimination, and Dalit resistance. They hence address the gaps, silences, and misrepresentations of mainstream media with regard to Dalit lived experiences and politics. The site is therefore a subversive chronicler, an archive, and additionally a source of social integration and network building, as it enables a sense of belongingness to a group whose members have common concerns. Essentially, Paul and Dowling define YouTube as a grassroots online community that can be reinvented as a tool for political resistance.[14]

Recognition of the radical possibilities of the internet is evident in my informants' narratives, and online harassment does not emerge as a threat. The internet is seen as a democratic space where Shahirs can reach wider audiences, allowing freedom of expression to thrive, even as repressive socio-political climates create hinderances in offline worlds. Affirming the same, KKM members Sachin Mali and Sheetal Sathe, after they were released on bail, resumed their activism through YouTube.[15] Banned from performing in certain districts of Maharashtra, facing recurring disruptions by right-wing groups, Mali and Sathe claimed the internet to be a powerful way of fighting oppression, as it could take them everywhere.

Jadhav and Randive talk about the uncongenial circumstances they often face during live performances. Policing, surveillance, obstructions to performance as singers are often not permitted to carry the duff, labels of various kinds (anti-national, Naxalite), and sections of audiences leaving, are common impediments, particularly when Shahirs seek out new spaces beyond their usual performance avenues.[16] Jadhav underlines the importance of digital spaces in this regard, claiming that YouTube takes his songs to every corner, and enables singers to navigate barriers that often hamper live performances. Moreover, he argues that, as a medium that does not recognize socio-political boundaries, YouTube is apt for operationalizing Lokshahirs' cultural aims, which seek to break the rigid social divides which confine people. He further says that, through YouTube, he intends to take his music to all the Dalit castes in Maharashtra, along with women, workers, and all the marginalized.

Dalit leaders have long recognized the importance of building horizontal ties between socially oppressed groups in the region at large. Ambedkar (1989, pp. 112–116) saw the failure of political attempts to build such solidarities as obstructing the eradication of untouchability. Furthermore, antagonisms and caste divisions within Dalit castes in Maharashtra have been noted by scholars (Paik 2007, p. 36; Waghmare 2010, p. 923; Waghmore 2013; Wankhede 2019, p. 12). Even as incidents of atrocities against Dalits spark collective outrage by Dalit organizations, and certain grassroots political-cultural initiatives seek to form collective identities, deep caste divides hinder the formation of a united Dalitness capable of serving as a united identity of protest (Paik 2007, pp. 173–185; Waghmore 2013, p. 9). Apart from occasional state-wide protests, attempts to forge and sustain political solidarities have largely failed. Dalit consciousness has registered itself primarily in non-political spheres, which contain possibilities of comprehensive struggles based on social justice (Wankhede 2019, p. 10).

Against this fragmented socio-political context, Lokshahirs transcend caste divides within Dalits, enable the creation and sustenance of unified struggles against caste inequalities, gender oppression, and labour exploitation, and posit Dalitness as an identity that seeks justice for all the exploited. Commenting on rifts within Dalit castes, Jadhav tells me about monopolization of icons by groups within Dalits. Ambedkar is considered to belong to the Mahars, Annabhau and Lahuji belong to the Matang castes, Ravidas belong to the Charmakars, etc. As a Shahir, akin to other Shahirs, he says that it is his responsibility to establish common ground between these communities, engendering an awareness about the humanist progressive strand that runs across these icons, the values they exemplify, etc., and YouTube comes in handy for the same.

On his channel, Jadhav's compositions make recurring references to progressive anti-caste leaders, thinkers, and poets. Ambedkar is posited as a leader who belongs, not just to the Mahars or any specific caste, but to every oppressed human being. The underlying idea is that Ambedkar should be reclaimed as the force that joins people together in resistance against Brahmanical domination, superstition, and all forms of discrimination. A key example is a song written by Jadhav himself, titled *Gyan Geleli Maansa* (People Who Have Lost Their Ability to Reason), with 4,226 views.[17] Composed after he saw some people performing Hindu rituals in an open space near Chaityabhoomi, this song is a more general interrogation of prevalent religious superstition and fanaticism, which drives people to kill. Jadhav calls upon his listeners to reject the hatred bred by fanaticism, embrace the rational and egalitarian outlook represented by Ambedkar, Jyotiba Phule, and Shivaji, and build solidarity, beyond social divides. The song ends with:

> *Rath Samatecha Odhuya, Mansa mansa la zodua*
> *Gana Bhima cha gaauni*
> *Gana Jyoti cha gaauni*
> *Gana Shivba cha gaauni*
> *Desh navya ne gadhauya ga maaye*
> Let's pull the chariot called equality
> Let's connect people in solidarity
> Singing the song of Bhim
> Singing the song of Jyotiba
> Singing the song of Shivba
> Let's rebuild the idea of India afresh[18]

In yet another song, Jadhav pays a tribute to Annabhau Sathe.[19] Sathe, a Matang Shahir whose ideological orientation straddled the Ambedkarite-Marxist divide, has been projected essentially as a Matang leader (Cybil 2013, p. 61; Naregal 2008). Singing about Annabhau and following up on his intention to popularize the common ground between key icons, Jadhav emphasizes his role in building rich literary resources that contested caste and class inequalities. The song goes on to highlight Annabhau's role in the *Samyukta Maharashtra Movement*, which he held to be a struggle of the working classes against the non-Marathi capital (Rege 2002, p. 1045). Jadhav sings:

*Bedya todlya gulaamichya tyana tadatada*
*Mothya shitafine ladhla toh Maharashtracha ladha*
*Sangato Annabhau tumhi zulmaala bhida*
Breaking the shackles of slavery with a force
He fought skilfully for Maharashtra
Annabahu tells us all, fight against injustice and exploitation

In the comments section below the popular video (with 11,373 views), a sense of solidarity across caste divides is discernible. "Jay Bhim, Jay Annabhau, Jay Lahuji," say several comments. Significantly, this comment—posted by numerous users—appears frequently below videos by several Lokshahirs, conveying a sense of unity across caste divides. Comments are key to the architecture of YouTube, constituting contexts where interactive communication takes place, users mark out their political positions, and political subjectivities take shape (Neumayer 2012, p. 56). Comments under Shahirs' videos give a sense of the unifying potential of these songs. "Let's all unite. Jai Bhim," is another comment appearing under several videos. Under Yalgaar's *Bahujan Hitay, Bahujan Sukhay*, a song presented as "Lockdown Work," a comment says: "Such songs are deeply needed to unite our community. Best wishes, Jai Bhim."[20] This sentiment is evident across comments under Lokshahirs' videos at large.

The need to build cross-caste convergences is noticeable in Yalgaar's sonic repertoire. In addition to Ambedkar Jayanti, the troupe performs regularly at Annabhau Sathe Jayanti. Singing Annabhau's popular song *Jag Badal Ghaluni Ghav* at a performance for the latter, Yalgaar member Siddharth intersperses the song with dialogue.[21] Telling the audience that Ambedkar has named two major enemies of the nation, *Brahmanvad* and *Bhandvalvad* (capitalism), he points out that Annabhau's song conveys the same point:

*Dhanvantanni akhand pilale*
*Dharmandhani tasech chhalale*
*Sangun gele mala Bhimrao*
The rich capitalists exploited us endlessly
The fanatics tortured endlessly
Bhimrao said to me

Echoing Jadhav's aforementioned views on deepening caste divides within Dalits and the appropriation of icons by different communities, Siddharth tells the audience that the present-day situation is such that every *mahapurush*, be it Ambedkar, Annabhau, or Ravidas, has been dragged into the divides between castes. He continues with Annabhau's song:

*Ekjutichya hya rathavarti, aarudh houni chal ba pudhati*
*Nav Maharashtra nirmun jagati, kari prakat nij naav*

Let's all sit on this chariot called solidarity, and move forward
A new India will rise, a new Maharashtra will rise
Giving birth to new affinities

Deploying Annabhau's lyrics, which emphasize solidarity and the need to strengthen ties, the group addresses a contemporary socio-political domain marked by caste divides, interspersing the song with pertinent commentary on the current fragmented political situation. While this video is a recording from a live performance, the group recently presented the performance of a *lok-natya* (folk-drama) written by Annabhau and titled *Aklechi Gosht*, as well as a performative rendition of another of his stories, called *Sapala*, on their channel, all as part of a digital cultural festival marking Annabhau's 100th Birth Anniversary. Implicit in every video is an emphasis on cross-caste solidarity between marginalized communities, which is considered a prerequisite for an egalitarian social order.

In their attempts to build unified struggles, gender issues form a significant part of Lokshahirs' cultural output, in live and digital performances. In this context, it is important to examine the relationship between Ambedkarite music and gender. Significantly, the upper-caste nationalist relegation of caste and women's question to the "cultural" and "private" realm in the late 19th century was challenged by songs of Satyashodhak and Ambedkarite Jalsas. Songs addressed to women disturbed the divide between the social/cultural and political, unsettling upper-caste/middle-class ideals of conjugality and companionate marriage, by prioritizing women's commitment to community over conjugality, seeking access to public space, political representation, etc. (Rege 2013, pp. 13–23). Sheetal Sathe, in an interview to Ajotikar (2018, p. 158), underscores the historical and continuing importance of *Stridasyanta* (end of women's servitude) in the Shahiri tradition.

In a video uploaded on Women's Day, Yalgaar members sing a parody, combining lyrics by poet Puneet Sharma with the tune of popular Hindi film song *Kajra Mohabbat Wala*.[22] They sing:

*Aurat hai Shaheen Baagi, Aisi hai inquilabi*
*Kehta hai saara yeh jahaan, hai re mein tere kurbaan*
*Apne gharon se nikli, aankhon mein khwaab leke*
*Gandhi ne jo sikhlaya, woh inquilab leke*
*Phule ne jo sikhlaya, who inquilab leke*
*Zulmi ke sab zulmon ka saara hisaab leke*
The woman is Shaheen Baagi, she rebels
She makes the world fall in love
She walks out of her house, harbouring dreams in her eyes
Bringing along the revolt taught by Gandhi
And that taught by Phule
Setting out to avenge all the wrongdoings of the bully

The song goes on to critique the Citizenship Amendment Act, 2019 (CAA), against which Yalgaar had actively registered opposition in rallies and demonstrations.

Interestingly, the song subverts the trope of the original song from the late 1960s, which fetishizes femininity. Stressing the role played by women in the anti-CAA protests-and in political demonstrations in general-this song fits squarely within the Lokshahir's broader feminist repertoire. As Sharmila Rege (2013, pp. 13–20) suggests, Shahirs' songs on Ambedkar's relationship with Ramabai throw light on her "invisible" yet major contributions to Ambedkar's political projects, her growing interest in the political movement, and call upon young women to follow. As stated earlier, songs contest Brahminical ideals of marriage, as Ramabai is not projected as an inherently sacrificing wife. She argues with Ambedkar, develops political convictions of her own, and plays a vital political role. Several songs by Lokshahirs on YouTube emphasize the importance of educating women, which is held to be necessary for developing a political consciousness. In a song by Jadhav, intended to be a tribute to his mother, he underlines the role played by her in inculcating Ambedkarite values into his childhood, as she persistently encouraged him to rebel against oppression. Songs highlight efforts taken by Savitribai, Jyotiba, and Lahuji, to educate women, and in videos, images of girls studying at school recur. Gender issues are hence foregrounded as key to anti-caste mobilization.

Furthermore, Lokshahirs' digital mobilization entails music on workers' lived realities, farmers' suicides, and tribal rights. As part of International Workers' Day 2020, Yalgaar presented a week-long series on their channel, aimed at honouring the labour of workers across the world. Talking about ways in which manual workers' everyday lives are affected by their caste and class status, and the low value attributed to their labour, singers critique the government's handling of the migrant crisis in the wake of the pandemic, stating that labourers figure on the margins of national priorities. In the opening video of the series, Pravin Khade, a member, invokes Annabhau's assertion that the earth is not balanced on the head of Vishnu's Sheshnag, it stands on the palm of the workers. This invocation is important, as, aiming at unified struggles against caste and labour exploitation, Annabhau foregrounded workers' concerns, holding Dalits as a distinct class whose labour lies at the socio-cultural foundation of the nation. Emphasizing the commonality of Dalit experiences of suffering, weaving different sub-castes into a Dalit community underlined by shared histories, Sathe provided a platform for all the oppressed (Awad 2004).

Khade goes on to sing Wamandada's *Sanga Amhala Birla Bata Tata Kuthe Aahe ho* (Tell us, where are Birla, Bata and Tata). In the song, Wamandada calls upon the capitalists, Tatas and Birlas, to tell the oppressed where their rightful share of wealth is.[23] Even as he represented the Ambedkarite trend within Shahiri, and was opposed to an alliance with the Communists, Wamandada's compositions called for an annihilation of castes and demanded a redistribution of resources (Rege 2002, p. 1045).

Akin to the series to mark International Worker's Day, taking cue from their antecedent Shahirs and aiming at comprehensive struggles of subaltern communities at large, Randive streamed a live video addressing tribal rights on *Adivasi Din*. Through a series of songs and recitations of poems written by Adivasi poets such as Jacinta Kerketta and the late Abhay Xaxa, Randive presented a sonic-poetic critique of their exoticization in mainstream cultural institutions, their objectification by academia, and of a corporatist development which ignores their livelihoods. Underlining these performances is a call for Adivasi-Dalit-Mazdoor solidarity.[24]

Discernible in Lokshahirs' songs is a definition of "Dalitness" as a united identity of protest, hinging on solidarities of the marginalized. To fully understand the unifying force of these songs, it is essential to get a sense of the significance of "Dalit" as a term that unites the oppressed. Ambedkar's definition of Dalit as a community oppressed by social, economic, cultural and political domination of Brahmanical ideology enabled a unity of ascriptive groups that were victims of discrimination, rather than those who only suffered economic hardship (Paik 2011, p. 228). Shailaja Paik (2011, pp. 228–230), citing narratives from her fieldwork, suggests that the term "Dalit" is not uncontested, because many among the lower castes reject it on grounds that it invokes a past marked by suffering and oppression, which these groups are seeking to escape. However, the term-as a marker of pride and rebellion-has gained widespread currency in Dalit politics, particularly following the rising tide of self-assertion in 1970s. Concomitantly, notions of "Dalitness" have expanded. Gangadhar Pantawane (1986, p. 79), founder-editor of *Asmitadarsh*, asserts that to him, Dalit is a symbol of revolution. As an adherent of humanism, the Dalits reject the existence of god, rebirth, sacred books that preach discrimination, etc., as these have enslaved them. Being a Dalit implies seeking justice for all mankind. The Dalit, as defined by Pantawane, represents every exploited individual in his country.

Presenting the most inclusive definition, the Dalit Panthers posited Scheduled Castes and tribes, Neo-Buddhists, the working people, the landless and poor peasants, women, and all those being exploited politically, economically and in the name of religion, under the all-encompassing category of "Dalit." The Dalit became a mobilizing slogan, including within its ambit all oppressed social groups and thereby forging a "solidarity of the oppressed" (Paik 2011, p. 229). A glance at the content of Shahirs' popular songs, their stated aims on social media and YouTube videos, and their prominent role in the events outlined in this section, reveals that they potentially build solidarities of the oppressed, representing Dalitness akin to Dalit Panthers' formulation of the category.

At this point, it is important to note that the Panthers' all-inclusive definition has been problematized, and wider questions have continually been raised regarding the possibilities of solidarities between Dalits and non-Dalits. Vivek Kumar (2005, pp. 516–517) presents a critique of the umbrella definition, arguing that it elides the specificity of ex-Untouchables' experience of oppression, marked by aggregation of political, economic, and socio-cultural forms of exclusion. Furthermore, Dalit/non-Dalit solidarities cannot neglect the question of "difference," or the ways in which the social context produces the consciousness of caste and class in different ways for Dalits and non-Dalits (Natrajan 2013, p. 16). Aspirations towards unity can often be part of ulterior political motives, with dominant groups making universal knowledge claims, failing to recognize difference, resulting in a silencing of the different knowledge claims that emerge from marginalized groups. Solidarities therefore become homogeneous spaces, glossing over structural inequalities or unequal power relations between different groups within these spaces. Against such a context, solidarities must build common ground, such that differences are acknowledged, even as they are not reified into separate enclaves. Solidarities therefore become spaces for dialogue and understanding, enabling people to articulate differences while working towards building an inclusive "we" (Nikunen 2019, pp. 22–23). The solidarities built by Lokshahirs can be viewed in this context. With repertoires that include songs composed by poets from diverse backgrounds (women, adivasis, workers, etc.), the inclusive spaces they forge are not homogenous. In seeking to build common ground between the marginalized at large, structural differences within the oppressed are not ignored.

## Conclusion

Through content, styles, sites, and contexts of performance, Lokshahirs therefore seek to build bridges across social divides and foment Dalitness as an inclusive identity of resistance. As a medium that can reach far and wide, YouTube offers possibilities to meet the aims of their cultural mobilization. The site also permits the development of an archive of Shahirs' productions. On a YouTube channel, one finds videos recorded by Shahirs throughout the years and across diverse sites. While the Shahirs' homes and rooms are often the locus of production in the digital age, they continually upload video recordings of live performances held at various points. As a result, the trajectories of their cultural politics, and their attempts at creating solidarities, remain documented on their YouTube channels. Moreover, YouTube's role as a social networking site, a comments section for feedback and building contacts, the possibility of finding other singers, poets and activists through the medium, only bolster Shahirs' cultural production.

Cautioning against an uncritical celebration of the internet as a constraint-free space, Shahirs claim that the thriving digital world, where the ideas they oppose flourish, serves as a constant reminder to them, making them aware of the urgency and difficulty of their cultural project. Moreover, as Chopra (2006, pp. 187–189) has argued, Dalit online discourse can mirror the Hindutva discourse, wherein both make claims to belongingness and cultural ownership of the nation on the basis of primordial territorial ownership of the region, rather than the grammar of citizenship. Nevertheless, the internet emerges as germane to Shahirs' artistic/political projects of creating solidarities of the oppressed, and opening dialogue across divisive socio-political forces, including the divisions that often mark progressive movements. It removes significant barriers, allows the performative tradition to reinvent itself, ensures that "Artists Without Borders" (as Yalgaar members represent themselves in a video) are able to reach audiences across social divides, and enables music to fight divisive political discourse. It permits singers to establish a direct link with individual listeners. The internet offers hope that at some point, Shahirs' songs and narratives will be mainstreamed. More importantly, it is considered to be an apposite domain for reaching the youth, whose minds have not been colonized by hatred yet, where these songs need to reach the most. Against a polarized socio-political context, and a fragmented Dalit political arena, Lokshahirs' cultural terrain emerges as a space pregnant with possibilities to build inclusionary narratives of Dalitness. Speaking to the oppressed at large, this music becomes the balm that can heal collective wounds.

## Notes

1 For the performance, see www.youtube.com/watch?v=kPAxcp3BgY0 (Last accessed 9/12/20)
2 For the song by Strings, see www.youtube.com/watch?v=LsyyR2Yo83M (Last accessed on 9/12/20)
3 For the song, see www.youtube.com/watch?v=ujyD746xtiM (Last accessed on 9/12/20)
4 Likewise, in Punjab, a genre of songs by Dalit singers, emerging in response to the dominant Jatt pop music, seeks to challenge narratives of upper-caste hegemony. Singers such as Ginni Mahi, a "YouTube sensation," through their songs, redefine the Dalit self and invest a sense of pride in Dalit identity. For more on this, see https://kractivist.org/the-caste-question-and-songs-of-protest-in-punjab/ (Last accessed on 10/01/21)
5 The *Kalapathaks* where these Shahirs performed were key sites for building solidarities during the Budhhist conversion movement. Buddhist iconography constitutes an important aspect of videos of Shahirs' songs, figuring alongside Ambedkar's photos in several YouTube videos. For more on this see http://sharmilarege.com/resources/Songsters_From_The_Mudhouse-ShramilaRege.pdf (Last accessed on 10/01/21).
6 For more on this, see www.youtube.com/watch?v=iMAEbXZslUQ (Last accessed 10/01/21).
7 It is important to note that these meanings are constrained by factors such as the object's inherent properties, and Prior (2018) cautions against assumptions that technology is open to limitless readings.
8 See www.youtube.com/watch?v=ItNYI6neS78 (Last accessed on 10/01/21).
9 In the song, mentioned at the beginning of this paper, Jai Bhim, representing an egalitarian society, is posited as belonging, not to any particular caste, but to every oppressed person.
10 See www.youtube.com/watch?v=IBjrId7Si6c (Last accessed 11/01/21).
11 The interview can be accessed here www.vice.com/en/article/a34b4j/a-dalit-protest-group-scales-the-walls-of-caste-with-song (Last accessed on 10/12/20)
12 The video, with 2,703 views, is available at www.youtube.com/watch?v=np_lcI1l_iU (Last accessed on 10/12/20)
13 Yalgaar's Aman Ke Rang can be viewed in this context.
14 Dalit Camera, and social media in general, was instrumental in grassroots mobilization during the protests that followed Rohith Vemula's suicide (Thakur 2004, Paul and Dowling 2018).
15 For more on the duo's activism, see www.mumbaitheatreguide.com/dramas/features/17/apr/features-channelising-resistance.asp# (Last accessed 11/12/20)
16 For instance, Yalgaar mentions several instances of disturbances in Maharashtra and beyond, and an incident when their songs caused several upper-caste audience members to leave. Similarly, Jadhav mentions the difficulties he faces when he seeks to take his songs to new avenues, such as the Jijabai Utsav, where he was labelled a "Naxalvadi."
17 This song is especially popular, sung by other Shahirs including Yalgaar, during their programmes. See www.youtube.com/watch?v=RtJK3Hp6ZoY (Last accessed 11/01/21).
18 All the translations in this paper are mine.
19 See www.youtube.com/watch?v=iANihnTcajQ (Last accessed on 11/01/21).

20 See www.youtube.com/watch?v=2nM5zzwR7iQ (Last accessed on 11/01/21).
21 See www.youtube.com/watch?v=uUIiIxlE9bo (Last accessed on 11/01/21)
22 See www.youtube.com/watch?v=GyMzPmgBTkI (Last accessed on 11/01/21).
23 See www.youtube.com/watch?v=MEuFk4LQZ8I (Last accessed 11/01/21)
24 See www.youtube.com/watch?v=de4LHfzTltM (Last accessed 11/01/21)

## Bibliography

Ajotikar, R. (2018) '"Our song impure, our voice polluted": Conversations with activist and musician Shital Sathe', *Feminist Review,* 119, p154–162.

Ambedkar, B.R. (1989) 'Problem of Isolation' in Moon, V., Borale P.T., Phadke B.D., Rege S.S., and Pawar D. (eds.) *Dr. Babasaheb Ambedkar: Writings and Speeches, Vol. 5.* New Delhi: Dr. Ambedkar Foundation, Ministry of Social Justice and Empowerment, Govt. of India, pp. 112–127.

Awad, M. (2004) *Annabhau Sathe's Life and Work: From Marx to Ambedkar.* MPhil Dissertation. Jawaharlal Nehru University.

Burgess, J. and Green, J. (2009) *YouTube: Online Video and Participatory Culture.* 1st edn. Cambridge: Polity Press.

Castells, M. (2015) *Networks of Outrage and Hope: Social Movements in the Internet Age.* 2nd edn. Cambridge: Polity Press.

Chopra, R. (2006) 'Global primordialities: Virtual identity politics in online Hindutva and online Dalit discourse', *New Media and Society*, 8(2), p187–206.

Cybil, K.V. (2013) 'Dalit Humanism, Literature and "Technologies of Deification"', *Economic and Political Weekly*, 48(51), p60–67.

Frith, S. (1966) 'Music and Identity', in Hall, S. and Paul, D.G. (ed.) *Questions of Cultural Identity*. London: Sage Publications, pp. 108–128.

Junghare, I. (1983) 'Songs of the *Mahars*: An Untouchable Caste of Maharashtra', *Ethnomusicology*, 27(2), p271–295.

Karkabi, N. (2018) 'Electro-*Dabke*: Performing Cosmopolitan Nationalism and Borderless Humanity', *Public Culture*, 30(1), p173–196.

Kumar, S. (2016) 'YouTube Nation: Precarity and Agency in India's Online Video Scene', *International Journal of Communication*, 10(2016), p18–29.

Kumar, V. (2005) 'Situating Dalits in Indian Sociology', *Sociological Bulletin*, 54(3), p514–532.

Kvetko, P. (2009) 'Private Music: Individualism, Authenticity and Genre Boundaries in the Bombay Music Industry' in Gokulsing, K.M. and Dissanayake, W. (eds.) *Popular Culture in a Globalised India.* New York: Routledge, pp. 111–125.

Maitreya, Y. (2019) 'From Shahiri to Sahitya', *Economic and Political Weekly*, 54(6), p71.

Matzner, D. (2014) 'Jai Bhim Comrade and the Politics of Sound in Urban Indian Visual Culture', *Visual Anthropology Review*, 30(2), p127–138.

Naregal, V. (2008) 'Marginality, regional forms and state patronage', *Seminar*, 588 [online]. Available at: www.india-seminar.com/2008/588/588_veena_naregal.htm (Accessed: 15 March 2019)

Natrajan, B. (2013) 'Punctuated Solidarities: Caste and Left Politics', *Economic and Political Weekly*, XLVIII(6), p16–19.

Nayar, P. (2014) 'The Digital Dalit: Subalternity and Cyberspace', *The Sri Lanka Journal of the Humanities*, XXXVII(1), p1–6.

Neumayer, C. (2012) 'Which Alternative? A Critical Analysis of YouTube Comments in Anti-Fascist Protest', *tripleC: Communication, Capitalism* and *Critique*, 10(1), p56–65.

Nikunen, K (2019) *Media Solidarities: Emotions, Power and Justice in the Digital Age*. 1st edn. London: Sage.

Masroor, Z. (2018) *A Dalit Protest Group Scales the Walls of Caste with Song* {Online}. Available at: www.vice.com/en/article/a34b4j/a-dalit-protest-group-scales-the-walls-of-caste-with-song (Accessed: 12 May 2021)

Paik, Shailaja. (2007) *Daughters of the Lesser God: Dalit Women's Education in Postcolonial Pune*. PhD Dissertation. University of Warwick.

Paik, Shailaja. (2011) 'Mahar-Dalit-Buddhist: The History and Politics of Naming in Maharashtra', *Contributions to Indian Sociology*, 45(2), p217–241.

Pantawane, G. (1986) 'Evolving a New Identity: The Development of a Dalit Culture' in Joshi, B.R. (ed.) *Untouchable!: Voices of the Dalit Liberation Movement*. London: Zed Books, pp. 79–87.

Paul, S. and David D. (2018) 'Digital Archiving as Social Protest', *Digital Journalism*, 6(9), p1–16.

Prior, N. (2010) 'The Rise of the New Amateurs: Popular Music, Digital Technology and the Fate of Cultural Production' in Hall, J.R., Grindstaff, L. and Lo, M. (eds.) *Handbook of Cultural Sociology*. London: Routledge, pp. 398–407.

Prior, N. (2018) *Popular Music: Digital Technology and Society*. 1st edn. London: Sage Publications.

Rege, S. (2002) 'Conceptualising Popular Culture: "Lavani" and "Powada" in Maharashtra', *Economic and Political Weekly*, 37(11), p1038–1047.

Rege, S. (2008) 'Interrogating the Thesis of "Irrational Deification"', *Economic and Political Weekly*, 43(7), p16–20.

Rege, S. (2012) *Songsters from the Mudhouse* [Online]. Available at: http://sharmilarege.com/resources/Songsters_From_The_Mudhouse-ShramilaRege.pdf (Accessed: 10 January 2021)

Rege, S. (2013) 'Introduction' in Rege, S. (ed.) *Against the Madness of Manu: B.R. Ambedkar's Writings on Brahmanical Patriarchy*. New Delhi: Navayana, pp. 13–56.

Small, C. (1987) *Music of the Common Tongue*. 1st edn. London: Calder Press.

Straw, W. (2004) 'Cultural Scenes', *Society and Leisure*, 27(2), p411–422.

Thakur, B. (2004) *Ambedkari Jalse*. 1st edn. Pune: Sugava Prakashan.

Thakur, A. (2019) 'New Media and the Dalit Counter-public Sphere', *Television and New Media*, 21(4), p360–75.

Thirumal, P and Tartakov, G.M. (2011) 'India's Dalits Search for a Democratic Opening in the Digital Divide' in Leigh, P.R. (ed.) *International Exploration of Technology Equity and the Digital Divide: Critical, Historical and Social Perspectives*. New York: Hershey, pp. 20–40.

Udupa, S. (2018) 'Gaali cultures: The politics of abusive exchange on social media', *New Media and Society*, 20(4), p1506–1522.

Waghmare, B.S. (2010) 'Reservation Policy and the Plight of Matangs in Maharashtra', *The Indian Journal of Political Science*, 71(3), p923–946.

Waghmore, S. (2013) *Civility Against Caste: Dalit Politics and Citizenship in Western India*. 1st edn. New Delhi: Sage Publications.

Wankhede, H. (2019) 'The Post-political Dalit Movement in Maharashtra', *Economic and Political Weekly*, 54(36), pp10–14.

Zelliot, E. (1995) 'The Folklore of Pride: Three Components of Contemporary Dalit Belief' in Sontheimer, G. (ed.) *Maharashtra: Culture and Society: Folk Culture, Folk Religion and Oral Traditions as a Component in Maharashtrian Culture*. New Delhi: Manohar Books, pp. 63–85.

# 20

# ENCOUNTERING THE DIGITAL IN FOLK SONGS AND ORAL HISTORY

## Tracing the History and Memory of Migration of Tea Plantation Labour Through Jhumur Songs*

*Devika Singh Shekhawat*

Music, when it speaks to us, often speaks for itself and takes us on a journey through space and time. The time, space, matter, and circumstances from which songs and music come are never really static and are always making and unmaking themselves—but what remains an interesting insight is the changes and unfolding of time, which bring about a change in the very fabric of social, everyday, and lived realities. These changes, upheavals, and the process of making and unmaking come to work in the ruptures of the social fabric, and it is in these fault lines that life truly comes to take meaning. It is in these fault lines of history that music is created and comes to life. Music takes a form and a life which tells a lot about living in a particular moment of time. The endless possibility of making music in a deeply fragmented society gives music the power to express and mobilize. *Jhumur* songs, which tell us so much about the making and unmaking of tea plantation workers, is one such genre of music which this chapter explores.

Tea plantations in Assam, much like in the rest of the world, were built on exploitative relations in the process of production. The social life of a tea plantation, its cultural realm, and the relational ties within it are built on the relations of power which play out in the tea estates. The historical trajectory of tea has a plethora of fragmented, violent, contradictory, and ambiguous histories. The Indian subcontinent, what is now the state of Assam, was one of the first sites of tea production. Tea is consumed in more than 100 countries, and India is one of the largest producers and consumers of tea in the world. Assam is the largest tea-producing state in India and contributes about 60% of the total production of tea in the country. Tea is an important agro-industry in Assam, which contributes to the state's economy.

"The romance of Assam is a romance of commerce, the history of a savage country brought under civilized rule through the cultivation, by alien labour, of a single product," wrote a European traveller in 1906 (Gupta 1986). Complex

DOI: 10.4324/9781003354246-26

processes of colonialism, imperialism, dispossession, the circulation of global capital, exploitation, resistance, local cultural formations, and contestations all make what is known as "Assam's Cup of Tea." Vast tracts of "virgin" forests in Assam were destroyed under the Waste Land Acts of 1838, after the official "discovery" of tea in December 1834 to make way for the establishment of the empire's glorious gardens through an endemic vision of conquest. The Indigenous tea plants that grew wildly to a height of 30 metres in Assam were tamed, ordered, and disciplined by the superior knowledge of Victorian science and experimentation for large-scale commercial cultivation and production for a global market, through which the British sought to break the Chinese monopoly on the ever-growing market for tea. The British enterprise of converting Assam from a seemingly wild, jungle-laden frontier with "primitive" practices of commerce and agriculture into an export-oriented tea industry built on "modern" ideals of "improvement," "advancement," and "progress" changed the physical and socioeconomic landscape of Assam forever (Gupta 1986). The abysmally low wages offered in the tea industry, in a context of a highly favourable land to man ratio and land fertility, meant that the colonial enterprise was unable to procure much participation of "local" labour for work in the plantations despite a number of measures which negatively affected agricultural populations. The locals came to be stigmatized as "lazy," "opium-addicted" masses disinterested in "economic advancement." The British employed local Kachari and Naga labour, but they came to be considered "rebellious" and difficult to retain due to proximity to their homeland or agricultural lands. By the 1860s, frustrated in its efforts to procure local labour, the tea enterprise, in collusion with the colonial state, started a quest for immigrant labour that was cheap, consistent, "docile," and easily "disciplined." Lured with promises of light work in "beautiful," "green" gardens, thousands of predominantly tribal migrants from across labour catchment areas in India were transported in inhuman conditions to Assam beginning in the mid-19th century. This continued for almost a century by a network of "legal," "para-legal," and "illegal" agents and actors engaged in various nefarious forms of coercion and outright violence (Behal 2014).

Migration by different communities in the recent past, such as the Nepalis and the different tea tribes, transformed Assam's socio-cultural terrain. According to Gogoi (1991), the tea garden community, composed of 100 sub-tribes, has added a new dimension to the cultural landscape of the region. Thus, a prolonged period of close contact and togetherness among the variegated cultural groups and their socio-cultural relationships, whether inter-tribal or tribal and non-tribal, helped in developing an integrated culture in Assam. The culture and livelihood of tea plantation workers and tea tribes, from whom *Jhumur* folk songs come, have a rich and dynamic existence in terms of religion, language, songs, dances, rituals, and numerous customs. In this context, the *Jhumur* folk culture can be perceived as a composite culture, and so is the wonderful folk musical repertoire that has grown around it. Though the term Assamese folk music refers to a single, obviously identifiable phenomenon, it is marked by diversity contributed to by various groups and communities and different regions. The regional diversities in music's traditions, too, have lent an exclusive dimension to Assamese folk music (Minakshi 2007).

*Jhumur* folk songs, as a genre, reflect a multiplicity of expressions and heterogeneous elements, which intermingle harmoniously. They reflect tribal and ethnic influences and also hint at affinities with their culture and music which might have been the result of socio-cultural, religious exchanges and social ties. As observed by Datta (1994), "tribal and non-tribal, the acculturated and the assimilated, the sanskritised and non-sanskritised, all coexisting in a remarkable state of juxtaposition."

*Jhumur* is one of the most famous dance forms of Assam. *Jhumur nach* is mainly performed by the tea tribes during the autumn season when they wish to take a break from their daily schedules, and during special festivals, too. During celebrations, and when communities come together, are the times when *Jhumur* is performed. *Jhumur* dances and songs now hold a very important and lively place in Assamese folk-cultural tradition, and they have even found their way into popular culture, with new *Jhumur* songs and remixes being released every other year. Performing *Jhumur* songs and dances has been a lively tradition in the identity of the tea tribes of Assam. The striking thing about the *Jhumur* dance is its steps, which are synchronized with *madal*, a popular two-headed hand drum. Accompanying the drum is a flute and pair of *taals* which help make the music more harmonious. During the dance, the dancers clasp each other's waists while following the precision of their footwork.

There are over 800 tea estates in Assam, and in each one of them *Jhumur nach* is performed on special occasions and festivals. *Jhumur nach* can be easily recognized by the costumes worn by the dancers, as they are quite different from the regular traditional costumes of the different tribal and ethnic groups of Assam. The male members wear long, traditional dresses, and women wear white sarees with broad red borders which end right above their ankles. The dresses are simple yet colourful, the songs full of melody and electrifying joy and energy. The range of themes covered in *Jhumur* songs has grown and expanded, but the essence of love, life, and all that comes with it are what one finds in *Jhumur* songs. Digging a little deeper into these songs and closely engaging with certain themes that these songs bring to life, and unravelling the fissures in the lives of tea plantation workers, tells us a lot about the lives of tea plantation workers and how a history of migration and exploitative labour relations mark their lives.

Kali Dasgupta, a renowned cultural activist who started his political involvement in India's independence struggle, built and worked for highlighting and challenging socioeconomic disparities in society and struggled against the feudal and political oppression of people during his years as an activist. The folk songs that Kali Dasgupta often performed and documented subtly yet resiliently bring questions of power and oppression to light with a tinge of softness as these songs dwell on the everyday experiences of those left at the margins of society. They also highlight people's love, life, desires, sufferings, and hardships. In the later part of his life, Kali Dasgupta travelled through England and the United States and shared his worldview and songs from the Assam valley with different people as he continued teaching and performing with his *dotara* (a four-stringed plucked instrument) and his *ektara* (a one-stringed instrument made of gourd). Kali Dasgupta's work brought Assam's folk music, especially *Jhumur* music, to the forefront, and gave it a new life and recognition as resistance music.

*Jhumur* songs are often not remembered as songs of resistance, but the varied themes which encompass *Jhumur* songs carry the spirit of resistance in the questions they raise about labour and the relationality of exploitation and oppression, which exist in the everyday lives of tea plantation workers. As Kali Dasgupta collected folk songs, especially *Jhumur* songs, he documented and highlighted the themes and expressions of work, life, love, oppression, and resistance that we find in these songs (Gregory 2001).

*Jhumur* songs have a dynamic personality of their own, and many including Kali Dasgupta have come to see them in their dynamism. Ethnographic work and different narratives and stories about tea gardens narrate the tales of womenfolk plucking tea in the tea gardens under the blue sky and singing *Jhumur* songs as they lift their spirit. The songs help them work hard, and smile with a sense of togetherness. Work or labour forms an inseparable part of folk life, and the songs associated with the working process are considered work songs. The origin and development of folk songs has been attributed to the productive and labouring process. Eminent folklorists and social scientists opine that men in the ancient time depended on magical acts and chanting to succeed in their work, and these prayers and chants were performed along with magical dances and songs now turned into folk songs (Goswami 1983). Traditional work songs are an attempt to reduce the drudgery during hard work, or to make the work process easier. They are created or sung by the workers with an intent of increasing their efficiency by timing the work, setting a steady work pace, or whiling away the tedium of the working hours (Brakeley 1984).

Records of work songs are roughly as old as historical records, and anthropological evidence suggests that all agrarian societies had work songs. According to Gioia (2006), work songs include both songs sung while working and songs about work, since the two are seen as interconnected. Referring to the comprehensiveness of folk songs, Biswas (2014) observes that folk music, in totality, is both the music of a toiling life and the desire for labour, and, when detached from labour and the fruits of labour, the music loses its character. He also observes that most of the love songs are indirectly associated with the cultivation process and magical imagination—even today—as they are deeply connected to the broader processes of production, fertility, work, and love. Hence, to cluster the songs having direct reference to work, or containing the rhythms of work, as work songs is erroneous as well as unscientific. The occupational pattern of the common folk songs of Assam, both tribal and non-tribal, is mostly associated with agriculture and other functions related to the field. Jhumur songs also find a place in such expressions. The work songs of Assam are mostly associated with the process of cultivation and also with some works such as fishing, boating, weaving, cow herding, and rice pounding. Jhumur songs much like Bihu songs of Assam exhibit the inseparable aspects of love, labour, and agricultural production, and they resonate with the rhythms of work, love, and nature. The *Ban ghoxas* are the songs of the cowherds, representing the wild expressions of young hearts in amorous language. The *Moishal* and *Maut* songs are associated with the occupations of buffalo herding and the elephant catching, reflecting the struggles of work life, and at the same time their agonizing experiences generated in the lovelorn hearts' (Minakshi 2007).

Thus, there are numerous categories of folk songs, associated with particular occupations or work representing different aspects of common human life. *Jhumur* songs also find a place in such expressions along with holding an important place in history as an oral tradition which tells the story of a community which has been long forgotten and sidelined. Listening closely to some of these songs gives a chance to trace the immersions of memory, migration, and nature of work in the songs and music.

The story of Assam tea and Assam tea plantation labourers, as remembered in *Jhumur* songs, keeps alive the memory of all that has shaped history and continues to unfold for the workers. Assam tea tribes' *Jhumur* songs often tell the story of tea garden workers, their history, their relation to the work that they do, and to the state of Assam. In a seamless manner, they tell the story of what this life means to the labourers, and lay out the history of tea plantations in Assam, tracing their origins to the colonial administration and providing a chance to listen to and understand how these memories live on in the tea tribes of Assam. Lending a close ear to these songs opens up horizons for understanding the gendered dimension of this history and analysing how female workers are placed in history and memory.

## An Analysis of Some *Jhumur* Songs

The popular *Jhumur* song *Ranchi che bhejali kuli* is from the tea plantations in Assam, which was documented by cultural activist Kali Dasgupta in the 1960s. This song provides a piercing glimpse of the universe and experiences of coolies on plantations in Assam.

*1*

*RANCHI CHE BHEJALI KULI*
*Rachi che bhejal kuli*
*Dedalai kalam churi Dale,*
*Dale Babu Nazara bhaithaise*
*laxe laxe laxe re Dale,*
*Dale Babu Nazara bhathaise*
*Kur mara chalak chuluk*
*Pata tula dogi dog*
*Aina dekhi khupa bandhe Ure je kapoor re*
*Rachi che bhejal kuli*
*Dedalai kalam churi*

*Rode barxhane maya pata ke Tulane*
*laxe laxe laxe re Dale*

Translation:

*FROM RANCHI WAS SENT THE COOLIE*

From Ranchi, was sent the coolie
And handed *kalam* knives
On every tree, on every branch
The babu places a gaze.
Slowly and slowly
On every tree, on every branch
The babu places a gaze.
Dig the earth in earnest haze
Pluck the leaves in haste.
Looking at the mirror
She ties her bun and drapes her cloth.
From Ranchi, was sent the coolie
And handed *kalam* knives.
Through the sunlight, through the rains
We are made to pluck leaves.

The song *Ranchi che bhejali kuli* is a famous *Jhumur* song, which takes us on a journey through the life of a tea plantation labourer who is brought to Assam to work on the plantation but cannot rest. The song captures the pulse of migration under the Colonial Raj and expresses the helplessness that the worker feels and is trapped in. This fear and helpless state find articulation as lines in the song point out that, if the coolie is not able to pick two leaves and a bud correctly, he will be beaten. The coolie curses the contractor who brought him to Assam. The song captures the loss of his freedom, and a longing for an end to the abyss that has become his life. The history of migration, and the bringing of indentured labour from the labour catchment areas of what is present-day Bihar, Jharkhand, Bengal, and Odisha, is now well documented, researched, and studied. But what remains interesting is that, as the forces of oppression were tightening their grip and countless workers were being made to travel to unknown land under false promises and hopes of a better life, it was through songs and music that the migrants' memories and experiences found expression and a voice, both of which live on to this day.

Not much has changed for the tea plantation workers today: the songs and their meaning still find resonance in the conditions of work and life of tea plantation workers. The *kalam* knives talked about in the song *Ranchi che bhejali kuli* are still very much a part of the lives of tea plantation workers, as they are often used for pruning the tea bushes and giving them the shape the manager wants.

The *nazar* of the *babu* on every move that the workers make comes to highlight the surveillance and constant check kept on them. In the tea plantations of Assam, the management negotiates and controls workers' conduct. The very need and nature of controlling the workers becomes excessively important for a tea plantation unit in maintaining its exploitative relations. Here, the conduct of the population, and relations of servitude, get established through an age-old, tried-and-tested system of regular checks on the lives of the workers, encompassing their movements, their livelihoods, and their relations. There is a constant check through the wandering eye of the manager, who monitors their movements and works through a system of reportage, punishment, and wage cuts. With such a stringent system in place, the workers find it difficult to live a life where their every move is not geared towards adding value to the production process, or even adding surplus. The song captures the multiple layers of control exercised on the worker. As workers try to live their lives, they are heavily scrutinized when they are seen walking near the plantation area, grazing their cattle, by the division-in-charge, and have to hear an earful from the manager, who also punishes repeat offenders by cutting their wages or, at times, even cutting their names from the list of permanent workers and shifting them to the temporary workers list. The looming eye or the babu's *nazar* remains a constant in the song *Ranchi che bhejali kuli*. The *chowkidars* and *sardars* who work as the guards, and are often appointed from among the workers, discipline the workers and bring them in for plucking, pruning, pesticide spraying, and irrigation. An intricate system of "surveillance raj" has been established for servitude, and this finds a voice in *Jhumur* songs.

The *kuli* in the song laments and recites the hardships of work and the monotonous and continuous nature of work, which includes pruning of tea bushes, digging the earth, and plucking leaves all day under the hot sun and in the rain. The song paints a picture of a woman *kuli* who ties her hair in a bun and drapes her work cloth around her waist as she works in the tea garden for long hours. A sense of alienation comes across in the last few lines of the song, as engaging in routine work over days and getting ready in work clothes is described in a lonesome, wearisome fashion, reflecting a worker who isn't just alienated from work but also from oneself. The *kuli* sings and laments her fate. The memory of migration and the plight of tea plantation workers finds articulation and expression in this song. *Jhumur* songs sung, performed, and enshrined in memory tell the story of workers who are often forgotten, sidelined, and marginalized.

The song *Chol Mini Assam Jabo* is a very popular folk song of Assam. Often remembered as a *Jhumur* song, it is also recognized as a Domkoich song which has gained massive popularity over the years, finding a place in popular films, music videos, protest gatherings, and remix versions, and has been sung throughout time. Kali Dasgupta also sang, documented, and performed the song, and so have different artists, cultural activists, and scores of other people. Every time the song is sung, it seems to gain a new life, and the sweet melodies of *Chol Mini Assam jabo* echo in a timeless fashion. A sense of sweetness remains attached to the tunes of the song as it explores themes of migrations, memories of loss and betrayal, and the hardships of working conditions in a tea garden which lies tucked away in the promised green land of Assam.

*2*

*CHOL MINI ASSAM JABO*
*Chol Mini Assam jabo*
*Deshe boro dukh re*
*Assam deshe re Mini*
*Chaa bagan horiya*
*Hor mara jaimon taimon*
*Pata tola taan bo*
*Hai joduram*
*Phaki diye cholai di assam*
*Eek poisar potima*
*Gaya golai tail go*
*Minie papa mangee Jodi*
*Aare dibo jhol ko*
*Sardar bole kaame kaam*
*Babu bole dhori aan*
*Sahib bulelibo pither chaal*
*Hai joduram*
*Phaki diye cholai di assam*

Translation:

Come Mini, we'll go to Assam
Misery abounds in our Desh
In Assam, my dear Mini
The tea-gardens are green and beautiful
There lies our future
The heavy digging is done somehow
Plucking leaves is very difficult
Oh Joduram!
You lied to us
And sent us to Assam
You fooled us
And lured us to Assam
It is difficult to earn one paisa
Just fetch some oil from the Marwari trader's shop
If Mini's father asks
He will get some more fish curry
The children are crying here and there
There is no water in the vessel

The menfolk, o ranjha
Are playing the murali
Sardar says "Work work!"
Babu says "Catch them"
Sahib says "Whip them hard"
Oh Joduram! You fooled
And brought us to Assam

The tea industry is highly labour-intensive, has a long history rooted in colonialism, and is well known for its exploitative working conditions. A tea plantation does not require many skilled workers, as the bulk of the work centres around plucking tea leaves. Tea-pluckers constitute nine-tenths of the total workforce. Plucking is mostly done by women workers; the strength of women labourers in a tea garden is almost equal to, and even surpasses, that of men (Kaniampady 2003). Till today, tea estates function with various dynamics of relationality that the workers share with the management, each other, and the increasingly seamless—yet oftentimes invisible—relations with the outside world. Various processes make and produce the labouring body, and the workers make and unmake a lot around them. A tea estate works as a unit of production, and the socioeconomic and cultural lives of the workers are tied to and controlled by this unit. The socioeconomic lives of those who live on the estates are closely related to production. The wages that the workers receive, the housing and sanitation facilities provided for them, the medical facilities in tea estates, ration provisions, provision of electricity and firewood, and permission for entertainment and cultural programs all come under the surveillance and control of the estate's management. The accessibility of resources and even the basic mobility of workers are all controlled by the production process. The management of the tea estates tries to control all aspects of workers' lives. The structures and relations of production configure the workplace, and that, in turn, frames the workers' lives. Power, and the process of production, operate at the everyday level—directly on the body of the worker, not just as exploitation of labour and appropriation of labour power, but also as a tool for managing social reproduction through the creation of chains of dependence and ensuring intergenerational servitude. The complex web of these relations, so often theorized and analysed in countless books and articles, finds expression in the popular *Jhumur* song *Chol Mini Assam Jabo*. The song highlights the history of migration and the painful memory of that migration when workers were tricked, promised, and lured to the green fields of Assam and brought in through the *joduram* or the agent of the colonial administration. The promises of a hopeful future in green tea gardens turn out to be lies, as the workers work tirelessly in the fields and dig the soil and pluck the leaves all through the day, all while under constant surveillance: the sahib (the manager) emphasizes that they need to work endlessly; the *babu*, or the clerk, takes on the responsibility of "catching" them and making sure that they don't run away; and the *sardar*, who is the division in charge, punishes and keeps them in check. The carefully crafted system of surveillance and servitude works to keep a complete check on the workers.

The everyday experiences of work, the journey to the wrenched green fields, and the everyday experiences of the workers find expression in the song. The experiences of the workers as they negotiate survival through attempts at procuring oil from the local Marwari trader's shop, or the hope that Mini's father might be able to come by some food and barter some fish for curry, are all highlighted in the song. These are narrations of life experiences, as the worker tells a lot about the lives that the workers carve out and the relations that are forged between communities. The Marwari's shop, which in the context of tea plantations in Assam has been looked at as a supplier of goods and services to the management as well as the labourers, seems to have long-standing ties with the tea estate community, and is mentioned in the song for the establishment of material relationality. The song paints a picture of life in the tea gardens, with the men folk playing the *murali* as water vessels lie empty. The song seamlessly brings out the different relations that a worker shares with the world, be it with the colonial administration and its agents, who have trapped him into servitude, the marwari shopkeeper from whom he buys some oil and some food, and, of course, the other workers who share the uncertainties that have become a part of life in the tea gardens as they play the *murali* and sing *Jhumur* songs together. Interestingly this song is massively popular in films, music, and cultural activism, and it remains rooted in the tea gardens' culture, as till today, women plucking tea leaves sing this song together as a symphony.

The complex history of migration and exploitation finds expression in *Jhumur* songs. *Axom deshor bagisare sowali* (the girl from the tea gardens of Assam) is a song from the national award-winning, mid-1960s Assamese movie *Saameli Memsahab*. The song is essentially remembered as a *Jhumur* song. In the song, a young girl named Saameli points to the complexities of her history and location; she has never known the land her ancestors came from, but does remember and experience the brutal surveillance and violence of the "Planter Raj." The song beautifully captures the complex history of migration of tea plantation labourers through memory, music, songs, folktales, oral history, and narratives. The history and narrative of *bagisare sowali* (the girl from the tea gardens of Assam) trace the intense and complex history of migration through cultural narratives that remain alive till today. These cultural narratives help understand the memories of migration and labour relations that remain alive in *Jhumur* songs, folktales, and oral narratives.

*3*

*AXOM BEKHOR BAAGISAARE SOWALI*
*Axom dekhor baagisaare sowali,*
*Jhumur tumur nassi koru dhemali*
*Hei Laxmi nohoi mure naam Saameli*
*Shiris paale dhorbi paahi*
*Paata lamba paabi buli*

*Naake pindhi naake phuli*
*Juwaan bulaali*
*Hei Sampaa nohoi mure naam Saameli*
*Choto choto chokori*
*Boro boro tokori*
*Morom abuj paatot tole dok dok*
*Jowaan bazar raakhide kore lok lok*
*Choto choto bowkhanaa kore dhok dhok*
*Ki bhaabes ore aamak chaheli*
*Mone raakh mur naam Saameli*
*Baap dada aasile kunuba mulukor*
*Sei aami bihu gaabo jaanu*
*Aaare paagli*
*Paagli nohoi mure naam Saameli*
*Birbolor beti mur naam Saameli*
*Axom dekhot aami phuru umoli*
*Sardar bole kaam kaam*
*Babu bole dhori aan*
*Sahib bulelibo pither chaal*
*O bideshi shaam*
*Phaaki diye aanilu Assam*

Translation:

I am a girl from the Gardens of Assam
Dancing *Jhumur*
in joyous glee,
No, my name is not Laksmee
I am Saameli.
I have pretty eyes and
Beautiful long legs that can run,
Wearing a nose-ring
I joyously dance in glee.
As the young young girls
Walk with their huge huge baskets,
they pluck tea leaves
The tender dry leaves
Rustle under their feet.
They are all my friends
Remember, my name is Saameli!
My forefathers came from
Some *muluk*
I don't know,
However, I have learnt now

To perform the Bihu dance.
"Aaaaare Paagli"
My name is not Paagli, I am Saameli
Birbal's daughter I am Saameli
I roam free and in glee though Assam
Sardar says "Work work"
Babu says "Catch them"
The Saheb says "Whip them"
Oh! You Bideshi,
you tricked and brought us to Assam!

The film *Saameli Memsaab* won the national award in 1975. It revolves around the love story of a British tea plantation manager and a tea garden worker. The film brings to the forefront complex historical dynamics and forces that have come to characterize female labour in tea plantations. In the video of the very famous song *Axom deshor bagisare sowali*, Saameli, the protagonist of the film, is seen with long black, flowing hair, dancing in joyous abandon, as she marks her difference as Saameli, versus the Hindu-equivalent-name, *Laksmee*. When she does a *Jhumur* dance, she asserts her Adivasi identity and culture. She also indicates her complicated relationship with her Assamese identity and nationalism when she confesses that she learnt to perform the Assamese folk dance *bihu*. She points to the complexity of her history and location, where she has never known the land her ancestors came from, but does remember and experience the brutal surveillance and violence of the "Planter Raj." She reiterates this in the last lines of the song, an excerpt taken from the popular *Jhumur* folk song *Chol Mini Assam jabo*.

However, even this apparently progressive film, whose music was directed by the legendary Bhupen Hazarika, comes to invisibilize Saameli's gendered labour, marking her as a sexualized subject, where desire is located in the construction of her "wild," "carefree," "simple," and almost "child-like" nature. Such a portrayal obscures the brutal history of exploitation of women plantation workers. Her *Jhumur* dance is not as much located in a subaltern culture as it is marked by a racialized and sexualized gaze—the same gaze that has historically characterized the imagery of her "nimble" fingers, on which depended the tremendous profit of one of history's most sought-after imperial products. The song brings to light, and at the same time invisibles, the context of the indentured labour which characterized labour control in the colonial world, including in the development of the tea industry in Assam. It erases the specific context of Assam's tea plantations and the processes and mechanisms of surplus labour extraction borne by women tea plantation workers, even though it retains Saameli's assertive manner, where she time and again clarifies that her name is not *Chameli*, or *Laksmee*, or *Pagali*, but Saameli. The song beautifully captures the history of migration, as Saameli sings that she does not remember where she comes from, but now finds herself in Assam and calls it her *desh*. She does not know or remember where her forefathers came from, but she is now a part of Assam and performs *bihu* with glee.

Saameli's invisiblization, in terms of her labour, provides glimpses of the nameless women workers, with bamboo baskets on their shoulders, looking up as they pluck the tea leaves to give a shy smile to the camera. These women, and their likenesses seemingly adorn all of Assam and Northeast India's tourism advertisements. Women pluckers never directly speak themselves; they are present solely in their absence. Their voices resound only through the gaps and the silences, through the fissures and the omissions, from the margins of non-existence. This borrowed existence comes through even in the two songs *Ranchi che bhejali kuli* and *Chol Mini Assam jabo*, where women workers who make up a major part of the workforce in tea gardens do not find a voice, but stay as silent entities, as women who tie their hair in buns and drape work clothes to go to work in *Ranchi che bhejali kuli*, or they remain a distant someone who is called upon as the cooli's journey is recited in *chol Mini Assam jabo*. The existence of women workers is a tussle where they might not have a voice but are important characters when the story of tea and all that comes with it is told in *Jhumur* songs. The woman is the eroticized, gendered labour, plucking the "world's sweetest leaves." She is one of those nameless people who colonial archives classify as "Class 1 Junglies," sought-after labour which was cheap, docile, industrious, easily reproducible, and thus enough to sustain the "Planter Raj."

The song *bagisare sowali* and its relation to production brings forth important questions about the processes of racialization and "otherness" seen through Saameli's character. She is portrayed as someone who is a "wild" Adivasi, *junglee* girl, not quite suited for the British Sahib. The feminisation of the commodity and fetishization of the female labourer, which operates in various complex and enmeshed ways to produce the feudal patronage system of the "Planter Raj," comes out starkly in the song, which is often sung and performed as a *Jhumur* song.

In some ways, the categorization of what actually makes *Jhumur* songs does not remain a static, well-defined category. It gets enmeshed in what comes through and gains recognition as *Jhumur* songs, but is often something which tells a story of the tea gardens of Assam and is reborn in remixes and popular culture or in what is sung, performed, and lives in the workers' memories. What remains true is that these songs allow us to understand the past in a way that colonial archives often do not. Songs, poems, oral narratives, and stories have lived through all these years; they talk about the varied experiences of tea garden workers and keep alive the experiences of migration and its inherent links to exploitation.

*Jhumur* songs of the Assam tea tribes have often told the story of tea plantation workers, their histories, the relation to the work they do, and to the state of Assam. They explore the dynamics of the system of colonial control and exploitation in the tea plantations of Assam through the memory of the migration of indentured labour (from the hills of the Chota Nagpur area to the green fields of Assam), and in the work environment of the system of "Planter Raj" of the colonial era that the workers had to endure. It engages with the long-forgotten history of workers in the tea plantations of Assam.

Oral narratives have lived on in the present day and age. The authorship, circulation, distribution, and performance of *Jhumur* songs has continued to shape memory and identity. As we try to understand and unravel these dynamics in the realm of the digital—as Jhumur music has begun to finds its place in the digital, electronic and remix music fields—there remains a complexity about the implications of the intermingling of *Jhumur* songs and music with popular culture and digital archiving; and, in a way, *Jhumur* has taken shape as a popular folk culture of Assam, with traditional and contemporary cultural significance for the tea plantation workers community. Such intermingling is to have implications with regard to memory and migration.

*Jhumur* songs confront the global structure of colonialism and indentured labour through the very local formations of experience and keep alive the memory of migration and exploitation. For example, the *Jhumur* song *Chol Mini Assam Jabo*, which traces the journey, life and experiences of a worker, seems to have become a statement in popular culture, with legends like Bhupen Hazarika singing renditions of the song, and the Adivasi youth from the tea tribe community remixing the song and uploading it on different music streaming sites. Similarly, the song *Axom Deshe Bagisare Sowali*, from the 1974 movie *Sameli Memsaab* and the *Jhumur* song *Ranchi Che Bhejar Kuli*, collected by cultural activist Kali Dasgupta in the 1960s, have also been able to mark their place in the digital realm, whether through archiving projects or finding a place in various remixes, and multiple covers by song artists. This digital song archiving gives the songs a new kind of popularity and space, as the terrain of oral traditions undergoes a shift to such a documentation process. A digital history through archiving and remixing of the *Jhumur* songs which in its very evocation finds an erasure of its history through the process of commercialization found in remixing where the history of colonialism is often romanticized and exploitative relations put on the backfoot through picturization of the song or remixing and removing of songs of migration from the genre of what comes under *Jhumur* music. In spite of such a process the remixing of *Jhumur* songs or making of electronic music in *Jhumur* folk culture provides an important site for assertion for the community largely recognized as tea tribes of Assam. At the same time, these songs stand as a testament of the history and memory of migration and exploitative relations and are very much part of a rich *Jhumur* oral tradition. Folk music and folk songs are an important part of the performing arts and literature. Memory, history, and literature come to survive in these new archives, and the digitization of the *Jhumur* songs and oral traditions finds a way to survive and relive in digital formulations.

The social, economic, and cultural politics in the history of migration of the tea plantation workers through people's stories, folktales, music, folk songs and dances, and its place in the digital, is an attempt in the production of knowledge of the voices and narratives, that mainstream history and contemporary hegemony silences, while acknowledging the difficult questions of representation, reality and ethics that a construction of marginalized narratives entails. The *Jhumur* songs and new tracks that come out every year continue to be played during festivals and at *Puja pandals* in tea plantations, and are often played alongside the latest Bollywood music, Assamese and Bihu songs, contemporary popular Bhojpuri music, and Bollywood music from the 1980s and 1990s.

The internet, digital achieving, and the online realm operate as a space for the continuity of oral narratives and the remix. The digital realm also brings about a new change in how songs are circulated and perceived. Exactly how it is perceived, and how it circulates with an ever-widening audience as memory unfolds through different ruptures in the social and cultural realm, is something which is ever-changing. What remains interesting, however, is that the songs *do* survive the test of time, as they persist in popularity, are reworked, and even remixed for digital consumption.

Remixes of *Jhumur* songs, or the work of digital and electronic remixing, has changed the terrain of digital archiving. It has also changed how songs are produced and circulated on different streaming networks, local television channels, online sites, and new-age social media. As the songs circulate with new fervour, it is difficult to unravel how the music is perceived, how its meaning and messages are transferred. *Jhumur* music speaks of community, the flora and fauna, love, livelihood, work and even—at times—resistance, yet the electronic digital realm produces newer songs on similar and varying themes, which finds a space not only in digital archives but also in different celebrations and festivals.

The digital space itself is rapidly transforming, and so are modes of communication and circulation, where the audience also has a strong space for interaction, with the option of commenting on videos and re-uploading various remix versions of songs and music. This change gave a new voice to the audience, and has brought the audience into the mix. This is interesting, as it allows the digital medium to be an important part of the realm of oral tradition that *Jhumur* folk music has been a part of. For the longest time, folk music has been an important part of oral history, passing on history and culture from one generation to another as it picks inspiration and change from different ruptures in time. The very tradition and culture of remixing thus actually finds itself in continuation with folk music, especially the *Jhumur* songs of the community of tea plantation workers, as it continues the oral tradition of the narrative, lived experiences, and the memory of their history and culture. Remixes and digital archiving, as we see it today, might be seen and understood as a particular phenomenon unique to present times. However, a deeper look into the genre signals a fundamental shift in not just how we look and understand contemporary music, whether as a commodity or a product produced by artists, but shifts the terrain to something which is a creation of a process, too. John Egenes has argued that remixing and remix culture are the 21st century's new folk process, a communal way of experiencing art and intellectual creations and a sense of mass ownership of creation (Egenes 2010). Different streaming sites and portals, such as YouTube, have emerged over the past decade. They have opened the space for the audience and the process of music to come closer together in the digital realm, giving it a particular nature of folk remixes. Many *Jhumur* songs find themselves remixed or digitally produced and the different themes of love, community, intimacy, the flora and fauna of a region, history and memory are often captured in these new remixes and digital productions. A continuation of *Jhumur* songs as that of memory and community finds space in the archiving of *Jhumur* songs, the new remixes and new digital productions.

Katherine MacDonald (2005) has discussed folk process as the process by which cultural artefacts are changed whether mildly or in a substantive manner to form new cultural products. The multiple renditions of the *Jhumur* song *Chol Mini Assam jabo*, which has, for around half a century, been remade and adapted multiple times by multiple artists with different renditions and tones, making a mark in mainstream music in Assam. It has long since reworked its way into the digital folk process. As the song or artefact itself changes in the digital realm, the digital culture also changes and widens, allowing tribal communities from the tea plantations of Assam to find a space for expression and articulation. In such a context, where the digital comes so close to musical personhood, McLuhan rightly notes that electric media enriches our musical world, and our music enriches our new technology and the lives of those who use it (McLuhan 1964). Though we do need to remind ourselves that remix music and the digital realm, with its streaming sites, algorithms, and corporate control, does work as a commodity, wherein its cultural value is often transformed into economic value (Duggar 2010).

Both the digital and the remix work as memory. A remix of a song actually asks the audience to rely on the memory of the song, and is dependent on a certain kind of love and affiliation for the original soundtrack (Duggar 2010). *Jhumur* music that presently circulates in the digital realm also draws from a memory, be it a memory of community, belonging, shared history, and collectivity. So, even though contemporary *Jhumar* music, while not necessarily needing clear overtones of memories of migration or colonial exploitation, is nonetheless based on the memories of such events. Different social, economic and political forces and dynamics that produce the fractured positionality of tea plantation workers in Assam find voice even in the new remixed and digital tracks of *Jhumur* music. They remain to be an exercise in reconstituting, imagining, and producing an understanding of the "past," in a process of engagement with *Jhumur* songs of the new digital realm. No matter how it changes, *Jhumar* music remains grounded in its themes of love, work, memory, and community ties, and continues to tie the genre to the tea plantation workers of Assam.

## Note

* The research was conducted under the Zubaan-Sasakawa Peace Foundation Writing Grant for Young Researchers from the North East 2019.

## Bibliography

Bahadur, G. (2013) *Coolie Woman: The Odyssey of Indenture*. London: Hurst & Company.

Behal, R. (2014) *One Hundred Years of Servitude: Political Economy of Tea Plantations in Colonial Assam*. New Delhi: Tulika Books.

Bhadra, M. (1992) *Women Workers of Tea Plantations in India*. New Delhi: Heritage Publishers.

Brakeley, T.C. (1984) *Funk and Wagnalls Standard Dictionary of Folklore, Mythology and Legend*, eds. Leach M. and Fried J. New York: HarperCollins Publishers.

Biswas, H.Y. (2014) *Asom Aru Bongar Loka—Sangeet Samiksha*. Nalbari, Assam: Journal Emporium.

Chatterjee, P. (2003) A *Time for Tea: Women. Labour and Post/Colonial Politics on an Indian Plantation*. New Delhi: Zubaan.

Datta, B. (ed.) (1994) A *Handbook of Folklore Material of North East India*. Guwahati: ABILAC.

Duggar, V. (2010) *The Hindi Film Song Remix: Memory, History, Affect*. MPhil Thesis, School of Arts and Aesthetics, Jawaharlal Nehru University: New Delhi.

Egenes, J. (2010) 'The Remix Culture: How the folk process works in the 21st century', *Prism Journal*, 7(4), p. 1–4.

Gioia, T. (2006) *Work Songs*. Durham and London: Duke University Press.

Gogoi, L. (1991) *Sah Bagisar Jivan Aru Sanskriti*. Assam: Assam Sahitya Sabha.

Goswami, P.D. (1983) *Essays on the Folklore and Culture of North-Eastern India*. Guwahati: Spectrum.

Gregory, M. (2001) *Kali Dasgupta, An Interview*. Available at: *http://kalidasgupta.com/index.html*. Accessed on October 20, 2019.

Gupta, R.D. (1986) 'From Peasants and Tribesmen to Plantation Workers: Colonial Capitalism, Reproduction of Labour Power and Proletarianisation in North East India, 1850s to 1947', *Economic and Political Weekly*, 21 (4), p. 2–10.

Jain, S. (1998) 'Gender Relations and the Plantation System in Assam, India', in Jain, S. and Reddock, R. (eds), *Women Plantation Workers: International Experiences*. Oxford & New York: Berg, pp. 107–128.

Jain, S. and R. Reddock. (eds.) (1998) *Women Plantation Workers: International Experiences*. Oxford & New York: Berg.

Kaniampady, E. (2003) *Status of Women Working in The Tea Plantation*. New Delhi: Akansha Publishing House.

Kar, B. (2008) 'Incredible Stories in the Time of Credible Histories: Colonial Assam and Translations of Vernacular Geographies', in Raziuddinand A. and Chatterjee P. (eds.), *History in the Vernacular*, New Delhi: Permanent Black, pp. 288–321.

Macdonald, K. (2005) *Reflections on the Modern Folk Process*. Unpublished Doctoral thesis, Bryn Mawr College, PA: Bryn Mawr.

Mcluhan, M. (1964) *Understanding Media: The Extension of Man*, 2nd edn. Corte Madera, CA: Ginko Press.

Minakshi, B. (2007) *Songs of Dr. Bhupen Hazarika: A Folklorist Study*. Guwahati, Assam: University of Guwahati.

Northrup, D. (1995) *Indentured Labour in the Age of Imperialism 1834–1922*. Cambridge: Cambridge University Press.

Perks, R. and Thomson A. (2016) *The Oral History Reader*. Oxon and New York: Routledge Publications.

Portelli, A. (1991) *The Death of Luigi Trastulli, and Other Stories: Form and Meaning in Oral and Public History*. Albany, NY: State University of New York Press.

Sarkar, R.L. and Lama M.P. (1986) *Tea Plantation Workers in the Eastern Himalayas*. Delhi and Lucknow: Atma Ram & Sons.

Savur, M. (1973) 'Labour and Productivity in the Tea Industry', *Economic and Political Weekly*, 8 (11), p. 551–559.

Sen, S. (2004) 'Without His Consent': Marriage and Migration in Colonial India, *International Labor and Working-Class History*, 65, p. 77–104.

Sharma, J. (2009) 'Lazy Natives, Coolie Labour and the Assam Tea Industry', *Modern Asian Studies*, 43 (6), p. 1287–1324.

Sircar, K.K. (1987) 'Coolie Exodus from Assam's Chargola Valley, 1921: An Analytical Study', *Economic and Political Weekly*, 22(5), p. 184–193.

Sameli Memsahab song *Axom Dexor Bagisare Suwali*. Available at: *www.youtube.com/watch?v=GAoA8iv7uUU*. Accessed on November 1, 2019.

Thompson, P. (2000) *The Voice of the Past: Oral History*. New York: Oxford University Press.

Tinker, H. (1975) *A new system of slavery: The export of Indian Labour Overseas 1830–1920*, New York: Oxford University Press, for the Institute of Race Relations.

# 21

# INFUSING DIGITAL MEDIA INTO THEATRE IN CONTEMPORARY INDIAN PERFORMANCES

*Tanya Jaluthria*

## Introduction

Like all other art forms, theatre has been constantly evolving with the passage of time. It is in this process of evolution that any art form survives. So, in the contemporary digital age, the intervention of digital media in theatre was inevitable. Theatre, like today's times, has also responded to the needs of a digital world driven by technology. It has been digitalized, blurring the boundaries and increasing its horizon. In fact, digital media not only complements the representational form of theatre, but it also feeds it to a great extent. This can be seen in the views of theatre director Robert Lepage, who also works in digital performance:

> The only way theatre can evolve and stay alive is to embrace the vocabulary of alternative ways of storytelling. We know that today's audience has really changed, right? They reach the end of the play before the actor does. They're conditioned by television and film idiom. They're influenced by the web, by video clips . . . nowadays, stories are told in many different ways. Our narrative vocabulary is highly sophisticated. So, if we want theatre to be at least up to speed with the audience, we must adopt those kinds of narrative idioms.
>
> *(NFB 2017)*

The term "digital" refers to electronic technology. This study explores how such technologies are not only used as digital tools intended to add to the magnificence of the visual, but also to be an integral part of the narrative of the play. A majority of contemporary performances focus on interactivity among different art forms in the production, between performers and the spectators, between traditional theatre styles and upcoming technology. This has resulted in the inclusion of almost all kinds of tools, which can be modified to fit into the ideological stance of the theatre artist and the aesthetics of the form.

DOI: 10.4324/9781003354246-27

## Presence of Digital Technology

Digital technology in theatre affects the form at the technical level and content at the thematic level. As opposed to popular views suggesting that the advancement of modern technology has hampered the flourishing of theatre, digital technology has helped add layers to the already-existing multimedia art form of theatre. Directors have been exploring the technological and digital domain with respect to theatrical performances through the use of projection, telematics, live telecast, highly customized digital sound, and light effects, web-cam, robots, and cyborgs, etc. Here, a few of those tools are studied and selected on the basis of their prominence in Indian performances.

It is crucial to identify and understand the transitional trends of any art form, so as to best understand the changes any society is going through and vice versa. This study is an attempt to do so. The chapter looks into how digital media represents theatrical culture and archives it through digital preservation. It blurs boundaries rendering theatre more interactive. The study was designed to take into consideration two aspects of digital media in performance practice in India. The first is that theatre incorporates digital media by extensively weaving it through the narrative of performance, which has been seen through the plays of Abhilash Pillai and Amitesh Grover. They are Indian theatre practitioners whose most works are Delhi-based. Second, the newly emerging form, cineplay, was largely introduced in India by the company named "CinePlay," established by Subodh Mascara and Nandita Das. A cineplay of this company has been referenced to understand how the realm of the cinematic, associated with the camera, is brought into the theatrical space. The digital technological tools that come up in these two domains are projections, cameras, digital lighting, and sound. Thus, these plays are read with specific foci on the uses of these digital tools, among the variety of digital media interventions widely used across borders.

Cinema came into existence primarily because of technological factors and with today's increasing technological advancements, cinema's reach is also increasing. Today, cinema can be spread across borders. It is available on mobile phones and computers because of the internet, digital media, and globalization. Moreover, because of these very reasons, a change in the sociological scenario can be observed, and many people are living a technologized existence. People today have the opportunity to sit comfortably in their homes and consume all that is available on the internet. If plays too are available online, through the medium of cineplay, people may savour them like films. A 2017 article in the daily *The Hindu* touches on the very purpose of the venture CinePlay,

> Cineplays were born out of a very clear-cut desire: to push the artistic envelope and experiment with a new form of storytelling. "The idea was to merge the language of cinema and theatre and see what hybrid emerges," says Subodh Mascara, co-founder and chairman of the eponymous enterprise CinePlay . . . on paper, cineplays can help expand the viewership and reach

> of theatre. "The plays of Tendulkar, (Habib) Tanvir and (Sombhu) Mitra have not been archived. This can make them accessible to a larger audience, beyond the urban elite," says Das. But for Mascara, it also shows the way ahead for filmmaking: how it should be driven by strong content, good storytelling and a tight budget.
>
> *(Joshi 2017)*

## Historical Overview

Theatre has taken up the tools, practices, and perspectives that arose in a gradually changing world. New technological innovations brought more digital tools, which then came to theatre. Steve Dixon, in the book *Digital Performance*, talks of Richard Wagner and his practice of *Gesamtkunstwerk* ("Total Artwork") in the 19th century. He says,

> Wagner's conception is central to the lineage of digital performance both in its advocacy for grand theatrical spectacle and in the paradigm of "convergence" that unites the *Gesamtkunstwerk* with contemporary understandings of the modern computer as a "meta-medium" that unifies all media (text, image, sound, video, and so on) within a single interface.
>
> *(Dixon and Smith 2007, p. 41)*

What is common between Wagner's theory and later digital performances is that both endeavour to create immersion in performance by removing the orchestra from the main stage, in order to prevent the "alienation effect" from happening to the audience. Digitally created projections also create such immersion, as discussed later in the chapter.

Studies have seen the 20th-century avant-garde movements of futurism, expressionism, and others as major influences on digital theatrical performances. These may be interpreted as precursors to digital theatre. The ideological stances that these movements upheld, and the way these artistic creations are represented, feed into the content and aesthetics of digital performances. For instance, the centrality of the machine is important to futurism. It imagines machines replacing live actors with computer-generated images; this is evident in the virtual actors of VR performances or robots in contemporary plays. As of this study, the centrality of the machine is evident in Pillai's *Blindside*, which will be talked about later. As for expressionism, the pattern of "distortion and exaggeration in visual forms" is a recurrent practice in digital performances (Dixon and Smith 2007, p. 70). Grover's *Strange Lines* is one such example of this occurrence, with its use of multiple images of fragmented faces. With this as the theoretical background of digital technology in art came the intervention of digital tools in theatre, starting with using projections in plays since the early 20th century. The second half of the 20th century saw an outburst of digital theatre (including projection and film) because of its accessibility and democratization. This was also because there was a transition coming in cultural perception, which moved towards the acceptance of technological innovations along with the ongoing computer development. The collaboration of digital technicians with artists led to new inputs in the theatre-making process by the 1990s, because they brought, in their new worldview, different knowledge into art. Globalization, too, has affected theatre in India, allowing domestic artists to experiment with digital media.

The referenced texts are *Blindside*, *Strange Lines*, and *Rahenge Sadaa Gardish Mein Taare*. *Blindside* is a 2019 play by Abhilash Pillai. Projections and live camera footage run throughout the narrative of the play. *Strange Lines* is a 2010 performance by Amitesh Grover, which uses the relationship between two friends to reveal Indian and Swiss lived experiences, cultures, and their problematic societal issues. These revelations are done through ample use of projections and camerawork which add visual imagery to the written narrative of the letters. *Rahenge Sadaa Gardish Mein Taare* is a cineplay based on the play *Gardish Mein Taare* directed by Saif Hyder Hasan. It is inspired loosely by the lives of Guru Dutt and Geeta Dutt.

Much research has been done focusing on the performance and production aspects of theatre along with thematic studies of the plays. However, most research has been done by Westerners, who keep Western theatre artists as their main focus. Technological patterns in the works of Indian theatre artists, conversely, have not been explored much. Through this study, the technological patterns and shifts in Indian theatre practice will be recognized and recorded for understanding the art form and its transitions.

As far as human history has been traced, theatre has been present in the cultural practices of people across borders. Since theatre, as an art form, has its own language to reflect its own stories, it is crucial to record such stories so that future generations can know what theatre was like. From the religious ceremonies of ancient Greece to shaping political history in the 20th century across the world, theatre has contributed substantially, with its potential to imagine, create, and bring change at a social level. However, theatre has shown a marked inability to preserve itself across generations. Written plays do survive time, but they are just scripts of the plays. They are not the plays. Theatre is a performative art and plays are written primarily to be performed. But what future generations have access to is just their scripts. The experience of watching a play can vanish with time because a performance is a lived experience for a specific period of time. One can only have an idea of what the performance could have been. This contrasts with cinema, which can preserve performances through camerawork and recording, thereby preserving the culture of cinema from any particular time. With cineplays, this preservation of theatrical culture can be done. Also, it is very important for any civilization to collect and archive the cultural practices of its times, especially regional theatres, which carry the immediate cultural traces of any region at the root level. Many don't have access to these narratives. And regional narratives are the core narratives of any nation. This is why theatre institutions and auditoriums started recording plays on camera and archiving them on CDs or DVDs for their personal records.

The subsequent aim of this chapter is to bring forth the potentials of cineplays, emphasizing the fact that when theatrical culture is recorded, the cultural practices of performers and people will be preserved, providing the masses access to regional theatres through digital media.

## Realizing the Digital–Theatrical Interface Through *Blindside* and *Strange Lines*

Dr. Abhilash Pillai is a play director, pedagogue, and scholar of contemporary Indian theatre, known for directing the play *Blindside*. The play's 2019 brochure, for instance, claims *Blindside* as "a digital devised performance." The play is based on the novel *Cut*, written by Sreemoyee Piu Kundu. *Cut* traces the life of a theatre artist and his relations with other people. Pillai, in the brochure, talks of the devising process of the play:

> [W]hile devising the play, we kept in mind that all the exercises and improvisations should have a digital intervention or interface. This intervention is made use of to give an immersive language into the performance making and also to explore how time and space is getting challenged in theatre. Digital theatre design and performance open up a chance for the spectator to come into contact with the artists and even participate in the creation.
>
> *(National School of Drama 2019)*

The play makes extensive use of digitally operated sound and lights, audio-visual projections showing recurring patterns of numeric designs, and the active presence of a web camera, footage from which is simultaneously broadcasted live on the projection screen.

The protagonist, Amitabh, is seen through other people's perspectives and experiences throughout the play. We never get to see the actual, physical self of the protagonist. This hits a chord in the overall dynamics of theatre because Amitabh's absence is shown by a handy camera that projects live footage onto the screen on the stage. Whatever the camera sees is what Amitabh sees, and those visuals are made available to the audience with the help of live projection of camera recordings. But Amitabh himself, physically, is never there. Hence, the camera becomes Amitabh's eye. The camera is carried by a technical team member, who is clearly recognizable as not a part of the play. This digital ploy enables Pillai to fulfil his purpose as he says in the brochure: "We wanted to take the challenge of the physical absence of Amitabh Kulasheshtra on stage, the main protagonist of the novel. So that this could be any theatre artist of this country who voices against the existing system" (National School of Drama 2019). It is evident that the reason why Pillai replaces the live actor with a camera is to bring a sense of universality to the play. By eliminating the face of the main character, Pillai manages to eliminate specificity by making Amitabh's struggle the struggle of all theatre artists. This way *Blindside* uses a digital camera to render the director's conceptual idea as an executed ploy, further fulfilling his aim.

An example of the execution of this idea of replacing the protagonist with a camera can be seen in the rehearsal scene of a theatre company that the protagonist visits for the first time. The technician holding the camera shoots the rehearsal, then zooms to the character with whom Amitabh is talking. This shot shows the man in the theatre approaching the camera, asking Amitabh what he is doing there. This scene indicates to the audience that the footage projected on the screen at the back of the stage is, in fact, what Amitabh is seeing, and that the man talking to the camera is actually talking to Amitabh.

When theatrical performances incorporate visuals projected live on-screen, they blur the boundaries of different art forms. This is because the use of screen and projection to create imagery is typically considered the domain of cinema, whereas live stage performance pertains to theatre. For instance, in Pillai's *Blindside*, a live actor talks to a woman in a video projected on the stage's wing. The live dialogue is coordinated with the dialogues in the projected video, and in this coordination lies the fudging of the two forms: the live dialogue delivery of theatre, and the recorded video of screen images. This interactivity is crucial to digital theatre. This novel juncture has produced a domain that does not fall into any specific category of either of the two forms but carries potential akin to what Steve Dixon refers to in his book *Digital Performance*. Therein, Dixon writes, "This sense of *in-between-ness*—a luminal space operating between the screen images and live performers—is often the essential kernel, what one might even call the 'metatext' of digital theatre production" (Dixon and Smith 2007, p. 337). The screen on which visuals are projected can deliver a similar experience to the theatre spectator like that of a viewer watching a film in a cinema hall. Usually, things are symbolically shown in theatre: the aura is created, or any huge spectacle that is needed, are all primarily done through symbolism. But projectors can add to this representation similar to cinema visuals. Projections help create a sense of immersion for the audience while still upholding the "suspension of disbelief." But with projection being run concurrently with live actors' performances, a contradiction comes to play. The audience looks at the projected visual, and then at the live actor, sometimes they have to be seen together. This makes the audience aware of both visuals: digital and live. With this awareness, the audience does not get completely lost in the experience; hence, some sense of distancing happens.

The projection screen, which is two-dimensional, can facilitate three-dimensional visuals. It is a tool that has the potential to let theatre bear multiple possibilities of spatial arrangement in theatre. Even if the stage setup is not there, it can be created by projecting the image. *Blindside* has minimum stage setup. For each scene, the play brings a few chairs, while projections are mainly used to (re) create the environment that the scene demands.

Unlike well-structured plays, which offer narrative division in the form of separate acts and scenes, this play, being adapted from a novel, does not offer the inherent narrative division to break up different scenes. This enables the director to use projection to demarcate scenes and create a new narrative structure. A recurring pattern in the play is that, after any scene, a blackout occurs, which is followed by newly projected visuals. These images tell the audience that the scene has changed. They are shown at the back of the stage, on the right and left wings, and on the floor and ceiling of the stage as well. The first scene changes with a gradual blackout and the video of a train passing is projected on the left wings of the stage, accompanied by the sound of the train passing by. This is a foreshadowing of the next scene, about a murder on the train. The next visuals that are projected on the back of the stage are jumbled images of chaos, violence, and clippings of news channels. This creates the aura of the implicit panic and dread of the events following the murder. In some of the other scene changes, we see digital patterns of lines, circles, etc., in projected visuals. These also show scene changes. This way, each consecutive scene is joined by the projection of images, clips, or live feed.

Another scene that requires critical attention is the scene of Sarla's monologue. This scene captures what one can accomplish using a camera, editing techniques, and video projection, and evidences how well digital technology can embrace theatre in order to enhance it. Sarla's monologue comes after her father decides that she will get married to Amitabh, which she doesn't want. We see Sarla's monologue projected on the screen; a close view of her face is visible as she speaks to Amitabh. The camera captures a close shot, with no space around her, showing the claustrophobic sense of her existence. This trick is considered notable in the field of cinema, as it brings out the trapped sense of the characters, coupled with grim lighting and restricted space. Pillai brings all of these elements into theatre. Sarla then cries, and, while her voice in the projected video increases, the image of her face splits into two. The image gradually gets more scattered with her shouting and wailing. The digital fragmentation of her face is representative of the fragmentation of her desires and self. Practically viewed, such a depiction would not have been possible to execute on stage with live actors. However, it could have been done symbolically by using voice modulation, gestures, or props, but not to the same extent as this precise depiction.

Another theatre director and performer, Amitesh Grover, translates his extensive knowledge of live and digital arts into his nuanced engagement with the digital medium and its fusion with theatre. *Strange Lines* (2010) is based on *When Kulbhushan Met Stockli*, a graphic novel anthology. The form of graphic novel capitalizes on drawings and imagery, duly brought into the theatrical space with the help of digital media. The illustrations were reshaped and delivered through projection and camerawork. The patterns and visuals that are projected on the screen throughout the play are more than splendid images to please the eye. Those are symbols of surrounding society, culture, and the events that happen in the daily lives of these characters, as well as the very source text translated into digital language.

The play makes ample use of live drawing and live camera footage, which is simultaneously projected on the screens over the three walls of the performing area. The premise of the play is that there are two pen friends who discuss a variety of things, getting to know each other and their respective cultures. The first half of the play is in the form of monologues that are originally the letters spoken by one character while the other sits in front of a fixed camera, the visuals from which are projected simultaneously. During the course of the play, they switch positions regularly to sit in front of the camera showing certain objects/body parts, as their close shots appear on the screen. The camera is fixed but the actors play with the frame of its eye by putting only half their faces in front of it so that the camera captures and projects a partial image of the actor's face. The image of this face is multiplied when projected and spread over all three walls of the staging area yet it is an incomplete image. Since faces are often recognized as integral to our identity, the split images which reach the audience suggest each character's incomplete sense of self. This is rendered by virtue of the camera delivering one-half of the actor's face, which would have been difficult to show otherwise in reality.

*Strange Lines* encapsulates the vast expanse of the two nations from which the characters hail: India and Switzerland. Issues ranging from politics, scientific innovation, hunger, state disputes, certain cultural traits, etc. are all brought up. The sense of plurality present in multicultural nations comes up in the text of the play, while the tools used in the play further showcase this plurality. This is done by capturing, through camerawork and projection, certain objects and images inherent to these cultures and nations. There is another sense of plurality in the use of digital technological tools maintained by Grover. The uses of camera, live projection, and live drawings show the plurality of the inputs he uses in his plays.

In an interview taken during the course of this research Amitesh Grover had said:

> I like to set up a tension between being very close and being very far at the same time. Camera as a mediation serve that purpose where even if the performer on stage is live, the mediation of camera sometimes can bring the performer very close and sometimes can throw the performer very far away. . . . I call this the degree of distance which needs to be kept elastic. It produces a double attitude. It's difficult to say which one to trust more or the third stage of being in audience which gets produced by the tension between these two.
>
> (*Grover 2020*)

This reveals Grover's intent and goals in shaping audience reactions when he uses such tools in theatre. In his plays, Grover maintains a balance between total immersion and distance on the part of the audience. This balance is achieved through the combined use of camera and projection, which are both woven into the narrative. This way, the audience experiences the presentation of his work at multiple levels, which are subjective and relative to each scene.

One scene shows two lines coming from the left and right wall screens towards the centre screen at the back. Both the characters follow it towards each other, but the lines don't meet. This is suggestive of the inability of the characters to unite. The coming of two lines closer to each other is a simple way to hint at the two characters getting closer, which is done not by using direct speech but through imagery. These are the "strange lines" of the title which add subtlety to the text. This pattern of lines coming towards each other is also shown in the end when the woman asks, "How do you see the future?" The man, in his response, points and touches the screen to imprint a mark. The woman too does it. Then a line connects these two marks. Their connection is evident in the meeting of these two marks. Thus, their union was shown symbolically through the projection and live drawing of those lines.

In the end, the woman takes up the position of the artist, who was drawing live. A camera is fitted onto the drawing table, which enables any movement made on the table to be projected with a magnified size. An image that is created using this technique is when the woman puts her hands (which seem to be huge on the screen) over the man's relatively small head (standing on the stage). The woman also creates the effects of fire and snowfall around the man, who is standing on stage in front of the screen. She constantly draws, erases, or makes a collage of a variety of images from cut-out pieces.

The audience receives different signals from each element present on stage: through the live actor, and the projected videos or images in Grover's multilayered plays. This causes different members of the audience to perceive the elements differently. Also, Grover mentions that he never allows each member of the audience to see everything (Grover 2020). The seating arrangement in his plays breaks the conventional pattern of proscenium seating because the performance area is scattered as is the seating area. Most of his plays work upon this premise. With regard to this, Grover says:

> It must be an interaction, a conflict and sometimes even a contradiction between two or three elements that are present on stage which are leading the audience into . . . different ways of experiences. . . . It introduces democracy of viewing as well. . . . That is only possible if there is no centre on stage. . . . Neither technology takes centre on stage nor the performer, but an evolving relationship of conflict, of use, of utility, but also an enquiry into each other.
>
> *(Grover 2020)*

Hence, Grover attempts to establish a de-centralization of anything present on stage. The performer no longer holds the power of performance. Neither is it given to technology solely. Instead, it is spread all over the elements in the play.

Web technology is another domain that constitutes a crucial part of the digital world. Artists across the world have been incorporating and experimenting with web technology and the internet for the past several decades. However, Indian artists and creators made limited use of such technologies until the pandemic partly forced theatre onto the digital platform. The Serendipity Arts Festival is a multidisciplinary forum spanning South Asia, that organized the Serendipity Arts Virtual (2020). Among other events scheduled for the festival, there was a performance directed by Grover which included live performance, film, sound, and coding named *The Last Poet.* Due to the sensitive conditions caused by COVID-19, Indian audiences saw for the first time the full festival online. Surely, the art changed through its presentation across new mediums. The performance was adapted to the features, benefits, and limitations of web technology. Artists and viewers were connected through the screen and the internet. This ensured safety while ensuring that theatre art does not stop completely due to lockdown. Theatre groups are continuously functioning despite the conditions. Some groups are performing plays that are telecasted live to audiences sitting in their houses while the actors are together in another space. Some other theatre groups do not meet in person at all; both actors and viewers participate through their own screens, whether performing or watching. Actors' individual acts, even in front of their own, small screens, are coordinated to create a collective, overall visual for the scene.

## Alternative Narratives Brought in Theatre and Cineplay via Camera

Both theatrical plays have taken up projection and camerawork as crucial inputs marking the essence of these productions, and, hence, they are central to these plays. As said by Nicholas T. Proferes in the book *Film Directing Fundamentals*, "Film is a language used to tell stories, and the narrator of those stories is the camera. Yes, the director is the ultimate storyteller, but the 'voice' she will use is that of the camera" (Proferes 2005, p. 40). Being the narrator, the camera can provide a third-person perspective, or a bird's eye view that sees everything, every time. This means that the audience is invited to get into an unbiased, holistic, and macro-type view of the characters. If the camera is used otherwise by the director or the actors, it can bring forth a completely different, personal point of view of the characters that would be, in effect, their first-person narrative: subjective and, perhaps, manipulated. This gives the audience alternate stories at the micro-level, all within the larger story. These multiple potentials of the camera as a narrative tool can add to the layers of understanding that the theatrical performance otherwise exhibits.

The camera is not merely placed in a position, recording and projecting the actor's performance from the director's point of view, with the actor being indifferent to the camera. Instead, the actors gradually develop a relationship with the camera. This shows, first, the dependency on the tool and, second, its ability to benefit and enrich performances. There is an interaction between the actors and the camera, as the actors now also respond to the camera to project themselves. The result juxtaposes the live actor performing on stage with the screen image produced by the camera. The audience now witnesses the cinematic rendering of the live actor and the actual live actor. This suggests that the camera, when inserted into the theatrical space, presents a play by creating its images within the larger play being performed. It may be in line with the theme of the plot yet presents it differently with an intermixing of the images it chooses to show and omit, what is focused upon, and what is eliminated on the projection screen, when the characters talk to the camera, when they speak to each other, and when they speak to the audience.

However, the audience can get alienated by the presence of the camera. They are confronted with too many things to pay attention to: the actual actors, the props, and the camera, are all visible to them, as are the close-ups and montages that the camera captures. They see how the actors move the camera to create specific camera angles or see actors carrying cameras and making live-time changes to better shoot scenes. They see the whole process in front of them. This may prevent them from being swayed or overcome by the emotions the play intends to generate. Due to this, theatre ceases to be the "piece of life" or truthful experience it was earlier assumed to be. Instead, the audience is reminded again and again that it is sitting in an auditorium, watching a theatrical performance that is in process in front of them. The audience does not get immersed in the performance but feels distanced enough to be aware of the fact that it is a fictional narrative performed in an auditorium. Suspension of disbelief is not exercised in the presence of the camera visible to the audience. Much of the discussion made earlier, regarding cameras and with regard to theatrical plays, also applies to the form of cineplay as mentioned forth.

A cineplay is a piece of art that blends theatre and cinema in such a manner that it would be unjust to draw a line where its theatrical aspect ends and where the cinematic charm takes off. "Cineplay is a new form which will show plays on films" said Nandita Das, who has acted and made such cineplays (Bollywood 99, 2015). Since it takes from both forms of performance, its horizon, scope, and its utilities regarding practical advantage, aesthetics, and style of both forms increase by an exponential level. In a cineplay, because the final product is in the form of a film, so the larger narrative is of the camera, because, in cinema, the camera is the narrating tool. Hence, a sense of omnipotence is associated with it. But in a cineplay, inside the camera's narrative, we see theatre's narrative. Thus, it is two languages: those of theatre and of film, two narratives that tell the story and collectively enrich the storytelling process by presenting the audience with both theatrical and cinematic languages to appreciate, enjoy, and decode.

## Dynamics of the Form Cineplay

It is originally a rehearsed play that is later shot on camera, so, the basic characteristic of a cineplay is that the acting style is not purely cinematic. That is, the facial expressions are not the actor's only or most important way to express emotion or convey feelings. Instead, the actors are supposed to be expressive through their body movements, gestures, positions, and facial expressions as well. Cineplay takes this aspect from theatre, in which the actors must make loud gestures to make everything visible even to the last benches. Hence, the acting style in a cineplay is to some extent dramatic.

From theatre, cineplay borrows the fixed stage space, the acting style, the coloured lights creating dramatic effects, and so on. Cineplay is performed on stage with a theatrical setting and then shot. So, the performance is captured and then rendered with all the cinematic techniques that cinema bears—focusing techniques; close, mid, and long shots; editing, background score, etc. Cameras in cinema can be placed in actual places, capturing realities not possible in theatre because the space that is used is that of an auditorium. It has to be imagined and (re)created as per the setting of the play.

As Susan Sontag writes in her essay *Film and Theatre*, "Films have been rather too often acclaimed as the democratic art, the art of mass society. . . . Theatre, by contrast, means dressing up, pretense, lies. It smacks of aristocratic taste and the class society" (Sontag 1966, p. 26). Often theatre has been associated with the bourgeois, elite classes because only they had the time, money, and education to cultivate their intellectual taste by going to performances. Cinema, conversely, has been seen as fodder for the masses, probably because the early period of cinema sold cheap tickets for films, as compared to that of the plays performed in theatres. So, the working classes too could savour the taste of a new art form, cinema. But the form cineplay has the potential to blur this demarcation. The art form associated with the elite is now available to the common masses.

The fact cannot be negated that cinema takes a lot from theatre. It was there before the advent of cinema, so it is inevitable that theatre didn't impact, to a large extent, the early period of cinema. Early filmmakers shot vaudeville acts, boxing matches, and "passion" plays about the life of Christ. Because they were originally theatrical performances that were later shot, they can be considered akin, in effect, to the cineplay. There is the active presence of the camera capturing individual shots and, second, the use of montage when the shots are compiled. This can be understood as a basic version of present-day editing. But this practice gradually ended with the advent of feature films. By the 1980s, television had reached households; so did this art form. Then, it was called the "Television Play" in the UK. These were plays that were broadcasted live on television. But it, too, gradually faded after television films gained more audience. The first Indian film released in India was *Shree Pundalik* (1912), a Marathi silent film by Dadasaheb Torne- a photographic recording of a play. Hence, this film and the form of cineplay are similar when it comes to their processes of shooting and performance. In 2019, Tata Sky launched a new channel named *Tata Sky Theatre*. It is as if the television plays have been revived with the same purpose of bringing theatre into houses. Also, the Indian company CinePlay says on its official website, "CinePlay is an innovation in cinema that presents timeless stories as a digitally-immersive experience, and is specially calibrated for all screen sizes" (CinePlay 2020). With this, theatre may now be presented as a digital experience after being shot as cinema.

Therefore, it is evident that this form of cineplay has been present for years and, if traced historically, it has some differences depending upon age and culture, whether such cineplay-type performances were recorded vaudeville acts, television plays, or India's *Shree Pundalik*. But the basic feature that remains the same is shooting a film out of a theatrical performance. Even today, theatre and cinema cannot be read in complete isolation. It is here, in cineplay, that two art forms evolving from completely different circumstances take shape of a unified being.

Keir Elam, in the book *Semiotics of Theatre and Drama*, mentions that Edward T. Hall distinguishes "three principal proxemic 'syntactic' systems" about proxemic relations. First, fixed feature, which involves static architectural structures like the theatres, the opera houses, and their structures. Second, the semi-fixed features include "movable but non dynamic objects," such as the set and props lights. The third is the informal proxemic mode, which "has as its units the ever-shifting relations of proximity and distance between individuals, thus applying, in the theatre, to actor-actor, actor-spectator and spectator-spectator interplay." Elam further says that "in the typical western bourgeois theatre then, the informal and semi- fixed-feature systems exist under the dominion of the fixed feature" (Elam 2002, pp. 56–57). But in the cineplay, these dynamics are flexible, and they are constantly changing. The proximity is customized with the help of the camera. Now the audience can enter the personal space of the actor. The space that is used to execute the whole play is that of an auditorium, the limited space that had to be made into a home, the same stage was made into a police station for the interrogation scene in *Rahenge Sadaa Gardish Mein Taare*. But unlike theatre, the audience no longer has any obligation to sit in one fixed position and watch the play from that point of view only. Because the eye of the camera will lead the eye of the audience in the final product (film), so the audience can be at any position which is subject to change any moment, providing the audience with multiple points of view. Following Proferes' take, "In cinema audience can be anywhere because camera can be anywhere" (Proferes 2005, p. 40).

Also, while watching a play, a person sitting in the audience can look at the extreme right of the stage while another may look in the opposite direction, as per their will. This is beyond the control of the theatre director. But cinema helps the film director lead the audience to look at one particular character/thing/prop with the help of focusing technique/close shots. With the camera, the director can show close-ups of the actors, both to make the audience feel closer to them and to understand them better. Because of technological advancements, even a 360° view is possible for the audience, because now the camera can go on the stage and shoot the actors from all sides-a feat which was not possible in a proscenium theatre, where the audience is in a seating area separated from the actors, sitting in front of the stage. This feature has received substantive investment and interest from both the theatre directors taken up in the study. With cinema comes the benefit of editing. It not only helps to sequence the scenes in a particular order and make a montage of shots from different angles consecutively, but it can also do miracles with the mistakes committed. This differs from live performances, where, once a fumble or some mistake is made, the audience can catch the glitch immediately. Also, cuts and retakes can be used to achieve the desired outcome which is impossible in live theatrical performances. However, with live theatrical performances comes coloured lights, which serve the purpose of throwing light on the actors not only to make them visible but also to create the illusion of day/night, or to increase the dramatic effect in certain, dramatically charged scenes. By the virtue of these features, cineplay tries to fetch the best of cinema and theatre.

Through the use of the camera, cinema equips its audience with the points of view of the characters through the POV shots; while theatre has its own techniques to do so. Here the characters deliver monologues, soliloquies, or "acts" in such a way as to tell the audience what their point of view is. Cineplay has access to both. There are many POV shots in *Rahenge Sadaa Gardish Mein Taare* which make the audience closer to the vision of the character, quite literally. The cinematography also makes ample use of overlapping of scenes through editing and pan shots where the camera rotates around the actors capturing close shots of their expressions. This further deploys the mise en scene, which is the arrangement of actors, props, and everything present on stage. It can be analysed to further understand the scene. In the confrontation scene between Bhawna and Dev, where Bhawna comes home drunk, the mise en scene of the scene is divided into two halves. The right half shows Dev sitting on a chair, and the left half shows Bhawna doing drunk talk, making loud body movements and gestures- a style of acting that falls much into the domain of dramatic acting practiced in theatre. The camera shifts attention, from time to time, from each half of the mise en scene by focusing on one half and de-focusing the other with respect to who is speaking. This way, the acting style that is brought in is theatrical, but the active presence of the camera makes the cineplay cinematic.

## Conclusion

The changes that occur in the art forms are symptomatic of the changes that the world around goes through; it is equally true for its opposite. This brings one to the conclusion that the increasing use of digital technology in theatre suggests the increasing presence of the same in the world. Hence, bringing forth the possibility that digital technology is gradually becoming a prominent factor in the cultural fabric of our society and human life.

The primary concern of this study was to understand the treatment of digital technology by theatre directors in their performances, and the impact of these on the audience with respect to the creation of spectacle in performance. As of the projections, *Blindside* uses digital technology to reveal the inner turmoil of the characters, their feelings, and fears. Sarla's face on the projection screen in *Blindside* gets digitally fragmented after the image of her close shot, suggestive of her claustrophobic and broken self. This surely adds to the spectacle for the audience, but it also puts forth the hidden psychological realm that was earlier inaccessible to the audience. Moreover, it uses projection to create the narrative structure of the play; hence, it goes beyond creating a spectacle or merely pleasing the senses of the audience.

Among many of the features that the camera carries with it, the one employed most efficiently by Pillai is the portability of digital cameras. Of course, its other features like focusing techniques, close shots, and pan shots were also invested in throughout the play. *Blindside* makes use of the potential of camera placement by replacing the physical presence of the protagonist with a video camera, whereby the camera's eye becomes Amitabh's eye. This simple camerawork gave life to multiple metaphorical resonances in the play. The introduction of the camera into theatre brings with it all its features, and these plays show how the realm of cinematic, associated with the camera, is brought into the theatrical space.

The centrality of images is inherent to the form of the graphic novel and, because Grover's *Strange Lines* was based on a graphic novel, the delivery of narrative is primarily done through images. Drawings are crucial to such novels, which could before only be shown pictorially. Thus, the projection of the camera's live feed and live drawings maintained a sense of the visual art of the source text in the adapted work, suggesting that technology is used strategically to both retain and reinvent, to some extent, the essence of the source text. This can be seen in the case of adaptations such as *Strange Lines*, and this applies to *Blindside*, too.

Cineplay blurs the boundaries between theatre and cinema, and the general associations they have with the elites and the common masses, respectively. Here, the stage is available on screen for people who didn't have access to theatre. Ideally, theatre should get a boost from this form, because theatre's reach will increase when plays are available through digital media. Also, people who do not regularly watch theatre will now watch it on their screens, just like they watch films. A whole new market will be opened for plays in the form of cineplay. Consequently, theatre will have a wider reach, and the technological benefits embedded in cinema will help theatre have a more nuanced language. By producing and distributing cineplays like movies, theatre practitioners will get profits, potentially resolving what has long been a major problem in the field. But, after entering the market, these cineplays might get commercialized like cinema, and their quality may deteriorate in order to accrue higher profits.

Plays are live performances that are lived for a certain, limited time period by the performers and the audience. Once the performance ends, the experience ends. The dramatic moments are created and then get lost in time. This serves both as a charm and a limitation. The cineplays fulfil the purpose of preservation of the theatrical culture for the next generations, who may get to know how drama was practised in past times.

Because the digital world can be created, customized, and played upon as per the requirements and wishes of theatre artists, it can help one to show directly, without any symbolism, that which was inaccessible to the audience- the impossible realms of the psychological state of the characters, and the imaginative ends of the play. However, it may not guarantee emotional or actual physical experiences. But for that, theatre artists still continue to create performances meant to gather and display human experiences and truths. While the "liveness" of actors in theatre cannot justifiably be replaced by digital technology, it can surely still complement theatre. What can be aimed for is a balance between the two by choosing the best of theatre and complementing it with the positives of digital media, thus enhancing the calibre of human art.

## References

*Blindside.* (2019) *Directed by Abhilash Pillai.* [National School of Drama, New Delhi. Play recording].

Bollywood 99. (2015) Nandita Das and Subodh Maskara opening night of their cineplay festival act 1–27.02.2015. *BNB News India* [Online Video], 10 March. Available at: www.youtube.com/watch?v=hmSrqnJt4Rk&t=1854s (Accessed: 15 November 2020).

CinePlay. (2020) About [Online]. Available at: http://cineplay.com/pages/cpabout.php (Accessed: 10 November 2020).

Dixon, S. and Smith B. (2007) *Digital Performance: A History of New Media in Theater, Dance, Performance Art, and Installation.* Cambridge, MA: The MIT Press.

Elam, K. (2002) *Semiotics of Theatre and Drama.* London and New York: Routledge, Taylor & Francis Group.

Grover, A. (2020) Telephone conversation with Tanya Jaluthria, 28 April.

Joshi, N. (2017) 'Is it Cinema? Is it Drama? Is it good?', *The Hindu*, 18 February [Online]. Available at: www.thehindu.com/entertainment/movies/is-it-cinema-is-it-drama-is-it-good/article17324475.ece (Accessed: 15 November 2020).

National School of Drama. (2019) Play- Blindside [Online]. Available at: https://nsd.gov.in/delhi/index.php/play-blindside/ (Accessed: 08 November 2020).

NFB. (2017) Robert Lepage [Online Video]. 4 April. Available at: www.youtube.com/watch?v=D4RQ0T2uDsg (Accessed: 21 October 2020).

Proferes, N. T. (2005) *Film Directing Fundamentals: See Your Film Before Shooting.* Amsterdam: Elsevier.

*Rahenge Sadaa Gardish Mein Taare* (2019) Directed by Saif Hyder Hasan [Film]. Chhoti Production. Available at: www.zee5.com/movies/details/rahenge-sadaa-gardish-mein-taare/0-0-92977 (Accessed: 2 April 2020).

Sontag, S. (1966) 'Film and Theatre', *The Tulane Drama Review*, 11 (1), p 24–37. www.jstor.org/stable/1125262

*Strange Lines.* (2010) *Directed by Amitesh Grover.* [National School of Drama]. New Delhi: Play Recording.

# AFTERWORD

## Rethinking Digital Colonialisms—The Limits of Postcolonial Digital Humanities

Digital humanities has opened up new vistas for the interpretation of literature, history, and other dimensions of culture, creating space for us to imagine an incredible array of new possibilities for methodologies to interpret the rich, vibrant digital cultures around us and to revisit traditional forms of cultural heritage in new ways. Recognizing the limits of bandwidth and Internet access, this work shows glimmers of the possibilities of the democratization of the cultural record—the historical, literary, and cultural texts that document humanity—as we construct a digital cultural record through open-access publications, digital archives, and digital exhibitions. Here, I offer a bit of reflection on how far digital humanities in South Asian contexts has come, as well as look forward to the challenges ahead.

My 2015 article, "South Asian Digital Humanities: An Overview," was commissioned by *South Asian Review* guest editors Jana Fedtke and Pranav Jani after the 2015 South Asian Literary Association conference, which featured a roundtable on digital humanities in South Asian studies (Risam 2015). I focused on the issue of digital literary studies, where we have seen—and continue to see—some of the most powerful work in South Asian digital humanities. The breadth and reach of this work is impressive—digitizing literary texts, strengthening regional language literary traditions, creating literary archives, and disseminating information.

Certainly, one of the most robust examples of this is the Bichitra: Online Tagore Variorum (2021), the collection of Rabindranath Tagore's work, which is arguably the most substantial archive of a writer in *any* language. Beyond volume alone, the project is particularly notable because it demonstrates the local, granular level of work in digital humanities that needs to be done to attend to the particularities of language and poetics. For example, the project attends to multilingual search functions and the need to develop new tools, like Bichitra's Prabhed collation tool that negotiates not only Tagore's multilingual writing but also his multigenre writing. Urdu language and literature is another area that has received significant attention—particularly through projects like the Iqbal Urdu Cyber Library (2021), which was the first digital collection of Urdu literature, grounded in the belief that the survival of Urdu literature relies on a robust web presence. Based on Project Gutenberg's goal of creating a digital library of free books, the Iqbal library publishes Urdu books in multiple formats.

But aside from the already impressive work of digitization and access alone, South Asian digital humanities projects have also developed ways to cut across boundaries—whether boundaries of high versus low culture, established versus emergent writers, and scholarship versus praxis. The project Rekhta (2021), for example, takes up the challenges of multiple scripts in the context of Urdu, with content available in Nastaliq, Devanagari, and Roman scripts. With a goal of making Urdu poetry accessible to those who do not read Nastaliq, the project boasts over 12,000 ghazals and nazms from more than 1,200 poets over three centuries. In addition to digitizing literature, the project provides a platform for young poets to create videos, which takes advantage of the affordances of the medium to cultivate continuity between literary history and the literary present. Seeing to transcend linguistic boundaries in the production of digital archives, Umang (2021), a project based in Karachi, provides a forum for discussing, exploring, and sharing poetics across languages. The site includes videos and documentaries that feature contemporary poets from Pakistan who write in Urdu, Sindhi, and Wakhi. It also focuses on access to full-text, translation to Urdu and English, and subtitles in English, Urdu, and transliterated Urdu. This is a critical example of how projects can foster transregional and even transnational connections.

Innovative and inventive programs have also blended cultural heritage preservation with workforce development, like Nitartha Digital Tibetan (2021), which created digital versions of Tibetan pecha texts, translated classical Buddhist texts into English, and has worked on Tibetan language preservation and word processing and data analytics software. Critically, the work took place in Kathmandu and incorporated training of young people in IT—thus serving local IT development needs. This is such an important and critical model of how digital humanities can have broader impact beyond the content alone.

Something that is also particularly impressive is that even though I wrote about these projects in an article that was written in 2015, they are all still live, which speaks to the care and attention to sustainability and maintenance that often bedevils digital humanities projects. Link rot—broken links—and missing websites can often be disappointing to encounter and speak to the need for building robust data management and sustainability plans as projects are being developed to increase the likelihood that they will have longevity.

The successes of this body of work—and these are just a few examples because there are many others—are evident: such projects have made primary literary and historical sources available for scholars. They transcend the geographical challenges of physical archives that circumscribe research within South Asia and the diaspora. They have made public the challenges and struggles of South Asia and its diasporas, laying claim to national identity as a rich site of study. These projects have also challenged linguistic hegemonies and have begun pointing us in the direction of considering the role digital humanities might play in challenging nationalist and elite historiographies that have erased subaltern voices.

While only seven years have passed since I wrote that article, the tremendous growth and flowering of digital humanities in South Asia is absolutely inspiring. The short-lived but significant South Asian Digital Humanities Network (SADH), an affiliate organization of Global Outlook::Digital Humanities, which fosters global connections among digital humanities practitioners around the world, brought together scholars within South Asia and South Asianists abroad who engaged with digital research methods. Padmini Ray Murray described SADH's aims as "to promote the digital scholarship and dissemination of scholars based in South Asia and elsewhere—and provide a space for this community of scholars whose work pertains to the region." In Ray Murray's words, SADH intended to address "questions of access, infrastructure, economic, and governmental policy; the exigencies of working in languages other than English, rate of technological growth and obsolescence, and our different institutional histories to broaden these horizons" (qtd. in Risam 2016). SADH gave rise to the formation of the Digital Humanities Alliance of India—now DHARTI—which has facilitated new directions for digital humanities in India—and has gained international recognition and admiration for its work.

Fortunately, after that first article, I had the opportunity to revisit the new, thriving work of digital humanities in South Asia, to see what had changed and how the body of scholarship had grown, when assembling a 2019 special issue on South Asian Digital Humanities for *South Asian Review* with Rahul K. Gairola. What we found was the phenomenal range of scholarly questions, theoretical insights, and practical considerations of digital humanities in South Asian contexts—and, perhaps more critically, how the work of South Asian digital humanities actually *transforms* what digital humanities makes possible.

Drawing on my conceptualization of postcolonial digital humanities and its possibilities for redressing the gaps and omissions in digital knowledge production that remain legacies of colonialism (Risam 2018) and drawing on Gairola's concept of "homelanding" (Gairola 2016), or the ways that postcolonial diasporas have transformed understandings of "home" and "belonging," we articulated how digital humanities in South Asian studies challenges and shapes notions of home, belonging, nation, identity, memory, and diaspora (Risam and Gairola 2019). This includes Nishant Shah's concept of the "post-access" subject of digital humanities in India, that attends not to those who are digitally *connected* but who are digitally *disconnected* (Shah 2019). We also incorporated Porter Olsen's work on the Salman Rushdie Born-Digital Archive, which raised critical questions about efforts to create computer-based emulations of the work of postcolonial writers (Olsen 2019). Tawnya Azar tackled Rushdie, in addition to Amitav Ghosh and Arundhati Roy, by examining how these writers use digital platforms—blogs and various forms of social media—to challenge the traditional landscape of publishing in the global literary marketplace (Azar 2019). Offering a look at Indian writers grapping with digital technologies to experiment with form and genre, Jana Fedtke examined two texts, *Priya's Shakti* and *Priya's Mirror* to examine how digital graphic novels examine violence against women (Fedtke 2019). We also featured A. Sean Pue's work on "Acoustic Traces of Poetry in South Asia," which examined how computational humanities methods can help us move beyond semantic meaning and the written word as sites of interpretation, to address oral performance and aural forms of recognition, as well as Amardeep Singh's work on developing the digital collection The Kiplings and India: A Collection of Writings from British India"—where he undertakes the crucial steps of balancing the colonialist voices of the Kiplings with writing by Indian reformers and activists of the late 19th and early 20th centuries, including Pandita Ramabai, Rukhmabai, and others (Pue 2019; Singh 2019). And we concluded with Dhanashree Thorat's work on transnational and historical dimensions of India's internet infrastructure, which links the development of the telegraph as a colonial technology to the undersea cable network that forms contemporary Internet infrastructure (Thorat 2019).

As it's clear—in just seven short years, the scope and contributions of South Asian digital humanities have blossomed—and this is just a very small fraction of the tremendous work that's being done.

But despite important work like Varsha Ayer's pioneering work leading digitization of the Ambedkar Papers, there is a noticeable absence in South Asian digital humanities—related to Dalits and denotified tribes or DNTs. And this raises the question of the extent to which South Asian digital humanities really is challenging digital colonialisms and addressing the hallmarks of colonialism in the digital cultural record—and extent to which it perpetuates digital colonialisms. Both of these things can be true simultaneously. At once, this body of work provides a challenge to the construction of digital scholarship of the Global North by asserting the importance of and making visible South Asian cultural heritage and tends to focus on dominant narratives in Indian literature, history and culture—specifically dominant narratives that render Dalits and DNTs invisible in digital cultural heritage.

While postcolonial studies as a body of thought has offered many wonderful insights on how we understand language and culture, what it has also, inadvertently done, is lead us to believe that representation—and more specifically representation in the eyes of the Global North—is enough. We cannot let this be a limit of postcolonial digital humanities too. Within the context of South Asian studies, we have the responsibility to ensure that the complexities of culture and history are rendered legible, that Dalits and DNTs become part of the digital cultural record—in their own voices and on their own terms.

This first way to start thinking about this begins with examining digital humanities practices as they have arisen in South Asian contexts to put at the foreground questions of epistemological power and epistemic violence. When working with materials or undertaking a project, the very first question must be: which epistemologies are being privileged, sanctioned, or valorized? Whose voices are likely to be authorized? Whose are disenfranchised—and how do you address that? In the context of working with digital archives, the crucial questions are: how was the archive constructed? What does it contain? What isn't there? Why is it not there? And, in this context, to what extent does this work reinforce Dalit and DNT oppression?

The question then becomes: what do we as practitioners have to do to avoid reproducing and amplifying these forms of archival violence? Is it feasible, for example, to offer a corrective? And, in the case of perspectives that may be unrecoverable—because we know that archival erasures can be permanent—how are practitioners addressing that absence?

What I'm arguing for here is an openness to a change in method. If we are going to fully realize the possibilities of postcolonial digital humanities, then methods are going to need change—and who gets to determine the methods needs to change. For example, supplementing a project with additional sources or resources that give voice to Dalit and DNT experiences doesn't mean representing *them* or speaking *for* them but providing Dalits and DNTs with the means—financial support and access to the means of production of knowledge—for self-representation on their own terms, rather than through a relation of extraction of value.

As a Kashmiri Sikh of the diaspora, particularly one who works at a very underfunded state university in the U.S., it has not been lost on me that institutions like the Indian Institutes of Technology have received a lot of money from the government to support digital humanities. And I would just ask, to what extent has that been treated in a way that is redistributive—or as Varsha Ayyar has voiced in recent talks—as reparations for Dalits? And I would add for DNTs to that issue as well.

One of the most dangerous dimensions of digital humanities is, in fact, the funding it attracts—because funding comes with strings attached and funding comes with possibilities of notoriety and recognition. I've seen this in a lot of different cultural contexts, and what often happens is that the funding and the notoriety accrue to people who are already in relative positions of privilege and power—giving them more and giving them access to academic prestige, nationally and internationally. It's incredibly seductive, but it's a trap—a trap to ensure that those who find themselves in those enviable positions keep doing what they're doing, keep upholding the status quo, keep upholding oppression, keep reproducing the conditions of academic knowledge production—rather than using the position to try and change the power dynamics of academic knowledge production.

This points us towards the importance of how we are articulate collaboration, particularly if we are going to use the affordances of digital humanities to avoid rehearsing colonialism, to avoid contributing to Dalit and DNT oppression. Often, academic work is constructed as working "on" a topic or, worse, "on" a particular group of people. Relationships between project developers with the money and the power and people whose stories and histories they may be working *on* are encumbered by power dynamics. This puts the onus on project directors to facilitate ethical collaboration—to build relationships with those affected by a project's concerns, to avoid equating having access to material resources to having control over the project itself, to shift from working *on* to working *with*. And this is particularly critical when collaborating with vulnerable communities. Furthermore, it places the burden on those with the ability to command resources to avoid positioning themselves as "saviors" rather than ethical collaborators.

If, we in fact, are striving to use digital humanities to challenge digital colonialisms, then it must start with representation of Dalits and DNTs—if they want, on their own terms—and must involve being willing to relinquish control and put redistribution at the centre of academic practices. Only then can the full possibilities of postcolonial digital humanities be realized.

Roopika Risam

## References

Azar, T. (2019) 'Inside and Outside the Literary Marketplace: The digital products of Amitav Ghosh, Arundhati Roy, and Salman Rushdie', *South Asian Review*, 40(3), pp. 190–205.

Bichitra: Online Tagore Variorum (2021). Available at: http://bichitra.jdvu.ac.in/index.php (Accessed: 25 January 2021).

Fedtke, J. (2019) 'Gender-based violence in contemporary digital graphic narratives from india', *South Asian Review*, 40(3), pp. 206–20.

Gairola, R.K. (2016) *Homelandings: Postcolonial Diasporas and Transatlantic Belongings*. Lanham, MD: Rowman and Littlefield.

Iqbal Cyber Library (2021). Available at: www.iqbalcyberlibrary.net/, (Accessed: 25 January 2021).

Nirtartha Digital Tibetan (2021). Available at: http://nitarthadigitallibrary.org/xtf/search (Accessed: 25 January 2021).

Olsen, P. (2019) 'Emulation as Mimicry: Reading the Salman Rushdie Digital Archive', *South Asian Review*, 40(3), pp. 174–89.

Pue, A.S. (2019) 'Acoustic Traces of Poetry in South Asia', *South Asian Review*, 40(3), pp. 221–36.

Rekhta (2021). Available at: www.rekhta.org (Accessed: 25 January 2021).

Risam, R. (2015) 'South Asian Digital Humanities: An Overview', *South Asian Review*, 36(3), pp. 161–75.

Risam, R. (2016) 'Diasporizing the Digital Humanities: Displacing the Center and Periphery', *International Journal of E-politics*, 7(3), pp. 65–78.

Risam, R. (2018) *New Digital Worlds: Postcolonial Digital Humanities in Theory, Praxis, and Pedagogy*. Evanston, IL: Northwestern University Press.

Risam, R. and Gairola, R.K. (2019) 'South Asian Digital Humanities Then and Now', *South Asian Review*, 40(3), pp. 141–54.

Shah, N. (2019) 'Digital Humanities on the Ground: Post-access Politics and the Second Wave of Digital Humanities', *South Asian Review*, 40(3), pp. 155–73.

Singh, A. (2019) 'Beyond the Archive Gap: The Kiplings and the Famines of British Colonial India', *South Asian Review*, 40(3), pp. 237–51.

Thorat, D. (2019) 'Colonial Topographies of Internet Infrastructure: The Sedimented and Linked Networks of the Telegraph and Submarine Fiber Optic Internet', *South Asian Review*, 40(3), pp. 252–67.

Umang (2021). Available at: https://umangpoetry.org/, (Accessed: 25 January 2021).

# INDEX